FINANCIAL STATEMENT ANALYSIS:
A VALUATION APPROACH

LEONARD C. SOFFER
UNIVERSITY OF ILLINOIS AT CHICAGO

ROBIN J. SOFFER
CONSULTANT

Prentice Hall
Upper Saddle River, NJ 07458

Library of Congress Cataloging-in-Publication Data

Soffer, Leonard C.
  Financial statement analysis: a valuation approach / Leonard C. Soffer, Robin J. Soffer.
    p. cm.
  Includes bibliographical references and index.
  ISBN 0-13-032834-0
  1. Corporations—Valuation. 2. Financial statements. I. Soffer, Robin J. II. Title.

HG4028.V3 S595 2002
332.36'2042—dc21

Acquisitions Editor: Thomas Sigel
Editor-in-Chief: PJ Boardman
Assistant Editor: Sam Goffinet
Developmental Editor: Elisa Adams
Senior Media Project Manager: Nancy Welcher
Executive Marketing Manager: Beth Toland
Marketing Assistant: Christine Genneken
Managing Editor (Production): Cynthia Regan
Production Editor: Kerri M. Limpert
Production Assistant: Joe DeProspero
Permissions Coordinator: Suzanne Grappi
Associate Director, Manufacturing: Vincent Scelta

Manufacturing Buyer: Diane Peirano
Design Manager: Maria Lange
Designer: Steve Frim
Interior Design: Pre-Press Company, Inc.
Cover Design: Steve Frim
Cover Illustration/Photo: Courtesy of Eric Perry/Amana America/Photonica
Illustrator (Interior): Matrix Publishing Service
Manager, Print Production: Christy Mahon
Composition: Suzanne Duda and Ashley Scattergood
Printer/Binder: Courier-Westford

Credits and acknowledgments for material borrowed from other sources and reproduced, with permission, in this textbook appear on the appropriate page within the text.

The information contained in this publication is of broad general usefulness to the accounting student and to those with an interest in accounting practices. However, it is sold with the understanding that the Publisher and the Authors are not engaged in rendering legal, accounting, investment, or other professional services or advice. If such advice is required, it should be obtained from a qualified professional. The examples used in this publication, and the references to or opinions expressed about financial reporting practices or companies identifed in this book, are intended to serve educational purposes, including encouraging classroom discussion, and are not intended to serve as examples of effective or ineffective or good or poor management practices.

Pearson Education LTD.
Pearson Education Australia PTY, Limited
Pearson Education Singapore, Pte. Ltd
Pearson Education North Asia Ltd
Pearson Education, Canada, Ltd
Pearson Educación de Mexico, S.A. de C.V.
Pearson Education—Japan
Pearson Education Malaysia, Pte. Ltd

10 9 8 7 6 5 4 3
ISBN 0-13-032834-0

To Robert Bakal, Roberta Bakal, and Shirley Soffer

and

Michael, Andrew, and Leah Soffer

and

In memory of Arthur Soffer

About the Authors

Leonard Soffer

Leonard Soffer is Associate Professor of Accounting at the University of Illinois at Chicago, where he teaches courses in Corporate Valuation and Advanced Accounting to both undergraduate and graduate students. He has also taught graduate students at the Kellogg Graduate School of Management and the University of Chicago Graduate School of Business, as well as executive education students at Kellogg and in an executive education program for a major accounting and consulting firm.

Professor Soffer has a B.S. in Accountancy from the University of Illinois at Urbana-Champaign, an M.B.A. in finance and information systems from the Kellogg Graduate School of Management, and a Ph.D. in Accounting from the University of California at Berkeley. He is a Certified Public Accountant and a winner of the prestigious Elijah Watt Sells Award for his performance on the C.P.A. exam. Professor Soffer is a member of the American Accounting Association, the American Institute of C.P.A.s and the Illinois C.P.A. Society. He serves on the Accounting Principles Committee of the Illinois C.P.A. Society.

Professor Soffer's research focuses on security analysis, the role of security analysts, and the use of financial statement information. His work has appeared in the *Journal of Accounting Research*, the *Review of Accounting Studies*, *Contemporary Accounting Research*, the *Journal of Accounting, Auditing and Finance*, *Accounting Horizons*, *Managerial Finance*, the *Review of Accounting and Finance*, and *Investor Relations Quarterly*. He is a member of the editorial board of the *Review of Accounting and Finance*. Professor Soffer's research has been cited in *Business Week*, *Crain's Chicago Business*, and *Worth Magazine*. He has appeared on the Chicago CBS television affiliate and on WebFN, a Web-based business news station, to discuss the state of the accounting profession, his research, and regulation of financial disclosures.

Prior to entering academia, Professor Soffer worked in accounting and corporate finance positions, most recently as manager of corporate development for USG Corporation, where he worked on acquisitions, divestitures and corporate strategy issues for the Chicago-based construction products firm. Professor Soffer has served on the board of directors of a not-for-profit corporation providing services to the developmentally disabled. He and his wife/co-author live in the Chicago area with their three children.

Robin Soffer

Robin Soffer is a consultant specializing in financial analysis and business strategy. As part of her consulting work, she runs the financial training programs at Quaker Food and Beverages, a division of PepsiCo. She has taught finance and accounting at the undergraduate and MBA levels at Dominican University, Concordia University and Keller Graduate School of Management.

Robin has a B.S. in Accountancy from the University of Illinois at Urbana-Champaign and an M.B.A. in finance and marketing from Northwestern University's Kellogg Graduate School of Management. She is a Certified Public Accountant and a winner of the prestigious Elijah Watt Sells Award and the Illinois Silver Medal for her performance on the C.P.A. exam.

Before becoming a consultant, Robin spent fourteen years at The Quaker Oats Company in finance, planning and general management. Her finance experience includes corporate and divisional financial analysis, strategic planning, cash management, international financing, pension and profit sharing investment management, and directing Quaker's acquisitions and divestitures. Her most recent position was Vice President and Assistant Treasurer. Robin was also the General Manager of Ghirardelli Chocolate, a Quaker division. In this position, she was responsible for all aspects of the business including sales, marketing, plant operations, and retail stores.

Robin lives with her husband/co-author and three children in the Chicago area.

Brief Table of Contents

PART I INTRODUCTION 1

Chapter 1 *An Introduction to Security Analysis* 2
Chapter 2 *Security Analysis and Efficient Markets* 20

PART II BUSINESS AND FINANCIAL STATEMENT ANALYSIS 39

Chapter 3 *Business Analysis* 40
Chapter 4 *Accounting Analysis and the Financial Statements* 66
Chapter 5 *Financial Statement Analysis* 98

PART III CASH FLOW BASED VALUATION 125

Chapter 6 *The Economic Balance Sheet and an Overview of Cash Flow Based Valuation Models* 126
Chapter 7 *Discount Rates in Valuation* 144
Chapter 8 *The Dividend Discount and the Flows to Equity Models* 170
Chapter 9 *Free Cash Flow Model and Analysis* 186
Chapter 10 *Forecasting Free Cash Flows* 210
Chapter 11 *The Adjusted Present Value Model* 250
Chapter 12 *The Residual Income Model* 266

PART IV SPECIAL TOPICS IN CASH FLOW BASED VALUATION 293

Chapter 13 *Using Income Tax Information* 294
Chapter 14 *Employee Stock Options and Valuation* 316
Chapter 15 *Valuation of Firms with Pension Plans and Other Postemployment Benefit Plans* 348

PART V MULTIPLES VALUATION 383

Chapter 16 *A "Theory" of Multiples* 384
Chapter 17 *PE Ratios and Earnings Growth* 406
Chapter 18 *Additional Issues in Multiples Analysis* 422

Table of Contents

Foreword xvii
Preface xix

PART **I** INTRODUCTION   1

Chapter 1   *An Introduction to Security Analysis*   2

1.1   Who Does Security Analysis?   3
1.2   Where Do Analysts Get Information?   4
1.3   Financial Reporting Environment   7
1.4   The Limitations of GAAP For Security Analysis   12
1.5   A Look At Security Analysis In Phases   14

Summary   17
Review Questions   17
Problems   18
My Case   19

Chapter 2   *Security Analysis and Efficient Markets*   20

2.1   Goal of Security Analysis   21
2.2   What is an Efficient Securities Market?   22
2.3   Implications of an Efficient Market for the Behavior
of Security Prices   23
2.4   The Role of Investors in an Efficient Market   28
2.5   Implications of Market Efficiency for Security
Analysis   29
2.6   Market Efficiency—Overview of Empirical
Evidence   31

Summary   35
Suggested Readings   35
Review Questions   36
Problems   37
My Case   38

PART **II** BUSINESS AND FINANCIAL STATEMENT ANALYSIS   39

Chapter 3   *Business Analysis*   40

3.1   External Analysis   43
3.2   Internal Analysis   54

Summary   60
Suggested Readings   60
Review Questions   61
Problems   61
My Case   65

Chapter 4   *Accounting Analysis and the Financial Statements*   66

4.1   Balance Sheet   68
4.2   Income Statement   72
4.3   Cash Flow Statement   77
4.4   Starbucks' Financial Statements   79

Summary   87
Suggested Readings   89
Review Questions   89
Problems   90
My Case   92

Appendix 4.1   *Accounting for Investments*   93

Appendix 4.2   *Accounting for Contingencies*   96

Chapter 5   *Financial Statement Analysis*   98

5.1   Common Ratios   100
5.2   Ratio Analysis   106
5.3   Cautions about Using Ratios   112

Summary   116
Suggested Readings   116
Review Questions   116
Problems   117
My Case   123

PART III CASH FLOW BASED VALUATION   125

Chapter 6   *The Economic Balance Sheet and an Overview of Cash Flow Based Valuation Models*   126

6.1   The Economic Balance Sheet   127
6.2   The Valuation Models   133

Summary   139
Suggested Readings   139
Review Questions   140
Problems   141
My Case   143

Chapter 7   *Discount Rates in Valuation*   144

7.1   The Cost of Equity   145
7.2   The Weighted-Average Cost of Capital   155

7.3   The Unlevered Cost of Equity   160
7.4   Issues With Private Companies   161

Summary   164
Suggested Readings   164
Review Questions   164
Problems   165
My Case   167

Appendix 7.1   *Averaging Estimated Betas Having Different Precisions*   168

Chapter 8   *The Dividend Discount and the Flows to Equity Models*   170
8.1   The Dividend Discount Model   171
8.2   The Dividend Discount Model Assumptions   172
8.3   Variants of the Dividend Discount Model   176
8.4   Applying the Dividend Discount Model   177
8.5   Flows to Equity Model   179

Summary   182
Suggested Readings   182
Review Questions   182
Problems   182
My Case   183

Appendix 8.1   *Circularity of the Dividend Discount Model*   184

Chapter 9   *Free Cash Flow Model and Analysis*   186
9.1   The Free Cash Flow Model   187
9.2   Differences Between GAAP Cash Flow and Free Cash Flow   189
9.3   An Organized Method for Making the Adjustments   192

Summary   203
Suggested Readings   203
Review Questions   203
Problems   204
My Case   209

Chapter 10   *Forecasting Free Cash Flows*   210
10.1 Model the Free Cash Flows   213
10.2 Set the Model Assumptions and Compute the Results   219
10.3 Refine the Model   229
10.4 Sensitivity Analysis   236

Summary   244
Suggested Readings   244
Review Questions   244
Problems   245
My Case   248

Chapter 11   *The Adjusted Present Value Model*   250

11.1 The Adjusted Present Value Model   251
11.2 Comparing the Free Cash Flow and Adjusted Present Value Models   252
11.3 The Modigliani-Miller Propositions and Value   254
11.4 How Leverage Affects Cost of Capital   258
11.5 Pros and Cons of the Adjusted Present Value Model   260

Summary   261
Suggested Readings   261
Review Questions   262
Problems   262
My Case   263

Appendix 11.1   *Derivation of the Modigliani-Miller Proposition with Taxes*   264

Chapter 12   *The Residual Income Model*   266

12.1 The Residual Income Model Defined   267
12.2 Starbucks' Valuation Under Residual Income   269
12.3 A Comparison of the Free Cash Flow and Residual Income Models   278

Summary   286
Suggested Readings   286
Review Questions   286
Problems   287
My Case   288

Appendix 12.1   *Derivation of the Residual Income Model*   289

Appendix 12.2   *Derivation of Perpetuity Value in the Residual Income Model*   290

PART IV SPECIAL TOPICS IN CASH FLOW BASED VALUATION   293

Chapter 13   *Using Income Tax Information*   294

13.1 Statutory, Marginal, and Effective Tax Rates   295
13.2 Review of Income Tax Accounting Concepts   297
13.3 The Structure of the Income Tax Footnote   304

13.4 Estimating the Effective Tax Rate on Core
        Operations 307

Summary 312
Suggested Readings 312
Review Questions 312
Problems 313
My Case 315

Chapter 14 *Employee Stock Options and Valuation* 316
    14.1 Stock Options 317
    14.2 Differences between Publicly Traded Options
          and ESOs 321
    14.3 Accounting and Tax Issues 324
    14.4 Cash Flow Valuation of Firms With ESOs 329

Summary 342
Suggested Readings 342
Review Questions 343
Problems 343
My Case 346

Appendix 14.1 *Summary of Employee Stock Option
               Terminology* 347

Chapter 15 *Valuation of Firms with Pension Plans and
             Other Postemployment Benefit Plans* 348
    15.1 Overview of Retirement Plans 349
    15.2 Financial Reporting for and Valuation of Defined
          Contribution Plans 354
    15.3 Financial Reporting for Defined Benefit Pension
          Plans and OPEB Plans 355
    15.4 Valuing Firms with Defined Benefit Pension Plans
          and OPEB Plans 364

Summary 372
Suggested Readings 372
Review Questions 373
Problems 374
My Case 377

Appendix 15.1 *Projected Benefit Obligation
               and Accumulated Postemployment Benefit
               Obligation* 378

PART V MULTIPLES VALUATION **383**
    Chapter 16 *A "Theory" of Multiples* 384
        16.1 What is the Multiples Approach? 386

16.2 Arguments For and Against the Multiples
      Approach   389

16.3 Importance of Using Comparable Firms   391

16.4 An Example Using PE   395

16.5 What to Do When Perfect Comparability
      is not Possible   396

Summary   398
Suggested Readings   398
Review Questions   398
Problems   399
My Case   403

Appendix 16.1 *Excerpts from Merrill Lynch Food Industry
                    Report (September 9, 1999)*   404

Chapter 17 *PE Ratios and Earnings Growth*   406

17.1 How Expected Earnings Growth Affects
      PE Ratios   407

17.2 Controlling for the Effect of Supernormal Earnings
      Growth Rates on PE Analyses   411

Summary   417
Suggested Readings   417
Review Questions   417
Problems   418
My Case   421

Chapter 18 *Additional Issues in Multiples Analysis*   422

18.1 Capital Structure and PE Ratios   423

18.2 Financial Reporting Differences
      and PE Ratios   428

18.3 PE Ratios and Firms with Near-Zero Earnings
      or Losses   431

18.4 Valuing Firms in Several Lines of Business   432

18.5 Using the Market/Book Ratio   434

Summary   439
Suggested Readings   439
Review Questions   440
Problems   440
My Case   443

Index   445

Foreword

Research over the last 10–15 years has documented the benefits from using accrual accounting numbers when projecting enterprise cash flows. These findings show that using GAAP financial statement data can improve financial analysis and security valuation. While this perspective is widely accepted today, for much of the 1990s, a deep understanding of financial statement numbers wasn't widespread. The prevailing procedural orientation of upper level financial reporting text materials set a "form over substance" tone that permeated both classrooms and accounting practice, to the detriment of both. This parochial focus had two major educational consequences: 1) many MBA programs downscaled the role of elective financial reporting courses in their curricula, and 2) undergraduate finance majors were often not required to take the procedurally oriented financial reporting courses.

The impact on professional practice was also profound. Auditors often lacked the requisite training and insight to undertake analytic and forensic reviews. Financial analysts, in turn, were trained to utilize only the most rudimentary accounting data. Professional and other books aimed at these audiences usually perpetuated the problem by avoiding the presumably deficient accounting skill base.

Clearly, a new pedagogical approach was needed to train future professionals in how to harness the power of financial reporting when undertaking financial analyses and valuations. Dan Collins, Bruce Johnson and I recognized this and began the process when we wrote *Financial Reporting & Analysis.** It is gratifying to see this book by Lenny and Robin Soffer arrive since it continues the growing emphasis on informed use of accounting in all facets of financial decision making. By firmly grounding their valuation approach on detailed, real-world disclosures, the Soffers make an important contribution to the study and practice of valuation. Their book will allow valuation students and professionals to achieve more fully the information potential of financial disclosures.

Lawrence Revsine
Evanston, IL
August 7, 2002

*L. Revsine, D.W. Collins, and B.W. Johnson, *Financial Reporting & Analysis,* Prentice-Hall, Inc., 1st ed. 1999, 2nd ed. 2002.

Preface

The collapse of Enron. The bankruptcy of WorldCom. Accounting irregularities at Qwest. These are just a few examples of how all of our lives have been affected by global business practices. These events have brought to our attention more than ever the significance of accounting. Hardly a day goes by that newspaper editorials do not lament the state of accounting and discuss its effect on capital markets. Being an informed user of financial statements was never unimportant. But today the need is more obvious than ever.

This book provides both a sound theoretical framework for financial statement analysis and corporate valuation and a thorough discussion of how valuations are actually done in the real world. It is targeted for people who are in, or intend to enter, investment banking, consulting, accounting, corporate finance, commercial banking, equity analysis or equity research. While of interest to the practitioner, this book is primarily designed for use in an **elective MBA course** or in a **capstone undergraduate course**. A draft of this book has been used successfully in the MBA programs at Northwestern University's Kellogg Graduate School of Management, the University of Illinois at Chicago and Dominican University. It has also been used for Masters in Accounting students and undergraduate students at the University of Illinois and in executive education at Kellogg. The book works well either in the accounting or the finance curriculum.

KEY FEATURES

- **Rigorous theory matched with a practice oriented approach** The book is rigorous in its coverage of valuation theory, but it is equally concerned with presenting the material in a practical way. Students must understand why valuations are done the way they are, and also be able to use real world information in their analyses. This book discusses the information sources used in building valuation models, financial statement quality issues, interpreting the information in a valuation context, dealing with the imprecision and vagueness that often accompany real disclosures, and avoiding common analysis pitfalls.

- **Focus on real financial statements and real business examples** Real world business examples and actual financial statements appear throughout the text and in the end of chapter material, adding realism and providing experience using these documents. It forces students to think critically and make assumptions and estimates when they encounter incomplete information in financial statements. The text explores the subtleties of accounting disclosures and shows how to incorporate this information in a valuation. We use the Starbucks financial statements throughout the book to show how financial statement analysis and valuation are applied to a real company.

- **Discussion of financial statement quality issues woven throughout all the chapters** Financial statement quality issues are very important in financial statement analysis and valuation. Rather than address these issues separately, earnings quality is discussed throughout the book, as each element of the analysis is developed.

- **Blend of accounting, finance and business strategy** This book covers the accounting, finance and business strategy concepts needed to prepare a valuation. These concepts are integrated so students see the connections among them. The book provides a framework for analyzing business strategy and discusses the link between strategy and valuation. Students learn about business strategy and how to relate a firm's strategic position to the assumptions in a valuation.

- **Unique and substantial end of chapter material** Each chapter includes a substantial number of review questions and problems. These serve to reinforce the material and allow students to test themselves using many real financial statements and disclosures. This material includes several innovative features, each of which is clearly labeled with an icon:

     To respond to the concern that students do not develop adequate writing skills, we have included a number of questions and problems requiring a **writing-intensive response.**

     In-class exercises are problems with opportunities for classroom debates and hands-on projects. All of these problems could also be used as regular homework problems.

     Each chapter includes an assignment that is part of a course-long project, called **My Case**, to analyze and value a company. This allows the student to prepare the appropriate part of his or her project immediately after covering the material for class. By the end of the book, the student has a complete analysis of the company, which can be turned in as a written document and/or presented orally to the class.

     Because students will be using **Internet research** in their jobs, we have included problems that require the use of common Internet research tools.

- **Innovative coverage of pension and employee stock option valuation** The book includes chapters on using financial statement disclosures to value companies with pension plans and companies with employee stock option plans.

- **Short sidebars on current topics** Most chapters include one or more short pieces on related topics, including practical information, academic research, and recent news stories. Called "A Closer Look," sample topics for these pieces include the Enron bankruptcy, accounting treatment of losses from the September 11 terrorist attacks, finding industry information, using government data sources, academic research on using multiples to value firms with no earnings, and Regulation FD.

- **Comprehensive coverage of all commonly used valuation models** The book covers all of the commonly used valuation models, including five models derived from basic discounted cash flow theory: the dividend discount model, the flows to equity model, the free cash flow model, the adjusted present value model, and the residual income model. The book also provides an unusually rigorous treatment of valuation with multiples.

- **Accounting Appendices** Some chapters include more detailed information on the accounting for certain items. For example, we include appendices on accounting for contingencies and accounting for investments.

- **Suggested Readings** The suggested readings provide additional resources and/or assignment material. The readings include both classic and recent articles and books. They also include current working papers available on the Social Science Research Network, which are highlighted with the SSRN logo.

SUPPLEMENTS

A complete package of supplements is available to assist students and instructors in using this book. These resources include:

Instructor Resources

- **Solutions Manual** Written by the authors, the Solutions Manual provides solutions to the review questions and problems at the end of each chapter. This manual is available in a printed version, or for easy accessibility, download the electronic files from **www.prenhall.com/soffer**. Professors will need to obtain a password from their Prentice Hall representative.

- **Test Item File** With questions ranging from easy to difficult, the test item files include multiple choice, true/false, and essay questions. An electronic version of these questions is also available.

- **Author Updates** Posted twice a year, remain current with author updates as they pertain to the book.

- **Custom Case Option** Would you like to offer pertinent cases drawn from Harvard, Ivey or Darden in addition to this text? For details go to **www.pearsoncustom.com** or ask your Prentice Hall book representative.

Instructor and Student Resources

- **Prentice Hall Companion Web site** The Companion Web site is an online learning environment for instructors and students developed to support this book. Log onto **www.prenhall.com/soffer** to access the following:

- **Power Point Slides**, prepared by Russell Madray of Clemson University, provide the instructor with a show ready for classroom use. Use the slides as they are, or edit them to meet your classroom needs. Students can also download these slides to use as a study aid.

- **Online Study Guide**, also prepared by Russell Madray of Clemson University, provides instructors and students with about 25 questions per chapter. Instructors may assign these or students may use the study guide as an enrichment and reinforcement tool.

- **Excel Spreadsheets and Templates**, prepared by the authors, provide additional detailed analyses and complex computations, such as a template pre-programmed to value employee stock options using the Black-Scholes option pricing formula.
- **Links to Pertinent Sites** Access pertinent Web sites relating to financial statement analysis and valuation.

ACKNOWLEDGEMENTS

We are grateful for the support and excellent suggestions we have received in the course of writing this book. We thank Larry Revsine, Northwestern University, for his endless support, advice and counsel. We thank Morley Lemon, University of Waterloo, for years of friendship and encouragement on this project. Thanks also to Ahmed Riahi-Belkaoui, University of Illinois at Chicago, for his helpful comments and suggestions. We thank Chris Jones, George Washington University, for the depth and insight with which he reviewed the manuscript.

We also appreciate the following professors for their detailed written reviews or comments on this book.

Charles Caliendo, *University of Minnesota*
Michele Daley, *Rice University*
WaQar I. Ghani, *Saint Joseph's University*
Paul A. Griffin, *University of California- Davis*
Bruce Johnson, *University of Iowa*
Frank Kopczynski, *Plymouth State College*
James A. Largay, *Lehigh University*
Charles M.C. Lee, *Cornell University*
Robert Lin, *California State University–Hayward*
Kenneth J. Martin, *New Mexico State University*
Charles McPeak, *Pepperdine University*
Krishnagopal Menon, *Boston University*
Lawrence Metzger, *Loyola University–Chicago*
The late Arijit Mukherji, *University of Minnesota*
Phil Shane, *University of Colorado*
Virginia E. Soybel, *Babson College*
Lloyd Tanlu, *Brandeis University*
Charles E. Wasley, *University of Rochester*
Joseph Weintrop, *CUNY–Baruch*
Clark M. Wheatley, *Florida International University*

Many thanks to the following business people for providing information used in the preparation of the manuscript:

Matt Bell, ACNielsen
Karl Brewer, William Blair
Janet Cooper
David Frank, Holland Capital Management
Andrew Goldstein, Watson Wyatt Worldwide
Mike Hayes, Watson Wyatt Worldwide

Anthony Kolovitz, Bear Stearns
Clive Lipshitz, TDA Capital Partners
Michael Mauboussin, Credit Suisse First Boston
Mary Ellen Ryan, ACNielsen

We also wish to thank the more than 1,000 students at the University of Illinois at Chicago, Dominican University and Northwestern University, who used various stages of the manuscript and helped us improve the materials.

A big thank you to the entire Prentice Hall team, including PJ Boardman, Editor-in-Chief; Thomas Sigel, Acquisitions Editor; Kerri Limpert, Production Editor; Steve Frim, Cover and Interior Designer; Elisa Adams, Developmental Editor; Annie Todd, Director of Marketing; Beth Toland, Executive Marketing Manager; and Anne Riddick, Chicago Area Sales Representative.

Leonard and Robin Soffer

PART I

INTRODUCTION

1 An Introduction to Security Analysis

2 Security Analysis and Efficient Markets

1

 **Where We Are:**

In this chapter, we discuss the jobs of the various financial professionals who do security analysis and we review their sources of information. We also discuss the financial reporting environment and the limitations of financial reports as well as present a framework for security analysis.

 **Where We Are Going:**

In Chapter 2, we will discuss the concept of efficient markets and explain how it affects security analysis. In later chapters, we will explain how to use our security analysis framework to value firms.

An Introduction to Security Analysis

LEARNING OBJECTIVES:

After studying this chapter, you will understand:

- The many kinds of financial professionals who use security analysis in their jobs and the types of analyses they do.

- The sources of information security analysts use to prepare their analyses.

- How the financial reporting environment affects security analysis and how regulators, management, and auditors influence financial reporting.

- Why analysts consider accounting method choices, accounting estimates, and disclosures when using financial reporting to prepare a valuation.

- What the limitations of generally accepted accounting principles are in presenting information for valuation purposes.

- How analysts assess the quality of financial information.

- How equity security analysis consists of four phases: business analysis, financial statement analysis, forecasting, and valuation.

This book explores techniques of security analysis and focuses on the analysis of equity securities. Many people do "security analysis," even those who do not have the title "security analyst." Anyone who values individual firms, makes buy/sell recommendations, or searches to find portfolios that will outperform the market is doing security analysis. This includes brokerage research analysts, investment bankers, corporate finance specialists, mergers and acquisitions analysts, venture capitalists, and individual investors. The material in this book is intended for all of these readers.

One of our goals is to provide you with a framework for analysis. We present the theory behind the methods explored in this book because it is critical that analysts understand what they are doing and why. Only then can they apply their knowledge to new and different situations. We also include examples using real companies to demonstrate how to apply the valuation methods.

Analysts must also understand how to get the information they need to be effective in their roles. Another one of our goals, therefore, is to discuss the many different sources from which analysts can obtain information. We explore the wealth of data available in published financial statements, as well as brokerage research reports and other information about firms.

Financial statements are a key input to security analysis. Therefore, analysts must understand the accounting model on which the financial statements are based. Importantly, they must also understand the incentives managers have to distort from the financial statements. So, a critical element of security analysis is to strip away any distortions. Our goal in a valuation is to estimate the value of the firm in a way that is not influenced by accounting distortions.

Section 1.1 discusses the different groups of people that do security analysis. Section 1.2 explores the sources of information available to security analysts. Section 1.3 discusses the financial reporting environment, including how generally accepted accounting principles (GAAP) are set. We outline the limitations of GAAP in Section 1.4 and provide an overview of the four phases of security analysis in Section 1.5.

1.1 WHO DOES SECURITY ANALYSIS?

People in many different jobs use security analysis. **Buy-side analysts** are professionals who analyze securities and make buy or sell recommendations for their firms' funds. For example, an analyst who works for a fund manager at a firm such as Fidelity Investments or Merrill Lynch & Company uses security analysis to help pick stocks that would be appropriate for a specific fund. A buy-side analyst also might work for a large pension fund that invests in equities, such as the California Public Employees' Retirement System, or CalPers. These security analysts carefully study equities before the fund purchases them, and they continue to study them to determine which stocks should remain in the portfolio.

Sell-side analysts work for brokerage firms, which execute trades on behalf of individuals and institutional investors. These analysts issue reports containing information about the companies they follow, their businesses, and their competitive situations. Sell-side analysts make buy, hold, and sell recommendations on the stocks they follow. They also provide earnings forecasts and additional information. Their reports are issued to the brokerage houses' clients. These clients include both individual customers and buy-side analysts employed by institutional investors.

Investment bankers advise clients on financial matters such as corporate restructurings, acquisitions, and divestitures. In addition to analyzing the strategic reasons for a particular transaction, an investment banker must also consider its financial implications and the price the firm should be willing to pay or should demand. In the case of an initial public offering of stock, the investment banker will prepare significant amounts of analysis to help market the offering. Thus, much of investment bankers' analysis revolves around equity valuation. **Corporate finance specialists, merger and acquisition analysts,** and **venture capitalists** may also be involved in these kinds of decisions.

Individual investors use security analysis to make investment decisions. An individual with some savings may want to buy stocks in the hope of increasing the value of his or her savings. Individuals use security analysis to determine which stocks to buy for their own investments and what price to pay for these stocks. They also use security analysis techniques to decide when to sell certain stocks. Individual investors may seek the advice of professional analysts, or they may collect data about investments on their own.

Employees and **potential employees** may also perform security analysis. Before joining the firm, the potential employee may want to be comfortable that the new employer is financially stable. He or she may also be interested in valuing a compensation package that includes stock or stock options. Once inside the company, the employee may use security analysis to determine whether to exercise stock options.

1.2 WHERE DO ANALYSTS GET INFORMATION?

Analysts need significant amounts of data to make good investment decisions. The primary source of information for security analysis is the financial statements and related disclosures of the firm under analysis. If the firm is publicly held,[1] its financial statements and related disclosures are published and freely available. The financial statements and disclosures will be prepared according to generally accepted accounting principles (GAAP) and will be audited. If the firm being analyzed is not publicly held, the financial statements may not be prepared in accordance with GAAP and may be unaudited. In this case, the analyst must determine what accounting conventions have been used and be aware that no one has attested to the reliability of the financial statements. If the purpose of the analysis is to consider an acquisition of the private company, an audit of financial statements prepared under GAAP may be a condition of the acquisition.

In addition to the financial statements, the analyst has many other sources of information about any particular firm. The analyst may get information directly from the company itself. Publicly traded firms often provide live conference calls accessible through the Internet. They also

---

[1]A "publicly held" firm is one that has many shareholders and usually has its shares actively traded on a stock exchange such as the New York Stock Exchange or the Nasdaq. Publicly held firms must provide annual and quarterly reports to their shareholders, as well as extensive disclosures to the Securities and Exchange Commission (SEC). All of these documents are available to the public. Annual and quarterly reports are available free of charge from the company. Many companies also make these documents available on their Web sites. There are also Web sites that collect and distribute electronic versions of annual reports, such as Report Gallery (**www.reportgallery.com**). Documents filed with the SEC can be obtained from the Commission's Web site at **www.sec.gov**.

A CLOSER LOOK

Technology and the Changing Role of the Sell-Side Analyst

Historically, a key role of sell-side analysts has been "information intermediary." These analysts develop relationships with the companies they follow, allowing them to obtain information about these firms, their prospects, their expected earnings, and so on. This information forms the basis for research reports these analysts send to their clients.

The analyst has been a sort of middleman, a wholesale distributor linking the producers of information (firms) with the ultimate consumers (investors). This has been an important role because of the expense to each firm of attempting to communicate directly with investors and the practical difficulties in reaching all investors. By following and reporting on many firms, the analyst has a distinct cost advantage in the dissemination of information, so it is not surprising that this role has developed over the years. This is not to say that analysts did no analysis. However, some analysts could survive and even prosper without doing much analysis, because there has been value added in the simple packaging and dissemination of information.

The breakthroughs in technology over the last decade have begun to change all that. Many firms now use the Internet to broadcast conference calls with analysts; e-mail information to investors; and post press releases, financial statements, and other information. Since 1994, virtually all public firms have submitted their Securities and Exchange Commission filings electronically, and investors can access these for free, 24 hours a day. Not only do firms have the capability to reach investors in these ways, but also more and more investors have the equipment necessary to access information via the Internet. The new structure provides investors with information in a much more timely fashion than hard-copy research reports distributed by security analysts, which might not reach investors until weeks after the information in them was obtained. This suggests that sell-side analysts are going to have to find new ways to add value. Unless there is something new and insightful in the analyst's report, it is old news to investors by the time they receive it.

As their role as information intermediaries becomes less important, analysts must provide insightful analyses of information, as opposed to simple dissemination of information, in order to continue to add value. Those who do will continue to find an audience for their reports. Those who do not, will find that investors are not very interested in what they have to say.

make public announcements of important information. The analyst may get information from stock analyst reports; newspaper and magazine articles; the firm's competitors and customers; competitors' annual and quarterly reports; economic data and purchased data services that provide information on sales, distribution, pricing, and so on. Analysts may also use industry experts or their own experience to draw conclusions about the company.

A CLOSER LOOK

Careers in Security Analysis

A good analyst has many different career options such as a portfolio manager or a private equity investor.

Portfolio Manager

Karl Brewer is a portfolio manager at William Blair. Karl and two coworkers run the William Blair Small Cap Growth Fund. Karl has a BA in economics from Washington and Lee University in Virginia and his MBA from Northwestern's Kellogg Graduate School of Management. Before working at William Blair, Karl worked at Lehman Brothers for six years. When he first joined William Blair, he was an analyst doing research to support portfolio managers.

In Karl's job as a portfolio manager, he must select stocks for his fund and determine when to sell stocks from his fund. To learn about the companies they invest in or are considering investing in, Karl and his coworkers meet with the companies; talk to other people such as the company's customers and competitors; read annual reports and other public filings, research reports, trade journals, newspapers, magazines, and other information; and do modeling and financial statement analysis. They use comparable company analysis, multiples analysis, and discounted cash flow. Karl tries to get behind the numbers and truly understand the business drivers. Karl feels that business analysis is key to valuing stocks and that the strategic review of the business can be the most important part of the analysis.

Private Equity Investor

Clive Lipshitz is an associate director of a New York–area global private equity firm. Clive screens for, identifies, and analyzes potential buyout candidates for his firm. Clive received his BA and MBA from Tel Aviv University. He is a CPA. Before taking his current position, Clive worked in corporate venture capital at PaineWebber, equity research at Schroders and Salomon Smith Barney, and was an accountant at Price Waterhouse.

To identify buyout candidates among publicly traded companies, Clive uses predominantly quantitative screens. The analysis of candidates has three stages: (1) initial review to identify suitability of the company for the types of deals his firm is considering; (2) detailed analysis, including modeling and valuation; and (3) development of a buyout model, with reference to capital structure. In the modeling and valuation stage, Clive develops detailed financial forecasting models, analyzing the company's historical financial performance with reference to revenue growth, cost structure, and capital structure. Clive uses both multiples methods and discounted cash flow analysis to value firms. To develop his forecasts further, Clive speaks with customers, suppliers, industry experts, and management and attends industry trade shows in order to assess demand for the company's product/service and future cost structure. Clive says that financial skills are only part of the important skills he uses; being able to make qualitative assessments of company management and industry dynamics is key.

A CLOSER LOOK

Regulation FD

In 2000, the Securities and Exchange Commission (SEC) adopted Regulation Fair Disclosure (FD). This regulation prohibits firms from providing information to security analysts and other market professionals unless that information is already in the public domain, or is broadly disclosed simultaneously. When first proposed, this regulation was met with opposition from the analyst community, which argued that unfiltered information was not useful to investors. Analysts felt that their superior access to information was justified, so that they could properly interpret the information before providing it to investors.

The SEC, however, was concerned that analysts were using their superior access to company-provided information to act essentially as "information gatekeepers," rather than as analysts. The Commission argued that this could lead to reduced confidence in security markets, as well as to companies threatening to limit access to information to induce analysts to write more positive reports.

Some analysts warned of a "chilling effect" from Regulation FD, wherein companies would refuse to provide any information at all, for fear of violating the regulation. However, there was little evidence of such an effect in the first year under Regulation FD. Although the new regime makes life somewhat more difficult for analysts, it has enabled investors to access information directly from companies on a more timely basis.

1.3 FINANCIAL REPORTING ENVIRONMENT

Because so much of the data analysts use is from financial statements, analysts need to understand the financial reporting environment. Managers use required financial reports to communicate with investors and potential investors in order to attract capital investment in the firm. In presenting information to these investors, however, managers face a problem known as **asymmetric information**. The managers know more about the firm than the investors do, and the investors may have no way of knowing whether the reports they receive fairly present the underlying economics of the business. Managers need a way to convince investors of the fairness of the financial reports. As a result, most highly developed countries such as the United States have established reporting rules and have mandated audits of publicly held companies. Reporting rules set acceptable accounting methods and also prescribe minimum levels of disclosure. Mandating audits helps to make the representations of managers credible, by having an independent expert attest to their fairness.[2]

The content of financial reports is determined by the interactions among capital market regulators, managers of firms preparing financial reports, and auditors. The Securities and Exchange Commission (SEC) has the statutory power to prescribe accounting methods used in financial reports

---

[2]Despite some recent highly publicized audit failures, audits still play an important role in the capital markets by attesting to the reliability of management's disclosures.

and to specify disclosure requirements for publicly held companies. For the most part, the SEC has delegated this responsibility to the Financial Accounting Standards Board (FASB). The pronouncements of the FASB and its predecessor organizations, together with accounting practices that have evolved over time, constitute generally accepted accounting principles, known as GAAP. The primary stated objective of GAAP is to ensure that the information in financial statements is useful to investors.

Management influences the financial statements through its choices of accounting methods and estimates, and by applying judgment in decisions that affect how information is presented and what amount of information is disclosed. Management's biases may affect these reporting decisions and therefore the quality of the information provided. Auditors influence financial reporting in that they are charged with independently attesting that the firm's financial statements are consistent with GAAP. In this process, auditors influence management's reporting.

Exhibit 1.1 summarizes these influences.

Influence of Regulators

The SEC and the FASB each have a role in setting accounting standards in the United States.[3] These standards significantly influence financial statements, because they affect how transactions are reported.

The Securitites and Exchange Commission

The Securities Act of 1933 was the first in a series of statutes designed to protect investors from fraud in the wake of the 1929 stock market crash. It requires firms to register securities with the SEC[4] before offering them for sale to the public.[5] The registration statement generally becomes a public document and includes financial statements and a number of disclosures about the registrant and the

EXHIBIT 1.1   Factors Influencing Financial Reporting

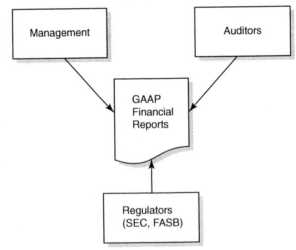

---

[3]Although the SEC and the FASB are the most important groups influencing reporting rules, the American Institute of Certified Public Accountants (AICPA) and other organizations do have an influence on reporting standards.

[4]The 1933 Act actually predates the SEC. The Federal Trade Commission administered the 1933 Act until creation of the SEC under the 1934 Act.

[5]The SEC has exempted small offerings, securities of governmental units, and certain other securities from the provisions of the Act.

securities being offered. The Securities Exchange Act of 1934 created the SEC and extended disclosure requirements to all firms whose securities are publicly traded. Companies listed on a national securities exchange now must provide updated information annually and quarterly, as well as in certain other circumstances.[6]

The SEC consists of five commissioners who are appointed by the president (subject to Senate consent) for staggered five-year terms, with one commissioner's term expiring each year. The president also designates one of the five commissioners to be chairman. The SEC staff is organized into divisions. From a financial reporting perspective, the three most important divisions are the

- Division of Corporate Finance, which reviews documents filed with the SEC
- Office of the Chief Accountant, which is the principal adviser to the SEC on accounting and auditing issues
- Division of Enforcement, which enforces the SEC rules

The Financial Accounting Standards Board

Although the SEC has full authority to impose financial reporting rules, it has delegated this role to the FASB. In most cases, the SEC does not interfere with the FASB's rule-setting process. On rare occasions, it has forced the profession to address certain issues. The SEC has only once rejected a FASB standard.

The FASB is therefore responsible for establishing accounting standards in the United States. It issues pronouncements, including Statements of Financial Accounting Standards (SFAS) and Interpretations thereof, Statements of Financial Accounting Concepts, and Technical Bulletins. However, the FASB does not have any authority or responsibility to enforce compliance with these standards. Compliance is left to company management, the accounting profession, the SEC, and the legal system.[7]

Before issuing an accounting standard, the FASB goes through a due process procedure, gathering public comment on the issues and a draft of the standard. This procedure allows all interested parties to provide input into the standard. Although the FASB is under no obligation to please any particular constituency, the political pressure brought to bear on the FASB during due process can be enormous. SFAS No. 106 (on accounting for postretirement benefits other than pensions) was adopted over tremendous opposition from business. The FASB backed down from its original proposal on accounting for compensation under stock option plans after an even more contentious fight, which involved both Congress and the president. The FASB altered its position on stock options because it could not overcome the political pressures. The result was a compromise statement (SFAS No. 123), which the FASB itself criticized in the appendix to the statement it issued. This example highlights how political pressure can result in accounting standards that do not provide the best information to investors. The analyst needs to be cognizant of such situations and may need to go beyond financial statement data to gather needed information.

Influence of Management on Financial Statement Quality

Management is responsible for the way in which it uses the business's assets, and financial reports are designed to inform shareholders of how managers are satisfying their fiduciary responsibilities.

---

[6]For a complete listing of forms filed with the SEC, along with descriptions of the contents, see the SEC's Web site at **www.sec.gov**.

[7]The current structure of the FASB and responsibility for compliance with accounting standards may change as a result of reforms proposed in the wake of the Enron bankruptcy.

Through accounting method choices, estimates, and decisions about levels of disclosure, management has significant influence over financial statements. This can create situations in which management's personal goals conflict with the goal of financial reporting to provide useful information to investors. Most managers like their firms to appear strong and profitable. Often, they own stock in their respective firms and would like the stock prices to increase. They may also have bonuses tied to their firms' reported income. And, the firms may have covenants in its debt agreements that require the maintenance of certain financial ratios. Whether these covenants are met may depend on accounting method choices and estimates. Because of these conflicts, managers may try to affect the financial statements. For this reason, the concept of conservatism underlies many GAAP reporting rules. It states that accountants should be biased toward estimates and assumptions that delay the recognition of income and accelerate the recording of losses. This principle puts limits on management's natural bias toward optimism. Independent audits also limit the effect of management bias. Nevertheless, managers can still influence financial reporting results, and in interpreting financial statements, the astute analyst must consider the possibility of management bias in financial reporting.

Accounting Method Choice

Although GAAP provide some consistency in financial reporting across firms, they still allow considerable flexibility. In many situations, management can select from among several acceptable accounting methods. For example, although GAAP require revenue to be recognized upon "substantial completion of the earnings process," different firms may define this as occurring at different points. Depreciation and inventory methods are other examples of management choices in accounting methods.

Accounting Estimates

In addition to determining what accounting methods to use, managers must make estimates to implement those methods. For example, management must estimate the proportion of accounts receivable that will not be collected. At the time this must be done, no one really knows which accounts will not be paid.[8] But, based on historical levels of uncollectibles, an understanding of credit policies, and an analysis of current collection rates, management must make an estimate of the dollar amount that will never be collected. Management also makes estimates in determining depreciable lives of fixed assets and in accruals for certain expenses, such as coupon redemptions, warranty expenses, and inventory obsolescence. The analyst must recognize that this information is based, to a large extent, on estimates.

Accounting Disclosures

GAAP set disclosure rules in addition to accounting methods. These disclosure rules are fairly detailed. However, firms still have some leeway in deciding exactly how much information to disclose. In most cases, GAAP prescribe minimum disclosures, and some firms will disclose more information. Firms may choose to provide additional or more detailed information so that investors will realize the full potential of the firm. However, the competitive environment often limits the amount of disclosure a firm will make. Even though a firm may want to tell investors about the potential of a new product, pricing strategy on a key product line, or detailed margin information about profitable items, it cannot tell investors about these matters without also telling competitors. If a disclosure would injure the firm's competitive position, the firm and its shareholders are better off not to make the dis-

---

[8] If they did, they would not have sold any goods to those customers.

A Closer Look

The Enron Bankruptcy

In late 2001, Enron Corporation sought protection from creditors under Chapter 11 of the Bankruptcy Code. In the ensuing months, it was learned that Enron used a vehicle called a special purpose entity (SPE) to keep billions of dollars of debt off its balance sheet. Although keeping debt off the balance sheet with SPEs is acceptable under GAAP, the way Enron structured these transactions appears to have violated GAAP.

Were there any red flags for investors? Although Enron was not the only company to use the techniques it did, there were some reasons for investors to be concerned. First, Enron's corporate structure was extremely complicated. Investors who did not want to invest in companies they could not understand had good reason to avoid Enron. Second, Enron had significant related party transactions. Related party transactions can be problematic because they are not necessarily done at arm's length, raising the possibility of overstated earnings or asset values. Third, the reported results may have been too good to be true. David Frank, a pension fund manager at Holland Capital Management, sold all his clients' Enron holdings by December 2000 because he simply did not believe Enron's growth and profitability figures made sense.

It is difficult to detect financial statement manipulation, especially when it is done in small amounts. Nevertheless, the Enron debacle may provide some lessons for the future. Complex corporate structures, related party transactions, and financial performance that is not only outstanding but also difficult to explain, indicate that the analyst should ask questions. In particular, the analyst should seek to understand:

- How the corporate structure works and why the company needed to make it so complicated
- How related party transactions were accounted for and whether any income was recognized on transactions that were not at arm's length
- What economic factors have led to the firm's strong financial performance

closure. At the other extreme, some firms may not want to disclose problems with a particular business line. To avoid highlighting the problem, the firm may report aggregated data so that the problem business is combined with a more profitable business. This firm may keep detailed disclosures to the required minimum. All of these choices affect the content of the firm's financial reporting.

Unraveling Management Distortions

A valuation analysis should be based on the underlying economics of a business. In principle, the result of a valuation should not depend on accounting choices managers make; yet in practice, this may be difficult to achieve.

As this book will cover, there are two basic ways to value a company: a discounted cash flow analysis (or equivalent method) and a multiples analysis. Accounting choices do not affect cash flow, suggesting that the discounted cash flow method will not be affected by accounting distortions. In reality, this is only partly true. Although analysts can always observe historical cash flow, they must forecast future cash flow. They often rely on income statement information to do this. There is no guarantee that their cash flow forecasts will not be influenced by the firm's accounting choices. In analyzing historical results, it is important to be especially aware of accounting choices that may have affected the results.

When analysts value a company using the multiples approach, they must also be careful to consider accounting distortions in earnings. They may restate earnings before using them in the multiples valuation.

The Role of the Auditor

We have said that one of the most important problems in financial reporting is asymmetric information, and the independent auditor is one of the most important solutions. By performing an audit, independent accountants provide a measure of reliability to the resulting reports. They examine the financial statements and determine that the methods the firm has followed are consistent with GAAP. They test the firm's internal control systems to establish that the likelihood of material errors[9] is small. They verify many of the financial statement assertions, such as the value of accounts receivable and cash in the bank and physically observe certain assets. Even if an audit uncovers no material errors, the fact that auditors are reviewing their work makes managers more careful in preparing financial statements.

One role of the auditor is to limit the distortions to financial reporting that arise due to managers' incentives to misstate certain items. These distortions can never be completely eliminated because there are ranges of acceptable estimates and accounting methods. Auditors attest to the reasonableness of the financial statements, not to their perfection.

From time to time there are audit failures. These are instances in which an audit failed to detect a material misstatement or departure from GAAP. Of course, the most notable recent example is Arthur Andersen's audit of Enron. However, there were many audit failures before Enron. Unfortunately, audits are not perfect and there will probably be more audit failures.

1.4 THE LIMITATIONS OF GAAP FOR SECURITY ANALYSIS

Even if management did not have any biases in preparing financial statements and audits never failed, there would be limitations to GAAP. Although GAAP are designed to help make financial statement information useful to investors, the information in financial statements does not always achieve this goal. GAAP are determined under a formal process that encourages many constituents to voice their opinions about proposed accounting standards. These constituencies include firms subject to GAAP reporting rules, security analysts, regulators, practicing accountants, credit analysts, employees, and academics. Each group has a different perspective, and the FASB's final decision may be a compromise intended to address the major concerns of each constituent group. The result is not necessarily financial statements that are ideal from the perspective of any particular group, such as security analysts.

Our primary goal in this book is valuation. GAAP are not perfect for our purposes, because financial statements were not designed solely for our use. In general, there are two differences

---

[9]An error is material if, given the circumstances, it is likely that a reasonable investor's judgment would be affected by the error.

A CLOSER LOOK

Is Regulation Necessary?

In the United States and most other developed economies, a governmental body such as the SEC or an independent private sector organization such as the FASB sets accounting standards. The government generally mandates audits of publicly held firms. Although these seem like reasonable rules to reduce the asymmetric information problem, whether these requirements are necessary is a matter subject to ongoing debate. Many financial professionals argue that firms should be free to determine their own accounting conventions and hire or not hire auditors as they see fit. Investors, who are free to invest or not invest, could make their decisions based on, among other things, whether the accounting disclosures are adequate and a respected auditor has attested to the financial statements.

Despite the debate, accounting standards and mandated audits are a fact of most well-developed capital markets. And, although there would undoubtedly still be a demand for independent audits and high-quality accounting disclosures even if they were not mandated, it is not clear that the disclosures or audits would be as complete as they are today.

between financial reporting rules and valuation analysis requirements that limit the usefulness of GAAP. First, important information may not be available under GAAP. Second, information may be available, but not presented in the same format as is required to do a valuation analysis.

Necessary Information Not Available Under GAAP

When the information we need to do a valuation is not provided in financial statements, we have to try to find it from other sources. For example, with few exceptions, GAAP financial statements are accounts of historical transactions. They tell us about the past. Valuation, on the other hand, is forward looking. When valuing an equity security, the analyst is interested in the value of the firm today, given what he or she thinks will happen in the future. The historical financial statements do not tell the analyst what to expect for the future, yet this is precisely the analyst's interest. Although this aspect of GAAP financial statements makes them imperfect for valuation, they still provide important information for valuations. An astute analyst knows how to use historical financial information as one input to help predict the future and estimate value, and how to acquire additional information elsewhere.

GAAP largely relies on a historical cost basis for financial statements. Although historical cost helps ensure consistency and conservatism in reporting, it may not always provide the information the analyst would like. For example, suppose a company has an investment in land. As part of the valuation, the analyst wants to determine the value of the land. Unfortunately, historical cost reporting shows the land at its original cost (or lower if it has decreased in value). The analyst needs to go to another source to determine the land's current value if it has increased. In determining values for elements of a business, analysts must understand that financial statement book values are often not good estimates of fair values or current values. Finally, financial statements provide mainly financial data. Nonfinancial information, qualitative data, industry information, and other important information must be found outside the financial reports.

Information Not in Appropriate Format

As we will see in this book, each valuation model requires the forecast of a specific performance measure. These measures are not the same as the financial statement items disclosed under GAAP. This does not mean GAAP financial statements are useless. Rather, to extract the information that is available in GAAP financial statements and use it properly, it is critical to be able to reorganize it for the particular model we are using.

GAAP financial statements focus on earnings, financial position, and cash flow in a prescribed format. The format and the accounting rules help achieve consistency. But the analyst is sometimes interested in financial measures other than earnings, or definitions of cash flow that differ from those in GAAP. For example, the most commonly used valuation technique is the free cash flow model. The definition of cash flow in this model is not equal to any component of the GAAP cash flow statement. To transform the GAAP financial statements into this information, analysts must thoroughly understand how GAAP statements are constructed so they can adjust them for their own use.

1.5 A LOOK AT SECURITY ANALYSIS IN PHASES

We examine security analysis in four phases: business analysis, financial statement analysis, forecasting, and valuation. Exhibit 1.2 shows each of these phases and their relationships to each other. Although we present these phases sequentially, in reality they need not follow a strict sequence. For example, business analysis and financial statement analysis may be done in either order or even concurrently.

Business Analysis

The first phase of security analysis is **business analysis**, in which the analyst tries to understand the key business drivers affecting the firm. The analyst will need to understand the internal environment of the firm, such as the firm's mission, products and services, pricing, marketing and selling strategies, manufacturing, research and development, distribution processes, financial health, and the human resource issues. To do this, the analyst collects much information about the firm.

EXHIBIT 1.2   A Picture of the Security Analysis Process

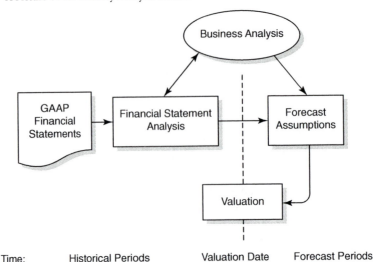

Of course, the analyst will focus significant attention on understanding the financial health of the firm. This will continue in the financial statement analysis phase. In this phase, the analyst will study the firm's accounting methods and choices, margin and capital structure, profitability, cash flow, and investment priorities.

Understanding how the external environment affects the firm is also important. Here the analyst attempts to understand the industry's economics and the firm's competitors and customers. Here are some issues to consider:

- Does the firm operate in an industry with many small players, or a few very large players, such as the computer software industry?
- What are the barriers to entering this industry?
- Will there be new competitors entering in the future?
- What are the growth prospects for the industry?
- Who are the firm's competitors and what are their products and strategies?
- Who are the key customers and how do they affect the firm's prospects?
- Are there regulations that affect the business operations?

Successful business analysis relies on the analyst's ability to understand all aspects of the internal and external environment of the business.

Financial Statement Analysis

The second phase of security analysis is **financial statement analysis**. In this phase, the analyst uses the historical financial statements to learn about the firm's profitability, growth, and resource needs. We attempt to understand the interrelationships between all of the financial variables of the entity, using historical data to understand the business dynamics of the firm and to consider how these relationships might change in the future. An important element of financial statement analysis is **accounting analysis**. In accounting analysis, we consider the entity's accounting policies and how its estimates, accounting choices, and judgments affect the reported numbers. We must strip away any management distortions in the financial statements. This is sometimes called a quality of earnings analysis, but we use a more general term, *accounting analysis*, because it pertains to all of the financial statements and disclosures. As part of this work, the analyst often recasts the financial statements in a format that is more closely aligned with a particular analytical framework than the GAAP financial statements. This may include adjusting the financial statements to exclude items that are not likely to recur and include items the GAAP framework ignores.

Exhibit 1.3 illustrates how accounting analysis is like peeling an onion. At the core of our analysis is the underlying economics of the firm. Financial statements allow us to see only the outside layer. As we learn more about the firm's accounting methods and choices, we get closer to understanding the business's economics.

The first two phases of security analysis, business analysis and financial statement analysis, are closely linked and either can be done first. The analyst may start with financial statement analysis, then do some of the business analysis, and then do further financial statement analysis. The results of the financial statement analysis will help the analyst understand the key business drivers. This will be included in the business analysis. The business analysis will highlight certain business drivers or risks that may be further analyzed in the financial statement analysis. For example, suppose that the analyst was studying the industry during the business analysis and determined that new price-based competitors would likely enter the market. The analyst might go back to the financial statement

EXHIBIT 1.3   Accounting Analysis

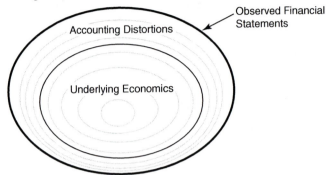

analysis to study further the effect this might have on the firm's profitability. Together, the business analysis and financial statement analysis provide the information the analyst needs to understand the business and to begin to project it into the future.

Forecasting

The third phase of security analysis is **forecasting**. In this phase, the analyst uses the information gathered about the business in the previous phases to predict financial results in the future. This requires a very thorough understanding of both the business environment and the entity. Depending on the valuation technique selected, the analyst may forecast different parts of the financial statements or financial ratios into the future. For example, in a free cash flow model, the analyst projects each component of "free cash flow," from sales through reinvestment requirements. He or she will use ratios such as the sales growth rate, operating margins, and investment to sales to construct the forecast. In another model, the residual income model, the analyst quantifies the same forecast of the future with a different set of variables. Although many of the same ratios used to build the forecast in the residual income model are also used in the free cash flow model, additional elements will enter into the residual income forecast.

Valuation

The fourth phase of security analysis is **valuation**. In valuation, the analyst uses the forecast and a valuation model to determine a value for the firm's equity. Many valuation methods are available. In this book, we will explore five variations of discounted cash flow models (dividend discount, flows to equity, free cash flow, adjusted present value, and residual income). Given consistent assumptions, each of these models produces the same value. Although the five models are theoretically equivalent, certain models are easier to implement than others are in particular circumstances. We will also examine multiples valuation, a popular valuation technique.

SUMMARY

Many people do security analysis. Buy-side analysts, sell-side analysts, investment bankers, corporate finance specialists, merger and acquisition analysts, venture capitalists, individual investors, and employees use security analysis to make investment decisions. These people use company data, such as financial statements and related disclosures, to prepare their analyses. They also use external data such as stock analyst reports, newspaper and magazine articles, competitive and customer data, industry data, and even industry experts to study the firm.

Analysts rely on GAAP financial reports, and they need to understand that this information is not perfect. Analysts must consider the many factors influencing these reports such as regulators, management, and auditors. Management can significantly influence reporting through accounting method choices, estimates, judgments, and biases. Furthermore, GAAP statements do not always include the information needed for security analysis. Even when the reports include the needed information, the analyst must often reorganize the data into a format appropriate for security analysis.

Analysts use four phases in their security analysis. In the business analysis, the analyst tries to understand the key business drivers of the firm. In financial statement analysis, the analyst uses historical financial statements to learn more about the firm's profitability, growth, and resource needs. The analyst also tries to understand the interrelationships of the financial variables. In the forecasting phase, the analyst uses the information collected in the prior phases to predict results in the future. The analyst uses these future projections in the valuation phase to determine a value for the firm's equity.

REVIEW QUESTIONS

1. A friend who is interested in doing equity security analysis would like to know what kind of jobs are available. Describe each of the possible jobs in which he might do equity security analysis.

2. What is the difference between a buy-side analyst and a sell-side analyst?

3. In addition to annual reports, what other sources would an analyst use to get information on a company?

4. A new financial analyst is reviewing an annual report. He says, "This financial report has a clean audit opinion, so I can use it in my analysis and be sure that the financial results are accurate." Respond to this comment.

5. Which regulators influence financial reporting? How does their work affect security analysis?

6. What is the asymmetric information problem? What has been done in the United States to reduce this problem?

7. Explain the three ways managers influence financial reporting. How does this affect how the analyst uses financial reporting in valuation?

8. Two firms with very similar transactions report very different financial statements. How can this happen? Provide an example.

9. What challenges do GAAP financial statements provide to the equity security analyst?

10. Provide three examples of data that an analyst might need in preparing a valuation that are not included in a financial report.

11. What is the primary objective of generally accepted accounting principles?

12. Explain the differing goals of GAAP reporting and valuation. How does this affect the analyst?

13. Describe the four phases of security analysis.

PROBLEMS

1. Generally accepted accounting principles provide rules for preparing financial statements and therefore have a great influence on financial reporting. When a firm is audited, the audit itself also affects the financial statements as the auditors provide a check on whether GAAP have been followed. Although GAAP and audits provide some rigor around financial statements, management's accounting method choices, management's accounting estimates, and management's disclosure decisions also influence financial statements. Describe the influence of these factors on the financial statements. Be sure to provide a detailed example of how each factor could influence one or more specific financial statements.

2. You are an equity security analyst assigned to analyze and value The Vermont Teddy Bear Company, Inc. Vermont Teddy Bear designs, manufactures, and sells teddy bears and related products. Over 85% of the company's sales come from its Bear-Gram service, which sends personalized bears to recipients for special occasions such as birthdays, weddings, Christmas, and Valentine's Day. The company sells a variety of bears and outfits for the bears. Consumers can order via a toll-free number or through the company's Web site. Vermont Teddy Bear also has a small retail factory store business and a small corporate/wholesale business. (*Source:* The Vermont Teddy Bear Company, Inc. annual report and 10-K for the year ended June 30, 2000.)

Prepare an outline showing what you plan to do in your analysis of The Vermont Teddy Bear Company. Be sure to cover each of the four phases of security analysis. If you need more information, access the company's SEC filings at **www.sec.gov**.

3. Suppose there is a proposal before the Securities and Exchange Commission that would eliminate the requirement that public companies be audited.

a. You are a lobbyist representing an industry group that wants audits no longer to be mandated. Draft a letter to the Securities and Exchange Commission explaining why audits should not be required.

b. You are the chief lobbyist for an organization of accounting professionals. Your organization opposes the proposal to eliminate mandated audits. Draft a letter to the Securities and Exchange Commission explaining your position.

 ## My Case

This is the first of a series of exercises in which you will prepare an analysis and valuation of a publicly traded company. Select a company for this project. Familiarize yourself with this company by accessing its Web site and getting and reviewing its annual report.

2

 Where We Have Been:

In the first chapter, we introduced the jobs of the various professionals who do security analysis and presented a framework for security analysis.

 Where We Are:

In this chapter, we discuss the goal of security analysis, introduce the concept of an efficient securities market, and discuss the implications of market efficiency for security prices. This chapter provides the background needed to understand the various valuation methods used in security analysis.

 Where We Are Going:

In Chapters 3 through 5, we will study business and financial statement analysis. We then move on to specific valuation techniques.

Security Analysis and Efficient Markets

LEARNING OBJECTIVES:

After studying this chapter, you will understand:

- The goal of security analysis.

- The concept of an efficient securities market and the differences between weak-form, semistrong-form, and strong-form efficient markets.

- The implications of an efficient market on the behavior of security prices.

- The key role investors play in an efficient market.

- What creates comparative advantage in security analysis.

- How investors' beliefs about efficient markets determine their style of investment analysis.

- The recent empirical evidence on efficient markets.

This chapter covers the goal of security analysis and the concept of an efficient market. These two subjects are closely related. Security analysis is an attempt to earn higher-than-average returns, whereas the efficient market hypothesis argues that this is not possible. Section 2.1 covers the goal of security analysis, whereas Section 2.2 explains the meaning of efficient markets and the three levels of efficiency. After this preparation, Section 2.3 covers the implications of efficient markets on the behavior of security prices, and Section 2.4 reviews the role of the investor in an efficient market. In Section 2.5, we discuss the implications of market efficiency for security analysis. Section 2.6 covers the empirical evidence about efficient markets.

2.1 GOAL OF SECURITY ANALYSIS

The ultimate goal of security analysis is to increase the returns[1] that an investor is able to earn. Successful security analysis identifies securities that are likely to have future stock returns above the returns of other equity securities of similar risk. This analysis also spots securities that are likely to have returns below that level. Assuming that incorrectly priced securities will eventually reach their true values, security analysis boils down to identifying securities that are priced higher or lower than their "true value." As a result, security analysis focuses on valuation. Successful security analysis allows us to earn above-market returns by investing in firms that are priced below their true values and reaping the rewards when the prices reach their correct values. Similarly, good analysis reveals which stocks are selling at too high a price, so we can avoid them or sell them short.[2]

The purpose of security analysis is to increase our investment returns. How high do these returns have to be for our analysis to be successful? The benchmark to beat is the return that we could have earned over the same period without doing any analysis. In most other endeavors in life, making no effort leads to extremely poor results. In investing, however, we can turn in an average performance without doing any work at all. By buying and holding a diversified portfolio or a mutual fund, we can generally earn very close to the market average return. (That is not too bad for no effort.) If we put significant effort and cost into security analysis and still earn the average market return, what is the point? So, the goal of security analysis is to beat the average market return.

By making the goal of security analysis to beat the average market return, we have set an extremely high hurdle to clear. Earning superior returns requires that we select undervalued securities. However, the **efficient market hypothesis** argues that securities are always priced correctly. If the efficient market hypothesis is true, then no one can earn consistently higher returns than the market average. Indeed, the efficient market hypothesis explains much of the behavior of security prices, and investing strategies that earn consistently above-market returns are extremely rare. Most mutual funds, which are managed by highly trained, experienced professionals, fail even to meet broad market averages consistently, let alone beat them. Thus, successful security analysis is a challenge.

Still, there is hope. There is growing evidence of "pockets of inefficiencies." Many researchers now believe that, even if security prices are correct most of the time, on occasion there are mispricings in the market. An analyst who is able to identify and trade on these mispricings will earn returns

---

[1] For a given level of risk.

[2] "Selling short" means selling borrowed shares of stock. The short seller hopes to profit from a decline in stock price by first selling borrowed shares when the stock price is high and later purchasing shares at a lower price, using those shares to replace the borrowed shares.

above the market average, or **abnormal returns**. To succeed, however, the analyst must be smarter than most everyone else or be faster to react to information than most everyone else or act more cost effectively than most everyone else.

2.2 WHAT IS AN EFFICIENT SECURITIES MARKET?

To evaluate whether a market is efficient, we must first specify an information set. A securities market is **efficient** with respect to a set of information *if prices in the market reflect that information.* For example, we can talk about a stock market being efficient with respect to corporate earnings announcements. This means that a security's price reflects the information you could discern about its value from earnings announcements. Similarly, a football betting market may be efficient with respect to player injury reports. This means that the point spread reflects the information you could discern about the outcome of the game from injury reports.

In an efficient market, prices react immediately and correctly to an update of the information. This generally requires that information is widely and cheaply available and that market participants understand it. There are no limits to investors' access to the information or their abilities to interpret it. When a corporate earnings announcement is made, the stock price in an efficient market reacts quickly and correctly to the announcement. Similarly, if the starting quarterback breaks his collarbone in practice on Wednesday, the point spread in an efficient market adjusts immediately.

Eugene Fama[3] proposed three levels of market efficiency, and these definitions are still widely used today. These are weak-form, semistrong-form, and strong-form efficiency. These levels are based on increasingly broad information sets.

- A market is **weak-form efficient** if market prices reflect all past stock price information. That is, the current price incorporates any relevant information from past prices, such as patterns, volatility, and trading volume.

- A market is **semistrong-form efficient** if prices reflect all publicly available information. In such a market, prices incorporate not only past price information but also corporate earnings announcements, security analyst reports, newspaper articles, implications of announcements by competitors, SEC filings, Internet postings, rumors, and so on.

- A **strong-form efficient** market is one in which market prices reflect all information, whether public or private. In addition to all the information incorporated in price in a semistrong-form efficient market, prices in a strong-form efficient market also reflect information that may be known to only a handful of insiders.

Exhibit 2.1 provides examples of the information in each of the three information sets above and the relationships among them. The inner circle represents prior stock price information, including prior price patterns, trading volume, and any other public stock price and volume information directly related to a stock's trading activity. It excludes information that is not directly related to trading in stock, such as earnings announcements and dividend announcements. A market is weak-form efficient if security prices reflect all the information in this circle. The outer circle represents all public information. In addition to the information in the inner circle, this also includes public information that is not related directly to the trading activity in a firm's stock. Earnings announcements and

---

[3]See Eugene F. Fama, "Efficient Capital Markets: A Review of Theory and Empirical Work," *Journal of Finance* 25 (1970):383–417.

EXHIBIT 2.1 Fama's Information Sets

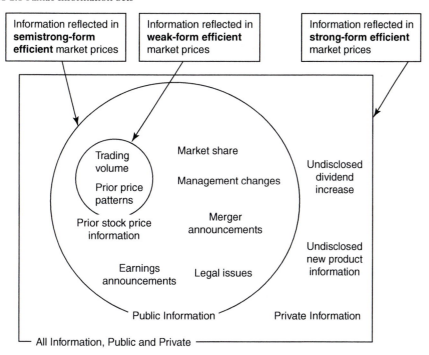

merger announcements are examples of information included in this circle that is not part of the inner circle. If security prices reflect all the information in this circle, the market is semistrong-form efficient. Note that if a market is semistrong-form efficient, it is also weak-form efficient because the outer circle includes the inner circle. Finally, the rectangle includes all information in the circles, plus all other information about a firm that has not been publicly disseminated, such as inside information about future dividend payments, new products, and so on. Prices in a strong-form efficient market reflect all this information. A strong-form efficient market would also be semistrong-form and weak-form efficient.

The market could be efficient with respect to some, but not all, of the information in a particular information set. For example, earnings and merger announcements are both public information, and semistrong-form efficiency would mean the market reacts efficiently to both these announcements, as well as to any other public information. However, the market could react efficiently to one of these announcements, say merger announcements, but not the other. In this case, the market would not be semistrong-form efficient because it does not react efficiently to all public information. Once again, we can only evaluate the efficiency of the market relative to a particular information set.

2.3 IMPLICATIONS OF AN EFFICIENT MARKET FOR THE BEHAVIOR OF SECURITY PRICES

We now understand the definition of market efficiency, but we also need to understand the implications of market efficiency for our work in security analysis.

Definition of Market Efficiency versus Implications of Market Efficiency

A common misconception is that an efficient market is *defined* to be one in which future stock returns are not predictable or in which prices fluctuate randomly. That is not the case. As seen in Section 2.2, we define efficiency in terms of the kind of information incorporated in price. An *implication* of this definition is that future price movements will be unpredictable; that is, they will *appear* to fluctuate randomly. Why? Prices constantly reflect expectations for the future. As those expectations change, so do prices. However, if the expectations are always unbiased, as market efficiency implies, then they are just as likely to be raised as lowered when new information arrives. Therefore, the change in expectations is unpredictable and, as a result, so are price changes. Price is unpredictable because the information causing price movements is unpredictable. However, price changes are not really random. They are caused by the arrival of unpredictable information.

For example, consider a security that will pay $1 for each of 100 coin tosses that turns up heads. The value of the security at the end of the 100 tosses will be between $0 and $100, with an expected value of $50 before the first toss is made. Suppose investors may trade this security at any time. For simplicity, further assume that all investors are risk-neutral, meaning they do not require an additional expected return to incur risk. Before the first toss, the security should trade for $50, its expected value. We will now consider how the price of this security will fluctuate after each toss, assuming the market is efficient with respect to the publicly known results of all the prior tosses.

After the first toss, the expected value of the security will differ from its initial expected value of $50. If the first toss is "heads," the expected value of the security will be $50.50 ($1 for the first heads rolled plus 99 remaining rolls times the 50% chance each will be heads times $1 for each head).[4] If it is "tails," the expected value will be $49.50 (99 × $1 × 0.5). Because we have assumed the market is efficient with respect to past tosses, the price of the security should be updated to the new expected value. So, the price moves from $50.00 to $50.50 if heads are tossed, and from $50.00 to $49.50 if tails are tossed.

Prior to the first toss, it is impossible to predict how the price will change after the first toss. Even though we could not predict the price movement before the toss, the price did not really fluctuate randomly. It reacted immediately to the information in the first toss, which changed the expected value of the security.

After the second toss, the price will be $49, $50, or $51, depending on whether there have been zero, one, or two heads. Again, the price would move to the updated expected value of the security that is revealed by the second toss. Just as in the first toss, an investor evaluating the investment before the second toss cannot predict how price will change. If the first toss were heads, the price after the second toss would be either $50 or $51. If the first toss were tails, the price after the second toss would be either $49 or $50.

The process continues until all 100 tosses are completed. Exhibit 2.2 shows one possibility for the series of tosses. Looking at the prices in the last column, we see that they appear to be random, but are actually based on the information in the prior rolls.

Exhibit 2.3 is the security's **price path**, the graph that results when prices are plotted after each flip. The market in our example is at least weak-form efficient because any information in past prices that might inform us about the value of the security is already reflected in the price of the security. Suppose you were given Exhibit 2.2 after the first 10 tosses and asked what you thought the value of

---

[4]The expected value of future rolls is equal to the number of rolls multiplied by the probability of rolling heads multiplied by the amount of winnings for each head. After the first roll, to get the total expected value we must add the existing winnings to the expected value of future rolls.

EXHIBIT 2.2 One Possible Outcome for 100 Coin Tosses

Toss	Result	Cumulative Heads	Expected Future Heads	Efficient Price
0		0	50.0	$50.00
1	H	1	49.5	$50.50
2	H	2	49.0	$51.00
3	T	2	48.5	$50.50
4	H	3	48.0	$51.00
5	T	3	47.5	$50.50
6	T	3	47.0	$50.00
7	T	3	46.5	$49.50
8	T	3	46.0	$49.00
9	H	4	45.5	$49.50
10	T	4	45.0	$49.00
.	.	.	.	.
.	.	.	.	.
.	.	.	.	.
99	H	53	0.5	$53.50
100	T	53	0.0	$53.00

the security was going to be. You would infer from each of the price movements the number of heads that have been thrown (4) based on the number of upward price movements. You would infer from this that the expected value of the security is $49 ($4 + 90 × 0.50 × $1). This value is also the price, so you would be unable to profit from the information. Further, any other analysis you might do on the pattern of past returns would be of no value, because it could not accurately tell you whether the price of the security would rise or fall in the future.

This market is also semistrong-form efficient, because in addition to the price-related public information, the nonprice public information (the history of tosses) is also reflected in the price of the security. You could obtain the history of the first 10 tosses and infer from this that the expected value of the security is $49. However, because the price reacted to the information in each coin toss immediately and completely as it was made, the price is equal to the expected value, and no profits are possible.

EXHIBIT 2.3 Price Path of Coin Toss Security

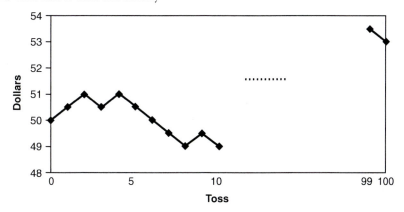

A CLOSER LOOK

Price Movements in a Political Futures Market

The University of Iowa's Tippie Graduate School of Business operates the Iowa Electronic Market (IEM). This is a real-money electronic market that trades contracts whose payoffs are based on, among other things, election outcomes. Examined here are the stock price movements in the McCain Nomination contracts, one of the contracts trading on the IEM during the presidential primary elections in the spring of 2000. The McCain contracts would have paid $1 each if Senator John McCain had won the Republican nomination and nothing otherwise. As one might expect, the price at which these contracts traded fluctuated with the senator's prospects. The McCain contracts began trading on November 12, 1999. The price of the contract fluctuated over the next two months, trading between 13 cents and 25 cents each. Exhibit 2.4 shows the daily closing prices for these contracts.

EXHIBIT 2.4 McCain Nomination Contract Prices

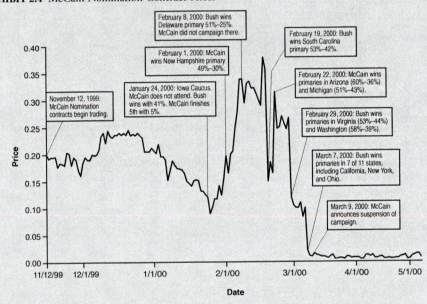

Sources: Contract prices are from the Iowa Electronic Market; election results are from **www.cnn.com**.

What is seen in the prices of the McCain contracts is an efficient market at work. There were major price movements when information arrived to suggest that the price of the security should be different from what it was. As unexpected good news for McCain's prospects came in, such as the large New Hampshire victory and the comeback in Michigan after the South Carolina defeat, the contracts increased in price very quickly. As bad news came in, such as the March 7 "Super Tuesday" defeat, the contracts quickly lost value. News items that had little or no impact on investors' perceptions about the likely outcome of the nominating process, such as the results in Iowa and Delaware, had little effect on contract prices.

Market Efficiency and Inference About Future Information

Before we leave the coin toss example, we will change the underlying assumptions a little bit to make one more point about semistrong-form efficiency. A semistrong-form efficient market is one in which prices reflect not only all public information per se but also everything that you can infer from that information. Let us say, for example, that we announce that the coin is double-sided. It has either two heads or two tails, but initially no one knows which. Therefore, the type of coin (double heads or double tails) is not public information. There is a 50–50 chance that it is double heads or double tails. The efficient price before the first toss is still $50, because this is the expected value of the security.

Suppose the first toss is heads. The efficient price is now $100.00, not $50.50 as it was in the original example. The reason is that after the first toss is heads, we know that the coin is double heads. We can now infer that the next 99 tosses also will be heads, even before these tosses are made and the results are announced. So, the expected value of the security, using all the information that we have, is $100.00. We inferred what the future tosses will be from the first toss.

If the price moved only to $50.50, it would not reflect all the available information, even though the market reacted to the toss. The market would have failed to infer from the available information what the future information was going to be. As a result, astute investors could predict future returns. They could purchase the security at $50.50, confident that the future returns would be positive as the price eventually moved to $100.00.

This example is similar to circumstances that we find in real markets. Information that is released on one date often should change our expectations for future information. For example, positive earnings surprises in one quarter are often followed by positive earnings surprises in the following quarter. After a positive earnings surprise, the price in an efficient market should reflect not only the higher earnings in the current quarter but also the increased likelihood of higher earnings in future quarters. If the price does not reflect this increased likelihood, then the market is not efficient.

Unpredictable Future Returns versus Random Prices

If future prices are unpredictable using available information, prices will *appear* to fluctuate randomly when analyzed against that information. For example, there was no way to relate future price movements in the original coin toss example to any past tosses. Based on such an analysis, future prices appear to be random. However, future prices did not really fluctuate randomly. Instead, they reacted to new information that deviated from the prior expectation.

Consider what would happen if prices really did fluctuate randomly. Truly random prices would move without regard to relevant information or changed expectations. Such a market is not efficient because prices do not reflect relevant information. Of course, such a market should not exist. Why? Because in that market, investors could profit by buying stocks that have fallen in price for no particular reason, and shorting stocks that have risen for no particular reason.

In the coin toss market, for example, a random fluctuation after a heads toss to any price other than $50.50 would create a mispricing. Astute investors would recognize this mispricing and try to profit from it by buying (shorting) the security if the price were below (above) $50.50. If enough investors recognized this mispricing and tried to make money from it, they would bid the price up if it were below $50.50 and down if it were above that point. Eventually the price would revert to the appropriate level. The price would then reflect the relevant information ("heads" on the first toss) and the price would again be efficient. Thus, at least in theory, a market whose prices are unrelated to relevant information about the underlying values of securities is not sustainable.

EXHIBIT 2.5 The Role of Investors in an Efficient Market

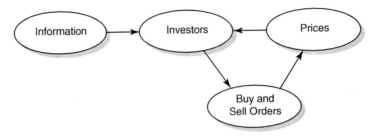

2.4 THE ROLE OF INVESTORS IN AN EFFICIENT MARKET

We have seen that an inefficient market, one that ignores relevant information, is not sustainable. However, is an efficient market sustainable? To answer that, let us consider *how* an efficient market gets to be efficient. What mechanism forces prices to their efficient levels? Investors gather information and, based on that information, they assess whether the price for a particular security is appropriate. If it is not, they place buy or sell orders. If there is a preponderance of investors wishing to buy, there is an order imbalance and the price increases. If more want to sell, the order imbalance causes the price to fall. After the price moves, investors reevaluate the relationship between price and their desire for the security. The process continues until investors believe the price is correct. Exhibit 2.5 illustrates how investors force prices to their correct levels.

We saw this process in the coin toss example. Investors observed the tosses and, based on the results, determined the "correct" price of the security. Had the price been above or below that level, they would have placed buy or sell orders to profit from the difference. As enough investors did this, order imbalances would occur in the market, and the price would adjust until the buy and sell orders were balanced. By finding, interpreting, and trading on information, these investors played a critical role in making the market efficient.

Yet finding information, analyzing it, and executing trades are costly activities, so in a truly efficient market, no one would ever do those things. In a truly efficient market, price and true value would always be equal, so all investors would expect to earn the same return no matter how hard they worked. As a result, investors would have no incentive to incur costs to try to do better, and no one would undertake security analysis. But without investors doing security analysis, mispricings would never be corrected, because the mechanism that corrects them would no longer exist. Thus, prices would not reflect relevant information. They would simply fluctuate randomly. This, in turn, would draw investors into the market to try to exploit mispricings. Thus, there is a paradox in the efficient market hypothesis because neither an efficient market nor an inefficient market is sustainable.[5]

How can we resolve this paradox? We do so by considering investors to be an integral part of the market's functioning. Investors will seek out information as long as there is enough inefficiency to cover their costs of doing so. We should expect markets to have *some* mispricing and therefore some abnormal returns from which astute investors can profit. Those returns should accrue to the investors who most quickly and cost effectively uncover and act on the mispricings. Their actions not only earn them profits but also force prices back toward their efficient levels.

---

[5]This argument is developed formally in S. Grossman and J. Stiglitz, "On the Impossibility of Informationally Efficient Markets," *American Economics Review* 70 (1980):393–408.

Since we expect markets to have some mispricing, a perfectly efficient market should not exist, even in theory. Still, the concept of an efficient market is a useful benchmark. Comparing a market to perfect efficiency can determine the extent to which a particular market is efficient. This is much like the concept of energy efficiency in gas furnaces. Energy efficiency is the percentage of the energy in the gas that is released into the home, rather than lost out the chimney or in unburned fuel. A 100% energy efficient furnace cannot exist, but the concept still provides a useful comparison to real furnaces, which might be labeled as 90% efficient, 95% efficient, and so on. Similarly, a market with less mispricing is "more efficient" because it comes closer to the ideal market in which prices are always correct.

2.5 IMPLICATIONS OF MARKET EFFICIENCY FOR SECURITY ANALYSIS

The implications of an efficient securities market for an analyst or investor are profound. If a market reflects a certain piece of information, then no one can profit from knowledge of that information. If, for example, the information indicates the price of a stock should be high, the price will be high. Thus, the investor in an efficient market is always doomed to pay a fair price, a high price when it should be high and a low one when it should be low, even if he or she has knowledge of all relevant information. When investors pay a fair price, their expected return is a **normal return**. Of course, investors will undoubtedly do better or worse than a normal return on any particular investment. They are likely to attribute worse-than-the-market returns to bad luck and better-than-the-market returns to incredible acumen. In an efficient market, however, the true determinants are bad luck and good luck. In the long run, investors will earn only a normal return, one that compensates them for the use of money (interest component) and the assumption of risk (risk component).

Because U.S. securities markets are highly efficient, it will be difficult for many, and impossible for most, to beat the market. The fact that a securities market can only approach efficiency, and only with the aid of investors and analysts finding information and trading on it, suggests that profitable analysis is possible. The questions are, who is likely to be able to earn abnormal returns, and how can they do it?

Security Analysis and Comparative Advantage

The concept of comparative advantage is common in microeconomics. Comparative advantage suggests that firms will operate in areas in which they have an advantage relative to others. The same is true of security analysts. This fact has two implications. First, security analysis will be done primarily by those who have some advantage, whereas those without any advantage will be passive investors, holding mutual funds, index funds, or their own diversified portfolios. Second, analysts will do whatever kind of analysis gives them a comparative advantage. Some sources of comparative advantage follow.

- *Faster access to data.* The first investor to obtain information is in a better position to exploit it than those who receive it later. Once a sufficient number of investors are trading on the information, the price will begin to correct. The first to trade can take a position before the price has completely corrected.

- *Superior ability to analyze data, due either to understanding of markets and firms or to ability to use statistical techniques.* Someone with years of experience in a particular industry might

EXHIBIT 2.6 Investor Beliefs and Security Analysis

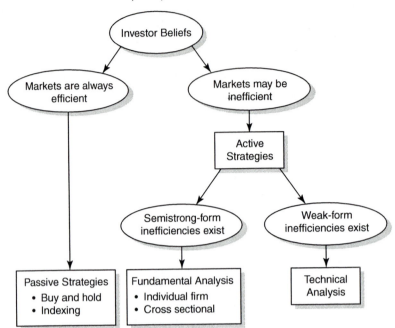

have superior insights about that industry and how certain events are likely to affect it. This person would be in a position to exploit information that others could not, because the others do not see all the implications of the information. Similarly, an analyst with a highly technical, statistical background might use complex statistical analyses to look for data that are good predictors of future stock returns. An analyst having the ability to unravel distortions in management's financial statements would have a distinct advantage. In all these cases, the analyst's advantage can be likened to knowing that the coin in the coin-flipping example is weighted and thus being able to infer what will happen on future tosses before anyone else does.

- *Lower transaction costs.* Transaction costs limit an investor's ability to exploit a mispricing. An investor with lower transaction costs will be able to exploit smaller mispricings, after others have found it unprofitable to do so.

- *Ability to keep trading rules proprietary.* Investors often develop **trading rules** that tell them when to buy or sell a stock. If a trading rule becomes well known, others are likely to use it as well, and prices will correct more quickly. For this reason, many investors and analysts try to avoid being too specific about how their trading rules work. Similarly, investors using a trading rule will try to keep their actual trades secret, to avoid having others observe the positions they are taking and copy their strategy.

Security Analysis and Beliefs About Market Efficiency

The kinds of activities an analyst perceives to be most profitable will depend on his or her beliefs about the circumstances in which the market might be inefficient. Exhibit 2.6 shows the relationship between an investor's beliefs and his or her likely approach to investing.

An investor who believes in market efficiency is likely to choose a **passive investment strategy**, one that minimizes implementation costs, because that investor believes he or she will not generate returns above what a passive strategy would earn anyway. Passive investors do not rely on information. Instead, they buy portfolios to satisfy particular risk preferences. An investor who believes the market may be inefficient is more likely to adopt an **active investment strategy**, which attempts to earn higher than normal returns. Such an investor believes that it is possible to find investments whose expected returns exceed the market average. One who believes in weak-form efficiency, but not semistrong-form efficiency, will be inclined to do **fundamental analysis**. This could be an analysis of an individual firm or a cross-sectional analysis of a portfolio of companies, which is the analysis of many stocks to find a characteristic that will identify the stocks that will perform better or worse than others. This is so because the investor believes that information in prior stock prices, but not all other public information, has been incorporated in the current price. Such an investor might use public information other than stock price movements to estimate the value of a particular firm, or search for information that predicts future abnormal returns for portfolios of firms having particular characteristics. Finally, an investor who believes markets are not even weak-form efficient will search for patterns in prior stock price movements that predict future movements. This investor believes that the information in those movements has not been reflected in the current price. This technique of using patterns in prior stock prices is often termed **technical analysis**.

There is good reason for many investors to be passive. Certainly those who believe in efficiency should invest passively. Even if markets are not always efficient, it may be so costly for many investors to obtain and analyze information, that it would be impossible for them to recover their information costs. Still others simply may not have the expertise to embark on an investment program of their own (although many investors are not deterred by this!). For these investors, a strategy of buying and holding a diversified portfolio, or investing in mutual funds or index funds, is also the most appropriate strategy.

For other investors, a more active approach may be appropriate. These investors use the techniques described in this book to estimate the values of firms in which they invest. We note that these investors will not always agree on what the correct valuation of a firm should be. It is for this reason that stock trades occur, as more optimistic investors acquire shares from more pessimistic investors.

2.6 MARKET EFFICIENCY—OVERVIEW OF EMPIRICAL EVIDENCE

What does the empirical evidence say about market efficiency? Academic experts have done significant amounts of research to determine whether mispricings exist. Doing such research is difficult, and the results are open to many interpretations.

It is virtually impossible to test whether a single stock is priced correctly. If we estimate a firm's value to be $50 and it trades at $40, we could interpret the result as due to either a mispricing or erroneous assumptions in our valuation. Further, if the stock later jumps to $50, it does not indicate that we were right. Such a jump could also be explained by changes in the company's prospects or a lucky guess on our part. It is also impossible to test for strong-form efficiency. Strong-form efficiency suggests that private, as well as public, information is reflected in prices. By definition, private information is not observable by the researcher. So, there is no way to know what information should be reflected in price in a strong-form efficient market.

A CLOSER LOOK

Post–Earnings Announcement Drift

A stock price "anomaly" is a case in which a factor appears to predict future stock returns. Such a factor is anomalous because it contradicts the efficient market hypothesis.

One of the best-documented and most robust anomalies is post–earnings announcement drift. This anomaly is that earnings announcements can be used to predict stock returns for nearly a year after an earnings announcement. Ray Ball and Philip Brown first documented this in a classic study published in the *Journal of Accounting Research* in 1968. Since then, dozens of other studies have confirmed that stock returns are predictable using information in an earnings announcement. Investors appear to react very slowly to that information, and abnormal returns drift, or continue in the same direction, for nearly a year after the initial reaction at the earnings announcement.

Although numerous researchers studied post–earnings announcement drift, for many years their focus was on replicating its existence with alternative techniques and data definitions, and confirming its existence in markets not included in the original study. It was not until 1990 that a plausible explanation for post–earnings announcement drift was offered. Vic Bernard and Jacob Thomas argued that investors fail to take into account the typical statistical pattern in earnings when forming their expectations for future earnings announcements. More often than not, good news is followed by more good news and bad news is followed by more bad news. Investors do not seem to use this information, so they are surprised in a way that someone with knowledge of the statistical pattern could predict.

Bernard and Thomas found two compelling results to support their argument. First, a disproportionately large amount of post–earnings announcement drift occurs in a few days around the subsequent earnings announcements. Second, their analysis predicts positive abnormal returns in the three quarters following good news and negative abnormal returns in the fourth quarter after good news, and the opposite pattern after bad news. They found this pattern in average abnormal returns, including the reversal in the fourth quarter.

Research continues to this day into why this apparent inefficiency has not been exploited to the point where it has disappeared.

Because of the difficulty of testing for mispricing of a single stock and for strong-form efficiency, market efficiency research relies on **cross-sectional tests** involving many securities, and it focuses on weak-form and semistrong-form efficiency. These tests examine whether firms with particular characteristics (based on prior price information and/or other public information) are mispriced on average. If they are, then investors who know about the mispricings could predict the returns of stocks based on their characteristics, because the prices will eventually correct. For example, if firms with high price-to-earnings (PE) ratios are overpriced, then their subsequent returns should be below the market average. Similarly, if low-PE firms are underpriced, their subsequent returns should be higher than the market average. These hypotheses can be tested either by grouping firms into portfolios based on their PE ratios and comparing average returns or by regressing returns on the PE ratios.

Cross-sectional tests have found evidence to suggest that there are systematic mispricings of equities in the United States. Further, their magnitude appears to be sufficient to compensate investors, especially institutional investors that incur low costs to gather information, process it, and trade, for the expense of finding and exploiting these mispricings. For example, it has been documented over the last 30 years that abnormal returns of as much as 5% to 6% can be earned over the 9 months following an earnings announcement, based only on the information in the earnings announcement. This is possible because investors appear to react very slowly to the information in those announcements. It has also been shown that such statistics as the PE ratio and the market-to-book ratio are related to subsequent returns. Evidence also shows short-term returns momentum (positive returns follow positive returns) and long-term returns reversals (negative returns follow positive returns). There even appear to be different returns associated with different calendar months, different days of the week, and firm size.

In Exhibit 2.5, we showed how investors, reacting to information, pushed prices toward their efficient level by trading when they perceived prices to be incorrect. We assumed implicitly that investors interpreted the information correctly; that is, their beliefs about the correct price, given the information they observed, were always correct. Suppose their beliefs are not correct. Suppose that there is information that investors are unable to interpret correctly, because of the complexity of the information or the imperfections of the human mind.

If most investors react to information in the same way, prices will reflect their beliefs. If those beliefs are systematically wrong (biased), then mispricings will occur. In the coin toss example, if most investors believed that a head on the first toss increased the probability of subsequent tails so that the expected value of the security was still $50.00, the security would trade at $50.00. An astute investor could profit by buying the security at $50.00 after a head is thrown. Over many such investments, he or she would earn an average of about $0.50 per investment. Although incorrect pricing of such a simple security is unlikely, in the much more complex evaluation of real equities, people's reactions to information could be systematically incorrect, resulting in mispricings and predictable future returns.

There is a growing literature called **behavioral finance** that attempts to explain inefficient prices with psychology. This literature argues that people often make decisions incorrectly. When most people interpret information in the same, incorrect way, prices will reflect those incorrect beliefs. This creates a mispricing that someone with knowledge of the mispricing could exploit.

Still, many highly respected researchers do not believe such inefficiencies exist. They argue that if some investors' errors result in mispricings, then other investors would find these mispricings and trade on them until they disappear. There is no adequate response to this argument.

Researchers who do not believe in inefficiencies also say that relationships between information and subsequent stock returns can be explained by econometric errors or by luck. For example, they would argue a statistic that consistently predicts high future stock returns must be a measure of risk. That is, characteristics that appear to predict higher than average returns consistently may simply indicate securities that are riskier, and the higher returns they earn are nothing more than an additional reward for accepting additional risk.

Some also argue that with enough researchers running enough regressions, something is bound to be associated with stock returns just by chance. Those analyses receive attention, but the thousands that produce no results do not. Those who do not believe that inefficiencies exist think that many documented "inefficiencies" are not inefficiencies at all and it is unlikely these studies will help predict future returns. For example, historically one of the most robust predictors of how the overall stock market will perform in a given year is the winner of the annual Super Bowl, which is played in January and determines the champion of the National Football League. An investor who had the foresight to base an investment strategy on this information over the last 30 years would be extremely wealthy today.[6] Although this is an obvious case of a lucky finding in an instance of no real relationship, it is quite possible that the results documented in the more plausible cases of inefficiency are also products of "torturing the data until it confesses."

---

[6]Buying or shorting the market for the year, depending on the outcome of the Super Bowl, would have outperformed a simple buy and hold strategy by a factor of six.

SUMMARY

Security analysis is the search for equity securities whose expected returns will exceed the overall market's return. This goal is difficult to achieve, largely because of the high degree of efficiency in U.S. security markets. If markets are efficient, then securities are always priced correctly and investors cannot consistently earn better than market returns.

When we call a market efficient, we must define the market as efficient with respect to a set of information. The market is efficient if prices in the market reflect that set of information. Fama defined three levels of market efficiency. A market is weak-form efficient if market prices reflect all past stock price information. A market is semistrong-form efficient if prices reflect all publicly available information. It is strong-form efficient if prices reflect all information, whether public or private.

A common misconception is that an efficient market is defined to be one in which stock prices fluctuate randomly. Efficiency is really about what information is incorporated into security prices. If prices constantly reflect unbiased expectations for the future, as new information arrives and these expectations go up and down, the price will go up and down. These price changes may appear to be random, but they are actually reflecting revisions in expectations for the future.

We see that investors are the mechanism that continually forces prices toward their efficient levels, and this happens only when it is profitable for investors to seek out and trade on information. Thus, markets cannot be perfectly efficient, even in theory. Our goal as security analysts is to use our techniques to search for mispriced securities. Our analysis will be most productive if we focus on those situations in which mispricings are most likely. Empirical evidence suggests these mispricings do exist in the U.S. securities market.

The concept of comparative advantage tells us that firms will operate in areas in which they have an advantage relative to others. Similarly, security analysis is primarily done by those who have such an advantage at it. Faster access to data, superior ability to analyze data, lower transaction costs, and the ability to keep trading rules proprietary are sources of comparative advantage in security analysis. People without such advantages generally should be passive investors, holding mutual funds, index funds, or diversified portfolios.

An investor's view of market efficiency affects his or her likely approach to investing. Investors who believe in market efficiency are apt to choose a passive strategy. Investors who believe that the market may be inefficient are more likely to adopt an active strategy.

SUGGESTED READINGS

Ball, R. and P. Brown. "An Empirical Evaluation of Accounting Income Numbers." *Journal of Accounting Research* 6 (Autumn 1968):159–178.

Bernard, V. and J. Thomas. "Evidence That Stock Prices Do Not Fully Reflect the Implications of Current Earnings for Future Earnings." *Journal of Accounting and Economics* 13 (1990):304–340.

Bernard, V., J. Thomas, and J. Whalen. "Accounting-Based Stock Price Anomalies: Separating Market Inefficiencies from Risk." *Contemporary Accounting Research* 14, 2 (1990):89–136.

Bodie, Z. and R. Merton. *Finance.* Upper Saddle River, NJ: Prentice Hall, 2000.

DeBondt, W. and R. Thaler. "Does the Stock Market Overreact?" *Journal of Finance* 40 (1985):793–805.

Fama, E. "Efficient Capital Markets: A Review of Theory and Empirical Work." *Journal of Finance* 25 (1970):383–417.

Grossman, S. and J. Stiglitz. "On the Impossibility of Informationally Efficient Markets." *American Economic Review* 70 (1980):393–408.

Malkiel, B. *A Random Walk Down Wall Street*, 6th ed. W. W. Norton, 1996.

Thaler, R., ed. *Advances in Behavioral Finance*. New York: Sage Foundation, 1993.

REVIEW QUESTIONS

1. What is the goal of security analysis and why is achieving this goal so difficult?

2. Define the following:
   a. Weak-form efficient market
   b. Semistrong-form efficient market
   c. Strong-form efficient market

3. Respond to this comment: "I believe that the U.S. stock market is efficient. Because it is efficient, the prices fluctuate randomly and cannot be predicted. So, I do not want to invest my savings in the stock market—anything could happen!"

4. How do investors help maintain efficient markets?

5. Explain how transaction costs affect the efficiency of security prices.

6. If markets are efficient, then it is useless to try to beat the market. In this case, no one would research companies to uncover mispriced securities and prices would become inefficient. However, if the market is inefficient, investors will have a reason to do security analysis and in the process will cause prices to become efficient. How can you explain this paradox?

7. Provide three examples of comparative advantage.

8. What is a passive investing strategy? What belief about market efficiency would a passive investor have? Provide an example of the type of investment the passive investor would be likely to make.

9. What is fundamental analysis? What belief about market efficiency would an investor doing fundamental analysis have? Provide an example of the type of investment the fundamental analyst would be likely to make.

10. What is technical analysis? How does technical analysis differ from fundamental analysis?

11. Index funds are popular investments today. An index fund attempts to match a particular broad index's performance. What type of investing strategy do index funds represent? What is an index fund investor likely to believe about market efficiency?

12. Some investors study individual firms. They analyze information from annual reports and news articles and review analyst reports. They hope to buy stock at a price lower than its true value. What belief about market efficiency do these investors have? How do we know this? What type of analysis is this?

PROBLEMS

1. There are three levels of market efficiency: weak-form efficient, semistrong-form efficient, and strong-form efficient. Here is some information about companies in the stock market.

   • Historical stock prices
   • Confidential company long-range plan
   • Public announcements of expected earnings
   • Historical stock trading volume
   • New-product introduction
   • Earnings announcement
   • Internal projections for sales for next five years
   • Undisclosed market test data
   • Announced dividend increase
   • Merger announcement
   • Public announcements of expected earnings
   • Internal memo on potential acquisition
   • Public announcement of management changes
   • Public announcement of downsizing

   a. If a market is weak-form efficient, which of the above information would be reflected in stock prices?
   b. If a market is semistrong-form efficient, which of the above information would be reflected in stock prices?
   c. If a market is strong-form efficient, which of the above information would be reflected in stock prices?

2. A retailer reported the following earnings per share amounts for 2001 and 2002.

	2001	2002
1st quarter	$1.25	$1.30
2nd quarter	$1.37	$1.28
3rd quarter	$1.31	$1.49
4th quarter	$1.81	$2.15

   The seasonal pattern in earnings in 2001 and 2002 is typical for this company, as well as for retailers in general. Do you think the company's stock price shows a similar seasonal pattern?

3. About 50% of all stock recommendations are "buys," whereas 40% are "holds," (neutral) and 10% are "sells." Does the skewness (more "buys" than "sells") of this distribution imply that the stock market as a whole is likely to increase in value?

4. Many investors "average down," meaning that after a stock they hold falls in price, they buy more. As a result, the average purchase price is lowered, and the stock does not have to gain back as much of its loss for the investor to be back to a breakeven position. In an efficient market, is this a sensible strategy?

5. Half of the investors in a market have "round-trip" transaction costs of 1%, meaning it costs 1% of a security's value to complete both a buy and a sell transaction. The other half have transaction costs of 0.2%. How close to "correct" values would you expect market prices to be?

6. The Iowa Electronic Market (IEM) operates a market in contracts whose payoffs depend on the Federal Reserve Board's Federal Open Market Committee (FOMC) meetings. Find the current prices for these contracts on the IEM's Web site (**www.biz.uiowa.edu/iem**). What do these prices tell you about the market's expectation for action at the next FOMC meeting? Why?

7. You have studied how firms' earnings change after large capital expenditures. You found that earnings usually increase substantially after large capital expenditures, because firms tend to make these when they expect strong demand for their products. Based on this finding, you have devised a strategy of buying companies' stocks when they announce major capital expenditures. Will your strategy work in a semistrong-form efficient market? Explain your answer.

8. Some experts believe the U.S. equity security market is efficient, whereas others believe it is not.

   a. Prepare an argument supporting market efficiency.
   b. Prepare an argument refuting market efficiency.

My Case

Obtain a graph of your company's daily stock price over the last three years. You may be able to use a stock charting service such as Bigcharts. You can find links to such services on our textbook Web site, **www.prenhall.com/soffer**. Also identify major news events affecting your company over this period. Relate price movements to these events.

PART II

BUSINESS AND FINANCIAL STATEMENT ANALYSIS

3 Business Analysis

4 Accounting Analysis and the Financial Statements

5 Financial Statement Analysis

3

Where We Have Been:

The first two chapters introduced the four phases of security analysis and the concept of efficient markets.

Where We Are:

In this chapter, we study the first phase of security analysis, business analysis. An in-depth business analysis is key to preparing a valuation. We break our discussion into two parts: external analysis and internal analysis.

Where We Are Going:

Chapters 4 and 5 discuss financial statements and financial statement analysis. Financial statement analysis is the next phase in security analysis and relates closely to the business analysis discussed in this chapter. In later chapters, we will use the insights gained from business analysis and financial statement analysis to forecast future performance and value firms.

Business Analysis

LEARNING OBJECTIVES:

After studying this chapter, you will understand:

- Why business analysis is crucial to security valuation.
- How to prepare an external analysis of the firm.
- How to prepare an internal analysis of the firm.
- Where to get information for business analysis.

In 1983, The Quaker Oats Company was widely praised for its astute analysis when it acquired Gatorade at a very attractive price.[1] Under Quaker's ownership, Gatorade grew from an approximately $100 million regional business to a $1.3 billion global brand in 11 years. In December 1994, Quaker acquired another beverage company, Snapple, for $1.7 billion. Shortly after the Snapple acquisition, Quaker disclosed problems with the Snapple distribution strategy. Observers concluded that Quaker had overestimated Snapple's sales growth and underestimated the complexity of its distribution channel. Two years and four months later, Quaker agreed to sell Snapple for $300 million. In addition to incurring this $1.4 billion loss, Quaker recorded large operating losses and restructuring charges during its two years of ownership.

How could Quaker make such a financially troubling acquisition just a few years after making one of the most successful food acquisitions in history? The Snapple story underscores both the difficulty and the importance of understanding a complex business. Even a major company, familiar with the beverage business and with an excellent acquisition track record, can have problems with business analysis.

The result of a valuation analysis depends entirely on the assumptions used in the valuation model. We make assumptions for projected sales, expenses, capital expenditures, and other items. To achieve a reasonable valuation, we must base these projections on an in-depth, forward-looking understanding of the firm's business and business environment.

We cannot accomplish the necessary level of understanding simply by looking at the firm's historical financial statements. We must study all aspects of the firm and its environment. This is the essence of business analysis, the topic of this chapter. Our goal in business analysis is to learn everything about the business, its industry, and its competitors that might somehow affect the future cash flow of the firm. This is a big task and perhaps the most important step in the valuation process. Without a strong understanding of what will drive the business in the future, even a careful, detailed financial statement analysis will be worthless.

Business analysis calls on skills learned in every one of your business school courses. We want to know about the industry and market outlook, the competitors, the various products, marketing and selling approaches, the human resources, the manufacturing process, purchasing, and the outlook for key ingredients, technology, research and development, investment opportunities, and more. We need to understand how all these aspects of the business come together to create value. We cannot cover all these subjects in depth in this chapter, but we will identify key issues to consider. You may also wish to consult the list of suggested readings at the end of the chapter.

How can we possibly begin to acquire all the knowledge needed for business analysis? How do we learn about unfamiliar industries? To take on such a task, we need a framework designed to help us apply sound business judgment to the firm we are studying. This chapter provides one framework as a starting point; in time, you will develop your own analytical approach. Your analysis will address the same issues we cover, although you may organize your thinking differently.

---

[1]Gatorade was purchased as part of the Stokely-Van Camp business.

A CLOSER LOOK

Managing Director, Chief U.S. Investment Strategist at Credit Suisse First Boston, on the Importance of Business Analysis

Michael Mauboussin is the Managing Director and Chief U.S. Investment Strategist at Credit Suisse First Boston in New York. Here are his thoughts about the importance of business analysis to security valuation: "Business analysis lies at the heart of security analysis. It is the most important aspect of valuing a stock. Without a firm grasp of a company's business model and its potential in the marketplace, you cannot begin to understand the value of the business."

Business analysis and financial statement analysis work hand in hand to help us understand the target firm's potential. Business analysis will highlight issues we need to study further in the financial statement analysis stage. Likewise, financial statement analysis identifies concerns that require more detailed business analysis. This is the reason for the two-way arrow between business analysis and financial statement analysis in Exhibit 3.1.

We break our discussion of business analysis into two parts, external analysis and internal analysis. As Exhibit 3.2 illustrates, the distinction between external and internal analysis is based on whether a particular item is within the firm's control.

The items within the circle in Exhibit 3.2 comprise internal analysis. These include goals and strategies set by the firm, such as its mission and products offered. The items outside the circle are the components of external analysis. These include factors that are not within the firm's control, such as government regulation and competitors.

EXHIBIT 3.1   A Picture of the Security Analysis Process

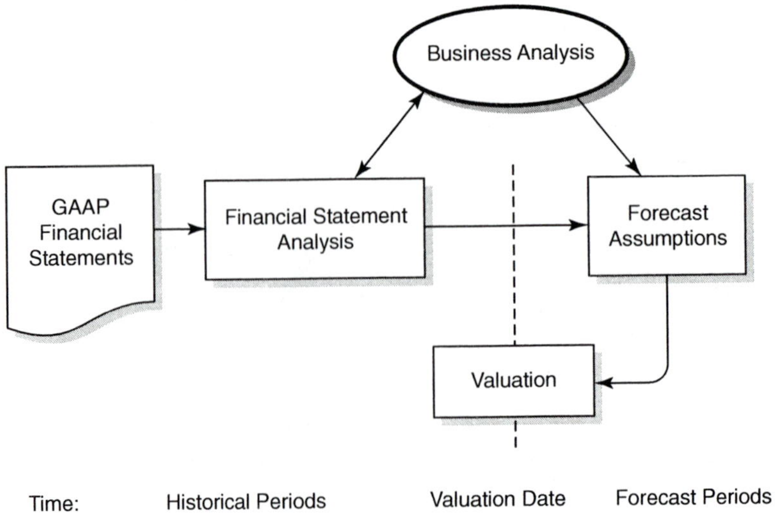

EXHIBIT 3.2   Business Analysis Framework

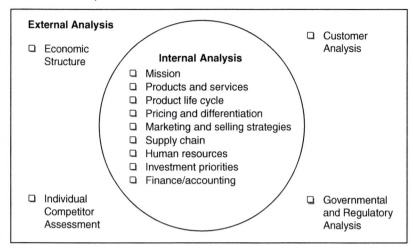

How do we use business analysis to help us value a firm? Even the best business analysis is not going to provide numerical answers for valuation assumptions. However, understanding of economic structure, competitors, customers, regulation, and the internal strengths and weaknesses of the firm will help us determine reasonable estimates of growth, margins, and capital requirements. When we evaluate historical financial ratios as benchmarks of firm performance, we will use the business analysis to assess how these ratios may change in the future. The business analysis will help us consider whether the firm can maintain profitability, become more profitable, or become less profitable. The business analysis should help us determine a range of reasonable assumptions for our valuation model.

Section 3.1 explains how to do external analysis. We will review the four components shown in Exhibit 3.2, the economic structure of the industry, individual competitor assessment, customer analysis, and regulatory analysis. Section 3.2 covers internal analysis, including all of the issues listed within the circle in Exhibit 3.2.

3.1   EXTERNAL ANALYSIS

In **external analysis**, we look at all the factors outside the firm's control that may affect its future. We study the economic structure of the industry, assess each individual competitor, learn about the current and future customer base, and examine the regulatory environment. The nature of the particular target business will determine which elements of the external analysis are most important to us. We usually start the external analysis with the economic structure of the industry, which provides a background to complete the other steps in the external analysis.

Economic Structure of the Industry

We want to understand the economic structure of the industry because it will, in part, determine the returns, profitability, and cash flow of our target firm. The more intense the competition, the lower

EXHIBIT 3.3   Porter's Five Forces Framework: Forces Driving Industry Competition

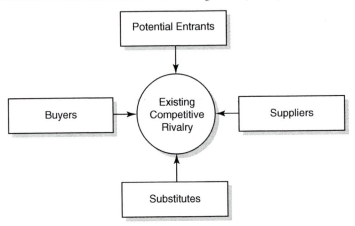

Source: Michael Porter, *Competitive Strategy* (New York: Free Press, 1980).

the expected industry return, and the lower the value of a given firm in the industry. If an industry has high returns, it is likely to attract investments from both new and existing firms, creating more competition and eventually lowering the industry return.

In his book, *Competitive Strategy* (1980), Michael Porter presents a systematic approach to studying the economic structure of an industry by analyzing five basic competitive forces that affect industry returns. In addition to helping us understand the industry's economic structure, Porter's framework provides a complete and organized structure for becoming knowledgeable about the industry. Exhibit 3.3 illustrates Porter's approach.

By considering the existing competitive rivalry and how it might change due to the actions of buyers, potential entrants, and suppliers, as well as the effects of substitute products, this framework helps us think about the firm's ability to generate cash flow in the future. Thus, it is a link between our analysis and the valuation models we will study later.

Existing Competitive Rivalry

At the center of the five forces framework and Exhibit 3.3 is existing competitive rivalry. At this point in the analysis, our goal is to understand the existing rivalry on a macroeconomic level, as opposed to knowing the details of each individual competitor's business strategies. In most cases, the greater the rivalry, the lower the profitability. Exhibit 3.4 shows the major factors that increase competitive rivalry among firms.

How strong is the rivalry? Are there many firms in the industry or just a few? When there are many firms, there is likely to be more price competition. Consider airline routes and fares. On routes

EXHIBIT 3.4   Factors Increasing Rivalry Among Existing Competitors

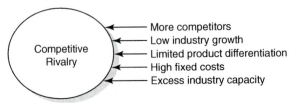

○ **A CLOSER LOOK**

U.S. Government Information for Business Analysis

The U.S. government publishes huge amounts of information that can be useful to the analyst doing business analysis. Here is a brief synopsis of some of the data sources. Most of these data are available on the Internet; the remainder should be available at your library.

- *Securities and Exchange Commission*. Filings include financial information on publicly held corporations. Much of these data are available through the EDGAR (Electronic Data Gathering, Analysis and Retrieval) database at the SEC's Web site, **www.sec.gov**.

- *Survey of Current Business*. Published by the Bureau of Economic Analysis of the U.S. Department of Commerce, the survey covers economic time series data and includes a monthly update of the business situation. Some of the data are broken down by industry. For example, the survey includes data on inventory, new plant and equipment, and production by specific industries.

- *U.S. Census*. This official count of people living in the United States that is done once every 10 years provides detailed demographic data.

- *The Federal Reserve Bulletin*. This contains aggregate economic data such as money supply figures, interest rates, and international exchange rates.

- *The Federal Reserve Bank*. This provides economic statistics including consumer and producer price indices, unemployment rates, labor costs, and personal income. The St. Louis Federal Reserve Bank's Web site, **www.stls.frb.org**, has detailed national economic data. For example, an analyst covering a company selling home building materials might be interested in the number of new one-family houses sold, as shown in the graph.

U.S. New One-Family Houses Sold, January 1990–July 2001

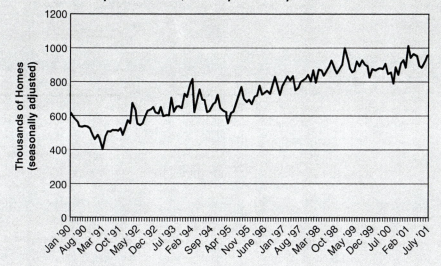

Source: St. Louis Federal Reserve Bank Web site at **www.stls.frb.org**.

that many carriers serve, such as Chicago to New York, airfares tend to be less expensive. If one carrier raises its price, consumers will switch to another airline, because there are so many choices. On routes serviced by a single airline, prices tend to be higher. Although there may be competition on these routes from other forms of transportation—automobile, bus, train—there is no direct competition. People who want to fly that route must pay the asking price. Similarly, if one or two major players dominate any industry, these players usually determine price leadership.

Industry growth also affects the intensity of competition. In slow-growing markets such as ready-to-eat cereals, the competition for market share is fierce. Price discounts, coupons, expensive promotions, and huge advertising budgets are common. This can cause lower profitability. In some very high-growth businesses, rivalry is less intense even though there are many competitors. The market growth can allow firms to expand without taking share away from others. In the early stages of the high-growth bottled water industry, for example, the industry had less advertising, promotional activity, and price discounts than other beverage categories because each firm's business was growing rapidly without the need for these expensive marketing techniques. Other high-growth markets, such as some Internet businesses, do compete on price. The analyst must consider how the industry growth will impact the intensity of competition and ultimately how this competition will affect the future of the business.

Limited product differentiation causes greater competitive intensity. If products are very similar, firms can compete only on price. For example, when you buy sugar in the grocery store, you probably select your brand based on price because all the brands of sugar seem so similar.

Cost structure affects competitive rivalry. When fixed costs are a relatively large proportion of costs, firms usually try harder to increase sales volume so that they can use all their manufacturing capacity and cover their fixed manufacturing costs. They can afford to lower prices to accomplish this because their variable costs are relatively low. Similarly, if there is excess capacity in the industry, competitors often reduce prices to attract more volume.

Potential Entrants

We cannot focus exclusively on the existing state of competitive rivalry. We are interested in what will happen in the future, so we must also consider the second of the five forces, potential new entrants. We want to know how many potential competitors there are and how they will affect competitive rivalry.

Barriers to entry, forces that prevent new firms from venturing into the market, influence the amount of new competition in the industry. Common barriers to entry are economies of scale, product differentiation, high capital needs, the difficulty of obtaining certain resources, access to distribution channels, cost disadvantages, and specialized technology or patents. The more powerful the barriers, the less the chance of increased competition. For example, a patented drug benefits from significant barriers to entry in its market, at least in the United States and until the patent on the drug expires. There will be little or no competition and prices will be high during the patent period. But an analysis of potential entrants must consider who will have the capacity and ability to compete when the patent expires, as well as who might be able to compete in countries that do not honor U.S. patents.

Substitute Products

There are very few products that do not have substitutes, and substitutes—the third of the five forces—can remove profits from the industry. If coffee prices get too high, for instance, you might replace your morning coffee with a cup of tea. If you are an analyst studying coffee businesses, you would certainly study the competitors selling coffee. But to understand what might happen in this industry, you also need to consider the available substitute products, such as tea.

A CLOSER LOOK

Finding Industry Information

Most industries have their own trade journals that cover important news in their industries. Trade journals may include articles about future expectations in the industry, market share information, and stories about individual firms. Sometimes articles even include information on typical or average profitability ratios. Many industries also hold annual conferences at which important issues are discussed and data are shared.

For example, someone analyzing a company in the bottled water industry might turn to *Beverage Industry* for information on the bottled water market. Here are some excerpts from a recent *Beverage Industry* article.

Bottled Water Comes of Age

Perhaps the biggest news in the bottled water industry is soft drinks, or rather the entry of major soft drink players Pepsi-Cola and Coca-Cola into the category. Both companies are putting their soft drink marketing savvy to work for Aquafina and Dasani, respectively, with well-financed media campaigns to boost sales of their waters.

According to a Pepsi spokesperson, Pepsi's beverage priorities include Pepsi, Mountain Dew and Aquafina, in that order. Aquafina went national just two years ago and is now the No. 1 brand of non-carbonated bottled water, according to Information Resources Inc., Chicago. The company has worked hard to take advantage of Coca-Cola's delay into the bottled water category, and has already sealed a number of sponsorship deals. Aquafina is the official bottled water of Major League Soccer, the PGA of America and the NCAA Championships. . . .

While the bottled water category has been growing in the double digits for years, the tremendous gains being made by Aquafina and Dasani have helped overall sales of bottled water. Sales of non-carbonated bottled waters rose more than 24 percent last year, to $1.8 billion in supermarket, mass merchandise and drug store outlets, according to IRI.

For sales of non-carbonated bottled water by outlet, mass merchandisers are showing the greatest gains, with a whopping 50 percent dollar sales gain and a 31 percent unit sales gain for the year ended May 21. Supermarkets with annual sales of more than $2 million enjoyed a 21 percent increase in dollar sales of non-carbonated bottled waters, while drug stores saw an 18 percent increase in the sale of water.

Total category sales, including carbonated, non-carbonated and distilled, were more than $2.4 billion in the three main channels.

Source: Beverage Industry, September 2000.

Buyers

If customers—the fourth of the five forces—have a strong bargaining position, they can affect industry profits by demanding quality improvements and price reductions. Customers, whether of consumer or industrial products, are more likely to have such power if they represent a large proportion of the industry's sales and can act in concert. If the product these customers purchase is not very differentiated and there are many suppliers, they will have an even easier time negotiating price improvements. When customers have the ability to negotiate price, industry profitability and cash flow will be reduced.

For example, groups of McDonald's franchisees buy buns from a single source. With McDonald's as a customer, the bun supplier has a huge source of steady business. But imagine the power of the customers, the McDonald's franchisees, to negotiate a good price from this supplier when there are many other bun suppliers who would also like to have this business!

Suppliers

Suppliers—the last of the five forces—generally have more bargaining power to raise prices or reduce quality if there are only a few of them and if there are not many substitutes for their products. If the supplier group has many customers and this particular industry does not generate a significant portion of its sales, the supplier group will also have more pricing flexibility with which to affect the industry profitability and cash flow.

An interesting example of supplier power is the Major League Baseball Players Association. This union negotiates collective bargaining contracts and all work rules with the two major leagues. Because of the athletic skill required in baseball, there is only a small supply of major league level players, all of whom belong to the union. The union therefore has a monopoly on the talent supply and has been able to negotiate strong minimum salaries and salary arbitration and free agency rules that have driven players' salaries to once unthinkable levels. These higher salaries in turn drive up the teams' operating costs, which are passed on to fans in the form of higher ticket prices.

Individual Competitor Assessment

Although the five forces framework helps us analyze the industry structure and profitability on a macroeconomic level, it does not address the specific strategies of key competitors on a microeconomic level. This task is done in the individual competitor assessment, the second element of the external analysis illustrated in Exhibit 3.2. We want to understand the competitors' strategies, products, marketing, supply chain, and profitability with an eye toward how each will affect our target company.

We will ask questions such as the following:

- How does this competitor approach the marketplace?
- What are the unique characteristics of its product or service?
- What are its competitive advantages?
- How does its pricing compare with the target company?
- What is its apparent marketing strategy?
- How do customers view the product or service?
- Is the competitor well positioned for future trends in the industry?
- Is this competitor profitable? Is it likely to invest more in the business if the competitive situation heats up?
- How does the competitor make or buy its product? Is the way it makes or buys its product a competitive advantage?

- How is the product distributed? Does the distribution method provide a competitive advantage?
- Is the business management a strength or weakness?

The answers to these questions result from studying information about the firm. For example, the firm may describe its competitive advantages in its annual report or in trade journal articles. Berkshire Hathaway is a conglomerate well known for having a competitive advantage in making astute acquisitions. It sets out its acquisition criteria each year in its annual report, including an admonition not to approach the company with an acquisition candidate that does not meet the criteria. In the 2000 annual report, Chairman Warren Buffett complains in the half-page description of the acquisition criteria that "if you advertise an interest in buying collies, a lot of people will call hoping to sell you their cocker spaniels."

Another example would be discerning a marketing strategy from advertising campaigns. The time slots of ads tell a lot about the target market. For example, Saturday morning ads are almost certainly aimed at children, whereas ads during prime-time dramas are more likely aimed at adults.

Sometimes an analyst can spend as much time studying competitors as he or she spends on the target company. Understanding each competitor's strengths will help us project the future for the target company. This is why security analysts working for retail brokerage firms are usually assigned to study a group of competitors. For example, one analyst might cover all the firms in the automotive industry, which means he or she must understand each competitor to be able to value any of them. Following a single industry also allows the analyst to be more efficient because only one external analysis is required, and each internal analysis becomes a competitor analysis for the other companies in the industry.

Customer Analysis

Earlier, we looked at the customer or buyer group as an economic factor affecting industry profitability. Now we turn to individual customers or groups of customers in an effort to understand how their needs drive demand. We must be able to understand customers' needs, from their perspective, to be able to project future trends. What aspects of our target firm's product are really important to the customer? Is price the key or is quality most important? Are buyers looking for customized product? How are the customers' needs likely to change in the future?

We study the customer because we will need to project future sales to customers and expenses for marketing to these customers. There are often two levels of customers and we must understand both levels to truly understand the business. Often, a firm sells products to a customer, who resells it to the consumer. In fact, most consumer products are sold this way. When that is the case, we must distinguish between the firm's immediate customer and the ultimate user. For example, Mattel sells to Toys "R" Us, which sells to the consumer. Mattel must market its products both to the ultimate consumer and to the retailers that carry its products, including Toys "R" Us. To understand Mattel, we need to understand both Toys "R" Us and the consumer.

The analyst studies consumers' needs and interests by looking at demographic trends, purchasing habits, attitudes and usage information, and other types of data. As you learned in your marketing courses, we might use demographic information to look at historical and projected trends in the size of the consumer base. For example, an analyst studying Mattel would be interested in the projected number of young families with children. Also, the analyst would look at purchasing habits in this group. How many toys are purchased on a shopping trip? How much more is purchased during the holiday season compared to the rest of the year? Attitude and usage data can be helpful in understanding consumers' feelings toward a brand, such as Mattel, or a type of toy, such as computer games.

In other businesses, the interested consumer group may grow along with ownership of a complementary product. Complementary products are products that are used together. For example,

A CLOSER LOOK

Procter & Gamble Admits to Searching Trash to Gain Hair-Care Information

Sep. 1—Talk about a bad hair day.

Procter & Gamble Co. has confessed to rifling through the trash to gain information on rival *Unilever's* hair-care business. A *Unilever* official confirmed Friday that the dumpster-diving took place outside its U.S. hair-care headquarters at 325 N. Wells in downtown *Chicago*.

The Cincinnati-based consumer-products giant used other means to get information from *Unilever* as well—without specifying what those might have been—but says it broke no laws. A spokeswoman now acknowledges that some of the activities, including searching garbage, undertaken by corporate detectives acting on its behalf were "outside our strict business information gathering policy."

The two companies, in an effort to avoid going to court over the incident, are in negotiations to resolve the matter. Nevertheless, P&G's tactics have ruffled *Unilever's* hair.

"You don't expect people to be going through your trash, do you?" said Stephen Milton, spokesman for *Unilever*. "We're not exactly Tom Cruise or Elizabeth Taylor."

But this is hardly the first time corporations have used dirty tricks to monitor rivals. In a highly publicized incident last year, software maker Oracle Corp. acknowledged that operatives it hired had offered to buy office trash from a technology trade group allied with rival Microsoft Corp.

Indeed, one corporate detective claims he has searched more than 2,500 dumpsters on behalf of clients in his 10-year career as an "intelligence practitioner."

"Dumpster diving is nothing; to me it doesn't even register on the offensive chart," said Marc Barry, founder of C3I Analytics in New York, who co-wrote a book called "Spooked: Espionage in Corporate America." "Now I have my minions do it for me."

Still, he says dumpster diving is one of the riskier ways to spy on business rivals. "If one of your agents gets caught, there's no plausible deniability," Barry said.

Barry used other tactics to help a rival of Kraft Foods Inc. In 1997, Schwan's Sales Enterprises hired him to find out when Northfield-based Kraft planned to launch a new rising-crust pizza. He set up bogus voice-mail and used an array of false names to throw Kraft off the track.

Barry has also spied on P&G. "Procter is targeted all the time by professional intelligence gatherers," he said.

But this time P&G was the one doing the spying. According to both companies, the spying on *Unilever* began last fall and continued into the spring. The espionage operation was first reported by Fortune magazine's Web site on Thursday.

When senior P&G officials became aware of the espionage, they halted the operation and informed *Unilever* in April, a P&G spokeswoman said. Since then P&G has

continued

continued

turned over more than 80 documents to **Unilever**, said Milton, of **Unilever**. P&G also fired three employees who were involved in the project

"We further assured **Unilever** that we have not nor will not use the information in our business plans," said Linda Ulrey, the P&G spokeswoman. "This is an unfortunate incident and we regret that it happened."

P&G and **Unilever** are two of the world's largest hair-care companies. P&G products include Head & Shoulders and the Pantene line. **Unilever** jumped into hair care in 1996 when the European conglomerate bought **Chicago**-based Helene Curtis Industries Inc. Its brands include Suave, Finesse and Salon Selectives.

Source: Chicago Tribune, September 1, 2001.

sales of computer software have grown as more households own computers. The projected growth of computer ownership might help us project the growth in computer software.

To be able to project the future profitability of the firm, it is vital to understand the channels used to get the product to the customer. Does the firm sell directly to the customer? For example, when you place a catalog or Internet order with L.L. Bean, you are a direct customer. When a manufacturer of specialized machines sends its own sales force to call on plant managers, these are also direct sales. In other cases, the manufacturer may hire representatives or brokers to sell its products, or it may sell machines to a distributor that resells them to the end customer. The choice of distributor, broker, or internal sales force varies from industry to industry, and the selection of the appropriate channel strategies can affect future sales and profitability of the firm.

Governmental and Regulatory Analysis

Laws and regulations can significantly affect the future of any firm, and so the final step in external analysis is to understand the governmental and regulatory environment of the firm. Of course, the extent and the type of regulation vary a great deal from one industry to the next. For example, drug manufacturers must prove the usefulness and safety of their products to the Food and Drug Administration before selling them. In contrast, consulting firms encounter few regulatory concerns. Government regulations and laws can limit or even foreclose entry into a market, such as in "dry" jurisdictions that do not permit alcohol sales. Laws can also proscribe certain forms of competition. For example, automobile dealers in Illinois must close on Sundays.

Regulation can also severely affect profitability. For example, California's recent power crisis can be traced to regulatory issues. The rates that California electric utilities may charge for power are regulated, but their costs of purchasing power were recently deregulated. So, the industry could not increase revenues sufficiently if costs were to increase by a large extent. This is just what happened in the spring of 2001 when electricity had to be "rationed" with rolling blackouts and voluntary use reductions.

Businesses can also incur significant expenses from adhering to licensing requirements, Occupational Safety and Health Administration (OSHA) rules, pollution standards, and Food and Drug Administration standards. For example, OSHA rules may require the firm to invest in costly special equipment or safety barriers in the manufacturing facility.

Who Buys Hot Cereal?

If you were an analyst studying a firm with a business in the hot cereals market, you would want to learn all about the hot cereals consumer. This would help you understand the potential sales growth for the firm. To answer your questions, you could purchase data about this consumer from a consulting firm. For example, ACNielsen is a leading market research firm that collects and sells data on retail sales, product movement, market share, distribution, and price of products sold in grocery stores, convenience stores, drugstores, and mass merchandise outlets.

The following table and list provide some information from ACNielsen about who buys hot cereal. What could an analyst conclude about the potential market growth for hot cereals?

HOT CEREALS MARKET GROWTH

	52 Weeks Ending January 3, 1998	52 Weeks Ending January 2, 1999	52 Weeks Ending January 1, 2000	52 Weeks Ending December 30, 2000
Dollars	4.4%	0.0%	9.2%	6.9%
Equivalized 16 ounce units	3.5%	-3.6%	6.5%	6.0%

Source: ACNielsen Category Planner™ Dec. 30, 2000 © 2001.

Hot Cereal Market Facts

- 65.5% of U.S. households purchased hot cereals at least once during the year.
- The average hot cereal–buying household spent $12 this year on hot cereal.
- The average hot cereal buyer spent $3.15 on each hot cereal–buying occasion.

Source: ACNielsen Homescan Consumer*Facts 2000 Report © 2001.

The following graphs help explain the demographics of hot cereal buyers. Each uses an index to distinguish heavy and light users. The index is calculated by taking the percentage of dollar sales contributed by the segment divided by the percentage of U.S. households in the segment, multiplied by 100. An index above 100 indicates that the segment is purchasing more than would be expected by the segment size alone.

The information shown is just a small sampling of the type of data available. Analysts would also look at market share for each of the brands, pricing, distribution data, regional information, and other data.

continued

External Analysis Summary

When we value a firm, we need to project its future profitability and cash flow. To make these projections, we need to have an in-depth understanding of its external environment. It is important to analyze the economic structure of the industry, the competitors, the customers, and the governmental and regulatory environment because of their influence on the future sales, costs, and capital needs of the firm.

continued

Hot Cereal Usage Based on Household Income

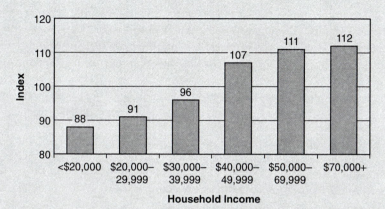

Source: ACNielsen Homescan Consumer*Facts 2000 Report © 2001.

Hot Cereal Usage by Household Size

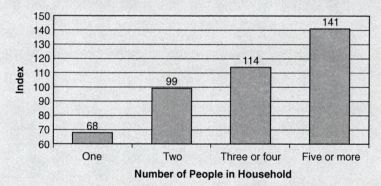

Source: ACNielsen Homescan Consumer*Facts 2000 Report © 2001.

Hot Cereal Purchase Index by Age of Children

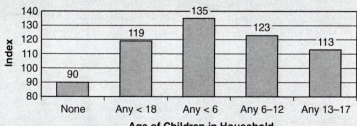

Source: ACNielsen Homescan Consumer*Facts 2000 Report © 2001.

3.2 INTERNAL ANALYSIS

So far, we have examined the firm's environment but not the firm itself. Now, in the internal analysis, we change our focus to understanding everything about the firm that may influence its future cash flow. As Exhibit 3.5, which is the inner circle from Exhibit 3.2, shows, we will examine the target's mission, products and services, product life cycle, pricing and differentiation, marketing and selling strategies, supply chain, human resources, investment priorities, and financial health.

We want to understand the target firm's competitive advantage. What makes this firm successful? What separates this firm from the competition? How long can this success continue?

Mission

A good starting point for an internal analysis is to understand the mission of the business. The **mission** is what the firm hopes to accomplish. For example, A&P, a large supermarket chain, includes the following mission statement in its annual report:

> To become the supermarket of choice
> > Where people choose to shop
> > Where people choose to work
> > Where people choose to invest

In its annual report, the company goes on to explain the strategies that will help it achieve this mission. Understanding the company's mission puts these business strategies and actions in perspective so that the analyst can better predict the firm's future.

Products and Services

Once you understand the business mission, you can study the products and services the firm offers. What do the products and services do? How does the customer use them? We also want to understand the market scope. The firm may define market scope in terms of a geographic area, a certain technology, or a customer type. For example, Mattel describes its market scope as world-

EXHIBIT 3.5   Internal Analysis

❑ Mission
❑ Products and services
❑ Product life cycle
❑ Pricing and differentiation
❑ Marketing and selling strategies
❑ Supply chain
❑ Human resources
❑ Investment priorities
❑ Finance/accounting

wide toys. Mattel puts no limits on where it will sell its products, but it does limit the scope of the products it will sell.

The analyst must be familiar with the depth and breadth of the firm's product lines. For example, Amazon.com offers great depth, with over 13 million book, music, and DVD/video items. The firm also achieves breadth by selling electronics, software, toys, video games, and kitchen, lawn, patio, tool, and hardware products. At the other extreme, William Wrigley Jr. Company focuses almost entirely on one product, chewing gum. The basic business information that helps us understand the product offerings is usually clear from reading the annual report, looking at the firm's Web site, and studying analyst reports and other information published by or about the company.

Product Life Cycle

Product "lives" generally go through four stages: introduction, growth, maturity, and decline. Although not all products follow this pattern, the concepts are still helpful in analyzing many businesses. Usually, sales grow rapidly through the introduction and growth stages, as shown in Exhibit 3.6. Sales remain fairly constant in the maturity phase and decrease in the decline phase.

Costs often vary with these stages, too. There are often significant research and development (R&D) and promotional costs in the introduction phase. Per unit production costs during introduction may be high, as the firm may not yet have achieved substantial economies of scale. In the growth phase, R&D and promotional expenses may still be high, but they are likely to be a lower proportion of sales than during the introduction stage. Production costs per unit are usually lower in the growth phase, too. In the maturity stage, production costs have been optimized and R&D costs are often low. Sometimes R&D in the maturity stage is focused on cost reduction rather than new-product development. In the final phase, decline, R&D and promotional costs are usually cut.

Although these stages are generalizations, they can still be helpful to consider the product life cycle possibilities when projecting future firm performance. For example, Exhibit 3.7 shows historical sales growth for Amazon.com through 2000 and two possible forecasted sales patterns beginning in 2001. The solid line depicts actual sales, whereas the dashed line is a simple extrapolation of prior sales growth. If you believe that Amazon is still in a strong growth part of its life cycle, you might project sales to grow in a pattern like the dashed line. However, if you believe that Amazon is getting closer to

EXHIBIT 3.6   Product Life Cycle

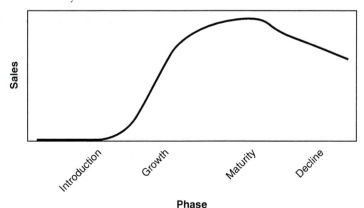

EXHIBIT 3.7   Amazon.com Historical and Projected Sales

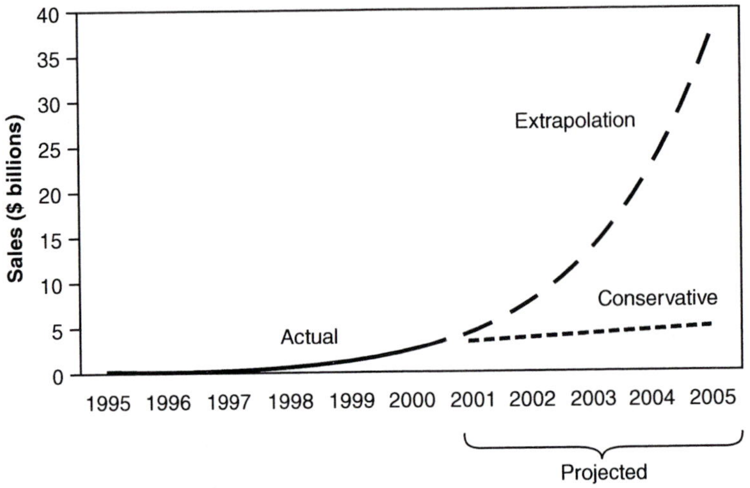

Source: 1995–2000 sales from Amazon.com annual reports.

the top of the product life cycle curve and the growth will slow, you might project the dotted line, a more conservative assessment of Amazon's likely sales pattern as the company matures. Your own business judgment about the particular product life cycle will be important in determining the future sales projections, and these projections will affect the valuation of the firm. Sales in 2001 would be $4.6 billion based on the extrapolation of the prior year's growth, but might be only $3.5 billion under a more conservative scenario. In later years, the sales forecasts would diverge by even more. In fact, Amazon's sales were $3.1 billion in 2001, an increase of only 13% over 2000, versus 68% growth in 2000 versus 1999. The lesson here is that simple extrapolation of growth rates is dangerous, especially for high-growth firms, because they are unlikely to sustain the same growth rates for very long.

Not all firms or industries follow this pattern. Some firms or industries grow, then decline, and then grow again. Firms or industries can spend different amounts of time in each phase. The most challenging aspect of analyzing product life cycles is that you never know for certain where you are on the curve while you are in business. If the business has been growing, we might expect more growth or we might think that growth will level out. Even if growth levels out for a few years, is that a temporary dip or a move toward maturity? We will not know for many years. So, although we recommend thinking about how the product life cycle may influence the future of your target firm, this should be only one piece of a much larger analysis.

Pricing and Differentiation

Economists often categorize products into those that compete based on differentiation and those that compete on price. Products can be differentiated based on the perceived quality, service, or function. Does the product or service offer something unique that customers will seek out? Is there a reasonable substitute for the product? The airline industry provides an example of a largely nondifferentiated business. Most of the time, airlines compete on price because their services are not substantially different. Over the years, however, many airlines have tried to differentiate to attract customer loyalty. Frequent-flier programs encourage travelers to stick with one carrier. Some airlines have tried offering more legroom, fully reclining seat backs, and newer aircraft. The Concorde differentiates with speed. Still, when faced with a choice of carriers, many travelers, especially nonbusiness travelers, choose based on price.

Some firms differentiate by selecting a small niche in the market and serving its very specialized needs. Whole Foods Market does not try to compete with the major grocery chains. Instead, it attracts the smaller but very profitable group of people who want natural foods. Convenience stores such as White Hen Pantry and 7-11 fill yet another niche. Smaller than traditional grocery stores, these retailers charge higher prices but attract people because they are conveniently located, are open early and late, and offer quick shopping.

Regardless of the type of differentiation, the more differentiated the product, the less competition focuses on price. In internal business analysis, it is helpful to understand the levels of differentiation and price competition and to think about how the balance between them might change in the future.

Differentiation and price are two ways in which a firm can position its product or product line. Positioning, on which companies usually spend much energy, identifies the target customer group, the kind of item against which the product will compete, and the unique characteristics or benefits the product offers. Thus it determines the type of advertising and other customer communication the firm will use. For example, although they are both retailers, Wal-Mart does not actually compete with Nordstrom. Wal-Mart's target consumer is the price-conscious family, and the company's unique characteristic is that it offers great prices on a variety of everyday items. Nordstrom, on the other hand, prides itself on great service and a good selection of high-quality clothing and accessories. Nordstrom's target consumer is much more upscale and its prices are correspondingly higher. Wal-Mart's and Nordstrom's positionings are clear from their widely different advertising, store designs, and locations.

Understanding the firm's positioning is important to valuation because the positioning can affect future sales and costs, and we need to be able to project these items. If we believe a firm has a successful positioning, such as Wal-Mart's and Nordstrom's, we would project strong future sales. We also want to understand how the firm's positioning can affect its future costs. For example, Nordstrom's capital expenditures for store fixtures are likely to cost much more per square foot of retail space than Wal-Mart's spending for these items.

Marketing and Selling Strategies

The success or failure of the firm's marketing and selling strategies has a profound impact on future sales and costs. Because of this, the analyst must understand the firm's strategy for bringing the product to the customer. Does the firm use advertising? Is the advertising on television, on radio, in magazines, in trade journals, by direct mailings, on the Internet, or by other means? Is the advertising seasonal? Some firms use other forms of promotion such as price discounts, free product, or customer incentives. It is vital to understand both the cost of these strategies and how they will affect future sales.

Supply Chain

The supply chain includes the combined efforts of purchasing, manufacturing, research and development, and distribution. It includes everything necessary from developing product prototypes to procuring ingredients or parts through getting the product to the customer, as shown in Exhibit 3.8. In an internal analysis, we try to understand how each part of the supply chain works to be able to project future cash flow.

For most firms, a large percentage of costs occur in the supply chain. Because we will project costs in our valuation, it is important that we understand the supply chain. The supply chain begins

EXHIBIT 3.8   The Supply Chain

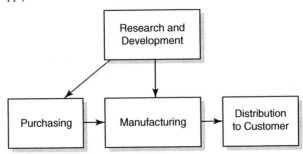

with the research and development group, which develops and improves products. The next step in the chain is purchasing. In purchasing, the firm tries to buy quality ingredients or components at the best possible price. If the firm has strong purchasing expertise and negotiating power, costs will be lower, which will translate into a higher valuation. Next, we consider the manufacturing process. Does the firm have an effective manufacturing process? Is the equipment modern and efficient? Are the costs of producing the product relatively low? What will be the amount of future capital spending for equipment? All of these questions will affect our cash flow forecast for the firm. Once the product is complete, we need to understand how it is distributed to the customer so that we can project the distribution costs.

A key element of understanding a company's supply chain is recognizing which parts of the supply chain are more important than others. For example, R&D is extremely important to pharmaceutical companies such as Pfizer. The distribution process, or fulfillment, has been key for Amazon.com. In other situations, distribution processes not only can be important but also can form the main reason for the firm's existence. For Peapod, a grocery delivery company, direct distribution to the consumer is the reason for being. Retailing focuses on the procurement and inventory management process. Wal-Mart has the ability to buy products at very low prices. It also uses information technology to track inventory and ship inventory daily so that product does not build up in warehouses. Analysts believe that competent supply chain management has contributed to Wal-Mart's tremendous success.

Human Resources

Underlying the marketing, selling, and supply chain are the firm's human resources. We need to understand the strengths and weaknesses on the people side. It is vital to know whether the firm has and will continue to attract employees with the appropriate skills and experience. How will the employee-related costs change in the future? We also want to have a grasp of the firm's relationship with its employees. Is the firm unionized? If so, how might this affect future costs?

Leadership ability and style are also important to the future of the firm. A company with a strong, successful leadership team is more likely to be profitable in the future. In addition to understanding the strength of the management team, it helps to know about the firm's bench strength. If the CEO retires, are there strong leaders in line to follow him or her? Warren Buffett has been among the most open and forthcoming chief executives, and his statements about executive succession are no exception. In the Berkshire Hathaway 2001 annual report, he writes about the management team that will succeed him.

Just who those managers will be, of course, depends on the date of my death. But I can anticipate what the management structure will be: Essentially my job will be split into two parts, with one executive becoming responsible for investments and another for operations. If the acquisition of new business is in prospect, the two will cooperate in making the decisions needed. Both executives will report to a board of directors who will be responsive to the controlling shareholder, whose interests will in turn be aligned with yours.

Finally, we need to understand the firm's **core competencies**, the special skills and abilities that allow it to be successful. For example, in its 2000 annual report, A&P states that customer service quality is the most important aspect of its business. The company expects superior customer service to be one of its core competencies.

Investment Priorities

Products, pricing and differentiation, marketing and selling strategies, supply chain, and human resources can all be important to the firm's future. To understand what makes a firm successful, we also must have a grasp of its investment priorities. Most firms have some business, sales region, or brand that they will ferociously defend. If a competitor tries to interfere with this business, the firm will fight with advertising, pricing, capital investment, legal maneuvers—whatever it takes to remove that competitor. Understanding this strategic priority can be the key to forecasting the firm's future. If another company launched a new, national cola brand with a large advertising campaign, Coca-Cola and Pepsi would probably defend their positions. They might invest in advertising or offer price discounts to force the new competitor into an unprofitable situation. Such activities affect future costs and sales and therefore can be important issues to consider in our forecast.

Finance/Accounting

Finally, we also need to understand the firm's financial health. We will do an accounting analysis to understand how the firm's accounting methods, estimates, and judgments affect the financial statements. Then, we must project the cost structure for our valuation forecast. Do profits stem from high margins as at Starbucks? Or does profit come from large volume as at McDonald's? It is also important to understand the need for capital in the business. This step will be covered in more detail in Chapters 4 and 5.

SUMMARY

The results of a valuation depend on the forecasts used in the valuation model. The key to developing forecasts is to understand the business. We cannot understand the future potential of a business by looking at only historical financial statements. We must use many information sources to learn about the external and internal environments of the firm. Business analysis is the challenging process of learning everything that might affect the future cash flow of the target firm. Business analysis requires skills and knowledge about all aspects of business, including sales, marketing, human resources, supply chain, and finance. This is often the most crucial part of security analysis.

Our framework breaks business analysis into external and internal analysis. In external analysis, we analyze the industry economics, the individual competitors, the customer, and governmental regulation. In internal analysis we study the workings of the firm, including the mission, products and services, product life cycle, pricing and differentiation, marketing and selling, supply chain, human resources, investment priorities, and finance. The business analysis will help us develop projections for our valuation model.

Business analysis goes hand in hand with financial statement analysis. Information from the business analysis will spark questions for the financial statement analysis. Data from the financial statement analysis will point out issues for further business analysis. Together, the business and financial statement analysis should provide a good understanding of the business. Without a true understanding of the firm, the analyst cannot possibly project the financial data needed for valuation.

Business analysis is the subject of entire books. Our treatment of it has been limited to highlighting important issues. We encourage students to utilize the suggested readings that follow to provide a more in-depth understanding of business analysis and strategy.

SUGGESTED READINGS

Besanko, David, David Dranove, and Mark Shanley. *Economics of Strategy*. New York: John Wiley, 1996.

Collis, David J. and Cynthia A. Montgomery. "Creating Corporate Advantage." *Harvard Business Review*, May–June 1998.

Collis, David J. and Cynthia A. Montgomery. *Corporate Strategy-Resources and the Scope of the Firm*. Chicago: McGraw-Hill, 1997.

Hamel, Gary. *Leading the Revolution*. Boston: Harvard Business School Press, 2000.

Hamel, Gary and C. K. Prahalad. *Competing for the Future*. Boston: Harvard Business School Press, 1994.

Porter, Michael. *Competitive Advantage: Creating and Sustaining Superior Performance*. New York: Free Press, 1985.

Porter, Michael. *Competitive Strategy*. New York: Free Press, 1980.

Prahalad, C. K. and Gary Hamel. "The Core Competence of the Corporation." *Harvard Business Review*, May–June 1990.

Rappaport, Alfred and Michael J. Mauboussin. *Expectations Investing: Reading Stock Prices for a Better Return*. Boston: Harvard Business School Press, 2001, Chapter 4.

Shapiro, C. and H. R. Varian. *Information Rules: A Strategic Guide to the Network Economy*. Boston: Harvard Business School Press, 1999.

REVIEW QUESTIONS

1. Why is business analysis important to security valuation?

2. How do business analysis and financial statement analysis affect each other?

3. Why do we need to understand the economic structure of the industry?

4. In our external analysis, we study our individual competitors. What should we learn about the firm's competitors?

5. Customer analysis is an important step in external analysis. What should we know about our customers to help us prepare our business analysis?

6. Why is regulatory analysis an important part of our external analysis? How can understanding the governmental and regulatory environment affect our forecast for the firm?

7. Prepare a brief summary of internal analysis and explain why it is important in security valuation.

8. How is the concept of product life cycles helpful in business analysis? What are the limitations of this concept for business analysis?

9. Why are we interested in understanding the amount and type of product differentiation for the target firm?

10. How can marketing and selling strategies affect our valuation forecasts?

11. Provide two examples of how human resource issues can affect our valuation forecast.

12. Why do we need to understand the target firm's investment priorities to complete our business analysis?

PROBLEMS

1. Select a firm that interests you and find its mission statement. What does this mission statement tell you about the company? How might this understanding affect your business analysis?

2. Analyzing the economic structure of the industry is one important part of the external analysis. Provide an explanation of the five forces that affect industry returns.

3. Throughout this text, we will use examples from Starbucks. Starbucks produces and roasts high-quality whole bean coffees and sells them, along with fresh-brewed coffees, espresso beverages, pastries, and coffee-related accessories and equipment, primarily through its company-operated retail stores. Refer to the Starbucks annual report and other information on the company's Web site, **www.starbucks.com**. Prepare an outline for an external analysis of Starbucks. Note some possible sources of information in your outline.

4. Here is some information about Starbucks' historical sales.

Fiscal Year	1994	1995	1996	1997	1998	1999	2000
Sales (in thousands of dollars)	284,923	465,213	697,872	975,389	1,308,702	1,680,145	2,169,218

What part of the product life cycle do you think Starbucks is in? Why is the product life cycle important to a valuation of Starbucks? How would you decide how to forecast sales into the future?

5. Home Depot is the world's largest home improvement retailer. Suppose you are valuing Home Depot. Review the graph on housing starts provided in A Closer Look: U.S. Government Information for Business Analysis on page 45. How could this type of data affect your Home Depot business analysis? Ultimately, how could this affect your valuation forecast?

6. Describe the supply chain. Why is understanding the supply chain important for our valuation forecast? Be sure to provide specific examples.

7. You are an analyst assigned to value a company that manufactures bicycles. In addition to the firm's financial statements, what sources of information would you use in your business analysis?

8. Refer to the information in A Closer Look: Who Buys Hot Cereal? on pages 52 and 53. How could these data be used to help forecast sales for a firm in the hot cereals business?

9. You are a new analyst assigned to cover the transportation industry. Your supervisor suggests you begin by reviewing the Swift Transportation Company. Swift is one of the largest publicly held national truckload carriers in the United States. Swift transports retail and discount department store merchandise, manufactured goods, paper products, nonperishable food, beverages and beverage containers, and building materials. Swift provides both regional and transcontinental service.

You will have the chance to meet with a more experienced analyst familiar with Swift in a few days. Prepare a detailed list of questions that you will ask to better understand this company prior to beginning your analysis. For more information, check the Swift Transportation Company, Inc. filings at the SEC's Web site, **www.sec.gov**.

10. Sirius Satellite Radio Inc. was organized in May 1990 to build a satellite radio broadcasting system. Once operational, subscribers will be able to obtain 100 radio stations on their specially designed car radios anywhere in the continental United States. Sirius' principal activities to date have included developing technology, obtaining regulatory approval, constructing and launching satellites, constructing a national broadcast studio, acquiring programming content, developing radios capable of receiving satellite broadcasts, strategic planning, market research, recruiting management, and securing financing.

One other company, XM Radio, is developing a similar system. Sirius and XM hold the only two licenses to operate satellite radio systems.

As of December 31, 2000, Sirius had yet to record any revenue.

The following information was excerpted from item 1 (business) of Sirius Satellite Radio Inc.'s 10-K filing for the year 2000. After reading this information, answer the questions that follow.

From our three orbiting satellites, we will directly broadcast up to 100 channels of digital quality radio to vehicles, homes and portable users throughout the continental United States for a monthly subscription fee, which we anticipate will be $9.95. We will deliver 50 channels of commercial-free music in virtually every genre, and up to 50 channels of news, sports, talk, comedy and children's programming. Sirius' broad and deep range of almost every music format as well as its news, sports and entertainment programming is not available on conventional radio in any market in the United States. We hold one of only two licenses issued by the Federal Communications Commission ('FCC') to operate a national satellite radio system.

Upon commencing commercial operations, we expect our primary source of revenues will be subscription fees, which we expect will be included in the sale or lease of certain new vehicles. In addition, we expect to derive revenues from directly selling or bartering limited advertising on our non-music channels.

We have exclusive agreements with Ford Motor Company, DaimlerChrysler Corporation and BMW of North America, LLC that contemplate manufacturing and selling vehicles that include radios capable of receiving our broadcasts. These alliances cover all brands and affiliates of these automakers, including Ford, Chrysler, Mercedes, BMW, Jaguar, Mazda and Volvo.

In addition, in the autosound aftermarket, we expect that radios capable of receiving our broadcasts will be available for sale at various national and regional retailers, such as Best Buy, Circuit City, Tweeter Home Entertainment Group and Good Guys. In 2000, 11 million car radios were sold through consumer electronics retailers.

We have entered into agreements with numerous consumer electronics manufacturers, including Alpine Electronics Inc., Clarion Co., Ltd., Delphi Delco Electronics Systems, Kenwood Corporation, Matsushita Communication Industrial Corporation of USA, Recoton Corporation, Sony Electronics Inc. and Visteon Automotive Systems, to develop radios capable of receiving our broadcasts. As these radios become available in commercial quantities, they will be sold to automakers for inclusion in new vehicles and consumer electronics retailers for sale in the autosound aftermarket.

We intend to program 50 channels of commercial-free music under our brand 'Sirius,' and to offer up to 50 additional channels of other formats, such as news, sports and talk programming.

Sirius' target market consists primarily of motorists. The Federal Highway Administration estimates that there were approximately 208 million registered private motor vehicles in the United States at the end of 2000. According to Radio Advertising Bureau, more than 40% of all radio listening is done in cars. According to Arbitron, a radio industry rating agency, in 2000 motorists listened to the radio an average of 50 minutes a day, despite the fact that 92% of cars have a CD or cassette player. In addition, according to Arbitron, in 1999 approximately 79% of total radio listening was to FM stations, which provide primarily music programming, as compared with AM stations, which devote a greater proportion of their programming to talk and news.

We expect that certain demographic groups are likely to have a high level of interest in Sirius, including commuters (over 100 million, including 34 million with extended commute times), niche music listeners (niche genres not generally available on radio were responsible for 33% of recorded music sales in 1999), Hispanic listeners (over 35 million Spanish-speaking Americans), sports enthusiasts (often underserved by limited regional broadcasts), truck drivers (over three million), recreational vehicle owners (approximately three million) and consumers in areas with sparse radio coverage (over 45 million).

Porter describes factors affecting the degree of competitive rivalry in an industry: number of competitors, industry growth, product differentiation, degree of fixed costs, industry capacity.

   a. Discuss how the number of competitors will affect the competitive rivalry Sirius should expect to face.

   b. Discuss how product differentiation will affect the competitive rivalry Sirius should expect to face.

 11. McDonald's is one of the largest and most popular fast food chains in the United States. You are working on a team preparing a business analysis on McDonald's.

   a. Your group is preparing the external analysis for McDonald's domestic business.

   1. Analyze the economic structure of the industry.
   2. Who are McDonald's most important domestic competitors? Are there other companies that may become important competitors? Analyze these competitors to determine how they will impact McDonald's future profitability.
   3. Analyze McDonald's customers. Who are McDonald's customers? What are the needs that bring them to McDonald's? What are the factors that will affect how much they spend per trip and how often they visit McDonald's? Provide some demographic information about McDonald's customers. What possible current and future trends will impact their future spending at McDonald's?
   4. What types of regulatory issues does McDonald's face?
   5. Putting together what you developed in 1 through 4, what are your conclusions from your external analysis? How will this affect your forecast for McDonald's future?

   b. You are working on a group preparing the internal analysis of McDonald's domestic business.

   1. What is McDonald's mission?
   2. Describe its current and planned products.
   3. Where do you think McDonald's is in its product life cycle? How will this affect your forecasting?
   4. How does McDonald's price its products? How does it differentiate itself from competitors?
   5. Analyze McDonald's marketing approach.
   6. What do we know about McDonald's supply chain? Is this a strategic advantage? Do we expect any changes in the future?
   7. What human resource issues does McDonald's face?
   8. Are there any financial or accounting issues that are key to McDonald's future? (Do not prepare a financial statement analysis, just identify major issues, if any.)
   9. Putting together what you learned in 1 through 8, what are the major issues that will affect your forecast for McDonald's future?

My Case

Prepare a business analysis for your company. Exhibits 3.2, 3.3, and 3.4 may help you outline your work. Possible sources of information include:

Annual report
Magazine articles
Newspaper articles
Company Web site
Government information
Industry information
Value Line, Standard & Poor's, Moody's, and similar investment advisory services
Analyst reports
Internet search

4

Where We Have Been:

In Chapter 3, we studied business analysis, the first phase of security analysis.

Where We Are:

In this chapter, we begin our study of the second phase of security analysis, financial statement analysis. We review the three primary financial statements—the balance sheet, the income statement, and the cash flow statement—so that we can interpret these statements in our financial statement analysis.

Where We Are Going:

In Chapter 5, we will continue our study of financial statement analysis. We will learn how to use financial statements to construct ratios for analyzing a firm.

Accounting Analysis and the Financial Statements

LEARNING OBJECTIVES:

After studying this chapter, you will understand:

- Why analysts must know how financial statements are prepared.
- The balance sheet, income and cash flow statements, and the relationships among them.
- The recognition criteria and valuation methods used for common balance sheet and income statement items.
- How management choices, estimates, and judgment affect the quality of the three primary financial statements.

Financial statement analysis, the second phase of security analysis, is an important tool for investigating a business in preparation for valuation. In this phase, we prepare an accounting analysis to understand the choices and estimates behind the financial statements. As part of our analysis, we may make adjustments to the financial statements. We then use the resulting financial statements to help us understand the business and identify issues for further research. This will help us prepare forecasts of the firm's future cash flow.

Exhibit 4.1 shows the security analysis framework introduced in earlier chapters. As this picture shows, the financial statement analysis portion of the process focuses on the historical periods, and the GAAP financial statements are the key input to the financial statement analysis.

In financial statement analysis, the analyst is like a detective and the financial statements contain many of the clues needed to solve the case. To uncover this information, we often use the financial statements to calculate ratios such as sales growth, profit margins, and reinvestment rates. These ratios help us characterize a firm in various ways. With these characterizations, and our predictions for them in the future, we can construct a forecast and value a firm.

An accounting analysis is the key to understanding the clues the financial statement ratios provide. An accounting analysis requires the analyst to know how the financial statements were prepared and how management's choices affected the statements. We refer to the effects of these choices as financial statement quality. How we incorporate financial statement information in our financial analysis depends on how the financial statements were constructed.

Section 4.1 describes the balance sheet and shows how to use accounting analysis to understand balance sheet quality. We review the income statement and earnings quality issues in Section 4.2 and the cash flow statement in Section 4.3. In Section 4.4, we examine Starbucks Coffee Company's financial statements and we will continue to use Starbucks as an example throughout the book. This

EXHIBIT 4.1   A Picture of the Security Analysis Process

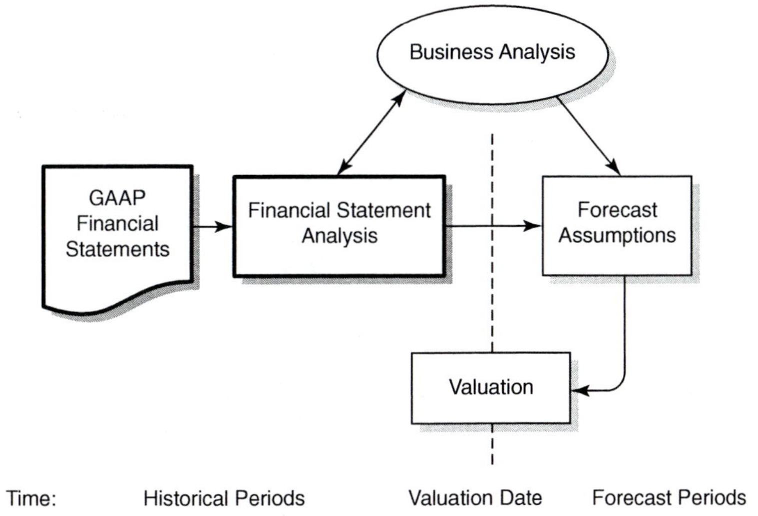

section also includes excerpts from AT&T's financial statements in situations in which Starbucks does not illustrate a particular accounting issue. Two appendices are also included. Appendix 4.1 describes various accounting treatments for investments in debt and equity securities of other firms, which is one of the more difficult financial reporting topics. Appendix 4.2 discusses accounting and disclosure rules for contingent liabilities.

4.1   BALANCE SHEET

The balance sheet describes a company's financial position at a point in time, called the balance sheet date. This statement presents the company's assets, liabilities, and shareholders' equity. The FASB, in its Statement of Financial Accounting Concepts No. 6, "Elements of Financial Statements," defines **assets** to be "probable future economic benefits obtained or controlled by a particular entity as a result of past transactions or events."[1] It defines **liabilities** to be "probable future sacrifices of economic benefits arising from present obligations of a particular entity to transfer assets or provide services to other entities in the future as a result of past transactions or events."[2] **Shareholders' equity**, a residual claim, is whatever is left over after offsetting liabilities against assets.

Assets, liabilities, and shareholders' equity are related to each other by the **accounting equation**, also known as the **balance sheet equation**:

$$\text{Assets} = \text{Liabilities} + \text{Shareholders' equity}$$

The accounting equation can also be written to highlight that shareholders' equity is a residual claim defined implicitly by **net assets**, or assets minus liabilities. Being a residual claim, shareholders' equity is essentially a "plug figure," the amount that makes the balance sheet balance.

$$\text{Shareholders' equity} = \text{Assets} - \text{Liabilities} = \text{Net assets}$$

Balance Sheet Content

Exhibit 4.2 is a balance sheet for Simple Company as of December 31, 2001. As is required in publicly issued annual reports, the firm also presents its balance sheet from the previous year. The

EXHIBIT 4.2   Simple Company Balance Sheet

In millions of dollars	December 31, 2001	December 31, 2000
Cash	$ 210	$ 150
Inventories	365	370
Property, plant, and equipment, net	840	815
Total assets	$ 1,415	$ 1,335
Long-term debt	$ 450	$ 500
Shareholders' equity	965	835
Total liabilities and shareholders' equity	$ 1,415	$ 1,335

---

[1] Financial Accounting Standards Board, Statement of Financial Accounting Concepts No. 6, "Elements of Financial Statements," Paragraph 25.
[2] Ibid., Paragraph 35.

A CLOSER LOOK

The GAAP Hierarchy

Generally accepted accounting principles are not a single set of rules. Rather, they are a hierarchy of rules set by several different regulating bodies after varying degrees of due process and with varying degrees of authority (see Exhibit 4.3). The American Institute of Certified Public Accountants (AICPA) established the GAAP hierarchy in Statement on Auditing Standards (SAS) No. 69 to make mandatory all accounting standards in the hierarchy that do not contradict a standard in a higher level. Until SAS No. 69, accounting pronouncements in what are now tiers 2 through 5 were voluntary.

EXHIBIT 4.3   The GAAP Hierarchy

Tier 1	Statements of Financial Accounting Standards and Interpretations thereof, Opinions of the Accounting Principles Board (APB), AICPA Accounting Research Bulletins
Tier 2	FASB Technical Bulletins, AICPA Industry Audit and Accounting Guides, AICPA Statements of Position
Tier 3	Consensus positions of the FASB Emerging Issues Task Force, AICPA Practice Bulletins
Tier 4	AICPA Accounting Interpretations, "Qs and As" published by the FASB staff, industry practices widely recognized and prevalent
Tier 5	Other accounting literature, including FASB Concepts Statements; APB Statements; AICPA Issues Papers; International Accounting Standards Committee Statements; Governmental Accounting Standards Board Statements, Interpretations and Technical Bulletins; pronouncements of other professional associations or regulatory agencies; AICPA Technical Practice Aids; accounting textbooks, handbooks and articles

Source: Statement on Auditing Standards No. 69.

The first tier of the hierarchy consists of major pronouncements, which receive a great deal of due process, and straightforward interpretations of those pronouncements. Due process for Statements of Financial Accounting Standards (SFASs) involves the issuance of proposals in various stages of development, called Discussion Memos and Exposure Drafts, on which the public comments through letters to the FASB and in public hearings.

Although the FASB is under no obligation to please any particular constituency, the political pressure brought to bear on the FASB during due process can be enormous. SFAS No. 106 on accounting for postretirement benefits other than pensions was adopted over tremendous opposition from business. The FASB backed down from its proposal on accounting for compensation under stock option plans after an even more contentious fight. The FASB did not alter its position on stock options because it was convinced that the proposal was improper accounting, but rather because it could not overcome the political pressure against significantly altering the

continued

continued

rules. The result was a compromise that the FASB itself criticized in the appendix to the statement it issued. FASB Interpretations are also in the first tier of the hierarchy and therefore carry the same weight as SFASs. However, they involve less due process because they are used to clarify existing SFASs, rather than to promulgate new standards or change existing practices substantially.

Pronouncements in the second tier of the GAAP hierarchy, consisting of Technical Bulletins and several non-FASB pronouncements, receive less due process and generally are not intended to develop new or different accounting practices, but rather to provide guidance on implementing existing rules.

The third and fourth tiers include pronouncements made by the FASB staff rather than the Board and involve no formal due process. The fifth tier includes other accounting literature, such as textbooks and professional handbooks.

Simple Company balance sheet satisfies the balance sheet equation at both dates. For example, at December 31, 2001, shareholders' equity of $965 million equals assets of $1,415 million less liabilities of $450 million.

Accounting standards include **recognition criteria**, or rules for determining what items are shown on the balance sheet as assets and liabilities. The standards also include **valuation rules** to determine the amounts at which assets and liabilities are to be reported. Each of the items appearing on the Simple Company balance sheet meets the criteria for recognition under GAAP, and each is valued based on a method prescribed or allowed by GAAP. Throughout the remainder of this chapter, we will build on this example to help illustrate the relationship between the balance sheet, the income statement, and the cash flow statement.

Accounting Analysis of the Balance Sheet

Before using balance sheet asset and liability information, we prepare an accounting analysis to understand how this information was developed. In our analysis, we focus on understanding the balance sheet recognition and valuation rules, try to assess the effect of management choices and estimates on the assets and liabilities, and identify assets and liabilities that are excluded from the balance sheet.

Recognition and Valuation

Managers have varying degrees of discretion in implementing GAAP recognition and valuation rules. In some cases, GAAP dictate an accounting method. In others, management selects from acceptable methods. In still other cases, the method depends on the facts and the circumstances. Exhibit 4.4 shows a continuum of ways in which recognition and valuation methods are determined.

Selected Methods   At the far right of Exhibit 4.4 are situations in which managers may set various recognition criteria or select from two or more valuation methods. For example, managers choose inventory (LIFO, FIFO, weighted-average) and depreciation (straight-line, accelerated) methods. In these situations, managers have significant influence over the reported results.

EXHIBIT 4.4   Continuum of Recognition Criteria and Valuation Method Determination

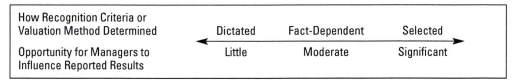

Dictated Methods   At the far left of Exhibit 4.4 are situations in which GAAP dictate specific recognition criteria and a single valuation method. For example, debt is accounted for under the effective interest rate method. Managers cannot deviate materially from that approach.[3]

Fact-Dependent Criteria and Methods   In the middle of the continuum of Exhibit 4.4 are fact-dependent recognition criteria and valuation methods. In these situations, GAAP have different recognition criteria or allow different valuation methods, but a particular method is required for a particular set of facts. For example, there are three different accounting treatments for marketable securities. GAAP require one treatment for securities expected to be held to maturity, another for trading securities, and a third for securities classified as available for sale. Management's plans for such securities determine the accounting treatment required. Appendix 4.1 reviews GAAP for investments. Similarly, there are two methods for translating foreign operations into U.S. dollars, with the required method depending on how the foreign subsidiary operates its business.

Theoretically, in these situations firms have no choice because the facts dictate the accounting method. In reality, they do have a choice for two reasons. First, firms can use their discretion in determining whether the criteria that require a particular method are met. In the marketable security case, what a firm *says* is its intention determines the accounting method. The opportunity for discretion here is clear.[4] Second, firms can structure transactions to obtain the desired accounting result. Prior to July 1, 2001, firms could use pooling of interests to account for acquisitions meeting 12 criteria. Many firms carefully structured transactions to meet these criteria and obtain an accounting treatment they viewed as more favorable.

Managers' discretion in a fact-dependent situation is not limited to valuation methods and estimates. There is even discretion in recognition. The most extensive situation in which this exists is with contingent liabilities. A **contingent liability** is a potential liability that may have been incurred as a result of a past transaction or event. Although GAAP include criteria under which contingent liabilities must be recognized, whether those criteria are met is very subjective. Appendix 4.2 discusses the accounting and disclosure rules for contingent liabilities.

Management Estimates

Regardless of whether an accounting method is dictated, fact-dependent, or selected, managers often have discretion in how to implement that method. Most accounting methods involve estimates, which are subject to management's discretion. For example, all firms must provide an allowance for estimated uncollectible accounts in valuing their accounts receivable. Within a reasonable range, management may essentially choose whatever estimate it wants, thereby influencing the valuation of its receivables and its equity. Similarly, firms also estimate some liabilities such as the accrual for coupon redemptions. These estimates provide room for **accruals management**. Because of the relationship between the balance sheet and the income statement, accruals management can be used to alter reported earnings.

---

[3]Managers may use a different method as long as it is not materially different. Thus, some discretion remains.
[4]However, not holding to maturity a security so classified may bar future use of that category.

Unrecognized Assets and Liabilities

Not every item that we would consider an asset or a liability appears on the balance sheet. This is because recognition criteria are not always consistent with the FASB's Statement of Financial Accounting Concepts No. 6, "Elements of Financial Statements." The expertise gained through a research and development program, the firm's human resources, and its brand names are all examples of valuable assets that generally do not appear on the balance sheet. Similarly, employee stock options represent probable future sacrifices of economic resources, but are not recognized as liabilities under GAAP.

Implications for Financial Statement Analysis

The various recognition criteria and valuation methods, the possibility of managers using their discretion to affect the financial statements, and the potential for unrecognized assets and liabilities all have important implications for analysts. Analysts must comprehend the accounting rules and how they were applied. They must understand when managers have latitude and interpret the financial statements and disclosures accordingly. Even in situations in which the accounting method is dictated, analysts must be careful to understand what the asset and liability amounts actually represent. For example, assets and liabilities recognized under the dictated GAAP method for retirement plans are not recorded at fair value. In fact, these amounts often deviate significantly from fair value. Analysts must also consider unrecognized assets and liabilities, both of which can have significant value.

4.2 INCOME STATEMENT

The income statement is usually considered to be more important to investors and creditors than the balance sheet. The FASB—in its Statement of Financial Accounting Concepts No. 1, "Objectives of Financial Reporting by Business Enterprises"—explains the importance of the income statement as follows:

> The primary focus of financial reporting is information about an enterprise's performance provided by measures of earnings and its components. Investors, creditors, and others who are concerned with assessing the prospects for enterprise net cash inflows are especially interested in that information.[5]

As this passage suggests, we often forecast future performance when doing financial statement analysis. The income statement, far more than the balance sheet, helps do this.

The income statement is closely related to the balance sheet. Why? We have seen that shareholders' equity is equal to net assets. This is true at *any* balance sheet date. So, it is also true that the *change* in shareholders' equity during a year is equal to the *change* in net assets in that year.

$$\text{Change in shareholders' equity} = \text{Change in net assets}$$

This equation is important because GAAP define net income implicitly, based on the change in shareholders' equity. Net income is the change in shareholders' equity that is not due to contributions of capital or distributions of capital.[6] To see the intuition behind this definition of income, consider your savings account. It increases when you make a deposit or earn interest. It decreases when you make a withdrawal or incur service fees. The net income from the savings account is the

---

[5]FASB, Statement of Financial Accounting Concepts No. 1, "Objectives of Financial Reporting by Business Enterprises."
[6]For now, we are ignoring the few situations in which firms are permitted to charge or credit a change in net assets directly to shareholders' equity, without recognizing anything on the income statement.

EXHIBIT 4.5   Reconciliation of Simple Company's Shareholders' Equity

($ millions)		
Shareholders' equity, December 31, 2000	$	835
Issuance of common stock		40
Dividends declared and paid		(20)
Net income		110
Change in shareholders' equity		130
Shareholders' equity, December 31, 2001	$	965

interest earned less the service fees. This is the total of all changes in the account balance that are not due to contributions of capital (deposits) or distributions of capital (withdrawals).

Similarly, GAAP define a firm's net income to be the change in its net assets, excluding stock issuances (contributions of capital) and dividends (distributions of capital). That means the balance sheet recognition and valuation rules directly affect net income. If the rules call for the net asset balance to increase, there is net income for the amount of the increase. If the rules call for net assets to decrease, there is a net loss for the amount of the decrease. For example, Simple Company's shareholders' equity and net assets increased by $130 million during 2001, from $835 million to $965 million. Suppose it sold stock for $40 million during the year and paid dividends of $20 million. Its net income for the year must be $110 million. Exhibit 4.5 explains the change in Simple Company's equity.

Although reconciling the shareholders' equity account determines the *amount* of net income, it does not provide much information about *how that income was earned*. This is where the income statement comes in.

Income Statement Content

The income statement summarizes the transactions that led to the firm's net income. Broadly speaking, the income statement contains five categories of items: revenues, expenses, gains, losses, and special items. These categories contain clues that are helpful in forecasting, because they relate to whether the item is likely to recur. The income statement in Exhibit 4.6 explains Simple Company's 2001 income of $110 million.

EXHIBIT 4.6   Simple Company Income Statement

For the year ended December 31, 2001 ($ millions)		
Sales	$	1,557
Cost of sales		(1,235)
Gross profit		322
Depreciation expense		(102)
Interest expense		(55)
Gain		15
Loss		(5)
Income before taxes		175
Income tax expense		(65)
Net income	$	110

Simple Company's income statement includes revenues (sales), expenses (cost of sales, depreciation expense, interest expense, income tax expense), a gain, and a loss. We explain each of these categories next.

1. **Revenues** include increases in net assets that result from selling goods and services in the normal course of business. Revenues also include other income that is not the result of selling a security or other asset. For example, royalties and interest income are considered revenues.

2. **Expenses** are decreases in net assets that result from activities related to preparing product for sale or delivering services in the normal course of business, or financing costs. Cost of goods sold, depreciation, advertising, salaries, rent, travel, interest, and taxes are examples of expenses.

3. **Gains**, like revenues, represent increases in net assets. However, they differ from revenues in an important respect. Gains do not arise in the ordinary course of business. For example, if a toy manufacturer sells one of its manufacturing plants for more than the amount shown on the balance sheet (its "book value") as of the date of sale, the firm would recognize a gain for the difference. Selling a plant is not part of the company's normal business of selling toys, so this inflow is not classified as revenue.

4. **Losses** are decreases in net assets resulting from transactions that are not part of the normal course of business operations. If the toy company sold the plant for less than its book value, the company would recognize a loss.

Simple Company does not have any special items, but we describe special items here for completeness.

5. Special items include extraordinary items, changes in accounting principles, and discontinued operations. These items are generally nonrecurring.
    a. **Extraordinary items** are gains and losses that are deemed to be both unusual and nonrecurring. Examples include losses from natural disasters, such as an earthquake or a tornado, assuming the location of the affected facility is not such that the disaster would be likely to recur.
    b. **Changes in accounting principles** arise when the firm switches from one accounting method to another. As of the first day of the year of the change, the firm revalues all its assets and liabilities to what they would have been had the firm always used the new accounting method. The resulting gain or loss is classified as a change in accounting principle. For example, if a firm switches from accelerated depreciation to straight-line, it revalues its net fixed assets to a higher amount, to reflect the amount at which its fixed assets would have been valued had the firm been using straight-line all along. This increase in fixed assets results in income recognition, which is classified as a change in accounting principle.
    c. **Discontinued operations** include all the items of income, expense, gain, and loss related to the operations of the firm's businesses that it intends to sell or otherwise dispose of. After Quaker Oats made the decision to dispose of its Fisher-Price toys unit, but before the transaction was complete, Fisher-Price was classified as a discontinued operation. All income statement items related to Fisher-Price were shown as profit or loss from discontinued operations.

The presentation of the various income statement components highlights whether each line item is likely to recur. Revenues and expenses relate to the normal course of business and generally recur every year. Gains and losses are not in the normal course of business, so we do not necessarily expect them to recur at the same level every year. However, they are not so unusual that we would not expect them ever to recur. Special items are much less likely to recur. The analyst can use these categorizations to develop better assessments of future profitability.

A CLOSER LOOK

Losses from Terrorist Attacks Not to Receive Extraordinary Item Treatment

Shortly after the attacks on the World Trade Center and the Pentagon on September 11, 2001, the Emerging Issues Task Force (EITF) decided that losses related to the attacks should not receive extraordinary item treatment. The EITF is a committee of accounting professionals organized by the FASB.

EITF Chairman Tim Lucas said,

> Because of the far-reaching effects of the September 11 events, coupled with a weakening economy that predated those events, it would be difficult to capture the resulting economic effects in companies' financial statements. As one example, the events impacted airlines in multiple ways. Air carriers were unable to fly for two days, suffered the effects of rerouting and initiated layoffs in anticipation of lower passenger demand. No single line item can capture all of those effects. Other companies representing a broad range of industries are experiencing similar impacts.

Source: FASB Press Release, October 1, 2001.

This decision followed a tentative conclusion a week earlier that losses arising directly from the attacks would be considered extraordinary. After deliberating about how to separate direct losses from indirect losses due to the resulting effect of the attacks on the economy, the EITF decided there was no feasible way to accomplish that task and ruled that no losses from the attacks should be treated as extraordinary. The economic effects of the attacks were simply too far-reaching for any entity reasonably to isolate them. For example, if equipment is idled due to an economic downturn precipitated by the attacks, is that an extraordinary loss from the attacks?

Although losses from the attacks will not be classified as extraordinary in the income statement, they were certainly extraordinary as that term is regularly used. Many firms discussed at length the effects of the attacks on their businesses in their annual reports. Presidents' letters to shareholders, management discussions and analyses, annual report texts, and financial statement footnotes included extensive analyses of how firms were affected by and are dealing with the attacks. An analysis of any firm should consider these discussions carefully and include in any projections the expected effect on the business.

Accounting Analysis of the Income Statement

Accounting analysis of the income statement often focuses on **earnings quality**. What is earnings quality? Different analysts use the term differently. Earnings quality can mean conservative accounting methods, earnings that are free of manipulation, and the exclusion of nonrecurring items.

Conservatism

Conservative accounting methods are those that tend to delay recognition of assets and accelerate recognition of liabilities or that tend to provide lower asset valuations and higher liability valuations.

Although conservative accounting methods generally lead to lower values for reported net assets, they do not necessarily result in lower reported earnings. Choosing a conservative accounting method usually lowers income in early years and increases it in later years. For example, using accelerated depreciation increases depreciation charges in the early years of an asset's life, but lowers them in later years. Similarly, choosing a higher level for the allowance for uncollectibles reduces income in one period, but increases it in the next.

Firms sometimes take a "big bath." In a year in which the firm is going to report lower earnings, the firm writes off additional assets, taking a charge to income. This is very conservative in that it provides a significantly lower asset valuation. However, this leads to *higher* income in future periods as depreciation charges are smaller.

Free of Manipulation

Some analysts say a firm has good-quality earnings if earnings are free of manipulation. This suggests that estimates, such as for the allowance for uncollectibles, be unbiased estimates of the underlying amounts. This is difficult to verify for a particular firm. Further, how can an analyst classify one depreciation method or inventory method as more free of manipulation than another? However, to the extent possible, the analyst should try to undo any management manipulation before using historical data.

The earnings manipulation issue has been in the news even more since the collapse of Enron in late 2001. In a story on the topic, the *Wall Street Journal* stated,

> Alan R. Ackerman, a veteran market strategist at Fahnestock & Co., says the multiplying accounting scandals are creating "a crisis of confidence among investors. Many people are moving money to the sidelines because of a high degree of concern about the quality of corporate earnings and how much accounting engineering is involved in producing those earnings."[7]

Excludes Nonrecurring Items

Sometimes earnings quality means earnings include only items expected to recur. Such a definition implies higher-quality earnings are those that are more useful for forecasting. For example, because extraordinary items are defined as unusual and nonrecurring, the analyst can usually ignore these items. A loss from an earthquake will not be forecasted to recur in the future. Similarly, analysts often exclude earnings from discontinued operations from their financial analysis.

Treatment of gains and losses in a forecast is more complex because there are many types of gains and losses. Should gains or losses be expected to recur in the future? Because gains and losses do not arise from the normal course of business, they are candidates for exclusion. However, gains and losses are not so unusual and nonrecurring to be considered extraordinary items. They can sometimes recur period after period. For example, McDonald's Corporation regularly acquires its franchised restaurants and later resells them to new franchisees. This creates gains and losses (usually gains) that appear regularly. The analyst must carefully consider each gain or loss in his or her analysis.

No one can determine a "true" historical earnings amount. In using historical income statement information to help us understand a business or develop a forecast, we need to assess the effect of choice in accounting methods, estimates, and nonrecurring items. These judgments will affect our own estimates of the firm's future performance.

---

[7]Michael Schroeder, Jerry Guidera, and Mark Maremont, "Accounting Crackdown Focuses Increasingly on Top Executives." *Wall Street Journal*, April 12, 2002.

4.3 CASH FLOW STATEMENT

The cash flow statement describes the reasons for the change in the firm's cash balance from the beginning to the end of the period. Virtually all cash flow statements use the **indirect method**.[8] Under this method, the cash flow statement begins with net income and then reconciles that amount to the change in cash. Simple Company's net income was $110 million, whereas its balance sheet shows that its cash increased by only $60 million, from $150 million to $210 million. Its cash flow statement begins with net income of $110 million and then has $50 million of net downward-reconciling items, to arrive at the $60 million increase in cash.

Cash Flow Statement Content

Exhibit 4.7 is Simple Company's cash flow statement for 2001. The GAAP cash flow statement divides cash flow into three categories: cash flow from operations, cash flow from investing, and cash flow from financing. **Cash flow from operations** includes the items that relate to the determination of net income. For example, producing or selling the firm's products or services is an operating activity. **Cash flow from investing** is the cash flow from activities in which the firm acquires or divests long-term assets or investment securities. Purchases of property, plant, and equipment; lending money or collecting principal on loans; and making investments in equity securities are investing activities. **Cash flow from financing** includes borrowing money from creditors and repaying debt, as well as obtaining funds from stockholders, paying dividends to stockholders, and repurchasing shares from stockholders.

EXHIBIT 4.7   Simple Company Cash Flow Statement

For the year ended December 31, 2001 ($ millions)		
Net income	$	110
Depreciation		102
Decrease in inventory		5
Cash flow from operations		217
Capital expenditures		(127)
Cash flow from investing		(127)
Issuance of common stock		40
Dividends declared and paid		(20)
Repayment of debt		(50)
Cash flow from financing		(30)
Net change in cash	$	60

---

[8]The other method for the cash flow statement is the direct method. Under the direct method, the firm reports gross cash receipts and cash disbursements related to operations. Receipts include such things as cash received from customers, interest, and dividends. Disbursements usually include cash paid to employees and suppliers of services, materials and equipment, interest, and income taxes. Very few companies actually use the direct method.

The Simple Company cash flow statement starts with net income of $110 million. The bottom line of the cash flow statement ($60 million) is equal to the change in the cash balance on the balance sheet ($210 million minus $150 million). Each reconciling item represents a reversal of a noncash component of income, a cash flow that has no income statement effect, or a difference between the amount of income statement recognition and cash flow on a particular group of transactions.

The first reconciling item is depreciation. Being a noncash expense, depreciation has no effect on cash flow, but it is subtracted in calculating net income. As a result, depreciation must be added back in the cash flow statement to reverse its effect in the income statement. The positive $5 million in the cash flow statement for the decrease in inventory indicates that cash flow from sales of products exceeded gross profit on the income statement by $5 million, because Simple Company did not replenish all the inventory that it sold. Capital expenditures are payments for new fixed assets. These payments are not expensed in the income statement, but they are cash outflows, so they appear on the cash flow statement. Issuance of stock is a cash inflow, whereas dividends and debt repayments are cash outflows.

As we will see in Chapter 9, the GAAP definitions of cash flow are not consistent with the typical definition of cash flow used in financial analysis. For example, cash flow from operations under GAAP includes interest income and interest expense, whereas one of the first lessons we learn in corporate finance is to segregate these items from operating cash flows. As a result, when we use the cash flow statement to do financial analysis, we often reclassify certain components of the GAAP cash flow statement to make the statement consistent with a financial analysis framework.

Accounting Analysis of the Cash Flow Statement

Quality issues are less problematic for the cash flow statement than for the income statement or balance sheet. Cash flow is simply the change in cash and this amount is not affected by accounting method choices or estimates. However, individual line items in the cash flow statement are affected. For example, a large write-off of a fixed asset does not affect cash flow but does reduce income, resulting in a positive reconciling item in the cash flow statement. The reconciling items on the cash flow statement may be a useful tool for identifying potential earnings quality issues. Large reconciling items are potential red flags and should be evaluated. For example, large negative reconciling amounts for changes in working capital could indicate that earnings are being propped up through accruals management, resulting in increases in the reported values of noncash assets or liabilities. If income is increased by extending depreciable lives of fixed assets, this fact will be highlighted in the cash flow statement, even if depreciation is not a separate line item in the income statement.

The Combined Income Statement and Cash Flow Statement

Although it is not the format prescribed by GAAP, it is possible to combine the income statement and cash flow statement into a single statement, simply by substituting the entire income statement for the first line of the cash flow statement, which is net income. Although this format contains no new information, it puts all the elements of cash flow in a single statement, rather than splitting them between the income statement and the cash flow statement. Thus, it is a convenient format in financial statement analysis and in valuation. Exhibit 4.8 is Simple Company's combined income statement and cash flow statement.

This format allows us to view all the elements of cash flow, whether included in income or not. It is a convenient format because as we adjust the financial statements to remove nonrecurring items, to deal with other quality issues, or to produce any particular analysis, it provides a natural check on our work. Our analysis cannot involve a change in the bottom line of this statement—the net change in cash.

EXHIBIT 4.8   Simple Company Combined Income Statement and Cash Flow Statement

For the year ended December 31, 2001 ($ millions)		
Sales	$	1,557
Cost of sales		(1,235)
Gross profit		322
Depreciation expense		(102)
Interest expense		(55)
Gain		15
Loss		(5)
Income before taxes		175
Income tax expense		(65)
Net income		110
Depreciation		102
Decrease in inventory		5
Cash flow from operations		217
Capital expenditures		(127)
Cash flow from investing		(127)
Issuance of common stock		40
Dividends declared and paid		(20)
Repayment of debt		(50)
Cash flow from financing		(30)
Net change in cash	$	60

4.4   Starbucks' Financial Statements

Actual financial statements are always more complicated than the Simple Company statements we have examined. To gain experience with real statements, we now examine Starbucks' financial statements. Although Starbucks is a good example of typical financial statements, every company's financial statements are unique. Because Starbucks' financial statements do not contain every element we would like to discuss, we also use AT&T's financial statements for part of the discussion.

As you work more with financial statements, you will notice the similarities and also become comfortable with the subtle differences among them. Various companies use slightly different terminology, format their disclosures in varying ways, and have different kinds of transactions. With experience, it will be easier to use and interpret financial statements of different companies.

Starbucks' Balance Sheet

The Starbucks' balance sheet, presented as Exhibit 4.9, is as of October 1, 2000, with the prior year's statement as of October 3, 1999, also presented.[9]

---

[9]Starbucks is on a 52-week/53-week year. This means that the fiscal year ends on the same day of the week every year and so some years are 52 weeks and others are 53 weeks.

EXHIBIT 4.9   Starbucks' Balance Sheet

In thousands except share data	October 1, 2000	October 3, 1999
ASSETS		
Current Assets:		
Cash and cash equivalents	$ 70,817	$ 66,419
Short-term investments	61,336	51,367
Accounts receivable, net of allowances of $2,941 and $1,227, respectively	76,385	47,646
Inventories	201,656	180,886
Prepaid expenses and other current assets	20,321	19,049
Deferred income taxes, net	29,304	21,133
Total current assets	459,819	386,500
Joint ventures	52,051	42,718
Other investments	3,788	25,342
Property, plant and equipment, net	930,759	760,289
Other assets	25,403	23,474
Goodwill, net	21,311	14,191
Total assets	$ 1,493,131	$ 1,252,514
LIABILITIES AND SHAREHOLDERS' EQUITY		
Current Liabilities:		
Accounts payable	$ 73,653	$56,108
Checks drawn in excess of bank balances	56,332	63,811
Accrued compensation and related costs	75,250	43,872
Accrued occupancy costs	29,117	23,017
Accrued taxes	35,841	30,752
Other accrued expenses	35,053	32,480
Deferred revenue	7,320	484
Current portion of long-term debt	685	673
Total current liabilities	313,251	251,197
Deferred income taxes, net	21,410	32,886
Long-term debt	6,483	7,018
Minority interest	3,588	400
Shareholders' equity:		
Common stock—Authorized 300,000,000 shares; issued and outstanding, 188,157,651 and 183,282,095 shares, respectively (includes 848,550 common stock units in both years)	750,872	651,020
Retained earnings	408,503	313,939
Accumulated other comprehensive loss	(10,976)	(3,946)
Total shareholders' equity	1,148,399	961,013
Total liabilities and shareholders' equity	$ 1,493,131	$ 1,252,514

Assets

Starbucks' balance sheet, like most balance sheets, separates assets into current assets and noncurrent assets. **Current assets** are assets that are expected to be converted into cash or used to satisfy a liability within one year.[10] These include cash and cash equivalents, short-term investments, accounts receivable, other receivables, inventory, and prepaid expenses. **Noncurrent assets** are assets that are not expected to be converted to cash or used to satisfy a liability within one year. Within the current asset and noncurrent asset sections of the balance sheet, items are generally placed in order of liquidity.

Examining the current asset section of Starbucks' balance sheet, we see the many different valuation methods used under GAAP. Cash is shown at its face amount, which is also its market value. Starbucks' short-term investments include corporate bonds, government bonds, municipal securities, common stock, and preferred stock. All investments in stock whereby the investor does not have influence over the investee, and any investments in debt that the firm does not intend to hold to maturity, are shown at market value. Accounts receivable are recorded at the amount due, but are reduced by management's estimate of the uncollectible portion. This adjustment reduces the value of accounts receivable to net realizable value. Inventories are generally valued at the lower of cost or market, a valuation method that illustrates a conservative bias. Prepaid expenses and deferred income tax assets are recorded at historical cost.

Starbucks' noncurrent assets are also valued under several different methods. Starbucks' joint ventures are accounted for under the **equity method**, which is used when the company is deemed to have substantial influence over the operations of the company it has invested in, known as the investee. In most cases, we assume substantial influence when ownership exceeds 20 percent.[11] Under the equity method, the company records its investment at cost. It adds its proportionate share of the investee's income to the investment and subtracts its proportionate share of the investee's loss from the investment. Dividends received are deducted from the investment. The $52,051,000 value shown for joint ventures is equal to Starbucks' initial capital contribution plus its share of the joint venture's income over the years, less the dividends Starbucks has received. Other investments include additional equity-method investments. For Starbucks, these are primarily investments in Internet companies, including living.com, Cooking.com, and Kozmo.com. Due to the decline in the values of Internet stocks, Starbucks recorded a loss and wrote off most of its investments in Internet companies in fiscal 2000. This accounts for the large decline in the amount shown for these investments, despite $35 million of additional investments in fiscal 2000. Property, plant, and equipment (PP&E), other assets, and goodwill are all recorded at cost. The property, plant, and equipment is depreciated. Goodwill was amortized through 2001, but effective in 2002, goodwill is no longer amortized.[12] So, balance sheet amounts for PP&E and goodwill are below historical cost.

---

[10]Or within one operating cycle if that is longer than one year. An operating cycle is the time from the commitment of cash for purchases until the collection of receivables from the sale of the finished product or service. For most firms, the operating cycle is less than one year. However, in certain industries, the operating cycle might be longer due to the extended amount of time it takes to manufacture a product. In winemaking, for example, the operating cycle is much longer than a year due to the time that the wine must sit before it is ready to be sold. For the discussion in this chapter, we assume the operating cycle is less than one year.

[11]Generally, when the firm owns less than 20% of another company's voting stock, the investment is classified as a marketable security and accounted for as either a trading security or a security available-for-sale, depending on management's intentions. As discussed in Appendix 4.1, both trading securities and securities available-for-sale are reported at market value.

Once the company owns more than 50% of another entity, the investment is consolidated into the investing company's financial statements. This means that the investee becomes a subsidiary, and all of its assets and liabilities are reported as if they were assets and liabilities of the parent. There is no longer an investment in the equity of the firm shown in the balance sheet.

[12]For calendar-year firms. The effective date of the change is slightly different for firms not on a calendar year. The change in this rule is prospective, meaning goodwill amortization will cease, but prior amortization will not be reversed.

A CLOSER LOOK

EDGAR

Today virtually all SEC filings are made electronically via the Electronic Data Gathering, Analysis, and Retrieval system, or EDGAR, and are available free of charge, 24 hours per day from the SEC's Web site at **www.sec.gov**.

Documents on EDGAR include the following:

- Form 10-K, the annual report to the SEC. This contains essentially the same information as in the company's annual report to shareholders, plus additional disclosures required by the SEC. In fact, many companies include the annual report to shareholders as an exhibit to the 10-K, and provide the additional disclosures in the form itself. Form 10-K must be filed within 90 days of the fiscal year end.
- Form 10-Q, the quarterly report to the SEC. This form must be filed within 45 days of the end of each of the first three fiscal quarters. It contains unaudited financial statements.
- Form 8-K, a current report to the SEC. It is filed whenever there are material events that must be disclosed publicly.

There are many more documents on EDGAR, and the full list of available forms is on the SEC Web site.

Obtaining information from EDGAR is easy. For example, to find Starbucks' Form 10-K for the year ended October 1, 2000, do the following:

- Go to the SEC Web site at **www.sec.gov**.
- Click on "Search for company filings."
- Click on "Quick forms lookup."
- In the company name field, enter one or more words from the company name, in this case Starbucks.
- Select the filing date range for the filings you wish to see. Because Starbucks fiscal 2000 10-K could have been filed in either late 2000 or early 2001, select the range 2000-2001 for the filing years.
- Click the "Search" button.
- Click the link for whichever document you wish to view.

Liabilities

Liabilities, like assets, are usually separated into current and noncurrent, depending on whether the liability must be satisfied within a year. Most liabilities are reported at historical cost. Although there are no revisions to market value for liabilities, there is a notable exception to the historical cost valuation. Debt instruments are accounted for under the **effective interest rate method**, which amortizes any bond premium or discount relative to par value over the bond's life.

Minority interest represents the portion of the book value of net assets of Starbucks' subsidiaries that is owned by shareholders other than Starbucks. At October 1, 2000, about $3.6 million of the net assets in Starbucks' balance sheet related to these minority shareholders. Although minority interest is equity, it is not equity in the parent company, but in one or more subsidiaries. Conceptually, it is not clear whether minority interest is a liability or equity. As a result, most firms present it in between liabilities and equity and include it in neither. For this reason, minority interest is sometimes referred to as being in the mezzanine. For simplicity of presentation, we include minority interest in liabilities.

Equity

Equity represents the ownership interests of shareholders. It is equal to net assets, or the difference between assets and liabilities. On the balance sheet, equity is broken down by class of stock. For example, in addition to common stock, a firm might have one or more **preferred stock** issues. Some firms even have more than one class of common stock, although that is fairly rare. Each class of stock represents a different set of claims on the firm's net assets. Generally, preferred stockholders have a prior claim on earnings. This means the preferred dividend must be paid before any common dividends can be paid. Preferred stockholders also have preference over common stockholders in a bankruptcy, but do not usually have voting rights. Starbucks has no preferred stock. If it did, the preferred stock would appear at historical cost and before common equity in the balance sheet. **Common equity** is the residual claim of the common stockholders. This is equal to net assets less preferred stock, if any. As is customary, Starbucks' common equity is further broken down into common stock, retained earnings, and accumulated other comprehensive income or loss. In financial analysis, the distinction among these components is generally not important.

Starbucks' Income Statement

We now turn to Starbucks' income statement, shown in Exhibit 4.10. As part of our analysis of Starbucks' income statement, we must consider which items are likely to recur. Most of the line items on Starbucks' income statement are revenues and expenses, which generally recur year after year. These are labeled with the letters R and E. Merger expenses and Internet-related investment losses are labeled L for loss. Although the former is called an expense, we classify it as a loss because it is not a recurring item, as indicated by the absence of any amounts for it in 1999 and 2000. In fact, Starbucks likely presented this amount as an individual line item to highlight the fact that about $9 million of its expenses in 1998 were nonrecurring. Starbucks has no gains or special items.

Earnings per Share

Analysts are often interested in **earnings per share (EPS)**, because it expresses the firm's income in the same units as its stock price. EPS is the amount of the company's net income attributable to each share of common stock.

As Starbucks' income statement shows, there are actually two earnings per share numbers, called basic EPS and diluted EPS. **Basic EPS** is net income available to common shareholders divided by the weighted-average number of common shares outstanding during the year. Net income available to common shareholders is net income less preferred dividends, if any. The weighted-average number of common shares outstanding is an average of the number of common shares outstanding over the entire period.

$$\text{Basic EPS} = \frac{\text{Net income} - \text{Preferred dividends}}{\text{Weighted-average number of common shares outstanding}}$$

Starbucks' income statement shows that in fiscal 2000 its net income was $94,564,000. On average, Starbucks had 185,595,000 common shares outstanding during the year.[13] It had no

---

[13] This is consistent with the balance sheet, which showed about 183.3 million shares outstanding at the beginning of the year and about 188.2 million shares at the end of the year.

EXHIBIT 4.10 Starbucks' Income Statement

In thousands, except earnings per share			
Fiscal year ended	October 1, 2000	October 3, 1999	September 27, 1998
R Net revenues	$ 2,169,218	$ 1,680,145	$ 1,308,702
E Cost of sales and related occupancy costs	953,560	741,010	578,483
Gross margin	1,215,658	939,135	730,219
R Joint venture income	20,300	3,192	1,034
E Store operating expenses	704,898	543,572	418,476
E Other operating expenses	78,374	54,566	44,513
E Depreciation and amortization	130,232	97,797	72,543
E General and administrative expenses	110,202	89,681	77,575
L Merger expenses			8,930
Operating income	212,252	156,711	109,216
R,E Interest and other income, net	7,110	7,315	7,134
L Internet-related investment losses	58,792		
Earnings before income taxes	160,570	164,026	116,350
E Income taxes	66,006	62,333	47,978
Net earnings	$ 94,564	$ 101,693	$ 68,372
Net earnings per common share—basic	$ 0.51	$ 0.56	$ 0.39
Net earnings per common share—diluted	$ 0.49	$ 0.54	$ 0.37
Weighted-average shares outstanding:			
Basic	185,595	181,842	176,110
Diluted	192,999	188,531	183,771
R = revenues, E = expenses, L = loss.			

preferred stock and, hence, no preferred dividends. Starbucks' basic earnings per share is therefore $94,564,000/185,595,000 shares = $0.51 per share.

Diluted EPS is a pro forma, which means "as if," calculation. It is the basic EPS the firm would have had if:

- All the convertible securities[14] it had outstanding were converted to common stock as of the first day of the period. The one exception to this rule is that if assuming conversion increases diluted EPS, it is ignored. Such conversions are called antidilutive.
- All outstanding warrants and stock options[15] were exercised as of the first day of the year, with the proceeds used to repurchase shares at the average market price during the year. Exercises are not assumed if the exercise price exceeds the market price.

---

[14]A convertible security is debt or preferred stock that can be exchanged for common shares at a fixed ratio at the option of the security holder.
[15]Warrants and options give the holder the right to purchase stock from the company at a fixed price, regardless of the stock's market price at the time.

EXHIBIT 4.11   Excerpt from AT&T's 1998 Income Statement

$ millions	Fiscal Year Ending December 31, 1998
Revenues	$ 53,223
Access and other interconnection	15,328
Network and other communications services	10,250
Depreciation and amortization	4,629
Selling, general and administrative	13,015
Restructuring and other charges	2,514
Operating Expenses	45,736
Operating Income	7,487
Other income—net	1,247
Interest expense	427
Income from continuing operations before income taxes	8,307
Provision for income taxes	3,072
Income from continuing operations	5,235
Discontinued Operations:	
Income from discontinued operations (net of taxes of $6)	**10**
Gain on sale of discontinued operations (net of taxes of $799)	**1,290**
Income before Extraordinary loss	6,535
Extraordinary loss (net of taxes of $80)	**137**
Net Income	$ 6,398

Because antidilutive (EPS-increasing) adjustments are not made, diluted EPS is always less than or equal to basic EPS. Starbucks has no convertible securities, so the only difference between its basic EPS and diluted EPS is the effect of the assumed exercise of its outstanding stock options. This would increase the weighted-average number of shares outstanding during 2000 by about 7.4 million, to 192,999,000, making diluted EPS $94,564,000/192,999,000 = $0.49.

Special Items

Although Starbucks has no special items, it is useful to see an example of them. Exhibit 4.11 is AT&T's 1998 income statement. AT&T has several special items. In 1998, AT&T sold its Universal Card Services, Inc. business. Universal became a discontinued operation and its income was shown separately. AT&T recorded a gain on the sale, which is also shown as part of discontinued operations. AT&T extinguished about $1 billion of debt prior to maturity, resulting in an extraordinary loss of $137 million, net of the related income tax benefit.[16]

Starbucks' Cash Flow Statement

We now turn to Starbucks' cash flow statement, shown in Exhibit 4.12.

---

[16]In April 2002, the FASB eliminated extraordinary item treatment for gains and losses early on extinguishment of debt.

EXHIBIT 4.12 Starbucks' Statement of Cash Flows

In thousands Fiscal year ended	October 1, 2000	October 3, 1999	September 27, 1998
OPERATING ACTIVITIES			
Net earnings	$ 94,564	$ 101,693	$ 68,372
Adjustments to reconcile net earnings:			
Depreciation and amortization	142,171	107,512	80,901
Internet-related investment losses	58,792	-	-
Provision for losses on asset disposals	5,753	2,456	7,234
Conversion of compensatory options into common stock	-	-	1,158
Deferred income taxes, net	(18,252)	794	2,125
Equity in (income) losses of investees	(15,139)	(2,318)	14
Tax benefit from exercise of nonqualified stock options	31,131	18,621	9,332
Cash provided (used) by changes in operating assets and liabilities:			
Net purchases of trading securities	(1,414)	-	-
Accounts receivable	(28,235)	3,838	(19,790)
Inventories	(19,495)	(36,405)	(23,496)
Prepaid expenses and other current assets	(700)	(7,552)	(2,497)
Accounts payable	15,561	4,711	4,601
Accrued compensation and related costs	30,962	7,586	9,943
Accrued occupancy costs	6,007	5,517	5,342
Accrued taxes	5,026	12,429	7,173
Minority interest	3,188	400	-
Deferred revenue	6,836	(53)	209
Other accrued expenses	1,818	10,366	1,590
Net cash provided by operating activities	318,574	229,595	152,211
INVESTING ACTIVITIES			
Purchase of available-for-sale investments	(118,501)	(122,800)	(51,354)
Maturity of available-for-sale investments	58,750	85,053	112,080
Sale of available-for-sale investments	49,238	3,633	5,138
Purchases of businesses, net of cash acquired	(13,522)	(15,662)	-
Investments in joint ventures	(8,473)	(10,466)	(12,418)
Purchases of other investments	(35,457)	(20,314)	-
Distributions from joint ventures	14,279	8,983	2,750
Additions to property, plant, and equipment	(316,450)	(257,854)	(201,855)
Additions to other assets	(3,096)	(6,866)	(3,184)
Net cash used by investing activities	(373,232)	(336,293)	(148,843)
FINANCING ACTIVITIES			
Increase/(decrease) in cash provided by checks drawn in excess of bank balances	(7,479)	29,512	4,846
Proceeds from sale of common stock under employee stock purchase plan	10,258	9,386	4,649
Exercise of stock options	58,463	33,799	20,755
Payments on long-term debt	(1,889)	(1,189)	(1,993)
Net cash provided by financing activities	59,353	71,508	28,257
Effect of exchange rate on cash and cash equivalents	(297)	(54)	(88)
Net increase/(decrease) in cash and equivalents	4,398	(35,244)	31,537
Cash and equivalents beginning of year	66,419	101,663	70,126
Cash and equivalents end of year	$ 70,817	$ 66,419	$ 101,663

Starbucks' cash flow statement begins with net earnings, and the numbers on this top line match the bottom line numbers from the income statement. The remainder of the operating activities section includes reversals of noncash components of income such as depreciation and amortization, as well as changes in various working capital items. The second section is investing activities. As the captions indicate, these items are purchases and sales of investments in marketable securities and similar assets, as well as purchases and sales of operating assets. The final section is financing activities. The cash flow in this section is usually dictated by the firm's financing needs, as determined in the first two sections. For example, a firm that has a negative cash flow from operations and investing is likely to have borrowed or issued equity to finance its capital needs. Similarly, a firm that has generated a great deal of cash is likely to have paid down debt or repurchased some of its stock. In fiscal 2000, Starbucks generated about $60 million through financing, which financed the roughly $55 million cash outflow from operations and investing.

The three components of cash flow, together with a downward revaluation of $297,000 of cash denominated in foreign currencies due to changes in foreign exchange rates, resulted in an increase of $4.4 million in cash during fiscal 2000.

Starbucks' Combined Income Statement and Cash Flow Statement

Exhibit 4.13 provides a combination income statement and cash flow statement for Starbucks for fiscal year 2000 only. This combined statement includes all the information in the income statement and the cash flow statement. As such, it provides the information necessary to form a base from which an analyst can forecast future cash flows. We will use this structure when we study valuation.

SUMMARY

Financial statements are the key input to financial statement analysis. To interpret financial statement information effectively, we must understand how the financial statements were constructed.

Accounting provides a system of three primary financial statements. These statements are linked together. The balance sheet presents assets and liabilities, with the difference between them being equity. Changes in equity that do not arise because of contributions to or withdrawals from the firm's capital are income. The cash flow statement presents a reconciliation of differences between income and the change in cash.

To be included in the balance sheet, an item must meet recognition criteria. Some items may not be recognized, even though they meet the conceptual definition of an asset or a liability. Once an item is recognized, accountants must determine how the item is to be valued on the balance sheet. Although people often refer to the balance sheet as being based on historical cost, historical cost is just one of many valuation bases found in the balance sheet. Other valuation bases include fair value, present value of future cash flows, amortized cost, lower of cost or market, and net realizable value.

GAAP sets balance sheet recognition criteria and valuation rules in three different ways. In some cases, it dictates the valuation methods. In other cases, firms select from among two or more methods, providing the manager with discretion. In still other cases, one of several methods is required, depending on the facts. This also provides the manager with discretion as the determination of the facts is not always clear.

Whether assets and liabilities are recognized and how they are valued affects income. An increase in an asset valuation, for example, results in the recognition of income. The income statement lists items that affected income in a period, and consists of five categories of items: revenues, expenses, gains, losses, and special items.

EXHIBIT 4.13   Starbucks' Combined Income Statement and Cash Flow Statement

In thousands Fiscal year ended	October 1, 2000
Net revenues	$ 2,169,218
Cost of sales and related occupancy costs	(953,560)
Gross margin	1,215,658
Joint venture income	20,300
Store operating expenses	(704,898)
Other operating expenses	(78,374)
Depreciation and amortization	(130,232)
General and administrative expenses	(110,202)
Operating income	212,252
Interest and other income, net	7,110
Internet-related investment losses	(58,792)
Earnings before income taxes	160,570
Income taxes	(66,006)
Net earnings	94,564
Adjustments to reconcile net earnings:	
Depreciation and amortization	142,171
Internet-related investment losses	58,792
Provision for losses on asset disposals	5,753
Deferred income taxes, net	(18,252)
Equity in (income) losses of investees	(15,139)
Tax benefit from exercise of nonqualified stock options	31,131
Net purchases of trading securities	(1,414)
Accounts receivable	(28,235)
Inventories	(19,495)
Prepaid expenses and other current assets	(700)
Accounts payable	15,561
Accrued compensation and related costs	30,962
Accrued occupancy costs	6,007
Accrued taxes	5,026
Minority interest	3,188
Deferred revenue	6,836
Other accrued expenses	1,818
Net cash provided by operating activities	318,574
Purchase of available-for-sale investments	(118,501)
Maturity of available-for-sale investments	58,750
Sale of available-for-sale investments	49,238
Purchases of businesses, net of cash acquired	(13,522)
Investments in joint ventures	(8,473)
Purchases of other investments	(35,457)
Distributions from joint ventures	14,279
Additions to property, plant, and equipment	(316,450)
Additions to other assets	(3,096)
Net cash used by investing activities	(373,232)

continued

continued

Decrease in cash provided by checks drawn in excess of bank balances	(7,479)
Proceeds from sale of common stock under employee stock purchase plan	10,258
Exercise of stock options	58,463
Payments on long-term debt	(1,889)
Net cash provided by financing activities	59,353
Effect of exchange rate on cash and cash equivalents	(297)
Net increase in cash and equivalents	4,398
Cash and equivalents beginning of year	66,419
Cash and equivalents end of year	$ 70,817

The accounting method and valuation choices firms make affect reported earnings. We often characterize how these choices affect earnings in terms of earnings quality. Quality can mean conservatism, absence of manipulation, or absence of nonrecurring items.

The cash flow statement reconciles net income to the change in cash. It consists of three sections: cash flow from operations, cash flow from investing, and cash flow from financing. Although not a GAAP statement, the combined income statement and cash flow statement provides a summary of all the items affecting cash flow and is useful in analysis.

Analysts use financial statements every day. In doing so, it is important that they consider how managers may have influenced the financial statements. The analysts must interpret the financial statements accordingly and often adjust them for a particular analysis.

SUGGESTED READINGS

Financial Accounting Standards Board. *Current Text Accounting Standards.* New York: John Wiley, 1999.

Fraser, L. and A. Ormiston. *Understanding Financial Statements.* Upper Saddle River, NJ: Prentice Hall, 2001.

Fridson, M. *Financial Statement Analysis: A Practitioner's Guide,* 2nd ed. New York: John Wiley, 1996.

Gordon, G. *Understanding Financial Statements.* Cincinnati, OH: South-Western, 1992.

Mulford, C. and E. Comiskey. *Financial Warnings.* New York: John Wiley, 1996.

Revsine, L., D. Collins, and B. Johnson, *Financial Reporting and Analysis,* 2nd ed. Upper Saddle River, NJ: Prentice Hall, 2001, Chapters 2, 4, and 17.

REVIEW QUESTIONS

1. Describe the relationship between the income statement and the balance sheet.
2. Describe the relationship between the cash flow statement and the balance sheet.
3. Why do some items that involve no cash flow, such as depreciation, appear on the cash flow statement?

4. What is the general definition of an asset?

5. Give an example of an asset.

6. Give an example of an item that meets the definition of an asset in question 4 but is not recognized as such on the balance sheet.

7. What is the general definition of a liability?

8. Give an example of a liability.

9. Give an example of an item that meets the definition of a liability in question 7 but is not recognized as such on the balance sheet.

10. Describe three possible interpretations of earnings quality.

11. Describe each of the following asset valuation methods:
    a. Historical cost
    b. Fair market value
    c. Present value
    d. Net realizable value
    e. Amortized cost

12. For each of the asset valuation methods in question 11, give an example of an asset typically valued on that basis.

13. In determining the value at which accounts receivable should be presented, managers must estimate the portion of the receivables that ultimately will not be collected. What should a manager consider in making that estimate?

14. Income statements sometimes have special items.
    a. Define the three types of special items found in income statements.
    b. If you are forecasting earnings for a company that has had each of these special items in the past, how would each affect your forecast?

PROBLEMS

1. PepsiCo, Inc.'s balance sheet as of December 30, 2000 includes an item called "accounts and notes receivable, net" of $1.8 billion. What does the word "net" mean in this caption?

2. PepsiCo reported two earnings per share amounts for the year ended December 30, 2000: $1.51 and $1.48. Which of these amounts is basic earnings per share and which is diluted earnings per share?

3. W. W. Grainger reported $1,707,258,000 in retained earnings at December 31, 1999, and $1,837,298,000 at December 31, 2000. It had net income of $192,903,000 in 2000. What amount of dividends did Grainger declare during 2000?

4. Grainger's 2000 cash flow statement includes a positive amount of $18,076,000 for "provision for losses on accounts receivable." Why is a provision for a loss a positive amount?

   The following was adapted from PECO Energy Company's income statement for 2000, 1999, and 1998. Use this statement for problems 5 and 6.

($ millions)	**For the Years Ended December 31,**		
	2000	**1999**	**1998**
Operating revenue	$ 5,950	$ 5,478	$ 5,325
Operating expenses:			
Fuel and purchased power	2,127	2,152	1,811
Operating and maintenance	1,791	1,454	1,198
Merger-related costs	248		
Early retirement and separation program			125
Depreciation and amortization	325	237	643
Taxes other than income	237	262	280
Total operating expenses	4,728	4,105	4,057
Operating income	1,222	1,373	1,268
Other income and deductions			
Interest expense	(457)	(396)	(331)
Company-obligated mandatorily redeemable preferred securities of a partnership, which holds solely subordinated debentures of the company	(8)	(21)	(31)
Equity in earnings (losses) of unconsolidated affiliates	(41)	(38)	(54)
Other, net	41	59	1
Total other income and deductions	(465)	(396)	(415)
Income before income taxes, extraordinary items, and cumulative effect of a change in accounting principle	757	977	853
Income taxes	270	358	320
Income before extraordinary items and cumulative effect of a change in accounting principle	487	619	533
Extraordinary items (net of income taxes of $2, $25, and $14 for 2000, 1999, and 1998, respectively)	(4)	(37)	(20)
Cumulative effect of a change in accounting principle (net of income taxes of $16)	24		
Net income	$ 507	$ 582	$ 513

5. Classify each item in PECO's income statement as revenue (R), expense (E), gain (G), loss (L), or special item (S).

6. Which items in the income statement do you not expect to recur?

7. People often say that GAAP financial statements are prepared on a historical cost basis. In reality, many valuation methods in addition to historical cost are used to prepare financial statements. Describe the various valuation methods used in GAAP financial statements. Be sure to include examples of which accounts are prepared with the various methods.

8. Use a search engine such as Yahoo! (**www.yahoo.com**) to search for "contingent liabilities." Choose one of the "hits" you found and read the disclosure.

   a. Does the company classify its contingencies as probable, reasonably possible, or remote? Explain your answer.
   b. Does the company classify its contingencies as estimable or not estimable? Explain your answer.

9. GAAP requires a dual disclosure for earnings per share—basic and diluted.

   a. Prepare arguments supporting the dual disclosure.
   b. Prepare arguments against the dual disclosure.

10. For each of the following situations, explain the appropriate accounting.

   a. A consumer organization warns that your product could injure children, although no such injury has occurred to date.
   b. A child is injured using your product. No lawsuit has been filed, but you expect one to be filed at some point in the future.
   c. A $50 million lawsuit has been filed against your company. Your lawyers think you have a strong case, but warn you there are no guarantees you will win.
   d. You lose the lawsuit for $50 million, but plan to appeal. In the meantime, you are negotiating a settlement with the plaintiff and expect to settle for around $10 million.
   e. You settle for $7 million.

11. In April 2002, the FASB eliminated extraordinary item treatment for gains and losses on early retirement of debt. Under the previous rules, all such gains and losses were shown as extraordinary items (if material), even if they did not meet the unusual and nonrecurring tests.

   a. Prepare arguments supporting extraordinary item treatment for these gains and losses.
   b. Prepare arguments supporting the elimination of extraordinary item treatment for these gains and losses.

My Case

Obtain the financial statements for your company.

   a. Confirm that the firm's income, dividends, and other capital transactions explain the change in equity for the most recent year. (You may need to consult the statement of shareholders' equity.)
   b. Confirm that the firm's cash flow statement begins with the same net income amounts found in the income statement.
   c. Confirm that the firm's cash flow statement shows a change in cash that is equal to the difference between cash shown on the balance sheet at the beginning and end of the year.
   d. Construct a combined income statement and cash flow statement.
   e. Does your company have any special items? What are they? Do you expect them to recur? Do they tell you anything about the business situation?
   f. What depreciation methods does the firm use? Have there been any changes?
   g. What inventory methods does the firm use? Have there been any changes?
   h. Does your firm have any significant contingent liabilities?

    i. Does your firm have any equity method investments? What are they?

    j. Does your firm have any minority interest (noncontrolling interest)?

    k. Review the historical cash flow statement. Are there any large reconciling items? What are they? What does this information tell you?

    l. Does your firm have an unqualified, clean audit opinion? If not, what was the exception?

    m. How would management choices, estimates, and judgment affect the financial statements?

APPENDIX 4.1 ACCOUNTING FOR INVESTMENTS

Firms often invest in another company's stock or debt securities. They may do this when they have excess cash available to invest for a period of time, or they may make a strategic investment for the longer term. In either case, the investing firm hopes to earn a return on its investment. In this appendix, we discuss the accounting for such investments, which Exhibit 4.14 summarizes.

As Exhibit 4.14 shows, when a firm invests in the stock of another company, the accounting treatment for the investment depends on the degree to which the investor can influence the operations of the investee. Investments that lead to control (through more than 50% of the voting stock) are consolidated. Investments that result in significant influence are accounted for under the equity method. Equity investments that do not result in significant influence, as well as investments in debt securities, are subject to the classifications and reporting rules of SFAS No. 115, "Accounting for Certain Investments in Debt and Equity Securities."

Controlling Equity Investment—Consolidation

Investments of over 50% of another firm are deemed to be controlling investments and are consolidated into the financial statements.[17] Under consolidation, the balance sheet reports all of the assets and liabilities of the subsidiary as if those assets and liabilities were the parent's own. Similarly, the income statement includes the revenues and expenses of the subsidiary, and the cash flow statement reports those items as if they were the parent's.

When a parent's ownership is less than 100%, there is a minority interest, also called a noncontrolling interest. All three statements report a reversal for the portion of the previous amounts in the statement that are attributable to the minority shareholders. For example, if a 90% owned subsidiary is consolidated, the income statement will include 100% of the subsidiary's sales, expenses, and so on, and near the bottom of the statement will subtract the 10% of the subsidiary's income not belonging to the parent.

Equity Investment with Significant Influence—Equity Method

If a firm owns between 20% and 50% of the investee, the accounting rules begin with a presumption that there is significant influence. That presumption can be rebutted by evidence to the contrary,

---

[17]The FASB is considering a broader definition of control that would include investment in less than 50% of the investee when effective control still exists. For example, a 49% investment when the remainder of the stock is widely held might be considered effective control.

EXHIBIT 4.14   Summary of Accounting for Investments

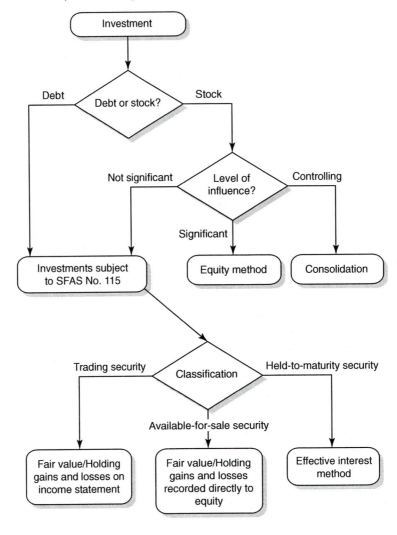

such as a failed attempt to gain board representation or more than 50% of the stock being held by another shareholder. When there is significant influence, the equity method is appropriate. Exhibit 4.15 summarizes the accounting for investments in stock under the equity method.

Under the equity method, the investing company records the investment at cost, adds its proportionate share of the investee's income, and subtracts its proportionate share of the investee's losses. The firm also subtracts the dividend received from the investment. The income statement will include the firm's proportionate share of the investee's income or losses. The investing firm will show an item on the cash flow statement reconciling income recorded and dividends received.

Investments Subject to SFAS No. 115

When one firm owns less than 20% of another, the accounting rules call for a presumption that there is no significant influence. However, if there is evidence to the contrary, such as a seat on the board of directors, that presumption can be overcome. So, it is possible, although not common, to have

EXHIBIT 4.15   Investments in Stock—Significant Influence

Balance Sheet Treatment	Original cost of investment + Proportionate share of income − Proportionate share of losses − Dividends received
Income Statement Treatment	Proportionate share of income or loss recognized
Cash Flow Statement Treatment	Difference between dividend received and income or loss is reconciling item

investments in less than 20% of another company accounted for under the equity method. Generally, such investments are subject to SFAS No. 115, as are investments in debt securities.

Investments subject to SFAS No. 115 are divided into three categories.

- **Trading securities**. These are debt and equity securities management plans to sell in the near term.

- **Available-for-sale securities**. These are debt and equity securities management plans to keep long term, but not until maturity.

- **Held-to-maturity securities**. These are debt instruments the firm plans to hold until maturity. This category is not an option for stock investments because there is no maturity for stock.

Management intent is critical to choosing the way investments are classified. The analyst must understand that management has a great deal of discretion in determining its intent.[18]

Exhibit 4.16 summarizes the accounting for marketable securities when there is no significant influence. Trading securities are reported at their fair value at the balance sheet date. Revisions in fair value are reported as gains and losses on the income statement. Interest and dividend income is also reported on the income statement. Unrealized gains and losses, being noncash components of income, are reversed on the cash flow statement.

Like trading securities, available-for-sale securities are reported at fair value. However, revisions in fair value are not reported as gains and losses on the income statement. Instead, shareholders' equity is increased or decreased directly. The increase or decrease is placed in an equity account called "other comprehensive income." Interest and dividend income is reported on the income statement. Because revaluations affect neither income nor cash, there is no effect on the cash flow statement.

EXHIBIT 4.16   Investments in Stock—No Significant Influence

Intent	To sell soon	To hold long term	To hold to maturity
Type of Security	Trading	Available-for-sale	Held-to-maturity
Balance Sheet Treatment	• Investment is reported at fair value.	• Investment is reported at fair value. • Unrealized gains and losses recorded directly into stockholders' equity.	• Investment is reported at amortized cost under the effective interest rate method.
Income Statement Treatment	• Interest and dividends recognized as income. • Unrealized gains and losses recorded as income.	• Interest and dividends recognized as income.	• Interest is reported as income.
Cash Flow Statement Treatment	• Unrealized gains and losses are noncash components of income, so they are reversed in the cash flow statement.	• Unrealized gains and losses do not affect the income statement, so there is no reversal in the cash flow statement.	• Amortization of discount or premium is a reconciling item.

---

[18]To deal with this problem, the FASB amended Statement No. 115, "Accounting for Certain Investments in Debt and Equity Securities," shortly after its issuance. As a result, if prior to maturity a firm sells investments that were classified as held-to-maturity, it will be barred from using the held-to-maturity classification in the future, except in certain circumstances.

Firms report held-to-maturity securities under the effective interest rate method at amortized cost, which is the original purchase price plus or minus the cumulative amortization of any discount or premium. The reported value of these securities may be different from the fair value. If interest rates have changed substantially since the security was purchased and the security is not near its maturity date, the difference may be quite large. As for available-for-sale securities, interest income is reported on the income statement. Amortization of discount or premium creates a difference between income and cash flow. As a result, it appears as a reconciling item on the cash flow statement.

APPENDIX 4.2 ACCOUNTING FOR CONTINGENCIES

A contingent liability, or contingency, is a potential liability that may have been incurred as a result of a past transaction or event. Although the event in question has occurred, there is uncertainty as to whether the event created a liability. That uncertainty will be resolved at some time in the future, often as a result of litigation. For example, the antitrust action against Microsoft represents a contingent liability for the company. Until the litigation is complete, uncertainty remains about the ultimate disposition of the case and the cost to the company.

It is important to distinguish contingent liabilities from potential future liabilities. If Microsoft is fined or pays to settle its antitrust case, it will be as a result of its *past* actions. However, the firm will not know until the end of the litigation whether there is such a liability. With a contingent liability, the future will resolve whether a liability has already been created. In contrast, there is a chance that an earthquake could destroy Microsoft's office at some time in the future. This is not a contingent liability because it would be the result of a future event, not a past event.

A contingent liability may also be due to uncertainty about the amount of a liability. This may be the case with an industrial or commercial accident. When the Exxon *Valdez* tanker spilled oil off the coast of Alaska, there was little doubt the company had incurred a liability; yet there was great uncertainty about the amount of that liability.

Understanding contingencies is an important part of the accounting analysis. Analysts must be aware of contingencies because the likelihood of a contingency ultimately leading to a use of resources, together with its potential magnitude, affects the company's financial position. SFAS No. 5, "Accounting for Contingencies," mandates disclosures about contingent liabilities. It requires firms to classify contingencies in two ways. First, the firm must classify each contingency based on the probability that a liability has been incurred. Second, the company must assess its ability to estimate the ultimate cost it might incur. These two classifications determine the recognition and disclosure requirements.

Firms classify contingencies as having a "probable," "reasonably possible," or "remote" chance of representing an actual liability. These are very subjective classifications, and the accounting standards provide no real guidance on what each means. In particular, no numerical probability cutoffs separate the three categories. Firms also classify contingencies as "reasonably estimable" or "not reasonably estimable." Estimability does not require an ability to determine a precise estimate, only an ability to arrive at a reasonable approximation of the ultimate cost. Exhibit 4.17 summarizes how these classifications determine the recognition and disclosure requirements for the contingencies.

EXHIBIT 4.17   Recognition and Disclosure Requirements for Contingencies

Estimability Classification		
Likelihood of Liability	Reasonably Estimable	Not Reasonably Estimable
Probable	Recognize liability and disclose	Disclose contingency and state that cost cannot be estimated
Reasonably possible	Disclose contingency and cost estimate	Disclose contingency and state that cost cannot be estimated
Remote	No disclosure required	No disclosure required

A contingency that is both probable and reasonably estimable must be recognized. Contingent liabilities that do not meet both of these criteria and are at least "reasonably possible" must be disclosed in the financial statement footnotes, along with an estimated loss if the estimate can be made. Remote contingencies need not be disclosed.

The contents of contingency disclosures vary substantially across firms, depending on the number and type of contingencies. Obviously, certain industries will be more prone to having lengthy contingency disclosures, such as those with environmental issues, for example, chemical and paint manufacturers. Contrast El Paso Electric's litigation footnote with that of R. J. Reynolds Tobacco Holdings Inc. El Paso wrote in its 2000 Form 10-K:

I. Litigation

The Company is a party to various claims, legal actions and complaints. In many of these matters, the Company has excess casualty liability insurance that covers the various claims, actions and complaints. Based on a review of these claims and applicable insurance coverage, the Company believes that none of these claims will have a material adverse effect on the financial position, results of operations and cash flows of the Company.

Source: El Paso Electric 2000 Form 10-K.

In contrast, the tobacco litigation section alone of Reynolds' 1999 contingency footnote runs nearly nine pages. Reynolds concludes that the results of litigation could materially affect the company, but that it cannot estimate the potential cost.

Contingent liabilities provide a challenge for the analyst. Management uses its judgment to determine whether a contingent liability meets the two recognition requirements. Management's natural inclination may be to keep liabilities off the balance sheet, which could influence their estimates of probability. Further, management may want to state that a potential liability is not estimable, even if it is. For example, if a firm is a defendant in a lawsuit and feels it is likely to lose a substantial judgment, it may not want to recognize, or even disclose, the estimated liability for fear the plaintiff will take that as a signal about the firm's expected loss. This could lead the plaintiff to play tougher in court or to demand a larger settlement.

5

 Where We Have Been:

In Chapter 4, we reviewed the structure of the financial statements.

 Where We Are:

In this chapter, we learn about using the financial statements for financial statement analysis. We present common financial ratios and review the cautions necessary for using these ratios in financial analysis.

 Where We Are Going:

In Chapters 6 through 12, we will study the next phases of security analysis: forecasting and valuation.

Financial Statement Analysis

LEARNING OBJECTIVES:

After studying this chapter, you will understand:

- How analysts use historical financial statements in financial statement analysis.

- How to calculate and interpret operating, credit, and investment ratios.

- How to prepare a trend analysis of a company's financial ratios.

- How analysts use financial statement analysis to help prepare a valuation forecast.

- The cautions analysts must consider when using financial statement analysis.

Analysts use financial statement analysis to answer questions about the business. The questions depend on the underlying purpose of their analyses but often include these:

- Is the business profitable?
- If so, which segments are most profitable?
- How does the profitability compare to that of the competition and why?
- What is changing in the business?
- Is the business growing?
- Are certain segments growing or declining more than others?
- Does the business generate cash?
- What are the cash needs for additional capital investments?

The focus of this book is business valuation. Much of our discussion in this chapter deals with using financial statement analysis not for its own sake, but as part of a valuation analysis. However, financial statement analysis is used for other applications as well. Competitors use financial statement analysis to judge the relative profitability of businesses in an industry, identify opportunities, and avoid unprofitable sectors. Managers use financial statement analysis to track their firms' performances. Credit analysts evaluate the creditworthiness of current and prospective borrowers, and customers and investors use certain ratios to screen potential investments.

Regardless of the underlying purpose of an analysis—whether it is competitive analysis, performance analysis, credit analysis, investment screening, or some other goal—analysts can gain a wealth of information about a business from studying its financial statements. In this way, financial statement analysis is inextricably linked to business analysis.

In financial statement analysis, we use the information provided in historical financial statements to calculate ratios. These ratios help us learn about such things as the firm's profitability, growth, and resource needs. Through this analysis, we detect and understand relationships among various financial statement items. These relationships, along with the information gained in the business analysis, will provide clues about the outlook for the business. We will use these clues to develop the forecasts needed in our valuation work.

As Exhibit 5.1 shows, financial statement analysis is based on historical results. Although we use data from the historical financial statements in our analysis, the purpose of financial statement analysis is not only to understand the history but also to use that information to forecast the future. For example, historical sales information helps us understand the business trends. When we combine this historical information with the market outlook derived in the business analysis, we will be able to develop sales forecast assumptions. The results of financial statement and business analyses lead to forecast assumptions that enable us to value the firm.

Section 5.1 presents ratios that analysts commonly study. Section 5.2 discusses the ways in which ratios are analyzed. Section 5.3 covers the cautions analysts must consider when using financial ratios.

EXHIBIT 5.1   A Picture of the Security Analysis Process

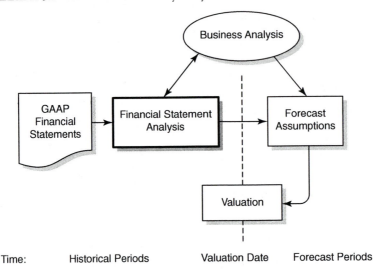

Time: Historical Periods   Valuation Date   Forecast Periods

5.1 COMMON RATIOS

In financial statement analysis, we study ratios that are helpful in interpreting business results. There is no "official" list of ratios nor "official" definitions of any ratios. Different analysts, firms, and textbooks define ratios differently. Despite these differences, analysts commonly use a number of ratios with fairly consistent definitions. We organize these ratios into three types: operating ratios, credit ratios, and investment ratios. **Operating ratios** help us understand the profitability and cash flow of the business operations. **Credit ratios** measure a firm's ability to repay obligations. **Investment ratios** measure a firm's total performance and are used, along with the operating ratios, to screen potential investments.

    We spend the most time on operating ratios, which are used much more extensively in the valuation process, and briefly discuss common credit ratios and investment ratios. Exhibit 5.2 is an outline of the ratios we will study.

Operating Ratios

Analysts use operating ratios to understand elements of a company's business, such as profitability and capital efficiency. This, in turn, will help forecast earnings and cash flows. Internal managers also

EXHIBIT 5.2   Financial Statement Ratio Outline

Operating Ratios	Credit Ratios	Investment Ratios
Analyze business profitability and cash flow	Measure ability to repay obligations	Screen investments
Revenue growth rate	Current ratio	Price-to-earnings ratio
Gross margin percentage	Quick ratio	Market-to-book ratio
Operating margin percentage	Debt to capital ratio	Return on capital
Effective income tax rate	Interest coverage ratio	Return on common equity
Days receivables outstanding		
Days payables outstanding		
Inventory turnover		

track operating ratios to help them understand business performance. If a ratio deviates significantly from its expected level, more detailed analysis may be needed to determine the source of the problem. Ultimately, this may lead to corrective actions, such as the replacement of a manager, an adjustment to pricing, or cost reduction measures.

Although we can define a ratio any way we want, ratios are most meaningful when the numerator and denominator are related to each other. Exhibit 5.3 presents some common operating ratios for Starbucks for fiscal 2000. In defining these ratios, we use Starbucks' terminology. Different companies use different terms, so you may see definitions that look slightly different as you study other companies. For example, Starbucks uses the term *gross margin* to refer to revenues less cost of sales. Other companies, such as Mattel, call this amount *gross profit*. Some use the term *gross margin* to refer to the ratio of gross profit to revenues.

Revenue growth rate is the change in revenues from the prior year to the current year, divided by revenues in the prior year. It measures the expansion or contraction of the business. Growth is better measured at the revenue level than at a profit level, such as net income. If growth were measured using net income, the result would mix the expansion or contraction of the business with changes in its profitability.

Gross margin percentage is gross margin divided by revenues, where gross margin is revenues less cost of goods sold. A key performance measure, it represents the amount per dollar of revenues available to pay other costs after the costs of the product sold have been met. Companies often analyze gross margin percentage when making pricing decisions.

Operating margin percentage, another key measure of operating profitability, is operating income divided by revenues. This percentage shows the profit from operating the business before any taxes and financing costs.

The **effective income tax rate** is income tax expense divided by earnings before income taxes.[1] We usually compare income tax expense to earnings before income taxes rather than to revenues because taxes vary most directly with earnings before income taxes. A ratio of income taxes to revenues would mix the effects of the income tax rate and profitability and end up telling us little about either.

In addition to the preceding ratios, which involve income statement items, analysts want to understand the business's working capital usage. To do so, analysts often study the three main working capital components. Each of the final three ratios in Exhibit 5.3 analyzes one component of working capital. **Days receivables outstanding** measures how well the company is collecting its receivables. The denominator, revenues/365, is the average daily revenue amount. Dividing the average accounts receiv-

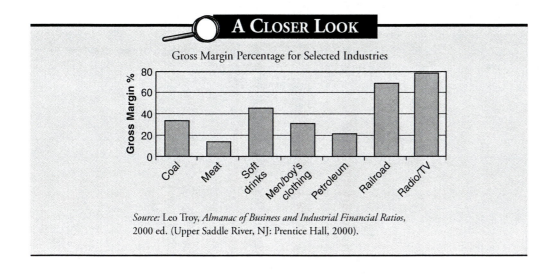

A CLOSER LOOK

Gross Margin Percentage for Selected Industries

Source: Leo Troy, *Almanac of Business and Industrial Financial Ratios,* 2000 ed. (Upper Saddle River, NJ: Prentice Hall, 2000).

EXHIBIT 5.3   Starbucks' Operating Ratios—Fiscal 2000

Ratio	Definition	Calculation	Value
Revenue growth rate	$\dfrac{\text{Current year revenues} - \text{Prior year revenues}}{\text{Prior year revenues}}$	$\dfrac{\$2,169,218,000 - \$1,680,145,000}{\$1,680,145,000}$	29.1%
Gross margin percentage	$\dfrac{\text{Gross margin}}{\text{Revenues}}$	$\dfrac{\$1,215,658,000}{\$2,169,218,000}$	56.0%
Operating margin percentage	$\dfrac{\text{Operating income}}{\text{Revenues}}$	$\dfrac{\$212,252,000}{\$2,169,218,000}$	9.8%
Effective income tax rate	$\dfrac{\text{Income taxes}}{\text{Earnings before income taxes}}$	$\dfrac{\$66,006,000}{\$160,570,000}$	41.1%
Days receivables outstanding	$\dfrac{\text{Average accounts receivable balance}}{\text{Revenues}/365}$	$\dfrac{(\$76,385,000 + \$47,646,000)/2}{\$2,169,218,000/365}$	10.4 days
Days payables outstanding	$\dfrac{\text{Average accounts payable balance}}{\text{Cost of sales}/365}$	$\dfrac{(\$73,653,000 + \$56,108,000)/2}{\$953,560,000/365}$	24.8 days
Inventory turnover	$\dfrac{\text{Cost of sales}}{\text{Average inventory balance}}$	$\dfrac{\$953,560,000}{(\$201,656,000 + \$180,886,000)/2}$	5.0 times

able balance by this amount gives the average number of days of receivables outstanding. Starbucks is mostly a cash business, so this ratio (10.4 days) is a low value.[2] The next ratio, **days payables outstanding**, is calculated in a similar way. It shows that Starbucks takes slightly less than a month to pay its payables, assuming the bulk of the payables relate to cost of sales. Too low a ratio indicates that the company is not using its available trade credit to its benefit. Too high a ratio indicates a problem in making payments. Common credit terms are 30 days, so 24.8 days is a reasonable value.

The **inventory turnover** ratio is equal to cost of sales divided by the average inventory balance. Starbucks turns over its inventory about five times per year, or about once every 73 days. Higher inventory turnover suggests greater efficiency. But if the ratio is too high (meaning inventory is very low relative to cost of sales), then the firm runs the risk of inventory stockouts, which are very costly when lost revenues result.[3] The inventory turnover ratio varies greatly by industry. Quite often, lower-margin businesses, such as grocery stores, have high inventory turnover. The only way for them to be profitable is to sell high volume relative to inventories, so they manage their inventory levels very carefully. For example, A&P's fiscal 2000 inventory turnover was 9.6 times. High-margin businesses, such as jewelry stores, will have much lower inventory turnover. Tiffany & Co., a major upscale jewelry retailer, had inventory turnover of only 1.2 times in fiscal 2000. Tiffany must carry enough inventory to have an adequate selection when the right buyer comes along because, unlike gallons of milk, no two diamonds are exactly the same. But Tiffany can afford large inventory holding costs because of the higher margins.

Credit Ratios

Credit analysts decide whether to extend credit to various businesses. They assess the ability of potential borrowers to repay obligations on a timely basis. A business's ability to repay obligations

---

[1]As we will see in Chapter 13, when doing a valuation, we will make some adjustments to both income tax expense and earnings before income taxes before calculating this ratio.

[2]If the information were available, it would be beneficial to use only credit sales in the denominator to get a better measure of how long it takes to collect a receivable.

[3]The cost is not limited to the revenues lost at the time of the stockout, because stockouts are likely to reduce customer loyalty and result in lost future revenues as well.

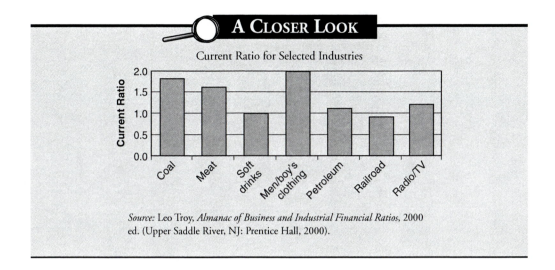

A CLOSER LOOK

Current Ratio for Selected Industries

Source: Leo Troy, *Almanac of Business and Industrial Financial Ratios*, 2000 ed. (Upper Saddle River, NJ: Prentice Hall, 2000).

will depend on its general health, its cash-generating abilities, and its existing credit commitments. To understand a business's general health and cash-generating ability, the credit analyst looks at the operating ratios. In addition, the credit analyst needs to understand existing credit commitments. The analyst will look at the debt to capital and interest coverage ratios to understand the existing credit commitments. Exhibit 5.4 shows common credit ratios for Starbucks for fiscal 2000.

The **current ratio**, current assets divided by current liabilities, measures liquidity. Generally, a higher current ratio signifies greater liquidity and thus an improved ability to pay short-term debts in a timely fashion. However, firms do not attempt to have extremely high current ratios, because it is costly to hold a greater amount of current assets than is necessary. An extremely high current ratio might indicate an inefficient use of working capital.

The **quick ratio** is like the current ratio, except that only cash, cash equivalents, and short-term investments are included in the numerator. This ratio measures the firm's ability to pay its obligations quickly. Again, firms do not attempt to have very high quick ratios because it is costly to hold additional assets. Starbucks' quick ratio is 0.4.

The **debt to capital ratio** is debt divided by total capital, with total capital consisting of debt, minority interest, and equity. This ratio measures the firm's financial leverage, the proportion of capital obtained from debt financing. Starbucks has very little debt in its capital structure; hence, its very low debt to capital ratio of 0.6%. Many firms have very little leverage, but many more have debt to

EXHIBIT 5.4   Starbucks' Credit Ratios—Fiscal 2000

Ratio	Definition	Calculation	Value
Current ratio	$\dfrac{\text{Current assets}}{\text{Current liabilities}}$	$\dfrac{\$459,819,000}{\$313,251,000}$	1.5
Quick ratio	$\dfrac{\text{Cash and short-term investments}}{\text{Current liabilities}}$	$\dfrac{\$70,817,000 + \$61,336,000}{\$313,251,000}$	0.4
Debt to capital ratio	$\dfrac{\text{Debt}}{\text{Debt} + \text{Minority interest} + \text{Equity}}$	$\dfrac{\$685,000 + \$6,483,000}{(\$685,000 + \$6,483,000) + \$3,588,000 + \$1,148,399,000}$	0.6%
Interest coverage ratio	$\dfrac{\text{Earnings before interest and taxes}}{\text{Interest expense}}$	$\dfrac{\$160,570,000 + \$1,363,000}{\$1,363,000}$	118.8 times

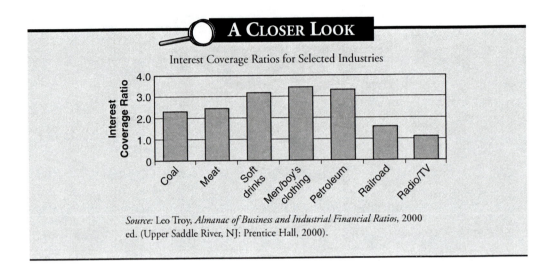

A CLOSER LOOK

Interest Coverage Ratios for Selected Industries

Source: Leo Troy, *Almanac of Business and Industrial Financial Ratios*, 2000 ed. (Upper Saddle River, NJ: Prentice Hall, 2000).

capital ratios of 40% or even more. For example, Superior Telecom, a wire and cable manufacturer, had a debt to capital ratio of 85% at December 31, 2000.

The **interest coverage ratio** measures the number of times interest expense has been earned. The higher the number, the better the firm's ability to make interest payments. It is generally higher for low-leverage firms such as Starbucks. An interest coverage ratio of less than one suggests that the company is not even earning enough to pay its interest requirements. Note that Starbucks does not disclose its interest expense separately, because it is not material. Instead, it nets interest expense against interest income. We needed to make an assumption about interest expense. We estimated its interest expense by using the amount from the company's fiscal 1999 income statement, in which it did separate interest income from interest expense. In making this estimate, we noted that interest income, net, did not change substantially from fiscal 1999 to fiscal 2000. In addition, Starbucks' debt level, which would have a direct bearing on its interest expense, remained approximately the same. Thus, we are confident that the estimate is reasonable.

Investment Ratios

Investors and managers use investment ratios to measure business performance and to screen potential investments. Many of these ratios combine information from the income statement and the balance sheet. Some combine financing and operating data to view a net result, whereas others focus only on the operations. Some measure stock valuation relative to earnings. For example, the price-to-earnings ratio is commonly used as a stock screen. A "value strategy" for investing in stock is one that focuses on buying stocks with low price-to-earnings ratios, presumably because they are better values. Exhibit 5.5 presents investment ratios for Starbucks for fiscal 2000.

The **price-to-earnings (PE) ratio** is a very popular valuation metric equal to the market price per share divided by earnings per share (EPS). Recall that there are two EPS numbers—basic and diluted. It is most common to use diluted EPS to compute the PE ratio.

The main purpose for the PE ratio is to get a sense of how expensive a stock is. However, the PE ratio depends on many things, including expected earnings growth, capital structure, and accounting methods. A high PE ratio does not necessarily mean a stock is expensive. For example, strong expected earnings growth or very conservative accounting methods could justify a high PE ratio.

The **market-to-book (MB) ratio** compares the market value of a company's common stock to the book value of its common equity. It gives information about the value of the firm relative to the recorded

EXHIBIT 5.5 Starbucks' Investment Ratios—Fiscal 2000

Ratio	Definition	Calculation	Value
Price-to-earnings ratio	$\dfrac{\text{Stock price}}{\text{Diluted earnings per share}}$	$\dfrac{\$40.0625}{\$0.49}$	81.8
Market-to-book ratio	$\dfrac{\text{Stock price}}{\text{Book value per share}}$	$\dfrac{\$40.0625}{\$1,148,399,000\,/\,188,157,651}$	6.6
Return on capital	$\dfrac{\text{Net income plus aftertax interest expense}}{\text{Average total capital}}$	$\dfrac{\$94,564,000 + \$1,363,000 \times (1-35\%)}{(\$1,155,567,000 + \$968,704,000)\,/\,2}$	9.0%
Return on common equity	$\dfrac{\text{Net income}}{\text{Average common equity}}$	$\dfrac{\$94,564,000}{(\$1,148,399,000 + \$961,013,000)\,/\,2}$	9.0%

value of its net assets. Many valuable assets are reported at historical cost and many are not reported at all, such as the benefits of research and development. The market-to-book ratio thus depends a great deal on the extent to which the balance sheet diverges from market values of the firm's assets.

Both **return on capital** and **return on common equity** measure return on investment. Return on capital measures return to all capital suppliers. By adding back interest expense, net of the related tax savings, to net income, the numerator represents profits before financing costs. This ratio compares these profits to the capital invested. Return on common equity measures the return to the common stockholders by comparing net income available to common shareholders to average common equity. For firms with little leverage, such as Starbucks, return on capital and return on common equity are usually very close to one another. For firms with more leverage, such as Federated Department Stores, return on capital will be significantly lower than return on common equity. Exhibit 5.6 shows that Federated, which operates Bloomingdale's, Macy's, and other department stores, had a debt to capital ratio of 47.3% at January 29, 2000. Federated's return on capital is 9.5%, similar to Starbucks' return on capital. However, due to its higher leverage, Federated's return on common equity is 13.0%, which is much higher than Starbucks' return on common equity.

Federated's return on common equity is higher than its return on capital, so leverage caused its return on common equity to increase. This will not always be the case. Additional leverage will increase the return on common equity only when return on capital is greater than the after-tax interest rate. Exhibit 5.7 illustrates how return on common equity and return on capital relate.

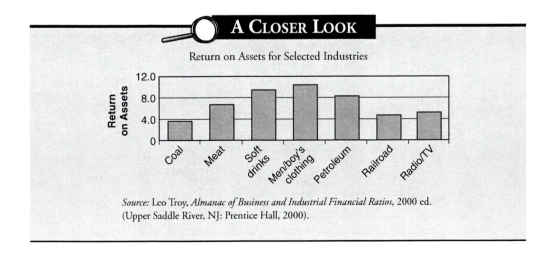

A CLOSER LOOK

Return on Assets for Selected Industries

Source: Leo Troy, *Almanac of Business and Industrial Financial Ratios*, 2000 ed. (Upper Saddle River, NJ: Prentice Hall, 2000).

EXHIBIT 5.6   Comparison of Federated Department Stores and Starbucks Return Ratios

Fiscal Year Ending	Starbucks October 1, 2000	Federated January 29, 2000
Debt to capital ratio	0.6%	47.3%
Return on capital	9.0%	9.5%
Return on common equity	9.0%	13.0%

The dashed line represents a firm with no debt. Its return on common equity is always equal to its return on capital. The more debt the firm has, the more the line relating its return on common equity and return on capital rotates counterclockwise. If the return on capital is greater than the after-tax interest rate, more debt means a higher return on common equity. If the return on capital is lower than the after-tax interest rate, more debt means a lower return on common equity.

5.2 RATIO ANALYSIS

A ratio has little meaning until it is compared to a benchmark. Financial analysts must therefore use some sort of benchmark in their analyses. The two common ways to do this are through trend analysis and cross-sectional analysis. **Trend analyses** look at changes in ratios over time. Here the benchmark is the same firm's prior performance. **Cross-sectional analyses** compare ratios across companies, usually from the same industry. The analyst will make comparisons to other companies serving as benchmarks.

Trend Analysis

In this section, we will study the trend analysis of Starbucks' operating ratios, as shown in Exhibit 5.8.

EXHIBIT 5.7   Relationship Between Return on Common Equity and Return on Capital

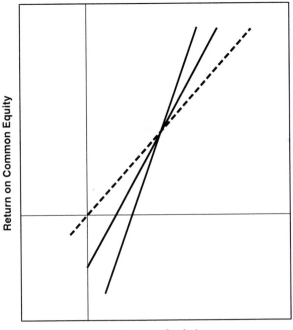

Return on Common Equity

Return on Capital

EXHIBIT 5.8   Starbucks' Operating Ratio Trend Analysis

Fiscal Year Ending	September 28, 1997	September 27, 1998	October 3, 1999	October 1, 2000
Revenue growth rate	39.8%	34.2%	28.4%	29.1%
Gross margin percentage	55.2%	55.8%	55.9%	56.0%
Operating margin percentage	8.8%	8.3%	9.3%	9.8%
Effective income tax rate	39.5%	41.2%	38.0%	41.1%
Days receivables outstanding	9.1	11.5	10.7	10.4
Days payables outstanding	35.6	32.3	26.1	24.8
Inventory turnover	4.3	4.4	4.6	5.0

Revenue Growth Rate

Exhibit 5.8 shows that Starbucks has had tremendous, but slowing, revenue growth. It is common for high-growth firms such as Starbucks, Amazon.com, and Wal-Mart eventually to experience declining revenue growth rates over time. Starbucks undoubtedly exploits its best investment opportunities first. For example, the first Starbucks location in downtown Chicago was probably the best Chicago location the company could find. The second and third were undoubtedly extremely desirable sites as well. Additional sites are likely to be less and less desirable. Otherwise, these sites would have been opened earlier. In addition, now that there are Starbucks locations only a few blocks apart in downtown Chicago, additional locations may not produce the same incremental revenue as they "cannibalize" revenue from existing locations. As a result, although we might expect each new investment to be good, it is not likely to be quite as good as the previous one. As new investments produce less incremental revenue, the result

A CLOSER LOOK

Starbucks Comparable Store Sales

In the management discussion and analysis section of the annual report, companies explain the reasons for changes in key financial items such as revenues, expenses, and certain assets and liabilities. In Starbucks' 2000 management discussion and analysis, the company explains revenue trends. It discusses "comparable store sales," a common concept used in financial analysis of retail businesses. Companies usually define comparable stores to be stores open for the full year for both years being analyzed. They can then compare 1999 comparable store sales to 2000 comparable store sales to understand the sales increase before considering new units. Here is an excerpt from the 2000 Starbucks management discussion and analysis describing revenue increases.

> As part of its expansion strategy of clustering stores in existing markets, Starbucks has experienced a certain level of cannibalization of existing stores by new stores as store concentration has increased. However, management believes such cannibalization has been justified by the incremental sales and return on new store investments. This cannibalization, as well as increased competition and other factors, may put downward pressure on the Company's comparable store sales growth in future periods.

is reduced revenue growth. Also, even if the level of new investment and incremental revenue stays relatively constant in dollar terms, it will fall in percentage terms as the revenue base grows.

When the information is available, the analyst often will look not only at overall revenue growth rates but also at revenue growth by business segment. The analyst may also be able to look at volume measures such as units sold or number of retail outlets. Some of the questions he or she might try to answer include the following:

- Is the key driver of the firm's growth its industry's growth or an increase in the firm's market share?
- Is volume growth or pricing the key driver of revenue growth?
- Is the growth strongly correlated with a certain economic statistic? If so, which one?
- Is the advertising and promotion causing the growth?

The analyst will study the information in the management discussion and analysis of the annual report to understand management's view of revenue growth and potential and do additional outside research to understand the industry and competitive trends. By combining all this information, the analyst will be able to understand the economics of the business and ultimately develop a range of projections of future revenue.

Exhibit 5.9 presents a more detailed analysis of Starbucks' revenues over the last three years. (Much of the data go back to only fiscal 1998 because Starbucks began providing segment data only recently.) An analyst might construct such an analysis to understand the factors affecting revenue growth more completely.

This analysis indicates that North American Retail's growth is lower than the rest of the company's. Because North American Retail is Starbucks' largest segment, the company's overall growth is closer to North American Retail's than to that of the other business units. A further breakdown of North American Retail reveals that virtually all of the segment's growth is coming from new stores. While the number of stores increased from 929 at the end of fiscal 1996 to 2,446 at the end of fiscal 2000, revenue per average number of stores open has increased by less than 3% over the last three years.

Gross Margin Percentage

From Starbucks' historical gross margin percentage, we see that the company has increased gross margin percentage slightly over the last three years. Because Starbucks' revenues and gross margin per-

EXHIBIT 5.9   Detailed Starbucks Revenue Trend Analysis

Fiscal Year Ending	September 29, 1996	September 28, 1997	September 27, 1998	October 3, 1999	October 1, 2000
Revenue growth					
North American Retail revenues			30.0%	27.7%	26.2%
All other business units			56.5%	34.3%	42.7%
Total Revenues			34.2%	28.4%	29.1%
Number of company operated North American Retail stores open at year-end	929	1,270	1,622	2,038	2,446
Sales per average number of North American Retail stores ($ thousands)		$ 753	$ 745	$ 751	$ 774
Increase in sales per North American Retail store			−1.1%	0.9%	3.0%

centage have both increased, its gross margin, which is equal to revenues times gross margin percentage, must also have increased in fiscal 2000. Starbucks' gross margin increased from $939,135,000 in fiscal 1999 to $1,215,658,000 in fiscal 2000.

How much of the gross margin increase results from the gross margin percentage increase and how much from the revenue increase? We can answer this question with a special type of trend analysis called **cause-of-change analysis**, which identifies the causes for a change in a specific item over some period. Exhibit 5.10 breaks out the components of the change in Starbucks' gross margin.

This analysis indicates that most of Starbucks' gross margin increase has been due to its revenue growth. As the company's revenue growth diminishes, we might expect its gross margin growth to do the same. On the other hand, if the gross margin percentage were increasing significantly, we might expect gross margin to continue to increase, even as revenues flatten out.

Additional analysis of gross margin would address questions such as the following:

- Is gross margin percentage increasing because of higher selling prices, a changing product mix, or lower costs?

- Are the changes sustainable in the future?

- Are competitive activities likely to affect Starbucks' ability to improve or sustain its gross margin percentage?

- Do any important commodities affect the company's gross margin percentage significantly?

- Can the firm increase price to offset increases in commodity costs?

- Can we obtain information about projected inflation for these commodities?

The answers to these questions will provide the business reasons for the change in gross margin. We will also consider whether these changes are likely to continue in the future, which helps in forecasting gross margin in our valuation forecast.

Operating Margin Percentage

Exhibit 5.8 showed that Starbucks' operating margin percentage grew from 8.8% to 9.8% from fiscal 1997 to fiscal 2000 and the gross margin percentage increased by about the same amount over the period. However, an investigation of the income statement components between gross margin and operating income reveals that the gross margin improvement was not the only change in operating income. Exhibit 5.11 is a trend analysis of gross margin, operating income, and all items in between as a percentage of revenues.

EXHIBIT 5.10   Starbucks Cause-of-Change in Gross Margin Analysis

($ thousands)		
Gross margin, fiscal 2000	$	1,215,658
Gross margin, fiscal 1999		939,135
Increase in gross margin	$	276,523
Increase in gross margin due to increase in sales, holding gross margin percentage fixed	$	273,373 (1)
Increase in gross margin due to increase in gross margin percentage		3,150 (2)
Total Increase in gross margin	$	276,523

(1) Gross margin percentage, fiscal 1999 × increase in revenues, fiscal 2000 vs. fiscal 1999 = 55.8961% × $489,073,000 = $273,373,000.
(2) Revenues in fiscal 2000 × increase in gross margin percentage = $2,169,218,000 × (56.0413% − 55.8961%) = $3,150,000.

EXHIBIT 5.11   Starbucks' Operating Income as a Percentage of Revenues

Fiscal Year Ending	September 28, 1997	September 27, 1998	October 3, 1999	October 1, 2000	Effect of Change on Operating Income % 1997–2000
Gross margin	55.2	55.8	55.9	56.0	0.8
Joint venture income	(0.2)	0.1	0.2	1.0	1.2
Store operating expenses	(32.2)	(32.0)	(32.4)	(32.5)	(0.3)
Other operating expenses	(2.7)	(3.4)	(3.3)	(3.6)	(0.9)
Depreciation and amortization	(5.4)	(5.6)	(5.8)	(6.0)	(0.6)
General and administrative expenses	(5.9)	(5.9)	(5.3)	(5.1)	0.8
Merger expenses	0.0	(0.7)	0.0	0.0	0.0
Operating Income	8.8	8.3	9.3	9.8	1.0
Operating income (excluding joint venture income and merger expenses)	9.0	8.9	9.1	8.8	(0.2)

Store operating expenses, other operating expenses, and depreciation and amortization (all as a percentage of revenues) have increased during this period, while general and administrative expenses have declined. From the management discussion and analysis, we learn that store operating expenses increased due to higher wage rates and a continual shift to more labor-intensive handcrafted beverages. Other operating expenses increased due to higher payroll-related expenses needed to accelerate the specialty business growth. General and administrative expenses declined due to lower payroll-related expenses as a percentage of revenues.

From Exhibit 5.11, we also see that joint venture income increased by over one percentage point. Although Starbucks includes joint venture income in operating income, it is really more of an investment than an operating item. To understand the operations of the business, we might remove this item. We also remove merger expenses, a one-time item in 1998, because these are not recurring business expenses. We recalculated the operating income percentage without joint venture income and merger expenses, and show the results on the bottom of Exhibit 5.11. The resulting ratio is virtually unchanged from 1997 to 2000. So, despite the increase in gross margin percentage using reported numbers, operating income (excluding joint venture income and merger expenses) as a percentage of revenues has been flat.

Our analysis highlights the importance of making adjustments to reported numbers to understand the business more completely. Note two things about the adjustments we made. First, in financial statement analysis we are not locked into either GAAP or the accounting policies of the companies that we study. We need not include joint venture income in operating income just because Starbucks does. Second, not all companies include joint venture income in operating income, so the adjustment we made to remove it will not always be necessary.

Effective Income Tax Rate

Starbucks' effective income tax rate has varied from year to year. These variations can occur for a number of reasons, including a change in the corporate income tax rate, a changing mix of taxing jurisdictions—states and foreign countries—with different tax rates, nondeductible expenses, or nontaxable income. We will discuss tax rates in Chapter 13.

A CLOSER LOOK

Finding Industry Financial Information

Investment advisory services such as Moody's/Mergents, Standard & Poor's, and Value Line provide company and industry data on publicly traded firms. The information is available in hard copy and online. Most public libraries have these services available. Moody's/Mergents provides historical financial data and prospects for about 1,000 companies in the *Moody's Handbook of Common Stocks. Moody's Industry Review* provides operating data, key financial ratios, and industry rankings for companies and by industry group. The *Value Line Investment Survey* provides a one-page detailed company summary that includes stock price history, historical financial results and ratios, some projections, ratings, and a qualitative commentary. Value Line also provides an industry summary covering the issues, prospects, and ratios for that industry. Standard & Poor's also provides company and industry data.

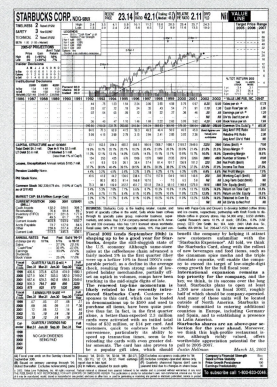

Source: Value Line, March 2002.

Dun & Bradstreet's *Key Business Ratios*, Robert Morris and Associates' *Annual Statement Studies*, and Prentice Hall's *Almanac of Business and Industrial Financial Ratios* also present industry ratios. When using any source for ratio comparisons, always check the ratio definition, as not all services use the same definitions.

Working Capital Ratios

The days receivables outstanding ratio in Exhibit 5.8 has been fairly stable over the period shown. Starbucks is paying its payables faster now than in prior years, as payables have fallen to 24.8 days of cost of sales. This has the effect of increasing working capital, because payables are a negative component of working capital. Finally, the company increased its inventory turnover from 4.3 times per year in fiscal 1997 to 5.0 times in fiscal 2000.

Cross-Sectional Analysis

In cross-sectional analysis, we compare two or more companies using financial ratios. We may also compare the companies' ratios to an industry average. This type of analysis is helpful in understanding the differences in results across companies. When comparing to a competitor, if our company has not performed as well as others, we can sometimes highlight areas of potential improvement. A competitor's ratio, if the firm is quite similar, can provide a goal for the firm.

Comparisons to competitive ratios can also highlight business differences. Suppose, for example, that firm A and firm B are two competitors in the same industry. Firm A selects a differentiated, high-quality strategy, and firm B selects a nondifferentiated, cost-focused strategy. A study of ratios for these two firms would probably find firm A to have a higher gross margin.

There are many published sources of industry and competitor ratios. Exhibit 5.12 shows a cross-sectional analysis from Mergent's Inc. *Industry Review*.

Common-Sized Income Statement

Whether doing a trend analysis or a cross-sectional analysis, analysts sometimes prepare common-sized income statements. These income statements are rescaled so that every line item is a percentage of revenues. This approach factors out size differences, increasing the comparability of the statements to each other. Exhibit 5.13 is a common-sized income statement for Starbucks for 1997–2000.

Because each element of the common-sized income statement is a percentage of revenues, various income amounts are just margin percentages. For example, the amounts shown for operating income are the operating income margins calculated in Exhibit 5.11.

Although common-sized income statements are useful in that they eliminate size differences across statements, they can also be misleading for items that do not vary with sales. The ratio of income tax expense to sales is less meaningful than the effective tax rate, because income tax is more closely related to income before taxes than to sales.

5.3 CAUTIONS ABOUT USING RATIOS

Although ratios can be a powerful tool, it is important to be very cautious when using them. Differences in accounting methods and estimates, as well as the existence of nonrecurring items, can cause ratio differences. Differences across industries and business environment changes can make interpreting ratios complicated. In addition, different disclosure levels across firms may make it impossible to calculate certain ratios for certain firms. Finally, analysts define ratios in various ways. Valuable ratio analysis requires the analyst to consider how a ratio was defined before interpreting its meaning.

Accounting Methods, Estimates, and Disclosures

An accounting analysis may uncover differences in accounting methods across firms or changes for a given firm. As a result, we may need to adjust the financial statement data to make ratios more mean-

EXHIBIT 5.12 Excerpt from Mergent's Inc. Industry Review on Jewelry

	Growth Rates													
COMPANY	Revenue Growth (%)			Earnings per Share Growth (%)			Operating Income Growth (%)			Share Price Growth (%)			No. of Employees	
	1 YR.	3 YRS.	5 YRS.	1 YR.	3 YRS.	5 YRS.	1 YR.	3 YRS.	5 YRS.	1 YR.	3 YRS.	5 YRS.	2000	1 YR. GROWTH (%)
Charles & Colvard Ltd.	4.17	…	…	30.47	d18.61	91.90	17.63	11.03	112.42	10.39	d45.59	d27.35	34	d69.31
Finlay Enterprises, Inc.	9.12	8.72	8.48	187.38	9.85	31.34	68.49	7.00	9.14	d23.99	d6.58	d12.47	3600	d30.83
Friedman's Inc.	20.16	15.46	20.17	18.53	0.74	6.76	21.47	3.63	13.12	59.91	d6.56	d11.21	4193	d4.59
Lazare Kaplan International, Inc.	d28.79	6.53	0.33	79.85	d15.67	d34.46	59.16	120.84	d10.22	28.91	d1.16	d18.59	205	…
Mayors Jewelers Inc.	15.43	d10.44	d6.75	d119.63	…	…	…	d72.60	…	d58.60	d19.53	d11.72	811	d119.23
Michael Anthony Jewelers, Inc.	d14.73	d1.37	d3.05	…	d13.03	…	…	d81.84	…	27.63	d10.25	d4.96	639	d3.69
Movado Group, Inc.	8.37	10.10	10.92	48.13	9.22	14.46	77.22	9.13	12.74	23.03	d10.90	5.57	838	d10.42
Reeds Jewelers, Inc.	d0.16	1.81	3.93	d404.31	d116.55	d74.27	d74.22	d12.57	d9.53	d5.13	d46.86	d24.98	902	3.27
Tiffany & Co.	13.20	16.47	14.61	25.02	30.80	29.15	24.25	29.92	28.18	d0.49	29.55	24.69	5960	10.46
Whitehall Jewellers Inc	11.84	21.04	19.94	d70.07	d3.81	d22.30	d51.32	0.13	7.39	44.21	d0.03	d0.02	2837	18.11
Zale Corp. (New)	14.25	15.13	11.96	d28.77	6.33	13.12	d40.56	d0.49	6.73	36.53	8.71	15.55	13000	43.08

d—deficit

Source: Mergent's Inc., February 1, 2002.

EXHIBIT 5.13 Starbucks' Common-Sized Income Statement, 1997–2000

Fiscal Year Ending	September 28, 1997	September 27, 1998	October 3, 1999	October 1, 2000
Net Revenues	100.0	100.0	100.0	100.0
Cost of sales and related occupancy costs	(44.8)	(44.2)	(44.1)	(44.0)
Gross margin	55.2	55.8	55.9	56.0
Joint venture income	(0.2)	0.1	0.2	1.0
Store operating expenses	(32.2)	(32.0)	(32.4)	(32.5)
Other operating expenses	(2.7)	(3.4)	(3.3)	(3.6)
Depreciation and amortization	(5.4)	(5.6)	(5.8)	(6.0)
General and administrative expenses	(5.9)	(5.9)	(5.3)	(5.1)
Merger expenses	0.0	(0.7)	0.0	0.0
Operating income	8.8	8.3	9.3	9.8
Interest and other income, net	0.6	0.6	0.5	0.3
Internet-related investment losses				(2.7)
Earnings before income taxes	9.4	8.9	9.8	7.4
Income taxes	(3.7)	(3.7)	(3.7)	(3.0)
Net earnings	5.7	5.2	6.1	4.4

ingful or comparable in a trend analysis or a cross-sectional analysis. Also, we must consider how management estimates affect ratios. These issues can be especially important if we are comparing ratios of different companies.

Because we often calculate ratios to help us project the future, we may need to make adjustments for items that will not continue into the future, being careful to identify what will and will not be recurring. For example, we often remove nonrecurring items such as extraordinary items from the income statement before calculating ratios involving net income.

In doing ratio analysis, we must recognize that different firms provide different levels of disclosure. For example, some firms supply significantly more detail about each business segment than is required, whereas others give only the bare minimum. In each case, we will combine the available financial information with the results of our business analysis to understand the firm. In many situations, computing ratios on more detailed segment data will produce better information. For example, by looking at revenue and operating margin trends in each segment, we can identify which segments are growing and profitable.

Industry and Business Differences

We must also carefully consider information about the firm's business, industry, and economic conditions as we analyze the meaning of the computed ratios. Ratios often vary substantially across industries, so comparisons across companies are usually done within an industry. Even within an industry, some firms are not comparable. Industry definitions can be rather general. For example, Starbucks is sometimes categorized in the restaurant industry. IHOP Corporation (International House of Pancakes), McDonald's Corporation, and Krispy Kreme Doughnuts, Inc. are also in this industry. Starbucks' unique business characteristics make it not comparable to these firms. It is extremely important to understand fully the business operations to determine when a competitive or industry comparison is meaningful.

Business Environment Changes

Once we decide on comparable companies, it is vital to consider the business and environmental changes that have occurred since the historical periods under study. While analyzing historical results, we have to remember that history does not necessarily repeat itself and ask what might change in the future. This requires understanding not only the financial statement analysis but also the changing environment of the business. The business analysis should provide clues about the potential changes in the business environment. For example, in the 1990s, the many start-up Internet companies created demand for Internet infrastructure products and services from technology companies such as Lucent Technologies and Cisco Systems. These infrastructure firms in turn experienced tremendous growth. However, when the growth of Internet firms subsided—and many even went out of business—Lucent, Cisco, and other firms also encountered a change in their businesses, which caused the growth patterns to change.

Ratio Definitions

If we use ratios prepared by others, it is important to keep in mind that analysts define ratios differently. For example, return on capital is income divided by capital, but income may be defined in many ways, such as operating income, income before tax, and net income. Total capital may or may not include minority interests. An analyst might use total capital as of the beginning of the period or an average balance, which could be computed using either annual balances or quarterly balances.

SUMMARY

In financial statement analysis, we begin with historical financial statements and use them to compute various ratios. However, simply calculating a set of ratios is not performing analysis. Analysis occurs when ratios are compared to those of other firms or across time, and are used to investigate questions about the company. This can be done in many contexts, including competitive analysis, performance analysis, credit analysis, and valuation.

Ratio analysis allows us to be creative. Not being bound by the rules of GAAP or any laws, we can calculate and analyze the ratio of *any* two financial statement items that will help us understand a financial relationship. Although we have presented one set of ratios, there is no official list of ratios. Each analyst can create the ratios needed for the situation. Still, analysts commonly use the ratios described in this chapter or similar ones. These fall into three broad categories: operating ratios, credit ratios, and investment ratios. Operating ratios are the most useful for valuation analyses.

Ratios are most meaningful when compared to a benchmark. Two types of analyses that provide benchmarks are trend analysis and cross-sectional analysis. A trend analysis examines a set of ratios over a period of time. This approach is often used when the ultimate goal of analysis is valuation. As part of our valuation approach, we will incorporate a trend analysis of the historical values of the ratios to forecast future performance. Analysts also commonly perform cross-sectional analyses, in which they compare ratios across firms.

Ratio analysis demands caution. We must consider the effects of accounting methods, estimates, disclosure levels, nonrecurring items, industry differences, and business environment changes. Sometimes we will need to make adjustments to our financial data before preparing ratios. We must also be careful to understand fully the definitions of ratios used in our analysis.

SUGGESTED READINGS

Bergevin, P. *Financial Statement Analysis: An Integrated Approach.* Upper Saddle River, NJ: Prentice Hall, 2002.

Ziebart, D., A. Feller, K. Malloy, and T. Omer. *An Introduction to Applied Professional Research for Accountants.* Upper Saddle River, NJ: Prentice Hall, 2002.

REVIEW QUESTIONS

1. How do analysts use financial ratios in the valuation process?
2. Describe operating ratios. How are they used?
3. Describe credit ratios and explain how they are used.
4. Describe investment ratios and explain how they are used.
5. John Jones is a credit analyst at a large commercial bank. In his training session, he received the list of credit ratios and their definitions used to evaluate loan applications. John asked his supervisor if these are the only ratios that affect credit risk. What should the supervisor tell him?
6. What is a gross margin percentage and how would a business manager use it?

7. What does the operating income margin percentage tell you?

8. What is trend analysis?

9. What is cause-of-change analysis?

10. What is cross-sectional analysis?

11. What does the current ratio tell you? Does the business manager want it to be higher or lower?

12. What does return on common equity tell you?

13. How would a business manager use the inventory turnover ratio to improve his or her business?

 14. Before beginning a ratio analysis, you must consider several important caveats. Explain these caveats and how they would affect your ratio analysis process.

PROBLEMS

The following information, adapted from Jacobson's fiscal 1999 annual report, will be used for problems 1 through 3. Jacobson's Stores Inc.'s 24 specialty stores in Michigan, Indiana, Ohio, Kansas, Kentucky, and Florida sell apparel and accessories for women, men, and children and home décor items.

Jacobson's Stores Inc. Summary of Operations
$ thousands, except per share data

Fiscal year	1999	1998	1997*	1996	1995	1994
Net sales	$448,075	$444,305	$447,471	$432,469	$414,267	$409,154
Cost of merchandise sold, buying and occupancy expenses	296,412	295,272	300,918	293,826	279,493	265,204
Selling, general, and administrative expenses	139,458	139,220	138,797	142,348	133,572	130,039
Interest expense, net	7,277	7,915	9,178	9,384	8,808	8,027
Nonrecurring charge (credit)	1,251			(340)	4,200	
Gains on sale of property	(1,717)	(617)	(2,987)		(1,065)	(504)
Earnings (loss) before income taxes	5,394	2,515	1,905	(17,289)	(6,541)	6,388
Provision (credit) for income taxes	1,888	880	691	(5,827)	(2,335)	2,300
Net earnings (loss)	$ 3,506	$ 1,635	$ 1,214	($ 11,462)	($ 4,206)	$ 4,088
Basic and diluted earnings per share	$0.61	$0.28	$0.21	($1.98)	($0.73)	$0.71

*53-week year

Jacobson's Balance Sheet

$ thousands	January 29, 2000 (Fiscal 1999)	January 30, 1999 (Fiscal 1998)
Current Assets		
Cash and equivalents	$ 722	$ 2,929
Receivables, net	32,142	32,151
Merchandise inventories	91,905	90,454
Prepaid expenses and other assets	1,472	1,370
Deferred taxes	5,494	4,894
Total current assets	131,735	131,798
Property and equipment, net	83,163	84,989
Other assets	18,766	20,088
Total Assets	$233,664	$236,875
Current Liabilities		
Current portion of long-term debt	$3,392	$3,719
Accounts payable	39,968	34,769
Accrued expenses	18,712	16,774
Accrued income taxes	1,670	442
Total current liabilities	63,742	55,704
Long-term debt	85,772	99,803
Deferred taxes	6,039	6,386
Other liabilities	3,668	4,045
Shareholders' equity	74,443	70,937
Total Liabilities and Equity	$233,664	$236,875

OTHER INFORMATION:

Jacobson's fiscal year ends in January of the following year. For example, fiscal 1999 ended January 29, 2000.

Jacobson's market price was $5.3125 per share as of January 29, 2000.

Jacobson's has authorized 15,000,000 shares of $1 par value common stock. 5,975,400 shares had been issued at January 29, 2000, and January 30, 1999. Shares issued include 187,200 shares in treasury at January 29, 2000, and January 30, 1999.

There is no preferred stock outstanding.

EXCERPTS FROM FOOTNOTES:

NONRECURRING CHARGE(CREDIT)

In the fourth quarter of 1999, the Company recorded a one-time charge totaling $1,251,000 to fully reserve its investment in a cooperative buying group made several years ago.

In early 1997, the Company closed three underperforming Michigan stores and incurred a related $4,200,000 pretax charge in fiscal 1996. Store closing activity was as follows:

($ thousands)	1999	1998	1997
Reserve at beginning of year	$125	$2,623	$4,200
Reserve related to properties sold		(2,210)	
Payments against reserve	(125)	(288)	(1,237)
Credit against reserve			(340)
Reserve at end of year	$ 0	$ 125	$2,623

At January 29, 2000, all closed facilities have been sold and all closing costs incurred. Store closing credits totaled $224,000 after-tax in 1997.

GAINS ON SALE OF PROPERTY

In fiscal 1999, the Company sold properties in Dearborn and East Lansing, Michigan, at a combined after-tax gain totaling $1,133,000. In fiscal 1998, the Company sold properties in Jackson and Kalamazoo, Michigan, at a combined after-tax gain totaling $407,000. In 1997, the Company sold its Store for the Home in Grosse Pointe, Michigan, and two nonoperating properties at a combined after-tax gain totaling $1,972,000.

1. A trend analysis compares ratios over time.

   a. Prepare a trend analysis of the following operating ratios:
      Revenue growth rate
      Gross margin percentage
      Operating margin percentage
      Effective income tax rate
   b. What conclusions can you make from this analysis?
   c. What other information would help you better understand the trends in operating income?

2. Inventory, receivables, and payables are key components of working capital.

   a. Calculate inventory turnover, days receivables outstanding, and days payables outstanding for fiscal 2000.
   b. If you were a financial manager at Jacobson's, what could you do to determine whether there was room for significant improvement in these ratios?
   c. If you were able to increase the inventory turnover, how would that affect cash flow from operations?
   d. If you were able to increase the inventory turnover, what business risk could be involved?
   e. If you were to increase days payables outstanding substantially by delaying payment of invoices, how would this affect cash flow from operations?
   f. If you were to increase days payables outstanding substantially by delaying payment of invoices, what business risks could be involved?

3. Calculate the following ratios for Jacobson's for the year ending January 29, 2000. (Assume a marginal income tax rate of 35%.)

   Return on capital
   Return on common equity
   Price-to-earnings ratio
   Market-to-book ratio
   Current ratio
   Quick ratio
   Debt to capital ratio
   Interest coverage

Problems 4 through 8 are based on the following information, which was adapted from Merck's 2000 annual report.

Merck & Co., Inc. and Subsidiaries Consolidated Balance Sheet

$ millions	December 31, 2000	December 31, 1999
Assets		
Cash and cash equivalents	$ 2,536.8	$ 2,021.9
Short-term investments	1,717.8	1,180.5
Accounts receivable	5,017.9	4,089.0
Inventories	3,021.5	2,846.9
Prepaid expenses and taxes	1,059.4	1,120.9
Current Assets	13,353.4	11,259.2
Investments	4,947.8	4,761.5
Property, plant, equipment, net	11,482.1	9,676.7
Goodwill and other	10,127.1	9,937.5
Total Assets	$ 39,910.4	$ 35,634.9
Accounts payable	$ 4,361.3	$ 4,158.7
Loans payable and current portion of long-term debt	3,319.3	2,859.0
Income taxes payable	1,244.3	1,064.1
Dividends payable	784.7	677.0
Current liabilities	9,709.6	8,758.8
Long-term debt	3,600.7	3,143.9
Deferred tax and noncurrent liabilities	6,746.7	7,030.1
Minority interest	5,021.0	3,460.5
Stockholders' equity	14,832.4	13,241.6
Total liabilities and stockholders' equity	$ 39,910.4	$ 35,634.9

Merck & Co., Inc. and Subsidiaries Consolidated Statement of Income

Years ended December 31 ($ millions)	2000	1999	1998
Sales	$ 40,363.2	$ 32,714.0	$ 26,898.2
Materials and production	22,443.5	17,534.2	13,925.4
Marketing and administrative	6,167.7	5,199.9	4,511.4
Research and development	2,343.8	2,068.3	1,821.1
Equity income from affiliates	(764.9)	(762.0)	(884.3)
Gains on sales of businesses			(2,147.7)
Acquired research and other, net	349.0	54.1	1,539.2
Income before taxes	9,824.1	8,619.5	8,133.1
Taxes on income	3,002.4	2,729.0	2,884.9
Net income	$ 6,821.7	$ 5,890.5	$ 5,248.2

Merck's interest expense in 2000 was $484.4 million, which was included in acquired research and other, net. Assume acquired research and other, net are not regular operating costs.

4. Calculate common-sized income statements.

5. Merck does not show a line item for operating income. Calculate operating income and operating margin percentage from the information provided.

6. Analyze Merck's operating income.

   a. What happened to Merck's operating margin percentage in this period?
   b. Prepare a cause-of-change analysis on the change in Merck's operating income from 1999 to 2000.
   c. What other sources would you want to check to better understand the changes in Merck's operating margin?

7. Calculate Merck's return on capital and return on common equity for 2000. For the return on capital calculation, assume a 35% tax rate to adjust interest to after-tax interest. Why is Merck's return on common equity so much higher than its return on capital?

8. Analyze Merck's working capital.

   a. Calculate Merck's days receivables outstanding, days payables outstanding, and inventory turnover for 2000.
   b. What does the information you calculated in (a) tell you?
   c. What other information would you want to have to assess the ratios calculated in (a)?

Problems 9 and 10 are based on the following information adapted from the 2000 PepsiCo, Inc. annual report.

PepsiCo, Inc. Information from the Income Statement

Fiscal Year Ended ($ millions)	December 30, 2000	December 25, 1999
Net sales		
New PepsiCo	$ 20,438	$ 18,244
Bottling operations	0	2,123
Total net sales	20,438	20,367
Cost of Sales	7,943	8,198
Selling, general and administrative	9,132	9,103
Amortization of intangible assets	138	183
Impairment and restructuring charges		65
Total costs and expenses	17,213	17,549
Operating Profit		
New PepsiCo	3,225	2,765
Bottling operations and equity investments	0	53
Total operating profit	$ 3,225	$ 2,818

PepsiCo, Inc. Information from Business Segment Data

Fiscal Year Ending ($ millions)	December 30, 2000	December 25, 1999
Net Sales		
Frito-Lay North America	$ 8,562	$ 7,865
Frito-Lay International	4,319	3,750
Total Frito-Lay	12,881	11,615
Pepsi-Cola North America	3,289	2,605
Pepsi-Cola International	1,842	1,771
Total Pepsi-Cola	5,131	4,376
Tropicana	2,426	2,253
New PepsiCo	20,438	18,244
Bottling operations/investments		2,123
	$ 20,438	$ 20,367
Operating Profit		
Frito-Lay North America	$ 1,851	$ 1,580
Frito-Lay International	493	406
Total Frito-Lay	2,344	1,986
Pepsi-Cola North America	833	751
Pepsi-Cola International	148	108
Total Pepsi-Cola	981	859
Tropicana	225	170
Combined segments	3,550	3,015
Corporate	(325)	(250)
New PepsiCo	3,225	2,765
Bottling operations/investments		53
	$ 3,225	$ 2,818

In 1999, PepsiCo completed four transactions creating four anchor bottlers. Through initial public offerings and other transactions, PepsiCo separated the bottling operations from its other businesses and retained a noncontrolling interest in the bottling operations. The segment information shown here is based on the new company structure. The bottling operations are separated into their own segment.

9. Create common-sized income statements for PepsiCo for 1999 and 2000.

10. Analyze the PepsiCo data.
   a. Which segments contribute the most income to PepsiCo? Show the analysis supporting your answer.
   b. Which segments showed the most sales growth in 2000?
   c. Calculate the segment operating profit margin percentages.
   d. How would an analyst use segment data to help forecast future cash flow?

 11. The following are common-sized income statements for five companies, whose names are not revealed. The information also shows the inventory turnover ratios for each company. The information is adapted from the most recent income statements and balance sheets of the five companies listed at the end of the problem. Review the information.

Based on the nature of each of the five companies' businesses, match each common-sized income statement with the appropriate firm.

(All amounts in percentages of sales)	A	B	C	D	E
Sales	100.00	100.00	100.00	100.00	100.00
Cost of sales	(43.32)	(71.64)	(16.59)	(76.26)	(76.68)
Gross profit	56.68	28.36	83.41	23.74	23.32
Selling, general and administrative	(35.64)	(23.84)	(49.70)	(45.27)	(17.55)
Research and development			(15.00)	(9.75)	
Operating profit	21.04	4.52	18.71	(31.28)	5.77
Losses from investments under equity method	(1.62)			(11.03)	(1.23)
Interest and dividend income and interest expense, net	(4.23)	(1.05)		(3.26)	(0.49)
Gains and losses	(3.03)			(5.16)	(1.80)
Other, net		(0.01)	0.84	(0.36)	
Earnings from continuing operations before taxes and minority interests	12.16	3.46	19.55	(51.09)	2.25
Income taxes	(5.51)	(1.38)	(6.93)		(1.24)
Minority interests	(0.33)		(0.05)		
Earnings from continuing operations	6.32	2.08	12.57	(51.09)	1.01
Discontinued operations	(1.75)		0.03		
Net income	4.57	2.08	12.60	(51.09)	1.01
Inventory turnover ratio	56.8	7.7	1.9	10.7	11.4

- Albertson's, Inc., one of the largest retail food and drug chains in the United States, operates more than 2,500 stores in 36 states.
- Amazon.com is an online seller of books, music, DVDs, videos, consumer electronics, toys, camera and photo items, software, computer and video games, tools and hardware, lawn and patio items, kitchen products, and wireless products.
- Pfizer Inc. is a research-based global pharmaceutical company.
- Tribune Company is engaged in newspaper publishing, broadcasting, entertainment, and the development and distribution of information and entertainment through the Internet.
- USX Corporation is engaged in exploration and production of crude oil and natural gas; refining, marketing, and transportation of petroleum products; other energy-related businesses; manufacture of steel mill products and coke and taconite pellets; management of mineral resources; coal mining; real estate development; and engineering and consulting services.

My Case

For your company:
a. Prepare a trend analysis of operating ratios.
b. If you adjusted for any nonrecurring items in part (a), explain the adjustments.
c. Use any other information in your company's annual report to explain the change in revenues, gross margin percentage, and operating margin percentage.
d. Find another company in the same industry and calculate two years of operating ratios for this company. Review the annual report and other information to understand this business. Compare the competitor's ratios to your company's ratios. Explain the similarities and differences between the ratios of your company and its competitor.
e. From your analysis, what areas do you need to evaluate further?

PART III

CASH FLOW BASED VALUATION

6 The Economic Balance Sheet and an Overview
of Cash Flow Based Valuation Models

7 Discount Rates in Valuation

8 The Dividend Discount and the Flows
to Equity Models

9 Free Cash Flow Model and Analysis

10 Forecasting Free Cash Flows

11 The Adjusted Present Value Model

12 The Residual Income Model

6

The Economic Balance Sheet and an Overview of Cash Flow Based Valuation Models

Where We Have Been:

In Chapter 5, we introduced financial statement analysis. To be meaningful, financial statement analysis must be applied in a decision-making context.

Where We Are:

In this chapter, we begin our study of valuation, a major application of financial statement analysis. To facilitate our valuation work, we introduce the concept of an economic balance sheet. We then provide an overview of the various valuation models and link them to the economic balance sheet framework.

Where We Are Going

In Chapter 7, we discuss the discount rates used in the various valuation models. In the remainder of Part III, we describe the cash flow valuation models in more detail and address implementation issues.

LEARNING OBJECTIVES:

After studying this chapter, you will understand:

- The concept of an economic balance sheet and how it differs from a GAAP balance sheet.

- How to create an economic balance sheet.

- How to relate each of the five components of the economic balance sheet to the appropriate cash flow stream.

- An overview of five valuation models.

- That all five of the valuation models produce identical results given identical assumptions.

- Why the models use different cash flow streams.

In this chapter, we examine five cash flow valuation models. Each is structured differently, valuing different flows and using different discount rates. Still, given identical assumptions, all five produce identical results.

To help in understanding these models, we introduce the economic balance sheet. The economic balance sheet is like a GAAP balance sheet in that it equates assets and claims, yet it differs in that it focuses on fair values rather than amounts reported under the accounting rules. The economic balance sheet provides a way of thinking about valuation. It also explains why each model works by valuing only some of the cash flows to the firm. A discussion of the economic balance sheet is in Section 6.1. Section 6.2 covers the five most common discounted cash flow valuation models.

6.1 THE ECONOMIC BALANCE SHEET

We have seen that a balance sheet presents a firm's assets, liabilities, and equity. If every economic asset and liability were recognized on the balance sheet and appeared at its fair value, equity would also represent fair value, or the amount you should be willing to pay for the firm's stock. However, we have seen that the balance sheet does not recognize all economic assets and liabilities, and values many at something other than fair value. This means that the GAAP value of equity is not its fair value.

The **economic balance sheet** is a statement showing the estimated fair values of all items that represent an economic asset or liability for the firm, along with the implied value of the firm's equity. A simple economic balance sheet might indicate that the equity in your house is equal to the house's value less the mortgage balance. This suggests that you can value the equity by valuing the house and then subtracting the outstanding debt. Similarly, a company's economic balance sheet provides insights into valuing the company's equity indirectly, by determining the values of other components of the economic balance sheet.

An economic balance sheet differs from a balance sheet prepared under GAAP in three important respects. (1) Economic balance sheet items are classified in a different way than under GAAP. (2) The economic balance sheet includes all items that are conceptually assets or liabilities. There are no recognition tests as there are under GAAP. (3) The economic balance sheet uses fair values for all items.

Economic Balance Sheet Classifications Differ from GAAP

Economic balance sheet items are classified according to whether they relate to the firm's core operations, nonoperating net assets, debt claims, other capital claims, or common equity claims, rather than on whether the items are assets or liabilities, or long-term or short-term.

Core operations are the assets and liabilities central to the basic business, which could not be easily separated from each other without affecting the cash-generating ability of the entity. For example, Intel Corporation has accounts receivable from its credit sales, inventory, manufacturing equipment, patents, technical expertise, land, and buildings used in its business operations. These are all economic assets related to Intel's core operations. None of these could be eliminated without affecting Intel's ability to operate its basic business. Similarly, Intel's trade payables, taxes payable, and unearned revenue are liabilities related to its core operations. As long as Intel is a going concern, these assets and liabilities have value because they contribute to the company's core operations.

We estimate the value of the core operations in the aggregate, using a valuation model, not line item by line item. To illustrate why, we can think about the value of a car. When we value a car, we do not add up the value of the tires, the windshield, the engine, and the other parts. Instead, we determine the value of the total based on its ability to provide reliable transportation. The tires, for example, create value because they are necessary to run the car, not because they have a certain value themselves. Assuming the car runs well, it is a going concern and gets its value from the combination of what all these parts can do together. This value is entirely different from what we would get if we sold each part for scrap. The core operations of a business are valued in the same way. The value of the core operations is not the sum of each asset and liability, but the value these assets and liabilities create as a whole.

Assets and liabilities that are not an integral part of the company's core operations are called **nonoperating net assets**. Generally, a company could separate nonoperating net assets from the rest of its business without any ill effects. Examples of nonoperating assets are marketable securities, investments in other companies, joint ventures, cash in excess of the amount required to operate the business, land not used in business operations, and so on. If Intel has vacant land that it does not use in its business operations, it can sell the land without affecting the cash flow generated by the core operations. Examples of nonoperating liabilities include environmental contingencies, such as might exist at a chemical manufacturer, and product liability lawsuits, such as those that were filed against tire manufacturer Bridgestone/Firestone. Even though nonoperating liabilities may arise out of a business's operations, the liabilities themselves are not integral to the operations. For example, Bridgestone/Firestone could value the liabilities separately from the rest of the business.

We can usually value a nonoperating asset or liability by appraisal, by doing a separate cash flow valuation, or by observing market value. For example, depending on our access to information, we might estimate the value of a company's excess land either by appraisal or by a discounted cash flow analysis of the rental income it generates.

Debt claims are the claims against the firm held by those who have loaned it money. These include long-term debt, capitalized leases, short-term debt, current maturities of long-term debt, and notes payable. **Other capital claims** include all claims on the firm's assets that are not common equity and are not included in core operations, nonoperating net assets, or debt claims. These consist primarily of preferred stock, employee stock options, warrants, and minority interest. As is done for nonoperating net assets, debt and other capital claims can usually be valued by separate analysis or by observing market value.

Common equity claim is the residual claim belonging to the common shareholders. This means that it comprises all of the firm's value after all other claims are satisfied.

Economic Balance Sheet Includes All Economic Assets and Liabilities

The second difference between a GAAP balance sheet and an economic balance sheet is that the economic balance sheet includes all items that are conceptually assets or liabilities. These assets and liabilities need not meet the GAAP recognition tests. Anything that would affect the price you should be willing to pay for the firm is part of the economic balance sheet. Three of the most common economic balance sheet items that are not recognized under GAAP are contingent assets, contingent liabilities, and employee stock options. A common contingent asset is the expected proceeds from a lawsuit. Although firms cannot recognize these amounts in a GAAP balance sheet, they would be included in an economic balance sheet, because the expectation of proceeds affects the amount we would be willing to pay for the firm. Similarly, contingent liabilities, such as potential litigation payouts, are not recognized unless the payout is sufficiently likely and reasonably estimable. Nevertheless, even potential payouts that do not meet the thresholds for recognition under GAAP affect the firm's value and must be included in the economic balance sheet.

The importance of contingent assets and liabilities is not lost on the stock market. During major litigation, stock returns can be associated with turning points in the case. For example, during the litigation between Texaco and Pennzoil in the 1980s, the two companies' market values moved in opposite directions as the trial played out and the expectations of the outcome changed. More recently, Microsoft's stock price changed as the antitrust proceedings against it unfolded.

In most cases, the accounting rules do not require firms to recognize an obligation for employee stock options. However, these options represent an obligation of the firm so they must be factored into a valuation and, therefore, included in the economic balance sheet.

Economic Balance Sheet Uses Fair Value

The third difference is that in an economic balance sheet we show all amounts at fair value, rather than the various measurement bases in a GAAP balance sheet.[1] In this book, we use the term **fair value** to mean the true underlying economic value of an asset or liability. On the economic balance sheet, core operations will be shown at the fair value we estimate with a valuation model, rather than the sum of the book values of the component assets and liabilities. The difference between the fair value of the core operations and its book value is likely to be very large. For some economic balance sheet items, we use an established market value to estimate fair value based on the assumption that the market prices the asset correctly. We might use the market value to value an investment in the equity of another firm. For example, Amazon.com owns stock in drugstore.com. We could estimate the value of this nonoperating asset by looking at the market value of the drugstore.com shares.

Starbucks' Economic Balance Sheet

We now illustrate the construction of an economic balance sheet for Starbucks Coffee Company. Exhibit 6.1 shows Starbucks' October 1, 2000 consolidated balance sheet under GAAP. At the far right of the exhibit, we classify each item as core operations (CORE), nonoperating net asset (NONOP), debt claim (DEBT), other capital claim (OCAP), or common equity claim (COMEQUITY). At the bottom of the exhibit are listed commitments and contingencies, and employee stock options, two items that are not part of the GAAP balance sheet yet appear in the economic balance sheet.

We classify short-term investments, joint ventures, and other investments as nonoperating. In contrast to accounts receivable, inventories, and other elements of core operations, these investments are separable from Starbucks' main business. We can value them separately, and their results are distinct from those of the core operations. Both the current portion of long-term debt and long-term debt are debt claims. Minority interest is the portion of Starbucks' subsidiaries' net assets not owned by Starbucks but rather by other shareholders. It is a component of other capital claims. Employee stock options are also other capital claims. We classify the commitments and contingencies as nonoperating. These are separable from the core operations in the same way that the investments are. All other elements of the balance sheet, other than common equity, are part of core operations. Each of these assets and liabilities is an integral part of Starbucks' operations.

To construct the economic balance sheet, we will do three things to the GAAP balance sheet. First, we will reorganize the balance sheet around the economic balance sheet classifications. In doing so, we can combine the elements of core operations into a single line, to reflect the fact that estimating the fair value of core operations is done for the entire operations, not element by element. Second, we will include all economic assets and liabilities whether they are recognized under GAAP

---

[1]In some circumstances we may use book value to approximate fair value. Book values are acceptable only when they approximate fair value.

EXHIBIT 6.1   Starbucks Coffee Company GAAP Balance Sheet

Starbucks Coffee Company Consolidated Balance Sheet October 1, 2000 (thousands of dollars)			
ASSETS			
Current Assets			
Cash and cash equivalents	$	70,817	CORE
Short-term investments		61,336	NONOP
Accounts receivable		76,385	CORE
Inventories		201,656	CORE
Prepaid expenses and other current assets		20,321	CORE
Deferred income taxes, net		29,304	CORE
Total current assets		459,819	
Joint ventures		52,051	NONOP
Other investments		3,788	NONOP
Property, plant, and equipment, net		930,759	CORE
Other assets		25,403	CORE
Goodwill, net		21,311	CORE
Total assets	$	1,493,131	
LIABILITIES AND SHAREHOLDERS' EQUITY			
Current Liabilities			
Accounts payable	$	73,653	CORE
Checks drawn in excess of bank balances		56,332	CORE
Accrued compensation and related costs		75,250	CORE
Accrued occupancy costs		29,117	CORE
Accrued taxes		35,841	CORE
Other accrued expenses		35,053	CORE
Deferred revenue		7,320	CORE
Current portion of long-term debt		685	DEBT
Total current liabilities		313,251	
Deferred income taxes, net		21,410	CORE
Long-term debt		6,483	DEBT
Minority interest		3,588	OCAP
SHAREHOLDERS' EQUITY			
Common stock		750,872	COMEQUITY
Retained earnings		408,503	COMEQUITY
Accumulated other comprehensive loss		(10,976)	COMEQUITY
Total Shareholders' Equity		1,148,399	
Total Liabilities and Shareholders' Equity	$	1,493,131	
Employee stock options	$	0	OCAP
Commitments and contingencies	$	0	NONOP

or not. As a practical matter, we need not add lines for unrecognized assets or liabilities that are part of core operations, because core operations have been collapsed to a single line anyway. For example, the value of brand names will be reflected in the value we estimate for core operations, because it will help contribute to the cash flows we use to value those operations. Third, we will use our best estimates of fair values, not GAAP book values. These estimates, of course, will be subject to error, but should be the best we can do with the information available.

As noted in the preceding discussion, in an economic balance sheet we do not value the items of core operations individually. Rather, we use a valuation model to estimate the aggregate value of core operations. Suppose we used a valuation model to estimate the value of Starbucks' core operations and arrived at $7.8 billion.[2] Exhibit 6.2 presents the resulting economic balance sheet for Starbucks, showing comparative GAAP amounts along with the economic values of each item.

We assume that for nonoperating items and debt, book value approximates fair value.[3] The information in the footnotes to Starbucks' financial statements indicated that the contingencies and commitments were immaterial, so here they have a value of zero. If one of these items were material, we would estimate the expected after-tax present value and include it in the economic balance sheet. We also included an estimated value for the employee stock options.[4]

Note how the three characteristics of the economic balance sheet discussed earlier apply to this example. (1) The classifications are based on the economic balance sheet format, not the GAAP for-

EXHIBIT 6.2   Starbucks Coffee Company Economic Balance Sheet

Starbucks Coffee Company Economic Balance Sheet October 1, 2000 (thousands of dollars)		
	Economic	GAAP
Core operations	$ 7,800,000	$ 1,041,980
Short-term investments	61,336	61,336
Joint ventures	52,051	52,051
Other investments	3,788	3,788
Commitments and contingencies	0	
Nonoperating net assets	117,175	117,175
Total core operations and nonoperating net assets	$ 7,917,175	$ 1,159,155
Current portion of long-term debt	$ 685	$ 685
Long-term debt	6,483	6,483
Debt claims	7,168	7,168
Minority interest	24,637	3,588
Employee stock options	347,304	
Other capital claims	371,941	3,588
Common equity	7,538,066	1,148,399
Total capital claims	$ 7,917,175	$ 1,159,155

[2]We will show how to estimate this value in later chapters.
[3]If these items were not at market value in the GAAP statement, they would need to be adjusted to market value.
[4]In Chapter 14 we show how to compute this number.

mat. (2) The Starbucks economic balance sheet includes items not recognized under GAAP. It shows commitments and contingencies, albeit at a value of zero in this example, as well as employee stock options. (3) We use estimated fair values, not book values. Core operations are valued at more than seven times book value.

Why are Starbucks' core operations worth $6.8 billion more than book value? A small part of the difference might be due to understated values of Starbucks' reported assets. However, the bulk of the difference is because Starbucks' value does not come from the assets themselves, but from the profits they generate when used together to operate the business. This additional value, called good-will, is not recognized in the balance sheet except when a company is acquired.

Debt and nonoperating items would also be presented at fair value. For simplicity we assumed book value approximated fair value for debt and nonoperating items. To complete the economic balance sheet, we needed to estimate the value of the minority interest, the portion of Starbucks' consolidated net assets owned by third parties. To do so, we assumed the ratio of minority interest to the total of core operations plus nonoperating net assets less debt would be the same on a fair value basis as a book value basis, as shown in Exhibit 6.3. This is equivalent to assuming the ratio of fair value to book value is the same for the subsidiaries in which there is a minority interest as for the rest of Starbucks. Although this may not be precisely true, it is certainly more accurate than using book value, and the more detailed information necessary to value individual subsidiaries is not generally available. We used the Black-Scholes option pricing formula to estimate the value of the employee stock options. Common equity is a "plug" figure, the amount that makes the economic balance sheet balance.

Linking the Components of the Economic Balance Sheet to the Firm's Cash Flows

Generally speaking, core operations and nonoperating net assets generate cash flows into the firm, whereas debt, other capital claims, and common equity claims result in cash outflows. Exhibit 6.4 shows the five components of the economic balance sheet, the value of each component in the Starbucks case, and the cash flows associated with each component.

The cash flow generated by the core operations is called **free cash flow**. Free cash flow is the net of the normal operating cash inflows—such as sales and collections of receivables—less the normal operating cash outflows—such as cost of sales; selling, general, and administrative expenses; and capital expenditures. Nonoperating net assets generate **nonoperating cash flows**. This includes interest income, dividend income, rental income on excess land, and lawsuit settlements. Debt claims generate **debt service**, consisting of the principal and interest payments (net of the related tax savings)

EXHIBIT 6.3   Calculation of Minority Interest Fair Value

($ thousands)	Economic (fair value)	GAAP
Total core operations and nonoperating net assets	$ 7,917,175	$ 1,159,155
Less: Debt claims	7,168	7,168
Net value	7,910,007	1,151,987
Minority interest (GAAP)		3,588
Ratio of minority interest to net value		0.0031146
Minority interest (economic)—0.0031146 × $7,910,007	$ 24,637	

EXHIBIT 6.4   Cash Flows and the Firm

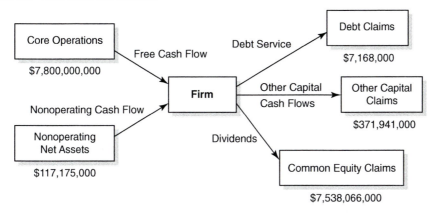

required to satisfy the debt. Other capital claims generate **other capital cash flows**. Common equity generates **dividends**. The use of the term *dividends* here broadly means net cash transactions with the equityholders, which would include stock repurchases and stock issuances as well.

A fundamental principal of finance is that the value of any asset or liability is the present value of the related cash flow stream. Thus, the value of the core operations is equal to the present value of the expected free cash flows. The value of nonoperating net assets is the present value of the expected nonoperating cash flows, and so on. This suggests we can value any of the components of the economic balance sheet as a present value. We can also use the notion that the economic balance sheet must balance to value economic balance sheet components indirectly, based on the value of other components.

Distinguishing Among the Elements of the Economic Balance Sheet

The question often arises how to distinguish among the five components of the economic balance sheet. For example, is an investment in a joint venture always nonoperating, or can it be considered part of the core operations if it is sufficiently related to them? As a practical matter, the way any particular item is classified is less important than the consistency between that decision and the categorization of cash flows. If we consider a particular asset or liability part of the firm's core operations, then the related cash flow must be included in free cash flow. Without this consistency, particular elements of the valuation may be either double-counted or erroneously ignored. In the Starbucks example, why is the investment in joint venture classified as nonoperating? We assumed the joint venture's operations were not commingled with Starbucks' main business. That is, we assumed its cash flows were separable from Starbucks' cash flows. For this asset, it is simpler to think of its value as separate from the rest of the business.

6.2 THE VALUATION MODELS

The economic balance sheet illustrates a fundamentally important corporate finance concept: The total value of all claims is equal to the total value of all assets they claim. This concept allows us to estimate the value of a firm's common equity in many different ways. Mathematically, the economic balance sheet means that:

$$CORE + NONOP = DEBT + OCAP + COMEQUITY \qquad (6.1)$$

where *CORE* is the value of the core operations, *NONOP* is the value of the nonoperating net assets, *DEBT* is the value of the debt claims, *OCAP* is the value of the other capital claims, and *COMEQUITY* is the value of common equity. Equivalently,

$$COMEQUITY = CORE + NONOP - DEBT - OCAP \qquad (6.2)$$

How does this relationship apply in valuation? The answer depends on which of the five basic models for estimating the value of *COMEQUITY* we use. In the **dividend discount model**, we estimate the value of *COMEQUITY* directly, by forecasting the expected dividend stream that the common equity will generate and calculating its present value. In the other four models, we estimate the value of *COMEQUITY* indirectly, by estimating or observing the values of the other amounts in the economic balance sheet and then calculating *COMEQUITY* using equation (6.2). These four methods are the **flows to equity model**, the **free cash flow model**, the **adjusted present value model**, and the **residual income model**. Given identical assumptions, all five models result in the same value for common equity. The differences among the models are in how the computation is done and what factors about the firm are highlighted in the process.

Before discussing the models, we note that all of them provide an estimate of the firm's value. Estimates are only as good as the assumptions on which they are built. In subsequent chapters, we will discuss ways to minimize estimation errors, though they can never be eliminated altogether.

Dividend Discount Model

The dividend discount model relies on the idea that the value of any security is the present value of the cash flows the security is expected to generate. The ultimate cash flow to the common shareholder is the common dividend stream. To determine the value of the common equity, we forecast the future dividend stream and discount it back to the present at the rate of return demanded by common equityholders, or the cost of common equity. This gives us the value today of all future common dividends, which must be equal to the value of the equity that claims them.

The bold arrow in Exhibit 6.5 illustrates that the dividend discount model considers only the cash flows out of the firm to the common shareholders. The dividend discount model is the only model of the five we will study that directly values this cash flow stream. Although all the other models are derived from the dividend discount model, they do not discount dividends directly.

Flows to Equity Model

Exhibit 6.6 shows that under the flows to equity model, we value the cash flows available to equityholders after the firm services its debt and other capital claims, whether or not the flows are paid out as dividends. The present value of this cash flow stream, discounted at the cost of common equity, is equal to the value of the core operations and nonoperating net assets, less debt and other capital claims, which is in turn equal to the value of common equity.

In the flows to equity model, rather than forecasting the dividend stream itself, we forecast the cash flows that would be available to fund the dividend stream. Because a firm can pay dividends only to the extent that it has generated cash to fund them, the values of the cash flow available to equity and the dividend stream must be equal. To the extent that the firm does not pay all

EXHIBIT 6.5   Dividend Discount Model

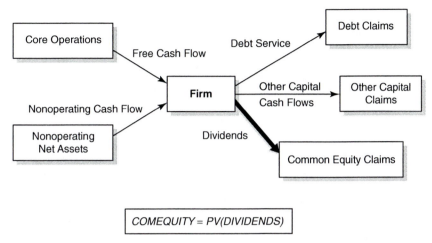

PV means present value.

the cash flow available to equityholders as a dividend in one year, it will be able to pay greater dividends in subsequent years.

Free Cash Flow Model

The free cash flow model is the most widely used valuation model in practice. The bold arrow in Exhibit 6.7 shows that in the free cash flow model, free cash flow is the only cash flow stream we value. We calculate the present value of free cash flow at the firm's weighted-average cost of capital, which blends the firm's costs of debt and equity. This gives us the value of the core operations. The bold boxes in the exhibit indicate that we add the fair value of nonoperating net assets

EXHIBIT 6.6   Flows to Equity Model

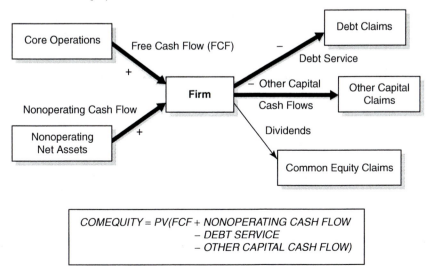

EXHIBIT 6.7 Free Cash Flow Model

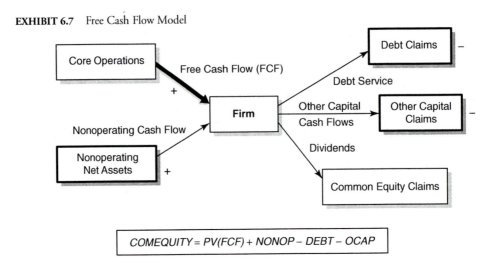

$$COMEQUITY = PV(FCF) + NONOP - DEBT - OCAP$$

to the value of the core operations and subtract the fair value of debt and other capital claims to arrive at equity value. By taking equation (6.2) and substituting the present value of free cash flow for the value of the core operations, the result is the free cash flow model.

Adjusted Present Value Model

The adjusted present value (APV) model is not as popular as the free cash flow model, but it is useful because it highlights the value the firm has created by using leverage in its capital structure. As Exhibit 6.8 illustrates, the APV model discounts free cash flow, the same cash flow stream used in the free cash flow model. In the free cash flow model, the free cash flows are discounted at the weighted-average cost of capital. If the firm created any value through the use of leverage, the weighted-average cost of capital would be lower than if the firm had no debt. As a result, the value of the core operations would be higher. In the APV model, the free cash flows are discounted to the

EXHIBIT 6.8 Adjusted Present Value Model

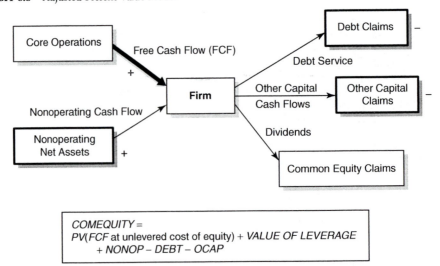

$$COMEQUITY = $$
$$PV(FCF \text{ at unlevered cost of equity}) + VALUE \text{ } OF \text{ } LEVERAGE$$
$$+ NONOP - DEBT - OCAP$$

A CLOSER LOOK

The Quaker Oats Company's Acquisition of Stokely-Van Camp

The Quaker Oats Company's acquisition of Stokely-Van Camp provides an example of the importance of nonoperating net assets in a valuation. When Quaker acquired Stokely-Van Camp, it was primarily interested in obtaining Stokely's Gatorade beverage business and the Van Camp and Wolf Brand bean businesses. Quaker planned to sell Stokely-Van Camp's regional grocery operations and industrial products business. Immediately before the acquisition, Stokely sold some of its vegetable businesses and had excess cash on hand from this divestiture.

Quaker used the free cash flow model to estimate the value of the Gatorade and bean businesses. Because these were the only Stokely businesses Quaker planned to keep, these were the core operations. The free cash flows included only the cash flows from the Gatorade and bean businesses. The businesses that Quaker planned to divest were treated as nonoperating net assets. Quaker estimated the divestiture proceeds from these businesses, net of transaction costs and taxes, and used that amount as a value for the nonoperating net assets. In addition, Quaker treated the excess cash it would acquire as a nonoperating net asset.

When Quaker managers spoke publicly after the acquisition, they explained that although the price of the deal was $238 million, the net price was really only $95 million. They provided three adjustments to the purchase price to get to the true cost of $95 million: the $123 million of Stokely's cash, the $70 million estimated value of the businesses Quaker would not keep, and the $50 million estimated market value of Stokely preferred stock and debt.

	MILLIONS	
Purchase price	$ 238	
Less: Stokely cash	(123)	Nonoperating asset
Less: Estimated proceeds from sale of Stokely businesses	(70)	Nonoperating asset
Plus: Estimated market value of Stokely preferred stock and debt	50	Debt claim
Net purchase price	$ 95	

Source: The Quaker Oats Company analyst presentation, October 31, 1983.

present at the "unlevered cost of equity," the hypothetical cost of common equity the firm would have if it had no leverage. This is generally higher than the weighted-average cost of capital, resulting in a lower value for the core operations. Once we determine this lower value for the core operations using the unlevered cost of equity, we add the dollar value created through leverage. This is the amount by which the value of the core operations is higher in the free cash flow model due to the use of a lower discount rate. We then add or subtract nonoperating net assets, debt instruments, and other capital claims, just as in the free cash flow model. In calculating value in this way, the APV model highlights the value created through leverage.

The Residual Income Model

The residual income model is another way to estimate the value of the firm.[5] Although it is not used much in practice, it provides some interesting insights about the relationships among the income statement, balance sheet, and cash flow statement. Exhibit 6.9 illustrates the residual income model.

The residual income model breaks the value of core operations into two components—current book value and the present value of future residual income. **Residual income** is income related to the core operations less base income. Base income is the product of beginning of period book value of core operations and the cost of capital. We add the current book value of core operations to the present value of expected residual income to obtain the value of the core operations. Just as in the free cash flow model, we adjust for nonoperating net assets, debt claims, and other capital claims.

Despite its name and the apparent lack of cash flows in the valuation formula, the residual income model is also a discounted cash flow model. Because of the interrelationships among the income statement, balance sheet, and cash flow statement, the residual income model actually does discount expected free cash flows to value core operations. Like the other models, it is derived directly from the dividend discount model and can also be derived from the free cash flow model. So, it is equivalent to all of the other models. However, the variables in the valuation formula are based on book values and earnings amounts.

EXHIBIT 6.9 Residual Income Model

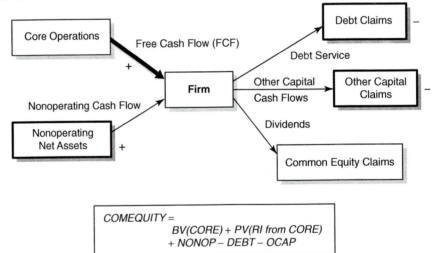

$$COMEQUITY = \\ BV(CORE) + PV(RI \text{ } from \text{ } CORE) \\ + NONOP - DEBT - OCAP$$

BV means book value.
RI means residual income.

[5]Just as the more traditional cash flow models can be done at the equity level (flows to equity model) or the operating level (free cash flow model), the residual income model can also be done at the equity level or the operating level. We will examine the residual income model at the operating level. It is simpler to implement than the residual income model at the equity level because it eliminates the need to forecast debt service.

SUMMARY

An economic balance sheet is similar to a GAAP balance sheet in that it always presents the firm's assets and claims in a way that balances. It differs from a GAAP balance sheet in three ways. (1) The economic balance sheet classifies assets and claims according to whether they are part of core operations, nonoperating net assets, debt claims, other capital claims, or common equity claims. (2) The economic balance sheet includes all economic assets and liabilities, even if they do not meet recognition tests under GAAP. (3) Amounts on the economic balance sheet represent fair values, or estimates of them, rather than book values. To create an economic balance sheet, we determine a value for core operations from a valuation model. We estimate the fair value of nonoperating net assets, debt, and other capital claims. The common equity value is equal to the core operations plus nonoperating net assets less debt less other capital claims.

Each of the five elements of the economic balance sheet (core operations, nonoperating net assets, debt claims, other capital claims, and equity claims) has a cash flow stream associated with it. The fair value of each component of the economic balance sheet is equal to the present value of the associated cash flow stream. We can value any of the components by forecasting and discounting to the present the related cash flow stream or by direct appraisal or observation of market value.

We discussed five valuation models. Each of the models arrives at an estimated value for a firm's common equity. Although each arrives at the result in a different way, all five are equivalent. Identical assumptions yield identical results for the five models. Some of the models differ from the others in terms of which elements of the economic balance sheet are valued by discounting cash flows versus direct observation or appraisal. The dividend discount model forecasts and discounts dividends. The flows to equity model forecasts and discounts all cash flows other than those to the common equityholders. The remaining three models all value core operations by forecasting and discounting, and use direct appraisal or observation for nonoperating net assets, debt claims, and other capital claims. These three models differ from each other in how they compute the value of the core operations. The free cash flow model forecasts free cash flows and discounts them at the weighted-average cost of capital. The adjusted present value model instead discounts the free cash flow at the hypothetical discount rate the firm would face if it were unlevered, and then adjusts the value for the fact that it is levered. The residual income model restates free cash flow in terms of book value and residual income, discounts the residual income forecast, and adds it to book value.

Although having five different models can be confusing, especially when trying to remember which cash flows are used in which models, keep in mind that every asset and every liability from the economic balance sheet must appear in the valuation exactly once. This is done *either* by incorporating the market or fair value of the item in the valuation *or* by including the cash flows the item generates in the cash flow stream to be discounted. By thinking about the economic balance sheet and which cash flows are related to each component, the cash flows to discount become clearer.

SUGGESTED READINGS

Courteau, L., J. Kao, and G. Richardson. The Equivalence of Dividend, Cash Flows and Residual Earnings Approaches to Equity Valuation Employing Ideal Terminal Value Expressions. Working paper, 2000.

Fernandez. P. Equivalence of the Different Discounted Cash Flow Valuation Methods: Different Alternatives for Determining the Discounted Value of Tax Shields and Their Implications for Valuation. Working paper, 2000.

Graham, B., D. Dodd, S. Cottle, R. Murray, and F. Block. *Graham and Dodd's Security Analysis*, 5th ed. New York: McGraw-Hill, 1988.

Lundholm, R. and T. O'Keefe. "Reconciling Value Estimates from the Discounted Cash Flow Model and the Residual Income Model." *Contemporary Accounting Research*, Summer 2001, 1–26.

Rappaport, A. *Creating Shareholder Value: The New Standard for Business Performance*. New York: Free Press, 1986.

Than, J. Equivalence Between Discounted Cash Flow (DCF) and Residual Income (RI). Working paper, 2001.

REVIEW QUESTIONS

1. In what three ways does an economic balance sheet differ from a GAAP balance sheet?

2. How is an economic balance sheet helpful in valuation?

3. What are the five components of the economic balance sheet?

4. What are the cash flow streams related to each of the five economic balance sheet components you listed in question 3?

5. Mark each of the following accounts as core operations (CORE), nonoperating net assets (NONOP), debt claims (DEBT), other capital claims (OCAP), or common equity claim (COMEQUITY).

___ Marketable securities

___ Preferred stock

___ Long-term debt

___ Accounts payable

___ Accrued expenses

___ Prepaid insurance

___ Forklift trucks

___ Goodwill

___ Short-term debt

___ Contingent legal liability

___ Cash used in operations

___ Raw materials inventory

___ Land used in manufacturing

___ Minority interest

___ Research and development facility

___ Income tax refund expected

___ Accounts receivable

6. The value of Jones Corporation's core operations is $100,000, the value of its nonoperating net assets is $50,000, the value of its debt is $60,000, and it has no other capital claims. What is the value of Jones' common equity?

 7. Briefly describe the dividend discount model.

 8. Briefly describe the flows to equity model.

 9. Briefly describe the free cash flow model.

 10. Briefly describe the adjusted present value model.

 11. Briefly describe the residual income model.

 12. Explain how the dividend discount model and the flows to equity model are related.

13. If land is classified as part of core operations, in what component of cash flow should the rental income it generates be included?

 14. How does an analyst use the free cash flow model to value equities? What are the steps the analyst would take?

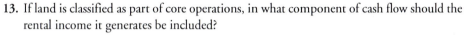

PROBLEMS

1. The Robbi Company manufactures hospital gowns. The firm has one plant built on company-owned land. Many years ago, the company purchased additional land for a planned expansion. More recently, the company decided not to expand, but to keep the land for investment purposes.

   The Robbi Company also owns a small amount of stock in Craig's Insurance Company because it believes this will be a good long-term investment.

   A recent appraisal determined the following market values for various assets and liabilities of Robbi's:

Land on which plant is located	$ 10,000,000
Land held for investment	$ 5,000,000
Debt	$ 40,000,000
Finished goods inventory	$ 7,000,000
Value of Craig's Insurance stock	$ 3,000,000

   The company has projected its free cash flow and determined the present value to be $100,000,000. What is the value of Robbi Company's common equity?

 2. Give an example of an asset that is part of core operations in one company and a nonoperating asset in another. Explain your answer.

   The following information pertains to problems 3 through 5.

   Saks Incorporated operates Saks Fifth Avenue stores, Parisian specialty department stores, traditional department stores, and Off 5th outlet stores. The following information is adapted from Saks' balance sheet as of January 29, 2000.

Saks Inc. Balance Sheet January 29, 2000

(In thousands of dollars)	
CURRENT ASSETS	
Cash and cash equivalents	$ 19,560
Accounts receivable	202,134
Merchandise inventory	1,487,783
Other current assets	122,983
Deferred income taxes	62,198
Total current assets	1,894,658
Property, plant, and equipment, net of depreciation	2,350,543
Goodwill and intangibles, net of amortization	578,001
Deferred income taxes	213,204
Other assets	62,546
Total assets	$ 5,098,952
CURRENT LIABILITIES	
Trade accounts payable	$ 235,967
Accrued expenses	436,478
Accrued compensation and related items	57,259
Sales taxes payable	46,387
Current portion of long-term debt	7,771
Total current liabilities	783,862
Long-term debt	1,966,802
Other long-term liabilities	139,945
Commitments and contingencies	
Common shareholders' equity	2,208,343
Total liabilities and shareholders' equity	$ 5,098,952

Saks has employee stock options outstanding, although they are not reported in its balance sheet.

3. Suppose you used the free cash flow model to value Saks' core operations at $3 billion. Further assume that the book value of debt approximates fair value, the value of the outstanding employee stock options is $75 million, and the commitments and contingencies are immaterial. There were 143.0 million shares of Saks outstanding on January 29, 2000. Estimate the value of a share of Saks' common equity.

4. Suppose you are an analyst at a major mutual fund and that your answer to problem 3 was $1.50 per share greater than the market value of Saks' stock. Draft a memo stating whether you think the fund should take a major position in Saks' stock and why.

5. Another analyst at your firm has also done an analysis of Saks. Her analysis used the residual income model and indicated that Saks' stock is worth $4 per share less than your analysis did. Indicate whether each of the following *could explain* why there is a difference between your results and hers. Explain your answer.

   a. You used more optimistic assumptions in your forecast.
   b. The residual income model generally produces more conservative results than the free cash flow model, even given the same assumptions.
   c. The other analyst has uncovered a contingent liability that you did not and incorporated it in her analysis.

6. Joey's Acting School has the following balance sheet (in millions of dollars) at December 31, 2001, prepared according to generally accepted accounting principles. The long-term debt, which was initially sold at par, is currently selling for 105% of par, plus accrued interest. The book values of all other items that are not part of Joey's core operations are reasonable estimates of fair market value, except the investment in Ross Paleontology, Inc., which is worth $800 million, and the common equity, which you are valuing.

Cash (all operating in nature)	$ 5.0	Accounts payable	$	6.0
Marketable securities	10.0	Wages payable		9.0
Computer equipment	40.0	Accrued interest		2.0
Other fixed assets	7.0	Long-term debt		300.0
Investment in Ross	100.0	Deferred taxes		7.0
Paleontology, Inc.		Common equity		548.0
Goodwill	710.0	Total liabilities and equity	$	872.0
Total assets	$ 872.0			

   a. Assuming the value of Joey's core operations (computed using a free cash flow model) is $2 billion ($2,000 million), what is the value of its common equity as of December 31, 2001?

   b. If you instead valued Joey using the flows to equity method and assumptions that are consistent with the assumptions in the preceding valuation, would the computed value of Joey's common equity be greater than, less than, or equal to the correct answer to part (a)?

 7. The following paragraph was taken from Arch Coal, Inc.'s 1999 annual report:

   The Company is a party to numerous claims and lawsuits with respect to various matters. The Company provides for costs related to contingencies when a loss is probable and the amount is reasonably determinable. As of December 31, 1999, the Company estimates that its probable aggregate loss as a result of such claims is $5.2 million (included in other noncurrent liabilities). The Company estimates that its reasonably possible aggregate losses from all currently pending litigation could be as much as $.5 million (before tax) in excess of the loss previously recognized. After conferring with counsel, it is the opinion of management that the ultimate resolution of these claims, to the extent not previously provided for, will not have a material adverse effect on the consolidated financial condition, results of operations or liquidity of the Company.

   The phrase "provides for costs" means that Arch Coal has recorded an expense and accrued a liability (without discounting for present values) for expected costs to be incurred related to past events. The phrase "will not have a material adverse effect on the consolidated financial condition, results of operations or liquidity of the Company" means it is unlikely the costs ultimately incurred will exceed the amount already accrued by a significant amount.

   You are estimating the value of Arch Coal using the free cash flow model. Discuss how the costs to which this disclosure refers should be handled in your valuation.

 ## My Case

For your company:

   a. For each item in the GAAP balance sheet, determine whether it is part of core operations, nonoperating net assets, debt claims, other capital claims, or equity claims.

   b. Determine whether any other items should appear on the economic balance sheet that were not in the GAAP balance sheet.

   c. Is there any information in the annual report or elsewhere that can help you value the nonoperating net assets, debt, and other capital claims?

7

Where We Have Been:

In Chapter 6, we introduced the economic balance sheet and the cash flow valuation models. Each of these models relies on a different discount rate.

Where We Are:

In this chapter, we will study the discount rates used in these cash flow valuation models.

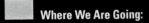

Where We Are Going:

In Chapters 8 through 12, we will study the valuation models in more detail.

Discount Rates in Valuation

LEARNING OBJECTIVES:

After studying this chapter, you will understand:

- Why different valuation models use different discount rates.
- The capital asset pricing model and how it relates to discount rates.
- How to estimate the discount rate for each model.
- How to alter the analysis of discount rates for private companies.

In discounted cash flow valuation models, we use various discount rates to calculate the present value of the forecasted flows. This chapter discusses how to compute the various discount rates we need to do valuations.

As seen in Chapter 6, different valuation models rely on different components of the firm's cash flows. These differences arise because different components of cash flow belong to different capital suppliers. In each model, we choose the discount rate that is a just sufficient expected return to compensate the relevant capital suppliers. Exhibit 7.1 shows each model, the capital supplier for the cash flow to be discounted, and the appropriate discount rate.

We begin in Section 7.1 with the cost of common equity.[1] We use the cost of equity in the dividend discount and flows to equity models because these models discount cash flows related to the common equityholders. The cost of equity is also a key building block for all other discount rates. Section 7.2 discusses the weighted-average cost of capital (WACC), which is used in the free cash flow and residual income models. These models rely on the cash flows available to all capital suppliers and so they use the WACC, which blends the costs of equity and other sources of financing. Section 7.3 discusses the unlevered cost of equity, which is used in the adjusted present value model. In this model, we use the cash flows available to all capital suppliers, but we separate the value created by leverage from the value of the cash flows if the firm were not levered. To do this, we use the unlevered cost of equity, the hypothetical cost of equity the firm would have if it were financed entirely with equity. We estimate this discount rate by applying an "unlevering" formula to the estimated cost of equity. Section 7.4 describes some special issues that arise when estimating a discount rate for private firms and certain public firms.

7.1 THE COST OF EQUITY

Estimating the cost of equity is difficult because common equity, unlike other sources of capital, has no *promised* rate of return. Equity prices are set based on investors' expectations of future cash flows and the expected rate of return they demand. Because we cannot observe this expected rate of return

EXHIBIT 7.1   Discount Rates

Model	Capital Supplier	Discount Rate
• Dividend discount model • Flows to equity model	Common equityholders	Cost of common equity
• Free cash flow model • Residual income model	Equityholders and debtholders	Weighted-average cost of capital
• Adjusted present value model	Common equityholders*	Unlevered cost of equity

*As if the debt were converted to equity.

---

[1]For simplicity, we will refer to the cost of common equity as the cost of equity.

directly, we must use an asset pricing model to infer the demanded rate of return. The most common is the capital asset pricing model, or CAPM.[2]

Capital Asset Pricing Model

The CAPM is a formal model relating risk and return. It assumes that investors are risk averse, meaning that all else being equal, they prefer less risk in their portfolios. However, investors will hold riskier portfolios if the expected return is sufficiently higher. The key concept is that the risk of the investor's *portfolio*, not the risk of any individual security in the portfolio, drives the risk–return trade-off.

As we will see, a fundamental insight of the CAPM is that stocks whose returns are highly correlated with the rest of the stock market contribute more to a portfolio's risk than do equally volatile stocks whose returns are not correlated very highly with the market. Thus, stocks that are highly correlated with the market command a higher expected return. In contrast, the volatility of an individual stock has virtually no effect on the volatility of a well-diversified portfolio, so highly volatile stocks (which are not highly correlated with the market) do not command a higher expected return.

A fundamental finding of the CAPM is that the cost of equity is

$$k_e = r_f + m \cdot \beta \tag{7.1}$$

where r_f is the risk-free interest rate, m is the equity risk premium, or the additional expected return an investor would need to hold an average-risk stock rather than the risk-free asset, and β is the degree to which the stock's returns are correlated with market movements, called *systematic risk*, often referred to simply as beta. Thus, to estimate a company's cost of equity, we need to estimate the risk-free interest rate, the equity risk premium, and the company's β.

Estimating the Risk-Free Interest Rate

A discount rate for calculating the present value of a set of cash flows should be related to the duration of the cash flows.[3] In a corporate valuation context, the cash flow stream generally has a fairly long duration, so we should begin with a long-term risk-free interest rate.

The yield on 30-year Treasury bonds, not surprisingly, is a good proxy for the risk-free rate.[4] The business section of any major newspaper provides yields on Treasury bonds. Exhibit 7.2 was taken from the October 26, 2001 issue of The *Wall Street Journal*. It shows that the longest-term Treasury bonds at the time, the bonds due in February 2031, were yielding 5.28%, which would be a reasonable proxy for the risk-free interest rate.[5]

Estimating the Equity Risk Premium

The most subjective task in determining the cost of equity is estimating the equity risk premium. The **equity risk premium** is the additional expected return above the risk-free rate that an investor requires

---

[2]This section is not intended to be a complete treatment of the CAPM, which can be found in a corporate finance text. Instead, it reviews the intuition behind the CAPM and then considers how to estimate the various parameters required to determine the cost of equity using the CAPM.

[3]Duration is the weighted-average time to maturity of the cash flows.

[4]With the Treasury Department eliminating the 30-year bonds, it appears that the benchmark for the long-term risk-free rate will be the 10-year bond. Because the yields on 10-year and 30-year bonds are usually similar, using the 10-year bond should have little effect on the cost of equity calculation. However, the 10-year yield is typically slightly lower than the 30-year yield.

[5]Note that the bonds due in April 2032 are inflation-indexed bonds (indicated by the note *i*), so the 3.38% yield is not the entire return that will be earned on these bonds. Inflation-indexed bonds should not be used as the risk-free rate unless all forecasted cash flows are inflation adjusted.

EXHIBIT 7.2   Treasury Bond Listing

TREASURY BONDS, NOTES & BILLS

Thursday, October 25, 2001

Representative Over-the-Counter quotation based on transactions of $1 million or more.

Treasury bond, note and bill quotes are as of mid-afternoon. Colons in bid-and-asked quotes represent 32nds; 101:01 means 101 1/32. Net changes in 32nds. n-Treasury note. i-Inflation-Indexed issue. Treasury bill quotes in hundredths, quoted on terms of a rate of discount. Days to maturity calculated from settlement date. All yields are to maturity and based on the asked quote. Latest 13-week and 26-week bills are boldfaced. For bonds callable prior to maturity, yields are computed to the earliest call date for issues quoted above par and to the maturity date for issues below par. *-When issued. Net changes unavailable.
Source: Associated Press

U.S. Treasury strips as of 3 p.m. Eastern time, also based on transactions of $1 million or more. Colons in bid-and-asked quotes represent 32nds; 99:01 means 99 1/32. Net changes in 32nds. Yields calculated on the asked quotation. ci-stripped coupon interest. bp-Treasury bond, stripped principal. np-Treasury note, stripped principal. For bonds callable prior to maturity, yields are computed to the earliest call date for issues quoted above par and to the maturity date for issues below par.
Source: Bear, Stearns & Co. via Street Software Technology Inc.

NOTICE TO READERS
Due to technical problems, Associated Press data are used for Treasury Bonds, Notes, Bills and Inflation-Adjusted Bonds.

GOVT. BOND & NOTES

TREASURY BILLS

U.S. TREASURY STRIPS

INFLATION-INDEXED TREASURY SECURITIES

RATE	MAT.	BID/ASKED	CHG.	*YLD	ACCR. PRIN

*-Yld. to maturity on accrued principal.
n.a.-Not available.

					ASKED
6⅛	Aug 29	111:06	111:08	n.a.	5.34
6¼	May 30	113:16	113:18	n.a.	5.32
5⅜	Feb 31	101:11	101:12	n.a.	5.28
3⅝	Apr 32i	99:25	99:27	n.a.	3.38

U.S. TREASURY STRIPS
ASKED

Source: Wall Street Journal, October 26, 2001.

A CLOSER LOOK

Treasury Department Eliminates 30-Year Bonds

In October 2001, the Treasury Department announced it would no longer sell 30-year bonds, also known as "long bonds." With a shrinking national debt, the government had actually been buying back some of its bonds and decided it no longer would need to issue long bonds. Traditionally, long bonds have earned a slightly higher return than bonds with shorter maturities, and the Treasury hoped to lower the government's borrowing cost with its move.

Although the discontinuation of the long bond is an important event for bond traders, it affects equity analysts as well. For many years, the long bond has been the standard indicator of the long-term, risk-free interest rate. As such, it has been a key input to the cost of equity calculation, which is so important in equity valuation. Analysts will have to switch to another benchmark, likely the widely traded 10-year bond.

Because the 10-year yield has usually been lower than the 30-year yield, the switch may cause analysts to estimate a slightly lower cost of equity, unless they adjust the 10-year yield upward for the typical difference. The November 16, 2001 yield curve shown here indicates the yield on the 10-year bond was about 0.4 percentage points below the 30-year yield.

EXHIBIT 7.2 Yield Curve, November 16, 2001

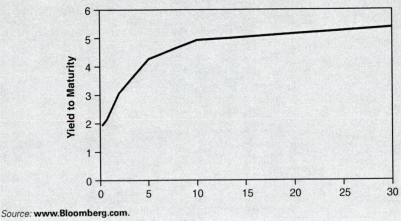

Source: **www.Bloomberg.com.**

to hold an average-risk stock rather than a Treasury bond. Many analysts simply use the average historical equity premium earned to estimate the expected premium. The **historical equity premium earned** is the excess return actually earned on stocks in a given period over (or under) the amount earned on the risk-free asset. Because the historical premium has averaged about 7% to 9%, depending on how the average is computed, many analysts use an equity premium in this range. Using the historical premium assumes that (1) the expected premium today is unchanged from what it was in the past and (2) the actual premium earned in the past is approximately what investors were expecting.

However, there are good reasons to believe the expected premium today is not the same as the historical premium that has been earned. As economic conditions and demographics change, risk preferences among investors might also change. It is entirely possible that the premium equity investors demand will change over time. Assuming that the premium today is the same as it was in the early part of the century therefore may not be appropriate.

The historical premium presents another problem. A shift in the expected equity risk premium causes stock prices to move in the *opposite* direction. If the expected equity risk premium falls in a particular year, stock prices will rise and therefore the actual premium earned in that year will be *higher* than what was expected. Thus, if the expected premium was falling over the years in which the historical premium was observed, the historical premium will overstate the expected future premium. The historical premium of 7% to 9% earned over the last 75 years could have been due to falling expected returns over that period. If that is the case, then the current expected return would be well below the 7% to 9% range.

Some researchers are now looking for ways to estimate the expected equity risk premium.[6] The procedure requires finding the risk premium that equates current stock prices with the present value of expected future cash flows. Of course, doing this depends on having an accurate estimate of the market's expectations of future cash flows. Deriving such an estimate is, to say the very least, extraordinarily difficult. Although the estimated risk premiums that researchers have found cannot be accepted as the final word on the matter, it is interesting to note that they are virtually all well below the historical average premium of 7% to 9%. Some researchers estimate the expected premium to be as low as 2% to 3%. Although there is no "right" answer to the question, the equity risk premium is probably quite a bit less than 7%. In our example, we will use 5% for the risk premium.

Understanding Beta

The final element of the cost of equity computation is beta, β, which measures a stock's correlation with the market. In order to understand what β means, we must formalize the distinction between correlation with the market and volatility. To do so, we consider a firm's stock returns to be described by equation (7.2).

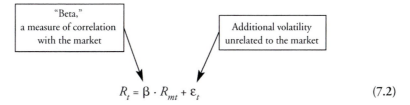

$$R_t = \beta \cdot R_{mt} + \varepsilon_t \tag{7.2}$$

where R_t is the firm's return on date t, R_{mt} is the market return on date t, and ε_t is a random variable with mean zero and some variance. ε_t is independent of the return on the market on date t, meaning that it is unaffected by whatever happens to the market on that date.

Beta represents the firm's sensitivity to market performance. For example, the expected return of a firm with a β of 1 is whatever the market's return was on that day. If β is greater than 1, the firm's expected return is greater than market movements in both directions. If β is less than 1, the firm's expected return is less severe than market movements. For example, Amazon.com has an estimated beta of 2.17,[7] meaning that on average, its return on any given day is 2.17 times the market's return.

[6]See, for example, J. Claus and J. Thomas, "Equity Premia as Low as Three Percent? Empirical Evidence from Analysts' Earnings Forecasts for Domestic and International Stock Markets." *Journal of Finance* 56, 5 (October 2001): 1629-66.
[7]Estimated from daily returns from the date Amazon.com went public until December 31, 2000.

General Motors, on the other hand, has an estimated beta of 0.83.[8] Its expected return is 0.83 times the market's. The average beta among all stocks is 1.00.

Beta, the firm's sensitivity to the market, measures **systematic risk**, which is the risk associated with the general market. Systematic risk cannot be eliminated by diversification, because a portfolio containing many different stocks would still be exposed to the risk of overall market movements.

On any given day, the return on a firm's stock will not be exactly its β times the return on the market because of ε_t. This component adds additional risk to the firm's return. Because the value of ε_t is unrelated to the return on the market on the same day, this element of the firm's risk is called **unsystematic risk**. Unsystematic risk can be eliminated through diversification, because in a portfolio containing many different stocks, the values of ε_t for various firms tend to offset each other, virtually eliminating this risk.

Exhibit 7.3 is a scatter plot of returns for Starbucks and the market over the five years 1996 to 2000. Each point represents one-day firm returns and same-day market returns. Starbucks' estimated β, which is the slope of the line through the data points, is 1.19. On average, Starbucks' return is 1.19 times the market's. On any given day, however, Starbucks' return deviates substantially from the line due to the unsystematic risk in its returns.

Exhibit 7.3 illustrates how the two components of risk affect Starbucks' returns. The first risk component is Starbucks' sensitivity to market volatility. The double arrow running horizontally along the bottom of the graph represents market volatility. The more volatile the market, the more spread out along the horizontal axis will be the market's returns. High market volatility translates into more volatile returns for Starbucks because Starbucks' returns are correlated with the market's.

EXHIBIT 7.3   Scatter Plot of Daily Starbucks' Returns and Market Returns—1996 to 2000

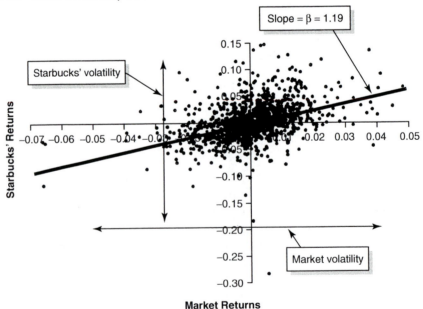

Market Returns

Source: Data extracted from Center for Research in Security Prices.

---

[8]Estimated from daily returns for the five years ended December 31, 2000.

How much more volatile the Starbucks returns will be depends on Starbucks' sensitivity to market performance, which is the slope of the line, or β.

The second component of the risk in Starbucks' common equity is company-specific or unsystematic risk. This volatility in Starbucks' returns is in addition to the effect of the market on Starbucks. It is represented by the dispersion in Starbucks' returns around the sloped line.

Consider now a portfolio of 100 different firms, each of which has a β of 1.19. If each also has the same level of unsystematic risk as in Exhibit 7.3, then the scatter plot of portfolio returns against market returns would look like Exhibit 7.4.

This portfolio's returns for a given day deviate much less from the expected return of 1.19 times the market return than do the returns for an individual company. The unsystematic risk has been nearly eliminated by holding a diversified portfolio. This fact is critically important. Because the unsystematic risk can be eliminated in a portfolio, and because it is the risk of the investor's *portfolio* that concerns him or her, the investor need not be rewarded for holding an individual stock that has unsystematic risk, no matter how great it is. Virtually all the risk in the portfolio represented in Exhibit 7.4 comes from volatility of the market, which is magnified by a factor of 1.19, the portfolio's β. There is essentially no risk in the portfolio related to the unsystematic risk of the 100 firms.

Of course, it would be unusual to find anyone holding a portfolio of stocks with identical betas. Consider a more likely example, in which the investor holds a diversified portfolio of 100 stocks. Suppose the average β of the 100 firms is 0.75. The scatter plot now looks like Exhibit 7.5.

Once again the unsystematic risk has been all but eliminated. However, this time the slope of the relationship is different. It is approximately 0.75 instead of 1.19, because the β of a portfolio is the average of the βs of the stocks in the portfolio. As a result, this portfolio will be less volatile than the market. Hence, we would expect a lower return on this portfolio than on the market as a whole.

The systematic risk of the portfolio is the average of the systematic risks of each stock in the portfolio. As a result, the systematic risk of every stock in the portfolio contributes to the portfolio's risk. As Exhibit 7.5 shows, diversification does not eliminate systematic risk. The portfolio return

EXHIBIT 7.4 Scatter Plot of Portfolio and Market Returns—Portfolio β Equals 1.19

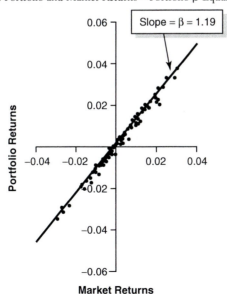

EXHIBIT 7.5 Scatter Plot of Portfolio and Market Returns—Portfolio β Equals 0.75

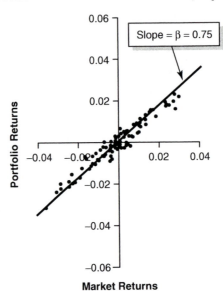

still varies with the market return. It is high or low on the same days the market return is high or low. However, the unsystematic risk is almost completely eliminated in the portfolio, as demonstrated by the fact that the points in Exhibit 7.5 are very near the sloped line. As a result, systematic risk must be rewarded with a higher expected return, whereas unsystematic risk is not.

Estimating Beta

Because β is the slope of the line that relates a firm's returns to the market's returns, we can estimate a firm's β by regressing its stock returns on the market's returns over a period of time. This is like fitting a line through the points in one of the figures we examined and then finding the slope of the line.

Before running the regression, we must make two choices. First, we must determine the length of the return interval to use—for example, daily returns or monthly returns. Second, we must determine the period over which to estimate the regression, such as trailing five years, one year, or some other period.

Return Interval

In general, a shorter return interval provides a more precise estimate of beta, all else being equal. This is so because for a given time period of data, using a shorter return interval increases the number of independent observations. For example, with five years of data, monthly returns provide 60 observations, while daily returns provide approximately 1,300. Thus, it is generally preferable to use daily returns to estimate beta.[9]

Estimation Period

To determine what length of estimation period to use, we must consider a trade-off. Examining a longer period increases the number of observations, which makes the estimate more precise.

---

[9]For thinly traded stocks it may be desirable to use a longer return interval to reduce the error that is induced in estimating beta for such stocks.

However, the further back in time we go, the more likely it is that the company was fundamentally different than it is currently. For example, it may have had a different capital structure or different kinds of investments many years ago. Even if a statistical software package reports that the estimate is more precise because of the greater number of observations, the estimate may actually be less accurate because much of the data was generated when the firm's β was different than it is today.

A common approach in estimating β is to go back in time five years. This provides enough daily observations to obtain reasonably narrow confidence intervals, without going back so far that most companies would be likely to have changed significantly. However, for companies that *have* changed substantially over the last five years, say through acquisition, divestiture, or recapitalization, a shorter estimation period is appropriate.

Interpreting Regression Results for Starbucks

Exhibit 7.6 shows the results of a regression estimating Starbucks' beta. The regression uses daily returns over the five-year period ending in December 2000. Starbucks' returns are regressed on an intercept (constant) term and market returns. Market returns are based on the value-weighted market index, which is a weighted average of all stocks' returns, with the weights based on market values. All data were obtained from the University of Chicago's Center for Research in Security Prices (CRSP).

The first section of Exhibit 7.6 shows summary regression statistics. The R-squared statistic of 0.1510 indicates that market returns explain about 15% of the variation in Starbucks' returns over the five-year period. About 15% of Starbucks' risk is systematic risk. The remaining 85% of the variance in Starbucks' returns is due to other factors. There are 1,263 observations in the regression, one for each trading day in the five-year period.

The second section of Exhibit 7.6 presents the regression coefficient estimates and related statistics. The top line shows information about the intercept. In this type of analysis, the intercept should be around zero. (If it is not, there may be a problem with the data.) In our example, the coefficient on the intercept term is very close to zero. We will not concern ourselves with the other information on the intercept; instead, we focus on the coefficient on the market return, R_{mt}, which is β.

The estimated value of β is 1.1891, or about 1.19. This is not Starbucks' actual β; it is an estimate of that value. Like any estimate, it carries a certain amount of error. The standard error is a measure of the likely magnitude of the estimation error. It represents the estimated standard deviation of the estimated value. Over many independent regressions to estimate Starbucks' β using the same number of observations, we would obtain many estimates of the true value. We would expect the standard deviation of those estimates to be 0.0794. This is a measure of how dispersed those estimates are likely to be. About two-thirds of all observations fall within one standard deviation of the true value.

EXHIBIT 7.6   Regression Results for Starbucks' Beta Using Daily Returns

Regression Statistics						
		R Squared	0.1510			
		Observations	1,263			
	Coefficients	**Standard Error**	**t-Statistic**	**p-Value**	**Lower 95%**	**Upper 95%**
Intercept	0.0009	0.0009	1.04	0.2967	−0.0008	0.0027
R_{mt}	1.1891	0.0794	14.98	0.0000	1.0333	1.3449

Source: Regression constructed from data extracted from the Center for Research in Security Prices.

The *t*-statistic (14.98) is the ratio of the coefficient estimate to its standard error. This is a standard element of any regression output. It is used to test the hypothesis that the coefficient estimate is not zero.[10] The greater the *t*-statistic (in absolute value), the more certain we are that β is not actually zero. We can best interpret what the *t*-statistic means with the *p*-value, which helps us to gauge how large the *t*-statistic is. The *p*-value in this regression is the probability that we would observe a *t*-statistic as high as 14.98 or higher (in absolute value) if the null hypothesis that $\beta = 0$ were true. The *p*-value is zero (when rounded to four decimal places), indicating that given the results, it is extremely unlikely that Starbucks' β is actually zero. The final two columns of Exhibit 7.6 give a 95% confidence interval for the estimate of β. Ninety-five percent of the time the true value of β will fall within the 95% confidence interval, so we are 95% confident that the true value of Starbucks' β is between 1.03 and 1.34.

Although this range is not large, it still leaves us with some uncertainty about the true value of Starbucks' β. This, in turn, implies uncertainty about the proper cost of equity. Because $k_e = r_f + m \cdot \beta$, using our estimates of the risk-free rate of 5.28% and the equity risk premium of 5%, we are 95% confident Starbucks' cost of equity is between 5.28% + 5% $\times$ 1.03 = 10.43% and 5.28% + 5% $\times$ 1.34 = 11.98%. This uncertainty about the cost of equity would add uncertainty to our estimate of Starbucks' value.

Although the potential error in our calculation may affect our results, this estimate is probably the best we can do. To reduce our uncertainty about the cost of equity, we would need more observations. But additional observations come with a price. We are already using daily data, so the only way to get more observations would be to use returns from more than the past five years. But Starbucks has seen tremendous growth and change in the past five years. Using data from more than five years ago would not necessarily give a true picture of the company in its current form, and the resulting cost of equity would not necessarily be a better estimate than what we already have.

As mentioned, using daily data provides a more precise estimate than using monthly returns, given the same estimation period. If we regress Starbucks' monthly returns on monthly market returns for the same time period, our standard error and our 95% confidence range are much larger. As Exhibit 7.7 shows, the coefficient estimate becomes 1.30, and the 95% confidence interval is from 0.58 to 2.03. This

EXHIBIT 7.7   95% Confidence Intervals for Starbucks' β Estimates

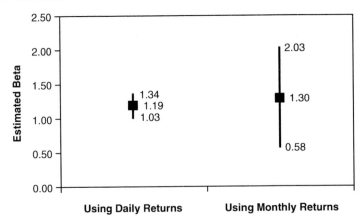

Source: Based on regression constructed from data extracted from the Center for Research in Security Prices.

---

[10]Our goal in this analysis is to estimate the value of β, not to test whether it is different from zero. We discuss the *t*-statistic and *p*-value only to complete the discussion of the regression output.

A CLOSER LOOK

BETAS OF SOME WELL-KNOWN COMPANIES

Company	Beta
Albertson's, Inc.	0.60
Dean Foods	0.60
Washington Post	0.75
Abbott Labs	0.85
Coca-Cola	0.90
Boeing	1.00
Land's End	1.00
Best Buy Co.	1.25
American Express	1.45
Bear Stearns	1.60
AOL Time Warner	1.65
Morgan Stanley	1.95

Source: *Value Line Investment Survey*, October 12, 2001.

much wider range is due to an increased standard error of 0.3618 using monthly data versus 0.0794 with daily data. Our cost of equity estimate would range from 8.18% to 15.43%. Clearly, we can be more confident that our estimate of β is near the true value when we use daily returns to compute it.

Starbucks' Cost of Equity

We have estimated the risk-free rate, the equity risk premium, and Starbucks' β. We use those estimates and (7.1) to estimate Starbucks' cost of equity:

$$k_e = r_f + m \cdot \beta = 5.28\% + 5\% \times 1.19 = 11.23\%$$

We use this cost of equity as the discount rate to apply under either the dividend discount model or the flows to equity model. It is also a component of WACC, which is used in the free cash flow and residual income models, and a component of the unlevered cost of equity, which is used in the adjusted present value model.

7.2 THE WEIGHTED-AVERAGE COST OF CAPITAL

We now examine the weighted-average cost of capital (WACC), which is used in the free cash flow model and the residual income model. First we discuss a simple case, in which the firm's economic balance sheet has only core operations, debt, and common equity. Then, we generalize the discussion to consider all firms, no matter how complicated the economic balance sheet.

Simple Case: Common Equity and Debt; No Nonoperating Net Assets

In a simple case, WACC is the weighted average of the after-tax cost of debt and the cost of equity. The weighting for debt is the proportion of debt to total capital, whereas the weighting for equity is

EXHIBIT 7.8 Easy Company Economic Balance Sheet

Easy Company			
Core operations	$	1,000	
	$	1,000	
			% of Capital
Debt	$	300	30%
Common equity		700	70%
	$	1,000	100%

the proportion of equity to total capital. These weightings are based on fair values, not book values, of debt and equity. In this simple case, we calculate *WACC* with the following formula:

$$WACC = d \cdot k_d \cdot (1 - \tau_c) + (1 - d) \cdot k_e \tag{7.3}$$

where d is the ratio of debt to total capital (based on market values), k_d is the pretax cost of debt, τ_c is the corporate marginal tax rate, and k_e is the cost of equity. For example, consider Easy Company. Exhibit 7.8 shows its economic balance sheet.

Assume Easy's pretax cost of debt is 7%, its marginal tax rate is 40%, the risk-free interest rate is 5.28%, the equity risk premium is 5%, and Easy's beta is 1.344. Easy's cost of equity is 5.28% + 1.344 · 5% = 12%. Easy Company's *WACC* is computed as follows:

$$\begin{aligned} WACC &= d \cdot k_d \cdot (1 - \tau_c) + (1 - d) \cdot k_e \\ &= 0.30 \times 0.07 \times (1 - 0.40) + (1 - 0.30) \times 0.12 \\ &= 0.0966 \end{aligned}$$

Note that the weights in this calculation sum to 100%. This is a standard feature of all weighted averages.

If the firm's core operations provide an after-tax return of 9.66%, it will be sufficient to provide both debtholders and equityholders with the returns they demand, 7% and 12%, respectively.

What we really want to know is the appropriate expected return for the cash flows we are going to discount, which relate to the core operations. This return depends on the risk profile of the core operations. We cannot observe that risk and therefore cannot estimate directly the required return on the firm's assets. However, because the debt and equity together are all the claims on the core operations, the combined risk of the debt and the equity must equal the risk of the core operations. Therefore, *the weighted average of the required returns on the debt and the common equity must be equal to the required return on the core operations.* We thus compute WACC as a way to infer the appropriate discount rate on the underlying assets, given their risk profile. This process is illustrated in Exhibit 7.9.

The reason we use the process illustrated in Exhibit 7.9 is subtle, but very important. The riskiness of the firm's core operations depends entirely on characteristics of those operations. There are many ways to divide that risk among debtholders and equityholders (via different capital structures), but how the risk is divided does not affect the assets' total risk. Therefore, *we are able to infer the appropriate expected return on the assets by examining the demanded returns on the combined claims against those assets.*

General Case

Consider now a more complicated case. Suppose Not So Easy, Inc., is identical to Easy Company except that, in addition to the assets and claims in the Easy example, Not So Easy holds $200 million

EXHIBIT 7.9 Computing WACC with No Nonoperating Assets: Easy Company

			Weight	After-Tax Cost	
Core operations	$	1,000		[0.0966]	
	$	1,000			
Debt	$	300	30%	0.042 ⎫	
Common equity		700	70%	0.120 ⎭ →	[0.0966]
	$	1,000			

of Treasury bonds that yield a 6% pretax return. As a result, the value of its claims is also $200 million higher. Assume that the firm has no more debt than it did originally, so the value of the equity claim is $200 million higher. Exhibit 7.10 is Not So Easy's economic balance sheet.

What would we expect the demanded returns to be for Not So Easy's core operations? The fact that the firm holds other assets does not affect the nature of its core operations. The core operations are the same as Easy Company's, so they must have the same risk level and hence the same required rate of return as before. We would still expect them to be priced to earn a return of 9.66%.

The problem is that applying the simple WACC formula (7.3) will no longer yield 9.66%. If we were to calculate the WACC under the same simple formula, the calculation would yield a lower discount rate. If we were to use this rate, we would erroneously conclude that the core operations are less risky than they actually are. Why? Because the debt and equity now claim core operations *and* Treasury bonds. So, the weighted-average demanded return on those securities will be equal to the average expected return on the core operations *and* the Treasury bonds. This average is lower than the demanded return on just the core operations.

We will compute the appropriate discount rate by treating such nonoperating securities as **negative debt**. The intuition behind the concept of negative debt is that if a firm holds equal amounts of debt and Treasury bonds, it is as if the firm is not levered at all. These two items offset, leaving only the core operations and equity in the economic balance sheet. It is only the *net* debt that matters. So, Not So Easy's economic balance sheet can be rewritten as shown in Exhibit 7.11.

Now we compute the weighted-average cost of capital using three elements of the capital structure: debt, Treasury bonds, and equity. The weights assigned to them would be the ratios of each item to total capital, 30%, (20%), and 90%, respectively.

Because Not So Easy, Inc. has Treasury bonds, it will have lower systematic risk and therefore a lower cost of equity than Easy Company. Suppose the cost of equity turned out to be 10.13%. Then our WACC computation is as shown in Exhibit 7.12.

EXHIBIT 7.10 Not So Easy, Inc. Economic Balance Sheet

Not So Easy, Inc.		
Core operations	$	1,000
Treasury bonds		200
	$	1,200
Debt	$	300
Common equity		900
	$	1,200

EXHIBIT 7.11   Not So Easy, Inc. Economic Balance Sheet

Not So Easy, Inc.			% of Capital
Core operations	$	1,000	
	$	1,000	
Debt	$	300	30%
Treasury bonds		(200)	(20%)
Common equity		900	90%
	$	1,000	100%

The result is that Not So Easy's WACC is the same as Easy's. This is because the core operations are the same and therefore should carry the same expected rate of return.

Although we selected the 10.13% cost of equity for Not So Easy so that it produced the same WACC as Easy's, this is what we would expect to happen.[11] The rates of return equityholders demand reflect the mix of assets to which the equityholders have a claim. The Not So Easy debtholders and equityholders claim a mix of risky core operations and riskless Treasury bonds. The rates of return they demand reflect this.

Although our illustration uses Treasury bonds, this approach to computing the WACC is appropriate whenever the firm has *any* nonoperating assets or liabilities. We estimate the discount rate for the core operations by taking a weighted average of the demanded return on all economic balance sheet items *other than the core operations*. Nonoperating assets receive a negative weight in this weighted average, but the weights must still sum to 100%.

In our example, failure to consider the effect of nonoperating assets would have caused an *understatement* in the discount rate for the core operations. This is not always the case. For example, if the nonoperating asset were a high-risk investment, say equity in a high-risk firm, then the firm's total cost of equity would be higher. If we failed to consider the extent to which the cost of equity were higher due to this high-risk nonoperating asset, we would overstate the discount rate for the core operations.

EXHIBIT 7.12   Computing Not So Easy's WACC

					Required Return
Core operations	$	1,000			0.0966
	$	1,000			
			After-Tax Cost	Weight	
Debt	$	300	0.0420	30%	
Treasury bonds		(200)	0.0360	(20%)	0.0966
Common equity		900	0.1013	90%	
	$	1,000		100%	

---

[11]More technically, this is approximately what we would expect to happen. As we will see when we study the adjusted present value model, capital structure may affect the weighted-average cost of capital, in which case Not So Easy's cost of equity would actually be slightly more than 10.13%.

Estimating Starbucks' Weighted-Average Cost of Capital

We just saw that a way to think about what is in the WACC calculation is to rearrange the economic balance sheet so that all of its components other than core operations are in the claims section. If we do this with the Starbucks economic balance sheet constructed in Chapter 6, we have Starbucks' capital structure, as shown in Exhibit 7.13. Note that at the time we estimate the cost of capital, we have not yet estimated the value of the firm. So, when we construct the economic balance sheet in order to find the appropriate weights to place on the various components of capital, we use the observed market value of equity.

Technically, the weighted-average cost of capital should combine the expected returns on each of the seven components shown in Exhibit 7.13. As a practical matter, because about 97% of Starbucks' capital is from common equity, its WACC will be very close to its cost of equity. Estimating expected returns for the other components is likely to be very cumbersome, especially for the employee stock options, and will still have very little effect on the cost of capital. We therefore use the cost of equity as an estimate of the weighted-average cost of capital. More generally, when we calculate WACC, we start with the entire economic balance sheet, but we can actually use just the material elements of it.

In order to provide an example in which the WACC is not approximately equal to the cost of equity, we imagine a company whose cost of equity is equal to that of Starbucks, but which has the following capital structure:

Debt	40%
Treasury bonds	(10%)
Common equity	70%
	100%

The firm's debt is priced to yield 8% and the Treasury bonds yield 6%, both before taxes. The marginal tax rate is 38%. The WACC is 9.47%, calculated as follows:

Debt	8% × (1 − 0.38) × 40%	1.98%
Treasury bonds	6% × (1 − 0.38) × (−10%)	(0.37%)
Common equity	11.23% × 70%	7.86%
		9.47%

The rates on the debt and the Treasury bonds are multiplied by one minus the marginal tax rate. Then the three components are combined using their weights of 40%, −10%, and 70%. We have

EXHIBIT 7.13 Starbucks' Capital Structure

Starbucks Coffee Company Economic Balance Sheet October 1, 2000 (thousands of dollars)		
Core operations	$ 7,800,000	
Debt claims	$ 7,168	0.1%
Employee stock options	347,304	4.5%
Minority interest	24,637	0.3%
Short-term investments	(61,336)	(0.8%)
Joint ventures	(52,051)	(0.7%)
Other investments	(3,788)	0.0%
Common equity	7,538,066	96.6%
Debt and other capital claims, net of nonoperating net assets	$ 7,800,000	100.0%

simply applied the notion that the appropriate discount rate for the core operations is the average expected return on all other components of the economic balance sheet.

7.3 THE UNLEVERED COST OF EQUITY

We now turn to the unlevered cost of equity. This is the cost of equity the firm would have if it were financed entirely with common equity. We will use this discount rate in the adjusted present value model.

Equation (7.1) indicated that the cost of equity depends on the risk-free interest rate, the equity risk premium, and the firm's beta. Because beta varies with a firm's capital structure, (7.1) is not the unlevered cost of equity; it is the cost of equity for the firm under its actual capital structure. To estimate the unlevered cost of equity, we need to find the **unlevered beta**, or the beta the firm would have if it were unlevered, all else being equal. We then estimate the unlevered cost of equity as:

$$k_U = r_f + m \cdot \beta_U \qquad (7.4)$$

where k_U and β_U are the unlevered cost of equity and the unlevered beta, respectively. We cannot estimate the unlevered beta directly from stock returns, because those returns are for the firm with its actual capital structure. But we can use the theoretical relationship among the unlevered beta, the levered beta, and the capital structure to infer the value of the unlevered beta from the levered beta and the capital structure.

Analysts use a formula to "unlever" betas. This formula converts the observed, levered beta to the beta the firm would have if it were unlevered. However, there are a number of *different* formulas for doing this task. The reason is that the relationship between a levered beta and an unlevered one depends on

- The pattern of the free cash flow stream
- Whether the debt will remain as a fixed dollar amount, a fixed percentage of capital, or follow some other pattern
- The beta on the firm's debt[12]

We present the most commonly used unlevering formula here.[13] It is based on a perpetuity for the free cash flow stream, a constant dollar amount of debt, and an assumed beta on debt of zero.

$$\beta_U = \beta_L \cdot \frac{1-d}{1-d \cdot \tau^*} \qquad (7.5)$$

where β_U is the unlevered beta, β_L is the levered beta, d is the current debt to capital ratio, and τ^* is the net gain in value per dollar of corporate debt as a result of income tax savings. We compute τ^* as $\tau^* = 1 - \frac{(1-\tau_c) \cdot (1-\tau_e)}{(1-\tau_d)}$, where τ_c is the marginal corporate tax rate, τ_e is the marginal tax rate on personal income derived from equity securities, and τ_d is the marginal tax rate on personal income derived from debt. We estimate $\tau^* = 0.14$ using the highest marginal rate for corporate taxes (35%) for τ_c, the maximum capital gains tax rate for individuals (20%) for τ_e, and the maximum

---

[12]The debt beta measures correlation between returns on debt and the stock market. For debt that does not have significant default risk, the beta is generally very low.

[13]For a description of several different unlevering formulae and the assumptions used to derive each, see R. Taggart, "Consistent Valuation and Cost of Capital Expressions with Corporate and Personal Taxes," *Financial Management* 20, 3 (1991): 8–20.

marginal tax rate for individuals (39.6%) for τ_d. Therefore, $\tau^* = 1 - \dfrac{(1 - 0.35) \cdot (1 - 0.20)}{1 - 0.396} = 0.14$.

This means that the firm creates about 14 cents of value for each dollar of debt in its capital structure.

Because Starbucks has so little debt, its unlevered cost of equity is essentially its cost of equity. So, we illustrate the unlevering process with Easy Company, for which we calculated the WACC earlier. Easy's beta is 1.344 and its capital structure is 30% debt and 70% equity. Its unlevered beta is 0.98, calculated as follows:

$$\beta_U = \beta_L \cdot \frac{1 - d}{1 - d \cdot \tau^*} = 1.344 \cdot \frac{0.70}{1 - 0.30 \cdot 0.14} = 0.98$$

Using (7.4), we then calculate the unlevered cost of equity to be

$$5.28\% + 5\% \times 0.98 = 10.18\%$$

This is lower than the original cost of equity of 12%, which was based on the levered beta of 1.344. This is as we expect, because levered equity is riskier than unlevered equity. But, the unlevered cost of equity is higher than the 9.66% WACC we calculated for Easy earlier. By levering itself, Easy has reduced its cost of capital from 10.18% to 9.66%.

7.4 ISSUES WITH PRIVATE COMPANIES

Estimating a discount rate for privately held firms adds complications that we do not face with public companies. First, we cannot observe security returns for private firms, so we cannot estimate beta with a regression. Second, when the private firm is a subsidiary of another firm, we have to consider the operating risk characteristics of the subsidiary together with the capital structure of the parent.

Inability to Estimate Beta Directly

It is not feasible to estimate beta for private companies from a regression of stock returns on market returns. The most common alternative is to examine betas of public companies in the same industry, which are likely to face similar economics. The analyst obtains the data necessary to estimate the betas of these public companies and averages them to obtain an estimated beta for the private company.

However, although companies in the same industry are likely to face similar operating risks, they may have different capital structures. As Exhibit 7.14 shows using the Easy Company example, capital structure affects beta, so the betas of other companies in the same industry may not be comparable. As a result, we must adjust the beta estimates of the comparable companies for the difference in capital structure. Our goal is to find the beta the comparable firm would have if it had the capital structure of the firm we are trying to value.

If the two firms are comparable except for capital structure, then their unlevered betas will be equal. Therefore, if we apply a bit of algebra[14] to (7.5), we conclude that

$$\beta_T = \beta_C \cdot \frac{1 - d_C}{1 - d_T} \cdot \frac{1 - d_T \cdot \tau^*}{1 - d_C \cdot \tau^*} \tag{7.6}$$

---

[14]We set the unlevered betas of the target and the comparable firm equal to each other:

$\beta_U = \beta_T \cdot \dfrac{1 - d_T}{1 - d_T \cdot \tau^*} = \beta_C \cdot \dfrac{1 - d_C}{1 - d_C \cdot \tau^*}$. Solving for β_T, we get (7.6).

EXHIBIT 7.14 Easy Company's Beta and Leverage

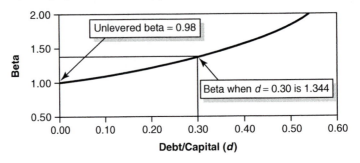

where the subscripts T and C refer to the target firm and the comparable firm, respectively. For example, if a comparable firm has a beta of 1.75 and a 45% debt to capital ratio, and the target firm has a 15% debt to capital ratio, we estimate the target firm's beta from the comparable firm's beta as follows (assuming $\tau^* = 0.14$):

$$\beta_T = 1.75 \cdot \frac{1 - 0.45}{1 - 0.15} \cdot \frac{1 - 0.15 \cdot 0.14}{1 - 0.45 \cdot 0.14} = 1.18$$

By using this formula, we take the information about operating risk from the comparable firm's beta, but adjust it for the less levered capital structure of the target firm. Instead of using the 1.75 beta of the firm with the more levered capital structure, we use the more appropriate value of 1.18. Now we would use the beta of 1.18 in our calculation of the target's cost of equity.

The analyst has two alternatives to the unlevering and relevering approach we have just shown. First, if possible, the analyst can choose a comparable firm with a capital structure similar to that of the firm being valued. This eliminates the need to adjust beta for the difference in leverage. For companies with close enough capital structures, the difference in beta due to a small difference in capital structure will be negligible. In this case, we can use the comparable beta in our cost of equity calculation. Second, the analyst could simply estimate the cost of capital for the comparable firm. That is, using the comparable firm's beta, cost of debt, and so on, the analyst would estimate the comparable company's WACC. Because WACC is less sensitive to capital structure than is beta or the cost of equity, we would use the comparable firm's WACC for the target company. None of these solutions deals perfectly with the problem of how to estimate the cost of equity and WACC when the firm's beta cannot be observed. Unfortunately, there is no perfect solution.

Averaging Betas of Different Precisions

In computing the estimated beta for a private firm, analysts often average the betas of several other firms and use this average to estimate the private firm's cost of equity. Recall that these betas are really estimates of each firm's true beta. The degree of precision of each of these estimates may differ. **Precision** is a statistical measure of accuracy, and it is equal to the reciprocal of the variance. When making an estimate by taking an average of several estimates, weighting the average on the precision of each component minimizes the error of the final estimate. Appendix 7.1 shows how to take such a weighted average for three estimates of beta.

Subsidiaries of a Company

Most companies, other than the smallest private ones, operate in a number of different businesses. Each of these business units faces different risks, and so the appropriate discount rate will vary across divisions, product lines, or subsidiaries, based on the risk profile of the particular business. As a result, discount rates should also vary across subsidiaries. In determining its cost of capital, the firm should estimate the beta separately for each division and compute the weighted-average cost of capital for each using the firm's capital structure and the division-specific equity costs implied by the betas at each division. Use of a single discount rate for the entire firm would overstate the value of high-risk divisions and understate the value of low-risk divisions.

Because individual divisions will not have equity traded on them, a division-specific beta requires the use of comparable companies, as noted in the preceding discussion. These betas may need to be unlevered/relevered for the company's capital structure using the previously discussed method.

SUMMARY

The discount rate we employ depends on the valuation model. The dividend discount model and the flows to equity model both use the cost of equity. The free cash flow and residual income models use the weighted-average cost of capital. The adjusted present value model uses the unlevered cost of equity. In each case, the discount rate is the expected return that is just sufficient for the pertinent capital suppliers.

The cost of equity is a building block for all other discount rates, so estimating any discount rate begins with an estimate of the cost of equity. We cannot observe the cost of equity directly but instead estimate it based on an asset pricing model, such as the capital asset pricing model. Estimating the cost of equity requires an estimate of beta, which is usually obtained from regression analysis, the risk-free rate, and an estimate of equity risk premium.

Estimating both the unlevered cost of equity and the weighted-average cost of capital begin with the estimated cost of equity. We apply an unlevering formula to the cost of equity to obtain the unlevered cost of equity. We average the estimated cost of equity with the costs of all other capital claims to obtain the weighted-average cost of capital. Although this appears to be a simple task, determining the appropriate WACC can be difficult for a firm with a complex capital structure. In calculating WACC, we must also consider nonoperating assets, which are given negative weights in the computation.

For private companies, betas cannot be estimated directly from stock returns. Instead, we use betas of comparable firms, adjusting for the capital structure differences, if necessary.

SUGGESTED READINGS

Bodie, Z. and R. Merton. *Finance.* Upper Saddle River, NJ: Prentice Hall, 2000.

Claus, J. and J. Thomas. "Equity Premia as Low as Three Percent? Empirical Evidence from Analysts' Earnings Forecasts for Domestic and International Stock Markets." *Journal of Finance* 56, 5 (October 2001):1629–66.

Lintner, J. "The Valuation of Risk Assets and the Selection of Risky Investments in Stock Portfolios and Capital Budgets." *Review of Economics and Statistics* 47 (February 1965).

Sharpe, W. "Capital Asset Prices: A Theory of Market Equilibrium." *Journal of Finance* 19 (September 1964).

Taggart, R. "Consistent Valuation and Cost of Capital Expressions with Corporate and Personal Taxes." *Financial Management* 20, 3 (1991):8–20.

REVIEW QUESTIONS

1. How do we choose the discount rate that is appropriate for any particular cash flow model?

2. The dividend discount and flows to equity models use the same discount rate. What rate is used and why?

3. The free cash flow model and residual income model use the same discount rate. What rate is used and why?

4. What rate is used in the adjusted present value model and why?

5. Under the capital asset pricing model, what drives the risk–return trade-off?

6. What is systematic risk and why is it important in estimating a firm's cost of equity?

7. What is unsystematic risk and why is it *not* important in estimating a firm's cost of equity?

8. How should we estimate the risk-free rate, r_f?

9. What is beta and why do we need to estimate it?

10. What does a beta of 1.50 mean? What does a beta of 1.00 mean?

11. How should you estimate a firm's beta?

12. What are the advantages of using daily returns instead of monthly returns to estimate beta?

13. How long of an estimation period should we use when gathering data to estimate beta?

14. What is the equity risk premium and why is it difficult to estimate?

15. How do we calculate the weighted-average cost of capital?

16. What is the unlevered cost of equity?

PROBLEMS

1. You are considering a stock repurchase and must value your own firm to determine an appropriate price. An analyst in your firm has computed the weighted-average cost of capital to use in the valuation. He estimated beta from historical returns for your stock and the market, and then applied the capital asset pricing model to arrive at a cost of equity. He then weighted the cost of equity and the after-tax cost of debt based on the relative market values of these two claims.

   You notice as you prepare your valuation that your firm holds a large amount of government bonds, and you plan to include them in your valuation by adding their fair value directly.

   To value the company's free cash flows, should you use a discount rate that is higher than, lower than, or equal to the discount rate computed by your analyst? Explain your answer.

2. According to the October 12, 2001, *Value Line*, American Express has a beta of 1.45 and Coca-Cola has a beta of 0.90.

   a. What would you expect the beta of a portfolio containing equal dollar amounts of these two stocks (and nothing else) to be?

   b. Of the three possible investments considered (American Express, Coca-Cola, American Express/Coca-Cola portfolio), which has the lowest systematic risk?

   c. Of the three possible investments considered (American Express, Coca-Cola, American Express/Coca-Cola portfolio), which has the lowest unsystematic risk?

   d. Of the three possible investments considered (American Express, Coca-Cola, American Express/Coca-Cola portfolio), which has the lowest cost of equity?

3. Your firm is considering an acquisition of a privately held toy manufacturer. Draft a memo for the chief financial officer describing how you would estimate the cost of equity for this business.

4. Vogelstein Beets, Inc. has the following economic balance sheet:

(thousands of dollars)		
Core operations	$	2,950
Long-term debt	$	700
Common equity		2,250
	$	2,950

Vogelstein's cost of debt is 7% before taxes. Its marginal tax rate is 40%. Assume the risk-free interest rate is 6%, the equity risk premium is 5%, and Vogelstein's beta is 1.20. Assume $\tau^* = 0.14$.

Compute the discount rate Vogelstein should use for the following:

a. the flows to equity or dividend discount model
b. the free cash flow or residual income model
c. the adjusted present value model

5. Here are the results of a regression of Microsoft's daily returns against market returns for the five-year period ending December 31, 2000.

Summary Output

Regression Statistics

R Squared		0.3687
Observations		1263

	Coefficients	Standard Error	t-Statistic	p-Value	Lower 95%	Upper 95%
Intercept	0.0005	0.00057	0.87	0.3825	−0.0006	0.0016
Market returns	1.3522	0.04983	27.14	0.0000	1.2545	1.4499

Source: Regression constructed from data extracted from the Center for Research in Security Prices.

a. What does the R-squared statistic mean?
b. What does the coefficient on the market returns mean?
c. Is the coefficient on market returns significantly different from zero?
d. What does the 95% confidence interval for Microsoft's beta mean?
e. Assuming a risk-free interest rate of 6% and an equity risk premium of 5.5%, calculate Microsoft's cost of equity.

6. You are trying to value Thomas' Publishing Company, a private firm. You have identified a publicly held publisher, P. J. Corporation, which is very similar to Thomas except that it has a more levered capital structure. You have estimated P. J.'s beta to be 1.30. Using the following information, estimate Thomas's beta.

- Thomas' debt to capital ratio is 16%.
- P. J.'s debt to capital ratio is 25%.
- $\tau^* = 14\%$.

7. Here is some information about Roosevelt Paper Company:

Roosevelt Paper Company Balance Sheet December 31, 2001

(in thousands of dollars)

Cash	$	50	Accounts payable	$	375
Accounts receivable		300	Debt		500
Inventory		500	Total Liabilities		875
Property, plant, and equipment		825	Preferred stock		200
Total assets	$	1,675	Common equity		600
			Total Liabilities and Equity	$	1,675

There are 200,000 shares of preferred stock outstanding, each paying a dividend of $0.15 per share. Preferred dividends are not tax deductible. There are 100,000 shares of common stock outstanding, currently paying a dividend of $1.00 per share. Roosevelt's beta is 1.10. Its marginal income tax rate is 40%, and its pretax cost of debt is 7%. Assume a risk-free interest rate of 5% and a market premium of 6%.

The fair values of certain assets and liabilities as of December 31, 2001, were:

Inventory	$	700,000
Debt	$	400,000
Preferred stock (per share)	$	1.50
Common stock (per share)	$	13.00

Calculate Roosevelt's weighted-average cost of capital.

8. You are the chief financial officer of a privately held firm. The chief executive officer wants to know more about the difficulties of estimating the cost of capital for a private firm. Discuss what issues are likely to arise and how to deal with them.

My Case

a. If your school has access to data from the Center for Research in Security Prices (CRSP)—for example, through Wharton Research Data Services[15]—pull the daily returns for your company and the value-weighted market index (including distributions). Run the appropriate regression to estimate beta. If your school does not have access to CRSP data, find the beta for your company from Value Line.

b. Estimate your company's cost of equity.

c. Estimate your company's weighted-average cost of capital.

d. Estimate your company's unlevered cost of equity.

[15]Many schools subscribe to this service, which permits instructors to establish class accounts for their students' use. The service provides an easy-to-use Web-based interface for obtaining CRSP data.

APPENDIX 7.1 AVERAGING ESTIMATED BETAS HAVING DIFFERENT PRECISIONS

Suppose we have three estimated betas from comparable firms and wish to average them. Because each of the three beta estimates contains errors, so will our average. To average them in a way that minimizes the error, we weight each estimate on its precision.

We have estimated betas for two companies in addition to the estimated beta for Starbucks of 1.19. The first two columns of Exhibit 7.15 show the estimated betas and standard errors. The next column shows the precisions of the beta estimates for the three firms. We compute these by taking the reciprocal of the variance (standard error squared). The weights are each firm's precision divided by the sum of the three firms' precisions. Finally, we compute the beta estimate. Although this is not the only possible weighted average, it is the one that minimizes the standard error of the resulting estimate.[16]

Most of the weight is put on the estimate with the smallest standard error. However, we do not put all of the weight on this estimate, because as we will see, the standard error of the weighted average is smaller than even the smallest standard error of the three individual estimates. The standard error of a weighted average of independent estimates is

$$SE(\overline{\beta}) = \sqrt{\sum_i w_i^2 \cdot SE^2(\hat{\beta}_i)} \qquad (7.7)$$

where $SE(\overline{\beta})$ is the standard error of the weighted average, w_i are the weights, which sum to 1, and $SE(\hat{\beta}_i)$ is the standard error of the i-th beta estimate. Exhibit 7.16 calculates the standard error of the estimated beta of 1.37 from Exhibit 7.15.

$$\text{Standard error} = \sqrt{0.001236} = 0.035$$

EXHIBIT 7.15   Weighted-Average Beta Estimate

	Estimated Beta	Standard Error	Precision	Weight	Beta × Weight
Starbucks	1.19	0.0794	158.62	0.196	0.233
Co. 2	1.30	0.0800	156.25	0.193	0.251
Co. 3	1.45	0.0450	493.83	0.611	0.886
			808.70	1.000	**1.370**

[16]The interested student with sufficient training in calculus may wish to verify that this is the optimal weighting scheme. To do so, set up a constrained optimization problem and use the Lagrangian multiplier method. Write out the expression for the variance of the weighted-average estimate. Then find the combination of weights that minimizes the expression, subject to the constraint that the weights sum to 1.

EXHIBIT 7.16   Standard Error of Weighted-Average Beta Estimate

	Standard Error	Weight	SE-squared $\times$ Weight-squared
Starbucks	0.0794	0.196	0.000242
Co. 2	0.0800	0.193	0.000238
Co. 3	0.0450	0.611	0.000756
		1.000	0.001236

The standard error of this estimate (0.035) is smaller than any of the individual standard errors, which range from 0.045 to 0.080. This is exactly the reason we use an average rather than any one of the individual estimates in the first place—it is more precise than any of the individual estimates.

Knowing the standard error of the estimate allows us to put a confidence interval around the estimate. Our estimate of 1.37 has a 95% confidence interval of about 1.30 to 1.44 ($\pm$1.96 standard errors).

8

 Where we have been:

In Chapters 6 and 7, we introduced the cash flow valuation models and their discount rates.

 Where we are:

In this chapter, we begin our detailed study of valuation models with the dividend discount and flows to equity models, two of the five cash flow models.

 Where we are going:

In Chapters 9 through 12, we will learn about the other cash flow valuation models.

The Dividend Discount and the Flows to Equity Models

LEARNING OBJECTIVES:

After studying this chapter, you will understand:

- The dividend discount model.
- The assumptions of the dividend discount model.
- The concept of a just barely sustainable dividend stream and its importance to the dividend discount model.
- The limitations of the dividend discount model.
- How the flows to equity model works.
- Why the flows to equity and dividend discount models are equivalent.

When you buy a share of stock, what do you expect to receive? Ask any investor this question and you are likely to get this answer: dividends and the appreciated (hopefully) price of my stock when I sell it. These two items comprise the cash flows equityholders expect to receive from a stock investment.

We begin our detailed study of discounted cash flow models with the dividend discount model because it is easy to understand and intuitive. The dividend discount model expresses the value of equity as the present value of the cash flows the equityholders expect to receive. It is the most direct application of discounted cash flow theory and the basis for all of the other cash flow models. This chapter also covers the flows to equity model, which is closely linked to the dividend discount model.

Exhibit 8.1 is our picture of the security analysis process. We now begin to focus on the valuation itself. The valuation depends on the forecast assumptions we make. These assumptions are based largely on the business analysis and financial statement analysis we have discussed in previous chapters.

Section 8.1 describes the dividend discount model. Section 8.2 analyzes the dividend discount model assumptions. Section 8.3 examines variants of the dividend discount model, and in Section 8.4, we apply the dividend discount model to a real company. Then Section 8.5 examines the flows to equity model.

8.1 THE DIVIDEND DISCOUNT MODEL

The dividend discount model is based on the idea that the value of any security is the present value of the security's expected future cash flows, discounted at the rate of return demanded by holders of that security. The holder of a share of stock will receive dividends over the holding period, plus the

EXHIBIT 8.1   A Picture of the Security Analysis Process

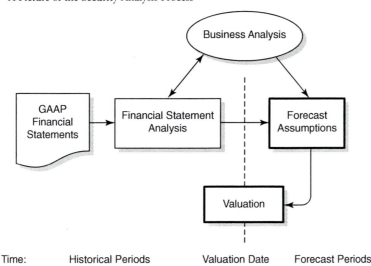

value of the stock when he or she sells it. So, the value of common equity is equal to the present value of the expected common dividend stream during the holding period plus the present value of the future stock price, discounted at the cost of equity. Algebraically,

Present value of future dividends during the holding period

Present value of stock at end of holding period

$$COMEQUITY = \sum_{t=1}^{T} \frac{DIV_t}{(1 + k_e)^t} + \frac{P_T}{(1 + k_e)^T} \qquad (8.1)$$

where DIV_t is the expected dividend at date t, P_T is the expected proceeds on sale of the stock at date T, and k_e is the cost of equity.

The expected value of the stock at time T is the present value of the expected dividend stream at that date. As a result,[1]

$$COMEQUITY = \sum_{t=1}^{\infty} \frac{DIV_t}{(1 + k_e)^t} \qquad (8.2)$$

As (8.2) shows, the value of the equity is the present value of all the expected future dividends, even for an investor whose investment horizon is shorter than the life of the firm. So, the value of the firm's equity is independent of the investor's investment horizon.

Although the dividend discount model is simple, forecasting the dividend stream correctly is complicated. We will now turn to the difficult task of forecasting the dividend stream.

8.2 THE DIVIDEND DISCOUNT MODEL ASSUMPTIONS

Exhibit 8.2 replicates Exhibit 6.5 from Chapter 6. It highlights the dividend stream, which is used to estimate value in this model.

Although the dividend discount model discounts only dividends, Exhibit 8.2 illustrates why we cannot forecast dividends without considering the net cash flows into the firm. These cash flows will provide the funds necessary to pay the dividends.

We now analyze the implications of the relationship between flows into the firm and its dividend stream. We first note from (8.2) that the dividend discount model requires a forecast for an infinite number of years, which is not feasible to do. As a result, analysts using the dividend discount model must make a simplifying assumption about the dividend stream's pattern. We will analyze the dividend discount model using a common assumption, that dividends will grow at a constant rate, g, per year. The dividend discount model can be adapted to other assumptions about dividend stream patterns, such as having two or three periods with different growth rates.

---

[1]Substituting $\sum_{t=T+1}^{\infty} \frac{DIV_t}{(1+k_e)^{t-T}}$ for P_T in (8.1) gives (8.2).

EXHIBIT 8.2   Cash Flows and the Firm—Dividend Discount Model

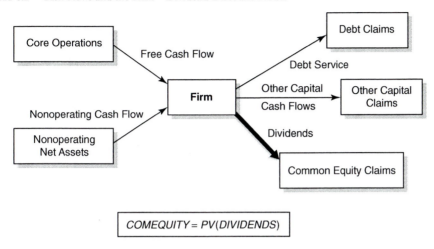

In the constant-growth case, also called the Gordon Growth Model, equation (8.2) reduces to[2]

$$COMEQUITY = \frac{DIV_1}{k_e - g} \tag{8.3}$$

as long as $g < k_e$. For example, if a firm is currently paying a dividend of $3 per share, has a cost of equity of 12%, and is expected to increase its dividend indefinitely by 5% per year, then the firm's value is $3/(0.12 − 0.05), or $42.86 per share.

The reasonableness of a dividend discount valuation depends on the reasonableness of the assumptions. The Gordon Growth Model has three assumptions: the initial dividend (DIV_1), the cost of equity (k_e), and the growth rate in the dividend (g). Let us examine each of them.

Initial Dividend

The initial dividend (actually, the expected dividend in the first year of the future dividend stream) is quite simple to determine. Newspapers, the annual report, and many other public sources all report dividend rates.

Cost of Equity

The cost of equity is a little bit more difficult to estimate. As we learned in Chapter 7, with the aid of an asset pricing model, such as the capital asset pricing model (CAPM), we can estimate a reasonable value for the cost of equity.

Dividend Growth Rate

In considering the dividend growth rate assumption, first we show how sensitive value is to this assumption. Then we introduce the concept of a just barely sustainable dividend growth rate and show that this is the appropriate growth rate to use in the model.

---

[2](8.3) is derived using (8.2) and the formula for a perpetuity with a constant growth rate.

EXHIBIT 8.3 Equity Value as a Function of Dividend Growth Rate

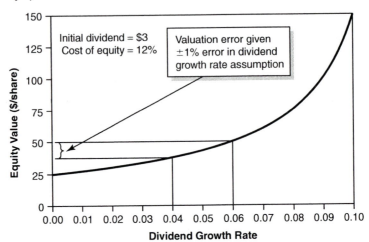

Sensitivity of Value to the Dividend Growth Rate

To illustrate the sensitivity of equity value to the dividend growth rate assumption, we calculated the value of equity in our example using various growth rates, holding the initial dividend and the cost of equity fixed at $3 and 12%, respectively. Exhibit 8.3 shows these values. As we saw before, when the dividend growth rate is 5%, the value is $42.86. However, for a ±1% difference in the growth rate, the values ranged from $37.50 to $50.00.

Exhibit 8.3 shows that the range of values is even more dramatic at higher growth rates.[3] When the growth rate is 8%, the value is $75. For a ±1% difference around the 8% growth rate, the values range from $60 to $100.

The Just Barely Sustainable Dividend Growth Rate

So which is the "right" growth rate? Is it 5%? Or 4%? Or some other rate? To answer that question, we must consider that the source of dividends is the firm's ability to generate cash. So, the appropriate dividend growth rate is the rate of growth in the dividend over the long run for which the firm would have sufficient resources to pay the specified dividend but would build up no excess cash. We will call this rate the **just barely sustainable growth rate**, and label it g^*. Assume that in valuing the firm using the dividend discount model, we used a growth rate greater than g^*, and consider the condition of the firm many years later if it adhered to this growth rate. At some point, the firm would not generate enough cash to fund the dividend stream, so it would need to borrow to make the dividend payments. Each year, it would have to borrow more and more to fund the dividend, as well as the ever-increasing debt-service payments, theoretically driving debt to an infinite level. Of course, eventually the firm could not obtain any more financing and as a result it could not sustain the dividend growth rate. The valuation would be based on an unsustainable dividend growth rate, and the resulting value estimate would be too high.

If instead we choose a dividend growth rate less than g^*, we would have the opposite problem. If the firm paid that dividend stream, then eventually it would build up an infinite amount of cash, which

---

[3]It is not a high dividend growth rate per se that causes greater sensitivity, but a small spread between the cost of equity and the growth rate. To see why, take the derivative of equation (8.2) with respect to g, which is $DIV_1/(k_e - g)^2$. Dividing this amount by $COMEQUITY$ gives $1/(k_e - g)$, which represents the rate of change in $COMEQUITY$ relative to the rate of change in g. When $k_e - g = 0.10$, $1/(k_e - g) = 10$, so a one percentage point error in g causes a roughly 10% error in $COMEQUITY$. For smaller spreads between k_e and g, the sensitivity is greater.

would never be paid out. By assuming this cash would grow within the firm, rather than being paid out as a dividend, we exclude its value from the valuation under the dividend discount model. This suggests that when a lot of cash builds up, the firm burns the cash rather than distributing it, which is an unreasonable assumption. Under this assumption, the estimate of firm value would be too low.

We properly value the firm only when $g = g^*$, the just barely sustainable growth rate. That is, the assumed dividend stream must be feasible given the cash flow stream coming into the firm, but just barely so.

Finding the Just Barely Sustainable Growth Rate   Even modest errors in the estimate of g cause large valuation errors. Therefore, estimates of g must be very close to the just barely sustainable growth rate (g^*) for the dividend discount model to be a reliable valuation method. We need to determine how to find accurate estimates of g^*. Because g^* is the dividend growth rate that makes excess cash tend toward zero over the long run, we can forecast the future cash flows (after dividend payments) for a very large number of periods and find the dividend growth rate such that the firm's cash balance in the last year is zero. For the cash balance to be zero at the end of this very long time period, the following must be true. (Appendix 8.1 derives this formula.)

$$\frac{DIV_1}{k_e - g^*} = C_0 + \sum_{t=1}^{\infty} \overbrace{\frac{FCF_t - DS_t}{(1 + k_e)^t}}^{\text{Cash flow before dividends}} \tag{8.4}$$

where C_0 is the firm's cash on hand at time 0, FCF_t is the free cash flow in period t, and DS_t is the debt service in period t.

Equation (8.4) represents the condition that must be true for g^* to represent the just barely sustainable dividend growth rate, the correct growth rate to use in the dividend discount model. Notice that the left-hand side of equation (8.4) is the same as the right-hand side of equation (8.3), using g^* for the growth rate.

Consider the implication of this. Because equation (8.3) shows how to calculate the value of equity, the left side of equation (8.4) is the value of the firm's equity. Therefore, the right side of equation (8.4) is also the value of the firm's equity. This suggests that to obtain the forecast of g^*, we should forecast cash flows *before considering dividends* and compute the value of the firm's equity from the expression on the right-hand side of (8.4). Once we do this, we can solve equation (8.4) for g^*. Then we can substitute g^* into equation (8.3) to obtain the value of the firm's equity. Once we compute the right-hand side of equation (8.4), we have the value of the firm's equity and there is no longer any need to know g^*. That is, to value a firm properly using the dividend discount model, we must value the firm using some other method first! This makes the dividend discount model of little practical value.

Despite this problem, some practitioners use the dividend discount model, usually without analyzing the just barely sustainable dividend growth rate. An analyst who uses the dividend discount model this way does not know whether the dividend stream he or she is valuing is just barely sustainable. The analyst also does not know the extent of the misvaluation if the assumed dividend stream is not just barely sustainable.

Why Not Just Estimate g^*?   At first glance, an analyst might suggest that picking a reasonable dividend growth rate, or one that approximates growth in the economy, is close enough. To show why this is not true, consider the following example. The cash on hand plus the present value of the stream of cash inflows for a firm is $100/share. The cost of equity is 15%. Because we know the cash on hand plus the present value of the stream of cash flows and the cost of equity, we can use equation (8.4) to determine

EXHIBIT 8.4   Implied Growth Rate at Various Year 1 Dividend Levels for $100 Share Price and 15% Cost of Equity

Year 1 Dividend	Implied Dividend Growth Rate
Low: $1/share	14%
Medium: $5/share	10%
High: $10/share	5%

what g^* must be for any level of year 1 dividend. Exhibit 8.4 presents values of g^* based on a low year 1 dividend of $1/share, a medium year 1 dividend of $5/share, and a high year 1 dividend of $10/share.

If the year 1 dividend is $1, a low payout, the just barely sustainable growth rate is 14%. If the year 1 dividend is $10/share, a high payout, the just barely sustainable growth rate is only 5%. The year 1 dividend has a major effect on the just barely sustainable growth rate. Simply selecting a "reasonable" growth rate will not be sufficient, because "reasonableness" cannot be determined without first valuing the firm using some other method and considering the year 1 dividend level relative to that value. The common approaches of using a historical dividend growth rate, the expected growth in the economy or industry, or the expected inflation rate, all are likely to lead to erroneous valuations.

8.3   VARIANTS OF THE DIVIDEND DISCOUNT MODEL

So far our analysis relies on a model with a single dividend growth rate. We could also specify dividend streams with less regular patterns. We could forecast dividends year by year until some point and then impose a Gordon Growth Model beyond that point in time. We could also specify several periods with different growth rates in each. In any case, it is still necessary to use a just barely sustainable dividend stream, a dividend stream that the firm's net cash inflows can support, but just barely.

We illustrate the dividend discount model with a slightly more complex pattern—a two-stage model. This model assumes dividends grow at one rate for a period of time, followed by a different growth rate that is sustainable indefinitely. Exhibit 8.5 illustrates this dividend pattern.

Although the valuation formula that follows does not require the stage 1 growth rate to be greater than the stage 2 growth rate, that is usually how we think of the model. For this reason, we call the stage 1 growth rate a supernormal rate and the stage 2 growth rate a normal rate. In this case, the value of equity is:

$$COMEQUITY = \sum_{t=1}^{\infty} \frac{DIV_t}{(1+k_e)^t}$$

$$= DIV_1 \cdot \frac{1 - \left(\dfrac{1+g_{SN}}{1+k_e}\right)^N}{k_e - g_{SN}} + DIV_1 \cdot \frac{(1+g_{SN})^{N-1} \cdot (1+g_N)}{(k_e - g_N) \cdot (1+k_e)^N} \tag{8.5}$$

Value of dividends during supernormal growth period

Value of dividends beyond supernormal growth period

where g_{SN} is the supernormal dividend growth rate projected through year N and g_N is the long-term sustainable growth rate. For example, consider a firm whose year 1 dividend rate is expected to be

EXHIBIT 8.5   Two-Stage Dividend Model

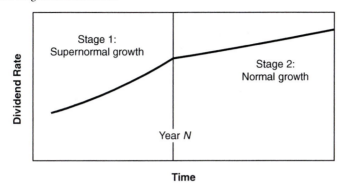

$10 per share. The firm expects to have supernormal dividend growth of 8% through year 5. After that, the just barely sustainable long-term growth rate is 3%. The cost of equity is 10%.

$$COMEQUITY = \$10 \cdot \frac{1 - \left(\dfrac{1.08}{1.10}\right)^5}{0.10 - 0.08} + \$10 \cdot \frac{(1.08)^4 \cdot (1.03)}{(0.10 - 0.03) \cdot (1.10)^5} = \$43.83 + \$124.30 = \$168.13$$

Like the Gordon Growth Model, the two-stage model is very sensitive to the assumed dividend growth rates. As before, accurately determining a combination of growth rates that is just barely sustainable requires the analyst first to estimate the value of the firm's equity using some other method. This information is then used to determine values of the two growth rates that set (8.5) equal to the value of the firm's equity. This makes the two-stage model, like the Gordon Growth Model, impractical. Other versions of the dividend discount model, such as a three-stage model, have the same fundamental problem.

8.4 APPLYING THE DIVIDEND DISCOUNT MODEL

Although the dividend discount model is not practical to use properly, we need to understand this model because it is the basis for all of the cash flow models. Also, it is important to understand the limitations of the model. To better understand these limitations, we will look at some practical issues—how to use the model on a real company and how the model could be used on a company that does not pay dividends.

Applying the Dividend Discount Model to Unitil Corporation

Unitil Corporation is a public utility holding company with subsidiaries providing electric and gas service in the northeastern United States. Exhibit 8.6 shows financial information for Unitil. Using

EXHIBIT 8.6   Unitil Corporation

Share price (December 29, 2000)	$26.50
Current annual dividend rate	$1.38
Average annual historical dividend growth (5 years)	1.5%

the Gordon Growth Model, we can determine the dividend growth rate implied by Unitil's current dividend and stock price. We assume a 12% cost of equity, k_e.

First, we calculate the dividend growth rate implied by Unitil's stock price. We use the formula for the Gordon Growth Model, (8.3), and substitute the $26.50 share price for $COMEQUITY$ and the 12% cost of equity for k_e. The current dividend is $1.38, so DIV_1 is $1.38 times $(1 + g^*)$.

$$COMEQUITY = \frac{DIV_1}{k_e - g^*} = \frac{\$1.38 \cdot (1 + g^*)}{0.12 - g^*} = \$26.50 \Rightarrow g^* = 0.0646$$

Assuming a 12% cost of equity, the current stock price and dividend imply a just barely sustainable dividend growth rate of 6.46%.

We now look at what happens if we value Unitil based on various reasonable estimates of the dividend growth rate. Likely choices for the growth rate would be the historical dividend growth rate, the expected inflation rate, and the expected growth rate in Unitil's earnings. We have already seen that the historical growth rate in Unitil's dividends has been 1.5%. We assume long-term inflation expectations are about 3.5%. Finally, suppose you have reviewed analysts' earnings forecasts for Unitil's earnings and found they are estimated to increase at about 8.0% per year. Exhibit 8.7 shows the valuation results assuming these growth rates.[4]

Although each of these assumptions for dividend growth appears to be reasonable and logical, there is no way of knowing whether any of these growth rates are just barely sustainable. Without that information, we cannot determine whether the appropriate price for Unitil should be around $13 or $37.

Using the same example, we can also use the two-stage growth model to value Unitil. Exhibit 8.8 shows some logical assumptions for the supernormal growth rate, the number of years at the supernormal rate, the long-term normal growth rate, and the resulting share values.

Cases 1 and 2 both illustrate just barely sustainable dividend streams, assuming the market value of $26.50 is a fair price. There are infinitely many just barely sustainable streams. Note the trade-off

EXHIBIT 8.7   Unitil Values Based on Various Dividend Growth Rates Using the Gordon Growth Model

Assumption for g	Dividend Growth Rate g	Per Share Value of Unitil
Historical dividend growth	1.5%	$ 13.34
Expected inflation rate	3.5%	$ 16.80
Analyst earnings growth estimates	8.0%	$ 37.26

EXHIBIT 8.8   Value of Unitil Based on Various Dividend Growth Rates Using the Two-Stage Model

CASE	Supernormal Dividend Growth Rate	Supernormal Growth Through Year	Normal Dividend Growth Rate	Per Share Value of Unitil
1	4%	5	7.13%	$ 26.50
2	20%	5	1.05%	$ 26.50
3	4%	5	2.00%	$ 15.27
4	6%	5	7.13%	$ 28.92

---

[4]DIV_1 is the dividend to be received one period from now, so in each case it is $1.38 \cdot (1 + g)$.

between growth in the supernormal period and in the subsequent years in cases 1 and 2. The higher the supernormal growth rate, the lower the normal growth rate. Compared to case 1, case 3 uses the same supernormal growth rate, the same number of years of supernormal growth, and a lower normal growth rate, 2% instead of 7.13%. The one change in assumptions creates a difference in value of $26.50 − $15.27 = $11.23, or 42.4%. Case 4 has the same normal growth rate as case 1, but a slightly higher supernormal growth, which increases the value by $28.92 − $26.50 = $2.42, or 9.1%.

How Do We Value Firms with No Dividends?

Many firms do not pay dividends, although not all for the same reasons. High-growth companies such as Amazon.com need to retain cash to fund expansion. Other companies, such as Berkshire Hathaway, do not believe that paying dividends is in the shareholders' best interests.

Does the dividend discount model apply to these firms? In theory, yes. Under the dividend discount model, the value of equity is the present value of future dividends forever. Just because a firm is not paying dividends now does not mean it never will. These dividends may come very far in the future and may be the result of the firm being acquired or liquidated. In any event, investors do expect some payout from the firm eventually. But, how could we ever accurately estimate the present value of a very distant dividend? Realistically, we would not use the dividend discount model. As we will see when we move on to the other valuation models, we value the dividend stream indirectly by valuing the cash flows coming into the firm rather than by valuing the dividends directly.

8.5 FLOWS TO EQUITY MODEL

The intuition of the flows to equity model is that the present value of the dividend stream must be equal to the present value of the net cash flows coming into the firm. Mathematically,

$$COMEQUITY = \sum_{t=1}^{\infty} \frac{FTE_t}{(1 + k_e)^t} \tag{8.6}$$

where FTE_t flows to equity in period t and k_e is the cost of equity. Cash flow to equity is equal to free cash flow plus nonoperating cash flow minus debt service and flows to other capital providers. The flows to equity model is simply all cash flow except dividends.

Exhibit 8.9 illustrates the flows to equity model. It shows that the value of the dividend stream, which is equal to the value of the common equity, is also equal to the present value of all the cash flows other than the dividend stream.

The following example also illustrates why the present value of the cash flows to equity must equal the present value of the dividend stream. Suppose a company has expected flows to equity of $100 per year over the next two years, its entire life. The cost of equity is 10%, and the firm pays the entire $100 of cash inflow out as a dividend each year. Obviously, this dividend policy is just barely sustainable. The dividend stream is identical to the flows to equity, so the present values must be the same as well. Both are $173.55 ($100/1.10 + $100/1.10² = $173.55).

But what would happen if the dividend stream did not match the flows to equity in each year? Suppose, for example, the period 1 dividend were delayed? If the firm has cash flow that it does not pay out as dividends, we assume this cash is invested in projects with zero net present value. The $100 of period 1 cash flow will grow to $110 in period 2. In period 2 the firm will have $210 ($110 + $100) available to pay as a dividend. The present value of this new dividend stream is $210/1.10² = $173.55, exactly equal to the value of the flows to equity and the original dividend stream.

A CLOSER LOOK

A Tale of Two Zero-Dividend Companies

Berkshire Hathaway Inc. is a holding company owning subsidiaries engaged in a number of diverse business activities, including property and casualty insurance, conducted on both a direct and reinsurance basis. Berkshire Hathaway has not paid a cash dividend since 1967 and has made it clear that it does not intend to pay dividends in the future. The Green Bay Packers, Inc. is a professional football team located in the smallest market in the National Football League. It also pays no dividends and is forbidden by its charter from doing so. What are the market values of shares of stock in each of these companies, and how do we reconcile these values with the dividend discount model?

Berkshire Hathaway closed trading on November 16, 2001 at $67,000 per share. Shares of the Packers have no market value, except as souvenirs, despite an estimate by *Worth* magazine in 1996 that the team was worth almost $36,000 per share.

How can Berkshire Hathaway, which pays no dividends and does not intend to start, be worth nearly $70,000 per share? Is not the present value of the expected dividend stream zero? The dividend discount model requires that a "just barely sustainable" dividend stream be used. Is Berkshire's current policy of paying no dividend just barely sustainable? No. That is why the market prices the stock as if eventually there will be some sort of payout to investors. It may not be in a regular cash dividend. It may come through a sale of the company or a liquidation. It may not come for many years, but eventually there will be a payout. Investors currently estimate the present value of that payout to be $67,000 per share.

Why does not the same hold true for the Packers? When this not-for-profit company needs capital, it sells shares, mostly to local fans. The shareholders receive no dividends or other tangible benefits, not even a ticket to a game. They also have no rights in a liquidation of the team. According to the Packers' corporate charter, if the team is sold, the proceeds must be used to build a new American Legion Hall. All these investors get is a stock certificate to hang on the wall and the satisfaction of helping keep the team in Green Bay.

Unlike the case for Berkshire Hathaway, the far-in-the-distance payoff if and when the Packers are sold will not accrue to the shareholders. So the shares have no value today. In the case of a share of the Packers, a dividend stream of zero every year forever, really is just barely sustainable.

In fact, for any one company *all* just barely sustainable dividend streams have the same value. No matter how management alters the dividend stream, as long as it is just barely sustainable, its value will still be $173.55. So, we could pick any just barely sustainable dividend stream to value the firm's equity. As we have seen, one possible just barely sustainable dividend stream is a payout exactly equal to the flows to equity each year. Therefore, the present value of the flows to equity must be the same as the value from the dividend discount model using any just barely sustainable dividend

EXHIBIT 8.9   Cash Flows and the Firm—Flows to Equity Model

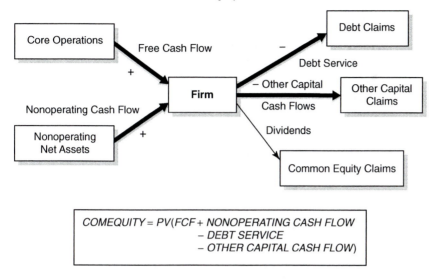

$$COMEQUITY = PV(FCF + NONOPERATING\ CASH\ FLOW \\ - DEBT\ SERVICE \\ - OTHER\ CAPITAL\ CASH\ FLOW)$$

stream. This means we can value the dividend stream and hence the equity by valuing the flows to equity. The intuition is that dividends are distributions of value. We can measure the value that can be distributed by measuring how much has been created.

Flows to Equity Valuation of Unitil

We now examine a valuation of Unitil using the flows to equity model. We have not yet studied forecasting, so we simply select a growth rate in flows to equity to illustrate the method. Unitil's 1999 flows to equity was $3,541,000. Assuming it grows at 5% per year indefinitely, and Unitil's cost of equity is 12%, its value is $\dfrac{\$3,541,000 \cdot 1.05}{0.12 - 0.05} = \$53,115,000$. With 4,712,001 common shares outstanding at December 31, 1999, this is a value of $11.27 per share.

SUMMARY

The dividend discount model is the most basic of the discounted cash flow models. Why? It is the only one that makes a direct link between the value of the firm's equity and the payoff to investors in that equity. The value produced by the dividend discount model depends on the dividend stream assumed. We showed that the appropriate dividend stream to use in a dividend discount valuation is one that is just barely sustainable. The need for a just barely sustainable dividend stream is a serious practical shortcoming in that it means it is not possible to forecast an appropriate dividend stream without a detailed analysis of the cash flows *into* the firm. However, once the analyst completes such an analysis, he or she effectively has the value of the firm and no longer needs to forecast the dividend stream.

Other valuation models are acceptable because they provide equivalent results to the dividend discount model. The flows to equity model discounts the cash flows available to equityholders. This model is equivalent to the dividend discount model because the present value of the net cash flows into the firm must equal the present value of the dividend stream.

SUGGESTED READING

Gordon, M. *The Investment, Financing and Valuation of the Corporation*. Homewood, IL: Irwin, 1982.

REVIEW QUESTIONS

1. What is the Gordon Growth Model?
2. What are the three key assumptions in the Gordon Growth Model?
3. What do we mean by a just barely sustainable dividend stream?
4. What happens if a firm increases dividends at a rate higher than its just barely sustainable growth rate?
5. What happens if a firm increases dividends at a rate lower than its just barely sustainable growth rate?

6. A consultant has proposed that you acquire another firm. He shows you a valuation he has done for this firm using the dividend discount model. He assumed a 3% growth rate in the dividend in perpetuity, contending the dividend would certainly keep pace with inflation. How do you respond?

7. Why is the flows to equity model equivalent to the dividend discount model?
8. Why do both the dividend discount model and the flows to equity model use the cost of equity for the discount rate?

PROBLEMS

Problems 1 through 4 pertain to the following information:

Figa Corporation expects to pay dividends of $2 per share in 2001, and it has a 12% cost of equity. Assume Figa pays all dividends on the last day of the year.

1. If Figa expects that it can sustain a dividend growth rate of 4% indefinitely, what is Figa's value per share at December 31, 2000?

2. Assume Figa's stock is trading for $40 per share on December 31, 2000. If the market agrees that Figa's cost of equity is 12%, what dividend growth rate does the market believe Figa can sustain?

3. How sensitive is Figa's equity value to the assumed dividend growth rate? That is, at what rate does the computed value change given a change in the assumed dividend growth rate?

4. Figa is generating cash of $5 per share and pays out dividends of $2 per share, so it has a dividend payout of 40%. Assuming its cash flow (before considering dividend payments or income on excess cash investments) is expected to grow at 4% indefinitely, what would the company's balance sheet look like in many years if its dividend grows at 4%?

5. What happens to the dividend growth rate implied by a firm's market price if the firm raises its dividend substantially? Assume this has no effect on expected future cash flows into the firm.

6. You start a new job as an analyst. Your supervisor asks you to value a firm using the Gordon Growth Model. The firm has a cost of equity of 15% and a current dividend of $2.50. Other analysts suggest growth rates for the firm of 5% to 10%. Prepare a memo to respond to your supervisor's request.

7. Wendy's International, Inc. is a large restaurant and franchise company that owns Wendy's Old Fashioned Hamburgers and Tim Hortons. Here is some information from the company's 2000 annual report:

	2000	1999	1998
Per Share Data			
Net income	$ 1.44	$ 1.32	$ 0.95
Dividends	$ 0.24	$ 0.24	$ 0.24
Market price at year end	$ 26.25	$ 20.81	$ 21.81

If Wendy's cost of equity is 11%, what dividend growth rate is implied by its 2000 market price? (Note: The 2001 dividend will be higher than $0.24 by the growth rate.)

8. Bob's Golf Carts, Inc. has forecasted flows to equity in 2002 of $10 million, which is expected to grow at 3% per year forever. Assuming Bob's has a cost of equity of 12%, what is the company's value?

9. Mirelman Company announced that it plans to increase its dividend. Assume that this announcement had no impact on investors' expectations of the company's future profitability or its operating cash flows, and that markets are efficient.

   a. What effect (increase, decrease, no effect) would the dividend increase have on the market price of Mirelman Company's stock immediately after the announcement?

   b. Consider the dividend growth rate that Mirelman Company could just barely sustain in perpetuity. Would this rate be higher, lower, or the same relative to the newly announced dividend rate than it was relative to the previous dividend rate? Explain your answer.

 ## My Case

What dividend growth rate does the market believe is sustainable for your company? (Note: If your company does not pay a dividend, how is the current market price still consistent with the dividend discount model?)

APPENDIX 8.1 CIRCULARITY OF THE DIVIDEND DISCOUNT MODEL

In this appendix, we show that to apply the dividend discount model correctly, we must first estimate the value of the firm's equity. However, once we have this value, we do not need to use the dividend discount model.

Recall that g^* is the just barely sustainable dividend growth rate, the growth rate that makes excess cash tend toward zero over the long run. We can forecast the firm's future cash flows, after dividend payments, for a very large number of periods and then find g, the value of the growth rate, such that the firm's cash in the last period is zero. We model this process with a "cash equation" (8.7), describing how the cash balance in each period is determined.

$$C_T = C_{T-1} \cdot (1 + k_e) + FCF_T - DS_T - DIV_T \tag{8.7}$$

where C_T is the firm's cash on hand at time T. We assume the firm can always find investments for its cash that return exactly the cost of equity. We call these "zero-NPV" investments because their net present value (NPV) is zero, meaning they have no effect on firm value. As a result of these zero-NPV investments during period T, cash at the end of the previous period, C_{T-1}, grows to $C_{T-1} \cdot (1 + k_e)$, where k_e is the cost of equity. In addition, cash increases by FCF_T, period T free cash flow, and decreases by DS_T, period T debt service flows, and by DIV_T, period T dividends.

Equation (8.7) is true in any period, so

$$C_{T-1} = C_{T-2} \cdot (1 + k_e) + FCF_{T-1} - DS_{T-1} - DIV_{T-1} \tag{8.8}$$

Substituting (8.8) into (8.7) and simplifying gives

$$\begin{aligned} C_T = {} & C_{T-2} \cdot (1 + k_e)^2 + \\ & \left[(FCF_T - DS_T) + (FCF_{T-1} - DS_{T-1}) \cdot (1 + k_e) \right] \\ & - \left[DIV_T + DIV_{T-1} \cdot (1 + k_e) \right] \end{aligned} \tag{8.9}$$

We can write C_{T-2} as a function of C_{T-3} and period $T-2$ free cash flow, debt service, and dividends. We can then substitute this into (8.9) to obtain an expression for C_T as a function of C_{T-3} and free cash flows, debt service, and dividends for periods $T-2$ through T. Then we can substitute in an expression for C_{T-3}, and so on. After making a total of $T-1$ such substitutions, the following results:

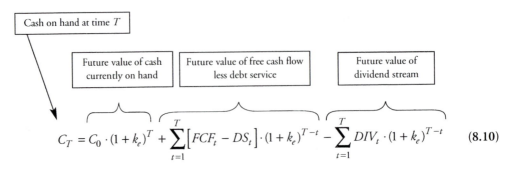

$$C_T = C_0 \cdot (1 + k_e)^T + \sum_{t=1}^{T} \left[FCF_t - DS_t \right] \cdot (1 + k_e)^{T-t} - \sum_{t=1}^{T} DIV_t \cdot (1 + k_e)^{T-t} \tag{8.10}$$

This equation illustrates that cash on hand at some future date T has three components. The first component is the future value of cash currently on hand, the amount to which this cash will accumulate after being invested in zero-NPV projects. The second component of period T cash is the future value of the free cash flow the business operations are expected to generate in excess of the debt service required. The third component is (the negative of) the future value of the dividend stream.

Under the Gordon Growth Model, $DIV_t = DIV_1 \cdot (1 + g)^{t - 1}$, so we can substitute this expression into (8.10), resulting in

$$C_T = (1 + k_e)^T \cdot \left[C_0 + \sum_{t=1}^{T} \frac{FCF_t - DS_t}{(1 + k_e)^t} - \frac{DIV_1}{1 + g} \cdot \sum_{t=1}^{T} \left[\frac{1 + g}{1 + k_e} \right]^t \right] \qquad (8.11)$$

Recall that g^* is the value of g that satisfies the above equation when $C_T = 0$ and T is large. Therefore, we can replace g with g^* and set $C_T = 0$. We also divide both sides by $(1 + k_e)^T$, and let T approach infinity. Then,

$$0 = C_0 + \sum_{t=1}^{\infty} \frac{FCF_t - DS_t}{(1 + k_e)^t} - \frac{DIV_1}{1 + g^*} \cdot \sum_{t=1}^{\infty} \left[\frac{1 + g^*}{1 + k_e} \right]^t \qquad (8.12)$$

Rearranging terms, we obtain

$$\frac{DIV_1}{1 + g^*} \cdot \sum_{t=1}^{\infty} \left[\frac{1 + g^*}{1 + k_e} \right]^t = C_0 + \sum_{t=1}^{\infty} \frac{FCF_t - DS_t}{(1 + k_e)^t} \qquad (8.13)$$

The summation term on the left-hand side of (8.13) is equivalent to $\dfrac{1 + g^*}{k_e - g^*}$. Substituting this expression into (8.13) gives

$$\frac{DIV_1}{k_e - g^*} = C_0 + \sum_{t=1}^{\infty} \frac{FCF_t - DS_t}{(1 + k_e)^t} \qquad (8.14)$$

The appropriate value of the dividend growth rate is the value of g^* that makes (8.14) true. Yet because the left side of the equation is the value of the firm's equity using the just barely sustainable growth rate, the right side of the equation also must equal the value of the firm's equity. So, once we evaluate the right-hand side of the equation, we know the value of the equity and no longer need to find g^*.

9

 Where We Have Been:

In Chapter 8 we discussed the dividend discount model, which values equity directly by discounting the expected dividend stream to be paid to shareholders, and the flows to equity model, which discounts net inflows available to equity-holders.

 Where We Are:

We now consider the most widely used valuation model — the free cash flow model. In addition to discussing the model itself, we show how to analyze a firm's free cash flow, the key input to this model.

 Where We Are Going:

In Chapter 10 we discuss free cash flow forecasting. We will use the free cash flow analysis from this chapter as a basis for our forecasting.

Free Cash Flow Model and Analysis

LEARNING OBJECTIVES:

After studying this chapter, you will understand:

- The free cash flow valuation model.

- The difference between free cash flow and GAAP definitions of cash flow.

- The definition of free cash flow equivalents and why they are included in the free cash flow model.

- How to derive a free cash flow statement from a historical combined GAAP income statement and cash flow statement.

The free cash flow model is the most commonly used valuation model in practice. Investment bankers and corporate finance and other financial professionals all use free cash flow models to value businesses. These people may be interested in value for a variety of reasons, including to take an equity position, to evaluate an acquisition proposal, or to consider a stock repurchase.

In the free cash flow model, we must forecast the free cash flow stream. We usually start the forecasting process by studying the firm's historical results. In this way, we can understand the relationships among the components of free cash flow. To do this, we must convert the combined GAAP income statement and cash flow statement to a free cash flow format.

In Section 9.1 we present the free cash flow model. Section 9.2 reviews GAAP cash flow definitions and discusses how these differ from free cash flow. Section 9.3 provides a spreadsheet approach to converting the combined GAAP income statement and cash flow statement to a free cash flow statement. In it, we develop a free cash flow statement for Starbucks for fiscal 2000. Our analysis shows how we obtain much of the information needed from the financial statement footnotes.

9.1 THE FREE CASH FLOW MODEL

As Exhibit 9.1 illustrates, the free cash flow model values core operations by discounting a forecast of the firm's expected free cash flow. We estimate the value of other nonequity components of the economic balance sheet directly, by observing market values or estimating fair values in other ways. To determine the value of the common equity, we add the value of core operations (the present value of the free cash flow) and the value of nonoperating net assets and subtract the value of debt and other capital claims. As the exhibit illustrates, the free cash flow forecast is a key input to the model. But how do we develop this very important component of a valuation? We will address this question in Chapter 10, when we will build a free cash flow forecast model, which is a set of equations that specifies how the components of free cash flow are related to each other and to the firm's environment.

Before actually preparing the forecast, we want to understand each of the components of historical free cash flow and the relationships among them. Because a forecast is forward looking, we are

EXHIBIT 9.1   Free Cash Flow Model

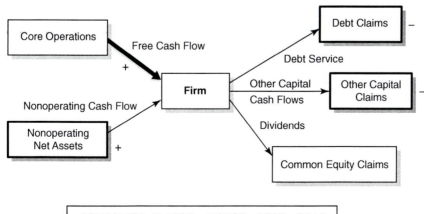

$$COMEQUITY = PV(FCF) + NONOP - DEBT - OCAP$$

interested in historical results not for their own sake, but because they are often good predictors of the future. For example, past sales growth rates and operating margins may be a guide to expected growth rates and margins. We also must understand how the business environment affects the components of free cash flow, in order to know how future relationships among the free cash flow components might differ from past relationships. Then we can consider which historical trends are likely to continue in the future and which will change due to changes in the business environment and in the firm.

In Exhibit 1.2 from Chapter 1 we provided a framework for security analysis. In Exhibit 9.2 we add additional detail to the process and tailor it to valuations using the free cash flow model. Exhibit 9.2 suggests how we might lay out a valuation on a spreadsheet. The area to the left of the valuation date illustrates the process of financial statement analysis. As we saw in Chapter 5, a central part of financial statement analysis is the computation of ratios. We want these ratios to quantify the relationships among the components of the historical free cash flow statements. For example, gross margin percentage is a ratio that quantifies how gross profit varies with sales.

The area to the right of the valuation date represents the forecast periods. Here we will create our free cash flow model and quantify our forecast assumptions with a set of ratios. These ratios, together with our free cash flow forecast model, lead to forecasted free cash flow statements, which we use to compute the value of the firm's core operations.

For the historical ratios we study to be useful for forecasting, we must calculate them in exactly the same way as the ratios we use to forecast free cash flow. However, GAAP financial statements mix transactions relating to core operations with transactions involving other elements of the economic balance sheet. As a result, we cannot calculate appropriate historical ratios directly from GAAP financial statements because these ratios would include the effects of transactions that are not related to core operations. So, the first step in financial statement analysis is to develop historical **free cash flow statements**. These statements separate free cash flows from all other cash flows. We use the components of free cash flow to calculate historical ratios that are defined in exactly the same way they will be used in the free cash flow forecast.

EXHIBIT 9.2   A Picture of the Security Analysis Process

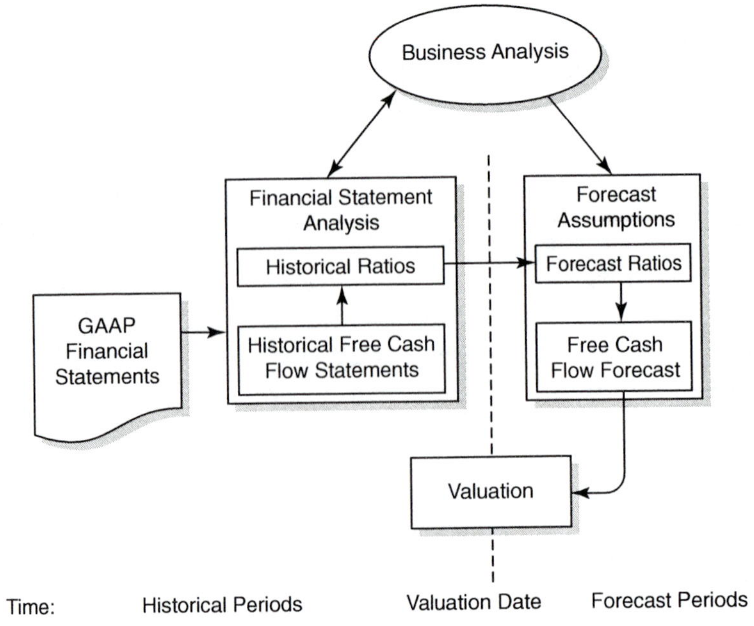

The ratios we use to quantify our assumptions are the link between the historical free cash flow analysis and the free cash flow forecast. Their historical values provide one input for forecasting future ratio assumptions. We combine these historical ratios with our knowledge of the business and environment, gained in the business analysis, to determine the forecast assumptions to use.

9.2 Differences Between GAAP Cash Flow and Free Cash Flow

In Chapter 6 we converted a GAAP balance sheet to an economic balance sheet format by reorganizing the line items to conform to the economic balance sheet classifications. The same reorganizing technique can be used to convert GAAP financial statements to free cash flow statements. We start with the combined GAAP income statement and cash flow statement covered in Chapter 4. We reorganize it to categorize the components in the same way that we think about them in a free cash flow valuation. This means that we must classify cash flows as free cash flow, nonoperating cash flow, and capital cash flow, where capital cash flow consists of flows between the firm and debtholders, other capital claimants, and equityholders.

The combined GAAP income statement and cash flow statement differs from the free cash flow statement in two ways, and these differences drive the way we do the analysis. First, GAAP categorizes cash flows in a different way than does the free cash flow statement. Second, GAAP does not report in the income statement or the cash flow statement certain noncash transactions that are included in the free cash flow statement. These transactions are called free cash flow equivalents.

GAAP Categories versus Free Cash Flow Categories

As discussed in Chapter 4, the GAAP cash flow statement is divided into three sections: cash flow from operations, cash flow from investing, and cash flow from financing. For valuation purposes, however, we need the cash flow categories to mirror the economic balance sheet. Thus we divide cash flows into free cash flow, nonoperating cash flow, and capital cash flow. Exhibit 9.3 illustrates that although the free cash flow breakdown differs from the GAAP cash flow categories, the net cash flow is exactly the same. It is simply the change that occurs in cash over the period. So, to derive a free cash flow statement from GAAP information, we must reorganize the line items in the combined GAAP income statement and cash flow statement into free cash flow, nonoperating cash flow, and capital cash flow.

EXHIBIT 9.3   Total Cash Flows Presented in GAAP and Free Cash Flow Statements

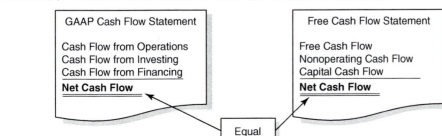

Free Cash Flow Equivalents

The second difference between GAAP financial statements and the free cash flow statement is that the free cash flow statement includes free cash flow equivalents. **Free cash flow equivalents** are transactions that have two components, one pertaining to core operations and the other pertaining to another element of the economic balance sheet, usually a component of capital. For example, if a company acquires a machine for debt rather than cash, the transaction has a component that affects core operations—the acquisition of new machinery—and another that relates to the firm's capital—the issuance of debt. Under GAAP, such transactions are not reported in the cash flow statement at all because they have no effect on cash.[1]

Transactions involving free cash flow equivalents are essentially two transactions, and the free cash flow statement reports the two transactions separately. Acquiring machinery in exchange for debt is equivalent to borrowing cash and immediately using the cash to acquire the machine. The free cash flow statement reflects these two transactions. The amounts of the two transactions perfectly offset, so there is no effect on cash. However, including the transaction does affect free cash flow.

In this example, if we do not include free cash flow equivalents in the free cash flow statement, we understate capital expenditures by the amount that was paid for with debt. If we used historical free cash flow statements that excluded these transactions as a basis for forecasting free cash flows, we would have an erroneous forecast.

Creating the Free Cash Flow Statement

Exhibit 9.4 presents the combined GAAP income statement and cash flow statement for Elementary Company for the year 2001. We will reorganize it into a free cash flow statement. We have indicated next to each item in the combined GAAP income statement and cash flow statement whether the item is part of free cash flow (FCF), nonoperating cash flow (NOPCF), or capital cash flow (CAPCF).

In addition to the cash flows described in the combined income statement and cash flow statement, Elementary Company acquired a building during 2001. There was no cash flow associated with the transaction. Elementary paid for the building by issuing $50 million of debt to the seller.

Sales; cost of sales; and selling, general, and administrative expenses all relate to the firm's core operations, so we classify them as part of free cash flow. Interest expense is a capital cash flow because it relates to the firm's debt. Marketable securities are nonoperating assets, so the interest income they generate is a nonoperating cash flow. The income tax expense pertains to all three components of the free cash flow statement. Assuming a 40% tax rate on all pretax income, the $128 million income tax expense consists of $140 million ($350 million times 40%) of tax on the operating earnings, a $40 million ($100 million times 40%) tax savings from the interest expense, and $28 million ($70 million times 40%) of tax on the interest income. The $140 million of tax on operating earnings is part of free cash flow. The $40 million tax savings from interest expense is part of capital cash flow. The $28 million of tax on interest income is part of nonoperating cash flow. We classify the $50 million addback for depreciation expense and the capital expenditures as free cash flow because they relate to the core operations. The debt issuances and dividend payments are both transactions with suppliers of capital, so we classify them as capital cash flows.

The purchase of the building in exchange for $50 million in debt is a free cash flow equivalent. Elementary has $50 million in capital expenditures in addition to the amount shown in its GAAP cash flow statement. It also has $50 million in additional cash inflow from the issuance of debt.

---

[1] If these transactions are material, they must be disclosed.

EXHIBIT 9.4 Elementary Company Income and Cash Flow Statements

		Elementary Company					
		Combined GAAP Income Statement and Cash Flow Statement					
		($ millions)					
		2001					
Sales	$	1,000	FCF				
Cost of sales		(400)	FCF				
Selling, general, and administrative expenses		(250)	FCF				
Operating earnings		350					
Interest expense		(100)	CAPCF				
Interest income		70	NOPCF				
Earnings before taxes		320		Tax provision on operating earnings	$	(140)	FCF
Income tax expense		(128)		Tax savings on interest expense		40	CAPCF
Net income		192		Tax provision on interest income		(28)	NOPCF
Depreciation		50	FCF		$	(128)	
Cash flow from operations		242					
Capital expenditures		(75)	FCF				
Cash flow from investing		(75)					
Issuance of debt		100	CAPCF				
Dividends paid		(200)	CAPCF				
Cash flow from financing		(100)					
Net change in cash	$	67					

When we reorganize the statement using the free cash flow statement classifications and include the free cash flow equivalent, we have the free cash flow statement shown in Exhibit 9.5. We now have **net operating profit after tax (NOPAT)** of $210 million rather than net income of $192 million. NOPAT represents what net income would be if the firm consisted of only core operations, and NOPAT excluded interest expense, nonoperating income, and the tax effects of both. The subtotals of cash flow are now free cash flow ($135 million), nonoperating cash flow ($42 million), and capital cash flow (−$110 million).

Based simply on their titles, the sum of GAAP cash flow from operations and GAAP cash flow from investing might seem to be the same as free cash flow. If that were true, the "adjustment" process to obtain free cash flow would be simply to add these two categories together. The Elementary Company example shows this is not the case, however ($242 − $75 = $167 ≠ $135). GAAP cash flow from operations includes interest expense and interest income (and their respective income tax effects), but free cash flow does not.

Still, summing GAAP cash flow from operations and GAAP cash flow from investing is a good starting point to derive free cash flow. Yet, because GAAP includes some nonoperating and capital cash flow items in cash flow from operations, we must remove those elements to arrive at free cash flow. As we work with more complicated examples, we will see that GAAP cash flow from investing

EXHIBIT 9.5   Elementary Company Free Cash Flow Statement

Elementary Company
Free Cash Flow Statement
($ millions)
2001

Sales	$ 1,000
Cost of sales	(400)
Selling, general, and administrative expenses	(250)
Operating earnings	350
Tax provision on operating earnings	(140)
Net operating profit after tax (NOPAT)	210
Depreciation	50
Capital expenditures	(125)
Free cash flow	135
Interest income	70
Tax provision on interest income	(28)
Nonoperating cash flow	42
Interest expense	(100)
Tax savings on interest expense	40
Issuance of debt	150
Dividends paid	(200)
Capital cash flow	(110)
Net change in cash	$ 67

← Same cash flow as on GAAP cash flow statement

also includes items that belong in nonoperating cash flow and capital cash flow, and we must remove those as well. In addition, free cash flow includes free cash flow equivalents, which are not reported under GAAP. We must add these transactions in order to arrive at free cash flow.

9.3 AN ORGANIZED METHOD FOR MAKING THE ADJUSTMENTS

When we convert the combined GAAP income statement and cash flow statement to a free cash flow statement, we move any cash flows related to nonoperating net assets, debt, common equity, or other capital out of free cash flow and into another section of the free cash flow statement. We also add in free cash flow equivalents. *Our goal is to derive a free cash flow statement that includes in free cash flow all the cash flows (and equivalents) related to the core operations and only these cash flows.* Using an organized worksheet simplifies the construction of a free cash flow statement. This approach lends itself nicely to a computerized spreadsheet, which can eliminate both tedium and mechanical errors.

A CLOSER LOOK

Why Not Construct the Free Cash Flow Statement from Balance Sheets?

In introductory accounting, you undoubtedly learned how to construct a GAAP cash flow statement from the balance sheets at the beginning and end of the year. By reconciling the change in each balance sheet account other than cash, you produced a cash flow statement. Why not use this approach to create the free cash flow statement instead of reorganizing the GAAP cash flow statement?

There are two reasons. First, the accountants have already done the hard work for you by analyzing the change in every balance sheet account to determine what the cash flow items are. These are the same cash flow items that you will use in the free cash flow statement, except that they are grouped differently. It is much simpler to rearrange the items from the GAAP cash flow statement than to re-create a cash flow statement from scratch.

Second, published balance sheets generally do not provide sufficient detail to create an accurate cash flow statement. The accountants who created the cash flow statement had access to much more detailed balance sheet information than you will. In fact, it is impossible to reproduce the cash flow statements in most annual reports exactly from the accompanying balance sheets. If you were to start with GAAP balance sheets and create the cash flow statement from scratch, you would essentially throw away useful information contained in the published cash flow statement.

The Free Cash Flow Worksheet

To construct a free cash flow worksheet:

- Lay out the combined GAAP income statement and cash flow statement, grouping cash flow from operations and investing as your first approximation to free cash flow.

- In the first column to the right of the GAAP numbers, place the adjustments to these numbers to get from your first approximation to the actual free cash flow amount. For each adjustment, determine how the item is treated under GAAP and how you want to treat it in the free cash flow statement. If those treatments differ, make an adjustment to convert the item from the GAAP basis to the free cash flow basis. Because we are not changing the total cash flow, only reorganizing it, every adjustment must sum to zero.

- The rightmost column sums the prior two columns and contains the free cash flow statement.

Exhibit 9.6 is a worksheet to derive Elementary Company's 2001 free cash flow from its combined GAAP income statement and cash flow statement. The first column is the combined GAAP income statement and cash flow statement from Exhibit 9.4. The second column contains the adjustments to get from the GAAP statements to the free cash flow statement. The third column is the free cash flow statement. Adjustments (1) and (2) move interest expense and interest income to capital cash flow and nonoperating cash flow. Adjustments (3) and (4) remove the portion of income tax expense pertaining to interest expense and interest income. We classify these amounts in the same place as the pretax amounts to which they relate. After adjustments (3) and (4), only the $140 mil-

EXHIBIT 9.6   Elementary Company Cash Flow Worksheet

Elementary Company
Cash Flow Worksheet
($ millions)
2001

GAAP Income and Cash Flow Statements		Adjustments		Free Cash Flow Statement		
Sales	$ 1,000			$ 1,000	Sales	
Cost of sales	(400)			(400)	Cost of sales	
Selling, general, and administrative expenses	(250)			(250)	Selling, general, and administrative expenses	
Operating earnings	350					
Interest expense	(100)	100	(1)	0		
Interest income	70	(70)	(2)	0		
Earnings before taxes	320			350	Operating earnings	
Income tax expense	(128)	(40)	(3)	(140)	Tax provision on operating earnings	
		28	(4)			
Net income	192			210	Net operating profit after tax (NOPAT)	
Depreciation	50			50	Depreciation	
Cash flow from operations	242					
Capital expenditures	(75)	(50)	(5)	(125)	Capital expenditures	
Cash flow from investing	(75)					
				135	**Free cash flow**	
		70	(2)	42	After-tax interest income	
		(28)	(4)			
				42	**Nonoperating cash flow**	
		(100)	(1)	(60)	After-tax interest expense	
		40	(3)			
Issuance of debt	100	50	(5)	150	Issuance of debt	
Dividends paid	(200)			(200)	Dividends paid	
Cash flow from financing	(100)			(110)	**Capital cash flow**	
Net change in cash	$ 67	0		$ 67	Net change in cash	

lion of income tax expense related to core operations remains in the income tax provision. Adjustment (5) records the free cash flow equivalent and offsetting issuance of debt in the free cash flow statement.

This example illustrates that it is critical to understand how GAAP treats the firm's transactions. To make the required adjustments, we must move certain elements of the combined GAAP income statement and cash flow statement to nonoperating cash flow and capital cash flow. Without a thorough understanding of GAAP, we could not identify the needed adjustments.

A CLOSER LOOK

How Do We Know What Adjustments to Make?

In converting the GAAP cash flow statement to a free cash flow statement, we remove from free cash flow any cash flows related to nonoperating net assets or cash flow between the firm and any capital claimants. We also record free cash flow equivalents. Each analysis will require different adjustments, depending on the kinds of transactions the firm has. However, there are common categories of adjustments. Although the following list will not include every situation, it is helpful as a checklist for your work. Remember that this list is not a substitute for understanding the business transactions of each individual company under analysis. The adjustments we make to accomplish this are grouped into five categories:

- Interest expense and related amounts
- Nonoperating cash flows
- Free cash flow equivalents
- Employee stock options (examined in Chapter 14)
- Defined benefit pension plans and other postemployment benefit plans (examined in Chapter 15)

Though we will use only components of historical free cash flow to calculate historical ratios, we continue both the GAAP cash flow statement and the free cash flow statement all the way down to the change in cash. By confirming that the change in cash is the same in both columns, we can double-check there are no errors and every item is accounted for.

Starbucks' Free Cash Flow

Exhibit 9.7 shows a free cash flow worksheet for Starbucks for fiscal 2000. Following the exhibit are explanations of each adjustment. Where the amounts necessary to make the adjustments are not taken directly from the income statement or the cash flow statement, the explanation refers to the source of the information in the Starbucks annual report. You may wish to obtain the financial section of the Starbucks annual report from the SEC's EDGAR Web site (**www.sec.gov**) or from the Starbucks Web site (**www.starbucks.com**).

Estimating Income Tax Effects

A number of the adjustments we will make for Starbucks have income tax effects. To determine the amounts of these tax effects, we must know the appropriate tax rate to use. Starbucks' marginal tax rate, the tax rate on an additional dollar of income or deduction, on income other than dividends is 38.7%. To determine the marginal tax rate, we referred to footnote 13 in the annual report. We used the federal income tax rate of 35% and the 3.7% state tax burden. Calculating marginal tax rates is discussed in more detail in Chapter 13.

EXHIBIT 9.7   Starbucks' Free Cash Flow Worksheet–Fiscal 2000

($ thousands)	GAAP	Adjustments		FCF
Net revenues	$ 2,169,218			$ 2,169,218
Cost of sales and related occupancy costs	(953,560)			(953,560)
Gross margin	1,215,658			1,215,658
Joint venture income	20,300	(15,139)	(2)	0
		(5,161)	(3)	
Store operating expenses	(704,898)			(704,898)
Other operating expenses	(78,374)			(78,374)
Depreciation and amortization	(130,232)			(130,232)
General and administrative expenses	(110,202)			(110,202)
Operating income	212,252			191,952
Interest and other income, net	7,110	(7,110)	(1)	0
Internet-related investment losses	(58,792)	58,792	(10)	0
Earnings before income taxes	160,570			191,952
Income taxes	(66,006)	2,752	(1)	(78,659)
		1,571	(5)	
		(16,976)	(11)	
Net earnings / NOPAT	94,564			113,293
Depreciation and amortization	142,171			142,171
Internet-related investment losses	58,792	(58,792)	(10)	0
Provision for losses on asset disposals	5,753			5,753
Deferred income taxes, net	(18,252)	(66)	(5)	(1,342)
		16,976	(11)	
Equity in (income) of investees	(15,139)	15,139	(2)	0
Tax benefit from exercise of nonqualified stock options	31,131	(31,131)	(12)	0
Net purchases of trading securities	(1,414)	1,414	(7)	0
Change in accounts receivable	(28,235)			(28,235)
Change in inventories	(19,495)			(19,495)
Change in prepaid expenses and other current assets	(700)			(700)
Change in accounts payable	15,561	(7,479)	(9)	8,082
Change in accrued compensation and related costs	30,962			30,962
Change in accrued occupancy costs	6,007			6,007
Change in accrued taxes	5,026			5,026
Change in minority interest	3,188	(3,188)	(13)	0
Change in deferred revenue	6,836			6,836
Change in other accrued expenses	1,818			1,818

FREE CASH FLOW

CASH FLOW FROM OPERATIONS

	CASH FLOW FROM INVESTING				FREE CASH FLOW	NONOPERATING CASH FLOW	CASH FLOW FROM FINANCING / CAPITAL CASH FLOW
Net cash provided by operating activities	318,574						
Purchase of available-for-sale investments	(118,501)	(7)	118,501	(7)	0		
Maturity of available-for-sale investments	58,750	(8)	(58,750)	(8)	0		
Sale of available-for-sale investments	49,238	(8)	(49,238)	(8)	0		
Purchase of businesses, net of cash acquired	(13,522)				(13,522)		
Investments in joint ventures	(8,473)	(6)	8,473	(6)	0		
Purchases of other investments	(35,457)	(7)	35,457	(7)	0		
Distributions from joint ventures	14,279	(4)	(14,279)	(4)	0		
Additions to property, plant, and equipment	(316,450)				(316,450)		
Additions to other assets	(3,096)				(3,096)		
Net cash used by investing activities	(373,232)				(62,892)		
Cash flow from operations and Cash Flow from Investing/Free Cash Flow	(54,658)						
Interest income, net of tax	4,358	(1)				4,358	
	5,161	(3)					
Distributions from joint ventures, net of tax	14,279	(4)				17,935	
	(1,505)	(5)					
Purchase of investments	(155,372)	(7)				(155,372)	
Sale and maturity of investments	107,988	(8)				107,988	
Investments in joint ventures	(8,473)	(6)				(8,473)	
Nonoperating Cash Flow						(33,564)	
Change in minority interest	3,188	(13)					3,188
Increase/(decrease) in cash provided by checks drawn in excess of bank balances	(7,479)	(9)					0
Proceeds from sale of common stock under employee stock purchase plan	10,258						10,258
Exercise of stock options	58,463		31,131	(12)			89,594
Payments on long-term debt	(1,889)						(1,889)
Net cash provided by financing activities /Capital Cash Flow	59,353						101,151
Effect of exchange rate changes on cash and cash equivalents	(297)						(297)
Increase in cash and cash equivalents	$ 4,398		0				$ 4,398
Marginal tax rate	0.387						

Adjustments

The adjustments to derive Starbucks' free cash flow are as follows:

1. Move interest and other income, net (which also includes interest expense) and its tax effect to the nonoperating section of the free cash flow statement. The tax effect is equal to the pretax amount multiplied by the marginal tax rate ($7,110,000 × 0.387 = $2,752,000).

2. The GAAP cash flow statement includes a line item that removes $15,139,000 of the $20,300,000 of joint venture income reported in the income statement. The $15,139,000 is the income Starbucks recognized from three of its joint ventures. This is a noncash component of income, so Starbucks reversed it in the cash flow statement. We offset the amount of this reversal against a similar amount in the income statement so that the free cash flow statement will not include this nonoperating item.[2]

3. Move the remaining $5,161,000 of joint venture income to nonoperating cash flow.

4. Move distributions from joint ventures to nonoperating cash flow.

5. Move the tax effects of the equity in income of investees and the related distributions from these joint ventures out of operating cash flow and into the nonoperating cash flow section of the free cash flow statement.

   - The income tax expense related to joint ventures included in the income statement is the tax on the $20,300,000 equity in income of investees. Because 80% of the income on this type of item is excluded from tax, the estimated tax effect is the 38.7% tax rate times 20% times $20,300,000, or $1,571,000. We removed $1,571,000 from income tax expense.

   - The $1,571,000 is the income tax expense on the investments, but not the actual tax paid, which is based on the distributions received. Again, 80% of the income is excluded from tax. The estimated tax actually paid is equal to the 38.7% tax rate times 20% times the $19,440,000 ($5,161,000 + $14,279,000) of distributions from joint ventures, or $1,505,000. This cash outflow is recorded in the nonoperating cash flow section of the free cash flow statement.

   - The difference between the tax expense and the tax paid is a deferred tax item. We removed this deferred tax item of $66,000 ($1,571,000 − $1,505,000) from operating cash flow.

6. Move additional investments in joint ventures to nonoperating cash flow.

7. Move purchases of trading securities and available-for-sale investments to nonoperating cash flow.

8. Move maturities and sales of available-for-sale investments to nonoperating cash flow.

9. Starbucks records its negative cash balance as a current liability called "checks drawn in excess of bank balances." The cash flow statement includes the change in this liability in the financing section. Because this is really an account payable, it is an operating item, and we reclassify the change in this account to be free cash flow. This is an example of an unusual situation in which an amount classified as a financing cash flow under GAAP is moved into free cash flow.

10. In adjustment (2), we removed both the noncash joint venture income and the reversal of it in the cash flow statement. Similarly, in this adjustment we remove the loss on Internet investments and the reversal of these losses. Starbucks took a write-down of investments for almost $59 million, but there was no cash outflow related to this write-down of nonoperating net assets. We do not want the free cash flow statement to reflect either the write-down or the reversal.

---

[2]Although there is no effect on free cash flow in total, it is still preferable to remove these two components so that we can completely ignore their effects when we forecast free cash flow.

11. Starbucks' income tax footnote indicates that it recorded a deferred tax asset of $22,635,000 related to the write-off of Internet investments. This was partially offset by a $5,659,000 contra-account, called a valuation allowance, for a net deferred tax asset of $16,976,000. This deferred tax asset arose because Starbucks did not receive a current tax deduction for the write-off—that will have to wait until Starbucks sells the investments. Still, it records the income tax benefit in the same period as the loss. As a result, Starbucks reduced its income tax provision by $16,976,000. This tax savings was reversed in the cash flow statement on the deferred income tax line. We remove both the reduction in the income tax provision and the reversal of it in the cash flow statement because both of these relate to nonoperating net assets.

12. Starbucks receives a tax deduction when its employees exercise stock options. As we will learn when we study employee stock options in detail, the tax savings from this deduction do not reduce income tax expense. Instead, the savings are credited directly to stockholders' equity. As a result, Starbucks reports the savings in the cash flow statement. We reclassify it to the capital cash flow section because it does not relate to core operations, but to how the firm is financed.

13. Finally, minority interest is the capital that Starbucks obtains from minority shareholders in consolidated subsidiaries. The change in minority interest, which appears in the cash flow statement, is reclassified to the capital cash flow section because it relates to how Starbucks is financed, not to core operations.

Analyzing Transactions to Derive Free Cash Flow

Although the Starbucks example illustrates many of the typical adjustments needed to derive free cash flow from a combined GAAP income statement and cash flow statement, it does not include every possible adjustment that could arise. The best way to know what to do when an unusual transaction is encountered is to (1) determine how the transaction is treated under GAAP, (2) determine how it should be treated in the free cash flow statement, and (3) adjust from GAAP to free cash flow. We illustrate this process with two additional types of transactions that did not appear in the Starbucks statements. These are amortization of bond discounts and premiums, and capitalization of interest. As you read these sections, focus not only on how we deal with these specific transactions but also the process by which we analyze the transactions and determine how to treat them.

Amortization of Bond Discount or Premium

As you will recall from intermediate accounting, when a bond is sold at a premium or discount to par value, the bond is initially recorded at the selling price. The difference between the selling price and par value is amortized over the life of the bond according to the effective interest rate method. For a bond sold at a discount, the liability increases each year due to the amortization, with a corresponding addition to interest expense. For a bond sold at a premium, the opposite occurs. The liability is reduced each year and there is a corresponding reduction in interest expense.

Like changes in interest payable, amortization of bond discount or premium is a difference between interest expense recognized and cash paid. So, it must also be moved to the capital cash flow section of the free cash flow statement. As an example, consider a firm that on December 31, 2001 issued $10 million face amount of 10-year bonds paying 6% interest annually each December 31. The bonds were priced to yield 7% to maturity, so they initially sold for $9,297,642, the present value of the interest payments ($600,000 per year) and the principal repayment ($1 million to be received in 10 years), discounted at 7%.

On December 31, 2002, the firm would pay $600,000 ($10 million × 6%) in interest, but it would recognize interest expense for the year 2002 of $650,835 ($9,297,642 × 7%). (It would claim

EXHIBIT 9.8   Analysis of Bond Discount Amortization

	GAAP	Adjustments	Free Cash Flow
Interest expense (included in income statement)	$ (650,835)	$ 650,835	$ —
Tax benefit (included in income tax expense in income statement)	260,334 *	(260,334)	—
Amount included in net income on cash flow statement	(390,501)		
Amortization of bond discount (reconciling item in cash flow statement)	50,835	**(50,835)**	—
Amount included in operating cash flow	(339,666)		
Free cash flow			—
Interest expense, net of tax		(650,835)	(390,501)
		260,334	
Amortization of bond discount		**50,835**	50,835
Capital cash flow			(339,666)
Net change in cash	$ (339,666)	$ 0	$ (339,666)

* Estimated by $650,835 × 40%.

an interest deduction on its tax return for the same amount.) The $50,835 difference between the expense and the payment is discount amortization. Exhibit 9.8 shows the amounts that would appear in the GAAP combined income statement and cash flow statement related to this debt instrument, the adjustments to a free cash flow basis, and the presentation in the free cash flow statement. (Note that this exhibit shows only the lines from the free cash flow worksheet related to this one item.)

As the exhibit shows, GAAP cash flow from operations includes a net outflow of $339,666 related to interest, a financing item. We move the interest expense and its tax effect to capital cash flow. If we stop there, however, free cash flow will still include the $50,835 amortization. Like the change in interest payable, the discount amortization must be moved into the capital cash flow section of the free cash flow statement along with the after-tax interest.

The amortization of a bond discount or premium appears as a reconciling item on the GAAP cash flow statement. However, companies often combine this amortization with depreciation of fixed assets and amortization of intangible assets, in which case it is not possible for us to discern the amount of the bond amortization directly from the cash flow statement. In that case, the debt foot-

EXHIBIT 9.9   Excerpt from Debt Footnote

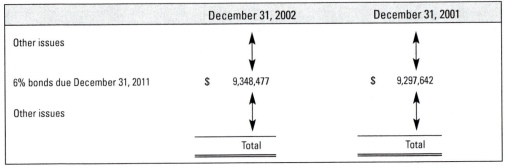

	December 31, 2002	December 31, 2001
Other issues	↕	↕
6% bonds due December 31, 2011	$ 9,348,477	$ 9,297,642
Other issues	↕	↕
	Total	Total

note can be used to determine the amount of bond amortization included in the depreciation and amortization line of the cash flow statement. Any change in the principal amount of debt during the year that is not explained by issuances or repayments is due to amortization. Exhibit 9.9 shows how the debt footnote for the company in the preceding example would indicate the existence of bond discount amortization. The increase in the principal amount for these bonds is $50,835 ($9,348,477 − $9,297,642), which is the amount of discount amortization during the year.

Capitalized Interest

Under GAAP, when a firm has long-term construction projects, it may capitalize a portion of its interest payments. The capitalized amount is charged to a fixed asset account rather than to interest expense. This amount appears on the cash flow statement as a capital expenditure, just as if it were a payment to acquire a machine. However, it is still an interest payment and not part of free cash flow. Therefore, we move capitalized interest out of capital expenditures, which is part of GAAP cash flow from investing, and into the capital cash flow section of the free cash flow statement. The Internal Revenue Code contains similar, although not identical, provisions for capitalized interest. Assuming for a particular company there is essentially no difference between capitalized interest for financial reporting and tax, there is no tax effect necessary in making this adjustment.

Consider the following example. A firm had $150 million of capital expenditures. In addition, it capitalized $20 million of the $100 million it incurred in interest during the year for both tax purposes and financial reporting. As a result, the company received a tax deduction for interest of only $80 million. Assuming a 40% marginal tax rate, the firm saved $32 million in taxes due to interest expense. Exhibit 9.10 shows the effect on the GAAP cash flow statement and the resulting adjustments.

The amount of interest that a firm may capitalize depends on the amount of its construction in progress. Construction in progress is the total accumulated cost of long-term construction projects that are not yet complete. The amount of interest that may be capitalized in a year is the average con-

EXHIBIT 9.10 Analysis of Capitalized Interest

	GAAP	Adjustments	Free Cash Flow
Interest expense (included in income statement)	$ (80,000,000)	$ 80,000,000	–
Tax benefit (included in income tax expense in income statement)	32,000,000 *	(32,000,000)	–
Amount included in net income on cash flow statement	(48,000,000)		
Capital expenditures	(170,000,000)	**20,000,000**	$ (150,000,000)
Amount included in operating and investing cash flow	(218,000,000)		
Free cash flow			(150,000,000)
Interest expense		(80,000,000)	(80,000,000)
Tax benefit on interest expense		32,000,000	32,000,000
Capitalized interest		**(20,000,000)**	(20,000,000)
Capital cash flow			(68,000,000)
Change in cash	$ (218,000,000)	$ 0	$ (218,000,000)

*Estimated by $ 80 million × 40%.

EXHIBIT 9.11   Estimate of Capitalized Interest from Construction in Progress

Construction in progress—beginning of year	$ 225,000,000
Construction in progress—end of year	275,000,000
Construction in progress—average	250,000,000
Average borrowing rate	0.08
Estimated capitalized interest	$ 20,000,000

EXHIBIT 9.12   Excerpt from Debt Footnote

7-1/2% bonds due in 2015	$ 1,000,000
7-3/4% bonds due in 2018	1,000,000
8-1/4% bonds due in 2020	3,000,000
Total long-term debt	$ 5,000,000

struction in progress balance during the year times the firm's average borrowing rate.[3] Sometimes, determining the amount of capitalized interest can be challenging. The amount of interest that was capitalized in a particular year may be disclosed in the footnotes or in the management discussion and analysis. If it is not, we estimate it by taking the estimated average borrowing rate times the average construction in progress balance for the year. Exhibit 9.11 shows how the $20 million of capitalized interest in our example might have been estimated from construction in progress and the borrowing rate.

We can estimate the average borrowing rate from information in the long-term debt footnote. We estimated the 8% average borrowing rate from the information in Exhibit 9.12. The average borrowing rate would be estimated as a weighted average of the borrowing costs of each issue: 7.5% × 0.20 + 7.75% × 0.20 + 8.25% × 0.60 = 8%.

---

[3]However, capitalized interest may not exceed the total interest cost incurred during the period. In other words, interest expense may not be reduced below zero.

SUMMARY

The free cash flow model values core operations by forecasting and discounting the expected free cash flows the core operations will generate. We then add or subtract other elements of the economic balance sheet, as appropriate, to arrive at equity value.

We start the forecasting process by studying historical cash flows. There is no requirement to make forecast assumptions that are the same as the historical results, and there is often good reason to make different assumptions. Still, historical results provide a frame of reference for constructing forecasts, and we must understand the historical results first.

It is important to examine historical results using the same structure we will use for the forecast. However, the structure of the GAAP cash flow statement is not consistent with free cash flow. The GAAP cash flow statement and the free cash flow statement categorize cash flows differently. In addition, the GAAP free cash flow statement includes free cash flow equivalents, which are noncash transactions having both an operating and a nonoperating or capital component. The GAAP cash flow statement ignores these transactions. We need to recast the historical combined GAAP income statement and cash flow statement in a free cash flow format.

This chapter provides a framework for deriving the free cash flow statement and an organized method for making the necessary adjustments. This method removes from free cash flow the nonoperating and capital components included in cash flow from operations and cash flow from investing under GAAP. It adds to free cash flow any free cash flow equivalents the firm has, with offsetting amounts elsewhere in the free cash flow statement. The resulting historical free cash flow statements will provide the analyst a starting point for making forecast assumptions, which is the topic of Chapter 10.

SUGGESTED READINGS

Hoyle, J., T. Schaefer, and T. Doupnik. *Advanced Accounting*, 6th ed. Burr Ridge, IL: McGraw Hill Irwin, 2001, Chapter 1.

Revsine, L., D. Collins, and B. Johnson. *Financial Reporting and Analysis*, 2nd ed. Upper Saddle River, NJ: Prentice Hall, 2001, Chapter 17.

REVIEW QUESTIONS

1. For valuation purposes, we prepare a free cash flow worksheet that separates the cash flows into three categories. Describe these categories. How are they different from the GAAP cash flow statement categories?

2. In which category of the free cash flow statement does each of the following belong?

   FCF: free cash flow

   CAPCF: capital cash flow

   NOPCF: nonoperating cash flow

   a. _____ Sales
   b. _____ Interest income
   c. _____ Depreciation (addback in cash flow statement)

d. _____ Cost of goods sold
e. _____ Tax on operating earnings
f. _____ Maintenance and repair expense
g. _____ Tax savings on interest expense
h. _____ Tax on interest income
i. _____ Preferred dividends paid
j. _____ Common dividends paid
k. _____ Capital expenditures (excluding capitalized interest portion)
l. _____ Capitalized interest portion of capital expenditures
m. _____ Selling expense

3. If a company has marketable securities, why do we need to move the interest income from these securities to the nonoperating cash flow section of the free cash flow statement?

4. If a company has marketable securities, why do we need to move the taxes associated with the interest income to the nonoperating cash flow section of the free cash flow statement?

5. In preparing a free cash flow statement for use in valuation, why can we not just use the cash flow from operations and cash flow from investing sections of the GAAP cash flow statement?

6. Why do we not recommend preparing a historical free cash flow statement from the beginning and ending balance sheets?

7. Why does the cash flow stream used in the free cash flow model exclude interest expense?

8. Why are the income tax effects of items not included in free cash flow also not included in free cash flow?

9. Why is the name of the first section of the GAAP cash flow statement, *cash flow from operations*, misleading?

10. The cash flow from investing section of the GAAP cash flow statement includes transactions related to the purchase and sale of property, plant, and equipment, as well as the purchase and sale of marketable securities and other investments. Why are these two types of transactions treated differently in the free cash flow statement?

11. What is a free cash flow equivalent?

12. Sidorow Corporation purchased machinery in 2002, paying for the machinery with an interest-bearing note payable rather than cash. Describe the two components of this transaction and why it should be treated as a free cash flow equivalent.

13. Why must the total in the adjustments column of the free cash flow worksheet be zero?

14. Why must the change in cash in the free cash flow statement be the same as in the GAAP cash flow statement?

PROBLEMS

1. Following is a combined income statement and cash flow statement for Jonathan's Tennis Clubs for 2002. Prepare a free cash flow statement for Jonathan's.

Jonathan's Tennis Club
Combined Income and Cash Flow Statement
For the year ending December 31, 2002 ($ thousands)

Revenues	$ 1,500.0
Salaries	500.0
Maintenance	300.0
Depreciation	75.0
Supplies	100.0
Other expense	50.0
Interest expense	50.0
Income before taxes	425.0
Taxes	161.5
Net Income	263.5
Plus: depreciation	75.0
Less: Increase in working capital	(100.0)
Cash Flow from Operations	238.5
Capital Expenditures	(80.0)
Cash Flow from Investing	(80.0)
Dividends paid	(150.0)
Repayment of debt	(50.0)
Cash Flow from Financing	(200.0)
Change in Cash	$ (41.5)

Jonathan's marginal tax rate is 38%. The company purchased a building and paid for it by issuing debt of $200,000. In accordance with GAAP, this transaction is not shown on the cash flow statement.

2. The following is a combined income statement and cash flow statement for Leah's Dance Studios, Inc. for 2002. Using this and the additional information that follows the statement, prepare a free cash flow statement for Leah's Dance Studios, Inc.

Leah's Dance Studios, Inc.
Combined Income Statement and Cash Flow Statement
For the Year Ending December 31, 2002 ($ millions)

Sales	$ 2,000
Cost of Goods Sold	(1,000)
Gross Profit	1,000
Selling Expense	(200)
General & Administrative Expense	(100)
Operating Earnings	700
Interest Expense	(200)
Interest Income	100
Earnings before taxes	600
Income Tax Expense	(175)
Net Income	425

continued

continued

Plus: Depreciation	25
Plus: Amortization	20
Less: Increase in working capital	(30)
Cash Flow from Operations	440
Capital Expenditures	(300)
Cash Flow from Investing	(300)
Repayment of debt	(120)
Issuance of stock	100
Dividends Paid	(130)
Cash Flow from Financing	(150)
Net Change in cash	$ (10)

The income tax expense shown on the income statement is comprised of $245 million tax on operating earnings (35% of $700 million), $70 million tax savings on the interest expense (35% of $200 million), and no taxes on interest income because this interest income is tax free.

3. The Dale Company has the following interest-related items on its combined GAAP income statement and cash flow statement:

Income Statement			Cash Flow Statement		
Interest expense	$	300	Increase in interest payable	$	50
Interest income	$	100			

Dale Company has a marginal tax rate of 35%. The interest income includes two items, $40 of interest income on municipal securities and $60 of taxable interest income.

What adjustments will you make to Dale's combined GAAP income statement and cash flow statement in preparing the free cash flow statement?

Problems 4 through 9 rely on the following information about Grossman Corporation: Grossman has an equity-method investment in another firm. It has the following GAAP income and cash flow statements (in millions of dollars):

INCOME STATEMENT:

Sales	$	5.0
Cost of sales		(3.0)
Gross profit		2.0
SG&A expense		(0.5)
Interest expense		(0.6)
Equity in earnings of affiliated company		1.3
Earnings before taxes		2.2
Provision for income taxes		(0.6)
Net income	$	1.6

CASH FLOW STATEMENT:

Net income	$	1.6
Depreciation		0.2
Deferred taxes		0.1
Excess of equity in earnings of affiliated		
company over dividends received		(0.7)
Change in inventory and receivables		(0.3)
Cash flow from operations		0.9
Capital expenditures		(0.5)
Cash flow from investing		(0.5)
Increase in debt		1.0
Dividends paid		(1.5)
Cash flow from financing		(0.5)
Net change in cash	$	(0.1)

Assume a 40% marginal tax rate and an 80% exclusion for dividends received.

4. What is the amount of the dividend received from the equity investment?

5. What is the amount of tax paid during the year related to the equity investment?

6. What is the amount of tax expense recognized in the income statement related to the equity investment?

7. What is the net effect (after taxes) of the investment on the current year's cash flow?

8. Identify the line items on the GAAP income and cash flow statements and the respective amounts related to the equity investment and its tax effects. (The total of these items should be the same as your answer to problem 7.)

9. What is Grossman's free cash flow?

10. Tucker Corporation's combined GAAP income statement and cash flow statement is shown below.

Sales	$	1,500.0
Cost of sales		(900.0)
Gross earnings		600.0
SG&A expense		(225.0)
Operating earnings		375.0
Equity in earnings of affiliate		80.0
Interest income		75.0
Interest expense		(130.0)
Earnings before taxes		400.0
Income tax expense		(91.6)
Net income		308.4
Depreciation expense (included in SG&A)		75.0
Deferred taxes		16.0
Excess of affiliated earnings over dividends received		(50.0)
Bond discount amortization		10.0
Change in interest payable		5.0
Change in other working capital		(40.0)
Cash flow from operations		324.4

continued

continued

Capital expenditures	(240.0)
Purchases of marketable securities	(280.0)
Cash flow from investing	(520.0)
Proceeds from debt issuances	275.0
Proceeds from equity issuances	100.0
Cash dividends paid	(80.0)
Cash flow from financing	295.0
Net change in cash	$ 99.4

In addition, you have discerned the following from footnotes to the financial statements:

- The marginal income tax rate on all income other than dividend income and interest income is 40%.
- Interest income is from municipal bonds and is not taxable.
- The company may exclude 80% of the dividends it receives from taxable income, so the marginal tax rate on this income is 8% (20% × 40%). This income is taxable when the dividend is received, but recognized in the financial statements under the equity method.
- Capital expenditures under GAAP include $40 million of capitalized interest.
- Capital expenditures under GAAP exclude new machinery for which the company issued additional preferred shares in lieu of any cash payment. The fair value of the preferred shares at the time they were issued was $10 million.

Prepare a free cash flow statement.

Problems 11 through 13 are based on the following combined income statement and cash flow statement, which was adapted from the GAAP statements in W. W. Grainger, Inc.'s 2000 annual report.

($ thousands)	1998	1999	2000
Net sales	$ 4,438,975	$ 4,636,275	$ 4,977,044
Cost of merchandise sold	(2,947,962)	(3,125,647)	(3,391,707)
Gross profit	1,491,013	1,510,628	1,585,337
Warehousing, marketing, and administrative expenses	(1,083,031)	(1,193,400)	(1,250,217)
Operating earnings	407,982	317,228	335,120
Interest income	1,560	1,606	1,891
Interest expense	(6,652)	(15,596)	(24,403)
Equity in loss of unconsolidated entities	0	0	(10,855)
Unclassified—net	(2,043)	512	29,842
Earnings before income taxes	400,847	303,750	331,595
Income taxes	(162,343)	(123,019)	(138,692)
Net earnings	238,504	180,731	192,903
Provision for losses on accounts receivable	10,310	13,585	18,076
Depreciation	58,256	72,446	81,898
Amortization of intangibles and goodwill	15,964	15,941	8,746
Amortization of capitalized software	4,645	9,840	16,249

(Gain) on sales of investment securities	0	0	(30,017)
Loss on unconsolidated entities	0	0	10,855
Change in accounts receivable	(21,349)	(109,269)	(66,332)
Change in inventories	(20,260)	(130,708)	54,468
Change in prepaid expenses	(3,192)	(6,333)	(7,163)
Change in deferred income taxes	(7,393)	(5,909)	(21,077)
Change in trade accounts payable	7,237	45,621	(37,944)
Change in other current liabilities	42,095	(23,530)	13,836
Change in current income taxes payable	(1,407)	(32,997)	28,920
Change in employment-related benefit costs	2,578	2,933	8,819
Change in other, net	5,493	4,889	5,520
Net cash provided by operating activities	331,481	37,240	277,757
Additions to property, buildings, and equipment	(132,857)	(111,900)	(65,507)
Proceeds from sale of property, buildings and equipment, net	4,315	4,387	1,701
Expenditures for capitalized software	(36,983)	(26,473)	(29,406)
Proceeds from sales of investment securities	0	0	31,665
Purchases of available-for-sale securities	(5,000)	(18,500)	(5,000)
Investments in unconsolidated entities	0	0	(26,862)
Other—net	(144)	(2,898)	(774)
Net cash (used) in investing activities	(170,669)	(155,384)	(94,183)
Net cash (used in) provided by financing activities *	(166,178)	135,783	(181,067)
Exchange rate effect on cash and cash equivalents	(687)	1,873	(1,806)
Net change in cash and cash equivalents	$ (6,053)	$ 19,512	$ 701

* Condensed from original statement.

Additional information: In 2000, Grainger made an investment in an unconsolidated subsidiary by issuing debt of $7,831,000. Because no cash was exchanged, the transaction was not reported in the GAAP cash flow statement. The marginal tax is 38%.

11. Prepare Grainger's free cash flow statement for 1998.

12. Prepare Grainger's free cash flow statement for 1999.

13. Prepare Grainger's free cash flow statement for 2000.

 ## My Case

Prepare a free cash flow statement for your company for at least three years. You may want to go back further. If your company has a line item for tax benefits on exercise of employee stock options, be sure that amount is not in free cash flow, but do nothing else with stock options. If your company has a defined benefit pension plan or a postemployment benefit plan, make no adjustments for those. (We will study employee stock options and retirement plans in Chapters 14 and 15.)

10

Where We Have Been:

In Chapter 9 we learned how to derive a free cash flow statement from a firm's combined GAAP income statement and cash flow statement. The free cash flow statement is a key input to the forecast and valuation.

Where We Are:

In this chapter we discuss forecasting free cash flow and using that forecast to estimate the value of the firm.

Where We Are Going:

In Chapters 11 and 12, we discuss the adjusted present value model and the residual income model, two more methods for estimating the value of the firm.

Forecasting Free Cash Flows

LEARNING OBJECTIVES:

After studying this chapter, you will understand:

- How to build a free cash flow valuation model.
- Why the assumptions that drive the valuation model must be reasonable and internally consistent.
- How to set assumptions for a valuation model.
- How to refine a valuation model.
- How to prepare a sensitivity analysis.

When General Electric's NBC subsidiary agreed to acquire Telemundo Communications Group for nearly $2 billion in October 2001, industry experts said NBC overpaid for the deal.[1] Whether the experts were correct remains to be seen. The fact is, many acquisitions are failures because the buyer simply overpays for the target firm, not because there are any particular operating problems with the acquired company. If a buyer uses an overly optimistic forecast to estimate the value of the target firm, it may pay too much for the acquisition. A more realistic forecast might lead the acquirer to negotiate a fairer price or at least to avoid a value-destroying acquisition.

One of the reasons forecasting is so difficult and prone to error is that it is very subjective. In fact, it is more of an art than a science. Forecasting requires the analyst to combine all the knowledge gained in the business and financial statement analyses to create a best guess as to the firm's future performance. In doing so, the analyst has no formula to provide the "right" answer. However, analysts use certain principles to improve their forecasts and their valuations. In this chapter, we discuss these principles in the context of forecasting free cash flow.

To illustrate, we develop a forecast and valuation for Starbucks. We develop this forecast under the assumption that we are outsiders valuing Starbucks using only publicly available information. This is actually the case for most valuation work. However, sometimes firms value themselves, say to determine whether a stock repurchase program is advisable. In these cases, the analyst has far more information available, which enables him or her to prepare a more detailed forecast and therefore a more accurate valuation.

In terms of our graphical representation of the valuation process, we are now in the portion to the right of the dashed line in Exhibit 10.1. We will use our business analysis, along with historical ratios we compute from the historical free cash flow statements, to determine a set of forecast assumptions. These assumptions will be the inputs to a forecast model, and the forecast will be the output. This forecast will determine the value of the core operations, which in turn determines the value of the common equity under the free cash flow model, as shown in equation (10.1).

$$COMEQUITY = \sum_{t=1}^{\infty} \frac{FCF_t}{(1 + k_c)^t} + NONOP - DEBT - OCAP \qquad (10.1)$$

where FCF_t is free cash flow in year t, k_c is the weighted-average cost of capital, $NONOP$ is the value of nonoperating net assets, $DEBT$ is the value of debt, and $OCAP$ is the value of other capital claims. Equation (10.1) is a direct application of the economic balance sheet using the present value of free cash flow to value core operations.

---

[1]According to "NBC Speaks Spanish," CNN Money Web page, October 11, 2001, **www.cnnmoney.com**.

EXHIBIT 10.1   Forecasting and the Valuation

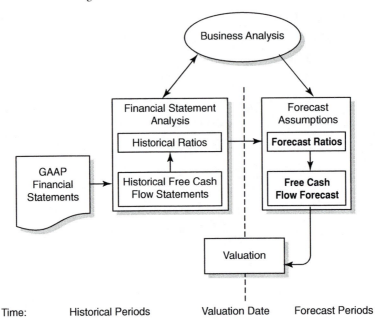

The forecasting and valuation process has four stages:

1. **Model the free cash flows.** We develop a set of equations to use in computing forecasted values for each component of free cash flow for each year in the forecast. Each equation uses an assumption, often in the form of a ratio. These equations are depicted in Exhibit 10.1 by the box labeled free cash flow forecast.

2. **Set the model assumptions and compute the results**. Each of the forecast assumptions is like a dial on a control panel, and we must determine where to set each dial. We estimate values for these assumptions by considering historical relationships, trends, expected changes in the business, and so on. We then calculate a base case or most likely case value. This is simple to do with a spreadsheet because once the model (worksheet formulae) is built and the assumptions entered, the computer does all the mechanical work very quickly. The valuation box in Exhibit 10.1 represents these results.

3. **Refine the model**. After building the model, the analyst often decides to refine it. For example, the forecast may be broken down by product line, or sales growth could be analyzed in more detail by forecasting price and volume changes. It is a good idea to get the skeleton of the model complete (step 1), and then add more detailed analyses and refinements that feed into the forecasts of particular components.

4. **Sensitivity analysis**. After developing a base case, the analyst is rarely sure that the assumptions are accurate. Will sales growth be higher or lower? Will capital needs change? In a sensitivity analysis, we recalculate the forecast and the resulting valuation under many different assump-

tions. We vary these assumptions so that we have calculated the entire range of cases that might reasonably occur, to gain an understanding of the potential upside and downside relative to our base case forecast. We also can use sensitivity analysis to determine the value of the security given some event we fear (or hope) might occur, or to determine the assumptions we would need to justify a particular stock price.

Sections 10.1 through 10.4 examine each of these steps in more detail. Although we discuss forecasting and valuing the firm in terms of the free cash flow model, the forecasting techniques presented also apply directly to the adjusted present value model, which discounts the same free cash flow forecast. The techniques we use will also be important in forecasting residual income in the residual income model. Although we quantify our forecast assumptions somewhat differently when we use the residual income model, we still make estimates about future performance and rely on similar forecasting techniques.

10.1 MODEL THE FREE CASH FLOWS

The first step in developing a free cash flow forecast is to model the components of free cash flow. The model is a set of equations, each of which defines the value of a particular line item in the free cash flow forecast, given the values of other forecast items, prior-year values, and additional assumptions. The assumptions that link one forecasted line item to other forecasted line items and prior-year values are usually quantified in ratios, but they could be other quantitative assumptions, such as dollar amounts, that drive the forecast.[2] Each ratio determines how one variable in the model affects another. For example, the equation defining sales might be prior year's sales increased by a growth rate.

The forecast must be both reasonable and internally consistent. **Reasonableness** means that the forecasted amounts are good estimates of the future values of the forecasted items. **Internal consistency** means the forecasted numbers are logical in relation to each other. Both reasonableness and internal consistency require that the forecasting ratios describe as direct a cause-and-effect relationship as possible. For example, if we project selling expense as sales times an assumed ratio of selling expense to sales, these expenses should actually vary with sales levels, perhaps due to commissions. If we change the sales forecast, the model will automatically change forecasted selling expenses, maintaining the internal consistency between these two items. In contrast, forecasting depreciation in the same way would not make sense, because depreciation does not vary with sales.

In creating a forecast to value a company, we usually define the free cash flow line items in a way that is consistent with the information the company provides, after adjusting to a free cash flow format as we did in Chapter 9. For example, if a company combines certain costs into a single line item such as selling, general, and administrative expenses, we would do so as well. However, there is no official way to forecast the line items in the free cash flow forecast. Rather, we use our understanding of the business to describe as best we can the relationships among the free cash flow line items.

The following is a free cash flow forecast model for Starbucks. View it as an example that shows one approach to one valuation. It does not contain every line item that might appear in a free cash flow forecast or every kind of analysis that may be used. Also, note that every company uses slightly different terminology. We construct the model using Starbucks' terminology, but in our discussion

---

[2]For convenience, we refer to all of our assumptions simply as ratios.

we also indicate the more standard terminology if it differs from Starbucks'. The items listed under ratio definitions represent parameters that we must set to particular values based on our analysis of their historical values and the business environment.

In this section, we focus on how to calculate each component of the forecast, given previously calculated components of the forecast, historical data, and forecast assumptions. In the following section, we discuss how to set the forecast assumptions. Exhibit 10.2 shows the forecast model.

Now let us discuss the model and its parameters.

Net Revenues—REV_t

Net revenues (sales) projections are often one of the most important variables affecting value. We modeled these (REV_t) using growth rates, gs_t, as assumptions. Revenue in the first year of the forecast depends on actual revenue in the most recent year and the assumed growth rate. In subsequent years, revenue depends on the prior year forecast and the assumed growth rate. Note that the model allows for a different growth rate in every year.

Cost of Sales and Related Occupancy Costs—COS_t

Cost of sales[3] is another key forecast component. We used gross margin percentage (gm_t), the ratio of gross profit (revenue minus cost of sales) to revenue, to project cost of sales (COS_t). We used this ratio because cost of sales has a cause-and-effect relationship with revenue. For the revenue and cost

EXHIBIT 10.2   Starbucks Free Cash Flow Forecast Model

Cash Flow Variable	Forecast Formula	Ratio Definitions
Net revenue	$REV_t = REV_{t-1} \cdot (1 + gs_t)$	gs_t = net revenue growth rate
Cost of sales and related occupancy costs	$COS_t = REV_t \cdot (1 - gm_t)$	gm_t = gross profit as a percentage of net revenue
Gross profit	$GROSS_t = REV_t - COS_t$	
Operating expenses	$OPX_t = REV_t \cdot a_t$	a_t = operating expenses as a percentage of net revenue
Operating income	$OP_t = GROSS_t - OPX_t$	
Income taxes	$TAX_t = OP_t \cdot \tau_t^{CORE}$	τ_t^{CORE} = effective tax rate on core operations
Net operating profits after taxes	$NOPAT_t = OP_t - TAX_t$	
Depreciation and amortization addback	$DEPR_t = DEPR_{t-1} + \Delta DEPR_t$	$\Delta DEPR_t$ = dollar change in depreciation and amortization in period t versus prior year
Deferred income taxes, net	$DEFTAX_t = TAX_t \cdot \delta_t$	δ_t = deferred tax as percentage of income tax provision
Change in working capital	$\Delta WC_t = w_t \cdot (REV_t - REV_{t-1})$	w_t = incremental working capital per dollar of incremental net revenue
Capital expenditures	$CAPEX_t = c_t \cdot DEPR_t$ $+ f_t \cdot (REV_t - REV_{t-1})$	c_t = ratio of replacement cost of fixed capital to historical cost f_t = ratio of expansion capital expenditures to incremental net revenue
Free cash flow	$FCF_t = NOPAT_t + DEPR_t$ $+ DEFTAX_t - \Delta WC_t - CAPEX_t$	

---

[3]Starbucks includes store rent in this item, although it is more common not to combine cost of sales with other expenses. For ease of exposition, we refer to this item simply as cost of sales.

of sales forecasts to be internally consistent, the cost of sales forecast must depend on revenue. The gross margin percentage defines that dependence. By linking the cost of sales forecast to sales,[4] we ensure that it will be automatically updated for any change in the sales growth assumption, and we will preserve the forecast's internal consistency.

Due to the way we have modeled sales and cost of sales, we can alter revenue growth without the gross margin becoming unreasonable and vice versa. Consider what would happen if we had instead forecast cost of sales using a growth rate (h_t) in cost of sales. The following would be the forecasting formulas for sales and cost of sales.

$$REV_t = REV_{t-1} \cdot (1 + gs_t)$$
$$COS_t = COS_{t-1} \cdot (1 + h_t)$$

Internally Inconsistent
Forecast

If we change one of the parameters and not the other, these equations will produce internally inconsistent forecasts. For example, if we increased the forecasted revenue growth without changing the growth in cost of sales, all the incremental revenue would be profit, meaning the margin assumed on an additional dollar of sales was 100%! This problem occurs in this form of the model because we have not modeled the cause and effect properly. Cost of sales do not simply grow at some rate independent of sales growth; rather, sales growth directly affects cost of sales. By modeling cost of sales using a margin, our forecast automatically incorporates sales growth in the cost of sales forecast. Changing the assumption for sales growth does not require us to change another assumption to maintain internal consistency.

Finally, our model implicitly assumes that cost of sales are entirely variable. This is reasonable for a business such as Starbucks, but might not be for a manufacturer with large fixed costs. In such a case, we could model cost of sales as a fixed component and a variable component where only the variable component was driven by the revenue forecast. For example, we might use $COS_t = FC_t + REV_t * (1 - VM_t)$, where FC_t is fixed costs in period t, and VM_t is the variable margin in period t.

Gross Profit—$GROSS_t$

Gross profit is net revenue less cost of sales.

Operating Expenses—OPX_t

We model OPX_t, operating expenses, using a percentage of revenues, a_t. Operating expenses usually include all expenses that occur in the normal course of operations except for those associated with preparing the product for sale, tax expense, and financing expenses. Examples include selling expense, marketing expense, rent of office space, and administrative expenses such as the accounting and legal departments. In this case, we assume that operating expenses, like cost of sales, depend on revenue levels. For some firms, this is a reasonable way to model operating expenses, whereas for others it is not. If operating expenses consist of rent on an office and some support staff, they are unlikely to vary with revenues, especially within a reasonable range of revenue levels. However, if they consist of sales com-

---

[4]These two ratios may need to be adjusted at some volume level due to economies of scale, which may cause a firm's margin to be higher when it has higher revenue growth. If this were an important enough issue for a particular company, the analyst could refine the model to specify cost of sales as a more complicated function of revenue.

missions, they are likely to be directly related to revenues. Because the kinds of expenses firms incur vary considerably, analysts may break them into components with different behaviors, if that information is available. For example, we could model operating expenses as having a fixed component and a variable component, similar to the alternative showed for cost of sales. The better we understand how costs actually behave, the closer to the true cause-and-effect relationship we can model the costs.

We modeled operating expenses as a percentage of revenues because, as we will see in Section 10.2, our historical analysis showed that Starbucks' operating expenses have been a fairly constant percentage of revenues, indicating this is likely to be a reasonable model of the cause-and-effect relationship. Much of this item is directly related to store operations, the largest part being store operating expenses. As Starbucks has expanded to more locations, this expense has grown in proportion to revenues. In addition, general and administrative expenses, another component, have grown as Starbucks has expanded and required a larger corporate staff and more facilities to house them.

Operating Income—OP_t

Operating income is gross profit less operating expenses. This subtotal is the basis for computing the income tax provision.

Income Taxes—TAX_t

Most analysts forecast the income tax provision by applying a tax rate (τ_t^{CORE}) to forecasted operating income (OP_t). Whenever we apply a tax rate, we use the tax rate that pertains to the associated income. In this case, we use the effective tax rate on core operations. This is our estimate of what Starbucks' effective tax rate would be if the firm consisted only of its core operations.

Net Operating Profits After Taxes—$NOPAT_t$

Once we have estimated the tax provision related to operating income, we can compute forecasted net operating profit after taxes (NOPAT). NOPAT is operating income less related income taxes.

We now turn to the components of free cash flow that come from the cash flow statement rather than the income statement. These are:

- The reversals of items included in NOPAT that are not cash flows, such as depreciation and amortization expense
- Cash flows related to core operations that are not included in NOPAT, such as capital expenditures and changes in working capital

Depreciation and Amortization Addback—$DEPR_t$

Depreciation ($DEPR_t$) relates to fixed asset balances or prior capital expenditures.[5] Some analysts project depreciation by examining historical changes in depreciation levels from year to year and forecasting analogous changes. In the absence of detailed fixed asset data, this approach is reasonable as depreciation is unlikely to change much from one year to the next. We take this approach by specifying a dollar amount for $\Delta DEPR_t$, the dollar change in depreciation from the prior year.

For a more detailed approach to forecasting depreciation, we could first separate future depreciation into depreciation on assets existing as of the valuation date and depreciation on forecasted capital expenditures. For existing assets, we usually project depreciation will remain equal to the prior

---

[5]Starbucks includes amortization in this line item. Yet because it has very few intangible assets, most of the line item is undoubtedly depreciation.

year's depreciation. For depreciation on new capital expenditures, we study the historical relationship between depreciation and capital expenditures and use the information in the footnotes to make educated assumptions about the depreciation methods and useful lives of the assets. By applying these rates and lives to capital expenditures, we can project future depreciation on new assets. Total depreciation will be equal to depreciation on existing assets plus depreciation on new assets. When enough detailed information is available, we can apply this process to classes of assets rather than to total fixed assets. For example, we could separate fixed assets into buildings and equipment, each with different depreciation patterns.

Deferred Income Taxes, Net—$DEFTAX_t$

This amount represents the deferred tax addback ($DEFTAX_t$). It is the portion of the income tax provision that is not a current obligation to the government. For most companies, the primary sources of this item are book/tax differences in depreciation. Analysts often model this amount as a percentage of the income tax provision, which we call δ_t. As long as the firm's growth pattern is stable, this ratio will generally stay about the same.

Change in Working Capital—ΔWC_t

The change in working capital (ΔWC_t) represents additional investment. This additional investment is generally related to revenue increases. As the firm expands its revenues, it needs additional accounts receivable, inventory, and other current operating assets (net of additional payables and other current operating liabilities). It is common to model the increase in working capital[6] as a percentage of the dollar increase in revenues over the prior period, w_t. The working capital formula says that it takes w dollars of additional working capital to support each additional dollar of revenue. Linking the change in working capital to the change in revenues forces internal consistency between the forecasted change in working capital and the revenue forecast. Changes to the revenue forecast will automatically alter the forecast of change in working capital.

Capital Expenditures—$CAPEX_t$

For Starbucks, we include additions to property, plant, and equipment and purchases of businesses, net of provision for losses on asset disposals, in the capital expenditures ($CAPEX_t$) line. The bulk of this amount is additions to property, plant, and equipment, or capital expenditures.

We usually forecast capital expenditures in two parts, maintenance capital expenditures and expansion capital expenditures. **Maintenance** capital expenditures are those expenditures required to maintain the existing level of productive capacity. We often assume depreciation is a reasonable estimate of maintenance capital expenditures. In doing so, we make three key assumptions. First, we assume that the cost of a unit of productive capacity does not change. If there has been substantial inflation during an asset's life, or if technological improvements have reduced the cost of productive capacity, this assumption will not be true. In either of these situations, we can apply a multiplier to depreciation to increase or decrease the amount of maintenance capital. c_t is the multiplier on depreciation to account for the changes in the cost of physical capacity due to inflation or technological improvements. $c_t \cdot DEPR_t$ represents maintenance capital expenditures. For example, if inflation has increased the cost of a unit of physical capacity by 50% from the time the depreciating assets were acquired, we can estimate maintenance capital expenditures as 1.5 times depreciation and c_t is 1.5.

---

[6]The change in working capital we refer to is related to core operations only and excludes all nonoperating items such as excess cash and short-term investments, as well as capital claims such as short-term debt and current maturities of long-term debt.

Similarly, if improvements in technology have reduced the cost of a unit of physical capacity by 70% from the time the depreciating assets were acquired, we can define c_t to be 0.3.

The second key assumption we make in using depreciation to estimate maintenance capital expenditures is that the firm used an accurate estimate of useful life to calculate depreciation. In analyzing the financial statements, we might find that the estimated depreciable lives are not realistic, perhaps because management wanted to report higher earnings. In this situation, using depreciation to estimate maintenance capital will not be reasonable. Again, we can use a factor to adjust depreciation so that it is a better estimate of maintenance capital expenditures.

The third assumption we make is that we will replace the asset evenly over its life. Although this is certainly not true for an individual asset, it is often approximately true on average for a company adding assets each year. Further, even if capital expenditures tend to be "lumpy" rather than smooth, as long as our total capital expenditure forecast is reasonable over a long period, we do not create a large valuation error. The difference in timing between a smooth pattern and a lumpy one will cause some difference in the present value of the free cash flow stream, but that error will be far less than if the total capital expenditures forecast were inaccurate.

Most firms will also have **expansion** capital expenditures, which are capital expenditures beyond those required to maintain existing productive capacity. If the free cash flow forecast includes real revenue growth (i.e., revenue growth beyond price increases), the firm will need additional manufacturing

---

◖ A CLOSER LOOK

Present Values of Lumpy and Smooth Capital Expenditures

Capital expenditures tend to be "lumpy," in that firms often have large expenditures in some years and smaller expenditures in other years. This occurs because it is not possible to build a fraction of a factory. Instead, a firm would build an entire factory and wait until it is operating at or near capacity before building another.

Although it is possible to forecast future capital expenditures, it is very difficult to forecast their exact timing. As a result, forecasts often treat capital expenditures as a smooth item, not a lumpy one. The following illustration shows that the effect of this simplification on the present value is not very large.

Consider Lumpy Company, which must build a factory at a cost of $100 million every fourth year, beginning two years from now. Assuming a discount rate of 10%, the present value of all of Lumpy's future capital expenditures is (in millions of dollars):

$$\frac{100}{1.10^2} + \frac{100}{1.10^6} + \frac{100}{1.10^{10}} + \cdots = 260.7$$

If the expenditures are forecasted correctly in total, but smoothly at $25 million per year, the present value is:

$$\frac{25}{1.10} + \frac{25}{1.10^2} + \frac{25}{1.10^3} + \cdots = 250.0$$

The difference is only 4.1% (10.7/260.7) of the present value of the capital expenditures.

facilities. f_t is the ratio of expansion capital expenditures to incremental net revenues. $f_t \cdot (REV_t - REV_{t-1})$ represents expansion capital expenditures. If we forecast no change in net revenues, then expansion capital expenditures are zero, and the only capital expenditures are for maintenance of physical capacity. If we forecast net revenues to increase, then expansion capital expenditures would be required to put enough physical capacity in place to produce the output in the net revenue forecast and maintain internal consistency in the forecast. Like w_t, the use of f_t forces internal consistency between the investment and net revenue forecasts.

Free Cash Flow—FCF_t

Free cash flow is NOPAT plus depreciation and the deferred tax addback less the change in working capital and capital expenditures.

10.2 SET THE MODEL ASSUMPTIONS AND COMPUTE THE RESULTS

To understand the difference between building the model and setting the model assumptions, let us return to our control panel analogy. In building the model, we determine what dials will be on the control panel and how any particular setting will affect the forecast. When we set the assumptions, we turn the control dials to particular positions.

In setting the model's assumptions, we must once again consider the issues of reasonableness and internal consistency. As we have seen, reasonableness and internal consistency require us to use cause-and-effect relationships to build the model. It is just as important to use reasonable assumptions for the forecasted ratios. For example, using a gross margin percentage is often a reasonable *way* to forecast cost of sales (and therefore gross profits), because gross profits tend to vary with sales for most companies. A good forecast also requires that we select a reasonable *value* for the gross margin percentage assumption.

If the model uses cause-and-effect relationships, it should be relatively easy to maintain internal consistency. However, not all cause-and-effect relationships are easy to model formally. We will have to consider explicitly the consistency of certain assumptions. For example, sales volume and price often vary in opposite directions. A firm may employ a high-price strategy and accept lower sales volume in return for higher margins, or it may cut price aggressively and earn very thin margins but enjoy higher volumes. If we do not formally model sales volume as a function of price, then it is important to consider whether the sales growth and gross margin assumptions are consistent with each other.

The Need for a Forecast Horizon

As we consider how to set the model's assumptions, we are faced with a practical problem. We value core operations as the present value of forecasted free cash flow from now until eternity. However, it is impossible to forecast free cash flow for an infinite number of periods. This is the same problem we encountered in the dividend discount model in Chapter 8. We solved that problem with the Gordon Growth Model. By using a regular pattern of cash flows, we were able to value an infinite series without literally summing an infinite number of terms. Similarly, in the free cash flow model, we forecast a finite number of periods explicitly and assume a regular pattern of cash flows after that point. Analysts often call the value of the regular cash flows after the finite forecast period the **terminal value** because it represents the value of the cash flows from periods after the explicit forecast terminates. Another common name for terminal value is **perpetuity value** because a perpetuity is a common way to value it.

We separate the value of the core operations into two parts, one representing the value of the free cash flows during the finite forecasting period and the other representing the terminal value, as follows:

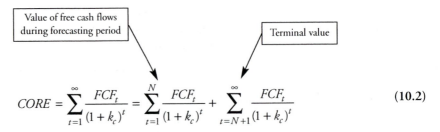

$$CORE = \sum_{t=1}^{\infty} \frac{FCF_t}{(1+k_c)^t} = \sum_{t=1}^{N} \frac{FCF_t}{(1+k_c)^t} + \sum_{t=N+1}^{\infty} \frac{FCF_t}{(1+k_c)^t} \qquad (10.2)$$

We forecast FCF_t explicitly for periods 1 to N. To determine the terminal value, we forecast free cash flow for period $N+1$ and assume a regular pattern for FCF_t after that point. We usually use a perpetuity for this regular pattern and sometimes include a constant growth rate, g_p. A constant growth rate means that we expect the free cash flow to continue growing forever at this rate after the forecasting period. The present value at date N of a perpetuity that begins with FCF_{N+1} at date $N+1$ and then grows at rate g_p is $FCF_{N+1}/(k_c - g_p)$. So, the value of the core operations is:

$$CORE = \sum_{t=1}^{\infty} \frac{FCF_t}{(1+k_c)^t} = \sum_{t=1}^{N} \frac{FCF_t}{(1+k_c)^t} + \frac{FCF_{N+1}}{(k_c - g_p) \cdot (1+k_c)^N} \qquad (10.3)$$

The last term in the perpetuity formula includes $(1+k_c)^N$ in the denominator in order to discount the terminal value back to date zero.

At this point most readers will ask what number do I use for N? How many years do I forecast explicitly before assuming a regular pattern of cash flows? There is no right answer to this question, but two principles guide our choice. First, the explicit forecast should be long enough for us reasonably to expect a regular pattern of cash flows starting at year $N+1$. For a young, growing company, N is likely to be larger than for a stable company in a mature industry. As many as 15 years may be appropriate for a start-up company, versus 5 years or less for a mature company.

Second, the forecast horizon should be long enough to capture the firm's potential positive net present value projects. Eventually, firms lose whatever competitive advantage they have. Extremely profitable firms will find new competitors entering their markets and driving profits down. How long this takes depends on the economic factors we studied in the external business analysis in Chapter 3. For example, firms that can maintain strong barriers to entry will enjoy a competitive advantage for a longer period of time. Once a firm has lost its competitive advantage, it will not be able to find positive net present value investments. If we extend the forecast horizon until the firm has lost its competitive advantage, we can reasonably assume that any incremental investments the firm makes in the perpetuity period are zero net present value projects. These investments have no effect on the value of the firm. As a result, we can actually ignore these investments altogether! This will permit us to forecast the perpetuity using a feasible free cash flow stream given the level of capacity in place at the end of the forecast horizon.

We now consider how to set assumptions for the ratios for the forecast horizon and the perpetuity period.

Forecasting During the Forecast Horizon

Historical relationships are usually a starting point for setting forecast assumptions. For example, to forecast sales growth, we might look at historical sales growth rates. Similarly, to estimate the gross margin percentage, we might look at the historical values. Thus, a first step (and an easy one with a spreadsheet) is to compute the historical values of all ratios that will be used as forecast assumptions.

If the historical ratios are to provide guidance for the forecast, we must compute them in precisely the same way we will use them in the forecast. For example, the tax rate we use in the free cash flow forecast is the effective tax rate applicable to the core operations. Therefore, the historical tax rate we examine must be the effective rate on income generated by the core operations. Because our forecast assumptions link components of free cash flow, we use the historical free cash flow statements to calculate the historical values of our forecast ratios.

A CLOSER LOOK

Forward-Looking Statements

In 1995, Congress enacted the Private Securities Litigation Reform Act with the purpose of making it less risky for firms to provide "forward-looking" information. Forward-looking information is information about the firm's future expectations, such as for earnings, prices, capital expenditures, and so on. The Act limited a firm's liability in the event its forward-looking statements turned out to be wrong, as long as they were made in good faith. By reducing litigation risk when companies provide information that goes beyond reporting historical results, the government hoped to encourage firms to provide investors with more useful information.

As a result of the Act, more and more firms have provided such information since 1995, both through press releases and in their annual reports. When they provide forward-looking information, companies include a statement that the information is subject to protection under the Act. For example, Starbucks' fiscal 2000 annual report contains the following statement:

Cautionary Statement Pursuant to the Private Securities Litigation Reform Act of 1995

Certain statements set forth in this Annual Report, including anticipated store and market openings, planned capital expenditures and trends in or expectations regarding the Company's operations, constitute "forward-looking statements" within the meaning of the Private Securities Litigation Reform Act of 1995. Such statements are based on currently available operating, financial and competitive information and are subject to various risks and uncertainties. Actual future results and trends may differ materially depending on a variety of factors, including, but not limited to, coffee and other raw materials prices and availability, successful execution of internal performance and expansion plans, the impact of competition, the effect of legal proceedings and other risks detailed herein and in the Company's annual and quarterly filings with the Securities and Exchange Commission.

Although historical ratios help us think about what the forecast ratios should be, there is no requirement that the forecast use the historical values. In fact, there often are good reasons not to do so. For example, Amazon.com had 68% sales growth in 2000 following several years of triple-digit growth. It would be unreasonable to assume Amazon's growth could continue at 68% per year, and a forecast of Amazon would likely show declining growth rates. Margins may also change as competitors enter a market and aggressive price increases become more difficult. Still, historical relationships provide a beginning point for quantifying the forecast assumptions, as long as you also consider the business knowledge gained in the business analysis.

As we learned in Chapter 4, we must consider the quality of financial statement data before using the data to help us build our forecast. We must consider whether to exclude any items that may be nonrecurring. We may also make adjustments to the historical data for other financial statement quality issues.

Valuing Starbucks

Exhibit 10.3 is a valuation of Starbucks. The historical information, together with the insights gleaned from a business analysis, help us set the assumptions for the free cash flow forecast. The shaded portion of the left side of Exhibit 10.3 presents five years of historical free cash flow statements. The 2000 free cash flow statement is the one constructed in Chapter 9. For all five years, we aggregate line items that are similar enough that we would want to forecast them together. For example, we forecast the change in working capital, rather than the change in each individual component of working capital. We also show net revenues for 1994 and 1995.

We present historical ratios above the free cash flow statements. These ratios are the historical values of the ratios that we will use to construct the forecast, computed in exactly the same way. On the right side of Exhibit 10.3, we show forecasted ratios. The resulting free cash flow forecasts appear below these ratios.

The boxes and arrows in Exhibit 10.3 illustrate the relationship between historical ratios and forecast ratios. We calculated the 28.4% revenue growth for 1999 using the 1998 and 1999 revenue amounts ($1,680,145,000 / $1,308,702,000 − 1 = 0.284). In 2003, the revenue growth forecast is 23%. This growth rate is analogous to the 28.4% rate in 1999, because both represent year-over-year growth. The 2003 net revenue forecast is computed as $3,443,634,000 × (1 + 0.230) = $4,235,670,000. This uses the revenue growth definition in exactly the same way we used it to calculate the historical value.

Determining the number of years in the forecast horizon is difficult. We chose five years because it appears that Starbucks' rapid growth is beginning to decrease. Our forecast assumes that it will be more difficult for Starbucks to find significant positive-NPV investments for much longer. Five years from now, Starbucks will have a much greater market penetration than it already does. In addition, it is possible that smaller coffee chains will merge, creating a more difficult competitive environment for Starbucks.

We now discuss how each assumption value was determined.

Revenue Growth

Starbucks has enjoyed tremendous growth in revenues over the past six years. As is common for any high-growth business, its rate of growth has been declining. Year-to-year growth was 50% in 1996 versus 29.1% in 2000. As young companies grow, it is impossible for them to maintain the same growth rate indefinitely. Despite a slight increase in the revenue growth rate in 2000, we expect Starbucks' revenue growth rate to continue to decline but that subsequent drops in the growth rate will be less severe. Our free cash flow forecast reflects this expectation. We project 2001 revenue growth at 27%, declining two percentage points per year thereafter. This is reasonable given the pattern in revenue growth over the last few years.

A CLOSER LOOK

Gathering the Information on Starbucks

How Did We Find Data on Starbucks?

To begin our business analysis, we wanted to learn as much as we could about Starbucks' business, its industry, and its competitors. We studied Starbucks' 1998 through 2000 annual reports, including a detailed review of the financial statements, the notes, and all the nonfinancial data. We also reviewed many analyst reports on Starbucks and read the *Value Line* report on Starbucks and its industry. We searched the Internet for news about Starbucks and information about its competitors and studied the information on Starbucks' Web site.

What Information Was Missing?

In most business analyses, some desired information will be unavailable. There is limited information about Starbucks' competitors, because there are no other major publicly traded coffee chains. Although there are many local competitors, there is no national chain with a large number of outlets and a large specialty business. As a result, most analysts place Starbucks in the restaurant industry. Although some restaurant trends may be helpful in understanding Starbucks, the company is different enough that restaurant industry data are of limited value.

Major Business Issues Affecting our Analysis

When we prepare a business and financial statement analysis of a company for use in a valuation, we work to develop many historical financial ratios and similar data. It is important to remember that all the quantitative data we compile are just measurements of the business results. We want to make sure that we are concentrating on understanding the business with the help of these numbers. To keep us focused on the business issues, we keep a log of business questions and issues uncovered during our analysis. We use this log as a "reality check" when finalizing our forecast and valuation, and we consider these issues during sensitivity analysis. Here is a summary of the business issues found during our Starbucks business and financial statement analysis.

- Starbucks has experienced tremendous growth. How does such a high growth level affect each of our projections? How long can this growth continue? Does the high growth mean that financial data from two or more years ago may not be representative for the future?
- Starbucks has many local competitors, but few national competitors. Will Starbucks' success attract new players into this market? Could the existing competitors merge or grow to be a more important force in the market?
- How much is the consumer willing to pay for a cup of Starbucks coffee? Will Starbucks be able to raise prices if coffee costs increase?
- Will Starbucks be able to staff its stores adequately? Historically, low unemployment rates have made attracting competent staff in low-paying food service positions difficult.

The answers we have for these questions are not necessarily right, but they do affect the value we place on the company. Our valuation model is a way to quantify the valuation implications of all our assumptions about what the future holds for this company.

EXHIBIT 10.3   Historical Analysis, Initial Free Cash Flow Forecast, and Valuation of Starbucks

	1994	1995	1996	1997	1998	1999	2000
				Historical Data			
Revenue growth (gs)		0.633	0.500	0.398	0.342	0.284	0.291
Gross margin percentage (gm)			0.518	0.552	0.558	0.559	0.560
Operating expenses to revenues (a)			0.434	0.462	0.468	0.468	0.472
Effective income tax rate on core operations (τ^{CORE})			0.378	0.389	0.385	0.386	0.410
Change in depreciation and amortization ($\Delta DEPR$)				19,426	22,037	26,611	34,659
Deferred taxes to income tax provision (δ)			0.206	0.165	0.052	0.022	(0.017)
Incremental working capital ratio (w)				0.055	0.046	(0.062)	(0.015)
Maintenance capital spending factor (c)							
Incremental fixed capital ratio (f)				0.421	0.341	0.461	0.372
Discount rate (k_c)							0.1123
Growth in perpetuity (g_p)							
($ THOUSANDS)							
Net revenues	284,923	465,213	697,872	975,389	1,308,702	1,680,145	2,169,218
Cost of sales and related occupancy costs	(336,658)	(436,942)	(578,483)	(741,010)	(953,560)	(1,214,914)	
Gross margin			361,214	538,447	730,219	939,135	1,215,658
Operating expenses			(302,704)	(450,206)	(613,107)	(785,616)	(1,023,706)
Operating income ***			58,510	88,241	117,112	153,519	191,952
Income taxes			(22,136)	(34,284)	(45,130)	(59,255)	(78,659)
NOPAT			36,374	53,957	71,982	94,264	113,293
Depreciation and amortization			39,438	58,864	80,901	107,512	142,171
Deferred income taxes, net			4,554	5,648	2,340	1,310	(1,342)
Change in working capital			55,361	(15,397)	(15,263)	23,083	7,205
Capital expenditures			(164,961)	(175,748)	(194,621)	(278,806)	(324,219)
Free cash flow			(29,234)	(72,676)	(54,661)	(52,637)	(62,892)

Present value of forecasted free cash flow (value of core operations)		2,150,709
Short-term investments		61,336
Joint ventures		52,051
Other investments	From economic	3,788
Current maturities of long-term debt	balance sheet.	(685)
Long-term debt		(6,483)
		2,260,716
Minority interest		(7,041)
Employee stock options		**
Value of common equity		2,253,675
Number of shares outstanding (thousands)		188,158
Value per share		11.98

---

* First year of perpetuity period.
** Ignored in this valuation. Employee stock options will be discussed in Chapter 14.
*** Before merger expenses in 1998.

		Forecast Data			
2001	**2002**	**2003**	**2004**	**2005**	**2006[*]**
0.270	0.250	0.230	0.210	0.190	0.040
0.559	0.559	0.559	0.559	0.559	0.559
0.469	0.469	0.469	0.469	0.469	0.469
0.385	0.385	0.385	0.385	0.385	0.385
36,000	38,000	40,000	42,000	44,000	0
0.030	0.030	0.030	0.030	0.030	0.000
0.020	0.020	0.020	0.020	0.020	0.020
1.000	1.000	1.000	1.000	1.000	1.000
0.400	0.400	0.400	0.400	0.400	0.000
					0.030
2,754,907	3,443,634	4,235,670	5,125,161	6,098,942	6,342,900
(1,518,643)	(1,867,930)	(2,260,196)	(2,689,633)	(2,797,219)	
1,539,993	1,924,991	2,367,740	2,864,965	3,409,309	3,545,681
(1,292,051)	(1,615,064)	(1,986,529)	(2,403,701)	(2,860,404)	(2,974,820)
247,942	309,927	381,211	461,264	548,905	570,861
(95,458)	(119,322)	(146,766)	(177,587)	(211,328)	(219,781)
152,484	190,605	234,445	283,677	337,577	351,080
178,171	216,171	256,171	298,171	342,171	342,171
2,864	3,580	4,403	5,328	6,340	0
(11,714)	(13,775)	(15,841)	(17,790)	(19,476)	(4,879)
(412,447)	(491,662)	(572,985)	(653,967)	(731,683)	(342,171)
(90,642)	(95,081)	(93,807)	(84,581)	(65,071)	346,201
(81,491)	(76,851)	(68,166)	(55,257)	(38,219)	2,470,693

Calculation of terminal value:

2006 free cash flow	346,201
Divided by cost of capital less perpetuity growth	0.0823
	4,206,574
Discounted five years to present	1.7025885
Present value of perpetuity	2,470,693

Minority interest:	
Book value of minority interest	3,588
Book value of core operations and nonoperating net assets less debt claims (net value)	1,151,987
Ratio of minority interest to net value	0.0031146
Fair value of core operations and nonoperating net assets less debt claims	2,260,716
Estimated fair value of minority interest	7,041

At this point, we have not done much detailed analysis of revenue growth. We simply start with some realistic projections and complete the model, believing it to be preferable to construct a base model like this first. In Section 10.3's discussion of model refinements, we will take a deeper look at Starbucks' expected revenue growth and replace our initial forecast with a more detailed one. We will use segment data, the management discussion and analysis from the 2000 annual report, and other public information to make a more detailed revenue forecast.

Gross Margin Percentage

Starbucks' gross margin percentage has been fairly stable historically, so we are comfortable with a projection around the average level of 55.9% over the last three years. When we refine our revenue growth forecast using segment data, we will also examine whether margin percentages vary by segment. If they do, and the segments are growing at different rates, we would expect changes in the overall gross margin percentage due to a "mix effect," even if margin percentages were not changing for any segment.

Operating Expenses to Revenues

The operating expenses to revenues ratio is stable in the historical periods. This suggests that these are mostly variable costs and that a percentage of revenue is a reasonable way to model them. Because most of these expenses are part of store operating expenses, we believe a stable percentage of revenue is a reasonable way to forecast these expenses. We use the average ratio over the last three years of 46.9%. Note that to calculate our historical ratios, we excluded merger expenses of $8,930,000 that Starbucks reported in 1998. By eliminating these nonrecurring expenses, we obtained a more realistic assessment of operating expenses in future periods.

Effective Income Tax Rate on Core Operations

Our free cash flow forecast captures only the core operations. So, the tax rate we use must be the effective tax rate on the income generated by the core operations. Rather than using Starbucks' overall effective tax rate, we use the ratio of income taxes on core operations to income from core operations. Our free cash flow analysis provides the necessary information to make this calculation.

In the free cash flow analysis, we eliminated all elements of income and the tax provision that do not relate to core operations. This left us with the portion of the income tax provision pertaining to core operations and the pretax earnings on those same core operations. These are the numerator and denominator we need to calculate the historical effective tax rate related to core operations. For Starbucks, this results in a fairly stable tax rate, mostly in the high 30s. We can use the information we get from the historical tax rate on core operations to project income taxes going forward. We use a forecasted tax rate of 38.5%, which is in line with recent years.

Note that in Chapter 5 we calculated Starbucks' effective tax rate in fiscal 2000 to be 41.1%, whereas Exhibit 10.3 shows a rate of 41.0%. This difference is because in Exhibit 10.3 we calculated the effective tax rate *on core operations*, not for the entire company. Although this is a minor difference, it illustrates that the company's effective tax rate and the effective tax rate on core operations are not the same thing. Further, this difference resulted from two larger, offsetting effects: the removal of joint venture income at a low marginal tax rate due to the dividend exclusion, and the removal of investment losses, a portion of which had no associated income tax benefit recorded due to the valuation allowance. The difference between the effective tax rate on core operations and for the firm as a whole can be larger.

Change in Depreciation

Depreciation is a difficult item to model formally, because doing so requires very detailed information about asset lives and depreciation methods. However, depreciation levels tend to be stable over time, because depreciation depends on prior capital expenditures and is not influenced by changes in the current operating environment. We note the recent year-over-year changes in depreciation and project depreciation to continue to grow at slightly increasing amounts. This growth in depreciation is consistent with the growth in fixed capital that we project via capital expenditures.

Deferred Taxes to Income Tax Provision

We model deferred taxes as a percentage of the income tax provision. We note this has been a fairly small ratio in recent years. Given that we do not expect a significant change in the kinds of assets Starbucks holds, we expect this ratio to remain fairly low. We forecast it at 3 percent of the income tax provision during the forecast horizon.

Incremental Working Capital Ratio

We model the change in working capital as a percentage of the change in sales. The retail operations, which is most of Starbucks' business, is a cash business, so the company's accounts receivable are low, and they do not increase significantly as the company's revenues increase. Therefore, we expect this ratio to be low. We project the change in working capital to be about 2 percent of the change in revenues.

Maintenance Spending Factor and Incremental Fixed Capital Ratio

Fixed capital is a much more important component of Starbucks' reinvestment requirements than is working capital. Most of the company's growth is through new stores, and each new store requires a substantial investment. We project a cost of 40 cents in incremental fixed capital to support each dollar of incremental revenues, consistent with the historical relationship between incremental fixed capital and revenue growth. We project maintenance capital costs to be equal to depreciation ($c = 1.00$), because there has not been substantial inflation since Starbucks put its fixed capital in place, and these assets are not subject to large technological improvements.

Forecasting the Perpetuity

As discussed earlier in this section, we assume that in the perpetuity period the firm maintains its physical capacity but makes no incremental investments. We then forecast a free cash flow stream that is feasible, given the level of physical capacity implied by the capital expenditure forecast as of the beginning of the perpetuity period. This does not mean that we actually expect growth to fall to this level or that there will be no growth in physical capacity. However, we assume that investments made in the perpetuity period are zero net present value projects, due to the eventual dissipation of competitive advantage. Any real growth for Starbucks would require an incremental investment. We assume that in the perpetuity period, the cost of the investment would be exactly equal to the present value of the cash flows it is expected to generate. The effect of these investments on Starbucks' value is zero. So, ignoring them does not affect the valuation, and it is far simpler to assume no real growth than to include these zero-NPV investments in the free cash flow forecast.

We have already forecast five years of free cash flow, from 2001 to 2005. We must now forecast a feasible free cash flow stream for 2006 and beyond. We will forecast 2006 explicitly and then set a perpetual growth rate for the years after that. We lowered revenue growth substantially in the perpetuity, to 4% for 2006 and to 3% in perpetuity after that. We assume no growth in physical capacity after 2005 and therefore no real growth in revenues. We assumed 3% inflation in the long run, which is consistent with the inflation expectations implicit in current interest rates. We forecast gross margin percentage, operating expenses as a percent of revenues, and the tax rate to hold steady in the perpetuity.

In the perpetuity period, we assume capital expenditures will consist of only maintenance spending. We accomplish this by setting the change in depreciation ($\Delta DEPR$) and the f parameter to zero in the perpetuity. We also set the maintenance capital expenditures factor c to 1, indicating that the cost of a unit of physical capacity has not changed. This results in capital expenditures equal to depreciation. If we believed that the cost to maintain productive capacity had changed since the depreciating assets were purchased, we would have set the parameter c to a different value, resulting in a different amount for capital expenditures.

We use a deferred tax parameter of zero in the perpetuity period, resulting in zero deferred taxes. Deferred taxes most often arise when the firm is growing and its tax depreciation, which is usually computed using an accelerated method, exceeds book depreciation. In the perpetuity period, growth is minimal, so deferred taxes will not arise. This does not mean the firm will not have a deferred tax liability, only that it will not be adding to it.

In most cases working capital increases will be required in the perpetuity period. If sales increase modestly due to inflation, the level of accounts receivable and other working capital items are likely to increase. We project w to remain at 2% in the perpetuity period. Some analysts set the w parameter, in addition to f and δ, to zero in the perpetuity period. When this is done, free cash flow is equal to NOPAT. As a result, a common procedure is simply to use NOPAT in the perpetuity and not to forecast anything below that line. Doing so relies on the assumption that all those parameters are zero and that c is 1. It is important to consider whether those are appropriate assumptions in the circumstances before simply using NOPAT in the terminal value calculation. A common misconception is that the free cash flow model is not really a cash flow model because it uses NOPAT in the perpetuity. In fact, the free cash flow model uses free cash flow in the perpetuity. Under the above assumptions, free cash flow and NOPAT are identical in the perpetuity period, so using NOPAT is the same as using free cash flow.

Computing the Results

Once we have the forecast model and assumptions, the spreadsheet calculates the value of the core operations using standard present value formulas. In Exhibit 10.3, we arrived at a value of $2,150,709,000 for the core operations. To arrive at the value of Starbucks' equity, we must add the value of nonoperating net assets and subtract the value of debt and other capital claims. After adding nonoperating assets and subtracting debt, we get a value of $2,260,716,000. This represents the combined value of Starbucks' equity, minority interest, and employee stock options. Using the procedure described in Chapter 6, we assume the ratio of minority interest to the total of core operations plus nonoperating net assets less debt is the same on a fair value basis and a book value basis. The calculation of minority interest of $7,041,000 is shown on the bottom right of Exhibit 10.3. After subtracting the minority interest, we have a value for Starbucks' equity of $2,253,675,000.[7] We divide this amount by the number of shares outstanding on the valuation date, 188,158,000, to arrive at a per share value of $11.98.[8]

Once we calculate these results, we should do a reasonableness check. Because we have focused on each of the separate assumptions, we want to be sure that the total results are logical. Do the projected results make sense given our business and financial statement analysis? Next, we are ready to analyze the results. We consider what assumptions are most important or are most likely to be inaccurate and consider ways to find more precise estimates.

---

[7] We have ignored the value of employee stock options for now. Because the value of an option depends on the value of the underlying stock and the value of the stock depends on the value of the employee stock options, calculating this value is rather complicated. We address this problem in Chapter 14.

[8] Note that we do not use the weighted-average number of shares outstanding from the earnings per share calculation, but the actual number outstanding on the valuation date.

A Closer Look

How Much History Is Adequate?

In our example, we studied five years of historical information. Is that the right amount? There is no clear answer to this question. Analysts may use three, five, ten, or even more years of data to help project the future. In considering how much historical data to obtain, we should first consider whether history will be indicative of the future. We must know enough about the firm, its market, and the industry to know whether past trends will continue. Is there a big change in the competitive environment, customer demands, or technology that will make history less relevant?

Historical information generally is less valuable for firms or industries in the early stages of development. For example, relying heavily on historical information for Amazon.com would not be sensible because this firm has seen tremendous change since its inception, due to tremendous growth, a move into additional product lines, and a change in the company's distribution strategy. Amazon's ratios are likely to continue to change until the company reaches a more mature and stable position. In contrast, historical information for USX Corporation, a 100-year-old steel company in a mature industry, might be more useful. Historical information also can be more useful for some variables than for others. Often, future margins and reinvestment ratios are more consistent with history than are sales trends. We saw that Starbucks' margins and reinvestment rates have been much more stable than its revenue growth and so relied more heavily on historical ratios for these parameters than for revenue growth.

10.3 Refine the Model

After initially building a basic model, we may find that we can do a better job of modeling the underlying causes and effects of one or more items in the model. We may then choose to refine the model by doing a more detailed analysis of part of it. For example, we could refine components of the Starbucks free cash flow forecast and valuation by:

- Separating the analysis into two or more business units using segment data
- Separating a ratio into two or more parts
- Linking the analysis to external or economy-wide forecasts

Exhibit 10.4 illustrates how two submodels will "feed into" our basic free cash flow forecast model for Starbucks. We will analyze revenues and costs of sales by segment and use these forecasts in our refined valuation model.

Every refinement has its costs and benefits. We will therefore want to put more detail into some parts of the model than others. Generally, the cost of a refinement is the need for more data and more complex modeling; the benefit is a more accurate forecast. These costs and benefits must be weighed against each other. In particular, a refinement will not be worth the cost when it has little impact on the forecast. For example, it is not useful to separate revenues and operating income fore-

EXHIBIT 10.4   Free Cash Flow Detailed Submodels

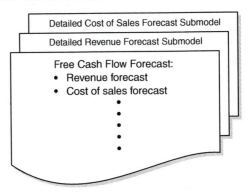

casts by product line when there is no reason to believe different product lines will have different revenues growth rates or margin percentages. We will arrive at the same forecast despite doing the additional work. Similarly, small product lines may have so little impact on the firm as a whole that considering them separately is not worth the effort.

In discussing sensitivity analysis, we will examine how changes in our assumptions affect the valuation. This analysis will also provide useful information about which components of the forecast to focus on and possibly refine. Assumptions that prove to have little effect on value need not be refined, whereas the more important ones are likely candidates for additional analysis.

Separating the Analysis into Two or More Business Units

For firms operating in more than one line of business, we may value each business unit separately and add the values. Even if we value the firm as a single entity, we may improve our valuation by separating the analysis by business unit or product line for key items in the forecast. For example, we might separate the sales forecast of a food products company into sales to grocers and sales to other food manufacturers. The forecast of grocery sales might be linked to population growth estimates, whereas sales to other food manufacturers might be linked to forecasts of that industry's growth. We would then re-aggregate our forecasts to arrive at the company's revenue and cost of sales forecasts. Meanwhile, the rest of the forecast can still be done as a single unit.

In order to forecast by business unit, we will want to study historical results by business unit. We can use segment reporting disclosures to disaggregate historical sales and margins by business unit. SFAS No. 131 requires firms to disaggregate financial information by segment and to identify segments the same way they do for internal management reporting and decision making. Firms must disclose detailed information any individual segment that meets at least one of the "10% tests,"[9] including the following:

1. Financial Information[10]
   - External revenue
   - Intersegment revenue

---

[9]The "10% tests" are:
- The segment's revenue is at least 10% of the combined revenues of all operating segments.
- The absolute amount of the segment's income or loss is 10% or more of the absolute amount of the greater of
  - the combined profit of all segments reporting a profit
  - the combined loss of all segments reporting a loss
- The segment's assets are 10% or more of the combined assets of all operating segments.

[10]This information is required if it is included in the measure of segment profit or loss. For example, if interest expense is not included in segment profit or loss, it need not be disclosed by segment.

- Depreciation, amortization, and depletion
- Significant noncash items other than depreciation, amortization, and depletion
- Interest expense
- Interest revenue
- Income tax expense or benefit
- Unusual items and extraordinary items
- Equity in net income of equity method investees
- Total assets
- Reconciliations to consolidated data

2. Descriptive Information
   - General information about the segment, including the factors used to identify reportable segments
   - Basis of measurement information (such as how intersegment transactions are accounted for)
   - Products and services

Some companies may provide more detail than the required disclosures. Many also provide segment data in other sections of their annual reports, such as the management discussion and analysis.

Separating Ratios

Rather than disaggregating by business unit (or perhaps in addition to it), we often separate a particular ratio into two or more component ratios. Using several different ratios to model an element of the free cash flow forecast may improve the forecast's accuracy. For example, rather than forecasting a revenue growth rate, we might forecast volume growth and price increases. In that case, the revenue forecast for period t would become

$$REV_t = REV_{t-1} \cdot (1 + v_t) \cdot (1 + p_t)$$

In this formula, v_t is the rate of growth in volume and p_t is the rate of growth in prices. Disaggregating the sales growth rate allows us to consider the two factors separately. If the two factors are likely to interact, it is important that they be internally consistent. For example, if we forecast large volume gains, then we need to consider how those gains will be achieved. If it is through price cuts, we must factor that into the forecast using the price parameter.[11] These assumptions also must be consistent with assumptions for other variables. If we forecast strong volume growth, there may be a need for substantial advertising expense. If price cuts are forecast, gross margin percentages will be lower.

If we model sales growth using volume and price growth rather than a single growth rate, then it may make sense to refine the computation of cost of sales as well. Obviously, volume growth will affect cost of sales. But price increases do not necessarily mean higher cost of sales, nor do price decreases necessarily mean lower cost of sales. If we expect cost increases that cannot be passed on to customers, then we would expect margin percentages to decline. If we expect the average cost of the product to decrease as sales grow, due to economies of scale, the cost of sales will not grow at the same rate as sales, and margin percentages will increase. Cost of sales could be forecast as follows:

$$COS_t = COS_{t-1} \cdot (1 + v_t) \cdot (1 + u_t)$$

---

[11]An advanced way to model volume and price would be to model the relationship between them. For example, one could write v_t as a function of p_t, rather than as a parameter to be set. This would ensure internal consistency between the two.

Here u_t is the growth rate in per unit cost of sales, and v_t is the same volume growth used in the revenue forecast.[12]

Linking the Analysis to External or Economy-Wide Forecasts

Another way to refine a forecast is to use information from the outside and an assumption about the relationship between this external item and a component of the free cash flow forecast. Analysts commonly use this approach for forecasting sales, because demand for many firms' products depends on outside factors such as gross domestic product, discretionary income, industry demand, and so on. Some possible ways to forecast sales using external information are listed here. Analysts may consider more than one of these approaches at a time and develop a forecast based on a combination of these methods.

- Use an economist's forecast of the growth in the total market demand for the firm's products and forecast the firm's market share. Sometimes the analyst develops a projection for market demand based on a combination of historical market trends, economic projections, and relevant population growth.

$$TOTALMARKET_t = TOTALMARKET_{t-1} \cdot (1 + gmd_t)$$
$$REV_t = TOTALMARKET_t \cdot ms_t$$

Here $TOTALMARKET$ is total market demand, gmd is an economic forecast of growth in the market demand, and ms is forecasted market share.

- Use an economist's forecast of a key indicator of demand for the firm's products to determine growth in sales. For example, a construction products firm such as Lafarge North America Inc. might base its sales forecasts on forecasts of housing starts. A supplier of steel pipe used by oil drillers such as Lone Star Technologies might link its sales forecasts to forecasts of the number of oil rigs operating.

- Use forecasts of sales for an industry that is a leading indicator of demand for your own. For example, automobile sales lead replacement battery demand in a fairly predictable way. For simplicity, say that 30% of batteries fail after three years, 30% after four years, and 40% after five years. We might forecast sales for the automotive replacement battery division of Johnson Controls as follows.

$$BATTERYMARKET_t = 0.3 \cdot AUTOS_{t-3} + 0.3 \cdot AUTOS_{t-4} + 0.4 \cdot AUTOS_{t-5}$$
$$REV_t = BATTERYMARKET_t \cdot ms_t \cdot PRICE_t$$

The firm first forecasts the total demand for replacement batteries using both actual and forecasted results for the number of automobiles sold. It then multiplies this total demand by forecasted market share and average price.

Refining the Starbucks Forecast

We now refine our forecast and valuation of Starbucks. First, we note from our original analysis that the most uncertain element of the forecast is revenue growth. We expect revenue growth to slow. We can gain an understanding of how quickly this is likely to occur by examining Starbucks' segment data, presented in Exhibit 10.5.[13] In addition, although margin percentages have held steady in the

---

[12]In some industries, it is possible to get price and volume information from publicly available sources. For example, information on retail grocery product sales is collected and sold. This data can be very useful in making forecasts using a more detailed model.
[13]The exhibit shows data from both the 1999 and 2000 segment disclosures.

past, if our segment analysis reveals different margins in different segments and different growth rates across segments, then we would expect a change in Starbucks' overall margin percentages.

For segment reporting, Starbucks divides its business into the North American retail segment and all other business units. North American retail includes all company-owned stores in North America. "All other business units"[14] includes licensed stores, company-owned stores outside North America, and a specialty business that sells coffee through grocery stores and other outlets, and licenses the Starbucks name for use on other food products containing Starbucks coffee. Historically, Starbucks' two business segments have had different growth rates and margin percentages.

Revenue Projections

Exhibit 10.6 summarizes disaggregated historical revenue information from Starbucks' 2000 annual report (Exhibit 10.5) and its 1999 annual report. Note that segment information is available only for 1997 to 2000. Starbucks adopted SFAS No. 131 in 1999 and provided only the required three years of historical data.[15] Exhibit 10.6 also shows forecasted revenue data by segment for 2001 to 2006.

EXHIBIT 10.5   Excerpts from Starbucks' 1999 and 2000 Segment Disclosures

Fiscal year ended	October 1, 2000	October 3, 1999	September 27, 1998	September 28, 1997
REVENUES:				
North American retail	$ 1,734,929	$ 1,375,018	$ 1,076,731	$ 828,074
All other business units	457,496	320,604	238,798	152,564
Intersegment revenues	(23,207)	(15,477)	(6,827)	(5,249)
Total revenues	$ 2,169,218	$ 1,680,145	$ 1,308,702	$ 975,389
OPERATING INCOME:				
North American retail	$ 249,924	$ 209,338	$ 161,334	$ 121,673
All other business units	97,100	55,998	45,943	29,566
Unallocated corporate expenses	(134,902)	(107,460)	(89,069)	(65,040)
Merger expenses			(8,930)	
Intersegment eliminations	130	(1,165)	(62)	
Interest and other income, net	7,110	7,315	7,134	5,111
Internet-related investment losses	(58,792)			
Total earnings before income taxes	$ 160,570	$ 164,026	$ 116,350	$ 91,310
DEPRECIATION AND AMORTIZATION:				
North American retail	$ 94,312	$ 72,252	$ 56,328	$ 42,526
All other business units	13,664	7,766	4,721	2,379
Unallocated corporate expenses	22,256	17,779	11,494	7,896
Total depreciation and amortization	$ 130,232	$ 97,797	$ 72,543	$ 52,801
INCOME (LOSSES) FROM EQUITY METHOD INVESTEES:				
All other business units	$ 15,139	$ 2,318	$ (14)	$ (2,760)
Intersegment eliminations	5,161	874	1,048	718
Total income from equity method investees	$ 20,300	$ 3,192	$ 1,034	$ (2,042)

[14]Under SFAS No. 131, operating segments not meeting any of the 10% tests are aggregated and reported as a single segment called "all other business units" or a similar name.

[15]Although there were segment disclosure rules prior to SFAS No. 131, Starbucks was not required to provide any disaggregated data under those rules.

EXHIBIT 10.6   Starbucks' Revenue Information by Segment

($ thousands)	Historical Data						
Net Revenues	1994	1995	1996	1997	1998	1999	2000
North American retail				828,074	1,076,731	1,375,018	1,734,929
All other business units				152,564	238,798	320,604	457,496
Intersegment revenues (1)				(5,249)	(6,827)	(15,477)	(23,207)
Total	284,923	465,213	697,872	975,389	1,308,702	1,680,145	2,169,218
REVENUE GROWTH							
North American retail					30.0%	27.7%	26.2%
All other business units					56.5%	34.3%	42.7%
Total		63.3%	50.0%	39.8%	34.2%	28.4%	29.1%
NUMBER OF STORES (2)							
North America:							
Company-operated	399	627	929	1,270	1,622	2,038	2,446
Licensed	26	49	75	94	133	179	530
Total	425	676	1,004	1,364	1,755	2,217	2,976
International:							
Company-operated	0	1	9	31	66	97	173
Licensed	0	0	2	17	65	184	352
Total	0	1	11	48	131	281	525
Grand Total	425	677	1,015	1,412	1,886	2,498	3,501
Average number of North American retail (company-operated) stores open during year		513.0	778.0	1,099.5	1,446.0	1,830.0	2,242.0
North American retail sales per average number of stores open				753	745	751	774
Growth in North American retail sales per average number of stores open					−1.1%	0.9%	3.0%
STORE GROWTH							
North American retail (company-operated)			48.2%	36.7%	27.7%	25.6%	20.0%

(1) Sales between Starbucks' business segments. These are eliminated from the consolidated totals because they are not transactions with outside entities.
(2) Historical information taken from "Selected Financial Data" section of Starbucks' annual report.

To analyze Starbucks' historical revenue data, we focus on North American retail and examine average sales per store and the average number of stores open using data from the Selected Financial Data section of the annual report. The analysis shows that Starbucks' tremendous revenue growth over the last several years is due almost entirely to the increase in the number of stores. The average number of North American retail stores has more than doubled from 1997 to 2000 (1,099.5 versus 2,242) while the average sales per store has held steady ($753,000 versus $774,000).

Starbucks' 2000 annual report states that the company plans to open at least 450 more company-operated stores in North America in fiscal 2001. We note that in 1999 Starbucks forecast that it would open at least 350 stores in North America in 2000, but the increase was actually 408. We forecast that Starbucks would repeat its 20% growth in North American retail stores, which translates to 489 new stores in the 2001.

	Forecast Data				
2001	2002	2003	2004	2005	2006
2,144,329	2,626,379	3,164,040	3,708,718	4,237,428	4,755,828
608,470	791,011	1,004,584	1,255,730	1,544,548	1,868,903
(30,424)	(39,551)	(50,229)	(62,787)	(77,227)	(93,445)
2,722,375	3,377,839	4,118,395	4,901,661	5,704,749	6,531,286
23.6%	22.5%	20.5%	17.2%	14.3%	12.2%
33.0%	30.0%	27.0%	25.0%	23.0%	21.0%
25.5%	24.1%	21.9%	19.0%	16.4%	14.5%
2,935	3,463	4,017	4,499	4,949	5,345
2,690.5	3,199.0	3,740.0	4,258.0	4,724.0	5,147.0
797	821	846	871	897	924
3.0%	3.0%	3.0%	3.0%	3.0%	3.0%
20.0%	18.0%	16.0%	12.0%	10.0%	8.0%

Based on the downward trend in the growth rate of stores in North America, we have slowed the growth in North American stores during the forecast horizon. We forecasted continuing nominal growth in sales per average number of stores open. We then used the forecasted average number of stores open and the forecasted sales per North American store to determine the forecasted sales level. For example, the average number of stores open in North America in 2001 would be 2,690.5 (average of 2000's and 2001's end-of-year stores of 2,446 and 2,935, respectively). At forecasted average sales of $797,000 per store, revenues for the segment are forecast to be $2,144,329,000, for a 23.6% growth in sales.

We forecast the "all other" business segment to grow at 33% in 2001 and then begin to drop the sales growth rate as the business matures. We used a percentage of all other to forecast intersegment sales, because these sales are related to the specialty business. Intersegment sales were about 5% of all other in 2000, and we used 5% of all other to forecast intersegment sales. This combination of growth provides an estimate that is just above 25% total revenue growth for 2001.

Operating Margin Projections

Exhibit 10.7 is an analysis of operating income based on Starbucks' segment data. It shows that Starbucks' consolidated operating margin has been stable over the past four years at about 9%. However, this stability has been the result of two offsetting effects. First, operating margin in all other has declined from 21.2% in 1997 to 17.9% in 2000. At the same time, revenues of the all other segment revenues have grown faster than those of North American retail. Despite its declining margin, all other still has higher margins than North American retail, so its higher growth rate has shifted the mix of Starbucks' revenue to the higher margins of the all other segment. The net effect has been stable margins on a consolidated basis.

We forecast continued stable operating income margin on North American retail at 15%. We forecast the operating income margin on all other to level off at 18%, and unallocated corporate expenses to be 6.4% of consolidated sales.

Exhibit 10.8 shows the revised Starbucks' valuation using these refined assumptions is $13.07 per share, versus $11.98 in our original analysis. In this case, the refinement had only a moderate effect (9%) on the value, because our growth and margin assumptions in the original analysis were not too far from what the more detailed analysis showed. This is not always the case. Refinements can have substantial effects on valuations.

10.4   SENSITIVITY ANALYSIS

Sensitivity analysis is a critical part of the valuation process. A valuation is only as good as the assumptions used to build the forecast, and we need to understand how a change in any of our assumptions affects value. For example, a new competitor in the market could cause a business to lose volume and force it to lower price, destroying value.

We calculate many sensitivities. This step provides a range of potential valuations based on different assumptions. Although it is possible to do a sensitivity analysis with either a very narrow or a very wide range of assumptions, sensitivity analysis is most meaningful when the range of assumptions covers the most extreme (both positive and negative) deviations from the base case that could reasonably occur. Thus we usually consider a very optimistic case and a worst case. Using our business judgment and analysis, we try to understand the likelihood of each case. This analysis allows us to consider the extent to which the correctness of our decisions depends on the possible errors in our analysis. The sensitivity analysis also quantifies the cost we will incur should these assumptions prove incorrect.

Analysts commonly use four types of sensitivity analysis: single-assumption sensitivity analysis, combined sensitivity analysis, scenario-based sensitivity analysis, and reverse valuation.

Single-Assumption Sensitivity Analysis

In its simplest form, sensitivity analysis might be done on single assumptions. For example, we might calculate what would happen if revenues were higher or lower than what we projected in the base case forecast. We would also compute similar sensitivities on other important forecast assumptions, such as operating margin. Using the refined Starbucks valuation as the base case, the sensitivities for revenues and margins would look like Exhibit 10.9.

In the first set of sensitivities, we changed revenues. For example, if we increased the revenues 10% over the revenue projection in the base case in every year of the forecast period, our value per share would be $13.88 instead of $13.07 in the base case.

A CLOSER LOOK

Qwest and U S WEST Merger Analysis

In 2000, Qwest Communications International Inc. and U S WEST, two large communication firms, merged. Prior to the merger, the firms' investment bankers each valued the transaction using the free cash flow model and the multiples model. The results of the free cash flow analysis, along with other financial analysis, were presented to shareholders before they voted on the merger agreement. Here are excerpts from the proxy.

This section discusses the valuation of U S WEST by Donaldson, Lufkin and Jenrette Securities Corporation (DLJ), for Qwest. The excerpt mentions EBITDA, which is earnings before interest, taxes, depreciation and amortization.

> Discounted Cash Flow Analysis. DLJ performed a discounted cash flow analysis of U S WEST based on the internal estimates of management of U S WEST in order to estimate the net present value of the unlevered, after-tax cash flows that U S WEST could generate for the remainder of fiscal year 1999 through fiscal year 2005. Applying discount rates of 9.0% to 11.0% and multiples of terminal year 2005 EBITDA of 8.0x to 10.0x, this analysis produced an implied equity reference range for U S WEST of approximately $76.00 to $109.00 per share, as compared to the equity value for U S WEST implied in the merger of approximately $69.00 per share based on the closing stock price of Qwest common stock on July 14, 1999.

This section reviews the valuation of Qwest by Merrill Lynch, Pierce, Fenner & Smith, Inc. and Lehman Brothers Inc., the investment bankers of U S WEST.

> Discounted Cash Flow Analysis. The U S WEST financial advisors performed a discounted cash flow analysis of the projected after-tax unlevered free cash flows of Qwest. The U S WEST financial advisors calculated a range of present values for Qwest based upon the discounted present value of the sum of the projected stream of after-tax unlevered free cash flows of Qwest and the projected terminal value of Qwest based upon a range of multiples of Qwest's EBITDA. Applying discount rates ranging from 10.0% to 12.0% and terminal value multiples of 12.0x to 14.0x, the U S WEST financial advisors calculated implied equity values per share of Qwest common stock ranging from $36.00 to $47.00, as compared to a market price per share of Qwest common stock of $34.00 on July 14, 1999.

Source: Joint proxy statement/prospectus, September 17, 1999.

In the second set of sensitivities shown in Exhibit 10.9, we adjusted the operating margin percentage. For example, if we increased the operating margin percentage by one point over the gross operating percentage in the refined base case in every year of the forecast period, the value per share will be $15.08.

Exhibit 10.9 indicates that the valuation is sensitive to these assumptions, especially to the margin assumption. A range of ±2% on margins gives a value range of $9.05 to $17.09 per share. We would compute similar single-assumption sensitivities on other variables as well.

EXHIBIT 10.7   Starbucks Operating Income Information by Segment

$ thousands	1997	1998	1999	2000
NORTH AMERICAN RETAIL				
Net Revenues	828,074	1,076,731	1,375,018	1,734,929
Operating Income	121,673	161,334	209,338	249,924
Operating Income Margin	14.7%	15.0%	15.2%	14.4%
ALL OTHER BUSINESS UNITS				
Net Revenues	152,564	238,798	320,604	457,496
Operating income as reported	29,566	45,943	55,998	97,100
Adjustment to remove joint venture (profits) and losses (2)	2,760	14	(2,318)	(15,139)
Operating Income	32,326	45,957	53,680	81,961
Operating Income Margin	21.2%	19.2%	16.7%	17.9%
INTERSEGMENT ELIMINATIONS				
Net Revenues	(5,249)	(6,827)	(15,477)	(23,207)
Operating Income	(718)	(1,110)	(2,039)	(5,031)
NET REVENUES				
North American Retail	828,074	1,076,731	1,375,018	1,734,929
All Other	152,564	238,798	320,604	457,496
Intersegment eliminations	(5,249)	(6,827)	(15,477)	(23,207)
Total Net Revenues (after intersegment eliminations)	975,389	1,308,702	1,680,145	2,169,218
OPERATING INCOME				
North American Retail	121,673	161,334	209,338	249,924
All other (net of joint venture profits and losses)	32,326	45,957	53,680	81,961
Intersegment eliminations	(718)	(1,110)	(2,039)	(5,031)
Subtotal	153,281	206,181	260,979	326,854
Unallocated corporate expenses	(65,040)	(89,069)	(107,460)	(134,902)
Operating Income (1)	88,241	117,112	153,519	191,952
Intersegment eliminations as % of all other revenues	−0.5%	−0.5%	−0.6%	−1.1%
Unallocated corporate expense as % of total revenues	−6.7%	−6.8%	−6.4%	−6.2%
Consolidated operating margin	9.0%	8.9%	9.1%	8.8%

(1) Before merger expenses in 1998.
(2) The amount of joint venture profit and loss assigned to the all other business unit was taken from Starbucks' segment disclosure. See Exhibit 10.5.

Combined Sensitivity Analysis

Although single-assumption sensitivities can be helpful, variables do not usually change one at a time. Changes in advertising affect sales volume and operating expenses. A new competitor can cause decreases in both margin and revenues. Combined sensitivities alter assumptions on two or more variables at the same time. For these sensitivities, we can prepare a matrix. This gives a different picture than the single-assumption sensitivities because many of the assumptions in a free cash flow

Forecast Data					
2001	2002	2003	2004	2005	2006
2,144,329	2,626,379	3,164,040	3,708,718	4,237,428	4,755,828
321,649	393,957	474,606	556,308	635,614	713,374
15.0%	15.0%	15.0%	15.0%	15.0%	15.0%
608,470	791,011	1,004,584	1,255,730	1,544,548	1,868,903
109,525	142,382	180,825	226,031	278,019	336,403
18.0%	18.0%	18.0%	18.0%	18.0%	18.0%
(30,424)	(39,551)	(50,229)	(62,787)	(77,227)	(93,445)
(6,085)	(7,910)	(10,046)	(12,557)	(15,445)	(18,689)
2,144,329	2,626,379	3,164,040	3,708,718	4,237,428	4,755,828
608,470	791,011	1,004,584	1,255,730	1,544,548	1,868,903
(30,424)	(39,551)	(50,229)	(62,787)	(77,227)	(93,445)
2,722,375	3,377,839	4,118,395	4,901,661	5,704,749	6,531,286
321,649	393,957	474,606	556,308	635,614	713,374
109,525	142,382	180,825	226,031	278,019	336,403
(6,085)	(7,910)	(10,046)	(12,557)	(15,445)	(18,689)
425,089	528,429	645,385	769,782	898,188	1,031,088
(174,232)	(216,182)	(263,577)	(313,706)	(365,104)	(418,002)
250,857	312,247	381,808	456,076	533,084	613,086
−1.0%	−1.0%	−1.0%	−1.0%	−1.0%	−1.0%
−6.4%	−6.4%	−6.4%	−6.4%	−6.4%	−6.4%
9.2%	9.2%	9.3%	9.3%	9.3%	9.4%

forecast may be interdependent. Exhibit 10.10 shows combined sensitivities of the Starbucks revenues and margin assumptions.

As is typical, value is much more sensitive to changes in revenue levels when operating margin percentage is high. If revenues are 20% higher than in the refined base case, value is $1.63 per share higher. But, when margins are two points higher, the same extra revenue results in $2.43 ($19.52 − $17.09) per share of additional value. Conversely, when margins are two points lower, the effect of the additional sales is only $0.83 ($9.88 − $9.05) per share.

EXHIBIT 10.8 Free Cash Flow Forecast and Valuation of Starbucks Using Refined Revenue and Margin Assumptions

				Historical Data			
	1994	1995	1996	1997	1998	1999	2000
Effective income tax rate on core operations (τ^{CORE})			0.378	0.389	0.385	0.386	0.410
Change in depreciation and amortization ($\Delta DEPR$)				19,426	22,037	26,611	34,659
Deferred taxes to income tax provision (δ)			0.206	0.165	0.052	0.022	(0.017)
Incremental working capital ratio (w)				0.055	0.046	(0.062)	(0.015)
Maintenance capital spending factor (c)							
Incremental fixed capital ratio (f)				0.421	0.341	0.461	0.372
Weighted-average cost of capital (k_c)							0.1123
Growth in perpetuity (g_P)							
($ THOUSANDS)							
Net revenues	284,923	465,213	697,872	975,389	1,308,702	1,680,145	2,169,218
Operating income ***			58,510	88,241	117,112	153,519	191,952
Income taxes			(22,136)	(34,284)	(45,130)	(59,255)	(78,659)
NOPAT			36,374	53,957	71,982	94,264	113,293
Depreciation and amortization			39,438	58,864	80,901	107,512	142,171
Deferred income taxes, net			4,554	5,648	2,340	1,310	(1,342)
Change in working capital			55,361	(15,397)	(15,263)	23,083	7,205
Capital expenditures			(164,961)	(175,748)	(194,621)	(278,806)	(324,219)
Free cash flow			(29,234)	(72,676)	(54,661)	(52,637)	(62,892)
Present value of forecasted free cash flow (value of core operations)							2,356,655
Short-term investments							61,336
Joint ventures							52,051
Other investments							3,788
Current maturities of long-term debt							(685)
Long-term debt							(6,483)
							2,466,662
Minority interest							(7,683)
Employee stock options							**
Value of common equity							2,458,979
Number of shares outstanding (thousands)							188,158
Value per share							13 .07

* First year of perpetuity period.
** Ignored in this valuation. Employee stock options will be discussed in Chapter 14.
*** Before merger expenses in 1998.

	Forecast Data					
	2001	2002	2003	2004	2005	2006*
	0.385	0.385	0.385	0.385	0.385	0.385
	36,000	38,000	40,000	42,000	44,000	0
	0.030	0.030	0.030	0.030	0.030	0.000
	0.020	0.020	0.020	0.020	0.020	0.020
	1.000	1.000	1.000	1.000	1.000	1.000
	0.400	0.400	0.400	0.400	0.400	0.000
						0.030
	2,772,375	3,377,839	4,118,395	4,901,661	5,704,749	6,531,286
	250,857	312,247	381,808	456,076	533,084	613,086
	(96,580)	(120,215)	(146,996)	(175,589)	(205,237)	(236,038)
	154,277	192,032	234,812	280,487	327,847	377,048
	178,171	216,171	256,171	298,171	342,171	342,17
	2,897	3,606	4,410	5,268	6,157	0
	(12,063)	(12,109)	(14,811)	(15,665)	(16,062)	(16,531)
	(419,434)	(458,357)	(552,393)	(611,477)	(663,406)	(342,171)
	(96,152)	(58,657)	(71,811)	(43,216)	(3,293)	360,517
	(86,444)	(47,411)	(52,183)	(28,233)	(1,934)	2,572,860

Calculation of terminal value:

2006 free cash flow	360,517
Divided by cost of capital less perpetuity growth	0.0823
	4,380,522
Discounted five years to present	1.7025885
Present value of perpetuity	2,572,860

Minority interest:

Book value of minority interest	3,588
Book value of core operations and nonoperatingnet assets less debt claims	1,151,987
Ratio of minority interest to net value	0.0031146
Fair value of core operations and nonoperating net assets less debt claims	2,466,662
Estimated fair value of minority interest	7,683

EXHIBIT 10.9   Single-Assumption Sensitivities for Revenues and Operating Margin Percentage

	Change in Revenues Relative to Refined Base Case				
	−20%	−10%	No Change	+10%	+20%
Value per share	$ 11.44	$ 12.25	$ 13.07	$ 13.88	$ 14.70
Deviation from base case	$ (1.63)	$ (0.82)	$ 0.00	$ 0.81	$ 1.63
	Change in Operating Margin Percentage Relative to Refined Base Case				
	−2 points	−1 point	No Change	+1 point	+2 points
Value per share	$ 9.05	$ 11.06	$ 13.07	$ 15.08	$ 17.09
Deviation from base case	$ (4.02)	$ (2.01)	$ 0.00	$ 2.01	$ 4.02

Exhibit 10.11 illustrates these sensitivities graphically. Note that the value (height of bar) increases more from either additional revenues or additional operating margin when the value of the other is higher.

Scenario-Based Sensitivity Analysis

In a scenario-based sensitivity analysis, we change our assumptions based on a specific event. Scenario-based sensitivity analysis requires an assessment of how every assumption might change given a different set of circumstances. If we were concerned that a new competitor might enter the market, we would recalculate the value of the firm using assumptions consistent with this scenario. Revenue growth and operating margin percentage might decline as the competitor takes market share and forces prices lower. Other operating expenses might increase as the firm responds by increasing its advertising and promotion.

EXHIBIT 10.10   Combined Sensitivity for Revenues and Operating Margin Percentage

	Share Values	Change in Revenues Relative to Refined Base Case				
		−20%	−10%	No Change	+10%	+20%
Change in Operating Margin Percentage Relative to Refined Base Case	−2 points	$ 8.23	$ 8.64	$ 9.05	$ 9.46	$ 9.88
	−1 point	$ 9.83	$ 10.45	$ 11.06	$ 11.67	$ 12.29
	No change	$ 11.44	$ 12.25	$ 13.07	$ 13.88	$ 14.70
	+1 point	$ 13.05	$ 14.06	$ 15.08	$ 16.09	$ 17.11
	+2 points	$ 14.65	$ 15.87	$ 17.09	$ 18.30	$ 19.52
	Deviations from Base Case	Change in Revenues Relative to Refined Base Case				
		−20%	−10%	No Change	+10%	+20%
Change in Operating Margin Percentage Relative to Refined Base Case	−2 points	$ (4.84)	$ (4.43)	$ (4.02)	$ (3.61)	$ (3.19)
	−1 point	$ (3.24)	$ (2.62)	$ (2.01)	$ (1.40)	$ (0.78)
	No change	$ (1.63)	$ (0.82)	$ 0.00	$ 0.81	$ 1.63
	+1 point	$ (0.02)	$ 0.99	$ 2.01	$ 3.02	$ 4.04
	+2 points	$ 1.58	$ 2.80	$ 4.02	$ 5.23	$ 6.45

EXHIBIT 10.11   Combined Sensitivity for Revenues and Operating Margin Percentage

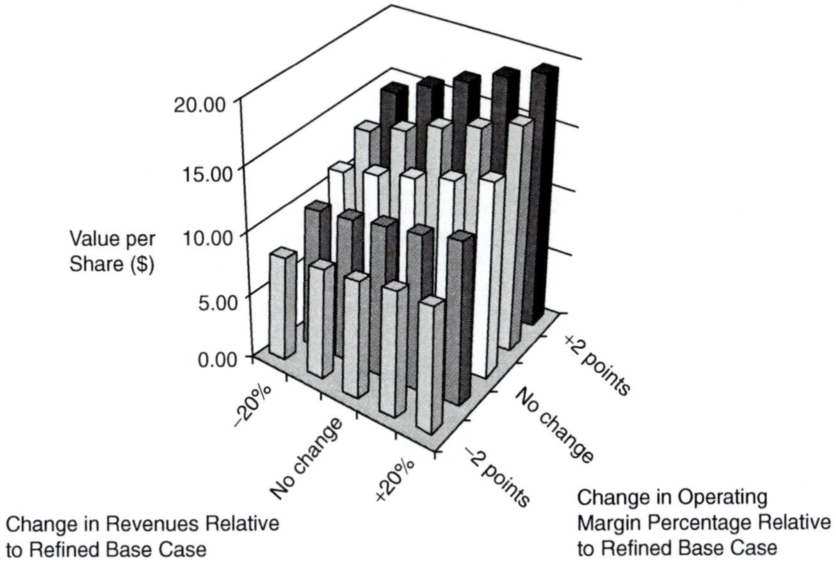

Reverse Valuation

Although we have focused on interpreting sensitivity analysis as a way to think about the potential error in our result, there is another way to use sensitivity analysis. In *Expectations Investing*,[17] Alfred Rappaport and Michael Mauboussin suggest a sort of reverse valuation approach. In this approach, you determine the assumptions that would justify the current stock price and then base the investment decision on whether such assumptions are reasonable. For example, Starbucks closed fiscal 2000 at $40.0625 per share. This suggests that the market is pricing Starbucks as if it will have higher growth, higher margins, and/or lower capital reinvestment requirements than in our projections, or with vastly different assumptions elsewhere in the analysis. This is not to say the market price is wrong. It illustrates only that the market has made different assumptions. If we assume eight years of positive-NPV projects rather than five, 30% revenue growth for the eight years, 9.5% operating margins, and a 10% fixed capital reinvestment rate, we get a value of about $40 per share.

---

[17]A. Rappaport and M. Mauboussin, *Expectations Investing: Reading Stock Prices for Better Returns* (Boston: Harvard Business School Press, 2001).

SUMMARY

A forecast valuation model is a set of equations that describe how each element of free cash flow behaves. The structure of the model, together with the assumptions that we make, determines the forecast, which, in turn, determines the estimated value of the firm. In a good model, the ratios that drive the model relate two components of the cash flow forecast that have a cause-and-effect relationship. By specifying the model in this way, we can change one assumption with the knowledge that other elements of the forecast that are affected will also change automatically.

In addition to creating a model, we must set the assumptions for the model. This is where we use our business judgment, together with the business analysis and an analysis of the historical relationships, to quantify our beliefs about the firm's future. The assumptions we make must be both reasonable and internally consistent, meaning each assumption must be a realistic assessment of the future and all assumptions must be realistic given all other assumptions. Internal consistency is most easily maintained when the model is as close as possible to specifying the actual cause-and-effect relationships among the components of free cash flow.

Once the basic model is designed, we may want to refine it. Refinements are additional, more detailed analyses about specific elements of the forecast. This might involve separating the analysis of operating earnings into separate business units, separating a particular assumption into two or more component assumptions, or linking the analysis to external forecasts about the economy as a whole or a particular product market.

Sensitivity analysis reminds us that although our spreadsheet produces a single amount for the valuation, we should think of it as a range of values. In a single-assumption sensitivity analysis, we calculate a range of values given optimistic and pessimistic values for the assumption. In a combined sensitivity analysis, we vary two or more assumptions simultaneously. In a scenario-based sensitivity analysis, we recalculate value given some event, such as a new entrant in the market. Finally, in a reverse valuation, we "back into" the assumptions that are consistent with the observed market price and assess whether these are reasonable.

SUGGESTED READINGS

Hanke, J., D. Wichern, and A. Reitsch. *Business Forecasting*, 7th ed. Upper Saddle River, NJ: Prentice Hall, 2001.

Rappaport, A. and M. Mauboussin. *Expectations Investing: Reading Stock Prices for Better Returns*. Boston: Harvard Business School Press, 2001.

REVIEW QUESTIONS

1. Describe the four stages of the forecasting and valuation process.
2. Forecasts should be both reasonable and internally consistent. What do these terms mean and why are they important for developing a good forecast?
3. How would you model cost of goods sold in a manufacturing firm?

4. How do we model capital expenditures?

5. How do we determine the number of years, N, for which we develop an explicit forecast?

6. How do we model the change in working capital?

7. How many years of history should we study in preparation for developing our forecasted ratios?

8. How can we use segment data to refine our forecast model?

9. What is sensitivity analysis and how does sensitivity analysis help us to develop a good valuation?

10. What are scenario-based sensitivities?

11. What is reverse valuation?

PROBLEMS

1. You are constructing a free cash flow model to value a possible acquisition target. Your manager has asked you to consider two ways to forecast sales as part of the free cash flow forecast. These are:

$$SALES_t = SALES_{t-1} \cdot (1 + gs_t)$$
$$SALES_t = SALES_{t-1} \cdot (1 + v_t) \cdot (1 + p_t)$$

gs_t is growth rate in sales in period t, v_t is growth rate in volume in period t, and p_t is growth rate in price in period t.

Draft a memo to discuss the pros and cons of each approach.

2. Suppose you are using the second of the two formulas in problem 1 to forecast sales. Draft a memo explaining how this choice would affect how you should forecast cost of sales.

3. Consider a firm in an industry in which technology improvements are constantly lowering its cost of physical capacity. On average, the cost to acquire a unit of physical capacity drops by about 15% per year and is expected to continue to do so for the foreseeable future. Fixed assets are depreciated on a straight-line basis over five years and, if not for the dropping cost of capacity, would represent a reasonable estimate of the amount of capital investment necessary to maintain capacity at the existing level.

   Construct formulas that could be used in a free cash flow forecast model to determine the amount of depreciation and capital expenditures in a given year. Assume that sales have already been forecasted and are represented by $SALES_t$.

4. Airlines are a mostly fixed cost business. That is, the cost of operating a flight is almost completely insensitive to the number of passengers on board. Thus, load factor, the percentage of seats sold, is a critical variable for airlines.

   Consider a revenue forecast for an airline that is constructed as follows:

   $REVENUES_t = FLIGHTS_t \cdot AVGSEATS_t \cdot LOAD_t \cdot AVGPRICE_t$, where
   $FLIGHTS_t$ = the number of flights in period t
   $AVGSEATS_t$ = the average number of passenger seats per flight in period t
   $LOAD_t$ = the average load factor (seats sold / seats available) in period t
   $AVGPRICE_t$ = the average ticket price in period t

a. For which components of the revenue formula do you think historical information will be most useful for forecasting?

b. How might you break out revenues by product line for a typical airline?

c. How would you forecast flight costs?

Following are the income and cash flow statements from The May Company's fiscal 1997 annual report. Use this information for problems 5 through 7.

Consolidated Statement of Earnings

(dollars in millions)	1997	1996	1995
Net Retail Sales	$ 12,352	$ 11,546	$ 10,402
Revenues	12,685	12,000	10,952
Cost of sales	8,732	8,226	7,461
Selling, general, and administrative expenses	2,375	2,265	2,081
Interest expense, net	299	277	250
Total cost of sales and expenses	11,406	10,768	9,792
Earnings from continuing operations before income taxes	1,279	1,232	1,160
Provision for income taxes	500	483	460
NET EARNINGS FROM CONTINUING OPERATIONS	779	749	700
Net earnings from discontinued operation	—	11	55
Net earnings before extraordinary loss	779	760	755
Extraordinary loss related to early extinguishment of debt, net of income taxes	(4)	(5)	(3)
Net earnings	$ 775	$ 755	$ 752

Consolidated Statement of Cash Flows

(dollars in millions)	1997	1996	1995
OPERATING ACTIVITIES:			
Net earnings from continuing operations	$ 779	$ 749	$ 700
Net earnings from discontinued operation	—	11	55
Extraordinary loss related to early extinguishment of debt, net of income taxes	(4)	(5)	(3)
Net earnings	775	755	752
Adjustments for noncash items included in earnings:			
Depreciation and amortization	412	374	333
Noncurrent deferred income taxes	58	45	42
Deferred and unearned compensation	8	10	15
Working capital changes*	265	142	(330)
Other assets and liabilities, net	8	(43)	(6)
Total Operating Activities	1,526	1,283	806

continued

continued

(dollars in millions)	1997	1996	1995
INVESTING ACTIVITIES:			
Capital expenditures	(496)	(632)	(801)
Dispositions of property and equipment	33	29	20
Goodwill	—	—	(89)
Other	—	—	(1)
Cash provided by (used in) discontinued operation	—	(24)	42
Total Investing Activities	(463)	(627)	(829)
FINANCING ACTIVITIES:			
Issuances of long-term debt	—	800	600
Repayments of long-term debt	(340)	(388)	(156)
Purchases of common stock	(394)	(869)	(71)
Issuances of common stock	65	49	57
Dividend payments	(297)	(305)	(296)
Total Financing Activities	(966)	(713)	134
INCREASE (DECREASE) IN CASH AND CASH EQUIVALENTS	97	(57)	111
CASH AND CASH EQUIVALENTS, BEGINNING OF YEAR	102	159	48
CASH AND CASH EQUIVALENTS, END OF YEAR	$ 199	$ 102	$ 159
*Working capital changes comprise:			
Accounts receivable, net	$ 262	$ 139	$ 29
Merchandise inventories	(53)	(211)	(321)
Other current assets	46	45	13
Accounts payable	(30)	180	(43)
Accrued expenses	26	(20)	(8)
Income taxes payable	14	9	—
Net decrease (increase) in working capital	$ 265	$ 142	$ (330)
Cash paid during the year:			
Interest	$ 319	$ 288	$ 268
Income taxes	355	380	448

5. Determine historical parameter values for fiscal 1996 and 1997 that relate incremental fixed capital to incremental sales. Assume depreciation is a reasonable estimate of the cost to replace physical capacity and that The May Company has no capitalized interest. Further assume that the amortization portion of "depreciation and amortization" in the cash flow statement is negligible. Treat the disposition of property and equipment as a "negative capital expenditure."

6. Assuming you forecast fiscal 1998 sales to grow by 10% and that depreciation will be $450 million in 1998, forecast capital expenditures (net of dispositions of property and equipment) for fiscal 1998 using the incremental capital to incremental sales approach. Use the historical parameter from fiscal 1996 to forecast 1998.

7. In converting the 1997 income statement and cash flow statement to a free cash flow basis, you removed the $299 million of interest expense from earnings (and therefore

from operating cash flow). You also must adjust the provision for income taxes for the related tax effect. In doing so, the $500 million income tax provision reported under GAAP becomes what amount on a free cash flow basis? (Assume a 39% marginal tax rate and no other adjustments to the income tax provision.)

8. Obtain the financial statements for a public company from the SEC's Web site (**www.sec.gov**). (Your instructor may select a company for the class.) Develop a forecast model for sales through operating income and set assumptions. Justify your assumptions.

My Case

Develop the forecast model and set assumptions for your company. Use the weighted-average cost of capital you developed in Chapter 7 to value the core operations. Adjust this value for nonoperating net assets, debt, and other capital claims to arrive at your company's equity value and value per share. Continue to ignore retirement plans and employee stock options.

11

 Where We Have Been:

We have studied the dividend discount, flows to equity, and free cash flow models.

 Where We Are:

We now examine the adjusted present value model. The adjusted present value model uses the same forecasted cash flow stream as the free cash flow model, but captures the effect of leverage on value in a different way. The adjusted present value model will result in the same value as the other cash flow models, given the same assumptions.

 Where We Are Going:

In Chapter 12, we examine the final cash flow model, the residual income model.

The Adjusted Present Value Model

LEARNING OBJECTIVES:

After reading this chapter, you will understand:

- How the adjusted present value model works.

- The different ways in which the free cash flow and adjusted present value models capture the valuation benefits of leverage.

- The Modigliani-Miller Propositions on capital structure irrelevance.

- How the "side effects" of leverage can affect firm value.

- How the relationship between the marginal corporate tax rate, the marginal tax rate on personal interest deductions, and the marginal tax rate on personal income from equity securities determine the tax benefits of leverage for a firm.

- How to estimate the value of leverage to a firm.

- How financial distress can affect a firm's value.

- The pros and cons of the adjusted present value model.

Having completed our discussion of the most commonly used valuation model, the free cash flow model, as well as the dividend discount and flows to equity models, we now examine the adjusted present value (APV) model. Some people prefer the APV model to the free cash flow model, even though the two give equivalent results, because APV highlights the extent to which the value of the firm has been enhanced by the use of financial leverage in the capital structure.

Although this model is used less often than the free cash flow model, practitioners do use it, and the analyst should understand it. Because the model highlights the value of leverage, understanding the model requires understanding the relationship between value and leverage.

In Section 11.1, we introduce the APV model. Section 11.2 shows the similarities and differences between the APV and free cash flow models. Because the APV model focuses on the effect of leverage, we must understand how leverage creates value. The keys to this are the Modigliani-Miller Propositions on the irrelevance of capital structure reviewed in Section 11.3. These propositions state that leverage itself does not affect firm value, but that certain "side effects" of leverage may affect value. The most important of these are taxes, the cost of financial distress, and operating effects of leverage. Section 11.4 examines these side effects and how they affect the cost of capital and the value of the firm. In Section 11.5, we discuss the pros and cons of the adjusted present value model.

11.1 THE ADJUSTED PRESENT VALUE MODEL

The APV model highlights the effect of financial leverage on the firm. **Financial leverage** is the use of debt in a firm's capital structure. Exhibit 11.1 illustrates the APV model.

EXHIBIT 11.1   Cash Flows and the Firm—The Adjusted Present Value Model

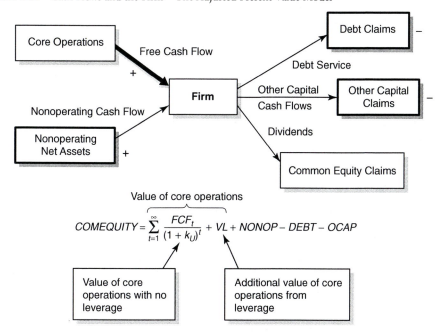

As the exhibit shows, the APV model estimates the value of core operations in two parts. The first is the value the core operations would have if the firm were unlevered, meaning it had no debt. To determine this amount, we discount the forecasted free cash flow stream at the unlevered cost of equity, k_U, the cost of equity the firm would have if it were financed entirely with equity. We saw how to estimate this rate in Chapter 7's discussion of discount rates. The second portion of the value of core operations is the additional value it has as a result of financial leverage.

11.2   COMPARING THE FREE CASH FLOW AND ADJUSTED PRESENT VALUE MODELS

We use the same cash flow forecast in the free cash flow and APV models. Given identical assumptions, the free cash flow and APV models produce identical results. The only difference between the two valuation models is the way they capture the value created by leverage. The APV model highlights the extent of the value created by leverage.

Exhibit 11.2 illustrates the similarities and differences between the free cash flow model and the APV model. The free cash flow model values the core operations by discounting the free cash flow stream at the weighted-average cost of capital (WACC). The APV model instead discounts these cash flows at the unlevered cost of equity and then adds the value that was created by leverage. In both cases, we add the value of nonoperating net assets and subtract the value of debt and other capital claims to reach the value of the firm's equity.

A simple example using the two models will illustrate how they are related. Exhibit 11.3 provides the assumptions for the example. Exhibit 11.4 shows that Schuler's equity is worth $5,000 under either model, even though the value is calculated in different ways.

EXHIBIT 11.2   Comparison of Free Cash Flow and Adjusted Present Value Models

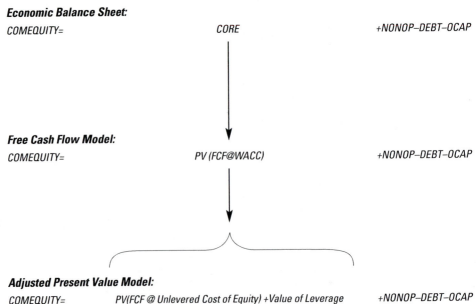

Economic Balance Sheet:

COMEQUITY=   CORE   +NONOP–DEBT–OCAP

Free Cash Flow Model:

COMEQUITY=   PV (FCF@WACC)   +NONOP–DEBT–OCAP

Adjusted Present Value Model:

COMEQUITY=   PV(FCF @ Unlevered Cost of Equity) +Value of Leverage   +NONOP–DEBT–OCAP

EXHIBIT 11.3 Schuler Company Valuation Information

Pretax cost of debt	7.69%
Corporate tax rate	35%
Weighted-average cost of capital	10%
Cost of common equity	15%
Unlevered cost of equity	10.753%
Value of nonoperating net assets	$0
Value of debt	$5,000
Value of other capital claims	$0
Value of leverage	$700
Annual free cash flow in perpetuity	$1,000

Under the free cash flow model, Schuler's value would be determined by (1) discounting the free cash flows at the weighted-average cost of capital, (2) adding the value of nonoperating net assets, (3) subtracting the value of debt, and (4) subtracting the value of other capital claims. In our example, because the annual free cash flow is constant, we can calculate its present value using a perpetuity. Schuler has no nonoperating net assets or other capital claims, so its equity value is just the $10,000 present value of free cash flow less the $5,000 of debt.

Under the APV model, we calculate value by (1) discounting the free cash flows at the unlevered cost of equity, (2) adding the value of leverage, (3) adding the value of nonoperating net assets, (4) subtracting the value of debt, and (5) subtracting the value of other capital claims. This time, the present value of free cash flow is only $9,300, because it does not reflect the lower cost of capital Schuler enjoys due to its use of leverage. We then add the $700 benefit from leverage to arrive at the same value for core operations as in the free cash flow model, again resulting in a $5,000 value for equity.

Note that the additional value attributed to leverage under the APV model ($700) is exactly equal to the increase in value from using the weighted-average cost of capital in the free cash flow model rather than the unlevered cost of equity ($10,000 − $9,300 = $700). This is the essence of the relationship between the two models. The value effect of leverage is always the same. The two

EXHIBIT 11.4 Schuler Company Valuation Example

Schuler Company Valuation				
	Free Cash Flow Model		APV Model	
Annual free cash flow in perpetuity	$	1,000	$	1,000
Divided by relevant discount rate		0.10		0.10753
Present value of free cash flow at relevant discount rate		10,000		9,300
Value of leverage				700
Value of core operations		10,000		10,000
Value of nonoperating net assets		0		0
Value of debt		(5,000)		(5,000)
Value of other capital claims		0		0
Value of equity	$	5,000	$	5,000

models just capture it in different ways. The free cash flow model does so by applying a lower discount rate, 10% instead of 10.753% in our example, to the free cash flow stream. The APV model does it through a separate addition of $700 to the value of the firm.

11.3   THE MODIGLIANI-MILLER PROPOSITIONS AND VALUE

As we have just seen, the adjusted present value model requires calculating a value for leverage. You may have asked: How do we calculate the value of leverage? To answer this question, we will first study the Modigliani-Miller (MM) capital structure irrelevance propositions. From these propositions, we will be able to derive a formula for the value of leverage.

The MM Propositions explain how the value of an asset relates to how that asset is financed. These propositions are perhaps the most profound insights in modern corporate finance. In its original formulation, under the assumption of no taxes, no costs to financial distress, and no operating effects to leverage, MM says that leverage does not create value. The proposition shows that the combined value of a firm's debt and equity is independent of its capital structure. This can also be written as (assuming for simplicity no nonoperating net assets and no other capital claims)

$$COMEQUITY_L = COMEQUITY_U - DEBT \qquad (11.1)$$

where $COMEQUITY_L$ is the value of equity if the firm is levered, $COMEQUITY_U$ is the value of the same firm's equity if it is unlevered, and $DEBT$ is the amount of debt the firm has when it is levered.

This idea is to corporate finance what the law of the preservation of mass is to physics. Just as matter can change its form but cannot be created or destroyed, MM shows that changing the form of capital cannot create or destroy value. As capital structure changes, the amount, timing, and riskiness of the firm's aggregate cash flows available to all security holders is constant, so the combined value of these securities is unchanged. Because total value does not vary with leverage, the discount rate that equates the present value of the total forecasted cash flows with the combined value of the firm's debt and equity also must be insensitive to leverage. Note the relationship between value creation (or lack thereof) and the cost of capital. If for some reason value were created by leverage, we would observe a lower cost of capital as we increased the firm's leverage. That is, to obtain a higher present value for the firm's unchanged cash flows, we would have to use a lower discount rate. But, in a world with no taxes, no costs to financial distress, and no operating effects to leverage, increased leverage does not affect the weighted-average cost of capital or the total value of the firm.

But what about these assumptions of no taxes, no costs to financial distress, and no operating effects to leverage? If these assumptions were true, we would not need an adjusted present value model because there would be no value to leverage. Of course, we know that these assumptions are not true. We do have taxes, and debt and equity are taxed differently, suggesting a potential advantage to one form of capital over another. Financial distress is costly. Bankruptcy proceedings can involve enormous legal costs. In addition, financial distress may affect a company's ability to deal effectively with customers and suppliers, and also divert management's attention away from its operations. Finally, leverage can affect operating decisions because of the constraints it places on managers.

These deviations from the original MM assumptions can affect firm value through side effects of leverage. Although leverage itself does not create value, the side effects of leverage caused by the fact that the simplifying assumptions do not hold in the real world, may create value. Still, capital structure irrelevance is a very useful concept. MM helps us understand that a particular transaction does not create value simply because it increases leverage. Instead, leverage may cause side effects that create value.

If there were no benefits to leverage, it would be surprising to see so many firms using so much of it. After the original MM capital structure irrelevance proposition was published, people searched for explanations for the existence of leverage. They began by exploring what the value-creating side effects of leverage might be. The focus was on those assumptions in the original MM analysis that might not be true.

Side Effects: Taxes, Interest Expense, and Firm Value

Because we do live in a world with taxes, we need to refine the MM Proposition for taxes. In Appendix 11.1 we derive the MM formula with taxes, assuming the current debt level is maintained indefinitely. It is

$$COMEQUITY_L = COMEQUITY_U - DEBT + DEBT \cdot \left(1 - \frac{(1 - \tau_c) \cdot (1 - \tau_e)}{(1 - \tau_d)}\right) \qquad (11.2)$$

where τ_c is the marginal corporate tax rate, τ_d is the marginal tax rate on personal interest deductions, and τ_e is the marginal tax rate on personal income derived from equity.

The MM Proposition without taxes, equation (11.1), showed that leverage creates no value. It simply substitutes debt for equity. The MM Proposition with taxes, equation (11.2), shows that leverage does create value. Exhibit 11.5 compares the two versions of the MM Proposition.

In the presence of taxes, the value of a levered firm's equity is higher by the difference between these two expressions. We call this the value of leverage (VL), and it is equivalent to

$$VL = DEBT \cdot \tau^* \qquad (11.3)$$

where $\tau^* = 1 - \dfrac{(1 - \tau_c) \cdot (1 - \tau_e)}{(1 - \tau_d)}$ represents the gain in value per dollar of debt in the capital structure.

To calculate the value of τ^*, we must estimate the three tax rates. If we assume the statutory corporate tax rate of 35% for τ_c, the capital gains rate of 20% for individuals for τ_e, and the 39.6% max-

EXHIBIT 11.5   Comparison of MM Propositions With and Without Taxes

MM with taxes:

$$COMEQUITY_L = COMEQUITY_U - DEBT + DEBT \cdot \left[1 - \frac{(1 - \tau_c) \cdot (1 - \tau_e)}{(1 - \tau_d)}\right]$$

MM without taxes:

$$COMEQUITY_L = COMEQUITY_U - DEBT$$

Difference:

$$VL = DEBT \cdot \left[1 - \frac{(1 - \tau_c) \cdot (1 - \tau_e)}{(1 - \tau_d)}\right]$$

EXHIBIT 11.6   Schuler Company Example—Tax Effects of Leverage and Value

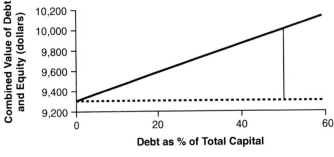

— Value of firm (debt and equity)
···· Unlevered value of firm

imum marginal income tax rate for individuals for τ_d, we find that $\tau^* = 0.14$. The increase in the value of the firm from leverage is 14% of the amount of debt incurred.

Exhibit 11.6 shows how the combined value of a firm's debt and equity varies with leverage as a result of tax benefits. This graph is based on the assumptions for the Schuler Company provided earlier in this chapter. It shows what Schuler's combined debt and equity value would be at various degrees of financial leverage. The horizontal dotted line represents the value Schuler would have if it were unlevered. In that case, it would not enjoy any of the tax benefits of leverage, and its equity would be worth $9,300. The solid line shows what Schuler's value would be at various levels of leverage. For example, at Schuler's actual 50% debt to capital ratio, its combined debt and equity is worth $10,000, resulting in $700 of value created.

Sample Calculation of the Value of Leverage—W. W. Grainger

W. W. Grainger, Inc., based in Lake Forest, Illinois, provides maintenance, repair, and operating supplies and related information to businesses and institutions. At December 31, 2000, W. W. Grainger, Inc.'s condensed balance sheet in millions of dollars was as shown in Exhibit 11.7. Assuming the book value of Grainger's debt approximates fair value, Grainger creates about $321.6 million times 14%, or $45.0 million of value due to its use of leverage. It had 93.9 million shares outstanding at December 31, 2000, so the value of leverage is about $0.48 per share, or 1.3% of its $36.50 stock price.

EXHIBIT 11.7   W. W. Grainger Condensed Balance Sheet

W. W. Grainger Condensed Balance Sheet December 31, 2000 ($ millions)		
Total assets	$	2,459.6
Debt	$	321.6
Other liabilities		600.6
Equity		1,537.4
	$	2,459.6

Side Effects: Financial Distress and Firm Value

Although we have explained how firms can create value by increasing leverage, we have a problem. If leverage adds value, we would expect to see many firms with nearly 100% leverage. Why is this not the case? Although the tax rate advantage might be pushing many firms toward more leverage, there comes a point where it is costly to become more levered. If one assumes that financial distress is costly,[1] due to legal costs and disruption of the business, then as the likelihood of financial distress increases with higher leverage, the higher expected financial distress costs offset the tax advantages of leverage. As the firm borrows more, increasing the probability of financial distress, the required expected rates of return increase to reflect these higher costs. Once financial distress is sufficiently likely that additional debt increases these expected costs by more than the value of the additional tax savings, additional leverage will actually reduce firm value. Thus, we would not expect to see many firms with near 100% leverage.[2]

One example of the costs of financial distress is that suppliers may not be willing to give trade credit. For example, after USG Corporation's leveraged recapitalization in 1987, it could not meet its financial obligations. Its suppliers may have required certified checks at the time material was delivered, so as not to become general creditors in a bankruptcy proceeding. This would be very disruptive to the firm's business.

Exhibit 11.8 shows the relationship between the combined values of debt and equity for Schuler Company when financial distress costs are considered. When leverage is low, there is little chance of distress, and the combined value of debt and equity (solid line) increases almost as much as if there

EXHIBIT 11.8 Schuler Company Example—Tax Effects of Leverage, Financial Distress, and Value

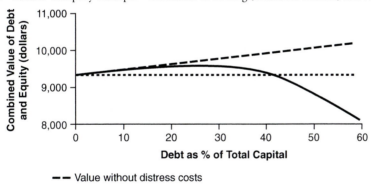

- -- Value without distress costs
- —— Value with distress costs
- ···· Unlevered value

---

[1]When we say financial distress is costly, this does not mean simply that the shareholders might lose their investment. Rather, we refer to net costs borne by all capital suppliers in the aggregate. A simple transfer of assets from shareholders to debtholders in a bankruptcy proceeding is not costly in this sense. It is the legal costs involved in resolving the situation, along with the disruption of the business that could occur, that make financial distress costly.

[2]In a leveraged buyout (LBO), the possibility of financial distress is very real. Investors are so concerned about possible financial distress costs that they will try to structure securities to minimize them. This is done by reducing differences in incentives among the various security holders, making it more likely that the firm would not be put into bankruptcy. In the extreme case, every capital supplier would hold both debt and equity in equal proportions to the proportions of total firm debt and equity. This gives capital holders the incentive simply to give the firm to the debtholders (themselves) or forgive debt to avoid insolvency, thereby incurring no legal or other costs in bankruptcy. This extreme case would be deemed to be an all-equity firm under Internal Revenue Service (IRS) rules, however; so LBO investors try to structure transactions to come as close to this ideal situation as possible without violating the IRS rules.

were no distress costs (dashed line). As leverage increases, so do distress costs, eventually lowering the combined value of debt and equity.

Once we consider financial distress, we see the firm no longer has an incentive to increase leverage indefinitely. At some point, the financial distress costs become large enough that they overshadow the tax benefits to leverage. Leverage beyond this point destroys value.

How does the side effect of financial distress costs affect the APV model? While we add the tax benefit of leverage to our valuation, we must also subtract this side effect of leverage, the cost of financial distress, at least in theory. Unfortunately, it is very difficult to quantify these costs and their effect on value. In practice, those analysts who use the APV model often ignore financial distress costs. This is not a significant problem for firms that are not highly levered and not likely to face financial distress. For highly levered firms or financially troubled firms, however, the APV model without consideration of financial distress costs overstates the value of equity.

Side Effects: Operating Decisions and Firm Value

The interaction between capital structure and operating decisions is another potential side effect of leverage. In financial analysis, we generally separate the analysis of capital structure or other purely financial decisions from operating decisions. Managers make financing decisions to minimize the firm's cost of capital, given its operating assets, and make operating decisions to maximize the value of the firm's cash flow stream, given its cost of capital. These two arenas are separate from each other, just as the decision on which mortgage loan to take is independent of which house you will buy.

However, there is evidence that capital structure can influence operating decisions. The tendency of firms to waste excess resources by investing in negative net present value projects such as unprofitable expansions and managerial perquisites is called the **agency cost of free cash flow**. For example, corporate jets, executive chauffeurs, and fancy meetings at resorts have questionable value to the firm. Highly levered firms reduce the agency cost of free cash flow because they precommit to return cash flows to capital providers through mandatory debt service payments. This forces firms that would otherwise waste excess cash to return the cash to investors, who presumably can invest the funds more profitably. On the other hand, highly levered firms may find themselves unable to obtain the resources to invest in positive-NPV projects they have access to. Thus, although capital structure may affect operating decisions, it is not always clear what that effect might be.

The analyst can include whatever effects he or she believes capital structure has on operating decisions under either the free cash flow model or the APV model. This is just a matter of forecasting free cash flows based on all the information the analyst has at hand, including how she perceives the capital structure to influence those operating decisions.

11.4 HOW LEVERAGE AFFECTS COST OF CAPITAL

We have seen that in the presence of taxes, leverage affects the value of the firm. This implies that any valuation ought to include the value the firm obtains from the tax benefit of its leverage, net of the expected financial distress costs and effects on operating decisions that result from its leverage. When we use the APV model, we do this by discounting the free cash flow stream at the unlevered cost of equity and then adding the value of the tax benefits, net of financial distress costs, to arrive

EXHIBIT 11.9   Schuler Company Example—Tax Effects of Leverage and Cost of Capital

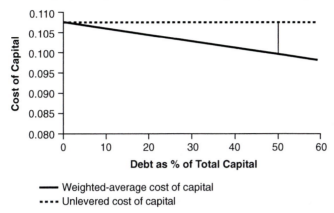

— Weighted-average cost of capital
···· Unlevered cost of capital

at the value of the core operations. The free cash flow model produces the same results as the APV model, so it must also capture the effect of leverage on value. It does so via the weighted-average cost of capital (WACC). Any benefits the firm captures from its financing will be reflected in a lower WACC and therefore a higher present value. So, we ought to observe a relationship between WACC and leverage that corresponds to the relationship seen between value and leverage.

We now explore graphically how leverage affects the cost of capital. Exhibit 11.9 illustrates how the cost of capital adjusts for the tax benefits of leverage. This plot ignores potential costs of financial distress. WACC, represented by the solid line, declines with leverage. The dashed line represents the unlevered cost of equity. This amount is the same as the firm's WACC when it is unlevered. The distance between the downward-sloping solid line and the horizontal dashed line at any degree of leverage represents the reduction in WACC due to leverage.

There is a direct relationship between the reduction in WACC as the firm levers, illustrated in Exhibit 11.9, and the increase in value, illustrated in Exhibit 11.6. As the required rate of return on the firm's assets (WACC) falls, the resulting value of the cash flows the assets will generate increases.

In Exhibit 11.10 we incorporate financial distress costs and reexamine how WACC varies with leverage. The horizontal line is still the unlevered cost of equity. The downward-sloping line is the WACC before considering financial distress. The U-shaped curve represents the WACC after

EXHIBIT 11.10   Schuler Company Example—Tax Effects of Leverage, Financial Distress, and Cost of Capital

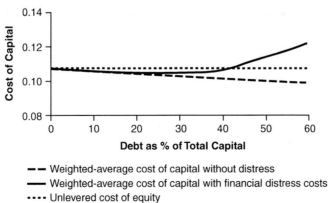

– – Weighted-average cost of capital without distress
— Weighted-average cost of capital with financial distress costs
···· Unlevered cost of equity

allowing for financial distress costs. After leverage becomes sufficiently high, the costs of financial distress become significant enough to outweigh the tax benefits to leverage. Thus, firms will not attempt to finance entirely with debt. Instead, they will try to be as close to the bottom of the U-shaped curve as possible. The trough of the curve is at the same level of leverage as the peak of the value curve in Exhibit 11.8. Choosing leverage to minimize the cost of capital is the same as choosing it to maximize value.

11.5   PROS AND CONS OF THE ADJUSTED PRESENT VALUE MODEL

The benefit of using the APV model is that it highlights the value created by leverage. If the analyst is interested in separating the value of leverage, the APV model provides this information, whereas the other cash flow models do not. In all other ways, the APV model is similar to the free cash flow model. Because the two models discount the same cash flow stream, the forecasting process cannot be any more or less difficult under one of these methods than the other.

One disadvantage of the APV model arises when the firm is levered enough that financial distress costs are an important consideration. In this case, some of the firm's cost of capital reflects the likelihood of incurring these financial distress costs. However, the formula used to estimate the unlevered cost of equity considers only the role of taxes, not the role of financial distress costs. As a result, the unlevered cost of equity will be misstated when potential financial distress costs are high, because the adjustment will not have eliminated the contribution of financial distress costs to the firm's levered cost of capital. In addition, estimating the dollar value of the financial distress costs to subtract from the leverage tax benefits is difficult. For example, an analyst valuing Polaroid or Bethlehem Steel in 2001 when these companies filed for Chapter 11 bankruptcy protection might have experienced the difficulty of estimating the cost of financial distress.

Finally, we can determine the value effects created by leverage and taxes without formally applying the APV model. If we equate the definitions of the free cash flow and adjusted present value models, we see that

$$\sum_{t=1}^{\infty} \frac{FCF_t}{(1+k_c)^t} = \sum_{t=1}^{\infty} \frac{FCF_t}{(1+k_U)^t} + VL \tag{11.4}$$

| Core operations under free cash flow model |

| Core operations under APV model |

Knowing this relationship, we can always infer the value of the free cash flows discounted at the unlevered cost of capital, $\sum_{t=1}^{\infty} \frac{FCF_t}{(1+k_U)^t}$, from the free cash flow model valuation, $\sum_{t=1}^{\infty} \frac{FCF_t}{(1+k_c)^t}$, and an estimate of the tax benefits and financial distress costs of leverage (VL). We need not actually calculate the unlevered cost of equity. This does not eliminate the need to estimate the tax benefits and financial distress costs if that is what we want to know, but it does reduce the complexity of calculating the unlevered value of the firm.

SUMMARY

The adjusted present value model focuses attention on the value created by leverage, because it incorporates this value as a dollar amount, rather than by applying a lower discount rate to the free cash flow stream. The APV model discounts the free cash flows at the cost of capital the firm would have if it had no debt and then adds the value obtained from leverage to get the value of core operations.

If properly applied, the free cash flow and adjusted present value models give identical results, and both reflect the value derived from the firm's financing strategy. Both models discount free cash flows. The free cash flow model incorporates the value of financing by using a lower weighted-average cost of capital than would otherwise be the case. The adjusted present value model incorporates the value directly as a dollar amount.

The key to understanding the APV model is understanding the Modigliani-Miller Propositions on capital structure irrelevance. MM argues that in the absence of taxes, financial distress costs, or operating effects of leverage, both value and the cost of capital are independent of capital structure. However, when one of these side effects exists, leverage can affect value and the cost of capital. The effect of leverage on value and the cost of capital are closely related. The free cash flow model captures these effects through the cost of capital, which affects value. The APV model captures the value directly.

The value of leverage comes primarily from the differential tax treatment of debt and equity capital, and depends on a combination of the marginal corporate tax rate, the marginal tax rate on personal interest deductions, and the marginal tax rate on personal income derived from equities. At current tax rates, the net value of leverage is about 14% of the value of the outstanding debt, assuming that debt is to remain outstanding indefinitely.

Financial distress costs and operating effects of leverage also can affect value. Financial distress costs are very difficult to estimate, and operating effects can be captured in the cash flows themselves.

SUGGESTED READINGS

Inselbag, I. and H. Kaufold. "Two DCF Approaches for Valuing Companies Under Alternative Financing Strategies (and How to Choose Between Them)." *Journal of Applied Corporate Finance* 10, 1(1997):114–122.

Miller, M. "Debt and Taxes." *Journal of Finance* 32 (May 1977):261–275.

Modigliani, F. and M. Miller. "Corporate Income Taxes and the Cost of Capital: A Correction." *American Economic Review* 53 (June 1963):433–443.

Modigliani, F. and M. Miller. "The Cost of Capital, Corporation Finance, and the Theory of Investment." *American Economic Review* 48 (June 1958):261–297.

Myers, S. "Interactions in Corporate Financing and Investment Decisions—Implications for Capital Budgeting." *Journal of Finance* 29 (March 1974):1–25.

Taggart, R. "Consistent Valuation and Cost of Capital Expressions with Corporate and Personal Taxes." *Financial Management* 20, 3(1991):8–20.

REVIEW QUESTIONS

1. What are the main differences between the adjusted present value model and the free cash flow model?

2. What is the main conclusion of the original Modigliani-Miller capital structure irrelevance proposition, which ignores taxes?

3. What are the side effects of leverage?

4. Describe the costs of financial distress.

5. How can leverage affect operating decisions?

6. Assuming no costs to financial distress, what happens to the weighted-average cost of capital when leverage increases?

7. Including the costs of financial distress, what happens to the weighted-average cost of capital when leverage increases?

8. Under what circumstances would an analyst prefer the adjusted present value model to the free cash flow model?

9. What is the disadvantage of the adjusted present value model?

10. What information do you need to know to calculate the value of leverage?

PROBLEMS

1. Calculate the value of leverage for Cruise Company and Kidman Company, whose economic balance sheets are shown. Assume the marginal corporate tax rate is 35%, the marginal tax rate on personal income derived from equity is 20%, and the marginal tax rate on personal interest deductions is 39.6%. Assume no costs to financial distress and no operating effects to leverage.

Cruise Company
Condensed Economic Balance Sheet
December 31, 2001

Assets	$ 1,000,000	Debt	$	700,000
		Equity		300,000
		Total Debt and Equity	$	1,000,000

Kidman Company
Condensed Economic Balance Sheet
December 31, 2001

Assets	$ 1,000,000	Debt	$	200,000
		Equity		800,000
		Total Debt and Equity	$	1,000,000

2. Here is the forecasted free cash flow for Smiley, Inc. for the next 10 years. Free cash flow is expected to grow at a rate of 3% per year beginning in year 11. Smiley's weighted-aver-

age cost of capital is 9%. The market value of its debt is $6,000,000. Assume the company has no nonoperating net assets or other capital claims.

Smiley, Inc.

Year	Forecasted Free Cash Flow
1	$ 1,000,000
2	$ 1,310,000
3	$ 1,200,000
4	$ 1,236,000
5	$ 1,273,000
6	$ 1,311,000
7	$ 1,051,000
8	$ 1,391,000
9	$ 1,432,000
10	$ 1,500,000

   a. Calculate the value of Smiley, Inc. using the free cash flow model.

   b. Calculate the value created by leverage. Assume $\tau^* = 0.14$.

   c. Using your answers to (a) and (b), what would be the value of Smiley if it were unlevered?

   d. Find the discount rate that equates the present value of Smiley's free cash flows with your answer to (c). (Use a computer spreadsheet to do this.) What does this discount rate represent?

3. The original Modigliani-Miller Proposition is based on certain assumptions. Explain these assumptions and discuss whether they are realistic.

4. Under current tax law, if you hold a stock for more than one year, the tax rate on the gain is 20% for most taxpayers, rather than the highest marginal rate of 39.6%. Suppose Congress repealed this special tax treatment, resulting in a 39.6% marginal tax rate on all income derived from equity securities. What would happen to τ^*?

5. Michael's Guitar Repair Service has an annual free cash flow of $100,000. This cash flow is expected to continue forever. Michael's unlevered cost of equity is 15% and the market value of its debt is $500,000. There are no nonoperating net assets. Calculate the value of Michael's equity using the adjusted present value model. Assume $\tau^* = 14\%$.

6. The Jones Company has an annual cash flow of $225,000, which is expected to continue forever. Jones' unlevered cost of equity is 10% and the market value of its debt is $500,000. There are no nonoperating net assets. Assume $\tau^* = 14\%$.

   a. What is the value of Jones Company's equity?

   b. What is the weighted-average cost of capital?

7. If the U.S. Congress adjusted the marginal corporate tax rate to 40% and the marginal tax rate on personal interest deductions to 42%, how would this affect the value of leverage? Why do the tax rates affect the value of leverage?

My Case

Calculate the value of your firm's equity using the APV model and the unlevered cost of equity you calculated in Chapter 7. (Note: The value may be slightly different from the value you calculated under the free cash flow model because your free cash flow pattern is probably not a perpetuity, so the unlevering formula is only approximately correct.)

APPENDIX 11.1 DERIVATION OF THE MODIGLIANI-MILLER PROPOSITION WITH TAXES

In order to see how leverage affects value in the presence of taxes, one must think of the firm and all its capital contributors as a single unit. If leverage reduces the total tax payments made by the firm and all its capital contributors, the value of the combined capital increases.

Under what circumstances will value be created in this way? How do we quantify the value created? To answer these questions, we analyze two investments that always result in the same cash flow stream to shareholders after all taxes are paid at both the corporate level and the investor level. The investments differ in that in one case leverage is incurred at the corporate level and in the other case at the investor level. This approach is the standard way to derive the Modigliani-Miller Proposition on capital structure including taxes.

For the first investment, we consider a company we will call Levco. This company obtains some of its capital from equity and some from debt, so it has a levered capital structure. For the second investment, which we call Unlevco, the firm is financed entirely with equity. The operating cash flows are always the same for the two companies, but their cash flows after paying interest costs and related taxes differ because of the different capital structures. We assume both companies distribute all of their cash flows to their shareholders.[3]

Suppose an investor acquires shares in Levco. Her annual, after-tax cash flow from the investment will be:

$$CF_L = \alpha \cdot (X - DEBT \cdot r) \cdot (1 - \tau_c) \cdot (1 - \tau_e) \qquad (11.5)$$

where α = proportion of Levco's shares owned by the investor, X = annual cash flows to Levco before interest and taxes, $DEBT$ = amount of debt incurred by Levco, r = interest rate, τ_c = corporate tax rate, and τ_e = tax rate on individual income derived from equity.

$(X - DEBT \cdot r)$ represents Levco's pretax cash flow after making interest payments. The term $(1 - \tau_c)$ reduces this to an after-tax amount. We multiply by α, the investor's ownership proportion, to get the cash flow to the investor before her taxes. We then multiply by $(1 - \tau_e)$ to remove taxes paid by the investor.

Suppose another investment always results in the same after-tax cash flow to the investor as this one. These two investments would sell for the same price. Otherwise, investors would buy one and sell the other short repeatedly, earning a riskless profit. This would continue until the two investments had the same price.

There is such an investment. The investor creates it with a combination of borrowing and an investment in Unlevco. To find just how much debt the investor in Unlevco must borrow to have a net investment that perfectly matches the investment in Levco, we first determine the cash flows to the Unlevco investor, which depend on the amount of debt the investor incurs. We then find the debt amount that equates these cash flows with the cash flows to the Levco investor.

---

[3]Although we are thinking of these as investments in two different companies with identical operating cash flows, another way to think about this example is the same company with two possible capital structures.

An investor who borrows and uses the proceeds along with some existing funds to acquire an interest in Unlevco has the following annual after-tax cash flow:

$$CF_U = \alpha \cdot X \cdot (1 - \tau_c) \cdot (1 - \tau_e) - DEBT^* \cdot r \cdot (1 - \tau_d) \tag{11.6}$$

where $DEBT^*$ = amount of debt incurred by the investor in Unlevco, and τ_d = tax rate on individual interest deduction.

Unlevco's cash flows are the same as Levco's, except that it has no interest payments. So, its after-tax cash flow is $X \cdot (1 - \tau_c)$. The proportion α of this is distributed to the investor, who pays tax on it at the rate τ_e, resulting in cash flows from Unlevco, but before considering the investor's interest payments, of $\alpha \cdot X \cdot (1 - \tau_c) \cdot (1 - \tau_e)$. Having borrowed $DEBT^*$, the investor pays interest of $DEBT^* \cdot r$ and receives a tax benefit at the rate of τ_d, for a net debt cost of $DEBT^* \cdot r \cdot (1 - \tau_d)$.

We now want to find the level of debt, $DEBT^*$, the Unlevco investor must take on so that the two investments' cash flows are *always* the same as each other. This does not mean that investors in unlevered companies have to take on debt for our analysis to be valid. We require only that they *could* do so. As long as investors could replicate one investment using another, those two investments should sell for the same price. By finding the level of $DEBT^*$ such that the Unlevco investor has replicated an investment in Levco, we will be able to then equate the values of the two investments.

We find the value of $DEBT^*$ that equates the cash flows in the two cases by setting (11.5) and (11.6) equal and solving for $DEBT^*$.

Cash flow to investor in Levco   Cash flow to investor in Unlevco

$$\alpha \cdot (X - DEBT \cdot r) \cdot (1 - \tau_c) \cdot (1 - \tau_e) = \alpha \cdot X \cdot (1 - \tau_c) \cdot (1 - \tau_e) - DEBT^* \cdot r \cdot (1 - \tau_d) \tag{11.7}$$

Equation (11.7) is satisfied when $DEBT^* = \alpha \cdot DEBT \cdot \dfrac{(1 - \tau_c) \cdot (1 - \tau_e)}{(1 - \tau_d)}$. When the investor in Unlevco borrows this amount, her cash flows are always equal to those of the investor in Levco. Therefore, the values of the cash flow streams to the two investors must be equal.

Thus, $\alpha \cdot COMEQUITY_L = \alpha \cdot COMEQUITY_U - DEBT^*$, where $COMEQUITY_L$ = value of Levco and $COMEQUITY_U$ = value of Unlevco, which implies that

$$COMEQUITY_L = COMEQUITY_U - DEBT \cdot \frac{(1 - \tau_c) \cdot (1 - \tau_e)}{(1 - \tau_d)} \tag{11.8}$$

Equation (11.8) can be rewritten as

$$COMEQUITY_L = COMEQUITY_U - DEBT + DEBT \cdot \left(1 - \frac{(1 - \tau_c) \cdot (1 - \tau_e)}{(1 - \tau_d)} \right) \tag{11.9}$$

Recall that under the original MM Proposition with no taxes, $COMEQUITY_L = COMEQUITY_U - DEBT$. This is the same as (11.9) without the last term, which represents the value created by the tax benefits of leverage. So, the benefit to leverage is $DEBT \cdot \tau^*$, where $\tau^* = 1 - \dfrac{(1 - \tau_c) \cdot (1 - \tau_e)}{(1 - \tau_d)}$.

12

Where We Have Been:

We have studied four of the five cash flow valuation methods.

Where We Are:

In this chapter we will study the last of our cash flow valuation methods, the residual income model.

Where We Are Going:

In the next part, we will cover three special topics in valuation: the income tax disclosure, employee stock options, and pensions and other postemployment benefits.

The Residual Income Model

LEARNING OBJECTIVES:

After studying this chapter, you will understand:

- How the residual income model works.
- How to determine residual income.
- Why the residual income model is a cash flow model.
- That the residual income model provides the same results as the other cash flow models, given the same assumptions.

This chapter examines the residual income valuation model, which uses projections of residual income and book value to calculate value. **Residual income** is the difference between income and **base income**, where base income is the discount rate times book value at the beginning of the period.

This model describes value as a function of book value and residual income, suggesting that it is not a cash flow model. However, because of the interrelationships among the income statement, the balance sheet, and the cash flow statement, the residual income model actually is a cash flow model. Value depends on the cash flow forecast implied by the book value and residual income, rather than on those amounts per se. Even though this is counterintuitive, accounting choices such as depreciation method and asset write-offs have no effect on value under the residual income model, even though they affect both book value and income.

Furthermore, any free cash flow forecast can be transformed into a residual income forecast. That residual income forecast will produce the same value under the residual income model as does the free cash flow forecast under the free cash flow model. The converse is also true. Any residual income forecast can be transformed into a free cash flow forecast, which will have an identical value. As long as the forecast assumptions are identical, the two models will produce the same value.

Section 12.1 defines the residual income model. In Section 12.2, we recast the Starbucks valuation from Chapter 10 using the residual income model. Section 12.3 compares various aspects of the free cash flow and residual income models.

12.1 The Residual Income Model Defined

As is the case with a valuation model based explicitly on cash flows, we can define the residual income model at either the equity level or the operating level. For example, the flows to equity model uses cash flows to the equityholders (equity level), whereas the free cash flow model uses cash flows to all the firm's capital contributors (operating level). Similarly, we can model residual income to the equityholders or to all the capital contributors.

Residual Income Model at the Equity Level

At the equity level, the residual income model is

$$COMEQUITY = BV_0 + PV(\text{residual income stream}) \tag{12.1}$$

where BV_0 is the book value of equity at the valuation date and PV represents present value. When we use the residual income model at the equity level, we use the cost of equity to discount the residual income stream.

Residual income equals net income less base income, where base income equals the cost of equity multiplied by the book value of equity at the beginning of the period. So, the formula for the residual income model at the equity level is

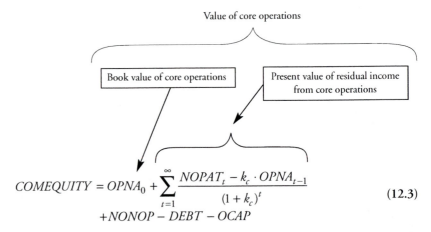

$$COMEQUITY = BV_0 + \sum_{t=1}^{\infty} \frac{NI_t - k_e \cdot BV_{t-1}}{(1 + k_e)^t} \qquad (12.2)$$

NI_t is forecasted net income in period t relative to the valuation date. k_e is the cost of equity. BV_{t-1} is the book value of equity at the beginning of period t. Base income is $k_e \cdot BV_{t-1}$ and represents the amount that net income would be if return on equity were equal to the cost of equity. Residual income equals net income less base income.

Residual Income Model at the Operating Level

At the operating level, we have a formula analogous to (12.2) for the value of core operations. It uses the core operations' book value, residual income related to core operations, and the weighted-average cost of capital for the discount rate. We then use the economic balance sheet to arrive at the value of common equity, much as we did with the free cash flow model:

$$COMEQUITY = OPNA_0 + \sum_{t=1}^{\infty} \frac{NOPAT_t - k_c \cdot OPNA_{t-1}}{(1 + k_c)^t} \qquad (12.3)$$
$$+ NONOP - DEBT - OCAP$$

$OPNA_0$ is the book value of core operations at the valuation date. $NOPAT_t$ is net operating profit after tax (NOPAT) in period t, as we defined it in Chapter 9. k_c is the weighted-average cost of capital, and $OPNA_{t-1}$ is the book value of core operations at the beginning of period t. *NONOP, DEBT,* and *OCAP* are the fair values of nonoperating net assets, debt claims, and other capital claims, respectively.[1]

In the remainder of the chapter, we focus on the residual income model at the operating level as shown in (12.3). Structuring the valuation in this way requires less forecasting than if we use the

---

[1]The residual income model is valid under all accounting methods, as long as they adhere to the concept of clean surplus. Clean surplus means there are no revisions to the forecasted book value of equity other than capital transactions such as purchases of stock, sales of stock, and dividends, and income or expense recognition. GAAP sometimes violate clean surplus, because revaluations of available-for-sale securities and certain foreign exchange adjustments are recorded directly in equity, not through income statement recognition. These usually do not present a problem because marketable securities are not part of core operations, and we usually do not forecast foreign exchange rate movements.

model at the equity level, because we need not forecast debt service. Appendix 12.1 formally derives the model and proves its equivalence to the free cash flow model. We work with examples, which are more intuitive, in the chapter itself.

12.2 STARBUCKS' VALUATION UNDER RESIDUAL INCOME

We now reconsider the Starbucks valuation using the residual income model. Exhibit 12.1 provides the additional information needed to use the residual income model with a forecast consistent with the Starbucks free cash flow forecast used in Chapter 10. Section A provides the free cash flow forecast from Exhibit 10.8. Section B derives forecasts of book value of core operations from the free cash flow forecast. Section C computes forecasted residual income.

Note in Section A that to forecast free cash flow, we forecasted NOPAT and then adjustments to arrive at free cash flow. Each of these adjustments is a change in an asset or liability account. So, free cash flow is equal to NOPAT minus any increases (plus any decreases) in the book value of core operations. We represent this relationship algebraically as

$$FCF_t = NOPAT_t - (OPNA_t - OPNA_{t-1}) \tag{12.4}$$

Rearranging terms, we find the book value of core operations is

$$OPNA_t = OPNA_{t-1} + NOPAT_t - FCF_t \tag{12.5}$$

In Section B, we use this relationship to forecast the book value of core operations. In 2001, the beginning book value of core operations, $OPNA_0$, is \$1,041,980,000. We obtain this amount by netting the book values of all the assets and liabilities in core operations. Forecasted NOPAT is \$154,277,000, whereas forecasted free cash flow is an outflow of \$96,152,000. We forecast the book value of core operations at the end of fiscal 2001 to be \$1,041,980,000 + \$154,277,000 − (−\$96,152,000) = \$1,292,409,000.

We calculate residual income in Section C. In each year, we subtract base income, which is the book value of core operations at the beginning of the period times the cost of capital, from NOPAT. For example, in fiscal 2001 residual income is

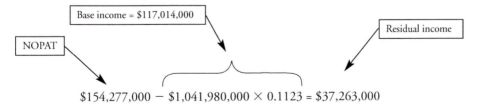

$$\$154,277,000 - \$1,041,980,000 \times 0.1123 = \$37,263,000$$

Three Terminal Value Assumptions

We now have our residual income projection for fiscal 2001 through 2006. Like the free cash flow model, the residual income model requires an infinite period forecast. So, we must make an assumption about residual income in 2006 and beyond. There are three possibilities. (1) We could use the same economic argument we did in the free cash flow model and assume that eventually competitive advantage dissipates. (2) We could assume residual income is zero. Some people argue that this is a logical

EXHIBIT 12.1   Forecasted Residual Income and Book Value of Core Operations for Starbucks

($ thousands)		2001		2002		2003		2004		2005		2006
Net revenues	$	2,772,375	$	3,377,839	$	4,118,395	$	4,901,661	$	5,704,749	$	6,531,286
Operating income	$	250,857	$	312,247	$	381,808	$	456,076	$	533,084	$	613,086
Income taxes		(96,580)		(120,215)		(146,996)		(175,589)		(205,237)		(236,038)
NOPAT	$	154,277	$	192,032	$	234,812	$	280,487	$	327,847	$	377,048
Depreciation and amortization		178,171		216,171		256,171		298,171		342,171		342,171
Deferred income taxes, net		2,897		3,606		4,410		5,268		6,157		0
Change in working capital		(12,063)		(12,109)		(14,811)		(15,665)		(16,062)		(16,531)
Capital expenditures		(419,434)		(458,357)		(552,393)		(611,477)		(663,406)		(342,171)
Free cash flow	$	(96,152)	$	(58,657)	$	(71,811)	$	(43,216)	$	(3,293)	$	360,517
Book value of core operations:												
Beginning balance	$	1,041,980	$	1,292,409	$	1,543,098	$	1,849,721	$	2,173,424	$	2,504,564
Plus NOPAT		154,277		192,032		234,812		280,487		327,847		377,048
Less free cash flow		(96,152)		(58,657)		(71,811)		(43,216)		(3,293)		360,517
Ending balance	$	1,292,409	$	1,543,098	$	1,849,721	$	2,173,424	$	2,504,564	$	2,521,095
Cost of capital 0.1123												
NOPAT	$	154,277	$	192,032	$	234,812	$	280,487	$	327,847	$	377,048
Base income		117,014		145,138		173,290		207,724		244,076		281,263
Residual income	$	37,263	$	46,894	$	61,522	$	72,763	$	83,771	$	95,785

Section A

Section B

Section C

extension of the first approach, and that return on capital will be equal to the cost of capital when competitive advantage dissipates. (3) We could forecast a perpetuity starting with the $95,785,000 of residual income in 2006 projected in Exhibit 12.1, perhaps allowing it to grow at some rate.

As we evaluate each of these approaches, we will rely on the following criteria:

- The terminal value approach should give the same value regardless of accounting method. This is because under the residual income model, accounting method does not affect value.

- The forecast must be feasible, given the capacity forecast to be in place by the end of the forecast horizon.

Assumption 1: Zero Net Present Value Investments

Our first assumption is based on the underlying economics of the industry. We assume that by the perpetuity period, the firm no longer has any competitive advantage. As a result, any additional capital investments it makes during the perpetuity period will have a net present value of zero. This assumption enables us to ignore these investments in the valuation and assume the firm would continue to operate indefinitely at the same level of capacity.[2] We allow for growth in the free cash flow stream at a nominal rate to account for expected inflation.

We derive the perpetuity value that is consistent with the assumption that incremental investment in the perpetuity period does not create value. To do so, we must calculate the expected residual income in each year of the perpetuity period. Exhibit 12.2 shows the residual income in the first six years of the perpetuity that is implied by our zero net present value investments perpetuity assumption. We begin with the projections for 2006 from Exhibit 12.1. We grow NOPAT and free cash flow at 3% each year, as we did when we used this assumption in the free cash flow model.

We could continue this spreadsheet for many years and take the present value of the residual income over those years. Eventually, the present value of the remaining years in the perpetuity would be very small, and we would have captured essentially all of the present value of the perpetuity period. But this approach is not practical. What we really need is a formula that calculates the present value of the residual income in the perpetuity period, much as we did in the dividend discount model and the free cash flow model. This turns out to be a bit tricky because the residual income does not grow at a constant rate, meaning we cannot use the standard perpetuity formula. The perpetuity formula for the residual income forecast that is consistent with our zero NPV investment assumption has a perpetuity with the following value:[3]

$$PERP = \frac{RI_{N+1} - [OPNA_{N+1} - (1 + g_P) \cdot OPNA_N]}{(k_c - g_P) \cdot (1 + k_c)^N} \tag{12.6}$$

where RI_{N+1} is residual income in the first year of the perpetuity, g_P is the sustainable growth rate in NOPAT and free cash flow in the perpetuity period, k_c is the weighted-average cost of capital, and $OPNA_N$ and $OPNA_{N+1}$ are the book values of the core operations at the beginning and end, respectively, of the first year of the perpetuity period. The perpetuity formula is more complicated than it was in the free cash flow and dividend discount models because OPNA does not grow at the same

---

[2]As was the case when we used this assumption in the free cash flow model, we do not actually assume the firm will not continue to expand in the perpetuity period. We assume only that if it does expand, it will do so via zero net present value investments. Ignoring those investments has no effect on the valuation.

[3]This expression is derived in Appendix 12.2.

EXHIBIT 12.2   Starbucks Residual Income in the First Six Years of the Perpetuity Period Given Zero-NPV Investment Assumptions

($ thousands)		2006		2007		2008		2009		2010		2011
Book value of core operations:												
Beginning balance	$	2,504,564	$	2,521,095	$	2,538,121	$	2,555,658	$	2,573,721	$	2,592,326
Plus NOPAT		377,048		388,359		400,010		412,010		424,370		437,101
Less free cash flow		360,517		371,333		382,473		393,947		405,765		417,938
Ending balance		2,521,095		2,538,121		2,555,658		2,573,721		2,592,326		2,611,489
Cost of capital	0.1123											
Growth in perpetuity	0.030											
NOPAT		377,048		388,359		400,010		412,010		424,370		437,101
Base income		281,263		283,119		285,031		287,000		289,029		291,118
Residual income	$	95,785	$	105,240	$	114,979	$	125,010	$	135,341	$	145,983

rate as NOPAT and free cash flow. As a result, neither does residual income. The bracketed term in the numerator of (12.6) accounts for this fact.

For Starbucks, the perpetuity value is

$$\frac{\$95,785,000 - [\$2,521,095,000 - 1.03 \cdot \$2,504,564,000]}{(0.1123 - 0.03) \cdot 1.1123^5} = \$1,101,824,000$$

as shown in Exhibit 12.3. The result is a value of $2,356,652,000 for Starbucks' core operations. After making adjustments for nonoperating net assets, debt, and other capital claims, the per share value is $13.07. Note that this value is equal to the value we found under the free cash flow model.[4] This is because our perpetuity assumption, zero net present value investments, and all our other assumptions, were the same in this valuation as in the free cash flow valuation.

Assumption 2: Residual Income Is Zero in the Long Run

If we assume residual income is zero in the perpetuity period, and we use the forecast for residual income from Exhibit 12.1, then the Starbucks valuation is as shown in Exhibit 12.4. The value of core operations is the book value of $1,041,980,000 plus the present value of the residual income over the forecast horizon, which is $212,848,000 for a total of $1,254,828,000. We then adjust for the values of nonoperating net assets, debt, and other capital claims, as we did in the free cash flow model in Chapter 10. The estimated value of Starbucks is $7.23 per share.

As discussed in Chapter 10, it is reasonable to assume competitive advantage dissipates in the long run, forcing returns on incremental investments down to the cost of capital. If we interpret the difference between return on capital and cost of capital as a measure of value creation, then we might expect residual income to be zero in the long run.

A CLOSER LOOK

Why Residual Income and Free Cash Flow Models May Give Different Results in Practice

We have seen that the residual income and free cash flow models are identical. In practice, however, these two models might produce different results. Why?

If the results differ, it must be because the underlying assumptions differ. An analyst who assumes residual income is either a perpetuity or is zero makes an assumption that implies a different free cash flow forecast than under the free cash flow model. It is this different assumption that creates the different result. In addition, an assumption of a perpetuity or zero residual income will give different results under different accounting methods, again because they imply different underlying cash flow streams. As long as identical assumptions, including the terminal value assumption, are used, the residual income and free cash flow models produce the same results.

---

[4]Core operations differ by $3,000 due to rounding differences.

EXHIBIT 12.3   Starbucks Residual Income Valuation Using Assumption 1—Competitive Advantage Dissipates

($ thousands except per share amounts)		2001	2002	2003	2004	2005	2006
Residual income		$ 37,263	$ 46,894	$ 61,522	$ 72,763	$ 83,771	$ 95,785
Cost of capital		0.1123					
Valuation summary:							
Book value of core operations	$	1,041,980					
Present value of residual income		1,314,672	37,903	44,706	47,536	49,202	1,101,824
Core operations		2,356,652					
Short-term investments		61,336					
Joint ventures		52,051					
Other investments		3,788					
Current maturities of long-term debt		(685)					
Long-term debt		(6,483)					
		2,466,659					
Minority interest		(7,683)					
Employee stock options		**					$ 3,588
		2,458,976					1,151,987
Number of shares outstanding (thousands)		188,158					0.0031146
Value per share	$	13.07					2,466,659
							$ 7,683

$$\$95{,}785 - \dfrac{[\$2{,}521{,}095 - 1.03 \cdot \$2{,}504{,}564]}{(0.1123 - 0.03) \cdot 1.1123^5} = \$1{,}101{,}824$$

Minority interest:

Book value of minority interest

Book value of core operations and nonoperating net assets less debt claims (net value)

Ratio of minority interest to net value

Fair value of core operations and nonoperating net assets less debt claims

Estimated fair value of minority interest

** Ignored in this valuation. Employee stock options will be discussed in Chapter 14.

EXHIBIT 12.4 Starbucks Residual Income Valuation Using Assumption 2—Long-Run Residual Income Is Zero

($ thousands except per share amounts)	2001	2002	2003	2004	2005	2006
Residual income	$ 37,263	$ 46,894	$ 61,522	$ 72,763	$ 83,771	$ 0
Cost of capital	0.1123					
Valuation summary:						
Book value of core operations	$ 1,041,980					
Present value of residual income	212,848	37,903	44,706	47,536	49,202	0
Core operations	1,254,828					
Short-term investments	61,336					
Joint ventures	52,051	Minority interest:				
Other investments	3,788	Book value of minority interest				$ 3,588
Current maturities of long-term debt	(685)	Book value of core operations and nonoperating net assets less debt claims (net value)				1,151,987
Long-term debt	(6,483)					
Minority interest	1,364,835	Ratio of minority interest to net value				0.0031146
Employee stock options	(4,251)	Fair value of core operations and nonoperating net assets less debt claims				1,364,835
	**					
	1,360,584	Estimated fair value of minority interest				$ 4,251
Number of shares outstanding (thousands)	188,158					
Value per share	$ 7.23					

** Ignored in this valuation. Employee stock options will be discussed in Chapter 14

Although intuitive, this interpretation is incorrect. Return on capital and cost of capital are not comparable (except in a very special case[5]). There are two reasons for this. First, return on capital is an annual amount; it relates to the results for a single year. Cost of capital is the internal rate of return a capital project must earn in order to neither create nor destroy value. When an investment is analyzed, there is one cost of capital. Over the life of the investment, there will be many returns on capital—one for each year. None of those returns measure value creation.

Second, return on capital is an accounting return, whereas cost of capital is the internal rate of return an investment must earn to be a zero net present value project. There is no reason these two values should be the same, either for a zero net present value investment or in the long run after the firm has lost its competitive advantage.

The fundamental problem with the zero perpetuity assumption is that it is not based on an underlying economic assumption about the firm or its industry. This means that we cannot draw any conclusions about a firm's profitability or its ability to create value by comparing the return on capital to the cost of capital. For example, from Exhibit 12.1, we see that Starbucks' forecasted return on (beginning of year) capital in fiscal 2001 is $154,277,000/$1,041,980,000 = 14.8%. The fact that this is above Starbucks' 11.23% cost of capital does not mean the company is forecasted to create value in 2001. That could be determined only by comparing the present value of the incremental expected cash flows due to investments made in 2001 to the costs of those investments. Further, if Starbucks were to write off $100 million of land, its subsequent wealth creation would not suddenly be higher due to an increased return on capital (to $154,277,000/[$1,041,980,000 − $100,000,000] = 16.4%).

More importantly, this approach violates our criteria for a reasonable terminal value calculation. The value we calculated depends on accounting methods, and we have no way of knowing such a forecast is feasible given the physical capital forecasted to be in place at the beginning of the perpetuity period.

Assumption 3: Residual Income Is a Perpetuity

We can assume that residual income is a perpetuity, perhaps growing at some constant rate. For example, if we assume that residual income grows at 3% per year after 2006, we have an additional $683,578,000, the value of the perpetuity. This also changes the value of the minority interest slightly. The revised calculation is shown on Exhibit 12.5. Starbucks' value per share under this assumption is $10.85.

The problem with this approach is that when NOPAT and free cash flow grow at stable rates, as we expect in the long run, OPNA does not grow at the same rate. As a result, residual income does not grow at the same rate, or even a constant one. So, we cannot just pick a rate near the expected inflation rate. More importantly, OPNA's growth rate depends on the firm's accounting methods, so for any given growth rate assumption, the calculated value will depend on the firm's accounting methods. Thus, this approach violates an important criterion we set for the perpetuity calculation. Like ignoring the perpetuity value, this approach is not based on an assumption about the underlying economics of the firm or the industry. It simply assumes a pattern in residual income that may or may not be reasonable.

---

[5]The special case when return on capital and the cost of capital can be compared occurs where the cash flows from a project will be a perpetuity with no growth, and the investment cost is not amortized or depreciated. In that case, the project has a positive present value if and only if the return on capital, which is now the same every year, is greater than the cost of capital. Few investment projects actually follow a pattern like this, and in the general case return on capital and cost of capital are not comparable. It is unfortunate that they have been given such similar names.

EXHIBIT 12.5 Starbucks Residual Income Valuation Using Assumption 3—Long-Run Residual Income Grows at 3%

($ thousands except per share amount)		2001	2002	2003	2004	2005	2006
Residual income		$ 37,263	$ 46,894	$ 61,522	$ 72,763	$ 83,771	$ 95,785
Cost of capital	0.1123						
Long-term growth rate in residual income	0.03						
Valuation summary:							
Book value of core operations	$ 1,041,980						
Present value of residual income	896,426	33,501	37,903	44,706	47,536	49,202	683,578
Core operations	1,938,406						
Short-term investments	61,336						
Joint ventures	52,051	Residual income in 2006				$ 95,785
Other investments	3,788	Divided by cost of capital minus growth rate				0.0823
Current maturities of long-term debt	(685)	Value of perpetuity at end of fiscal 2005				1,163,852
Long-term debt	(6,483)	Divided by 1.1123[5]				1.70259
	2,048,413	Present value of perpetuity				$ 683,578
Minority interest	(6,380)						
Employee stock options	**	Minority interest:					
	2,042,033	Book value of minority interest				$ 3,588
Number of shares outstanding (thousands)	188,158	Book value of core operations and nonoperating net assets				1,151,987
Value per share	$ 10.85	less debt claims (net value)				0.0031146
		Fair value of core operations and nonoperating net assets				
		less debt claims				2,048,413
		Estimated fair value of minority interest				$ 6,380

** Ignored in this valuation. Employee stock options will be discussed in Chapter 14.

Conclusion on Terminal Value Approach

Based on our analysis, we recommend using the first terminal value assumption of zero net present value investments, (12.6), to calculate the perpetuity value when using the residual income model. This provides an amount that is founded on a basic economic assumption, rather than simply assuming a pattern in residual income. It is consistent with an eventual loss of competitive advantage, and the value it produces does not depend on the firm's accounting methods.

12.3 A COMPARISON OF THE FREE CASH FLOW AND RESIDUAL INCOME MODELS

There has been a fair amount of debate as to whether the residual income model or the free cash flow model is "better." However, no one disputes that the two models are algebraically equivalent. Whatever errors arise in one model would exist in the other and affect the valuation by exactly the same amount, assuming consistent assumptions are used. In terms of accuracy, neither model can be better. Which method is better for an individual comes down to personal preference about how to structure the analysis.

We now compare various aspects of the two models. To understand the residual income model, we explore how the Starbucks valuation would change if we changed either the company's accounting or the forecasted cash flow stream.

Accounting Differences and Residual Income Valuation

Would a change in accounting methods affect the value determined by the residual income model? The answer is no. A change in accounting method, with no change in cash flow, has no effect on value, even though it will affect both book value and residual income. This is due to the interrelationship between the income statement and the balance sheet, and to the use of residual income rather than net income in the model. Assuming there is no concurrent change in the free cash flow forecast, the effects of changes in book value and residual income on the computed value always perfectly offset each other.

To illustrate, we recast the Starbucks residual income valuation again, this time changing the accounting without changing the forecasted cash flows. Suppose Starbucks wrote down its land by $100 million immediately before the valuation date. The book value of its core operations would be $100 million lower at the valuation date and at every date thereafter. Exhibit 12.6 provides the revised residual income valuation.

Although book value is $100 million lower, the present value of the residual income stream is now larger by exactly the same amount. This is so because the lower book value results in increased residual income each year by $100 million times the cost of capital in perpetuity. The increase in the present value of the residual income is the annual increase in residual income divided by the cost of capital, which brings us back to $100 million. The result is that book value is actually irrelevant to the model. We could arbitrarily choose *any* number to be the book value as of the valuation date and arrive at the same value for the firm.

For simplicity, we provided an example that did not affect subsequent depreciation. Even if we had assumed a write-off of depreciable property, which would result in revisions of subsequent depreciation, there would have been no change in the value. In addition, any other accounting changes not involving a change in the cash flow forecast would result in no change in the computed value. For example, changing any accounting method to any other accounting method would not affect value. Despite the use of book value and residual income in the model, free cash flow actually drives the value.

Cash Flow Differences and Residual Income Valuation

We have seen that changing accounting numbers without changing cash flows does not affect value under the residual income model. We now show that changing the free cash flow forecast does change the value, regardless of whether the change in cash flow affects income. Consider what happens if we increase Starbucks' forecasted free cash flow in fiscal 2004 by $100 million. The present value of that amount is $100 million/$1.1123^4$ = $65,330,000. The value of the core operations must be higher by this amount.

If the $100 million is recognized as part of NOPAT, the valuation becomes as shown in Exhibit 12.7. Book values are unchanged throughout the valuation. The additional income recognized in fiscal 2004 is "thrown off" as cash, resulting in no increase in operating net assets. The residual income is higher in fiscal 2004 by exactly the $100 million increase in cash flow. As a result, the present value of the residual income and Starbucks' value are higher by $100 million/$1.1123^4$ = $65,330,000.

What if the additional cash flow is not recognized as income? Suppose, for example, the incremental cash flow in fiscal 2004 were due to the removal of working capital from the operations. Exhibit 12.8 shows the valuation in this case. This time, there is no effect on NOPAT. However, book value is $100 million lower at every balance sheet date after the working capital reduction. This causes an increase in residual income in every year beginning in fiscal 2005. The amount of the annual increase is $100 million $\times$ 0.1123 = $11,230,000. The present value of the increase in residual income is $11,230,000/0.1123/$1.1123^4$ = $65,330,000.

These examples show that when free cash flow changes, value changes, regardless of whether there is any effect on NOPAT.

Portion of Value in Terminal Value in Residual Income Valuation

Generally, a greater portion of value will be attributed to the terminal value in a free cash flow valuation than in a residual income valuation. We might conclude from this fact that residual income valuations are more precise, because of the uncertainty surrounding cash flows that are very far out in the future. It is difficult, however, to reconcile this conclusion with the fact that the two models always produce the same result. How could one model be more precise than another model to which it is identical?

The answer is that it is not more precise. It is true that the residual income model usually has a smaller terminal value. However, a smaller terminal value does not mean the model is more precise, because the potential error in the terminal value is not proportional to the terminal value's size. Consider our Starbucks valuation. Suppose there is a possible error in gross margin percentage in the perpetuity period of ±1%. Assuming a marginal tax rate on this income of 38.5%, NOPAT and free cash flow in fiscal 2006 could be in error by as much as $6,531,286,000 $\times$ 1% $\times$ (1 − 0.385) = $40,167,000. This is $40,167,000/$360,517,000 = 11% of fiscal 2006 free cash flow.

However, our ability to forecast gross margin is not any better if we use the residual income model. The potential error in gross margin is still $40,167,000. This is $40,167,000/$95,785,000 = 42% of residual income. Although it is true that a greater portion of value is in the terminal value under free cash flow, the potential error in the valuation as a percentage of the amount being used to calculate the perpetuity is much smaller. The net effect is that the potential error in the valuation is identical under the two methods.

EXHIBIT 12.6   Revised Residual Income Valuation of Starbucks After Land Write-off

($ thousands except per share amounts)		2001
Net revenues	$	2,772,375
Operating income		250,857
Income taxes		(96,580)
NOPAT		154,277
Depreciation and amortization		178,171
Deferred income taxes, net		2,897
Change in working capital		(12,063)
Capital expenditures		(419,434)
Free cash flow	$	(96,152)
Book value of core operations:		
Beginning balance	$	941,980
Plus NOPAT		154,277
Less free cash flow		(96,152)
Ending balance	$	1,192,409
Cost of capital	0.1123	
Growth in perpetuity	0.030	
NOPAT	$	154,277
Base income		105,784
Residual income	$	48,493
Valuation summary:		
Book value	$	941,980
Present value of residual income	1,414,672	43,597
Core operations	2,356,652	
Short-term investments	61,336	
Joint ventures	52,051	
Other investments	3,788	
Current maturities of long-term debt	(685)	
Long-term debt	(6,483)	
	2,466,659	
Minority interest	(7,683)	
Employee stock options	**	
	2,458,976	
Number of shares outstanding (thousands)	188,158	
Value per share	$	13.07

Each of these amounts is $100,000 lower.

**Ignored in this valuation. Employee stock options will be discussed in Chapter 14.

	2002	2003	2004	2005	2006
	$ 3,377,839	$ 4,118,395	$ 4,901,661	$ 5,704,749	$ 6,531,286
	312,247	381,808	456,076	533,084	613,086
	(120,215)	(146,996)	(175,589)	(205,237)	(236,038)
	192,032	234,812	280,487	327,847	377,048
	216,171	256,171	298,171	342,171	342,171
	3,606	4,410	5,268	6,157	0
	(12,109)	(14,811)	(15,665)	(16,062)	(16,531)
	(458,357)	(552,393)	(611,477)	(663,406)	(342,171)
	$ (58,657)	$ (71,811)	$ (43,216)	$ (3,293)	$ 360,517
	$ 1,192,409	$ 1,443,098	$ 1,749,721	$ 2,073,424	$ 2,404,564
	192,032	234,812	280,487	327,847	377,048
	(58,657)	(71,811)	(43,216)	(3,293)	360,517
	$ 1,443,098	$ 1,749,721	$ 2,073,424	$ 2,404,564	$ 2,421,095
	$ 192,032	$ 234,812	$ 280,487	$ 327,847	$ 377,048
	133,908	162,060	196,494	232,846	270,033
	$ 58,124	$ 72,752	$ 83,993	$ 95,001	$ 107,015
	46,980	52,866	54,873	55,798	1,160,558

Each of these amounts is $100,000 × 0.1123 = $11,230 lower.

Each of these amounts is $11,230 higher.

Residual income is higher by $11,230 per year in perpetuity. The present value is higher by $11,230 / 0.1123 = $100,000.

$$\frac{\$107,015 - [\$2,421,095 - 1.03 \cdot \$2,404,564]}{(0.1123 - 0.03) \cdot 1.1123^5} = \$1,160,558$$

Minority interest:	
Book value of minority interest	$ 3,588
Book value of core operations and nonoperating net assets less debt claims (net value)	1,151,987
Ratio of minority interest to net value	0.0031146
Fair value of core operations and nonoperating net assets less debt claims	2,466,659
Estimated fair value of minority interest	$ 7,683

EXHIBIT 12.7   Revised Residual Income Valuation of Starbucks After $100 Million Increase in Fiscal 2004 NOPAT

($ thousands except per share amounts)		2001
Net revenues		$ 2,772,375
Operating income		250,857
Income taxes		(96,580)
Additional NOPAT in illustration		
NOPAT		154,277
Depreciation and amortization		178,171
Deferred income taxes, net		2,897
Change in working capital		(12,063)
Capital expenditures		(419,434)
Free cash flow		$ (96,152)
Book value of core operations:		
Beginning balance	No change in book values, because	$ 1,041,980
Plus NOPAT	additional income is "thrown off" as cash.	154,277
Less free cash flow		(96,152)
Ending balance		$ 1,292,409
Cost of capital	0.1123	
Growth in perpetuity	0.030	
NOPAT		$ 154,277
Base income		117,014
Residual income		$ 37,263
Valuation summary:		
Book value of core operations	$ 1,041,980	
Present value of residual income	1,380,002	33,501
Core operations	2,421,982	
Short-term investments	61,336	
Joint ventures	52,051	
Other investments	3,788	
Current maturities of long-term debt	(685)	
Long-term debt	(6,783)	
	2,531,689	
Minority interest	(7,885)	
	2,523,804	
Number of shares outstanding (thousands)	188,158	
Value per share	$ 13.41	

	2002		2003		2004		2005		2006
$	3,377,839	$	4,118,395	$	4,901,661	$	5,704,749	$	6,531,286
	312,247		381,808		456,076		533,084		613,086
	(120,215)		(146,996)		(175,589)		(205,237)		(236,038)
					100,000				
	192,032		234,812		380,487		327,847		377,048
	216,171		256,171		298,171		342,171		342,171
	3,606		4,410		5,268		6,157		0
	(12,109)		(14,811)		(15,665)		(16,062)		(16,531)
	(458,357)		(552,393)		(611,477)		(663,406)		(342,171)
$	(58,657)	$	(71,811)	$	56,784	$	(3,293)	$	360,517
$	1,292,409	$	1,543,098	$	1,849,721	$	2,173,424	$	2,504,564
	192,032		234,812		380,487		327,847		377,048
	(58,657)		(71,811)		56,784		(3,293)		360,517
$	1,543,098	$	1,849,721	$	2,173,424	$	2,504,564	$	2,521,095
$	192,032	$	234,812	$	380,487	$	327,847	$	377,048
	145,138		173,290		207,724		244,076		281,263
$	46,894	$	61,522	$	172,763	$	83,771	$	95,785
	37,903		44,706		112,866		49,202		1,101,824

Residual income in fiscal 2004 is higher by $100,000. The entire increase in free cash flow is reflected here.

Core operations is higher by $65,330 the present value of the increase in free cash flow.

$$\frac{\$95,785 - [\$2,521,095 - 1.03 \cdot \$2,504,564]}{(0.1123 - 0.03) \cdot 1.1123^5} = \$1,101,824$$

Minority interest:	
Book value of minority interest	$ 3,588
Book value of core operations and nonoperating net assets less debt claims (net value)	1,151,987
Ratio of minority interest to net value	0.0031146
Fair value of core operations and nonoperating net assets less debt claims	2,531,689
Estimated fair value of minority interest	$ 7,885

EXHIBIT 12.8 Revised Residual Income Valuation of Starbucks After $100 Million Removal of Working Capital in Fiscal 2004

($ thousands except per share amounts)		**2001**
Net revenues		$ 2,772,375
Operating income		250,857
Income taxes		(96,580)
NOPAT		154,277
Depreciation and amortization		178,171
Deferred income taxes, net		2,897
Change in working capital		(12,063)
Capital expenditures		(419,434)
Free cash flow		$ (96,152)
Book value of core operations:		
Beginning balance		$ 1,041,980
Plus NOPAT		154,277
Less free cash flow		(96,152)
Ending balance		$ 1,292,409
Cost of capital	0.1123	
Growth in perpetuity	0.030	
NOPAT		$ 154,277
Base income		117,014
Residual income		$ 37,263
Valuation summary:		
Book value of core operations	$ 1,041,980	
Present value of residual income	1,380,002	33,501
Core operations	2,421,982	
Short-term investments	61,336	
Joint ventures	52,051	
Other investments	3,788	
Current maturities of long-term debt	(685)	
Long-term debt	(6,783)	
	2,531,689	
Minority interest	(7,885)	
	2,523,804	
Number of shares outstanding (thousands)	188,158	
Value per share	$ 13.41	

	2002	2003	2004	2005	2006
	$ 3,377,839	$ 4,118,395	$ 4,901,661	$ 5,704,749	$ 6,531,286
	312,247	381,808	456,076	533,084	613,086
	(120,215)	(146,996)	(175,589)	(205,237)	(236,038)
	192,032	234,812	280,487	327,847	377,048
	216,171	256,171	298,171	342,171	342,171
	3,606	4,410	5,268	6,157	0
	(12,109)	(14,811)	84,335	(16,062)	(16,531)
	(458,357)	(552,393)	(611,477)	(663,406)	(342,171)
	$ (58,657)	$ (71,811)	$ 56,784	$ (3,293)	$ 360,517
	$ 1,292,409	$ 1,543,098	$ 1,849,721	$ 2,073,424	$ 2,404,564
	192,032	234,812	280,487	327,847	377,048
	(58,657)	(71,811)	56,784	(3,293)	360,517
	$ 1,543,098	$ 1,849,721	$ 2,073,424	$ 2,404,564	$ 2,421,095
	$ 192,032	$ 234,812	$ 280,487	$ 327,847	377,048
	145,138	173,290	207,724	232,846	270,033
	$ 46,894	$ 61,522	$ 72,763	$ 95,001	$ 107,015
	37,903	44,706	47,536	55,798	1,160,558

Book value is lower by $100,000 starting at the end of fiscal 2004.

Residual income is higher by $100,000 × 0.1123 = $11,230 in every year beginning in fiscal 2005.

Core operations is higher by $11,230/0.1123/1.1123^4 = $65,330.

$$\frac{\$107,015 - [\$2,421,095 - 1.03 \cdot \$2,404,564]}{(0.1123 - 0.03) \cdot 1.1123^5} = \$1,160,558$$

Minority interest:	
Book value of minority interest	$ 3,588
Book value of core operations and nonoperating net assets less debt claims (net value)	1,151,987
Ratio of minority interest to net value	0.0031146
Fair value of core operations and nonoperating net assets less debt claims	2,531,689
Estimated fair value of minority interest	$ 7,885

SUMMARY

The residual income model is another way to express the value of a firm. It can be implemented at either the equity level or the operating level. If implemented at the equity level, the model produces the value of the common equity. If implemented at the operating level, the model produces the value of the core operations. We then make the same adjustments that we made to the free cash flow result to obtain the value of the common equity, adjusting for nonoperating net assets, debt, and other capital claims. The residual income model is generally easier to implement at the operating level, because it allows us to avoid forecasting debt service and nonoperating flows.

We focused on the residual income model at the operating level. This model requires a forecast of essentially the same items as in the free cash flow model. The combination of a NOPAT forecast and a free cash flow forecast allows us to derive a forecast for book value of core operations. We can then use the NOPAT forecast, the book value forecast, and the cost of capital to derive the residual income forecast. We then add the present value of the forecasted residual income to current book value to arrive at the value of the core operations.

The residual income model is equivalent to the free cash flow model, despite the fact that it is expressed with only book value and income numbers. Changing book value or income has no effect on the result unless the change is accompanied by a change in the free cash flow forecast.

A practical problem with any model is how to estimate the perpetuity value. We showed that when using the residual income model it is best not to assume a value of zero for the perpetuity. Such an approach is based on an incorrect assumption that we should expect return on capital to approach the cost of capital in the long run. Despite their similar names, these measures are not comparable. It is also not appropriate to use a standard perpetuity formula, because under the economic assumptions we generally employ in the perpetuity period, the book value of core operations will not grow at the same rate as NOPAT and free cash flow. Hence residual income does not grow at a constant rate. We should instead use the perpetuity assumption that is consistent with dissipation of competitive advantage, resulting in investments in the perpetuity period providing a zero net present value.

SUGGESTED READINGS

Feltham, G. and J. Ohlson. "Valuation and Clean Surplus Accounting for Operating and Financial Activities." *Contemporary Accounting Research* 11 (Spring 1995):698–731.

Lo, K. and T. Lys. "The Ohlson Model: Contribution to Valuation Theory, Limitations, and Empirical Applications." *Journal of Accounting, Auditing and Finance* 15 (Summer 2000):337–367.

Ohlson, J. "Residual Income Valuation: The Problems." Working paper, May 24, 2000.

Ohlson, J. "A Synthesis of Security Valuation Theory and the Role of Dividends, Cash Flows, and Earnings." *Contemporary Accounting Research* 6 (Spring 1990):648–676.

REVIEW QUESTIONS

1. What is base income?
2. How do you calculate residual income?

3. Compare and contrast the residual income model with the other cash flow models.

4. We can use the residual income model at the equity level or at the operating level. What is different and what is similar between these two approaches?

5. Describe the recommended perpetuity assumption for the residual income model.

6. What is the problem with assuming a simple long-run growth rate for residual income?

 7. The residual income model uses book value of assets and net income to determine value. Despite the use of these accounting numbers, this is really a cash flow model. Explain.

8. Why are cost of capital and return on capital not comparable measures?

 9. An analyst argues that a write-off of assets involving no income tax benefits must still affect the value of the firm, because the residual income model states that value is equal to book value plus the present value of the residual income stream. The write-off reduces book value, so it must reduce the firm's value. Explain why the analyst's logic is incorrect.

PROBLEMS

Following is a free cash flow forecast for Egon's Paranormal Investigations Corporation. Use this information for problems 1–3.

($ millions)	2002	2003	2004	2005
NOPAT	20.0	22.0	25.0	28.0
Free cash flow	(2.0)	15.0	10.0	20.0

1. You expect NOPAT to grow at 3% per year and for free cash flow to be equal to NOPAT, beginning in 2006. The book value of Egon's core operations at December 31, 2001 is $100 million and its weighted-average cost of capital is 9%.

   a. Forecast Egon's book value of core operations for 2002–2006.
   b. Forecast Egon's residual income for 2002–2006.
   c. Calculate the value of Egon's core operations as of December 31, 2001, using the residual income method.

2. Confirm your answer to problem 1(c) by taking the present value of Egon's forecasted free cash flows.

3. Redo problem 1 assuming the book value of Egon's core operations at December 31, 2001 is only $80 million.

4. Using the zero net present value investments assumption for the perpetuity period, calculate the value of the perpetuity (terminal value) under the residual income model under the following assumptions.

	In thousands, except %
Residual income in first year of perpetuity period	$ 10,000
Sustainable growth rate in NOPAT	2%
Weighted-average cost of capital	10%
Book value of core operations at beginning of first year of perpetuity period	$ 205,000
Book value of core operations at end of first year of perpetuity period	$ 217,000
Number of years in forecast horizon	7 years

5. Consider two companies, Butch and Sundance. These companies are identical except they use different depreciation methods for financial reporting, although they use the same depreciation methods for tax purposes. For each of the following models, are the calculated values for Butch and Sundance the same or not? If not, which is higher?

   a. Free cash flow model
   b. Residual income model

6. Consider two companies, Thelma and Louise. The companies are identical except Thelma is forecasted to remove some working capital during the forecast horizon. This will not affect Thelma's NOPAT. For each of the following models, are the calculated values for Thelma and Louise equal or not? If not, which is higher?

   a. Free cash flow model
   b. Residual income model

7. Take a residual income valuation that a student in class has calculated. Change the initial book value of the core operations to his or her social security number. What happens to the value of the equity?

My Case

Recalculate the value of your firm using the residual income model.

APPENDIX 12.1 DERIVATION OF THE RESIDUAL INCOME MODEL

As seen in Chapter 4, the income statement, balance sheet, and cash flow statement are interrelated. You relied on those relationships in learning how to construct a cash flow statement in introductory accounting. The residual income model also relies on the relationship among the three statements, which enables us to restate the free cash flow model in terms of only income statement and balance sheet amounts.

To derive the residual income model, we start with a first principle of security analysis: The value of any asset is the present value of the expected cash flow stream it will generate. As we have seen, this implies that the value of the firm's core operations is equal to the present value of the expected free cash flows it will generate, or

$$CORE = \sum_{t=1}^{\infty} \frac{FCF_t}{(1+k_c)^t} \tag{12.7}$$

Let $OPNA_t$ be the book value of the net assets related to core operations. Note that this is the book value—the amount reported in the balance sheet—not the fair value of these net assets. The subscript represents time t relative to the valuation date. When t is zero, we are referring to the valuation date. When t is greater than zero, we are referring to a forecasted date t years from the valuation date. So, $OPNA_t$ is the forecasted book value of the core operations' net assets t years after the valuation date. This forecasted amount must be consistent with the free cash flow forecast.

By adding and subtracting $OPNA_0$, we can rewrite (12.7) as follows:

$$\boxed{= -OPNA_0}$$

$$CORE = \sum_{t=1}^{\infty} \frac{FCF_t}{(1+k_c)^t} + OPNA_0 + \overbrace{\sum_{t=1}^{\infty} \frac{OPNA_t}{(1+k_c)^t} - \sum_{t=0}^{\infty} \frac{OPNA_t}{(1+k_c)^t}} \tag{12.8}$$

We now let the index in the last summation run from 1 rather than from zero and change the expression in the summation accordingly.

$$CORE = \sum_{t=1}^{\infty} \frac{FCF_t}{(1+k_c)^t} + OPNA_0 + \sum_{t=1}^{\infty} \frac{OPNA_t}{(1+k_c)^t} - \sum_{t=1}^{\infty} \frac{OPNA_{t-1} \cdot (1+k_c)}{(1+k_c)^t} \tag{12.9}$$

This allows us to combine the three summation terms.

$$CORE = OPNA_0 + \sum_{t=1}^{\infty} \frac{FCF_t + OPNA_t - OPNA_{t-1} \cdot (1+k_c)}{(1+k_c)^t} \tag{12.10}$$

We are now ready to use the relationship among the three financial statements to rewrite free cash flow in terms of income statement and balance sheet amounts.

Recall that a free cash flow statement arrives at NOPAT, and then adds and subtracts changes in operating net assets. An increase in operating net assets is a free cash outflow and a decrease is a free cash inflow. As a result,

$$FCF_t = NOPAT_t - (OPNA_t - OPNA_{t-1})$$ (12.11)

When we substitute this expression into (12.10) and simplify, we get:

$$CORE = OPNA_0 + \sum_{t=1}^{\infty} \frac{NOPAT_t - k_c \cdot OPNA_{t-1}}{(1+k_c)^t}$$ (12.12)

After adjusting for other elements of the economic balance sheet, we have

$$COMEQUITY = OPNA_0 + \sum_{t=1}^{\infty} \frac{NOPAT_t - k_c \cdot OPNA_{t-1}}{(1+k_c)^t} + NONOP - DEBT - OCAP$$ (12.13)

This is the residual income model.

APPENDIX 12.2 DERIVATION OF PERPETUITY VALUE IN THE RESIDUAL INCOME MODEL

In this appendix, we derive the formula for the terminal value in the residual income model that is consistent with the assumption that the firm has no competitive advantage in the perpetuity period. This assumption allows us to ignore incremental investments and assume that the firm operates at a constant level of capacity. This constant level of capacity results in growth in NOPAT and free cash flow at a nominal rate to account for inflation, which we call g_P.

The perpetuity value is

$$PERP = \sum_{t=N+1}^{\infty} \frac{NOPAT_t - k_c \cdot OPNA_{t-1}}{(1+k_c)^t}$$ (12.14)

where $NOPAT_t$ is NOPAT in period t, k_c is the weighted-average cost of capital, and $OPNA_{t-1}$ is the book value of core operations at the beginning of period t.

Unfortunately, OPNA does not grow at the same rate as NOPAT and free cash flow except in the special case where $OPNA_N = \dfrac{NI_{N+1} - FCF_{N+1}}{g_P}$ and NI_{N+1} is net income in period $N+1$.

In fact, OPNA does not even grow at a constant rate except in this special case. So, residual income also does not grow at a constant rate, and we cannot apply a simple perpetuity formula to the year $N+1$ residual income.

Let $OPNA_N = \dfrac{NI_{N+1} - FCF_{N+1}}{g_P}$ be the value of $OPNA_N$ that gives the special case in which OPNA grows at the same rate g_p as NOPAT and free cash flow in the perpetuity period and let $OPNA^*_t$ be the book value under this special case at any time $t \geq N$. We can rewrite (12.14) as

$$PERP = \sum_{t=N+1}^{\infty} \frac{NOPAT_t - k_c \cdot OPNA^*_{t-1}}{(1 + k_c)^t} + k_c \cdot \sum_{t=N+1}^{\infty} \frac{OPNA^*_{t-1} - OPNA_{t-1}}{(1 + k_c)^t} \quad \text{(12.15)}$$

Because NOPAT and OPNA* both grow at the same constant rate g_P, the first summation is a simple perpetuity with growth. Its value is

$$\frac{NOPAT_{N+1} - k_c \cdot OPNA^*_N}{(k_c - g_P) \cdot (1 + k_c)^N}$$

In any given period, the changes in $OPNA^*$ and $OPNA$ are the same, $NI_t - FCF_t$. Therefore, $OPNA^*_t - OPNA_t$ is constant for all $t \geq N$. So, we can substitute $OPNA^*_N - OPNA_N$ for the numerator in the second summation term and take it outside the summation. These two substitutions give

$$PERP = \frac{NOPAT_{N+1} - k_c \cdot OPNA^*_N}{(k_c - g_P) \cdot (1 + k_c)^N} + k_c \cdot (OPNA^*_N - OPNA_N) \cdot \sum_{t=N+1}^{\infty} \frac{1}{(1 + k_c)^t} \quad \text{(12.16)}$$

The summation is equal to $\dfrac{1}{k_c \cdot (1 + k_c)^N}$, so

$$PERP = \frac{NOPAT_{N+1} - k_c \cdot OPNA^*_N}{(k_c - g_P) \cdot (1 + k_c)^N} + \frac{OPNA^*_N - OPNA_N}{(1 + k_c)^N} \quad \text{(12.17)}$$

This simplifies to

$$PERP = \frac{NOPAT_{N+1} - k_c \cdot OPNA_N - g_P \cdot (OPNA^*_N - OPNA_N)}{(k_c - g_P) \cdot (1 + k_c)^N} \quad \text{(12.18)}$$

Together, the first two terms in the numerator are period $N + 1$ residual income. Further, $g_P \cdot OPNA^*_N = OPNA^*_{N+1} - OPNA^*_N = OPNA_{N+1} - OPNA_N$. Substituting $RI_{N+1} = NOPAT_{N+1} - k_c \cdot OPNA_N$ and $g_P \cdot OPNA^*_N = OPNA_{N+1} - OPNA_N$ into (12.18) gives

$$PERP = \frac{RI_{N+1} - [OPNA_{N+1} - (1 + g_P) \cdot OPNA_N]}{(k_c - g_P) \cdot (1 + k_c)^N} \quad \text{(12.19)}$$

This is the formula one should use for the terminal value in a residual income valuation.

PART IV

SPECIAL TOPICS IN CASH FLOW BASED VALUATION

13 Using Income Tax Information

14 Employee Stock Options and Valuation

15 Valuation of Firms with Pension Plans
and Other Postemployment Benefit Plans

13

Where We Have Been:

We have completed the basic material on cash flow valuation.

Where We Are:

We now begin our study of special topics in valuation by examining how to use income tax information.

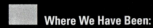

Where We Are Going:

In the remainder of Part IV, we address additional special issues in valuation.

Using Income Tax Information

LEARNING OBJECTIVES:

After reading this chapter, you will understand:

- The differences between statutory, marginal, and effective tax rates.
- The basic financial reporting and disclosure standards for income taxes.
- What loss carrybacks and loss carryforwards are.
- How loss carryforwards affect a valuation.
- How to use the income tax footnote to gather information for a valuation analysis.
- How to calculate the effective tax rate on core operations.

Most U.S. corporations pay about one-third of their pretax income to various governments in taxes. This makes taxes one of the most important elements of the cost structure and cash flow of almost every firm, and so it is not surprising that taxes are also a critical component of any valuation analysis. This chapter demonstrates how income taxes are reported[1] and shows how to incorporate them in a valuation analysis.

Recall from Chapter 10 that to prepare a valuation we need to forecast income taxes related to core operations. We do this by applying a forecasted effective income tax rate on core operations to forecasted operating income. We use the historical effective tax rate on core operations to develop the forecasted effective tax rate. In this chapter, we learn how to use income tax information to determine these historical effective tax rates.

We begin in Section 13.1 by identifying the very different meanings of statutory, marginal, and effective income tax rates. Section 13.2 reviews income tax accounting concepts. We discuss the distinction between permanent and temporary differences, as well as between current and deferred income taxes. We also review the treatment of loss carryforwards and carrybacks. Understanding these concepts is critical to being able to do a valuation, because of their effect on free cash flow and residual income. Section 13.3 analyzes the income tax footnote. This footnote helps us make the adjustments on the historical free cash flow worksheet. One of the assumptions we need for our free cash flow worksheet is the marginal tax rate for each adjustment item. We will show how to use the income tax disclosure to determine these marginal rates. Finally, in Section 13.4, we show how to estimate the effective tax rate on core operations.

13.1 STATUTORY, MARGINAL, AND EFFECTIVE TAX RATES

A tax rate can mean different things in different contexts. For that reason, in using the term in this book, we will precede it with the word *statutory, marginal,* or *effective.* We now define each of these kinds of tax rates.

The **statutory tax rate** is the tax rate that has been set by law (statute). In the United States, the federal statutory tax rate for major corporations is currently 35%. This rate changes from time to time, most recently when it increased from 34% to the current level in 1994. Many states also have a corporate income tax, and the state statutory tax rate varies by state. Because state income taxes are deductible on the federal tax return, the net effect of a state income tax is the state statutory rate times one minus the federal statutory rate. For example, the state corporate income tax rate in Illinois is 7.3%, so the net state cost is $7.3\% \times (1 - 0.35) = 4.745\%$. Most companies operate in many states, so the reported state tax burden will be an average state rate (net of the federal benefit) for all the states in which the firm operates.

---

[1]This chapter is not intended to be a complete treatment of income taxes or the financial reporting for them, but to explain basic tax concepts and the basics of financial reporting for them. It should provide a sufficient understanding so that an analyst can incorporate income taxes in a valuation for a typical company without particularly complicated or unusual tax issues. An analyst working on a valuation involving an unusual tax issue should consult an appropriate income tax text or a tax professional for advice. However, the analyst must understand how to incorporate what he or she learns from those sources into the analysis, based on the general principles discussed in this chapter.

The amount of income tax owed is figured by multiplying the statutory tax rate times the firm's taxable income. **Taxable income** is the amount of a firm's income that is subject to tax. It is not necessarily all the firm's income, and in the United States it is almost never the same as the firm's **pretax income**, the amount of income the firm reports (before taxes) in its GAAP income statement.

The **marginal tax rate** is the tax rate that applies to the next dollar of income. The marginal tax rate is not the same for all types of income, because different kinds of income are taxed differently.

The **effective tax rate** is the income tax provision divided by pretax income. We use a particular type of effective tax rate, the **effective tax rate on core operations**, in our valuation forecasts. This is the income tax provision that is related to core operations, divided by pretax income related to core operations. To determine the effective tax rate on core operations, we use the information in our cash flow worksheet. After adjusting to a free cash flow basis, we take the income tax provision and divide by operating income.

Suppose Lone Star Company, a Texas corporation, has $10 million of pretax income in 2001, $1 million of which is from municipal bond interest. Municipal bond interest is exempt from federal income tax. Suppose $2 million of the pretax income is from dividends received from another U.S. corporation in which Lone Star holds 3% of the outstanding shares. Under U.S. tax law, 70% of these dividends may be excluded from taxable income. The remaining $7 million of operating income consists of $9 million of operating income before depreciation less $2 million of depreciation. For now, we assume financial reporting and income tax depreciation are the same. (We will alter this assumption later in the chapter.) Lone Star's pretax income, taxable income, and income tax provision are as shown in Exhibit 13.1.

Lone Star's taxable income excludes all the municipal bond interest and $1.4 million (70%) of the $2 million of dividend income. Thus, Lone Star's taxable income is $7.6 million, even though its pretax income is $10 million. There is no state corporate income tax in Texas, so we apply the federal statutory rate of 35% to Lone Star's $7.6 million of taxable income. The firm will have to pay a total of $2,660,000 in income taxes for the year.

We will now compute the marginal tax rate for each component of Lone Star's income. All the firm's operating income is subject to income tax. The marginal tax rate on operating income is thus the same as the statutory rate, 35%. The municipal bond interest, unlike the operating income, is not subject to income tax, so, the marginal tax rate on that is zero. The dividends are subject to tax. However, with the 70% dividend exclusion, only 30% of the dividends are actually taxed. If dividends increased by $1, taxable income would increase by only 30 cents. Income tax would increase

EXHIBIT 13.1   Lone Star Company's 2001 Pretax Income, Taxable Income, and Income Tax Provision

	GAAP Pretax Income	Taxable Income and Income Tax Expense
Operating income before depreciation	$ 9,000,000	$ 9,000,000
Depreciation	(2,000,000)	(2,000,000)
Operating income	7,000,000	7,000,000
Municipal bond interest	1,000,000	0
Dividend income	2,000,000	600,000
Pretax income	$ 10,000,000	
Taxable income		7,600,000
Statutory tax rate		0.35
Federal income tax		$ 2,660,000

by 30 cents times the statutory rate of 35%, or 10.5 cents. Thus, the marginal tax rate on the dividend income is 10.5%.

As we can see on Exhibit 13.2, Lone Star's effective tax rate is 26.6%, which is computed by dividing the income tax provision ($2,660,000) by pretax income ($10 million). This is a weighted average of the firm's various marginal rates and the tax rate that would apply to additional income that had the same mix of characteristics as the firm's total income. If Lone Star increased its income by one dollar in the same proportions as its original income (i.e., 70% operating income, 10% municipal bond interest, and 20% dividends), income taxes would go up by 26.6 cents.

13.2 REVIEW OF INCOME TAX ACCOUNTING CONCEPTS

Understanding income tax accounting concepts is important to valuation because we use the tax information in the financial statements to develop our free cash flow or residual income analysis. Here we will take a moment to review the basic tax concepts from earlier financial reporting courses. This background should be sufficient to do the kinds of analyses in this book.[2]

Differences Between Financial Reporting Rules and Income Tax Law

Financial reporting standards and income tax laws have different underlying purposes and different rules. Financial reporting is designed to provide information for investors who are making financial decisions about a firm. Income tax law is designed to determine how much each company must pay in income taxes. Further, managers often make different accounting choices for financial reporting and tax reporting. They may benefit (or at least perceive that they benefit) from reporting higher income to shareholders, while they benefit from reporting lower taxable income to the IRS. The difference between financial reporting and tax reporting leads to the question of how the financial statements should report income taxes.[3]

The underlying concept in accounting for income taxes is the matching principle. This principle, when applied to income taxes, states that the income tax provision should be reported in the income statement in the same period as the income that causes it. The tax implications, if any, related to income recognized in the income statement in a particular period are reported in the income statement in the same period, regardless of when income tax law recognizes the income or deduction.

EXHIBIT 13.2   Lone Star Company Marginal and Effective Tax Rates in 2001

	GAAP Pretax Income	Tax Rate		Tax
Operating Income	$ 7,000,000	35.0%	(M)	$ 2,450,000
Municipal bond interest	1,000,000	0.0%	(M)	0
Dividend income	2,000,000	10.5%	(M)	210,000
Pretax income	$ 10,000,000	26.6%	(E)	$ 2,660,000

(M) Marginal tax rate
(E) Effective tax rate

---

[2]The interested student should consult a financial reporting text, such as L. Revsine, D. Collins, and B. Johnson, *Financial Reporting and Analysis*, 2nd ed. (Upper Saddle River, NJ: Prentice Hall, 2002), for a more detailed discussion of financial reporting for income taxes.

[3]Some countries have "book-tax conformity," meaning the same accounting methods and estimates must be used for financial reporting and income tax calculations. This greatly simplifies accounting for income taxes.

To apply the matching principle to income taxes, we must distinguish between two kinds of differences between financial reporting rules and income tax law: permanent differences and temporary differences.

Permanent Differences

A **permanent difference** between financial reporting rules and income tax law is a difference in whether an item is recognized as income or expense for financial reporting and income taxes. It is not just a matter of *when* the item is recognized, but whether it *ever* is recognized. For example, municipal bond interest is a permanent difference because the interest is reported as income in the income statement, but it is *never* recognized as income by the tax authorities. The dividend exclusion discussed earlier is also a permanent difference because a portion of the dividend is *never* taxed.

Temporary Differences

A **temporary difference** arises when financial reporting rules and income tax laws treat an item the same way, but in *different periods*. Examples of temporary differences include

- Accelerated depreciation for tax purposes and straight-line depreciation for financial reporting
- Expense under SFAS No. 106 for a postemployment benefit plan recorded over employment life for GAAP and deducted when paid for tax purposes

Suppose Lone Star used a more accelerated depreciation method for tax purposes than for financial reporting, resulting in depreciation for tax purposes that is greater than financial reporting depreciation by $1 million in 2001. Because total depreciation is the same for book and tax purposes over the entire life of the firm, this difference will reverse in a subsequent period. Hence, it is a temporary difference.

Under the matching principle, Lone Star's 2001 income tax provision is based on the depreciation it reports in its financial statements in that year, even though its tax payment is based on its tax depreciation in that year.

Reconciling Pretax Income Under GAAP with Taxable Income: Lone Star Example

Exhibit 13.3 reconciles Lone Star's GAAP pretax income with taxable income. This reconciliation helps us understand the computation of the income tax provision and its components. Recall that in addition to the depreciation difference, Lone Star has two other items that are treated differently for GAAP purposes and tax purposes: the $1 million of municipal bond interest and the dividend income of $2 million.

The reconciliation begins with GAAP pretax income, which consists of $7 million of operating income, $1 million of municipal bond interest, and $2 million of dividend income. We then remove any expense or income items included in pretax income that will never have a tax effect. We remove the municipal bond interest, which is not subject to tax, and the 70% of the dividend income not subject to tax. The resulting amount, GAAP pretax income that will ever be taxed, represents that portion of pretax income that will be recognized by the tax authorities, regardless of when. Next, we remove that portion of GAAP pretax income that will ever be taxed, but whose tax effect is not in the current year, that is, temporary differences. The depreciation difference is the only temporary difference in this example.

The result is 2001 taxable income, the amount that would have appeared on the company's 2001 tax return and on which its 2001 tax is based. Although the $1 million of additional tax depreciation reduced the 2001 income tax payment, it was not deducted to arrive at pretax income that will ever be taxed. In subsequent years, tax depreciation will exceed financial reporting depreciation

EXHIBIT 13.3   Reconciliation of Lone Star's 2001 GAAP Pretax Income and Taxable Income

GAAP operating income	$ 7,000,000
GAAP municipal bond interest	1,000,000
GAAP dividend income	2,000,000
GAAP pretax income	10,000,000
PERMANENT DIFFERENCES:	
Municipal bond interest	(1,000,000)
70% dividend exclusion	(1,400,000)
GAAP pretax income that will ever be taxed	7,600,000
TEMPORARY DIFFERENCE:	
Depreciation	(1,000,000)
Taxable income	$ 6,600,000

by $1 million, so this is a temporary difference, not a permanent difference, and it does not reduce GAAP pretax income that will ever be taxed.

Computing the Income Tax Provision and Its Components

The matching principle calls for the income tax provision to be recognized in the same period as the income that caused it, regardless of whether the tax will actually be paid in that period. However, items of income and expense that will never have a tax implication do not have any income tax effects recognized in the financial statements. This means that the income tax provision is based on

A CLOSER LOOK

LIFO Conformity Rule

In general, firms may choose different accounting methods for financial reporting and income tax reporting. (This freedom is what causes there to be deferred taxes.) For example, many firms use straight-line depreciation in their financial statements and accelerated depreciation for income tax purposes.

A notable exception to this freedom is inventory reporting. Under the LIFO Conformity Rule, if a firm uses LIFO (last in, first out) for tax purposes, it must also use LIFO for financial reporting. LIFO usually minimizes the present value of income tax payments (assuming inventory costs are rising) because the most recent costs are expensed first. To get this tax benefit, firms must also report the lower income to their shareholders.

LIFO firms usually report, in a footnote, information about inventories that is sufficient to calculate a pro forma (as if) cost of sales amount, and therefore income as well, as if FIFO (first in, first out) had been used. This permits LIFO firms almost to have their cake and eat it, too.

EXHIBIT 13.4   Computation of Lone Star's 2001 Income Tax

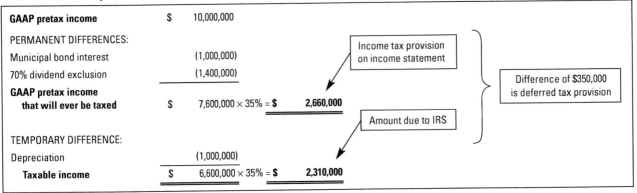

GAAP pretax income that will ever be taxed. Meanwhile, the IRS is going to base the tax due this period on the year's taxable income.

Exhibit 13.4 shows the computation of Lone Star's 2001 income tax provision and income tax payment, assuming a 35% statutory tax rate. The income tax provision is $2,660,000. This is the $7.6 million of pretax income that will ever be taxed, times the 35% statutory tax rate. Of the $2,660,000 income tax provision recognized in the income statement, only $2,310,000 will actually be paid currently. This $2,310,000 is the **current income tax provision**. The $350,000 difference between the income tax provision and the current income tax provision is called the **deferred income tax provision**. The current and deferred tax provisions sum to the **total income tax provision**, also sometimes called income tax expense. Thus, the $2,660,000 income tax provision consists of $2,310,000 of current tax provision and $350,000 of deferred tax provision.

Financial Statement Effects of Income Taxes

Let us take the income tax computations from Exhibit 13.4 and look at how Lone Star's financial statements reflect these amounts. Exhibit 13.5 summarizes the financial statement effects for the year. First, the income statement includes Lone Star's income tax provision, reducing net income by $2,660,000. However, it will pay only the $2,310,000 current tax provision to the IRS. Lone Star must therefore set up a liability for the deferred portion of the tax provision, $350,000, which it reports in the balance sheet.[4] (We have assumed here that there were no other temporary differences left over from prior periods.) This liability arises because Lone Star reports an income tax provision that is greater than the amount it actually pays in cash. In a subsequent period, the temporary difference will reverse. Lone Star will pay more than its income tax provision and relieve the deferred tax liability.

Income taxes also affect the cash flow statement. The cash flow statement begins with net income of $7,340,000, which includes the $2,660,000 income tax provision. However, the bottom line of the cash flow statement, change in cash, includes only the $2,310,000 actually paid. Thus, there must be a reconciling item in the cash flow statement. The $350,000 increase in the deferred tax liability is a difference between income recognized and cash flow, so it explains some of the income–cash flow difference and appears as a reconciling item in the cash flow statement.

---

[4]Note that temporary differences can also cause the income tax provision to be less than income tax payable. This would result in a deferred income tax asset on the balance sheet instead of a deferred income tax liability.

EXHIBIT 13.5   Financial Statement Effects of Lone Star's 2001 Income Taxes

INCOME STATEMENT:	
Operating earnings before depreciation	$ 9,000,000
Depreciation	(2,000,000)
Operating earnings	7,000,000
Municipal bond interest	1,000,000
Dividend income	2,000,000
Pretax income	10,000,000
Income tax provision	**(2,660,000)**
Net income	$ 7,340,000

BALANCE SHEET:	
Total assets	X
Deferred tax liability	**$ 350,000**
Other liabilities	X
Equity	X
Total liabilities and equity	X

CASH FLOW STATEMENT:	
Net income	$ 7,340,000
Depreciation	2,000,000
Increase in deferred tax liability	**350,000**
Change in cash	$ 9,690,000

Loss Carryforwards and Carrybacks

The Lone Star case was a basic example showing common tax accounting issues. Now we will explore a more complex tax issue: loss carryforwards and loss carrybacks. When a firm has a loss for tax purposes, it may use the loss to offset either prior or future taxable income. The firm can elect to carry back a loss against income in prior years in which it paid tax,[5] or the firm can carry forward the loss to future years. Tax law allows carrybacks against taxes from the prior two years.[6] Carryforwards are applied against the next 20 years. If a carryback does not use up all the available loss, the remainder is carried forward.

Suppose Rollercoaster Company had $2 million and $3 million of taxable income in 1999 and 2000, respectively, and a taxable loss of $4 million in 2001. Assume Rollercoaster has a 35% marginal tax rate. It can carry back the $4 million loss in 2001 against income earned in 1999 and 2000, as shown in Exhibit 13.6. Rollercoaster would claim an income tax refund of $4 million × 0.35, or $1.4 million. The refund would result from carrying back the 2001 loss first against 1999 and then applying the remainder of the loss against 2000.

Companies can also carry forward their losses. Suppose Rollercoaster had only $1 million of taxable income in 1999 and 2000. This income would not have used up the entire 2001 loss of $4 mil-

---

[5]Almost all firms with losses will elect to first carry back because this provides an immediate cash benefit, whereas benefits from carryforwards are delayed and therefore have a lower present value. In rare circumstances, such as when income tax rates are scheduled to increase, firms may elect not to carry back.

[6]The Job Creation and Worker Assistance Act of 2002, which was signed into law on March 9, 2002, extends the carryback period to 5 years for losses arising in 2001 and 2002. This change is temporary and the carryback period reverts to 2 years in 2003.

EXHIBIT 13.6　Rollercoaster Example 1—Carryback

	1999	2000	2001
Taxable income (loss) before carryback	$ 2,000,000	$ 3,000,000	$ (4,000,000)
Carryback	(2,000,000)	(2,000,000)	4,000,000
Taxable income after carryback	$ 0	$ 1,000,000	$ 0

lion. If the company returned to profitability, it could apply the unused portion of the loss against future income, as in Exhibit 13.7. Rollercoaster would first carry back its loss against 1999 and 2000, and receive a tax refund of $2 million × 35%, or $700,000. The company would still have $2 million of unused loss remaining to carry forward. It would pay no taxes in 2002 by using $1 million of the remaining loss to offset all its taxable income. It would then use the remaining $1 million of loss to reduce its 2003 taxes by $1 million × 35% = $350,000.

Loss Carryforwards and Financial Reporting

Loss carryforwards are temporary differences because the tax benefit is reported in the income statement in the year the carryforward arises (the loss year), even though the benefit is not realized until some future period, if it is ever realized. By recording the carryforward in the loss year as a deferred tax asset, firms report an income tax benefit (negative income tax provision), which increases income. Rollercoaster's income statement, cash flow statement, and deferred tax asset for 1999 through 2001 would be as shown in Exhibit 13.8.

Rollercoaster's income and cash flow were $650,000 in 1999 and 2000. In 2001, the company reported a pretax loss of $4 million. It recorded a tax benefit of 35% of this amount, or $1.4 million, so the net loss was only $2.6 million. Of this $1.4 million tax benefit, only $700,000 was received currently, when Rollercoaster carried back $2 million of its loss and received a refund of its 1999 and 2000 income taxes. So, Rollercoaster's cash outflow in 2001 is the $4 million loss less the $700,000 refund, or $3.3 million. This is reported as $2.6 million of net loss, minus the $700,000 of the income tax benefit not realized currently, which is equal to the increase in the deferred tax asset, for a total cash outflow of $3.3 million.

Although deferred tax assets are always recorded, in certain circumstances they are effectively removed from the balance sheet through a **valuation allowance**. The accounting rule governing when a valuation allowance must be recorded is SFAS No. 109, "Accounting for Income Taxes." It

EXHIBIT 13.7　Rollercoaster Example 2—Carryback and Carryforward

	1999	2000	2001	2002	2003
Taxable income (loss) before carryback/carryforward	$ 1,000,000	$ 1,000,000	($ 4,000,000)	$ 1,000,000	$ 3,000,000
Carryback/carryforward	(1,000,000)	(1,000,000)	4,000,000	(1,000,000)	(1,000,000)
Taxable income after carryback/carryforward	$ 0	$ 0	$ 0	$ 0	$ 2,000,000

EXHIBIT 13.8   Rollercoaster Example 2—Income Statement, Cash Flow Statement, and Deferred Tax Asset

	1999	2000	2001
INCOME STATEMENT:			
Pretax income (loss)	$ 1,000,000	$ 1,000,000	$ (4,000,000)
Income tax (provision) benefit	(350,000)	(350,000)	1,400,000
Net income (loss)	$ 650,000	$ 650,000	$ (2,600,000)
CASH FLOW STATEMENT:			
Net income (loss)	$ 650,000	$ 650,000	$ (2,600,000)
Less increase in deferred tax asset			(700,000)
Change in cash	$ 650,000	$ 650,000	$ (3,300,000)
Deferred tax asset (from balance sheet)	$ 0	$ 0	$ 700,000

states that if it is "more likely than not" that a deferred tax asset will not be realized, then a valuation allowance, a contra-account, should be recorded. Although SFAS No. 109 provides some guidance as to factors providing positive and negative evidence that the asset will be realized, to a large extent the valuation allowance decision is a management judgment, subject to approval by the firm's auditors. In the Rollercoaster example, if the company believed it was unlikely it would be profitable in the next 20 years and that the carryforward would expire unused, the income and cash flow statements and deferred tax asset would appear as shown in Exhibit 13.9.

In this case, Rollercoaster records only a $700,000 tax benefit in its 2001 income statement, the cash refund it receives immediately. As a result, the net loss is $3.3 million rather than $2.6 million. The $700,000 deferred tax asset is offset by a valuation allowance of the same amount. Note that the change in cash is the same regardless of whether a valuation allowance is recorded. The valuation allowance affects income and the amount reported as a deferred tax asset, but it does not affect the change in cash.

EXHIBIT 13.9   Rollercoaster Example 2—Income Statement, Cash Flow Statement, and Deferred Tax Asset with Valuation Allowance

	1999	2000	2001
INCOME STATEMENT:			
Pretax income (loss)	$ 1,000,000	$ 1,000,000	$ (4,000,000)
Income tax (provision) benefit	(350,000)	(350,000)	700,000
Net income (loss)	$ 650,000	$ 650,000	$ (3,300,000)
CASH FLOW STATEMENT:			
Net income (loss)	$ 650,000	$ 650,000	$ (3,300,000)
Less increase in deferred tax asset			0
Change in cash	$ 650,000	$ 650,000	$ (3,300,000)
Deferred tax asset	$ 0	$ 0	$ 700,000
Valuation allowance			(700,000)
Net deferred tax asset on balance sheet	$ 0	$ 0	$ 0

Loss Carryforwards and Valuation

Loss carryforwards have an important effect on firm valuation. They reduce the amount of future income taxes the firm would otherwise have to pay and therefore increase the expected free cash flow stream. The value of loss carryforwards depends on the

- Magnitude of the carryforwards
- Certainty with which they will be used
- Speed with which they will used

The importance of the magnitude of carryforwards is clear. The larger the carryforward, the more the reduction in future income tax payments. The certainty factor is more subtle. Carryforwards are valuable only if the firm has otherwise taxable income prior to the expiration of the carryforwards. For firms that may not become profitable, carryforwards are less valuable, because they may not result in any tax savings. The speed with which the carryforwards are expected to be used also affects their value, because the present value of saving a dollar of taxes is greater the sooner the savings occur.

Suppose it is the end of 2001. After carrying back $2 million of its $4 million loss, Rollercoaster has a $2 million loss carryforward. Exhibit 13.10 shows how its free cash flow forecast and valuation would be structured to capture the value of the carryforward. The valuation assumes a 10% discount rate and 3% growth in perpetuity. The carryforward enters into the value of the firm by increasing the free cash flow in years 2002 and 2003, relative to what it would have been without the carryforward. The effect on value is the present value of $0.35 million discounted one year, plus the present value of $0.35 million discounted two years. The spreadsheet also includes a carryforward reconciliation to determine when the carryforward has been used up.[7]

Regardless of whether the firm applies a valuation allowance, the net operating loss should be used to offset any forecasted income tax provision to maintain consistency with the rest of the forecast. If the valuation is based on the assumption the firm will become profitable, then it should also assume the operating loss carryforward is used, even if the firm applies a valuation allowance.

13.3   THE STRUCTURE OF THE INCOME TAX FOOTNOTE

The income tax footnote provides information we can use to determine the amounts of certain adjustments in the free cash flow analysis. It also provides important information on loss carryforwards and valuation allowances.

The income tax footnote generally has three tables.

- **Tax provision summary**. This table shows the income tax provision, broken out by the portions that are current and deferred.
- **Deferred tax asset and liability summary**. This table summarizes the temporary differences that have not yet reversed as of the balance sheet date, and the amounts each contributed to the firm's deferred tax asset or liability.
- **Reconciliation of the statutory rate to the firm's effective rate**. This table provides a reconciliation that explains differences between the statutory tax rate and the firm's effective tax rate. This reconciliation can be done in terms of rates, or the tax provision in dollars. If the reconciliation is

---

[7]If a firm with carryforwards is heavily levered, the analyst might wish to use the flows to equity method, because interest expense will reduce taxable income and delay the realization of the benefits from the carryforwards. The flows to equity method will capture the effect of this delay.

EXHIBIT 13.10 Rollercoaster Example 2—Company Valuation

($ millions)	2002	2003	2004	2005	2006	2007 (P)
Sales	$ 10.00	$ 15.00	$ 20.00	$ 24.00	$ 27.00	$ 35.00
Cost of sales	(7.70)	(11.00)	(15.00)	(16.00)	(17.20)	(19.00)
SG&A expenses	(1.30)	(1.00)	(1.20)	(1.60)	(1.80)	(2.20)
Operating income	1.00	3.00	3.80	6.40	8.00	13.80
Income tax provision before use of loss carryforward	(0.35)	(1.05)	(1.33)	(2.24)	(2.80)	(4.83)
Tax reduction from use of loss carryforward	**0.35**	**0.35**	**0.00**	**0.00**	**0.00**	**0.00**
NOPAT	1.00	2.30	2.47	4.16	5.20	8.97
Other free cash flow items (assume none)	0.00	0.00	0.00	0.00	0.00	0.00
Free cash flow	$ 1.00	$ 2.30	$ 2.47	$ 4.16	$ 5.20	$ 8.97
Present value (at 10%)	$ 0.91	$ 1.90	$ 1.86	$ 2.84	$ 3.23	$ 79.57
Total present value	$ 90.31					
Beginning carryforward	$ 2.00	$ 1.00	$ 0.00	$ 0.00	$ 0.00	$ 0.00
Carryforward used	1.00	1.00	0.00	0.00	0.00	0.00
Ending carryforward	$ 1.00	$ 0.00	$ 0.00	$ 0.00	$ 0.00	$ 0.00
Tax savings from use of carryforward (Carryforward used × 35%)	$ 0.35	$ 0.35	$ 0.00	$ 0.00	$ 0.00	$ 0.00

(P) First year of perpetuity

based on rates, it begins with the federal statutory rate, which is currently 35%. It then explains why the effective income tax rate is different from this amount, by showing each component of pretax income that is not taxed at the statutory rate and the effect that this had on the effective rate. If the reconciliation is done in dollars, it begins with what the income tax provision would be if all of the pretax income were taxed at the federal statutory tax rate. It then explains why the income tax provision is different from this amount by showing each item that had a tax effect other than 35%, and the dollar effect this different tax effect had on the income tax provision.

Exhibit 13.11 is Lone Star's 2001 income tax footnote. Although most companies show only one format for the tax rate reconciliation, we provide both the dollars and the rates for the purpose of illustration. The first table in Exhibit 13.11 summarizes Lone Star's income tax provision. It shows the breakdown between the current and deferred portions of the income tax provision. The second table summarizes the deferred tax assets and liabilities. The amounts shown in the table represent the tax effects of temporary differences that have not yet reversed. As of the balance sheet date, Lone Star has a cumulative temporary difference of $1 million, resulting in a $350,000 deferred tax liability.

The third table is the tax rate reconciliation, which deals with the effects of permanent differences. The dollar format of the reconciliation explains why the income tax provision is not simply the statutory tax rate times pretax income. It begins with the hypothetical income tax provision Lone Star would have recorded if all the firm's pretax income were subject to the statutory tax rate. It reconciles this amount to Lone Star's actual income tax provision, by showing how various permanent differences caused the income tax provision to be something other than the statutory rate times pretax income. Lone Star's permanent differences were the municipal bond interest and the dividend income. The municipal bond interest was not taxed. The income tax provision was $350,000 ($1 million × 35%) lower than it would have been if the income had been taxed at the statutory rate. Recall that 70% of the $2 million of dividend income was excluded from taxable income. The income tax provision was therefore $490,000 ($2 million × 70% × 35%) lower than it would have

EXHIBIT 13.11   Income Tax Footnote: Lone Star Example

INCOME TAX PROVISION:		
Current	$	2,310,000
Deferred		350,000
Total income tax provision	$	2,660,000
DEFERRED TAX ASSETS AND LIABILITIES:		
Deferred tax assets	$	0
Deferred tax liabilities:		
Depreciation		350,000
Total deferred tax liabilities		350,000
Net deferred tax asset (liability)	$	(350,000)

TAX PROVISION RECONCILIATION:		Dollars	Rate
Tax provision at statutory rate (35%)	$	3,500,000	35.0
Municipal bond interest		(350,000)	(3.5)
Dividend exclusion		(490,000)	(4.9)
Income tax provision/ Effective tax rate	$	2,660,000	26.6

been if the entire amount of dividend income were subject to tax. Note that if the municipal bond interest and dividend income amounts were not separately disclosed in the income statement, we could determine those amounts from the information in the reconciliation.

The tax rate format of the reconciliation begins with the federal statutory tax rate. It then adds and subtracts the effects of the permanent differences on the effective rate. Each of these items is the dollar effect of the permanent difference on the tax provision divided by pretax income.

13.4 ESTIMATING THE EFFECTIVE TAX RATE ON CORE OPERATIONS

In a valuation, the effective tax rate on core operations is a key assumption. All the tax analysis we do in this chapter prepares us to calculate this rate. In Chapter 9, we determined income from core operations by making adjustments to remove income not related to core operations. Using the appropriate marginal tax rates, we made similar adjustments to remove the portion of the tax provision not related to core operations. The remaining tax provision represents the tax provision on income from core operations. From the results of the free cash flow worksheet, we calculated the effective tax rate on core operations by dividing the tax provision on income from core operations by income from core operations.

Finding the Information for Tax Adjustments

To make the appropriate adjustments to the income tax provision in a free cash flow analysis, we need to know or estimate the tax effects of each of the adjustments affecting pretax income. In some cases, the firm will disclose the dollar amount of the tax effect of a particular item, either in the financial statement footnotes or elsewhere in the annual report. This is most likely to occur when there is a gain or loss that we are removing. In such a case, we use the disclosed tax effect, as this is more precise than any estimate we could make.

More often, we must estimate the tax effect using an estimated marginal tax rate for the item. The marginal tax rate we apply depends on the nature of the income. We use our knowledge of income tax law and the firm's footnote to estimate the marginal tax rate on various types of income. We use a marginal tax rate of 0% for interest income from municipal bonds. Unless we have other information, we assume that other interest income and interest expense are taxed at the combined federal and state statutory rates.

Calculating the marginal tax rate on dividend income requires an additional step. Tax law allows corporations that receive dividends from other U.S. corporations to exclude either 70% or 80% of the dividend income in calculating taxes, depending on the percentage of ownership involved. If Big Company owns less than 20% of Little Company, then Big may exclude 70% of the dividends received in calculating its taxable income. If Big owns 20% or more of Little, then Big may exclude 80% of the dividends received from Little.[8] This means the marginal tax rate on dividend income is either 30% (1 − 0.70) or 20% (1 − 0.80) of the combined federal and state statutory tax rates. For example, if Big's state income tax rate is 3%, and the federal statutory tax rate is 35%, then the effective tax rate on corporate dividends received would be either 11.085% or 7.39%, as shown in Exhibit 13.12.

Analyzing Starbucks' Income Tax Footnote

Let us now examine how to use the information in Starbucks' income tax footnote disclosure. Exhibit 13.13 shows the income tax footnote from Starbucks' fiscal 2000 annual report. Note that Starbucks presents the three tables in a different order than is typical.

---

[8]The dividend exclusion is 100% when ownership exceeds the threshold for filing a consolidated tax return, which is 80%.

EXHIBIT 13.12   Calculation of Marginal Tax Rates on Dividend Income

	Ownership %	
	Less than 20%	20% or Greater
Tax rates in percents		
Federal statutory tax rate	35.000	35.000
State tax rate	3.000	3.000
Federal benefit from state taxes (35% × 3%)	(1.050)	(1.050)
Combined federal and state tax rate before dividend exclusion	36.950	36.950
Taxable portion of dividend	0.300	0.200
Marginal tax rate on dividends received	11.085	7.390

What Information Is Included in Starbucks' Footnote?

Section A of the footnote reconciles the federal statutory tax rate to Starbucks' effective tax rate. Although the federal statutory rate was unchanged during the three years presented, Starbucks' effective rate fluctuated between 38.0% and 41.2%. In fiscal 1998, when nondeductible losses and merger costs were reported, the effective tax rate was higher. By recording these losses and expenses, Starbucks reported less income than it otherwise would have, but with no associated reduction in the income tax provision. Its income tax was higher than it would have been had the losses been tax deductible, increasing the effective tax rate. In fiscal 2000, Starbucks increased its valuation allowance. This caused an increase in the income tax provision with no corresponding increase in reported pretax income, which also increased the effective tax rate. State taxes, net of the federal benefit, and other items, net also caused Starbucks' effective tax rate to differ from 35%.

Section B of the footnote shows Starbucks' income tax provision, broken out between the current and deferred provisions. For example, in fiscal 1999 Starbucks recorded an income tax provision that was $794,000 higher than the amount it was required to pay in taxes that year, recording a deferred tax liability in the process. In fiscal 2000, the company paid $18,252,000 more in income taxes than the amount it reported as its income tax provision. This occurs either when a company's previously recorded deferred tax liabilities reverse or when it records a deferred tax asset. Section B also provides a breakout of the amount paid in taxes between federal and state jurisdictions.

Section C and the paragraph that precedes it provide information about Starbucks' deferred tax assets and liabilities as of its balance sheet date. It shows that Starbucks had $58.4 million of deferred tax assets at October 1, 2000. The largest single deferred tax asset relates to loss on investments. This indicates that although Starbucks recorded a tax benefit from the loss, thereby reducing the income tax provision, it did not receive the benefit in cash because the loss will not be deductible until a future period. We also see from this section that Starbucks recorded a valuation allowance, and the paragraph preceding the table indicates the valuation allowance is related to the loss on investments deferred tax asset. This valuation allowance effectively removed $5.7 million of the deferred tax asset from the balance sheet, increasing the income tax provision in fiscal 2000 when the valuation allowance was recorded.

Starbucks also has deferred tax liabilities. The single largest deferred tax liability is related to depreciation. Starbucks, like many companies, uses a more accelerated depreciation method for income tax reporting than for preparing its financial statements. Cumulatively, Starbucks has paid $36.2 million less in income taxes than it would have if it used its financial reporting depreciation method for tax purposes. However, this is a temporary difference, as the depreciation on any given

EXHIBIT 13.13 Starbucks' 2000 Income Tax Footnote

A reconciliation of the statutory federal income tax rate with the Company's effective income tax rate is as follows:

Fiscal year ended	A	October 1, 2000	October 3, 1999	September 27, 1998
Statutory rate		35.0%	35.0%	35.0%
State income taxes, net of federal income tax benefit		3.7	3.7	3.8
Nondeductible losses and merger costs				2.6
Valuation allowance change from prior year		3.5		
Other, net		(1.1)	(0.7)	(0.2)
Effective tax rate		41.1%	38.0%	41.2%

The provision for income taxes consists of the following (in thousands):

Fiscal year ended	B	October 1, 2000	October 3, 1999	September 27, 1998
Currently payable				
Federal		$ 71,758	$ 52,207	$ 39,267
State		12,500	9,332	6,586
Deferred (asset) liability, net		(18,252)	794	2,125
Total		$ 66,006	$ 62,333	$ 47,978

Deferred income taxes (benefits) reflect the tax effect of temporary differences between the amounts of assets and liabilities for financial reporting purposes and amounts as measured for tax purposes. The Company will establish a valuation allowance if it is more likely than not these items will either expire before the Company is able to realize their benefits, or that future deductibility is uncertain. At October 1, 2000, the Company established a valuation allowance of $5.7 million as a result of the losses incurred on Internet-related investments. The tax effect of temporary differences and carryforwards that cause significant portions of deferred tax assets and liabilities is as follows (in thousands):

	C	October 1, 2000	October 3, 1999
Deferred tax assets:			
Loss on investments		$ 22,635	$ 0
Accrued rent		10,321	8,234
Accrued compensation and related costs		6,710	5,622
Inventory related costs		3,550	2,067
Other		15,222	9,900
Total		58,438	25,823
Valuation allowance		(5,659)	0
Total deferred tax asset, net of valuation allowance		52,779	25,823
Deferred tax liabilities:			
Depreciation		(36,249)	(29,826)
Investments in joint ventures		(4,616)	(3,990)
Other		(4,020)	(3,760)
Total		(44,885)	(37,576)
Net deferred tax asset (liability)		$ 7,894	$ (11,753)

Taxes currently payable of $17.9 million and $16.3 million are included in "Accrued taxes" on the accompanying consolidated balance sheets as of October 1, 2000, and October 3, 1999, respectively.

asset is the same over its entire life under any depreciation method. As a result, the income tax provision is based on the financial reporting depreciation amount. The resulting income tax provision is thus higher than the amount paid to the government, resulting in a liability.

How Do We Use This Information?

First, we see that Starbucks' combined federal and state tax rate was 38.7% in fiscal 2000 and 1999, and 38.8% in fiscal 1998. In our free cash flow analysis, we used these rates on all adjustments where there was no reason to suggest that the item received unusual tax treatment, such as an item that is not deductible. For example, from the footnote we also see that the merger costs are not tax deductible. When we remove the merger costs from free cash flow in the adjustment process, the appropriate marginal income tax rate to apply to the adjustment is zero. These costs had no effect on the income tax provision, and no portion of the income tax provision needs to be reversed as a result of them. We also see from the footnote the exact amount of the tax effect of the investment losses. This was the $22,635,000 deferred tax asset that was created, net of the $5,659,000 valuation allowance, or $16,976,000. We do not need to estimate this tax effect using a marginal tax rate because we have the exact amount. Further, the disclosure tells us that the entire tax effect of these losses was deferred. As a result, when we removed them from the income tax provision, we removed an equal amount, but having the opposite sign, from the deferred tax addback on the cash flow statement.

Just as important as what is in Starbucks' income tax reconciliation is what is *not* there. Unlike Lone Star, Starbucks did not have significant municipal bond interest income. If Starbucks had municipal bond interest income, we would have seen an item related to this in the reconciliation, because it would have reduced the company's effective income tax rate. We therefore know we should apply a marginal rate of 38.7%, not zero, to the interest income adjustment that we make.

Tax Adjustments in the Starbucks' Cash Flow Worksheet

Exhibit 13.14 shows part of the Starbucks' cash flow worksheet from Exhibit 9.7 in Chapter 9. (We show the worksheet only down to the computation of NOPAT.) This worksheet indicates that Starbucks' effective tax rate on core operations was $78,659,000/$191,952,000 = 41.0%. In our historical analysis we will calculate several years of analyses as in Exhibit 13.14 to have several years of historical effective tax rates on core operations. We use these to forecast the effective tax rate on core operations going forward, also taking into account any reasons why the effective tax rate might change in the future.

Analyzing Income Taxes When There Are Foreign Operations

Starbucks does not have any substantial foreign operations, which can affect the income tax disclosure because foreign tax rates are often different from U.S. rates. We now consider the income tax analysis for a firm with foreign operations, using Wal-Mart Stores, Inc.'s tax rate reconciliation. Exhibit 13.15 is Wal-Mart's tax rate reconciliation for the year ended January 31, 2000. Wal-Mart provided the reconciliation in terms of tax rates. We have converted it to dollars by multiplying each item in the reconciliation by the pretax income of $9.083 billion Wal-Mart reported in its income statement.

From this and other footnote information, we can determine the effective tax rate for foreign operations. This is important because if we project increases in foreign income, we must know the appropriate tax rate to use. The tax rate reconciliation tells us that foreign taxes were $67 million lower than they would have been at 35%. Elsewhere in the footnote, Wal-Mart reported a foreign tax provision of $74 million. Therefore, had all foreign jurisdictions used the 35% rate, Wal-Mart's foreign provision would have been $74 million + $67 million = $141 million. This tells us that foreign

EXHIBIT 13.14 Starbucks' 2000 Cash Flow Worksheet Through NOPAT

($ thousands)	GAAP	Adjustments	FCF
Net revenues	$ 2,169,218		$ 2,169,218
Cost of sales and related occupancy costs	(953,560)		(953,560)
Gross margin	1,215,658		1,215,658
Joint venture income	20,300	(15,139)	0
		(5,161)	
Store operating expenses	(704,898)		(704,898)
Other operating expenses	(78,374)		(78,374)
Depreciation and amortization	(130,232)		(130,232)
General and administrative expenses	(110,202)		(110,202)
Operating income	212,252		191,952
Interest and other income, net	7,110	(7,110)	0
Internet-related investment losses	(58,792)	58,792	0
Earnings before income taxes	160,570		**191,952**
Income taxes	(66,006)	2,752 / 1,571 / (16,976)	**(78,659)**
Net earnings/NOPAT	94,564		113,293

(Left margin label: CASH FLOW FROM OPERATIONS; Right margin label: FREE CASH FLOW)

Effective tax rate on core operations:

$$\frac{\text{Tax on income from core operations}}{\text{Income from core operations before taxes}} = \frac{78{,}659}{191{,}952} = 41.0\%$$

pretax income is $141 million divided by 0.35, or $403 million. The $74 million provision is 18.4% of this amount, so Wal-Mart has an 18.4% effective tax rate on foreign income.

What do we know from this reconciliation? First, Wal-Mart has very little nontaxable income. Its effective rate of 36.75% is a reasonable approximation for the marginal rate on our adjustments. Second, Wal-Mart has a lower marginal tax rate on foreign income than on domestic income. If Wal-Mart expands internationally in the same countries in which it already operates, then we would expect its total effective tax rate to decline. The marginal tax rate on its foreign income is only 18.4%. If a forecast presumes international expansion, this income will become a larger percentage of Wal-Mart's overall income. When forecasting the effective tax rate on core operations, we should consider how this mix of income might change.

EXHIBIT 13.15 Wal-Mart Stores' Tax Rate Reconciliation for Year Ended January 31, 2000

	Millions of Dollars	Tax Rate
Tax provision at statutory rate	$ 3,179	35.00%
State income taxes, net of federal income tax benefit	198	2.18
International	(67)	(0.74)
Other, net	28	0.31
Tax provision	$ 3,338	36.75 %

SUMMARY

We commonly refer to three distinct types of income tax rates. The statutory tax rate is the rate set by law. This rate is used in conjunction with taxable income to compute the amount due to the government. The marginal tax rate is the rate applicable to the next dollar of income or deduction. This rate differs for different kinds of income. The effective tax rate is the average rate for the firm or for a group of assets. For example, we use the effective income tax rate on core operations in valuation.

Financial reporting rules are based on the matching principle. This results in income statement recognition of the income tax consequences of all pretax items, regardless of when the tax consequences affect taxes paid. Items for which the timing of recognition differs between financial reporting and tax rules give rise to temporary differences and deferred tax assets or liabilities. If it is more likely than not that the future benefit of a deferred tax asset will not actually be realized, then a valuation allowance is applied to it, effectively removing it from the balance sheet. Items that are recognized for income tax purposes but not financial reporting, or vice versa, are permanent differences.

Loss carrybacks occur when a firm reports a loss on its income tax return and uses it to offset taxable income from the prior two years, generating an immediate refund of previously paid taxes. Additional losses beyond the amount carried back may be carried forward up to 20 years. From a valuation perspective, loss carryforwards are an important deferred tax asset because they reduce future tax payments and therefore increase future cash flows.

The income tax footnote is an important source of information about a firm's income taxes. We can use it to estimate the appropriate marginal tax rates for our adjustments in the cash flow worksheet.

After we have completed our cash flow worksheet, we can calculate the effective tax rate on core operations by dividing the tax provision on income from core operations by the income from core operations. We consider the historical effective tax rates on core operations and what might change in this tax rate and develop an assumption for the forecasted effective tax rate on core operations. This rate will be a key assumption in the valuation forecast.

SUGGESTED READINGS

Anderson, K., T. Pope, and J. Kramer. *Prentice Hall's Federal Taxation 2003: Corporations, Partnerships, Estates and Trusts.* Upper Saddle River, NJ: Prentice Hall, 2003.

Revsine, L., D. Collins, and B. Johnson. *Financial Reporting and Analysis,* 2nd ed. Upper Saddle River, NJ: Prentice Hall, 2002.

Scholes, M., M. Wolfson, M. Erickson, and E. Maydew. *Taxes and Business Strategy: A Planning Approach,* 2nd ed. Upper Saddle River, NJ: Prentice Hall, 2002.

REVIEW QUESTIONS

1. What is a statutory tax rate?
2. What is a marginal tax rate?
3. What is an effective tax rate?

4. Assume Morley Corporation has a marginal tax rate of 35% and an effective tax rate of 30% due to the exclusion from taxable income of its municipal bond income. If Morley's pretax income increases by $1 million, by how much does its income tax provision increase in the following circumstances:

   a. the income is related to core operations
   b. the income is municipal bond interest

5. Distinguish between temporary differences and permanent differences.

6. Give an example of a permanent difference.

7. Give an example of a temporary difference.

8. What is a valuation allowance?

9. When is a valuation allowance recorded?

10. What is a tax loss carryback?

11. What is a tax loss carryforward?

12. Why does a tax loss carryforward affect a firm's value?

13. What are the three sections of a typical income tax footnote? What information is included in each?

PROBLEMS

The following information pertains to problems 1 and 2. You have obtained the following analysis of Wolfman Radiological Systems, Inc.'s pretax income and income tax provision.

($ millions)	Pretax Income	Tax Rate	Tax
Operating income	$ 1,000	0.350	$ 350.0
Municipal bond interest	70	0.000	0.0
Interest expense	(85)	0.360	(30.6)
Dividend income	60	0.105	6.3
Tax credit			(8.0)
Total	$ 1,045	0.304	$ 317.7

This analysis shows that different elements of Wolfman's pretax income are taxed at different rates. Operating income and interest expense are taxed at slightly different rates due to jurisdictional differences. Municipal bond interest is not taxed. Dividend income is taxed at a lower rate due to the corporate dividend exclusion. The tax credit reduces the firm's tax as a result of its investing in certain areas targeted by the state for development. This tax credit is related to the firm's core operations.

1. What is Wolfman's income tax provision related to core operations?

2. What is Wolfman's effective income tax rate from core operations?

3. Blimpie International franchises and licenses quick-service sandwich restaurants. As of June 30, 2000, Blimpie reported a $243,000 deferred tax liability related to trademark amortization. Has Blimpie recorded more trademark amortization for financial statement purposes or tax purposes?

4. As of June 30, 2000, Blimpie reported a $117,000 deferred tax asset for allowance for doubtful accounts. Which does Blimpie record sooner, bad debt expense for its financial statements or on its tax return?

5. Are the items referred to in problems 3 and 4 permanent differences or temporary differences?

6. The following was adapted from the Bally Total Fitness 1999 income tax footnote: The income tax provision consists of the following:

(in thousands of dollars)	1999	1998	1997
Deferred	$ 16,950	$ 6,180	
Reversal of valuation allowance	(16,950)	(6,180)	
State and other (all current)	870	525	$ 300
	$ 870	$ 525	$ 300

Bally reported pretax income of $43,314,000 in 1999.

a. What was Bally's effective tax rate in 1999?

b. What would Bally's effective tax rate in 1999 have been if the company had not previously recorded a valuation allowance?

7. As of June 30, 1999, America Online (AOL) reported a $2.7 billion deferred tax asset related to its net operating loss carryforward.

a. Assuming a statutory tax rate of 35%, what amount of net operating loss can AOL carry forward to offset future taxable income?

b. If AOL were forecasted to generate $1 billion of taxable income per year (before applying carryforwards) in the foreseeable future, what would be the value to the firm of the net operating loss carryforwards? Assume a discount rate of 12%.

8. The following tax rate reconciliation was adapted from the income tax footnote in General Motors' 2000 annual report.

(in millions of dollars)

Years ended December 31,	2000	1999	1998
Tax at U.S. federal statutory income tax rate	$ 2,507	$ 3,166	$ 1,730
Foreign rates other than 35%	78	(109)	1
Taxes on unremitted earnings of subsidiaries		138	92
Tax credits	(45)	(207)	(203)
Subsidiary settlement of affirmative claim with IRS			(92)
Other adjustments	(147)	130	108
Total income tax	$ 2,393	$ 3,118	$ 1,636

a. Estimate General Motors' pretax income in each of the three years presented.

b. In which year(s) was the average tax rate on General Motors' foreign income greater than 35%?

c. Did the settlement with the IRS increase or decrease General Motors' net income in 1998?

d. What is General Motors' effective income tax rate in each of the three years presented?

9. In its fiscal 2001 annual report, Circuit City Stores, Inc. reported an effective income tax rate of 38%, consisting of the 35% federal statutory tax rate and 3% for state taxes, net of the federal benefit.

   a. What is the average state tax rate before the federal benefit for Circuit City?
   b. Does Circuit City have any significant municipal bond interest income?
   c. Circuit City reported interest expense of $19,383,000 in fiscal 2001. In adjusting its income statement and cash flow statement to a free cash flow basis, what is the amount of the related income tax adjustment you would make? Would this adjustment increase or decrease the income tax provision?

10. The following is adapted from the income tax footnote in Johnson and Johnson's 2000 annual report.

   A comparison of income tax provision at the federal statutory rate of 35% in 2000, 1999, and 1998, to the Company's effective tax rate is as follows:

	2000	1999	1998
Statutory tax rate	35.0%	35.0%	35.0%
Puerto Rico and Ireland operations	(5.2)	(5.5)	(5.5)
Research tax credits	(0.6)	(0.6)	(0.3)
Domestic state and local	0.7	0.9	1.0
International subsidiaries excluding Ireland	(3.0)	(2.4)	(3.3)
In-process research and development	0.3		1.3
All other	0.3	0.2	
Effective tax rate	27.5 %	27.6 %	28.2 %

   The reduction in the 2000 worldwide effective tax rate was primarily due to a greater proportion of the Company's taxable income derived from lower tax rate countries offset by the Company's fourth quarter purchased in-process research and development charge which is not tax deductible.

   During 2000, the Company had subsidiaries operating in Puerto Rico under a tax incentive grant expiring December 31, 2007. In addition, the Company has subsidiaries manufacturing in Ireland under an incentive tax rate effective through the year 2010.

   a. Assuming all debt is in the United States, what is the marginal tax rate that should be used for interest adjustments for Johnson and Johnson in each of the three years presented?
   b. In determining the appropriate assumptions to use for the free cash flow forecast, how would you forecast the effective tax rate on core operations?

My Case

Analyze your company's income tax footnote. If appropriate, reconsider any of the marginal tax rate estimates in your historical analysis.

14

Where We Have Been:

We have learned how to construct valuations by forecasting and discounting free cash flows.

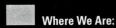
Where We Are:

In this chapter we examine how to structure a valuation of a company that has an employee stock option plan.

Where We Are Going:

In the next chapter, we will apply similar logic to pensions and other postemployment benefit plans.

Employee Stock Options and Valuation

LEARNING OBJECTIVES:

After studying this chapter, you will understand:

- What stock options are and why they are valuable.

- How the Black-Scholes option-pricing formula works.

- Why companies grant employee stock options.

- How employee stock options differ from publicly traded options.

- How the financial reporting for employee stock options works.

- How employee stock options affect income taxes.

- How to generalize valuation theory to deal with employee stock options.

O n June 30, 2001, Microsoft employees held nearly 900 million options to purchase Microsoft stock from the company, most of these options at prices well below Microsoft's $73 stock price, and some as low as 56 cents. At some point in the future, Microsoft will be forced to sell hundreds of millions of shares of its own stock for less than fair market value. This expected transfer of value from the firm to employees has a very large effect on how much investors should be willing to pay today for a share of Microsoft stock. As a result, we must consider employee stock options (ESOs) in our valuation.

This chapter explains how to value a firm that has an ESO plan. Section 14.1 discusses what stock options are and how they are valued. We present a simple example to show why options are valuable and then introduce the Black-Scholes option-pricing formula. Section 14.2 discusses why firms grant ESOs to their employees, how ESOs differ from publicly traded stock options, and why these differences affect option values. This section also discusses how an option-pricing formula such as Black-Scholes can be adapted to account for these differences. Section 14.3 examines the accounting for ESOs and the relevant tax law. Section 14.4 generalizes the valuation theory developed in prior chapters to incorporate ESOs and illustrates using Starbucks' ESO disclosure. Appendix 14.1 summarizes definitions used in this chapter.

14.1 STOCK OPTIONS

A stock option is a contract between the option holder and the option writer. It gives the **option holder** the right, but not the obligation, to buy stock from the **option writer** at a fixed price, called the **strike price**.[1] If the option holder **exercises** the option, the holder forces the option writer to sell shares to him or her at the strike price. The option holder's right to exercise the option expires at a fixed time, called the **expiration date**.

Thousands of different options are traded on option exchanges such as the Chicago Board Options Exchange (CBOE). Those who wish to buy options and those who wish to write them place orders with the exchange, which matches orders and executes trades, much like a stock exchange does. Exhibit 14.1 illustrates how an option transaction might take place on the CBOE. After the trade is executed, the purchaser receives an option and becomes an option holder. The option writer becomes obligated to sell stock if the option holder exercises, and the option holder pays the option writer (through the exchange and with transaction costs withheld) the price of the option.

Why Are Options Valuable?

To obtain the option in the transaction illustrated in Exhibit 14.1, the option holder had to pay a price to the option writer. Why? Because the option is valuable. Let us look at why options are valuable.

Recall the option strike price is the price at which the option holder may buy shares of stock. The amount by which the market value of the stock exceeds the option strike price is called the amount the option is **in the money**, or the **intrinsic value** of the option. For example, suppose a firm's stock is trading at $45 per share, and you hold a call option on that stock with strike price $40. Your option is in the money by $5. This means that you could exercise the option, permitting you to buy a share of

---

[1]Throughout this chapter, when we refer to **stock options**, we mean **call options**, which give the right to buy shares at a fixed price. Another type of stock option, called a put option, gives the holder the right to sell shares at a fixed price. Employee stock options are always call options, not put options.

EXHIBIT 14.1 Executing an Option Trade

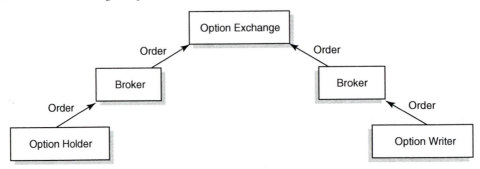

stock for $40 and immediately sell the share for $45, netting a $5 profit. A stock option is worth at least the amount it is in the money. Because the stock price could increase over time, an option that is not close to expiration generally is worth more than the amount it is in the money, as the following example illustrates.

Suppose your option has three months until it expires. During each of the next three months, the price of the stock will either increase to 1.05 times the prior month's price or decrease to 1/1.05 times the prior month's price. Further suppose that price increases and decreases are equally likely. Exhibit 14.2 is

EXHIBIT 14.2 Price Tree for Stock

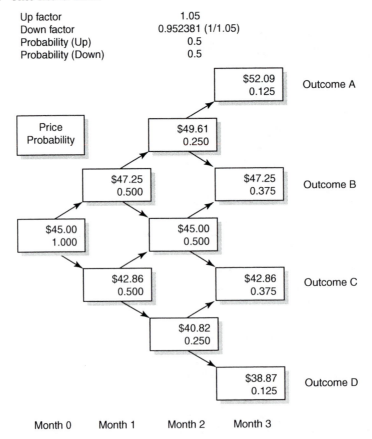

EXHIBIT 14.3 Expected Value of Option

Outcome	Probability	Stock Price	Option Value (Stock price − $40, but not less than $0)	Probability × Option Value
A	0.125	$ 52.09	$ 12.09	$ 1.51
B	0.375	$ 47.25	$ 7.25	2.72
C	0.375	$ 42.86	$ 2.86	1.07
D	0.125	$ 38.87	$ 0.00	0.00
			Total	$ 5.30

a price tree showing all possible stock prices at the end of each month, along with the probability that each possible price will be the actual price at that particular date.

We know that if you exercise your $40 option today you net a $5 profit, so the option would have produced $5 of value. Let us consider the expected value of your option if you intend to hold it for the entire three months until it expires. There are four possible outcomes for the month-3 price, which we have labeled outcomes A through D on Exhibit 14.2. For example, there is a 12.5% chance of three consecutive up months, in which case the stock price would be $52.09 (outcome A). Exhibit 14.3 summarizes the probability and option value for each outcome. In the case of outcome A, the option will be worth $52.09 − $40.00 = $12.09. In the case of outcome D, the option would be **out of the money**, meaning the strike price exceeds the stock price. The option holder would not exercise the option in this case, and it would be worthless. At expiration, an option is worth the amount it is in the money or zero if it is out of the money.

To determine the expected value today of the option at expiration, we multiply the probability of each outcome by the option's value at expiration and sum the products. The last column of Exhibit 14.3 shows the result is $5.30. An investor should be willing to pay up to $5.30 for this option,[2] even though it would be worth only $5.00 if exercised immediately. This $0.30 difference is called the **option premium**. It arises because holding an option allows an investor to benefit from increases in stock price while limiting the losses if the stock price falls, because a rational investor would never exercise an option that is not in the money.[3]

The Black-Scholes Option-Pricing Formula

The development of an option-pricing formula was one of the most important breakthroughs in finance. Myron Scholes won the Nobel Prize in 1997 for the **Black-Scholes option-pricing formula**, first published in 1973.[4] The formula is based on a continuous-time version of the price tree shown in Exhibit 14.2, meaning it involves infinitely many price movements over infinitely small periods. Black and Scholes showed that, assuming stock returns follow a log-normal distribution[5] and firms pay no dividends, call options have the following value:

---

[2]For simplicity, we have ignored the required interest for the three months.

[3]In the example, note that exercising the option when the stock price was $38.87 would result in paying $1.13 more for the stock than it would have cost on the open market. No rational investor would do this.

[4]Scholes' coauthor, Fischer Black, died before the Prize was awarded for this work. Because the Nobel Prize is not awarded posthumously, Black was not officially recognized by the Nobel Prize Committee.

[5]This means that the natural log of returns has a normal distribution. If we were to construct a price tree with infinitely many price movements over infinitely small periods, the returns would have a log-normal distribution.

$$C = S \cdot N(d_1) - X \cdot exp(-r \cdot t) \cdot N(d_2), \text{where:}$$

S = per share value of the firm's stock
X = strike price
t = time to expiration
σ = expected standard deviation of returns o
r = risk-free interest rate
$N(\cdot)$ = cumulative normal distribution functioi
$$d = [\log(S/X) + r \cdot t] / (\sigma \cdot \sqrt{t})$$
$$d_1 = d + \sigma \cdot \sqrt{t} / 2$$
$$d_2 = d - \sigma \cdot \sqrt{t} / 2$$

Exhibit 14.4 shows how Black-Scholes call option values vary with stock price.[6]

The solid curve represents the value of a call option as a function of stock price. The dashed, kinked line represents the amount the option is in the money as a function of stock price. The graph illustrates the following:

- Call option values increase with stock price.

- For options that are very far out of the money (the left side of the graph), the increase in option value is very small as stock price increases. This is so because when an option is far out of the money, the likelihood it will be in the money before expiration is very small. Hence, the option is almost certain to be worth zero at expiration.

- For options that are very far in the money (the right side of the graph), option value increases nearly dollar-for-dollar with stock price, because these options are virtually certain to remain in the money.

EXHIBIT 14.4   Black-Scholes Call Option Values and Stock Price

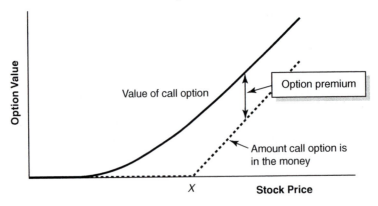

_____

[6]For firms that pay dividends, the Black-Scholes formula is more complicated. It is $C = S \cdot exp(-y \cdot t) \cdot N(d_1) - X \cdot exp(-r \cdot t) \cdot N(d_2)$, where y is the dividend yield and $d = [\log(S/X) + (r - y) \cdot t] / (\sigma \cdot \sqrt{t})$. d_1 and d_2 are as defined in the original Black-Scholes formula.

- The value of an option is always greater than the amount it is in the money[7] (except when the stock price is zero, in which case the option is worthless). The vertical distance between the curve and the kinked line represents the difference between the option's value and the amount the option is in the money. This is the option premium.

- The option premium is greatest when the option is **at the money**, meaning the stock price and strike price are equal.

14.2 Differences Between Publicly Traded Options and ESOs

Employee stock options (ESOs) differ from publicly traded options in two ways. First, ESOs are usually subject to restrictions that do not apply to publicly traded options. Second, the employer firm, not some independent party, is the option writer on an ESO.

ESO Restrictions

Employees cannot buy ESOs. Instead, many firms **grant** ESOs to employees as part of their compensation packages. ESOs align employees' incentives with those of the shareholders. Employees are more likely to take actions that will increase stock price if they too can benefit from stock price increases. Holding stock options causes employees to behave more like shareholders.

In order to ensure that ESOs are properly aligning incentives, firms generally place restrictions on them. Typical restrictions include the following:

- Employees may not sell ESOs. If employees sold their options, the desired effect of aligning incentives would be eliminated because employees would no longer directly benefit from a stock price increase.

- Employees may not hedge their options. An employee may not sell stock short (sell borrowed shares), buy put options (options to sell stock at a fixed price), or write (be the obligated party on) call options. These investments all benefit when the stock price declines and thus could be used to offset the risk of holding ESOs. Permitting such hedging would reduce the incentive alignment just like a sale of ESOs.

- ESOs are not exercisable until the employee has remained with the company through a **vesting period**. Employees who leave the company must forfeit any nonvested ESOs they hold. Employees also must exercise or forfeit any vested ESOs they hold upon leaving the company. Vesting provisions encourage employees not to leave the company.

Restrictions on ESOs make them different from a typical stock option, and reduce their value relative to that of similar publicly traded options. Why? Consider an employee holding an ESO with a $50.00 strike price when the stock price is $55.00. Exhibit 14.5 shows the value of the option, the amount it is in the money, and the option premium. The option is $5.00 in the money but has a value of $20.14. Thus, the option premium is $15.14.

---

[7]We refer here to an option that has time left until expiration. For an option that is at expiration, the option value is equal to the amount the option is in the money; that is, there is no option premium and the option price curve coincides with the kinked line.

A CLOSER LOOK

Stock Option Overhang

Use of employee stock options has grown tremendously in the last decade. This increase has attracted interest in employee stock options from financial advisers and consultants. One such consulting firm is Watson Wyatt Worldwide. Watson Wyatt, with offices in Reigate, England, and Washington, DC, provides consulting services in employee benefits, human resources technologies, and human capital management. Watson Wyatt has studied stock option overhang, which measures the usage of employee stock options. Watson Wyatt defines stock option overhang to be stock options granted, plus those remaining to be granted, as a percentage of the total number of shares outstanding. These data show option overhang was 5.4% of total shares outstanding in 1989. By 2000, stock option overhang had grown to 13%.

The following charts show how overhang has grown over time and how it varies by industry. Overhang in 2000 was almost two and a half times overhang in 1989. It is also much more common in technology and health care than in other industries.

Stock Option Overhang by Year

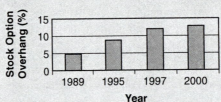

Stock Option Overhang by Industry (1999)

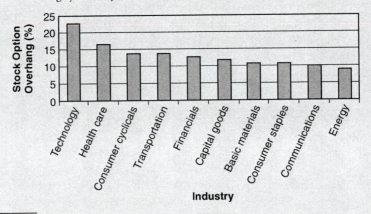

Source: Watson Wyatt Worldwide, Stock Option Overhang: Shareholder Boon or Shareholder Burden? The 2001 Study.

EXHIBIT 14.5   Black-Scholes Call Option Values—Option Premium Versus Amount in the Money

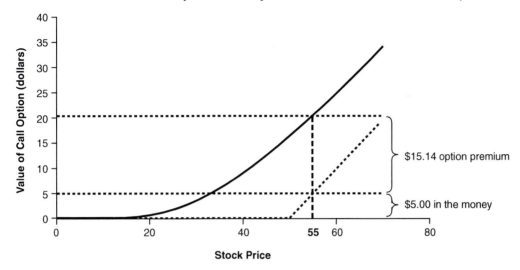

If this were a publicly traded option and the holder of the option no longer wanted to hold the investment, the holder could sell the option on an exchange and obtain for it the fair value at the time ($20.14).[8] The employee holding an ESO cannot do this, however. If the employee wants to change jobs, obtain cash, or reduce risk, he or she must exercise the ESO, sell the stock acquired upon exercise, and realize only the $5 the option is in the money. In essence, the employee gives up the $15.14 option premium implied by the Black-Scholes option value. Further, if the option were not yet vested, an employee changing jobs would have to forfeit the option and receive no value in return.

Due to the possibility of forfeitures and early exercises, it is likely that employees will not realize the full Black-Scholes value of ESOs, making the options worth less than the values we obtain using Black-Scholes.[9] Recently, academic research has examined how to incorporate the restrictions on ESOs in an estimate of the value of an ESO. This research shows that using Black-Scholes, but replacing the actual time to expiration with the expected time the option will be held, provides reasonable estimates of value. For example, we can estimate the value of an ESO with eight years to expiration and an expectation that it will be held five more years by treating the option as a regular call option that will expire in five years. This approach is the method the FASB required for valuation of ESOs when it mandated disclosures about ESO values.

The Firm as Option Writer

Another difference between ESOs and publicly traded options is the identity of the option writer. The top panel of Exhibit 14.6 shows that with a publicly traded option on Starbucks' stock, an independent third party writes an option and sells it to an investor. If the investor exercises the option, the independent option writer must sell Starbucks stock to the investor at the strike price. This transaction has no effect on Starbucks; it is between two independent parties.

---

[8]Less transaction costs.

[9]Another characteristic of employee stock options makes them more valuable than otherwise similar publicly traded options. Some firms will reprice ESOs downward if the stock price falls sufficiently far below the strike price. This increases the value of the option and would never be done with a publicly traded option.

EXHIBIT 14.6   Parties to Option Transactions

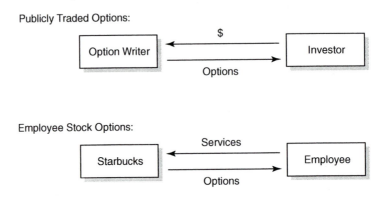

The bottom panel of Exhibit 14.6 shows that when the option is an ESO, Starbucks is the option writer. If the option is exercised, Starbucks must sell its own stock at less than fair value. This dilutes the other shareholders' ownership and reduces the per-share value of Starbucks' equity.[10] The existence of ESOs, unlike publicly traded options, has a direct effect on the value of the firm's stock. And, because ESO values depend on the value of the underlying stock, this also reduces the value of the ESOs.

A simple example will illustrate. Suppose Opco Inc. has assets worth $10,000 and 100 common shares outstanding. If not for its ESOs, Opco's stock would trade for $100 ($10,000/100) per share. Suppose further Opco has 50 ESOs outstanding. These ESOs have a strike price of $40 and are about to expire. Undoubtedly, these options will be exercised. Opco employees will pay a total of 50 × $40 = $2,000 to the company and receive 50 shares in return. A share of stock will be worth ($10,000 + $2,000)/(100 + 50) = $80. Knowing that after the options are exercised the stock price will be only $80, a rational investor would pay no more than $80 today for a share of stock, not $100. Because the stock is worth only $80 per share, the options are worth only $40. In contrast, if the $40 options were publicly traded options and Opco were not the option writer, the option exercise would not affect Opco and the stock value would be $100 per share. The options would be worth $60 each. When we incorporate ESOs in the valuation in Section 14.4, we will have to consider this aspect of ESOs.

14.3   ACCOUNTING AND TAX ISSUES

We now turn to accounting and tax issues related to ESOs. It is important to understand the accounting for ESOs because we will use financial statements and financial statement footnotes to obtain much of the information needed to incorporate ESOs in a valuation. We must understand ESO tax law because it affects the cost of an ESO and hence the firm's value.

Accounting for ESOs

Most firms follow the **intrinsic value method** of accounting for ESOs. Under that method, the expense that must be recognized at the time an option is granted is the intrinsic value, or the amount the option is in the money. Because few options are issued in the money, financial statements rarely

---

[10]Firms can eliminate the dilution in existing shareholders' percentage ownership by buying back shares and issuing those shares to employees who exercise ESOs. However, firms must acquire the shares at market value and receive only the option strike price when they reissue the shares. As a result, the dilution in the value of the existing shareholders' shares is unchanged by this strategy.

EXHIBIT 14.7   Financial Statement Treatment of ESOs Issued at the Money or out of the Money

	At Grant Date	At Exercise
Income Statement	—	—
Balance Sheet	—	Cash and common stock both increase by $500 million (amount of cash received, not value of stock issued).
Cash Flow Statement	—	Cash flow from financing (sale of common stock) increases by $500 million.

recognize any cost related to ESOs. When ESOs are exercised, the firm simply records a sale of stock for the amount of proceeds it receives. For example, say Michael Corporation granted 10 million ESOs in 1995. Each ESO has a strike price of $50, the price of the stock at the time of the grant. The ESOs expire in 10 years and are estimated to be worth $20 each at the time of the grant. Suppose further that the ESOs are exercised five years later, after the stock price has risen to $120 per share.

Exhibit 14.7 summarizes the effect of these transactions on Michael's financial statements. At the time of the grant, the intrinsic value of the options is zero, so Michael records nothing in its financial statements, despite the fact that it has distributed $200 million (10 million × $20) of value to its employees. At the time of the exercise, Michael issues stock worth $1.2 billion (10 million × $120) and receives only $500 million (10 million × $50) in return. It still recognizes no cost. Instead, it records a sale of shares for $500 million, as if $500 million were the fair value. Michael's balance sheet and cash flow statement simply report a sale of stock for $500 million.

The Accounting Principles Board (APB) adopted the intrinsic value accounting method in Opinion No. 25 in 1972 because, at the time, the Board could not establish a reasonable way to measure the value of stock options. (The decision was prior to the Black-Scholes option-pricing breakthrough.) In light of the new ability to value options, the FASB recently reconsidered the accounting for ESOs. There was much controversy over whether the cost of these options should be recognized in the financial statements. Millions of dollars were spent lobbying against any change in the rules, and even the president and members of Congress weighed in on this issue. The resulting compromise pronouncement, **SFAS No. 123**, "Accounting for Stock-Based Compensation," does not require firms to recognize ESO costs. Rather, it permits and encourages recognition. Nevertheless, virtually all firms still use the APB Opinion No. 25 accounting and report no cost related to ESOs.

A CLOSER LOOK

Coca-Cola to Expense Stock Option Costs

In July 2002, in the wake of accounting scandals at other firms that refocused attention on accounting for employee stock options, Coca-Cola announced that it would begin following the preferred method of accounting for stock options described in SFAS No. 123, which is not mandatory. Coke said that it expected the effect of the change on 2002 earnings to be one cent per share.

In making the change, Coke joined a very small group of firms that follow SFAS No. 123 accounting, Boeing and Winn-Dixie Stores being the only prominent firms in that group. With sentiment growing that firms not following SFAS No.123 are misstating earnings, more such announcements may follow. And, a change in the standard that would mandate use of SFAS No.123 may not be far behind.

The Fight over Accounting for Employee Stock Options

If there was ever any doubt that setting accounting standards is an inherently political process, that doubt was put to rest by the deliberations over SFAS No. 123, "Accounting for Stock-Based Compensation." When the FASB proposed that an expense should be recorded for the cost of ESOs, business leaders waged a battle to stop this action.

Letters of protest poured into the FASB. The following excerpts illustrate the hostility that the FASB ignited:

> From back there in sad decaying rustbelt Connecticut it is obviously difficult to comprehend the vibrant, dynamic entrepreneurship of Silicon Valley. Otherwise, how could you propose a change in accounting standards which will crush an industry which reclaimed its world leadership in 1993. . . . Look what you've done to the East Coast. A once beautiful state is full of some of the ugliest decaying slums in America. Leave us alone! We won't go down without a fight.
>
> Have you guys taken leave of your senses? The entire business community, including employees, are (sic) upset about your proposed accounting for stock options. This proposed opinion has the potential for disastrous economic consequences.
>
> *Source:* Excerpted from letters received by Financial Accounting Standards Board.

And, in an article about the proposal, *Upside*, a technology magazine, stated:

> Dennis R. Beresford and James J. Leisenring came to the Red Lion Inn on a hot August morning with a simple goal: to explain a change in an accounting rule. Before it was over they were lucky to have escaped the first lynching in San Jose in a half-century. Measuring out the rope were 300 seriously (ticked)-off Silicon Valley CEOs and other senior execs who could see the ruin of their lives' work because some glorified bean counters in Washington had decided to count sacrifice flies as home runs.
>
> *Source:* Michael S. Malone, Upside, "Lifeline" November 1, 1993.

Even politicians entered the fray. In early 1993, Senator Carl Levin (D-Michigan) introduced the Corporate Executives' Stock Option Accountability Act, which would have required the cost of stock options to be expensed. Six months later, Senator Joseph Lieberman (D-Connecticut) introduced the Equity Expansion Act of 1993, which would have prohibited a charge against income for stock options.

Ultimately, the FASB relented and made the provisions of SFAS No. 123 voluntary. Firms may charge income for the cost of stock options, but are permitted to continue to follow APB Opinion No. 25, "Accounting for Stock Issued to Employees." However, these firms must disclose in a footnote what income under SFAS No. 123 would have been. Virtually all public firms follow APB Opinion No. 25, which does not require a charge to income except in certain rare circumstances.

SFAS No.123 has been broadly criticized for lacking representational faithfulness.[*] In fact, the FASB itself made this criticism in the appendix to SFAS No. 123 and said that its decision was essentially a political one, not one based on sound accounting principles. Many believe that the forces opposing the FASB were so powerful and determined that the FASB would not have continued to exist had it adopted the proposed rule.

Throughout the debate, the only prominent business leader to support the FASB proposal was Warren Buffett, chairman of Berkshire Hathaway Inc. In a letter to Senator Christopher Dodd (D-Connecticut), who chaired the Securities Subcommittee of the Senate Committee on Banking, Housing and Urban Affairs, Mr. Buffett called the exclusion of stock option costs from the income statement "(t)he most egregious case of let's-not-face-up-to-reality behavior by executives and accountants." He also likened keeping the cost of options off the books to changing the value of pi from 3.14159 to 3.0 in order to make math simpler for students.

---

*Representational faithfulness is correspondence between a measure and the underlying phenomenon it purports to measure.

Earnings Quality and ESOs

Because the APB Opinion No. 25 approach keeps an economic cost of the business off the income statement, it represents an earnings quality issue. Analysts who believe earnings should reflect these costs would view the use of APB Opinion No. 25 as a manipulation of earnings, albeit a very common one. In this case, unlike many others, the effect of the choice is clearly disclosed. SFAS No. 123 requires footnote disclosure of pro forma earnings as if the firm used the recommended accounting. In addition, firms must disclose the estimated value of ESOs granted in each of the last three years, and enough information about outstanding ESOs that an astute analyst can make a reasonable estimate of the value of those ESOs.

ESO Tax Law

ESO tax treatment is important to valuation because any ESO-related tax deductions a firm receives reduce the cost of the ESOs. Whether a firm receives a tax deduction for ESOs depends on characteristics of the options.

Tax law recognizes two types of ESOs. **Incentive stock options** (ISOs) provide employees with tax-favored treatment, whereas **nonqualified stock options** (NSOs) do not.[11] An option must meet certain requirements to be an ISO, including that it was not in the money when granted and that the employee does not sell the shares received for at least one year after exercise. Options that are issued in the money or that do not meet one of the other requirements for ISO treatment are NSOs. Further, if an employee exercises an ISO and sells the stock received within one year, the sale is deemed to be a **disqualifying disposition**, which causes the ISO to be treated as an NSO for tax purposes.

To illustrate the employer tax consequences of ESOs, we return to the Michael Corporation example. In that example, Michael granted 10 million ESOs in 1995. Each ESO had a strike price of $50. The ESOs were exercised in 2000, after the stock price had risen to $120 per share.

The classification of ESOs as ISOs or NSOs determines whether Michael Corporation gets a tax deduction when the ESOs are exercised. Exhibit 14.8 summarizes how the employer's tax conse-

---

[11]Whereas employees receive more favorable tax treatment for ISOs than for NSOs, employers receive more favorable tax treatment for NSOs than for ISOs.

EXHIBIT 14.8 Tax Consequences of Employee Stock Options

Incentive Stock Options (ISOs)		
Date	Employer Tax Consequences	Example: Michael Corporation
Grant Date	No deduction allowed	—
Exercise Date	No deduction allowed	—
Sale of stock (if not a disqualifying disposition)	No deduction allowed	—
Sale of stock (if considered a disqualifying disposition)	Deduction for compensation expense for difference between fair value of stock at exercise and strike price	Deduction of $1.2 billion − $500 million = $700 million

Nonqualified Stock Options (NSOs)		
Date	Employer Tax Consequences	Example: Michael Corporation
Grant Date	No deduction allowed	—
Exercise Date	Deduction for compensation expense for difference between fair value of stock at exercise and strike price*	Deduction of $1.2 billion − $500 million = $700 million
Sale of stock	No deduction allowed	—

*If the option can be sold on an organized exchange, then the employer receives a deduction for the amount the option is in the money at the time of the grant. In that case, there are no tax consequences at the exercise date. In most cases, however, ESOs are restricted and cannot be sold on an exchange.

quences depend on whether the options are ISOs or NSOs. ISO exercises do not lead to employer tax deductions unless there is a disqualifying disposition. In contrast, all NSO exercises result in a tax deduction at the exercise date. Whether due to a disqualifying disposition or the exercise of an NSO, the amount of the deduction is the amount the option was in the money when it was exercised. Exhibit 14.9 summarizes the amount of the firm's tax benefits per exercised option, assuming only in-the-money options are exercised.

In Exhibit 14.9, τ_c is the corporate marginal tax rate, S_E is the stock price at the exercise date, and X is the option strike price. Assuming Michael's marginal tax rate is 35%, it would save $700 million times 35%, or $245 million in taxes in the ISO with disqualifying disposition case and the NSO case.

Accounting for ESO Tax Benefits

We have seen that firms do not generally recognize any expense in their income statements for ESOs. Still, they may generate income tax savings through tax deductions. This raises the question of how to report the tax benefit.

EXHIBIT 14.9 Summary of Employer Tax Benefits Realized per Exercised Option

Option Type	Tax Benefit per Option
ISO with no disqualifying disposition	0
ISO with disqualifying disposition	$\tau_c \cdot (S_E - X)$
NSO	$\tau_c \cdot (S_E - X)$

Under the matching principle, a fundamental accounting concept, income tax consequences are recognized in the same period and in the same manner as the transactions that generate them. So, because no expense is ever recognized for ESOs, the income tax benefit is not recognized on the income statement. Instead, it is credited directly to equity. Suppose Michael had $1 billion of pretax income before its $700 million tax deduction related to ESOs. It would pay ($1 billion − $700 million) × 35% = $105 million in income taxes. However, its income statement would not reflect the $245 million of tax savings due to the ESOs. Instead, its income statement would be as shown in Exhibit 14.10. Michael would actually pay only $105 million in taxes. Its balance sheet would reflect an increase in equity of $245 million. Because Michael pays a different amount in taxes than the tax provision it recognizes in the income statement, Michael will have a reconciling item in its cash flow statement, as shown in Exhibit 14.11.

The net income amount of $650 million is after subtracting the $350 million income tax provision. However, the change in cash includes as an outflow for taxes only the $105 million actually paid to the IRS. Thus, there is a reconciling item of $245 million in the cash flow statement. This reconciling item appears in the cash flow from operations section in the GAAP cash flow statement.

14.4 CASH FLOW VALUATION OF FIRMS WITH ESOs

We have discussed how ESOs work and their accounting and tax implications. We are now ready to consider how to use this information in a valuation. Recall from Chapters 9 and 10 that we value the core operations by calculating the present value of the expected free cash flows. We estimate common equity by adding the values of the core operations and the nonoperating net assets, and subtracting the values of debt and other capital claims, as shown below:

$$COMEQUITY = \underbrace{\sum_{t=1}^{\infty} \frac{FCF_t}{(1 + k_c)^t}}_{\text{Present value of expected free cash flows}} + NONOP - DEBT - OCAP \qquad (14.1)$$

where FCF_t is the expected free cash flow in period t and k_c is the weighted-average cost of capital.

EXHIBIT 14.10 Michael Corporation Income Statement (Assuming NSO or ISO with Disqualifying Disposition)

(millions of dollars)		
.	.	
.	.	
.	.	
Pretax income	$	1,000
Income tax provision		(350)
Net income	$	650

EXHIBIT 14.11 Michael Corporation Cash Flow Statement (Assuming NSO or ISO with Disqualifying Disposition)

(millions of dollars)		
Net income	$	650
.	.	
.	.	
Tax benefit from ESO exercises		245
.	.	
.	.	
Net change in cash	$	xxx

Also recall the concept of free cash flow equivalents from Chapter 9. Free cash flow includes some outflows that are paid not in cash but by issuing a capital claim on the firm's assets. ESOs are a capital claim on the firm's assets, and the issuance of ESOs is one type of free cash flow equivalent. Thus we can incorporate ESOs in the valuation by considering outstanding ESOs to be capital claims and expected ESO grants to be free cash flow equivalents.

Some ESO exercises generate a tax deduction. Our valuation must reflect not only the effect of ESOs but also the tax benefits the exercises generate. When we value the firm, we must do so in a way that reflects these tax benefits. This means the amounts we include in our valuation for both outstanding ESOs and expected grants must be on an after-tax basis.

When we add the outstanding ESOs and yet-to-be-granted ESOs, as well as their tax effects, the free cash flow valuation formula generalizes to

$$COMEQUITY = \sum_{t=1}^{\infty} \frac{FCF_t^*}{(1+k_c)^t} - \sum_{t=1}^{\infty} \frac{GRANT_t \cdot (1-\tau_{ESO})}{(1+k_c)^t} + NONOP - DEBT - ESO \cdot (1-\tau_{ESO}) - OCAP^* \quad (14.2)$$

where FCF_t^* is free cash flow in period t *before considering ESO grants*, $GRANT_t$ is the grant date value of option grants expected to be made in period t, ESO is the value of outstanding ESOs at the valuation date, τ_{ESO} is the marginal tax rate on ESOs, and $OCAP^*$ is other capital claims, but excluding ESOs. Thus, to incorporate ESOs in a valuation, we need a forecast of yet-to-be-granted ESOs, an estimate of the value of outstanding ESOs, and an estimate of the marginal tax rate on ESOs.

Three factors make it difficult to apply equation (14.2), and we deal with these problems in the following sections. First, only some ESOs give rise to a tax deduction, so the appropriate tax rate (τ_{ESO}) is a weighted average of zero and the firm's marginal tax rate. The second complicating factor is that $GRANT_t$ represents the expected grant-date value of options that have not yet been issued. Because the number and terms of these options have not been set, the values of these options cannot be computed with an option-pricing model such as Black-Scholes. The third complicating factor is that the value of ESOs outstanding depends on, among other things, $COMEQUITY$. Thus, equity value is a function of option value and vice versa. So, we actually have a simultaneous equation system.

Estimating τ_{ESO}

In Section 14.3, we saw that firms receive a tax deduction for NSOs and for ISOs followed by disqualifying dispositions, but not for ISOs that are not followed by disqualifying dispositions. We can estimate the historical value of this weighted-average tax rate with the following formula.

$$\tau_{ESO} = \frac{TB_E}{n_E \cdot (S_E - X)} \quad (14.3)$$

where TB_E is the tax benefit generated by ESO exercises, n_E is the number of options exercised, S_E is the stock price at the exercise date, and X is the option strike price. The numerator of (14.3) is the amount of tax benefits received, and the denominator is an estimate of what the tax deduction would be if all options were NSOs or ISOs with a disqualifying disposition. Therefore, the ratio is an estimate of the marginal tax rate on ESO exercises. It is a weighted-average of zero and the firm's marginal tax rate, with the weights equal to the proportions of options that do and do not receive a tax deduction. Assuming the mix of NSOs and ISOs does not change much from year to year, we can use the historical values of τ_{ESO} to forecast subsequent values.

How do we obtain the elements of (14.3) that we need to estimate τ_{ESO}? As we discussed earlier, TB_E, the tax benefit on exercise, is reported in the operating section of the cash flow statement.[12] SFAS No. 123 requires the number of options exercised (n_E) and their average strike price (X) to be disclosed in the footnotes. We must estimate the remaining component of (14.3), the average stock price at exercise (S_E).

Estimating Starbucks' Historical τ_{ESO}

Exhibit 14.12 provides Starbucks' cash flow statement. It shows Starbucks' tax benefits from ESO exercises were $31,131,000, $18,621,000, and $9,332,000, in fiscal 2000, 1999, and 1998, respectively. We obtain the number of options exercised (n_E) and the average strike prices of the exercised options (X) from Starbucks' SFAS No. 123 disclosure. Exhibit 14.13 provides relevant excerpts from the disclosure. It provides the reconciliation of outstanding options, which shows how the number of options outstanding has changed over the last three years.

Finally, we need to estimate the average stock prices at exercise (S_E). We do so based on Starbucks' stock price range during each year, which is provided in the annual report and also available from other sources. We assumed more options were exercised when the stock price was relatively high. Thus, the estimates of S_E are near the respective annual highs. The reason for this assumption is that when employees exercise early, they forego expected value equal to the option premium. As we saw in Exhibit 14.4, the higher the stock price, the lower the premium on an in-the-money option. Thus, as the stock price rises, it is less costly (in terms of foregone option premium) for employees to exercise early. So, they are more likely to do so.

In Exhibit 14.14, we use the preceding information to estimate Starbucks' historical τ_{ESO} in fiscal 1998, 1999, and 2000. The estimates of the historical values of τ_{ESO} in fiscal 1998 to 2000 are 13%, 21%, and 26%, respectively. Based on these results, we will use a forecasted τ_{ESO} value of 20%, the mean of the three historical values.

Estimating the Value of Yet-to-Be-Granted ESOs

Recall (14.2) is

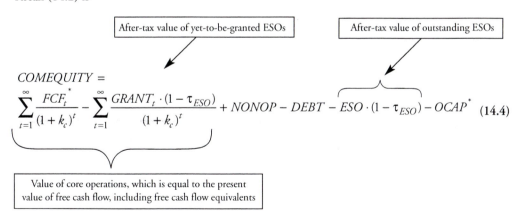

$$COMEQUITY =$$
$$\sum_{t=1}^{\infty} \frac{FCF_t^*}{(1+k_c)^t} - \sum_{t=1}^{\infty} \frac{GRANT_t \cdot (1-\tau_{ESO})}{(1+k_c)^t} + NONOP - DEBT - ESO \cdot (1-\tau_{ESO}) - OCAP^* \quad (14.4)$$

After-tax value of yet-to-be-granted ESOs

After-tax value of outstanding ESOs

Value of core operations, which is equal to the present value of free cash flow, including free cash flow equivalents

---

[12]Classification in the operating section of the cash flow statement was mandated by the Emerging Issues Task Force (EITF) of the FASB in Consensus 00-15, "Classification in the Statement of Cash Flows of the Income Tax Benefit Realized by a Company upon Employee Exercise of a Non-Qualified Stock Option." The consensus was issued in July 2000 and was effective for quarters ending after July 20, 2000. After the effective date of the consensus, cash flow statements also show the tax benefit in the operating section of the cash flow statement for all prior years presented, even those that predate the consensus. For reports issued prior to the consensus, the tax benefit is usually in cash flow from financing and may be added to the proceeds from option exercises in the cash flow statement.

EXHIBIT 14.12   Starbucks' Cash Flow Statement

Consolidated Statements of Cash Flows			
In thousands			
Fiscal year ended	October 1, 2000	October 3, 1999	September 27, 1998
OPERATING ACTIVITIES:			
Net earnings	$ 94,564	$ 101,693	$ 68,372
Adjustments to reconcile net earnings to net cash provided by operating activities:			
Depreciation and amortization	142,171	107,512	80,901
Internet-related investment losses	58,792		
Provision for losses on asset disposals	5,753	2,456	7,234
Conversion of compensatory options into common stock			1,158
Deferred income taxes, net	(18,252)	794	2,125
Equity in (income) losses of investees	(15,139)	(2,318)	14
Tax benefit from exercise of nonqualified stock options	31,131	18,621	9,332
Cash provided (used) by changes in operating assets and liabilities:			
Net purchases of trading securities	(1,414)		
Accounts receivable	(28,235)	3,838	(19,790)
Inventories	(19,495)	(36,405)	(23,496)
Prepaid expenses and other current assets	(700)	(7,552)	(2,497)
Accounts payable	15,561	4,711	4,601
Accrued compensation and related costs	30,962	7,586	9,943
Accrued occupancy costs	6,007	5,517	5,342
Accrued taxes	5,026	12,429	7,173
Minority interest	3,188	400	
Deferred revenue	6,836	(53)	209
Other accrued expenses	1,818	10,366	1,590
Net cash provided by operating activities	318,574	229,595	152,211
INVESTING ACTIVITIES:			
Purchase of available-for-sale investments	(118,501)	(122,800)	(51,354)
Maturity of available-for-sale investments	58,750	85,053	112,080
Sale of available-for-sale investments	49,238	3,633	5,138
Purchase of businesses, net of cash acquired	(13,522)	(15,662)	
Investments in joint ventures	(8,473)	(10,466)	(12,418)
Purchases of other investments	(35,457)	(20,314)	
Distributions from joint ventures	14,279	8,983	2,750
Additions to property, plant, and equipment	(316,450)	(257,854)	(201,855)
Additions to other assets	(3,096)	(6,866)	(3,184)
Net cash used by investing activities	(373,232)	(336,293)	(148,843)

continued

continued

FINANCING ACTIVITIES:						
Increase/(decrease) in cash provided by checks drawn in excess of bank balances		(7,479)		29,512		4,846
Proceeds from sale of common stock under employee stock purchase plan		10,258		9,386		4,649
Exercise of stock options		58,463		33,799		20,755
Payments on long-term debt		(1,889)		(1,189)		(1,993)
Net cash provided by financing activities		59,353		71,508		28,257
Effect of exchange rate changes on cash and cash equivalents		(297)		(54)		(88)
Net increase/(decrease) in cash and cash equivalents		4,398		(35,244)		31,537
CASH AND CASH EQUIVALENTS:						
Beginning of year		66,419		101,663		70,126
End of year	$	70,817	$	66,419	$	101,663

In (14.4), the value of core operations has been separated into the present value of free cash flow before considering yet-to-be-granted ESOs, and the present value of the yet-to-be-granted ESOs.

Chapter 10 discussed how to forecast $\sum_{t=1}^{\infty} \dfrac{FCF_t^*}{(1 + k_c)^t}$. We now move on to the second component,

$$\sum_{t=1}^{\infty} \frac{GRANT_t \cdot (1 - \tau_{ESO})}{(1 + k_c)^t}.$$

How do we determine $GRANT_t$? As of the valuation date, the grant date stock prices, and the number and terms of these options are unknown. Further, the number and terms of the future options granted are likely to depend on the grant date stock prices. As a result, direct use of an option-pricing model to determine $GRANT_t$ is not possible. One method to simplify the difficult problem of determining the present value of yet-to-be-granted ESOs is to estimate the aggregate dollar value of the grants. The SFAS No. 123 disclosure provides the number and weighted-average dollar value of ESO grants for each of the most recent three years. We can use these to compute the aggregate dollar values of prior ESO grants, using them as a reference to forecast the aggregate dollar value of future grants. The following formula lets us calculate the present value of yet-to-be-granted ESOs, assuming the dollar value of the grants grows at a constant rate in perpetuity:

$$\sum_{t=1}^{\infty} \frac{GRANT_t \cdot (1 - \tau_{ESO})}{(1 + k_c)^t} = \frac{GRANT_0 \cdot (1 + g_{ESO}) \cdot (1 - \tau_{ESO})}{k_c - g_{ESO}} \tag{14.5}$$

where g_{ESO} is the estimated growth rate in the aggregate value of the ESO grants.

Estimating the Value of Starbucks' Yet-to-Be-Granted ESOs

To estimate the value of Starbucks' yet-to-be-granted ESOs, we examine the values of ESO grants in the past three years. We return to Starbucks' SFAS No. 123 disclosure. The reconciliation of grants, exercises, and cancellations (forfeitures) in Exhibit 14.13 shows that Starbucks granted 4.71 million in fiscal 2000, 8.05 million in fiscal 1999, and 6.51 million ESOs in fiscal 1998.

EXHIBIT 14.13   Excerpts from Starbucks' Employee Stock Option Footnote

The Company maintains several stock option plans under which the Company may grant incentive stock options and nonqualified stock options to employees, consultants, and nonemployee directors. Stock options have been granted at prices at or above the fair market value on the date of grant. Options vest and expire according to terms established at the grant date. The following summarizes all stock option transactions from September 28, 1997, through October 3, 2000.

n_E	Shares Subject to Options	Weighted-Average Exercise Price Per Share	Shares Subject to Exercisable Options	Weighted-Average Exercise Price Per Share
Outstanding, September 28, 1997	17,907,322	$ 9.66	7,427,352	$ 5.43
Granted	6,508,632	18.52		
Exercised	(3,683,078)	6.13		
Cancelled	(1,229,478)	11.79		
Outstanding, September 27, 1998	19,503,398	13.10	7,560,806	8.49
Granted	8,051,998	22.97		
Exercised	(3,522,908)	9.53		
Cancelled	(1,461,937)	18.99		
Outstanding, October 3, 1999	22,570,551	16.84	12,080,825	13.55
Granted	4,705,165	24.84		
Exercised	(4,471,785)	13.07		
Cancelled	(1,859,068)	21.41		
Outstanding, October 1, 2000	20,944,863	$ 19.10	10,165,370	$ 15.65

EXHIBIT 14.14   Starbucks' τ_{ESO}

	1998	1999	2000	Symbol	Source
Stock option income tax benefits ($ thousands)	9,332	18,621	31,131	TB_E	Cash Flow Statement
Number of options exercised (thousands)	3,683	3,523	4,472	n_E	Footnote
Average stock price at exercise ($) (adjusted to reflect 2-for-1 stock split on March 19, 1999)	25	35	40	S_E	Estimated from Price Range
Average strike price of exercised options ($)	6.13	9.53	13.07	X	Footnote
Estimated tax deduction if all option exercises were deductible ($ thousands)	69,498	89,731	120,431		$= n_E \cdot (S_E - X)$
Marginal tax rate on ESOs	**0.13**	**0.21**	**0.26**	τ_{ESO}	$= \dfrac{TB_E}{n_E \cdot (S_E - X)}$

The last paragraph of Starbucks' ESO footnote includes the following statement: "As required by SFAS No. 123, the Company has determined that the weighted-average estimated fair values of options granted during fiscal 2000, 1999 and 1998 were $10.74, $8.86 and $7.20 per share, respectively."[13] Thus, the aggregate values of options granted in fiscal 2000, 1999, and 1998 were $50.6 million (4.71 million × $10.74), $71.3 million (8.05 million × $8.86), and $46.9 million (6.51 million × $7.20), respectively.

---

[13]Note that the prices shown in the reconciliation itself are average strike prices, not fair values of the options granted.

Our estimated value of Starbucks' yet-to-be-granted ESOs assumes the aggregate dollar value of ESO grants will grow 3% annually. The cost of capital is assumed to be 11.23%, as estimated in Chapter 7. As discussed earlier, we estimate τ_{ESO} to be 0.20. Given these assumptions, the present value at October 1, 2000, of the forecasted future option grants, after considering tax benefits, is about $506.6 million, computed as follows:

$$\sum_{t=1}^{\infty} \frac{GRANT_t \cdot (1 - \tau_{ESO})}{(1 + k_c)^t} = \frac{GRANT_{2000} \cdot (1 + g_{ESO}) \cdot (1 - \tau_{ESO})}{k_c - g_{ESO}}$$

$$= \frac{\$50.6 \ million \cdot 1.03 \cdot (1 - 0.20)}{0.1123 - 0.03} = \$506.6 \ million$$

Valuing Outstanding ESOs in a Free Cash Flow Model

We also must value the outstanding ESOs as of the balance sheet date. Recall equation (14.4) was

$$COMEQUITY =$$

$$\sum_{t=1}^{\infty} \frac{FCF_t^*}{(1 + k_c)^t} - \sum_{t=1}^{\infty} \frac{GRANT_t \cdot (1 - \tau_{ESO})}{(1 + k_c)^t} + NONOP - DEBT - ESO \cdot (1 - \tau_{ESO}) - OCAP^* \quad \textbf{(14.6)}$$

ESO is the value of outstanding ESOs, before considering tax effects, so

$$ESO = CALL(COMEQUITY) \quad \textbf{(14.7)}$$

where $CALL$ is the sum of the values of the outstanding call options as a function of the underlying equity value. As discussed in Section 14.2, the value of an ESO is less than the value obtained from the Black-Scholes model, due to restrictions placed on ESOs. However, we can approximate ESO values using a modified Black-Scholes model in which we replace the actual time to expiration with the expected time to exercise. The SFAS No. 123 disclosures provide the information needed to estimate the value of outstanding ESOs with such a model.

Equations (14.6) and (14.7) comprise a simultaneous equation system. However, we cannot solve this system algebraically. Instead, we must use a numerical search technique (sophisticated trial and error) to obtain values for ESO and $COMEQUITY$ that satisfy both equations. One such technique is illustrated next.

Estimating the Values of Starbucks' Outstanding ESOs and Common Equity

The following illustration focuses on the valuation effect of the options, so it does not include a complete free cash flow forecast. Rather, we begin with the value of Starbucks' free cash flow, $2,356,655,000, as estimated in Exhibit 10.8 from Chapter 10. The valuation uses the Black-Scholes model with expected time to exercise substituted for actual time to expiration to estimate the value of the outstanding ESOs.

Exhibit 14.15 is a revised valuation of Starbucks that incorporates the ESOs. We begin with the present value of free cash flow before ESO grants. This amount is $2,356,655,000, the same as the present value of free cash flow in Exhibit 10.8. We subtract the present value of forecasted ESO grants, net of tax, of $506,600,000, to get a revised value of core operations of $1,850,055,000. After considering nonoperating net assets, debt and other capital claims, we obtain $1.95 billion as the combined value of common equity and outstanding ESOs. For the first iteration, in panel A, we use a value of zero as a first approximation of the value of Starbucks' outstanding ESOs. This results in a per-share common equity value of $10.38. We then use the $10.38 equity value to estimate the value of the outstanding ESOs as of the valuation date. Each of the five columns in the option valuation section of panel A in Exhibit 14.15 represents a set of outstanding ESOs at October 1, 2000, and is based on information obtained from the ESO footnote, the relevant portions of which are shown in Exhibit 14.16. For example, there were 3,046,798 outstanding options having strike prices between $0.75 and $9.41, and an average strike price of $7.14. For these options, we used an average time to expiration of 3 years rather than the actual average time to expiration of 4.04 years, to reflect the likelihood of early exercises. Using the Starbucks-provided 55% standard deviation of returns and 6.25% risk-free interest rate (the average of the disclosed range), and the previously estimated $10.38 per share value of stock, we can calculate that these options are worth $5.67 each. Assuming τ_{ESO} = 0.20, the value of each option after considering tax benefits is $4.54. Thus, these 3,047,000 options have an aggregate after-tax value of $13,823,000. The same computation for the other four sets of outstanding options shows when the equity value is $10.38 per share, the outstanding options have an aggregate after-tax value of about $78.6 million. This is inconsistent with the initial assumption that the options were worth zero, so we do not have a solution.

In the second iteration, in panel B of Exhibit 14.15, we use the estimated after-tax option value from the first iteration. This shows if the options are worth $78.6 million, then the equity is worth $9.97 per share. The revised equity value implies the options are worth only $73.6 million after tax. This is still not a solution, but the $4,950,000 error is considerably smaller than the $78.6 million error in the first iteration. With a numerical search technique such as this one, the error is smaller with each iteration. Eventually, it will be trivial, and we can stop the process. Exhibit 14.17 shows the result after repeated iterations. In it, the options are worth $73.9 million after taxes, or about 4% of the value of the common equity of $1.9 billion ($9.99 per share).

For companies with few ESOs relative to the number of shares outstanding, two iterations are likely to be sufficient. Valuations of companies with a greater number of ESOs will require more iterations to obtain a small error. Note that the relatively small error we found after two iterations is just the error caused by using the option value implied by the first pass at equity valuation, and then adjusting the equity for the option value. This does not mean we can ignore ESOs altogether without a large error. Indeed, ignoring Starbucks' options would have caused two major valuation errors. First, core operations would have been valued $506.6 million too high, due to the exclusion of the cost of yet-to-be-granted ESOs. Second, no value would have been allocated to the nearly 21 million ESOs that were outstanding at the valuation date. As we saw in Chapter 10, the resulting common equity value would have been about $13.07 per share, rather than $9.99, an overvaluation of about 31%.

Valuing ESOs in a Residual Income Valuation

The task of incorporating ESOs in a residual income valuation is similar to what we have done in this chapter for free cash flow valuations. As we saw in Chapter 12, the residual income valuation is identical to a free cash flow valuation, except we express the value of the core operations using the book value of the core operations and its residual income.

$$COMEQUITY = OPNA_0 + \sum_{t=1}^{\infty} \frac{NOPAT_t - k_c \cdot OPNA_{t-1}}{(1 + k_c)^t} + NONOP - DEBT - OCAP \quad (14.8)$$

We simply generalize this expression, in the same way as we did for the free cash flow model, to be

$$COMEQUITY = OPNA_0^* + \sum_{t=1}^{\infty} \frac{NOPAT_t^* - k_c \cdot OPNA_{t-1}^*}{(1 + k_c)^t} - \sum_{t=1}^{\infty} \frac{GRANT_t \cdot (1 - \tau_{ESO})}{(1 + k_c)^t}$$
$$+ \ NONOP - DEBT - ESO \cdot (1 - \tau_{ESO}) - OCAP^* \tag{14.9}$$

Once again, the superscripts (*) indicate the amount is to be defined without regard to any ESOs. As we estimate $OPNA_{t-1}^*$ for each period in the forecast, we must exclude any of the forecasted ESO exercises, even though those would increase the firm's book value.[14] Similarly, $NOPAT_t^*$ must not include any charge for the ESOs. Once we have valued the core operations, incorporating the ESOs is the same under residual income valuation as it was for the free cash flow model, and the result is identical.

---

[14]Including the ESO exercises would violate the "clean surplus" assumption so critical to a residual income valuation.

EXHIBIT 14.15 Valuation of Starbucks Including ESOs

(thousands of dollars, except per share amount)	Panel A—Iteration 1		
Present value of free cash flow before ESO grants	$ 2,356,655	From Exhibit 10.8	
Forecasted ESO grants (net of tax)	(506,600)		
Core operations	1,850,055		
Short-term investments	61,336		
Joint ventures	52,051		
Other investments	3,788	From Exhibit 10.8	
Current maturities of long-term debt	(685)		
Long-term debt	(6,483)		
Combined value of equity, minority interest and outstanding ESOs	1,960,062		
Minority interest	(6,105)		
Combined value of equity and outstanding ESOs	1,953,957		
Outstanding ESOs	0		
Value of equity	1,953,957		
Number of shares outstanding (thousands)	188,158		
Value per share	$ 10.38		
Computed value of existing options at above share value:			
Range of exercise prices	$ 0.75–9.41	$ 9.69–18.41	$ 19.42–22.69
Number of options (thousands)	3,047	6,943	5,531
Average exercise price (dollars)	7.14	16.92	21.52
Time to expiration (years)	3.0	5.5	6.5
Standard deviation of returns	0.55	0.55	0.55
Risk-free interest rate	0.0625	0.0625	0.0625
Black-Scholes value per option (dollars)	5.67	4.61	4.55
Marginal tax rate on ESOs	0.20	0.20	0.20
After-tax option value per option (dollars)	4.54	3.68	3.64
After-tax option value (thousands of dollars)	13,823	25,583	20,145
Total after-tax value of all options (thousands of dollars)	78,566		
Error (assumed ESO value − computed ESO value) (thousands of dollars)	78,566		
Minority interest:			
Book value of minority interest	3,588		
Book value of core operations and nonoperating net assets less debt claims	1,151,987		
Ratio of minority interest to net value	0.0031146		
Fair value of core operations and nonoperating net assets less debt claims	1,960,062		
Estimated fair value of minority interest	6,105		

	Panel B—Iteration 2	
$	2,356,655	
	(506,600)	
	1,850,055	
	61,336	
	52,051	
	3,788	
	(685)	
	(6,483)	
	1,960,062	
	(6,105)	
	1,953,957	
	(78,566)	
	1,875,391	
	188,158	
$	9.97	

$ 23.25–35.31	$ 36.06–40.75	$ 0.75–9.41	$ 9.69–18.41	$ 19.42–22.69	$ 23.25–35.31	$ 36.06–40.75
5,197	227	3,047	6,943	5,531	5,197	227
25.60	38.13	7.14	16.92	21.52	25.60	38.13
7.0	8.0	3.0	5.5	6.5	7.0	8.0
0.55	0.55	0.55	0.55	0.55	0.55	0.55
0.0625	0.0625	0.0625	0.0625	0.0625	0.0625	0.0625
4.40	4.00	5.31	4.31	4.27	4.12	3.75
0.20	0.20	0.20	0.20	0.20	0.20	0.20
3.52	3.20	4.25	3.45	3.41	3.30	3.00
18,288	727	12,951	23,953	18,886	17,145	681
		73,616				
		(4,950)				

EXHIBIT 14.16 Excerpts from Starbucks' Employee Stock Option Footnote

Range of Exercise Prices			Options Outstanding			Options Exercisable	
			Shares	Weighted Average Remaining Contractual Life (Years)	Weighted Average Exercise Price	Shares	Weighted Average Exercise Price
$ 0.75	$	9.41	3,046,798	4.04	$ 7.14	2,872,310	$ 7.01
9.69		18.41	6,942,673	6.54	16.92	4,007,553	16.15
19.42		22.69	5,530,507	8.17	21.52	2,681,621	21.48
23.25		35.31	5,197,385	8.93	25.60	603,886	27.49
36.06		40.75	227,500	9.75	38.13	—	—
$ 0.75	$	40.75	20,944,863	7.23	$ 19.10	10,165,370	$ 15.65

The Company accounts for its stock-based awards using the intrinsic value method in accordance with Accounting Principles Board Opinion No. 25, "Accounting for Stock Issued to Employees" and its related interpretations. Accordingly, no compensation expense has been recognized in the financial statements for employee stock arrangements.

SFAS No. 123, "Accounting for Stock-Based Compensation," requires the disclosure of pro forma net income and net income per share as if the Company adopted the fair-value method of accounting for stock-based awards as of the beginning of fiscal 1996. The fair value of stock-based awards to employees is calculated using the Black-Scholes option-pricing model with the following weighted average assumptions:

	Employee Stock Options		
	2000	1999	1998
Expected life (years)	2–6	1.5–6	1.5–6
Expected volatility	55%	50%	45%
Risk-free interest rate	5.65–6.87%	4.60–6.21%	5.28–6.05%
Expected dividend yield	0.00%	0.00%	0.00%

The Company's valuations are based upon a multiple option valuation approach and forfeitures are recognized as they occur. The Black-Scholes option valuation model was developed for use in estimating the fair value of traded options, which have no vesting restrictions and are fully transferable. In addition, option valuation models require the input of highly subjective assumptions, including the expected stock-price volatility. The Company's employee stock options have characteristics significantly different from those of traded options, and changes in the subjective input assumptions can materially affect the fair value estimate.

As required by SFAS No. 123, the Company has determined that the weighted-average estimated fair values of options granted during fiscal 2000, 1999, and 1998 were $10.74, $8.86, and $7.20 per share, respectively.

EXHIBIT 14.17   Valuation of Starbucks—Consistent Equity and Option Values

(thousands of dollars, except per share amount)					
Present value of free cash flow	$ 2,356,655				
Forecasted ESO grants (net of tax)	(506,600)				
Core operations	1,850,055				
Short-term investments	61,336				
Joint ventures	52,051				
Other investments	3,788				
Current maturities of long-term debt	(685)				
Long-term debt	(6,483)				
Combined value of equity, minority interest, and outstanding ESOs	1,960,062				
Minority interest	(6,105)				
Combined value of equity and outstanding ESOs	1,953,957				
Outstanding ESOs	(73,939)				
Value of equity	1,880,018				
Number of shares outstanding (thousands)	188,158				
Value per share	$ 9.99				
Computed value of existing options at above share value:					
Range of exercise prices	$ 0.75–9.41	$ 9.69–18.41	$ 19.42–22.69	$ 23.25–35.31	$ 36.06–40.75
Number of options (thousands)	3,047	6,943	5,531	5,197	227
Average exercise price (dollars)	7.14	16.92	21.52	25.60	38.13
Time to expiration (years)	3.0	5.5	6.5	7.0	8.0
Standard deviation of returns	0.55	0.55	0.55	0.55	0.55
Risk-free interest rate	0.0625	0.0625	0.0625	0.0625	0.0625
Black-Scholes value per option (dollars)	5.34	4.33	4.29	4.14	3.77
Marginal tax rate on ESOs	0.20	0.20	0.20	0.20	0.20
After-tax option value per option (dollars)	4.27	3.47	3.43	3.31	3.01
After-tax option value (thousands of dollars)	13,006	24,060	18,969	17,220	684
Total after-tax value of all options (thousands of dollars)	73,939				
Error (assumed ESO value − computed ESO value) (thousands of dollars)	0				
Minority interest:					
Book value of minority interest	3,588				
Book value of core operations and nonoperating net assets less debt claims	1,151,987				
Ratio of minority interest to net value	0.0031146				
Fair value of core operations and nonoperating net assets less debt claims	1,960,062				
Estimated fair value of minority interest	6,105				

SUMMARY

Stock options give the holder the right, but not the obligation, to buy stock from the writer of the option at a fixed price up until the expiration date. Options are valuable because they enable the holder to profit from increases in the stock price while limiting the exposure to losses if the stock price falls. The Black-Scholes option-pricing formula is the most common way to estimate the value of stock options.

Many companies grant ESOs to their employees as part of their compensation packages. Companies do this to align employees' incentives with those of the shareholders in an attempt to make employees act in the shareholders' interests. Although ESOs are stock options, they generally come with restrictions that reduce their value relative to otherwise similar publicly traded options.

The income tax effects of an ESO depend on whether the option is classified as an incentive stock option or a nonqualified stock option for tax purposes. Firms receive a tax deduction for the amount a nonqualified option was in the money at the time of exercise. There is no tax deduction related to incentive stock options, unless the employee disposes of the stock received within one year of exercise.

Financial reporting largely ignores employee stock options, and in general no cost is ever charged against income for them. Nevertheless, ESOs have an important effect on the value of the firm and must be considered in a valuation. In fact, for many companies, ESOs are a very large claim on the firm. Failure to consider ESOs can lead to a material overstatement of equity value.

To value a company with employee stock options, we must subtract the value of forecasted ESO grants (net of tax) as they are free cash flow equivalents, to arrive at the value of the core operations. We also must determine the value of ESOs that are outstanding as of the valuation date, and subtract it (net of tax) along with the other claims against the firm's assets. When we determine the value of the outstanding ESOs, we must do it simultaneously with finding the value of the firm's common equity, because the value of each affects the value of the other. We do this with a numerical search technique that finds consistent values for these two amounts.

SUGGESTED READINGS

Aboody, D. and R. Kasznik. "CEO Stock Option Awards and the Timing of Corporate Voluntary Disclosures." *Journal of Accounting and Economics* 29, 1 (2000):73–100.

Black, F. and M. Scholes. "The Pricing of Options and Corporate Liabilities." *Journal of Political Economy* 81, 3 (1973):637–654.

Carpenter, J. "The Exercise and Valuation of Executive Stock Options." *Journal of Financial Economics* 48 (1998):127–158.

Core, J., W. Guay, and S. P. Kothari. The Economic Dilution of Employee Stock Options: Diluted EPS for Valuation and Financial Reporting. Working paper. University of Pennsylvania and Massachusetts Institute of Technology, 1999.

Hemmer, T., S. Matsunaga, and T. Shevlin. "Estimating the 'Fair Value' of Employee Stock Options with Expected Early Exercise." *Accounting Horizons* 8 (December 1994):23–42.

Huddart, S. "Employee Stock Options." *Journal of Accounting and Economics* 18 (1994):207–231.

Huddart, S. and M. Lang. "Employee Stock Option Exercises: An Empirical Analysis." *Journal of Accounting and Economics* 21 (1996):5–43.

Kulatilaka, N. and A. Marcus. "Valuing Employee Stock Options." *Financial Analysts Journal* 60 (November–December 1994):46–56.

Matsunaga, S., T. Shevlin, and D. Shores. "Disqualifying Dispositions of Incentive Stock Options: Tax Benefits versus Financial Reporting Costs." *Journal of Accounting Research* 30 (Supplement 1992):37–68.

Soffer, L. "SFAS No. 123 Disclosures and Discounted Cash Flow Valuation." *Accounting Horizons* 14, 2 (2000):169–189.

REVIEW QUESTIONS

1. What is a stock option?

2. Why is a stock option valuable?

Questions 3–5 are based on the following information: Garber Corporation's stock is trading for $30 per share. Each month, the stock price will increase to 1.03 times the prior month's price or decrease to 1/1.03 times the prior month's price. Increases and decreases are equally likely.

3. Construct a price tree for Garber's stock for four months.

4. What are the probabilities of each outcome in the price tree?

5. What is the expected value today of the final value of a $30 option on Garber's stock?

6. What is the Black-Scholes option-pricing formula?

 7. Your company is considering adding an employee stock option plan to its benefit package. Draft a memo discussing reasons why the company should have an employee stock option plan.

8. How do employee stock options differ from publicly traded options?

9. In general, is any expense ever recognized in the financial statements for ESOs?

10. Do companies receive any income tax benefits related to ESOs? If so, when and how much?

11. The marginal tax rate on ESOs is a weighted average of zero and the corporate marginal tax rate. For a particular company, what determines whether the marginal tax rate on ESOs is closer to the corporate marginal rate or to zero?

12. How is the free cash flow model generalized to deal with ESOs?

13. How does the concept of free cash flow equivalents relate to ESOs?

14. In a valuation, why do we multiply the value of outstanding ESOs by $(1 - \tau_{ESO})$ before subtracting them, even though we do not consider a tax effect before subtracting debt obligations?

15. Why must we find the values of outstanding ESOs and common equity at the same time?

PROBLEMS

1. Belkaoui Corporation granted 2 million ESOs with a strike price of $30 in 2000. All of the options are nonqualified. Belkaoui's stock price at the time was $30 per share. One million of the options were exercised in 2003. At the time, Belkaoui's stock price was $50 per share. Belkaoui follows APB Opinion No. 25 and has a marginal tax rate in general of 35%.

   a. How much expense did Belkaoui recognize in 2000 related to the ESOs?
   b. How much expense did Belkaoui recognize in 2003 related to the ESOs?
   c. How much total cash flow did Belkaoui have (including income tax effects) in 2000 related to the ESOs?

    d. How much total cash flow did Belkaoui have (including income tax effects) in 2003 related to the ESOs?

    e. What line items of Belkaoui's 2000 and 2003 income statements were affected by the ESOs and by how much?

    f. What line items of Belkaoui's 2000 and 2003 cash flow statements were affected by the ESOs and by how much?

2. Gross Corporation employees exercised 80 million ESOs in 2000. Gross reported in its cash flow statement that it had $400 million of income tax benefits due to ESO exercises. On average, exercises in 2000 were completed when the stock price was $30 per share. The average strike price of the exercised shares was $7.

    a. What is Gross's τ_{ESO} in 2000?

    b. Assuming that in general Gross faces a marginal tax rate of 35%, what proportion of the exercises in 2000 were of nonqualified options?

3. You are valuing McLelland Company using a free cash flow model. McLelland has forecasted future ESO grants and outstanding ESOs at the valuation date, and you have correctly incorporated the effects of both of these in your valuation.

    Based on additional analysis, you have decided your forecasted operating margins should be higher. You revise your forecast accordingly, resulting in an increase in the value of core operations of $100 million.

    a. After you revise your forecast, will the value of McLelland's common equity be greater than or less than it was in the original valuation?

    b. Is the change in the value of the common equity greater than, equal to, or less than $100 million?

4. You have just completed a valuation of Walther Corporation. You now realize that you did not consider Walther's employee stock options in the valuation. You ignored both the outstanding options as of the valuation date and the expected granting of additional options in the future. The rest of your valuation, however, is correct. It shows Walther's common equity is worth $1 billion.

    You have determined that as of the valuation date, the present value of Walther's future option grants, net of the appropriate tax benefits, is $100 million. The following table shows the value of Walther's outstanding employee stock options, net of the appropriate tax benefits, as of the valuation date, assuming various values for Walther's common equity. For example, if common equity is worth $1.2 billion, the ESOs are worth $173.5 million.

($ Millions)	
Common Equity	Outstanding ESOs (net of tax)
$ 1,200	$ 173.5
1,150	165.0
1,100	156.6
1,050	148.1
1,000	139.8
950	131.4
900	123.1
850	114.8
800	106.6
750	98.5
700	90.4

Indicate between which two values of common equity in the preceding chart that Walther's common equity falls.

The following information pertains to problems 5 through 7.

Enron Corporation filed for protection under Chapter 11 of the U.S. Bankruptcy Code in December 2001. Just a year earlier, at the end of 2000, its shares traded for $83.125. At that time, Enron had nearly 100 million ESOs outstanding, most of them substantially in the money.

The following table was adapted from Enron's 2000 annual report.

Range of Exercise Prices	Options Outstanding			Options Exercisable	
	Number Outstanding at 12/31/00 (thousands)	Weighted-Average Remaining Contractual Life	Weighted-Average Exercise Price	Number Exercisable at 12/31/00 (thousands)	Weighted-Average Exercise Price
$ 6.88 to $20.00	15,368	4.7 years	$ 16.72	14,001	$ 16.54
20.06 to 34.81	24,091	6.8 years	24.79	18,304	24.13
35.03 to 47.31	21,520	6.8 years	40.52	8,731	40.27
50.48 to 69.00	13,965	6.5 years	60.18	4,072	61.81
71.06 to 86.63	21,119	5.6 years	79.69	1,647	72.36
	96,063	6.2 years	$ 44.24	46,755	$ 29.85

5. Estimate the amount Enron's ESOs were in the money in the aggregate at December 31, 2000, using the weighted-average exercise price of $44.24.

6. Was the value of Enron's ESOs at December 31, 2000 greater than, less than, or equal to your answer to problem 5?

7. Assume the following parameters and use the Black-Scholes option-pricing formula (with dividends) to estimate the fair value of Enron's outstanding ESOs at December 31, 2000, based on the stock's market price.

   Volatility (σ) = 0.223
   Risk-free interest rate (r) = 0.058
   Dividend yield (y) = 0.024

   The Black-Scholes formula with dividends is

   $$C = S \cdot exp(-y \cdot t) \cdot N(d_1) - X \cdot exp(-r \cdot t) \cdot N(d_2), \text{where:}$$
   $$y \text{ is the dividend yield}$$
   $$d = [\log(S/X) + (r - y) \cdot t] / (\sigma \cdot \sqrt{t})$$
   $$d_1 = d + \sigma \cdot \sqrt{t} / 2$$
   $$d_2 = d - \sigma \cdot \sqrt{t} / 2$$

   Note: Use an expected remaining life for each tier of options equal to 80% of the weighted-average remaining contractual life.

The following information pertains to problems 8 and 9.

The Coca-Cola Company had 2.5 billion shares outstanding at December 31, 2000.

The following information was adapted from Coca-Cola's 2000 employee stock option footnote:

	1998	1999	2000
Number of ESOs exercised (millions)	16	6	12
Average strike price of exercised ESOs	$ 18.93	$ 26.12	$ 26.00
Tax benefits from ESO exercises (millions of dollars)	$ 97	$ 72	$ 116

Risk-free interest rate	5.8%
Stock price volatility	31.7%
Dividend yield	1.2%

		Options Outstanding			Options Exercisable	
Range of Exercise Prices	Shares	Weighted-Average Remaining Contractual Life	Weighted-Average Exercise Price		Shares	Weighted-Average Exercise Price
$10.00 to $20.00	2	0.8 years	$ 15.37		2	$ 15.37
$20.01 to $30.00	11	3.1 years	$ 23.41		11	$ 23.41
$30.01 to $40.00	10	4.8 years	$ 35.63		10	$ 35.63
$40.01 to $50.00	10	5.8 years	$ 48.86		9	$ 48.86
$50.01 to $60.00	65	8.9 years	$ 56.31		17	$ 57.06
$60.01 to $86.75	14	7.8 years	$ 65.87		11	$ 65.90
$10.00 to $86.75	112	7.4 years	$ 51.23		60	$ 46.57

Assume the average stock prices at the time ESOs were exercised were $65, $60, and $58 in 1998, 1999, and 2000, respectively.

8. Calculate Coca-Cola's τ_{ESO} for each of the three years presented.

9. Suppose you have determined the value of Coca-Cola's core operations plus its nonoperating net assets less all capital claims other than common equity and employee stock options is $180 billion at December 31, 2000. This calculation properly took into account forecasted ESO grants. Calculate the value of Coca-Cola's ESOs (net of related tax savings) and its common equity (see problem 7 for the Black-Scholes formula). Assume an expected remaining life for outstanding ESOs of 80% of the remaining contractual life.

10. Download the Excel spreadsheet containing a graph of the Black-Scholes option price versus stock price from the book's Web site. Adjust each of the Black-Scholes input parameters and try to guess how the graph will shift.

My Case

If your company has an ESO plan, incorporate it in your valuation. Be sure to consider both forecasted ESO grants and outstanding ESOs.

APPENDIX 14.1 SUMMARY OF EMPLOYEE STOCK OPTION TERMINOLOGY*

At-the-money option   An option whose strike price is equal to the price of the underlying stock.

Black-Scholes   A formula for valuing call options as a function of stock price, expected volatility of the underlying stock, the risk-free interest rate, time to expiration, and strike price.

Call option   The right, but not the obligation, to buy stock at a fixed price, called the strike price, up until the expiration date of the option.

Disqualifying disposition   The sale of stock received from an exercise of an incentive stock option within one year of the exercise date. Disqualifying dispositions cause such options to be treated as nonqualified stock options for tax purposes.

Employee stock option (ESO)   An option on the employer's stock granted to an employee as part of his or her compensation package.

Exercisable ESOs   ESOs that have passed the vesting period and may be exercised by the option holder.

Exercise   Demanding the option writer sell stock to the option holder at the option strike price.

Expiration date   Last date on which an option may be exercised.

SFAS No. 123   Statement Number 123 of the Financial Accounting Standards Board, which governs the accounting for ESOs. It allows firms to ignore the cost incurred when ESOs are granted.

Forfeiture   The giving up, without compensation, of an ESO. Generally, employees forfeit their unexercised ESOs if they leave the company.

Grant   The act of an employer giving ESOs to an employee.

Incentive stock option (ISO)   An ESO meeting the requirements of the Internal Revenue Code for favorable tax treatment for employees.

In-the-money option   An option whose strike price is below the price of the underlying stock.

Intrinsic value   The amount an option is in the money.

Nonqualified stock option (NSO)   An ESO not meeting the requirements to be an incentive stock option under the Internal Revenue Code.

Option holder   The owner of the option, at whose sole discretion the option may be exercised.

Option premium   The excess of the option value over the amount the option is in the money. This premium is lost if the option is exercised early.

Option writer   One who issues options to another and becomes obligated to sell at the strike price should the option holder exercise.

Out-of-the-money option   An option whose strike price is above the price of the underlying stock.

Stock option   The right, but not the obligation, to either buy (if a call option) or sell (if a put option) stock at a fixed price, called the strike price, up until the expiration date.

Strike price   The price at which the holder of an option has the right to buy stock.

Vesting period   The period of time after the grant of an ESO that an employee must remain with the company before the ESO may be exercised.

---

*Unless specifically noted otherwise, all the definitions in this appendix are based on call options.

15

 **Where We Have Been:**

In Chapter 14 we used the concept of free cash flow equivalents to apply valuation theory to firms with employee stock options.

 **Where We Are:**

In this chapter we extend our analysis to retirement plans. We rely on the concept of free cash flow equivalents to understand how to apply valuation theory to pension and other postemployment benefit plans. This chapter completes our discussion of discounted cash flow techniques.

 **Where We Are Going:**

In Part V, we move on to valuation using multiples.

Valuation of Firms with Pension Plans and Other Postemployment Benefit Plans

LEARNING OBJECTIVES:

. . . .

After studying this chapter, you will understand:

- The difference between defined contribution and defined benefit plans.

- The meaning and importance of economic ownership.

- How defined contribution and defined benefit plans are reported in financial statements and footnotes.

- How a valuation incorporates defined contribution and defined benefit plans.

- What plan assets are and why they are nonoperating assets in a valuation.

- What benefit obligations are and why they are capital claims in a valuation.

- How to adjust plan assets and benefit obligations for income tax effects before including them in a valuation.

- What service costs are and why they are free cash flow equivalents.

Companies compensate their employees in many ways, including through retirement plans, some of which are enormous. General Motors' retirement plan assets as of December 31, 2001, for example, totaled $79 billion. This amount was dwarfed by GM's even larger obligation to pay retirement benefits, which the company estimated to be $139 billion at December 31, 2001.

Because retirement plans can be so large, failure to consider them in a valuation is likely to lead to major errors. When WHX Corporation acquired Handy and Harman in 1998, a Lehman Brothers analyst suggested one reason for the acquisition was the market had overlooked the value of Handy and Harman's overfunded pension plan. The analyst was saying that by failing to consider Handy and Harman's retirement plan, the market had made a valuation error.

In this chapter, we examine how to incorporate retirement benefits in a valuation. Section 15.1 describes the two most common types of retirement plans—defined contribution plans and defined benefit plans—and introduces the concept of economic ownership. Section 15.2 examines the financial reporting for and valuation of defined contribution plans. Because of the complexity of defined benefit plans, we break our discussion of them into two sections, with Section 15.3 focusing on financial reporting and Section 15.4 on valuation.

15.1 OVERVIEW OF RETIREMENT PLANS

There are two types of retirement plans. A **defined contribution plan** specifies the amount an employer must contribute to the plan. A **defined benefit plan** specifies the benefits retirees will receive from the plan. This one characteristic—whether a plan defines contributions or benefits—determines both the financial reporting rules and the way we incorporate the plan into a valuation analysis.

Defined Contribution Pension Plans

A defined contribution pension plan specifies only the amount the employer must periodically contribute to the plan on behalf of each employee and does not guarantee employees any particular amount at retirement. The assets in the plan build up in value, depending on the investment results, and employees receive the funds in their respective accounts at or during retirement. As a result, employees reap the rewards and bear the risks of investing the assets in the plan.

Exhibit 15.1 illustrates the flow of funds through a defined contribution pension plan. It shows that the employer contributes funds to the plan during employees' working years. Those funds, and earnings on them, provide benefits for the employees during their retirements. The thick vertical line represents the point at which the risks and rewards associated with investing change hands. Once the firm has made its contribution, those risks and rewards belong to the firm's employees and retirees. The pension plan is on the same side of the thick vertical line as the retirees, indicating that the employees and retirees, not the firm, bear the risks and rewards associated with the invested assets.

Starbucks maintains a defined contribution plan, under which employees may contribute a percentage of their compensation, up to certain limits. The firm matches 25% of each employee's contributions, also up to certain limits. Starbucks promises to make its contribution, but makes no promises to the employees about how much will be available to them at retirement. Once the company contributes the required amounts, it has no further obligation to employees. Each employee directs the way

Growth in Pension Contributions and Assets, 1977–1996

Pension plans have become increasingly important over the last 20 years. During this period, the baby boom has accumulated enormous wealth in various types of plans. The following graph shows annual contributions to pension plans, which were almost $170 billion in 1996. Note the tremendous growth in contributions during the robust times of the 1990s. This was a period of strong economic growth and low unemployment.

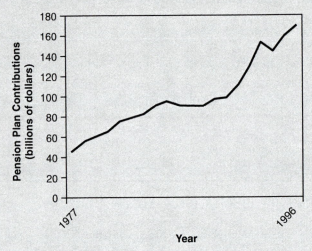

Source: Department of Labor. Private Pension Plan Bulletin Number 9, Winter 1999–2000.

Aided by strong stock market performance in the 1990s, the amount of assets in pension plans grew even more dramatically than contributions, as the following graph shows. By 1996, pension plans held more than $3 trillion in assets.

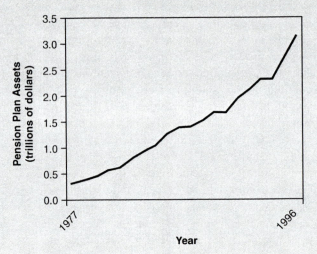

Source: Department of Labor. Private Pension Plan Bulletin Number 9, Winter 1999–2000.

EXHIBIT 15.1   Flow of Funds Through a Defined Contribution Pension Plan

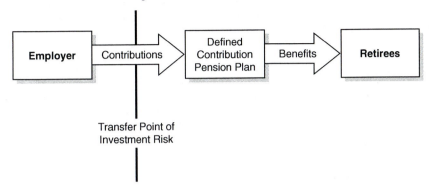

in which his or her funds are invested, usually by choosing among various options having different levels of risk, and each is entitled to whatever funds are in his or her account at retirement. Positive returns on an employee's account increase the amount available to that employee at retirement, while negative returns decrease it. Each Starbucks employee bears the risks and reaps the rewards of investing. The employees' investment returns have no effect on the amount of Starbucks' future contributions.

Defined Benefit Plans

Because a defined benefit plan dictates the amount of benefits retirees will receive, employers have no guarantee as to the amounts they will ultimately have to contribute to fund the plan. The amount of funding required will depend on how well the plan's investments perform; factors affecting employees' annual benefits, such as salary level and years of service; and how long retirees live. There are two main forms of defined benefit plans—defined benefit pension plans and other postemployment benefit plans.

Defined Benefit Pension Plans

A **defined benefit pension plan** provides retirement funds for employees. A formula determines the amount of benefits due to each employee. This formula varies by plan, but is usually based on years of service, terminal or average salary, age at retirement, and so on. The employer contributes funds to the plan, which invests the funds until they are needed to pay benefits to retirees. Because the plan specifies retiree benefits rather than employer contributions, the amount of benefits to which an employee is entitled does not depend on the return on the plan's investments. So employees bear no investment risk and are not rewarded if the plan's investments do especially well; instead the employer bears the risk and the reward. If the investment returns are poor, the employer must make larger contributions to the pension, because it is obligated to contribute sufficient funds to pay the benefits promised to the retirees. Similarly, positive investment returns reduce the amount of future contributions the firm must make.

Exhibit 15.2 shows the flow of funds through a defined benefit pension plan. Although this chart looks similar to the defined contribution plan illustrated in Exhibit 15.1, there is an important difference. The plan's assets are now on the employer's side of the thick vertical line, which illustrates where the risks and rewards transfer. The risks and rewards of investing pension plan assets belong to the company.

Other Postemployment Benefit Plans

Many firms provide additional retirement benefits beyond a pension. These additional benefit plans are called **other postemployment benefit plans**, or **OPEBs**. The most important of these plans is the

A CLOSER LOOK

Relative Use of Defined Contribution and Defined Benefit Pension Plans

Both defined contribution and defined benefit pension plans are common in the United States. Defined contribution plans outnumber defined benefit plans, and there has been a distinct shift toward defined contribution plans in recent years. However, defined benefit plans are still quite popular among large firms, as the following graph shows.

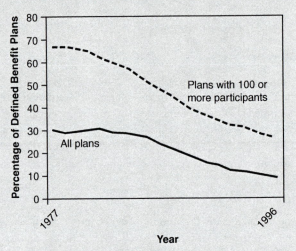

Source: Department of Labor. Private Pension Plan Bulletin Number 9, Winter 1999–2000.

Although there are more defined contribution plans than defined benefit plans, there are more assets in defined benefit plans because they tend to be larger. The following graph shows the proportion of assets in defined benefit plans by year. Even with the steady shift toward defined contribution plans, more than half of all pension assets in 1996 were in defined benefit plans.

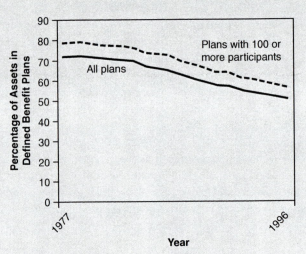

Source: Department of Labor. Private Pension Plan Bulletin Number 9, Winter 1999–2000.

EXHIBIT 15.2   Flow of Funds Through a Defined Benefit Plan

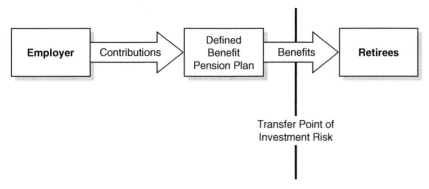

provision of health insurance. Although OPEB plans are not pensions, they are similar to defined benefit pension plans because they specify benefits, not contributions.

However, there are two practical differences between OPEB plans and defined benefit pension plans. First, in a defined benefit pension plan, at retirement the amount of the annual benefit to be paid is known, even if the length of time the retiree will live is not. In an OPEB plan, the annual cost of the benefits is unknown and depends on the employee's health and the cost of health care. Second, OPEB plans often do not entail a fund that invests contributions. Instead, the employer pays benefits directly to retirees (or to their insurers and health care providers) as they come due.

Exhibit 15.3 illustrates the flow of funds through an OPEB plan, assuming that it is not funded. Because there is no fund with invested assets, there is no investment risk. Employers must still make payments to fund whatever the benefits turn out to be, but they do so on what is called a pay-as-you-go basis. For funded OPEB plans, the picture looks like Exhibit 15.2 instead.

Economic Ownership of Retirement Plans

We have seen defined contribution and defined benefit plans differ as to when the risks and rewards of investing transfer from the employer to employees. To understand the significance of this difference, we must distinguish between legal ownership and economic ownership. **Legal ownership** belongs to the entity that holds legal title to an asset. A retirement plan generally is a separate legal entity, and it, not the employer or the employee, is the legal owner of the plan's assets. In contrast, **economic ownership** belongs to the entity whose welfare is affected by changes in the value of the asset. The economic owner is the one enjoying the economic benefits and incurring the investment risks generally associated with ownership.

In a defined contribution pension plan, each employee's retirement account balance depends on the returns his or her portion of the plan's assets earns. Employees are the economic owners because they enjoy the benefits and bear the risks associated with ownership of these assets, even if they do not hold legal title to them. In contrast, under a defined benefit pension plan or a funded OPEB plan, investment returns affect the employer, not the employee. Employers are the economic owners of those plan assets, because they enjoy the benefits and bear the risks related to the assets.

EXHIBIT 15.3   Flow of Funds Through an Unfunded OPEB Plan

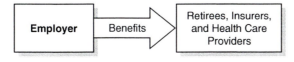

Exhibit 15.4 summarizes the differences among retirement plans. It shows that economic ownership depends on whether the plan specifies the amount of contributions or the amount of benefits. The accounting for a retirement plan depends on the concept of economic ownership, resulting in very different accounting treatments for defined contribution and defined benefit plans. Similarly, valuation analysis of retirement plans depends on economic ownership. The remainder of this chapter explores the accounting for and valuation analysis of retirement plans.

15.2   FINANCIAL REPORTING FOR AND VALUATION OF DEFINED CONTRIBUTION PLANS

From the employer's point of view, contributions to a defined contribution plan are like salary payments. Once the employer makes the required payment, it has no further obligation to the employee. Both the financial reporting for defined contribution plans and the way we incorporate them into the valuation are based on this concept.

Financial Reporting for Defined Contribution Plans

Contributions to defined contribution plans are expenses in the firm's income statement, like salary payments, and are usually categorized in selling, general, and administrative expense. These contributions are generally tax deductible when made, which reduces the firm's income tax provision by the amount of the contribution times the firm's marginal income tax rate. As a result, the income statement includes the contributions to the plan, net of the related income tax benefits. The cash flow statement, which begins with net income, also reflects this amount.

Because the employer has no obligation beyond making the required contribution, there are no balance sheet items related to a defined contribution plan. The plan's only effect on the company's balance sheet is to reduce cash and retained earnings for the amount of the contributions, net of tax. This is the same effect as if the contributions were salary payments.

Starbucks contributed about $1.1 million to its defined contribution plans in fiscal 2000, and its expenses include these contributions. Assuming a 38.7% marginal tax rate, Starbucks saved about $426,000 in taxes due to these contributions. Its income tax expense reflects this savings. Starbucks' 2000 net income and cash flow are about $674,000 ($1.1 million less $426,000) lower due to the contributions.

Valuing Firms with Defined Contribution Pension Plans

Because contributions to defined contribution plans are like salary payments, we incorporate a defined contribution plan in a valuation by including the periodic contributions in the forecast, just like salary expenses. Similarly, we include the related tax benefits as a reduction in the income tax

EXHIBIT 15.4   Summary of Types of Retirement Plans

	Defined Contribution Pension Plans	Defined Benefit Pension Plans and Funded Other Postemployment Benefit Plans	Unfunded Other Postemployment Benefit Plans (Defined Benefit)
Plan determines amount of:	Employer contributions	Retiree benefits	Retiree benefits
Economic owner (bearer of risk) of plan assets:	Employee	Employer firm	Not applicable

provision. These contributions are unaffected by the plan's investment results, so forecasting them is easy, at least relative to defined benefit plans. For example, if we know that a defined contribution plan calls for contributions of 5% of salary, then we can forecast contributions from salary forecasts.

In many cases, sufficiently detailed financial statements may not be available to permit the analyst to model contributions to defined contribution plans explicitly. However, because operating expenses in the income statement include contributions to defined contribution plans, it is unnecessary to consider these contributions explicitly. For example, the free cash flow forecasts we have done for Starbucks already took into account the company's defined contribution plans, because we based our forecasts on historical results that included these costs and the related tax benefits. Our analysis of the historical relationship between operating expenses and sales already includes the effect of the defined contribution pension costs.

15.3 FINANCIAL REPORTING FOR DEFINED BENEFIT PENSION PLANS AND OPEB PLANS

Unlike defined contribution plans, for which no special analysis is needed, valuing a defined benefit plan does require substantial analysis. For this analysis, we use information from the financial statements and footnotes. So, we need to understand the accounting for these plans.

SFAS Nos. 87, 106, and 132 provide the accounting and disclosure rules for defined benefit pension plans and OPEB plans. Taken together, these rules prescribe a means for measuring the economic position of a plan, called the funded status, and its annual economic cost. The funded status and the economic cost are often volatile from one year to the next, and the accounting rules contain additional provisions to reduce the reported volatility. The mechanism for this is a series of smoothing adjustments that delay the balance sheet recognition under GAAP of certain changes in a plan's funded status until future periods, thereby also delaying income and expense recognition.

Throughout this chapter, we will illustrate with Circuit City Group's defined benefit pension plan. We use Circuit City rather than Starbucks because Starbucks does not have a defined benefit plan. Exhibit 15.5 illustrates how the funded status and GAAP liability of Circuit City's pension plan varied over a five-year period.

EXHIBIT 15.5   Circuit City Group—Funded Status and Related GAAP Liability

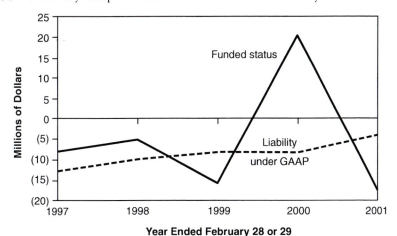

This chart shows that Circuit City's funded status was quite volatile. Conceptually, this funded status represents either an asset or a liability, depending on its sign. As of February 29, 2000, Circuit City's funded status was positive $20 million—an economic asset. Nevertheless, under GAAP the company reported a liability of almost $10 million. Even though the funded status position shifted dramatically in 2001 to negative $17 million, the GAAP liability was actually cut in half.

The difference between the solid and dashed lines in Exhibit 15.5 at any point in time represents the balance sheet smoothing adjustments as of that date. At February 29, 2000, there was a downward balance sheet smoothing adjustment of nearly $30 million. The following year, there was an upward smoothing adjustment of just over $13 million. Note that smoothing adjustments tend to offset sharp movements in the funded status, leaving the reported asset or liability under GAAP more stable over time.

The funded status, economic cost, GAAP asset or liability, and expense reported under GAAP are all closely related. Exhibit 15.6 illustrates how defined benefit pension plans and OPEB plans affect the financial statements. It shows that each of the amounts presented in the financial statements is equal to an economic amount plus smoothing adjustments. Beginning with the balance sheet, we see the economic amount, the funded status, plus the balance sheet smoothing adjustment equals the pension asset or liability reported under GAAP. Similarly for the income statement, the economic cost of the plan plus the change in the balance sheet smoothing adjustments equals the reported expense under GAAP.

EXHIBIT 15.6 Economic Amounts and GAAP

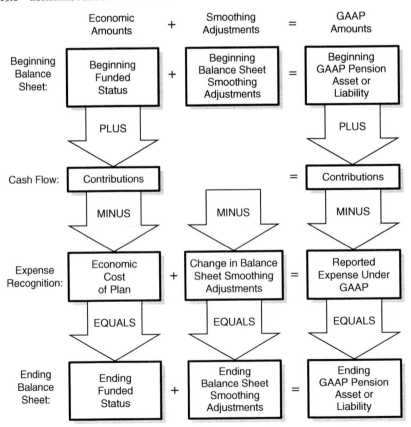

The exhibit also shows for both the economic amounts and the GAAP amounts, the plan's expense is equal to the change in the balance sheet amount not due to contributions to the plan. The economic cost of a plan is the change in funded status not due to contributions. The GAAP expense is the change in the reported asset or liability not due to contributions. As a result, the income statement effect of smoothing adjustments is equal to the change in the balance sheet smoothing adjustments.

As part of our free cash flow analysis, we will need to remove the pension and OPEB smoothing adjustments, so we must be able to identify them. Because our objective is to remove the effects of smoothing adjustments from the financial statements, we will focus on identifying the smoothing adjustments.[1] We are fortunate to have footnote disclosures that make it fairly easy to identify the smoothing adjustments.

To understand the financial reporting for defined benefit plans, we will first examine how the economic amounts affect the financial statements. Then we will discuss how smoothing adjustments change these amounts before they are reported under GAAP. For the remainder of this chapter, we will refer to Circuit City Group's pension footnote from its annual report for the year ended February 28, 2001, presented in Exhibit 15.7.

Economic Amounts

We first examine the economic amounts related to a defined benefit pension plan, which are represented by the first column of Exhibit 15.6.

Economic Amount on the Balance Sheet: Funded Status

The GAAP balance sheet includes either an asset or a liability related to a defined benefit plan. As we have already learned, this asset or liability consists of an economic component, called the funded status, and smoothing adjustments. The **funded status** is the difference between the plan assets and the projected benefit obligation. The term **plan assets** means the market value of the investments held by the plan. The **projected benefit obligation**, commonly referred to as the **PBO**, is the present value of the future retirement benefits, to the extent that employees have earned them.[2] Actuaries estimate the value of the PBO, and Appendix 15.1 examines how they do so.

The funded status, which is a main focus of accounting for defined benefit plans, may be either positive or negative. If plan assets exceed the PBO, the funded status is positive and the plan is **overfunded**. Economically, this excess is an asset, because it will permit the firm to contribute less to the plan in future years. If plan assets are less than the PBO, the funded status is negative and the plan is **underfunded**. A firm with an underfunded plan has an economic liability. Its future contributions will have to be higher to make up the deficit.

Exhibit 15.8 illustrates the relationship between plan assets and the PBO for overfunded and underfunded plans. Because the economic cost of the plan is equal to the change in the funded status not due to contributions, we examine the items that cause changes in the funded status, before moving on to the income statement.

---

[1]The reader interested in a detailed discussion of how these adjustments are computed should see L. Revsine, D. Collins, and B. Johnson, *Financial Reporting and Analysis*, 2nd ed. (Upper Saddle River, NJ: Prentice Hall, 2002).

[2]When referring to OPEBs, the technically correct term is **accumulated postemployment benefit obligation**, or **APBO**, not PBO. The APBO is the identical concept for OPEBs as is the PBO for defined benefit pension plans. It is the present value of future benefits, to the extent that they have been earned. The APBO takes into account a forecast of changes in health care costs, as well as all the other actuarial assumptions (such as employee turnover, mortality, etc.) that go into estimating the PBO.

EXHIBIT 15.7   Circuit City Group Pension Footnote

The Company has a noncontributory defined benefit pension plan covering the majority of full-time employees who are at least age 21 and have completed one year of service. The cost of the program is being funded currently. Plan benefits generally are based on years of service and average compensation. Plan assets consist primarily of equity securities and included 160,000 shares of Circuit City Group Common Stock at February 28, 2001 and February 29, 2000. Eligible employees of the Circuit City Group participate in the Company's plan. Pension costs for these employees have been allocated to the Circuit City Group based on its proportionate share of the projected benefit obligation.

The following table sets forth the Circuit City Group's share of the Pension Plan's financial status and amounts recognized in the balance sheets as of February 28 or 29:

(Amounts in thousands)	2001	2000
CHANGE IN BENEFIT OBLIGATION:		
Benefit obligation at beginning of year	$ 109,337	$ 110,001
Service cost	12,617	13,428
Interest cost	8,690	7,384
Actuarial loss (gain)	20,262	(17,325)
Benefits paid	(2,994)	(4,151)
Benefit obligation at end of year	$ 147,912	$ 109,337
CHANGE IN PLAN ASSETS:		
Fair value of plan assets at beginning of year	$ 129,638	$ 94,125
Actual return on plan assets	(10,396)	28,166
Employer contributions	14,103	11,498
Benefits paid	(2,994)	(4,151)
Fair value of plan assets at end of year	$ 130,351	$ 129,638
RECONCILIATION OF FUNDED STATUS:		
Funded status	$ (17,561)	$ 20,301
Unrecognized actuarial loss (gain)	13,922	(27,924)
Unrecognized transition asset	(199)	(398)
Unrecognized prior service benefit	(281)	(421)
Net amount recognized	$ (4,119)	$ (8,442)

The components of net pension expense are as follows:

(Amounts in thousands)	Years Ended February 28 or 29		
	2001	2000	1999
Service cost	$ 12,617	$ 13,428	$ 10,479
Interest cost	8,690	7,384	6,135
Expected return on plan assets	(10,914)	(8,919)	(7,675)
Amortization of prior service cost	(140)	(132)	(104)
Amortization of transitional asset	(199)	(199)	(199)
Recognized actuarial (gain) loss	(274)	10	
Net pension expense	$ 9,780	$ 11,572	$ 8,636

continued

continued

Assumptions used in the accounting for the Pension Plan were:

	Years Ended February 28 or 29		
	2001	2000	1999
Weighted average discount rate	7.5%	8.0%	6.8%
Rate of increase in compensation levels	6.0%	6.0%	5.0%
Expected rate of return on plan assets	9.0%	9.0%	9.0%

The Company also has an unfunded nonqualified plan that restores retirement benefits for certain senior executives who are affected by Internal Revenue Code limitations on benefits provided under the Company's Pension Plan. The projected benefit obligation under this plan and allocated to the Circuit City Group was $9.9 million at February 28, 2001, and $6.3 million at February 29, 2000.

- **Employer contribution** is the amount the firm contributed to the plan during the period. Most firms contribute to their defined benefit pension plans every year, but they do not necessarily have to do so.[3] The funded status increases due to employer contributions.

- **Service cost** is the increase in the PBO that occurs as employees earn additional benefits. The PBO is the present value of the portion of future retirement benefits employees have earned. As a result, the PBO increases as employees earn additional benefits, reducing the funded status.

- **Interest cost** is the increase in the PBO that occurs with the passage of time. With the passing of each year, each future benefit payment is one year closer and therefore discounted for one year less, increasing the PBO and decreasing the funded status.

- **Return on plan assets** is the amount by which the market value of the plan's assets increased or decreased during the year. When return on plan assets is positive, it increases the funded status. When return on plan assets is negative, it decreases the funded status.

EXHIBIT 15.8 Plan Assets, Projected Benefit Obligation, and Funded Status

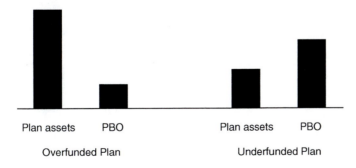

---

[3]The Employee Retirement Income Security Act (ERISA) requires a minimum contribution, based on the funded status of the plan. Yet a sufficiently overfunded plan might have a minimum contribution of zero. There is also an effective maximum contribution. Federal income tax law allows for a tax deduction for contributions to defined benefit plans only up to a point, often referred to as the deductible ceiling. Contributions beyond the ceiling are not tax deductible in the current period. Firms rarely contribute beyond the deductible ceiling.

- **Plan amendments** are changes in the formula that determines benefits. Amendments can be either **sweeteners**, which increase the benefits, or **curtailments**,[4] which reduce them. Amendments increase or decrease the PBO because they change the expected future benefit payments, thereby changing the funded status.

- **Actuarial gains and losses** are changes in the PBO due to changes in how it is measured, rather than changes in the terms of the plan. Actuaries estimate the PBO using many assumptions about the future. As time passes, they have access to actual results, as well as to new and more precise estimates of the future. When actuaries revise their estimates, the PBO changes. If the PBO declines, the change is an actuarial gain. If the PBO increases, it is an actuarial loss. These gains and losses cause changes in the funded status.

Economic Amounts on the Income Statement

All of the items in the preceding list, except contributions, are components of the economic cost of the plan. Exhibit 15.9 shows how Circuit City's funded status changed during fiscal 2001 and illustrates the relationship between this change and the economic cost of the plan. We obtain the numbers in this exhibit from the first table in Exhibit 15.7, which shows the change in benefit obligation and the change in plan assets as well as the funded status.

The funded status fell by $37,862,000, from a $20,301,000 overfunded position to a $17,561,000 underfunded position. From the change in plan assets section of Exhibit 15.7, we see that contributions increased the funded status by $14,103,000. However, the funded status fell by $51,965,000 due to the economic cost. This consisted of the other items in the change in benefit obligation and change in plan assets sections of the first table in Exhibit 15.7: service cost, interest cost, a *negative* return on plan assets, and an actuarial loss that occurred when the company changed underlying assumptions that go into computing the value of the PBO. Benefits paid reduced both the PBO and the plan assets and thus had no effect on the funded status.

If not for the smoothing aspect of the pension accounting rules, Circuit City would report a $17,561,000 liability at February 28, 2001, and an expense for the year of $51,965,000. We now examine the effect of smoothing adjustments on Circuit City's pension accounting.

GAAP Amounts and Smoothing Adjustments

If we were to use these economic amounts in financial statements, there would be very volatile effects on earnings from one year to the next. Returns on plan assets, the effects of plan amendments and actuarial gains and losses are unlikely to be stable from year to year. The FASB sought to smooth reported earnings when it devised the pension accounting rules. It did so by deferring certain changes in the funded status. Instead of recognizing an economic cost (or benefit) immediately upon a change in funded status, GAAP might recognize it slowly over a period of years, or not recognize it at all, simply allowing subsequent changes in the funded status that are in the opposite direction to offset them.

GAAP Amounts and Smoothing Adjustments on the Balance Sheet

We begin our analysis of GAAP amounts and smoothing adjustments by discussing the effect of smoothing adjustments on the balance sheet asset or liability reported under GAAP. We saw that the

---

[4]Firms generally do not curtail pension benefits without the permission of the employees, who may do so as part of a collective bargaining agreement, especially with a financially troubled firm. Occasionally firms curtail OPEB plans, where they often do not have a contractual obligation to provide the benefits or to continue them at existing levels. Curtailments were common just after the FASB issued Statement No. 106, perhaps because once firms were forced to measure the cost of these plans, they decided they were too expensive.

EXHIBIT 15.9 Economic Amounts and Circuit City's Pension Plan

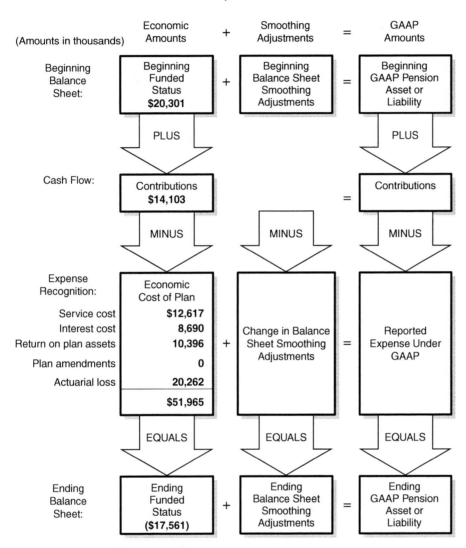

funded status changes due to contributions, service cost, interest cost, return on plan assets, plan amendments, and actuarial gains and losses. Of these changes, contributions, service cost, and interest cost are not smoothed. Changes in the funded status due to any of these three items are immediately recognized in the pension asset or liability reported under GAAP. The remaining three types of changes in funded status are smoothed, as discussed next.

Return on Plan Assets   Under GAAP, the pension asset or liability increases by the *expected* return on plan assets rather than the actual return. To the extent that the actual return differs from what was expected, there is an unrecognized gain or loss. Over the years, these differences accumulate, creating a difference between the funded status and the GAAP pension asset or liability. The differences may tend to offset from one year to the next, in which case the difference between funded status and the GAAP asset or liability due to unrecognized gain or loss on plan assets will be small.

However, after a protracted period of unusually high or unusually low returns, the difference could be substantial.[5]

Plan Amendments Although plan amendments immediately change the funded status, these changes are not reflected immediately on the GAAP balance sheet. Rather, they are recognized over subsequent years. If the amendment is a sweetener, as is usually the case, this decrease in the funded status, which remains unrecognized on the balance sheet, is called a prior service cost.

Actuarial Gains and Losses Actuarial gains and losses occur when the PBO, and hence the funded status, changes due to a change in an assumption used to calculate the PBO, such as a change in the discount rate or the expected growth rate in salaries. Actuarial gains and losses are not recognized immediately, but are amortized over a number of years subsequent to the year in which they arise.

One special type of actuarial gain or loss is the transition asset or obligation. When firms first adopted the current pension rules or OPEB rules, there would have been a funded status as of the date of adoption. Firms did not immediately recognize the funded status as an asset or a liability under GAAP. Instead, the funded status at the date of adoption, called the initial net asset or obligation, or transition amount, went unrecognized on the GAAP balance sheet initially and amortized onto the balance sheet over a period often extending 15 years.[6] Until the amortization is complete, the unamortized portion of the transition amount creates a difference between the funded status and the balance sheet asset or liability.[7]

GAAP Amounts and Smoothing Adjustments on the Income Statement

The pension expense reported under GAAP is equal to the change in the reported pension asset or liability that is not due to contributions. As Exhibit 15.6 showed, this relationship is similar to the relationship for the economic component of pensions. Also, because contributions are not smoothed, the difference between reported pension expense and the economic component of pension expense is equal to the change in the balance sheet smoothing adjustments. Therefore, smoothing adjustments follow the same pattern as the economic component of pensions and GAAP. Income statement smoothing adjustments are equal to the change in balance sheet smoothing adjustments. These income statement smoothing adjustments may result from either the deferral of current period funded status changes or the reversal (through amortization) of previously deferred funded status changes.

In Exhibit 15.10, we again examine Circuit City's defined benefit pension plan, now incorporating the smoothing adjustments and GAAP amounts as well.

Under GAAP, Circuit City reported a pension liability of $8,442,000 at the beginning of the year. This consisted of a $20,301,000 overfunded plan and $28,743,000 of downward smoothing adjustments. The company contributed $14,103,000 to the pension plan during the year, thereby increasing the funded status and reducing the pension liability by that amount. The economic cost of the plan was $51,965,000, consisting of $12,617,000 of service cost, $8,690,000 of interest cost, $10,396,000 of loss on plan assets, and $20,262,000 of actuarial loss. In contrast, Circuit City reported pension expense of only $9,780,000 under GAAP. Although service cost and interest cost were both included in GAAP expense, other components of the economic cost were not. Instead of

---

[5]In this case, the rules call for the firm to recognize a portion of the gains or losses that otherwise go unrecognized.

[6]Under SFAS No. 106, firms had the option to recognize the transition amount immediately when they adopted the OPEB rules.

[7]Although most firms are at or near the end of the amortization period for pension transition amounts, amortization of OPEB transition obligations not immediately recognized continues.

EXHIBIT 15.10   Economic Amounts, Smoothing Adjustments, and GAAP Amounts for Circuit City

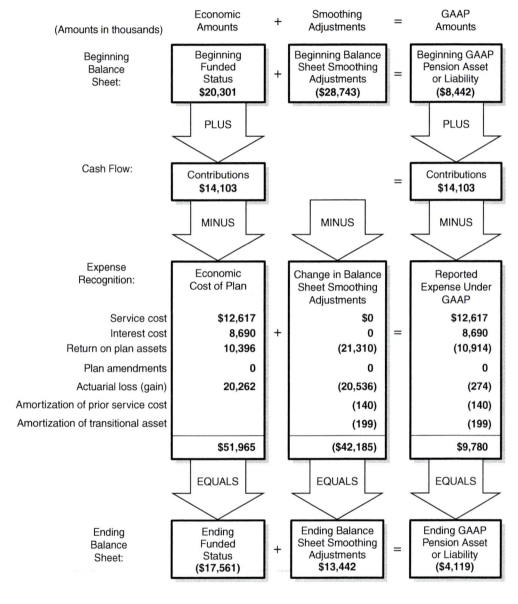

reporting the company's actual loss on plan assets of $10,396,000, GAAP pension expense was reduced by the expected *positive* return of $10,914,000, a $21,310,000 difference from the actual results. This upward adjustment to income was accomplished by adding a $21,310,000 upward smoothing adjustment to the balance sheet. Circuit City also reported an actuarial gain of $274,000 under GAAP, instead of the $20,262,000 actuarial loss that it incurred during the year. This, too, was achieved by an upward smoothing adjustment to both income (through a reduction to pension expense) and the balance sheet (through a reduced liability). This smoothing adjustment was $20,536,000. Finally, changes in funded status that previously went unrecognized were recognized in the current year. These amounts were $140,000 for amortization of prior service cost and $199,000 for amortization of the transitional asset. When Circuit City reduced its plan benefits, the resulting increase in funded status was not recognized under GAAP immediately, but amortized over subsequent periods; and $140,000 of that amortization took place in the current year. When Circuit City first adopted the current pension rules, it had an overfunded plan. That overfunding was not immediately recognized as an asset under GAAP. That asset is being recognized over time through amortization, $199,000 of which was in the current year.

GAAP Amounts and Smoothing Adjustments on the Cash Flow Statement

Exhibit 15.11 illustrates the pension-related components of the GAAP cash flow statement. The GAAP cash flow statement begins with net income, which includes pension expense as defined by GAAP, $9,780,000. This $9,780,000 is a combination of $51,965,000 in economic costs and $42,185,000 in income increasing smoothing adjustments. The cash flow statement ends with the change in cash, which includes the contributions of $14,103,000. Note that the smoothing adjustments have no effect on this amount. The cash flow statement reconciles net income and the change in cash, and the change in the GAAP pension liability is a reconciling item. This change in pension liability consists of the $37,862,000 decrease in funded status and the $42,185,000 increase in balance sheet smoothing adjustments.

Now that we understand the elements of defined benefit plan financial reporting, we are ready to consider valuation of firms with such plans. Then, we will use our knowledge of financial reporting to extract important information from defined benefit plan disclosures.

15.4 VALUING FIRMS WITH DEFINED BENEFIT PENSION PLANS AND OPEB PLANS

Because OPEB plans are similar to defined benefit pension plans, we incorporate them in a valuation in much the same way. Therefore, although we will generally talk in terms of a defined benefit pension plan, this discussion also pertains to OPEB plans.

Applying Discounted Cash Flow Theory to Defined Benefit Plans

A company that has a defined benefit plan is ultimately responsible for providing sufficient funds to satisfy the PBO. Thus, the PBO is really a financial claim against the firm. Taxes create a difference between the PBO and typical financial claims. For a typical financial claim, there is no tax deduction when the principal is repaid. However, when the PBO principal is repaid via contributions to the plan, there will be a tax deduction. For each dollar paid, the firm will save one dollar times its marginal tax rate in taxes. Hence, the value to the firm of the PBO is its reported value *multiplied by one minus the marginal tax rate*.

The company also enjoys the rewards and bears the risks related to the plan's investments. In economic terms, the company owns the plan assets, even if that is not an accurate legal description. The

EXHIBIT 15.11 Circuit City—Effect of Pension on GAAP Cash Flow Statement

($ thousands)	Economic Component		Smoothing Adjustments		GAAP
Pension expense (in net income)	$ (51,965)	+	$ 42,185	=	$ (9,780)
Change in pension asset/liability	37,862	+	(42,185)	=	(4,323)
Change in cash	$ (14,103)	+	$ 0	=	$ (14,103)

plan assets are therefore nonoperating assets. Taxes also create a difference between plan assets and typical nonoperating assets. When the firm uses funds from the plan to pay benefits, it will forego a tax deduction it would otherwise be entitled to if it paid the benefits directly. By using these assets, the firm avoids a cash outflow of only one dollar times one minus the marginal tax rate for each dollar of benefits paid. Hence, the plan assets are worth their fair value *times one minus the marginal tax rate*.[8]

A valuation must also consider forecasted future issuances of financial claims to pay operating costs, because they are free cash flow equivalents. Because the PBO is a financial claim, the issuance of additional PBO is a free cash flow equivalent. The amount of this free cash flow equivalent is the present value of the future payments that were earned that period. As we learned earlier in the chapter, this is the service cost. Thus, a valuation must include service costs, net of their related tax benefits, in the free cash flow forecast. Importantly, the free cash flow forecast should include no other amounts related to pensions.

Exhibit 15.12 shows the elements of the economic balance sheet. When a firm has a defined benefit pension plan, nonoperating assets include the plan assets, other capital claims include the PBO, and free cash flow includes service cost. All three of these amounts are net of tax.

From Exhibit 15.12, we see that we can rewrite the value of the firm's equity as

$$
\begin{aligned}
COMEQUITY = \;& PV(FCF_{-DB} - SERVICECOSTS_{FUTURE} \cdot (1 - \tau)) && \text{free cash flows and} \\
&&& \text{equivalents} \\
& + NONOP + PLANASSETS \cdot (1 - \tau) && \text{nonoperating assets,} \\
& - DEBT - OCAP - PBO \cdot (1 - \tau) && \text{including} \\
&&& \text{plan assets}
\end{aligned}
\tag{15.1}
$$

where FCF_{-DB} is forecasted free cash flow, excluding any cash flow related to defined benefit plans, $SERVICECOSTS_{FUTURE}$ is the stream of expected service costs after the valuation date, PV is the present value operator, $PLANASSETS$ is the fair value of the plan's investments at the valuation date, PBO is the projected benefit obligation at the valuation date, and τ is the marginal income tax rate.

EXHIBIT 15.12   Cash Flows and the Firm

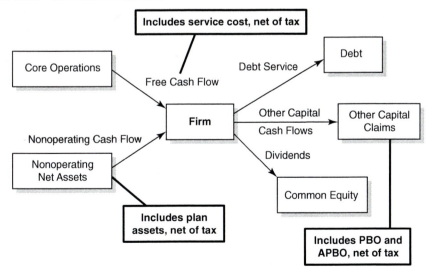

---

[8]It may appear that the firm loses money by using plan assets to pay benefits. That is not the case. When the firm contributed funds to the trust, it received a tax deduction. So, for each dollar in the trust, the firm also has one dollar times the marginal tax rate in additional cash from the tax savings. This is reflected in a higher cash (or lower debt) balance.

Equation (15.1) states that we treat service costs (net of tax) as free cash flow equivalents, plan assets (net of tax) as nonoperating assets, and the PBO (net of tax) as a financial claim.

Using the Information in the Defined Benefit Pension and OPEB Disclosures

The three pension-related items in (15.1) are plan assets, the PBO, and service costs. We now discuss where to find this information and how to use it in our analysis. We first discuss obtaining information about plan assets and the PBO. We then discuss service costs.

Plan Assets and PBO

The financial statement footnotes include disclosures of plan assets and the PBO. So, we can take these amounts directly from the retirement benefit footnote. We adjust these amounts for their tax effects and incorporate them in the valuation. Exhibit 15.13 shows how these amounts affect a valuation of Circuit City. We assume a 38% marginal tax rate.

    We take the plan assets and PBO directly from the pension footnote (Exhibit 15.7). We reduce each by the related tax effect. Although Circuit City's plan is underfunded by about $17 million, this reduces Circuit City's equity value by only about $11 million, due to the tax savings the firm will enjoy when it funds the plan. Note that if Circuit City had an OPEB plan, we would take comparable amounts from that plan as well.

Service Cost

As we have seen, pension expense for defined benefit plans consists of service cost, other changes in the funded status of the plan not due to contributions, and smoothing adjustments. Equation (15.1) tells us that in a valuation we must forecast free cash flow as if it included only the service cost portion of pension expense. We want no other cash flows related to defined benefit pension or OPEB plans in free cash flow. Although we must forecast future service costs, the financial statement footnotes disclose only historical values. However, this historical information about service costs will be very useful for forecasting future service costs. Unlike contributions, service costs are not discretionary. Thus, they are much easier to forecast reliably from historical information. In analyzing historical cash flows, we adjust the GAAP income and cash flow statements to a free cash flow basis. To do that, we must remove all components of pension expense other than service cost. We also must remove the cash flow statement reconciling item for the change in pension asset or liability. So, we make the following adjustments.

EXHIBIT 15.13   Effect of Plan Assets and Projected Benefit Obligation on Circuit City Valuation

($ thousands)		
Plan assets	$ 130,351	
Less: Tax effect	49,533	
Plan assets, net of tax	$ 80,818	Include as nonoperating asset
PBO	$ 147,912	
Less: Tax effect	56,207	
PBO, net of tax	$ 91,705	Include as financial claim

EXHIBIT 15.14   Components of Circuit City's Combined Income Statement and Cash Flow Statement

($ in thousands)	
Pension expense	$ (9,780)
Change in pension asset/liability	(4,323)
Change in cash (contribution)	$ (14,103)

1. Eliminate defined benefit pension and OPEB expense from the income statement and replace it with service cost.
2. Remove any adjustment in the cash flow statement for the change in the pension and OPEB asset/liability from free cash flow.
3. Replace the tax effect of the defined benefit plan in the income statement with the income tax provision related only to the service cost.
4. Remove the deferred tax effect of the pensions and OPEBs.

These adjustments leave only the service costs, net of the tax effect, in free cash flow.

Pension items usually are not separate line items on the financial statements but instead are aggregated with other items. For example, pension expense often is included in selling, general, and administrative expenses, and the pension asset or liability often is part of other assets or accruals. We use the pension footnote to determine the pension amounts included in the GAAP financial statements and then adjust those amounts to a free cash flow basis.

We used the Circuit City pension footnote to determine that the pension items included in the combined income statement and cash flow statement under GAAP included $9,780,000 of pension expense and the $4,323,000 decrease in pension liability, for a total contribution of $14,103,000, shown in Exhibit 15.11 and repeated here as Exhibit 15.14.

The pension expense of $9,780,000 and the $14,103,000 contribution are both taken from the pension footnote. We then compute the change in pension asset/liability, which must be the difference between these two amounts. There is one other amount needed to complete the analysis, which is the service cost. Circuit City's service cost is $12,617,000, and it also is obtained from the pension footnote in Exhibit 15.7.

Adjustments 1 and 2   In adjustment 1 we replace the $9,780,000 of pension expense with the $12,617,000 of service cost. This requires an adjustment to increase pension expense (thereby decreasing income) $2,837,000. In adjustment 2, we remove the $4,323,000 reconciling item in the cash flow statement for the change in pension asset/liability, leaving only service cost in the free cash flow. These two amounts are moved to the portion of the free cash flow statement appearing below free cash flow. Exhibit 15.15 summarizes the effects of adjustments 1 and 2 on free cash flow.

EXHIBIT 15.15   Effect of Adjustments 1 and 2 on Circuit City's Free Cash Flow

($ thousands)	GAAP	Adjustments	
Pension expense	$ (9,780)	(2,837)	(1) Adjusts pension expense to be equal to service cost of $12,617
Change in pension asset/liability	(4,323)	4,323	(2) Removes change in pension asset/liability
Contribution	$ (14,103)		

Together, these two adjustments convert the pretax amounts in the combined income statement and cash flow statement from a GAAP basis to a free cash flow basis, which includes service cost but no other pension-related cash flows.

Adjustments 3 and 4   We also need to consider how the income tax effects of the pension affect the combined income statement and cash flow statement under GAAP, and convert them to a free cash flow basis. The resulting free cash flow amounts should include the tax effect of service costs, but no other income tax effects. We will use an approach similar to the one used for pretax pension cash flows.

The income tax deduction related to pensions is based on contributions. The cash tax savings in any particular year is the marginal tax rate times the amount of contributions made in that year.[9] Assuming a 38% marginal tax rate, Circuit City would have saved about $5,359,000 in taxes by deducting its $14,103,000 contribution to the plan on its tax return.

The reported pension expense generally differs from the amount of contributions. Over the entire life of a pension plan, the amount of contributions is equal to the pension expense, so any difference between reported pension expense and contributions (the expense for tax purposes) is a temporary difference. Reported income tax expense is therefore the marginal income tax rate times the reported pension expense. For Circuit City, this is $3,716,000 on its $9,780,000 of pension expense. Any difference between this amount and the cash tax effect will increase or decrease the deferred tax liability.

Circuit City's combined income statement and cash flow statement includes the tax items related to pensions shown in Exhibit 15.16. The deferred tax amount must have been $1,643,000, because it reconciles the tax effect on the income statement, which is $3,716,000, to the cash tax effect of $5,359,000.

Free cash flow should include the income tax effect of the service cost, but no other amounts related to the income tax effects of pensions. This is the $12,617,000 service cost times 38%, or a $4,794,000 tax benefit. We need to replace the reported income tax benefit of $3,716,000 with the $4,794,000 tax benefit related to service cost, resulting in an adjustment of $1,078,000. The change in deferred taxes related to the pension plan also must be removed from free cash flow. Reversing this entire amount of $1,643,000 leaves only the tax effect of the service cost in free cash flow. As with adjustments 1 and 2, both these amounts are moved below the free cash flow line in the free cash flow statement. Exhibit 15.17 summarizes the effects of adjustments 3 and 4.

EXHIBIT 15.16   Tax Items in Circuit City Combined Income Statement and Cash Flow Statement

($ thousands)		
Income tax benefit	$	3,716
Deferred taxes		1,643
Cash tax savings	$	5,359

---

[9]We assume the firm's contributions have not exceeded the maximum allowable tax deduction. This is reasonable because firms rarely contribute more than the deductible amount.

EXHIBIT 15.17   Effect of Adjustments 3 and 4 on Circuit City's Free Cash Flow

($ thousands)	GAAP	Adjustments	
Income tax benefit	$ 3,716	1,078	(3) Adjusts tax benefit to be tax benefit related to service cost, $4,794
Deferred taxes	1,643	(1,643)	(4) Removes change in deferred tax liability
Cash tax savings	$ 5,359		

Transferring the Adjustments to the Free Cash Flow Worksheet

Exhibit 15.18 shows Circuit City's combined income statement and cash flow statement for 2001 and the adjustments to these to put the retirement costs on a free cash flow basis.[10] Adjustments 1 and 2 are the defined benefit pension plan adjustments. These adjustments remove from compensation and benefits all pension expense other than the service cost, as well as the reconciling item in the cash flow statement. Adjustments 3 and 4 are the related tax adjustments. These adjust the income tax provision to reflect only the tax benefit related to the service costs and eliminate the deferred tax effect. We also show offsetting amounts below the free cash flow line so we can check that the net effect of our adjustments on the change in cash is zero.

Using the Footnote Information to Make OPEB Adjustments

Disclosures for OPEB plans are virtually identical to defined benefit pension plans, so the analysis is very similar. OPEB plans often are unfunded, in which case there are no plan assets and no return on plan assets. In such an instance, we simply set plan assets and actual and expected return on plan assets to zero. Also, think of contributions and benefit payments as being equal, as if contributions are made to the plan and immediately paid to beneficiaries. Then the analysis of OPEBs is identical to the analysis of defined benefit pension plans.

Making Adjustments Under APV and Residual Income Models

We have discussed valuing companies with defined benefit plans in the context of the free cash flow model. The cash flow analysis is identical under the APV model because that model discounts the same cash flow stream. The plan assets and PBO (both net of tax) also are nonoperating assets and other capital claims, respectively, just as in the free cash flow model. Under the residual income model, the analysis is again the same, except the adjustment to convert pension expense to service cost affects the residual income stream in a different way than the adjustment to remove the change in the pension asset or liability. The adjustment to convert pension expense to service cost affects NOPAT, directly affecting residual income. The adjustment to remove the change in the pension asset or liability affects residual income through its effect on book value of core operations. Further, because we treat the plan assets and PBO as not part of core operations, the book value of core operations should not include these amounts.

---

[10]Adjustments other than those relating to retirement plans are not shown.

EXHIBIT 15.18   Circuit City Free Cash Flow Worksheet with Pension Adjustments

($ thousands)	GAAP	Adjustments	
Net sales and operating revenues	$ 10,458,037		
Cost of sales, buying, and warehousing	(7,964,148)		
Appliance exit costs	(28,326)		
Gross profit	2,465,563		
Selling, general, and administrative expenses	(2,270,745)	(1)	(2,837)
Appliance exit costs	(1,670)		
Interest expense	(7,273)		
Earnings before income taxes and intergroup interest in the CarMax Group	185,875		
Provision for income taxes	(70,637)	(3)	1,078
Earnings before intergroup interest in the CarMax Group	115,238		
Net earnings related to intergroup interest in the CarMax Group	34,009		
Net earnings	149,247		
Net earnings related to intergroup interest in the CarMax Group	(34,009)		
Depreciation and amortization	126,297		
Loss on sales of property and equipment	4,259		
Provision for deferred income taxes	11,007	(4)	(1,643)
Decrease in deferred revenue and other liabilities	(17,442)		
Decrease in net accounts receivable	12,950		
Increase in merchandise inventory	(4,910)		
Increase in prepaid expenses and other current assets	(41,964)		
Decrease in other assets	588		
Decrease in accounts payable, accrued expenses, and other current liabilities	(68,074)	(2)	4,323
Net cash provided by operating activities of continuing operations	137,949		
Purchases of property and equipment	(274,722)		
Proceeds from sales of property and equipment	100,189		
Net cash used in investing activities of continuing operations	(174,533)		
Decrease in allocated short-term debt, net	(1,240)		
Decrease in allocated long-term debt, net	(156,402)		
Equity issuances, net	38,123		
Dividends paid	(14,346)		
		(1)	2,837
Pension contributions in excess of service cost		(2)	(4,323)
		(3)	(1,078)
Tax benefit on excess pension contributions		(4)	1,643
Net cash used in financing activities of continuing operations	(133,865)		
Cash used in discontinued operations	(26,174)		
Decrease in cash and cash equivalents	$ (196,623)		0

EXHIBIT 15.19   Circuit City Valuation Summary

($ thousands)	
Present value of free cash flow *	$ 10,200,000
NONOPERATING NET ASSETS:	
Investment in CarMax	50,000
Fair value of pension assets, net of tax [$130,351,000 × (1 − 38%)]	80,818
FINANCIAL CLAIMS:	
Long-term debt, including current maturities	(215,000)
PBO, net of tax [$147,912,000 × (1 − 38%)]	(91,705)
Equity value	$ 10,024,113

* Based on a forecast that includes service costs, net of tax, but no other pension-related items.

Valuation Summary

We now summarize the structure of a valuation allowing for retirement plans using the Circuit City example. Exhibit 15.19 shows the valuation of Circuit City. We assume reasonable values for the nonpension items, for the sake of illustration.

We compute the first item, the present value of the forecasted free cash flow, in the way we described in Chapter 10. Free cash flow is defined to include service costs (net of tax) for any defined benefit pension plans and OPEB plans the company has, and nothing else related to these plans. It also includes forecasted contributions to any defined contribution plans, although including the contributions usually need not be done explicitly, because the historical financial statements already include the contributions in compensation expense. As in any valuation, we add the value of nonoperating net assets and subtract the value of capital claims other than equity. Now the nonoperating net assets include plan assets from defined benefit pension plans and OPEB plans. Both of these amounts are net of tax. Capital claims include the benefit obligations, also net of tax.

SUMMARY

Retirement plans may be defined contribution plans or defined benefit plans. Defined contribution plans specify how much the firm must contribute to employees' retirement funds. Defined benefit plans specify the benefits employees are to receive. Defined benefit plans may be pensions or other postemployment benefit plans, which primarily consist of health care plans.

Economic ownership refers to who reaps the rewards and bears the risks of investing. Employees are the economic owners of the assets in defined contribution plans and employers are the economic owners of the assets in defined benefit plans. Economic ownership determines both the accounting and the valuation approach for retirement plans.

Defined contribution plans require no special analysis because contributions are generally linked to salary and reported as expenses in the income statement. The free cash flow analysis we developed in earlier chapters already considers defined contribution plans. Defined benefit plans require substantial analysis because the accounting consists of an economic component and smoothing adjustments. In addition, the economic component contains a mixture of free cash flow equivalents, nonoperating cash flows, and capital cash flows, requiring adjustments to obtain the appropriate measure of free cash flow.

Defined benefit plans contain investment assets, which we treat as nonoperating assets in the valuation. Defined benefit plans also have benefit obligations, which are treated as capital claims. Because these assets and claims both have future income tax implications, we show these amounts net of taxes in the valuation.

Service cost, one component of pension expense, represents the free cash flow equivalent related to defined benefit plans. Service cost, net of tax, is the only item related to defined benefit plans that should appear in the free cash flow statement or free cash flow forecast.

SUGGESTED READINGS

Amir, Eli and Elizabeth Gordon. "Firms' Choice of Estimation Parameters: Empirical Evidence from SFAS 106." *Journal of Accounting, Auditing and Finance* 11, 3 (1996):427–448.

Bodie, Zvi and E. Philip Davis, eds. *The Foundations of Pension Finance.* Edward Elgar, 2000. London.

Bodie, Zvi, Alan Marcus, and Robert Merton. "Defined Benefit versus Defined Contribution Plans: What Are the Real Tradeoffs?" in *Pensions in the U.S. Economy*, Zvi Bodie, John Shoven, and David Wise, eds. Chicago: University of Chicago Press, 1988.

Bulow, Jeremy. "Analysis of Pension Funding under ERISA." National Bureau of Economic Research (NBER) Working Paper No. W0402, 1979.

Dhaliwal, Dan. "Measurement of Financial Leverage in the Presence of Unfunded Pension Obligations." *The Accounting Review* (October 1986):651–661.

Mozes, Haim. "The Shift in Emphasis from Defined Benefit Plans to Defined Contribution Plans in the 1980s: A Contracting Explanation." Working paper, 1997.

Revsine, Lawrence, Daniel Collins, and Bruce Johnson. *Financial Reporting and Analysis.* Upper Saddle River, NJ: Prentice Hall, 2002, Chapter 14: Pensions and Postretirement Benefits.

REVIEW QUESTIONS

1. What is the difference between a defined contribution plan and a defined benefit plan?

2. General Electric Company describes its pension plan as follows: "The GE Pension Plan provides benefits to certain U.S. employees based on the greater of a formula recognizing career earnings or a formula recognizing length of service and final average earnings." Is GE's plan a defined contribution plan or a defined benefit plan?

3. Who is the economic owner of plan assets under a defined contribution plan?

4. Who is the economic owner of plan assets under a defined benefit plan?

5. What amounts, if any, appear on the balance sheet related to a defined contribution plan?

6. What amounts, if any, appear on the balance sheet related to a defined benefit plan?

7. How is the amount of expense recognized for a defined contribution plan determined?

8. How is the amount of expense recognized for a defined benefit plan determined?

9. Eastman Kodak's 2000 proxy statement states the following about its pension plan: "For an employee with up to 35 years of accrued service, the annual normal retirement income benefit is calculated by multiplying the employee's years of accrued service by the sum of (a) 1.3% of APC, plus (b) 0.3% of APC in excess of the average Social Security wage base. For an employee with more than 35 years of accrued service, the amount is increased by 1% for each year in excess of 35 years." APC refers to average participating compensation, a measure of earnings during an employee's years at the company. Is Eastman Kodak's plan a defined contribution plan or a defined benefit plan?

10. General Electric's 2000 pension footnote includes the following statement: "Experience gains and losses, as well as the effects of changes in actuarial assumptions and plan provisions, are amortized over the average future service period of employees." Explain what this means.

11. What amount related to a defined contribution plan should be included in a free cash flow forecast?

12. What amount related to a defined benefit plan should be included in a free cash flow forecast?

13. Why are plan assets from a defined benefit plan included in a valuation as a nonoperating asset?

14. Why is the projected benefit obligation from a defined benefit plan included in a valuation as a financial claim?

15. You have prepared a valuation of a company with a defined benefit plan. You included plan assets and the projected benefit obligation as a nonoperating asset and a financial claim, respectively, in the valuation. Before including these amounts in the valuation, you multiplied each by one minus the firm's marginal income tax rate. Your supervisor has asked you to explain why you applied the income tax factor to these amounts.

PROBLEMS

1. Bestfoods' defined benefit plan calls for annual benefit payments beginning at age 62 equal to 1.2% of average annual compensation times the number of years of service, up to a total of 30 years. If an employee retires from Bestfoods at age 62 after 35 years of service, what will be her annual pension benefit?

Problems 2 through 6 are based on the following information: Pelletier-Sale Figure Skating Corporation has a defined benefit pension plan. It has only one employee, who is expected to retire on December 31, 2005, and receive an annual pension of $75,000. Benefit payments are to be made annually, with the first payment coming on December 31, 2006. The employee is expected to live for 20 years after retirement. Assume a discount rate of 8%, and that as of December 31, 2002, the employee has earned 80% of her future benefits. (Note that problems 4 through 6 are independent of each other.)

2. What is the present value of the employee's future benefit payments as of December 31, 2002?

3. What is the value of the PBO as of December 31, 2002?

4. Suppose on December 31, 2002, the discount rate were adjusted to 8.5%.

   a. What would be the amount of the actuarial gain or loss?
   b. Would the amount in (a) be recognized immediately under GAAP?

5. Suppose on December 31, 2002, the plan were amended, resulting in this employee expecting an annual pension of $85,000.

   a. What would be the effect on the PBO?
   b. Would the amount in (a) be recognized immediately under GAAP?

6. Suppose on December 31, 2002, mortality tables were revised so that the employee's life expectancy was 25 years after retirement.

   a. What would be the amount of the actuarial gain or loss?
   b. Would the amount in (a) be recognized immediately under GAAP?

The following was adapted from the footnotes in General Electric's 2000 annual report. Use this information for problems 7 through 12. Assume GE's marginal income tax rate is 38%.

RETIREE HEALTH AND LIFE BENEFITS

The effect on operations of principal retiree benefit plans is shown in the following table.

Effect on Operatons (in millions)	2000	1999	1998
Expected return on plan assets	$ (178)	$ (165)	$ (149)
Service cost for benefits earned	165	107	96
Interest cost on benefit obligation	402	323	319
Prior service cost	49	8	8
Net actuarial loss recognized	40	45	39
Total cost	$ 478	$ 318	$ 313

Changes in the accumulated postretirement benefit obligation for retiree benefit plans follow:

Accumulated Postretirement Benefit Obligation (APBO) (in millions)	2000	1999
Balance at January 1	$ 4,926	$ 5,007
Service cost for benefits earned	165	107
Interest cost on benefit obligation	402	323
Plan amendments	948	—
Actuarial loss/(gain)	534	(62)
Benefits paid	(553)	(475)
Other	—	26
Balance at December 31	$ 6,422	$ 4,926

Changes in the fair value of assets for retiree benefit plans follow:

Fair Value of Assets (in millions)	2000	1999
Balance at January 1	$ 2,369	$ 2,121
Actual return on plan assets	(85)	355
Employer contributions	300	368
Benefits paid	(553)	(475)
Balance at December 31	$ 2,031	$ 2,369

GE recorded a net liability for retiree benefit plans as follows:

Retiree Benefit Liability/Asset December 31 (in millions)	2000	1999
Accumulated postretirement benefit obligation	$ 6,422	$ 4,926
Deduct unrecognized balances		
Prior service cost	(999)	(100)
Net actuarial loss	(818)	(61)
Fair value of plan assets	(2,031)	(2,369)
Net liability	$ 2,574	$ 2,396

Actuarial assumptions used to determine costs and benefit obligations for principal retiree benefit plans follow:

Actuarial Assumptions December 31	2000	1999	1998
Discount rate	7.5%	7.75%	6.75%
Compensation increases	5.0	5.0	5.0
Health care cost trend (a)	10.0	9.0	7.8
Return on assets for the year	9.5	9.5	9.5

(a) For 2000, gradually declining to 5% after 2009.

PENSION BENEFITS

Details of the effect on operations of principal pension plans, and the total effect on cost of postemployment benefit plans, follow:

Effect on Operations (in millions)	2000	1999	1998
Expected return on plan assets	$ 3,754	$ 3,407	$ 3,024
Service cost for benefits earned	(780)	(693)	(625)
Interest cost on benefit obligation	(1,966)	(1,804)	(1,749)
Prior service cost	(237)	(151)	(153)
SFAS No. 87 transition gain	154	154	154
Net actuarial gain recognized	819	467	365
Cost reduction from pension	$ 1,744	$ 1,380	$ 1,016

Changes in the projected benefit obligation for principal pension plans follow:

Projected Benefit Obligation (in millions)	2000	1999
Balance at January 1	$ 25,522	$ 27,572
Service cost for benefits earned	780	693
Interest cost on benefit obligation	1,966	1,804
Plan amendments	1,155	—
Actuarial loss/(gain)	970	(2,790)
Benefits paid	(1,858)	(1,757)
Balance at December 31	$ 28,535	$ 25,522

Changes in the fair value of assets for principal pension plans follow:

Fair Value of Assets (in millions)	2000	1999
Balance at January 1	$ 50,243	$ 43,447
Actual return on plan assets	1,287	8,472
Employer contributions	85	81
Benefits paid	(1,858)	(1,757)
Balance at December 31	$ 49,757	$ 50,243

GE recorded assets and liabilities for principal pension plans as follows:

Prepaid Pension Asset December 31 (in millions)	2000	1999
Fair value of plan assets	$ 49,757	$ 50,243
Add (deduct) unrecognized balances		
Prior service cost	1,617	699
SFAS No. 87 transition gain	—	(154)
Net actuarial gain	(12,594)	(16,850)
Projected benefit obligation	(28,535)	(25,522)
Net prepaid pension asset	$ 10,245	$ 8,416

Actuarial assumptions used to determine costs and benefit obligations for principal pension plans follow:

Actuarial Assumptions December 31	2000	1999	1998
Discount rate	7.5%	7.75%	6.75%
Compensation increases	5.0	5.0	5.0
Return on assets for the year	9.5	9.5	9.5

7. Using a format similar to Exhibit 15.10, reconcile the economic and GAAP amounts for the retiree health and life benefits plans. Then answer the following questions.

   a. What is the funded status at December 31, 1999?
   b. What is the funded status at December 31, 2000?
   c. What was the amount of balance sheet smoothing adjustments at December 31, 1999?
   d. What was the amount of balance sheet smoothing adjustments at December 31, 2000?
   e. How does the difference between your answers to (c) and (d) relate to the income statement?

8. Using a format similar to Exhibit 15.10, reconcile the economic and GAAP amounts for the pension benefits. Then answer the following questions.

   a. What is the funded status at December 31, 1999?
   b. What is the funded status at December 31, 2000?
   c. What amount would GE have reported as pension expense if GAAP had not allowed smoothing adjustments?

9. In 2000, GE reduced the discount rate it used to compute the APBO and PBO from 7.75% to 7.5%.

   a. In what direction should the APBO and PBO change as a result of the revised assumption?
   b. Does this create an actuarial gain or an actuarial loss?
   c. Find the related gain or loss in each of the two footnotes.

10. Your supervisor has been studying GE's pension plan and found that GE has pension income rather than pension expense. This is labeled "cost reduction from pension" in the pension benefits footnote. He has asked you to explain how a pension plan could generate income rather than expense.

11. Determine the adjustments you must make to convert GE's combined income statement and cash flow statement to a free cash flow basis, taking into account the retiree health and life benefits plans as well as the pension plans.

12. Determine the amounts of nonoperating assets and financial claims related to the retiree health and life benefits plans and pension plans that would be included in a valuation of GE.

13. Your company is considering adding a pension plan to its benefits. Management is trying to determine whether to adopt a defined contribution plan or a defined benefit plan. Draw up a list of arguments supporting each of the pension types.

My Case

If your company has a defined benefit plan and/or an OPEB plan, revise your valuation to take these plans into account. To do so, you will need to:

   a. Adjust your historical free cash flow statements to include service cost, net of tax, and no other cash flows related to the plans.
   b. Adjust your forecasted operating margins, if necessary, to reflect the updated historical results.
   c. Include nonoperating assets and financial claims to reflect your company's funded status in the valuation.

APPENDIX 15.1   PROJECTED BENEFIT OBLIGATION AND ACCUMULATED POSTEMPLOYMENT BENEFIT OBLIGATION

The projected benefit obligation (PBO) is the portion of future benefits from a defined benefit pension plan that employees have earned. Determining the value of the PBO is very difficult because many uncertainties surround future benefit payments. How much will each employee be entitled to receive during retirement? How high will future salary increases be? How many employees will remain with the firm until retirement? How long will employees live once they retire? The accumulated postemployment benefit obligation (APBO) is similar to the PBO, but pertains to other postemployment benefit plans. Determining the value of the APBO is also difficult and subject to even greater uncertainty than is the PBO. In addition to the uncertainty that surrounds the PBO, the APBO also depends on assumptions about future health care costs.

Actuaries estimate the values of the PBO and the APBO using forecasts for the unknown elements of the computations. To understand how, we will use a simple example of a defined benefit pension plan with a single employee. As of December 31, 2002, this employee has worked for 10 years and is expected to work for 20 more, after which she is projected to receive a $50,000 annual pension. Based on current mortality tables, the actuaries expect her to live for 15 years after retirement. Assume the appropriate discount rate for this kind of obligation is 7.25%. This rate is based on the **settlement rate**, which is the rate at which the obligation would be valued by a third party agreeing to take responsibility for it.

Because the PBO is the portion of the present value of future benefits that have been earned, before determining the amount of the PBO we must know the present value of all future benefit payments, whether earned or not. Exhibit 15.20 provides this information. Column 5 shows the present value of the employee's expected future benefit payments as of all dates from her hiring until her death. Based on our assumption that the employee will receive 15 annual payments of $50,000 beginning in 2023, at the time of her retirement in 2022 the present value of the expected benefit payments is $448,291. Taking this present value back 20 more years to 2002 (the valuation date), the present value of these payments is $110,564.

In addition to showing the present value each year, Exhibit 15.20 also shows how the present value changes each year, by presenting an amortization table in columns 2 through 5. The amortization table is similar to those you have constructed for long-term debt and is based on the present value of the 15 benefit payments of $50,000. Column 2 is the present value of the future benefit payments at the beginning of each year. This is simply the present value of the future benefit payments at the end of the prior year (column 5 of prior row). Column 3 shows the increases in present value due to the passing of time. For example, in 1993, the $3,981 increase in the present value is equal to the beginning present value of $54,909 times 7.25%. Column 4 shows the reduction in the present value due to the benefit payments, which do not begin until 2023. As with any amortization table, at the end of the life of the obligation, the present value is zero.

The PBO is not the present value of all future benefit payments, but only the portion of them that has been earned. We will assume the employee earns her benefits evenly over the 30 years of employment (in present value terms). Column 6 shows the portion of the benefit payments earned as of each year. This fraction is zero when the employee is first hired. It increases over the employment life and reaches 100% at retirement.

EXHIBIT 15.20 PBO Calculation for a Single Employee (discount rate = 7.25%)

	1 Date	2 Beg. PV	+	3 Increase in PV Due to Time	−	4 Benefit Payments	=	5 Ending PV	×	6 Portion Earned	=	7 PBO
Hire	December 31, 1992							54,909		0/30		0
	1993	54,909		3,981				58,890		1/30		1,963
	1994	58,890		4,269				63,159		2/30		4,211
	1995	63,159		4,579				67,738		3/30		6,774
	1996	67,738		4,911				72,649		4/30		9,687
	1997	72,649		5,267				77,916		5/30		12,986
	1998	77,916		5,649				83,565		6/30		16,713
	1999	83,565		6,058				89,624		7/30		20,912
	2000	89,624		6,498				96,121		8/30		25,632
	2001	96,121		6,969				103,090		9/30		30,927
Valuation Date	2002	103,090		7,474				110,564		10/30		36,855
	2003	110,564		8,016				118,580		11/30		43,479
	2004	118,580		8,597				127,177		12/30		50,871
	2005	127,177		9,220				136,397		13/30		59,106
	2006	136,397		9,889				146,286		14/30		68,267
	2007	146,286		10,606				156,892		15/30		78,446
	2008	156,892		11,375				168,267		16/30		89,742
	2009	168,267		12,199				180,466		17/30		102,264
	2010	180,466		13,084				193,550		18/30		116,130
	2011	193,550		14,032				207,582		19/30		131,469
	2012	207,582		15,050				222,632		20/30		148,421
	2013	222,632		16,141				238,773		21/30		167,141
	2014	238,773		17,311				256,084		22/30		187,795
	2015	256,084		18,566				274,650		23/30		210,565
	2016	274,650		19,912				294,562		24/30		235,649
	2017	294,562		21,356				315,918		25/30		263,265
	2018	315,918		22,904				338,822		26/30		293,645
	2019	338,822		24,565				363,386		27/30		327,047
	2020	363,386		26,345				389,732		28/30		363,749
	2021	389,732		28,256				417,987		29/30		404,054
Retirement	2022	417,987		30,304				448,291		30/30		448,291
	2023	448,291		32,501		50,000		430,792		30/30		430,792
	2024	430,792		31,232		50,000		412,025		30/30		412,025
	2025	412,025		29,872		50,000		391,897		30/30		391,897
	2026	391,897		28,412		50,000		370,309		30/30		370,309
	2027	370,309		26,847		50,000		347,156		30/30		347,156
	2028	347,156		25,169		50,000		322,325		30/30		322,325
	2029	322,325		23,369		50,000		295,694		30/30		295,694
	2030	295,694		21,438		50,000		267,132		30/30		267,132
	2031	267,132		19,367		50,000		236,499		30/30		236,499
	2032	236,499		17,146		50,000		203,645		30/30		203,645
	2033	203,645		14,764		50,000		168,409		30/30		168,409
	2034	168,409		12,210		50,000		130,619		30/30		130,619
	2035	130,619		9,470		50,000		90,089		30/30		90,089
	2036	90,089		6,531		50,000		46,620		30/30		46,620
Death	2037	46,620		3,380		50,000		0		30/30		0

Column 7 shows the resulting PBO. This is equal to the portion earned (column 6) times the ending present value (column 5). On December 31, 2002, after 10 years of employment, the PBO is one-third (10 years / 30 years) of the $110,564 present value of future benefits, or $36,855. By retirement on December 31, 2022, the fraction is 100% (30 years / 30 years), and the PBO is equal to the present value of future benefits. From that point on, the PBO is equal to the entire present value of future benefits. Exhibit 15.21 illustrates the relationship over time between the present value of future benefits and the PBO.

The upper curve in Exhibit 15.21 represents the present value of the future benefit payments. It grows over the employment life, then falls during retirement as benefit payments are made. The lower curve is the PBO. This amount is the present value of the future benefits times the portion of the benefits that have been earned.

Explaining the changes in the PBO is key to the economics of pensions. Ignoring for now plan amendments and changes in actuarial assumptions, the year-to-year change in the PBO has three components: the interest cost, the service cost, and the benefit payment.

Exhibit 15.22 shows how the PBO changes for the employee illustrated in Exhibit 15.20. Column B shows the beginning-of-the-year PBO and column F shows the end-of-the-year PBO, both from Exhibit 15.20. Columns C, D, and E show the changes in the PBO each year. Column C is the interest cost. With the passing of each year, the present value of future benefits increases, as all the future cash flows that go into the present value of future benefits computation are discounted for one year less. Because the PBO is a portion of this present value, the PBO increases by the same percentage, in this case 7.25%.[11] The interest cost is equal to 7.25% times the beginning PBO. For example, interest cost in 2002 is $30,927 times 7.25%, or $2,242. Column D shows the increase in the PBO due to service cost. Each year during the employee's working years, an additional 1/30 of the future benefits is earned. The resulting increase in the PBO is service cost. Column D is equal to

EXHIBIT 15.21   Present Value of Future Pension Benefits and PBO

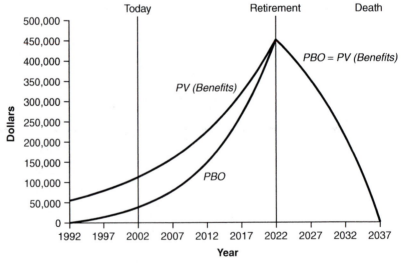

[11]The increase in the present value due to time (column 3 in Exhibit 15.20) is the increase in the present value of *all* benefit payments, whereas the interest cost is related only to the increase in the PBO. Thus, these amounts are not equal.

EXHIBIT 15.22   PBO: Analysis of Changes for Single Employee

	A Date	B Beginning PBO +	C Interest Cost (7.25%) +	D Service Cost –	E Benefit Payment =	F Ending PBO	G Ending PV
Hire	December 31, 1992					0	54,909
	1993	0	0	1,963		1,963	58,890
	1994	1,963	142	2,105		4,211	63,159
	1995	4,211	305	2,258		6,774	67,738
	1996	6,774	491	2,422		9,687	72,649
	1997	9,687	702	2,597		12,986	77,916
	1998	12,986	941	2,786		16,713	83,565
	1999	16,713	1,212	2,987		20,912	89,624
	2000	20,912	1,516	3,204		25,632	96,121
	2001	25,632	1,858	3,436		30,927	103,090
Valuation Date	2002	30,927	2,242	3,685		36,855	110,564
	2003	36,855	2,672	3,953		43,479	118,580
	2004	43,479	3,152	4,239		50,871	127,177
	2005	50,871	3,688	4,547		59,106	136,397
	2006	59,106	4,285	4,876		68,267	146,286
	2007	68,267	4,949	5,230		78,446	156,892
	2008	78,446	5,687	5,609		89,742	168,267
	2009	89,742	6,506	6,016		102,264	180,466
	2010	102,264	7,414	6,452		116,130	193,550
	2011	116,130	8,419	6,919		131,469	207,582
	2012	131,469	9,531	7,421		148,421	222,632
	2013	148,421	10,761	7,959		167,141	238,773
	2014	167,141	12,118	8,536		187,795	256,084
	2015	187,795	13,615	9,155		210,565	274,650
	2016	210,565	15,266	9,819		235,649	294,562
	2017	235,649	17,085	10,531		263,265	315,918
	2018	263,265	19,087	11,294		293,645	338,822
	2019	293,645	21,289	12,113		327,047	363,386
	2020	327,047	23,711	12,991		363,749	389,732
	2021	363,749	26,372	13,933		404,054	417,987
Retirement	2022	404,054	29,294	14,943		448,291	448,291
	2023	448,291	32,501		50,000	430,792	430,792
	2024	430,792	31,232		50,000	412,025	412,025
	2025	412,025	29,872		50,000	391,897	391,897
	2026	391,897	28,412		50,000	370,309	370,309
	2027	370,309	26,847		50,000	347,156	347,156
	2028	347,156	25,169		50,000	322,325	322,325
	2029	322,325	23,369		50,000	295,694	295,694
	2030	295,694	21,438		50,000	267,132	267,132
	2031	267,132	19,367		50,000	236,499	236,499
	2032	236,499	17,146		50,000	203,645	203,645
	2033	203,645	14,764		50,000	168,409	168,409
	2034	168,409	12,210		50,000	130,619	130,619
	2035	130,619	9,470		50,000	90,089	90,089
	2036	90,089	6,531		50,000	46,620	46,620
Death	2037	46,620	3,380		50,000	0	0

1/30 times the ending present value of retirement benefits in each year (column G). Column E shows the benefit payments, which reduce the PBO. If the actuary exactly predicts the employee's date of death, the PBO will be zero at that date.

If actuarial estimates were always perfect and the terms of defined benefit plans never changed, service cost, interest cost, and benefit payments would account for all changes in the PBO. However, actuarial estimates are not perfect. As a result, actuaries constantly revise their estimates of employee mortality, future salary increases, and the discount rate each year as more precise information becomes available. These revisions result in changes in the PBO. In addition, the terms of defined benefit plans may change, resulting in changes in the forecasted benefit payments and hence in the PBO.

When the PBO changes due to changes in actuarial assumptions, there is an actuarial gain or loss. Suppose on December 31, 2002, the firm in our example determined the appropriate discount rate should now be 6.75% rather than 7.25%, due to a decline in interest rates. The PBO would immediately increase. This would create an actuarial loss, because the value of an obligation is increasing.

Suppose instead the firm sweetened its pension plan, so our employee's benefits would be estimated to be $55,000 per year, rather than $50,000. The interest rate is unchanged, and the employee is still expected to retire on the same date and has the same life expectancy. Again the PBO would increase. This increase in the PBO would be due to plan amendments.

In either of the above examples—actuarial gains and losses or plan amendments—the PBO would be revised. New schedules like Exhibits 15.20 and 15.22 would be set up, and the PBO would continue to be accounted for as it was before, unless and until there were another actuarial change or plan amendment.

PART V

MULTIPLES VALUATION

16 A "Theory" of Multiples

17 PE Ratios and Earnings Growth

18 Additional Issues in Multiples Analysis

16

Where We Have Been:

So far in this book, we have learned about business and financial statement analysis and discounted cash flow methods of valuation.

Where We Are:

In this chapter, we begin our study of multiples valuation methods. We present a general framework for multiples analysis. Just as with discounted cash flow methods, we will use our knowledge of business and financial statement analysis in applying multiples. We will also see that multiples can be used as a shortcut for cash flow valuation models.

Where We Are Going:

In Chapters 17 and 18, we will further explore the price/earnings multiple, introduce the price-earnings to growth and market/book ratio valuation approaches, and discuss some complicating issues in multiples valuation.

A "Theory" of Multiples

LEARNING OBJECTIVES:

After studying this chapter, you will understand:

- How and why analysts use the multiples approach to value companies.

- What are the arguments for and against using multiples to value companies.

- Why the multiples approach requires that firms be comparable.

- How to identify comparable firms.

- How earnings quality issues affect comparability in the multiples approach.

- How the multiples approach can be an acceptable shortcut to discounted cash flow valuation.

Anyone who reads the popular business press has seen reference to the multiples approach to valuation. The multiples approach is controversial because, despite very strong theoretical arguments against it, recent empirical research has actually shown that multiples such as the price/earnings and market/book ratios can be used to predict future stock returns. This suggests firms with low multiples are undervalued and multiples can be used to rank investments.

Although most academics would argue that discounted cash flow methods are preferred for valuation, in practice many analysts use the multiples approach. Practitioners like the multiples approach because it is quick and relatively easy to implement. In this chapter, we discuss the arguments for and against the use of the multiples method. With sufficient analysis, the multiples approach can be an acceptable shortcut to discounted cash flow valuation, given the same assumptions.

In earlier chapters, a graphical representation explained the security analysis process. Exhibit 16.1 shows that representation, adapted to the multiples approach. In using the cash flow methods of valuation, we analyzed the financial statements, prepared our accounting analysis, and developed a business analysis before forecasting and using the selected valuation model. Multiples analysis is another type of valuation model. To prepare a good multiples analysis, we use the same steps. However, rather than forecasting many variables as we do in the cash flow models, in the multiples valuation the forecast is summarized in one ratio called the multiple.

In Section 16.1, we explain the use of the multiples approach and the underlying assumptions in a multiples valuation. Section 16.2 discusses the pros and cons of multiples valuation. Section 16.3 explores the notion of *comparability*, the art of choosing firms to determine the appropriate ratio in a multiples analysis, so the underlying assumptions are valid. Section 16.4 illustrates the multiples approach with a simple valuation problem. Section 16.5 discusses what to do when perfect comparability cannot be achieved.

EXHIBIT 16.1   A Picture of the Security Analysis Process

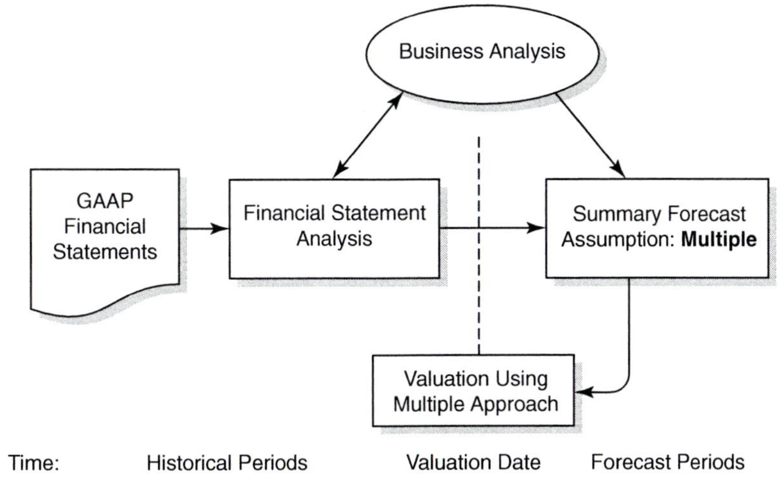

16.1 WHAT IS THE MULTIPLES APPROACH?

In the multiples approach, we assume the ratio of value to some firm-specific variable is the same across firms. We call this ratio the **multiple**. The firm-specific variable is the **value driver**. The analyst estimates value by multiplying the multiple times the value driver. The most common multiple is the price/earnings (PE) ratio. Other common multiples include the market/book (MB) ratio and the price/sales (PS) ratio.

The multiples approach is based on the idea that similar assets sell at similar prices. We expect two firms in the same industry, with the same earnings, sales, and growth prospects to sell for similar prices. However, if two firms are similar, but one is twice as big as the other is, we expect the larger one to have a value about twice that of the smaller one. These firms are not the same, but they are **comparable** because they differ only in terms of size. We use the term comparable to mean the firms are similar in terms of business, growth prospects, operating margins, and cash flow needs, but not necessarily size. When firms are comparable, we can use the multiples approach to determine the value of one firm based on the value of the other because the multiples approach controls for differences in value due solely to size.

When we use the multiples approach to value one firm, the target, based on the observed multiple of another, the comparable firm, the formula is

$$V_{TARGET} = \left(\frac{V_{COMP}}{X_{COMP}} \right) \cdot X_{TARGET} \tag{16.1}$$

where the Multiple is $\frac{V_{COMP}}{X_{COMP}}$ and the Value driver is X_{TARGET}.

where V means value, X means value driver, and the subscript indicates whether the amount pertains to the target or the comparable firm. In order for (16.1) to work both mathematically and logically, we always must have consistency between the multiple and the value driver. There are two requirements for this consistency:

- The value driver and the denominator of the multiple must be based on exactly the same definition. For example, if the denominator of the multiple is net earnings, the value driver must also be net earnings. If the multiple is based on pretax earnings, pretax earnings must be the value driver. If the multiple is based on book value, so is the value driver.

- Both the multiple and the value driver must be for the same period or as of the same date. If the multiple is based on 2001 earnings, the value driver must be 2001 earnings. If the multiple is end of 2000 book value, so is the value driver.

If the consistency requirements are not met, our analysis compares "apples and oranges" and the results are meaningless.

Using Multiples

To use the multiples approach, we need to observe the value of the comparable firm and the value drivers of both the target and comparable firms. We then compute the comparable firm's observed multiple and apply it to the target firm's observed value driver.

An example from the real estate business can help explain how to use multiples and how multiples control for size differences across firms. Suppose you have completed your education and decide to open your own company. You need to rent about 1,500 square feet of office space. You visit several similar vacant spaces in your neighborhood: the first one is 1,400 square feet and rents for $700 per month; the second is 1,500 square feet and rents for $750 per month; and the third is 1,600 square feet and rents for $800 per month. Each of these rents includes all your taxes and utilities, and each space is in good condition and has similar views. The spaces are comparable. From your visits, you conclude that good office space in your community rents for about 50 cents per square foot per month. If you were to look at another comparable space that was 1,300 square feet, you would expect it to rent for $0.50/ft^2 × 1,300 ft^2 = $650 per month. You estimate rent for similar spaces by applying the multiple, $0.50 per square foot, to the value driver, the number of square feet being rented. The multiple controls for size and, in conjunction with the value driver, determines the value of a particular space.

This procedure is valid as long as you hold constant all the other variables that affect rental rates, such as the neighborhood, the expenses included in the rent, the general condition of the space, the views, and so on. You could ignore the color of the carpeting or the brand of doorknobs in doing your analysis, because there is no reason to believe these things would affect rental rates. But, in a different neighborhood, or in a building in poor condition, rental rates (the multiple) would be different and could not be used to make a comparison.

When we use a multiple to estimate the value of a company's equity, we take the same steps as we did in this example. The multiple will be a ratio such as price/earnings, market/book value, or price/sales. We find comparable companies to determine an appropriate multiple, just as you looked at comparable spaces to determine the typical rent per square foot. We apply the appropriate value driver to the multiple, that is, earnings to the price/earnings ratio, book value to the market/book value ratio, or sales to the price/sales ratio.

Sometimes, multiples of seemingly comparable assets are not identical. We may not even be aware of small differences in the assets that affect their relative values. As long as the multiples are reasonably close, however, you can average them and then use the average as the multiple in your analysis. Returning to the real estate example, suppose you had located the same three office spaces, but their rents were as shown in Exhibit 16.2.

A friend who was also looking at office space asked you what he should expect to pay to rent a similar office space of 1,550 square feet in your neighborhood. To answer his question, you might take the average rent per square foot for the three known offices, ($.49 + $.56 + $.54)/3 = $.53. You would then multiply $.53 by 1,550 square feet to determine an estimated rent of $821.50.

Similarly, when there are several comparable firms, their multiples are unlikely to be identical. We can use the averaging approach to determine the appropriate multiple. For example, we can average the PE ratios for the comparable firms to determine a single comparable PE. We use this average PE as the multiple in the valuation. To determine an estimated value for the target company, we multiply this average PE by the earnings of the target firm. For example, assume you are trying to value a firm. You have the information about two comparable firms shown in Exhibit 16.3.

EXHIBIT 16.2   Comparable Rentals

	Square Feet	Rent	Rent per Square Foot
Space 1	1,400	$ 686	$ .49
Space 2	1,500	$ 840	$ .56
Space 3	1,600	$ 864	$ .54
Average			$ .53

EXHIBIT 16.3   Comparable Firm Data

	Price per Share	Earnings per Share	PE Ratio
Adamms Company	$ 30	$ 1.50	20
Munster, Inc.	$ 63	$ 3.00	21
Average			20.5

The target firm has earnings of $10 per share. So, we estimate its per-share value by multiplying its earnings per share by the average PE of the two firms. The value of the company is the per-share value times the number of shares outstanding.

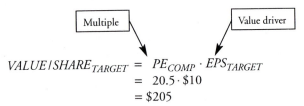

$$VALUE/SHARE_{TARGET} = PE_{COMP} \cdot EPS_{TARGET}$$
$$= 20.5 \cdot \$10$$
$$= \$205$$

Although averaging is a common and reasonable approach in multiples valuation, it is important to understand the implicit assumption involved, that the target firm is most similar to the *average* of the comparable firms. If the multiples of the firms are very different from each other, the firms may not be truly comparable. It may be more reasonable to assume the target is like *one* of the comparable firms, rather than the average. So, when firms' multiples are very different from each other, a better approach than averaging is to try to understand which of the firms are truly comparable and which are not, and then limit the analysis to the truly comparable firms.

In the preceding example, suppose a third firm in the same industry had a price of $45 per share and earnings of $1 per share. A strict averaging approach would result in the valuation shown in Exhibit 16.4. By adding this one additional firm to the group before averaging, we increase the valuation of the target firm from $205 to almost $287 per share, a jump of 40%. The large difference between the PE ratio of the Three Stooges Company and those of the first two firms suggests that Stooges is not similar to the other two. So, it is better to discover why its PE ratio is different and then determine whether the target is more similar to Adamms and Munster, or to Stooges. It may be that Stooges took a large write-off in the current year, reducing its reported earnings, while Adamms and Munster and the target did not. In that case, it is more reasonable to use the average PE of Adamms and Munster to value the target or to add back Stooges' write-off before calculating its PE.

EXHIBIT 16.4   Comparable Firm Data and Valuation

	Price per Share	Earnings per Share	PE Ratio
Adamms Company	$ 30	$ 1.50	20
Munster, Inc.	$ 63	$ 3.00	21
Three Stooges Co.	$ 45	$ 1.00	45
Average			28.667
Target Earnings per Share			$ 10.00
Target Valuation (average PE ratio × target EPS)			$ 286.67

Stooges may be in a high-growth segment of the industry, as is the target, whereas Adamms and Munster may be in the slower-growth end. In that case, the more appropriate multiple to use is Stooges' PE of 45, rather than either of the previous two average PEs.

Why Do Analysts Use the Multiples Approach?

The main reason analysts use the multiples approach for valuation is it is much quicker than discounted cash flow techniques. Discounted cash flow models require explicit assumptions for sales growth, margins, tax rates, reinvestment rates, cost of capital, and so on. So, if we could find an easier method to estimate a similar value, we would most certainly consider using such an approximation. The multiples approach generally requires only one explicit assumption, that the companies' multiples are equal. Once we identify comparable firms, the valuation process is quite simple. If a multiples approach can be structured so that it captures discounted cash flow theory's predictions about how multiples should vary, then it could be just as valid as using discounted cash flow.

Do we avoid all the discounted cash flow assumptions in a multiples valuation? Not really. The reason we would expect two firms' multiples to be the same is that we expect their future cash flow streams to be similar. In fact, if this assumption were not true, we would expect different multiples. So, it is not that we avoid all the discounted cash flow assumptions. Rather, we assume they are the same for both firms. The multiples approach permits the analyst to make discounted cash flow assumptions *implicitly*, rather than *explicitly*. Many analysts who use the multiples approach may not even realize they are making implicit discounted cash flow assumptions. They may simply believe the firms they are comparing should have the same multiple. However, their belief is reasonable only if the two firms have the same underlying cash flow streams, that is, if their discounted cash flow assumptions are the same.

16.2 ARGUMENTS FOR AND AGAINST THE MULTIPLES APPROACH

Over the years, experts have debated about whether it is appropriate to use a multiple to estimate value. We now summarize these arguments and offer a view that addresses the concerns of both sides.

Arguments Against the Multiples Approach

Many academics argue that the multiples approach is not valid because value is determined by expected future cash flows. The only correct way to calculate firm value, in their view, is to project the firm's cash flows and discount them to their present value. They argue that, relative to discounted cash flow, the multiples approach suffers from two shortcomings. First, accounting earnings, not cash flows, drive the multiples approach. Second, the multiples approach uses only one year of results, rather than all the expected future cash flows of the firm.

Problems with Using Earnings Instead of Cash Flow: Earnings Quality

The criticism that it is incorrect to use accounting earnings instead of cash flow in a valuation has merit.[1] Value is not related to earnings per se, but to cash flow. As discussed in Chapters 1 and 4, earn-

---

[1] The residual income model is not subject to this criticism because, as we saw, the combination of a residual income forecast and current book value is equivalent to a free cash flow forecast.

ings depend on the many choices the firm's accountants make when they calculate earnings, and so we must consider earnings quality issues when using the multiples approach. The accountants choose among different methods for depreciation, amortization, inventories, and revenue recognition, just to name a few. They also make many estimates that affect the reported amount of bad debt expense, income tax expense, promotional expense, warranty expense, various write-downs, and other expenses. Two economically identical firms could report very different earnings amounts if they made different accounting choices. Some academic researchers believe earnings are commonly "managed." There is evidence that managers choose accounting methods and estimates judiciously to achieve desired reporting results, such as achieving profit goals, beating analysts' earnings estimates, reaching bonus targets, and avoiding debt covenant violations. Just as with all the other valuation models, we cannot use the multiples approach without first doing our accounting analysis. We may need to adjust a firm's earnings to make them truly comparable to that of the comparable firm.

Problems with Using a Single Year of Earnings

Using a single year's results to estimate value creates another problem with multiples. This procedure effectively ignores all the expected results beyond the first year. As we will see in Chapter 17, earnings growth after year one should have a large effect on value. For example, if one firm were expected to have constant earnings of $5 million per year, whereas another were expected to see its earnings grow from $5 million to $15 million over the next several years, the two firms should have different values. But if we applied the same multiple to the first year of earnings of each firm, we would arrive at the same value.

Some firms may have unusual or extraordinary items included in their earnings in a particular year, another consideration in evaluating earnings quality. This causes a problem in a multiples analysis. One-time items are likely to have a different multiple associated with them than are items expected to recur. For example, a $1 million item of income that is a one-time windfall will increase value by $1 million. If the item is expected to recur every year forever, the effect on value is much greater, even if the income effect in the year being used as the value driver is only $1 million.

Arguments for the Multiples Approach

Proponents of the multiples approach have a very simple argument. Because this approach is used so much, the value of many firms in the marketplace may actually be based on multiples. Regardless of any theoretical arguments about why this should not be the case, multiples end up determining the values of many firms in the market, and the approach is considered valid because it is so commonly used.

Of course, the logical flaw in this argument is that if everyone else were valuing companies incorrectly, you could become very wealthy by valuing them appropriately and trading against the others. You would be able to find firms that the multiples approach undervalues, take positions in those firms, and reap large profits when the cash flows were realized. Nevertheless, enough people use multiples that it is at least worth considering the circumstances under which it might be a valid valuation tool.

Which Argument Is Right?

The arguments for and against the use of multiples seem directly opposite. One is based on a theoretical argument about how investors *should* value firms, and the other on a practical argument alleging how investors *do* value firms. In fact, both these arguments can be correct when placed in the proper context. People do use the multiples approach in practice; however, they do not apply it in a simple, mechanistic way. If investors applied the PE method in a very simple fashion, then all stocks would trade at the same PE ratio, and prices would change only when an earnings announcement were made, or about once every three months. Obviously, this is not what is happening. There are many different values for PEs and prices change constantly, even in the absence of news about earnings.

If investors use the multiples approach, why do firms trade at different PE ratios? Investors consider many factors in selecting the appropriate PE for valuing a firm, the same factors that influence a discounted cash flow valuation. For example, we will see in Chapters 17 and 18 that multiples are correlated with both expected earnings growth and accounting methods. If you laid out a discounted cash flow valuation in a spreadsheet and added a computation at the end of it to determine the PE ratio, the PE would change as earnings growth changed. In fact, actual PE ratios are related to earnings growth in exactly the way such a discounted cash flow analysis would predict. Our discounted cash flow analysis would also produce different PEs under different accounting methods. This, too, is what we observe in actual PE ratios. Further, analyst reports on companies often focus on earnings growth, accounting methods, and earnings quality when comparing PEs of several companies. They base what they believe to be an appropriate multiple on the same factors that affect a discounted cash flow valuation.

So, even if investors actually use multiples, they apply different multiples to different firms, and those multiples vary in the way discounted cash flow predicts. Investors must consider the same factors we consider in a formal discounted cash flow analysis and must incorporate them into the multiples they apply, even if they do not actually calculate detailed discounted cash flow valuations. In effect, these multiples-based investors are using multiples *as a shortcut to discounted cash flow valuation*.

It is possible for both arguments to be correct. We can use multiples, but doing so is only valid as long as *we understand that cash flow actually creates value and that multiples analysis is a shortcut to valuing cash flow*. We must carefully select multiples appropriate for the underlying value drivers, taking into account the accounting methods, earnings growth, and capital structure of the firm we are valuing, as well as any other factors that might affect the multiple.

Is the multiples approach less accurate than a discounted cash flow approach? This is a difficult question. In a perfect world, in which we could accurately project the cash flows for the future, discounted cash flow would certainly be better. Then, a multiples valuation would be as accurate as discounted cash flow only if the multiple were determined by doing a discounted cash flow analysis first and then "backing into" the correct multiple by dividing the discounted cash flow value by the value driver. However, in the real world, we need many assumptions to develop the discounted cash flow valuation. The discounted cash flow valuation is only as good as these explicit assumptions, which may be quite inaccurate. The multiples approach sounds less scientific, because it does not involve the same number of assumptions. But, in fact, the multiples valuation requires exactly the same scope of assumptions as the discounted cash flow valuation. By equating the multiples of two firms, the analyst assumes all their discounted cash flow assumptions are the same.

16.3 IMPORTANCE OF USING COMPARABLE FIRMS

Identifying comparable firms is a key step in a successful multiples valuation. Returning to our rental office space example, it was relatively easy for our young graduate to determine the going rate for office space. Identifying comparable firms, however, is more challenging. Many variables differ across firms, suggesting their multiples should be different. Yet, to be comparable, firms

A CLOSER LOOK

A Sampling of PE Ratios

The following graphs plot earnings per share and the PE ratio for Starbucks, Enron, Ford, and McDonald's from 1991 through 2000. Earnings per share is shown with bars and the scale appears on the left. The PE ratio is shown with a line and the scale appears on the right.

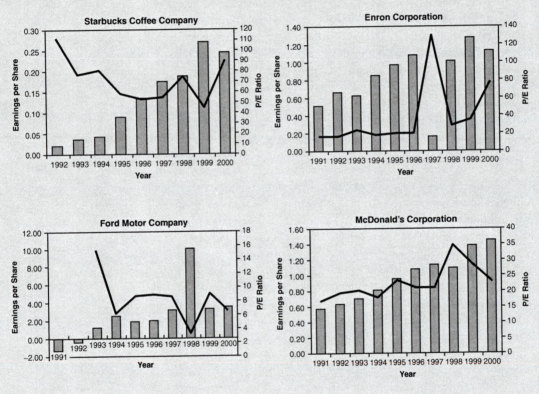

Source: Compustat.

In addition to having PEs that are different from each other, the four companies' PEs vary over time. This is especially true in a year in which earnings are unusually low (Enron in 1997) or high (Ford in 1998). When earnings are temporarily low, price does not decrease proportionately, resulting in a higher PE ratio. Similarly, when earnings are temporarily high, price does not increase proportionately, resulting in a lower PE ratio.

must have similar values for all these variables. Consider Exhibit 16.5, which plots PE ratio against expected earnings growth.

Tiger Company and Nicklaus Company are two firms in the same industry. Tiger Company, the target, has an expected earnings growth rate of 10% and a PE ratio of 15. Nicklaus Company has an expected earnings growth rate of 20% and a PE ratio of 25. Nicklaus' PE ratio is appropriately higher, because its expected earnings growth is higher. Suppose we mistakenly select Nicklaus to be the comparable firm, without considering the fact that it is a higher-growth firm

EXHIBIT 16.5   PE Ratio as a Function of Expected Earnings Growth

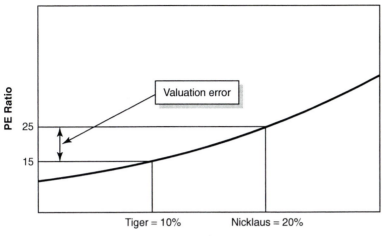

than Tiger. We observe Nicklaus' PE ratio, which is 25, and assume Tiger should have the same PE. With this assumption, we create a valuation error, represented by the difference between the two horizontal lines in Exhibit 16.5. To avoid a valuation error, it is thus important for the two firms to have similar expected earnings growth rates. In addition, the two firms should have similar values for *any* variables that affect the PE ratio. The more sensitive the PE ratio is to a particular variable (the steeper the slope of curve), the more important it is to match closely on the variable.

There are also many variables that do not affect a given multiple. Comparable firms need not be similar with respect to these. To illustrate, consider a second example, the relationship between PE and the number of letters in the CEO's last name. A plot of the expected relationship is shown in Exhibit 16.6.

EXHIBIT 16.6   PE Ratio as a Function of the Number of Letters in the CEO's Last Name

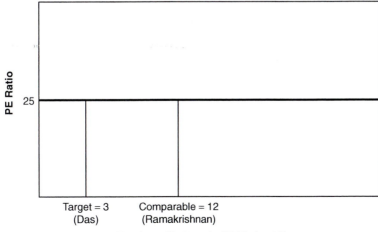

Suppose the average PE in the industry is 25. We do not expect any relationship between PE and the number of letters in the CEO's last name. Therefore, our best estimate of the PE of any firm in the industry, regardless of the number of letters in the CEO's last name, is the same, 25. Further suppose that the target's CEO's last name is Das. The comparable firm's CEO is named Ramakrishnan. We do not expect a valuation error as a result of the mismatch on the length of the names. Because failure to match on this variable does not create an error, there is no need to match on it.

These two examples show it is critically important to understand which variables affect the PE and why different firms should have different PEs. Understanding the variables that affect PE will allow us to minimize valuation errors by *matching* firms on important variables. In the example in Exhibit 16.5, we could reduce the valuation error by picking a comparable firm whose expected earnings growth is closer to Tiger's.

Finding Comparable Companies

Ultimately, the value of the firm is related to the cash flows it will generate. Truly comparable firms are therefore those whose cash flow streams are similar. However, identifying firms with identical cash flow projections would require us to develop those cash flow projections. This would defeat the purpose of using multiples valuation as a shortcut to discounted cash flow valuation. Once we went to the trouble of projecting cash flows to identify comparable firms, we might as well use those cash flow projections to value the firm! To make multiples valuation useful, we need to find a method of identifying firms likely to have similar cash flow patterns, without actually projecting the cash flows.

How do analysts find comparable firms? Often, the first step in identifying comparable firms is to match the firms on industry. The idea is that firms in the same industry (e.g., having the same Standard Industrial Classification, or SIC) are likely to have similar growth prospects, reinvestment requirements, margins, and so on. The U.S. government publishes SIC codes in the *Standard Industrial Classification Manual*, and this information is also available from other published sources, such as Standard and Poor's Compustat. Often, identifying industry classification is not enough, and good judgment is required to identify a segment of an industry as most comparable, because firms can vary substantially within an industry. The analyst will need to have some knowledge of the business of the target firm and the group of potential comparable firms. The market segment, size of the market segment, market share, firm's potential for growth, similarity of product lines, and earnings history are all factors that might be considered in identifying comparable firms.

In-depth knowledge of the target and the potentially comparable firms may be difficult to achieve. In some circumstances, industry experts can help identify comparable firms. Large investment companies often have industry experts on staff who closely monitor certain industries. Security analyst reports can also be helpful in identifying comparable firms. In addition to reviewing individual company prospects, these reports often compare the company to a group of firms in the industry. They often include information about economic factors that make these firms comparable. Even if an analyst does not cover a target firm, you can use a company report or an industry report to identify comparable firms.

Another source of comparable firms is the firm's own proxy statement. The **proxy statement** is a document sent to the firm's shareholders and filed with the SEC ahead of the annual shareholders' meeting. Its main purposes are to describe the business to be carried out at the meeting and to provide shareholders with a way to vote without attending the meeting. The proxy statement includes a disclosure describing the firm's stock performance over the past five years as well as a comparison to a group of peer companies. The list of peers is a good place to find comparable firms.

16.4 An Example Using PE

We now illustrate a valuation using multiples. Elisa is an analyst trying to use the PE ratio to value a private company that manufactures and sells ready-to-eat cereals and other food products to grocery stores. Elisa is looking for comparable companies and decides to review a Merrill Lynch report on food companies. As part of its advisory services, Merrill Lynch prepares research reports on equities for its clients. Appendix 16.1 shows excerpts from one of these reports.

Elisa's first step is to identify comparable companies. The Merrill Lynch report provides a good list of possibilities, but Elisa should not assume all these companies are truly comparable. The companies should be comparable to the target company in terms of the following:

1. Economics of underlying businesses

2. Projected earnings growth rates

3. Accounting methods

4. Earnings (there should not be any very unusual items)

5. Capital structures

Elisa is particularly concerned about comparability because Ralcorp's relative PE (its PE divided by the S&P 500 PE) is substantially lower than those of the rest of the group. After reviewing the various companies' annual reports and industry data, she decides to remove Ralcorp from the comparable group, because its business is entirely "private label," meaning it produces store brand goods for major grocery retailers. The economics of private label products are very different from those of branded products, which often leads to a different multiple. Elisa determines that the target company is similar to, even though it is smaller than, the remaining companies in the Merrill Lynch report. She uses the quarterly and annual reports for each company to perform an accounting analysis. This step ensures there are no unusual accounting methods and the earnings in the Merrill Lynch report do not include any special adjustments or one-time items in earnings. She also verifies the earnings estimates by looking at recent results and estimates from each company. The PE ratios for the three comparable firms are shown in Exhibit 16.7. All the firms have similar business characteristics and reasonably close PE ratios. Therefore, Elisa feels comfortable that using the average would result in a reasonable valuation.

To determine the target company's value, Elisa needs an estimate for its 1999 and/or 2000 earnings. She must also be sure that the target company's earnings do not have any unusual items. Exhibit 16.8 shows the valuation. To estimate the target company's value, Elisa multiplies the earnings estimate by the comparable firms' average PE ratio. Note that she uses the total earnings rather than earnings per share. The PE ratio can be applied to total earnings to get total value or to EPS to get

EXHIBIT 16.7   Comparable Ready-to-Eat Cereal Manufacturers

	Price per Share		1999E EPS		2000E EPS		1999E PE[*]	2000E PE[**]
General Mills	$	84.13	$	3.81	$	4.19	22.1	20.1
Kellogg	$	37.94	$	1.49	$	1.63	25.5	23.3
Quaker	$	65.75	$	2.67	$	2.96	24.6	22.2
Average							24.1	21.9

[*] Current price divided by estimated 1999 earnings per share.
[**] Current price divided by estimated 2000 earnings per share.

EXHIBIT 16.8   Valuation of Private Ready-to-Eat Cereal Manufacturer

	1999E	2000E
Target company's earnings estimate	$ 15 million	$ 15.5 million
Comparable group average PE	24.1	21.9
Valuation of target company	$361.5 million	$339.5 million

value per share. Because the target company is a private firm with only one shareholder, it is unlikely to calculate EPS. In this case, it is easiest to apply the PE multiple to the total earnings to get a valuation for the total company. Also note Elisa is careful to maintain consistency between the earnings definition in the multiple and the value driver. She multiplies estimated *1999* earnings by the comparable firms' average PE ratio, computed using *1999* earnings in the denominator. She also multiplies estimated *2000* earnings by the comparable firms' average PE ratio, computed using *2000* earnings in the denominator. The value of the company is estimated to be between $339.5 million and $361.5 million.

16.5 WHAT TO DO WHEN PERFECT COMPARABILITY IS NOT POSSIBLE

Despite an analyst's best efforts, it is probably impossible to find a perfectly comparable firm. Although we can usually find firms in a similar industry with similar products, there are likely to be differences in their growth potential, accounting methods, or capital structures that make them different from the target firm. Thus, we need a strategy for dealing with situations in which perfect comparability is not possible. Three approaches are to *adjust the multiple* for differences in important variables, *redefine the multiple* to be less sensitive to the differences in the important variables, and *adjust the value driver* for differences in accounting.

Adjusting the Multiple

Recall that in Exhibit 16.5 we determined that we needed to match on earnings growth, because failure to do so would cause a valuation error. However, suppose we cannot find a comparable firm with the same earnings growth prospects. What else can we do? If we know how the multiple changes as the variable in question changes, we can adjust the multiple for the difference in the variable. If we know how the PE varies with the earnings growth rate, and we know Nicklaus' and Tiger's growth rates, we can estimate what Nicklaus' PE would have been at Tiger's growth rate. We can adjust Nicklaus' PE ratio before we multiply it by Tiger's earnings. In Chapter 17, we will use this technique to adjust the PE ratio for the effects of expected earnings growth.

Redefining the Multiple

Another approach to dealing with comparability problems is to redefine the multiple we are using so it is less sensitive to the variable on which we cannot match very well. For example, the PE ratio is very sensitive to leverage. As we will see in Chapter 18, we can redefine the PE to be on an unlevered basis; that is, we can make it a ratio of debt plus equity to earnings before subtracting financing costs.

Two firms that are comparable in all other ways will have the same unlevered PE ratio,[2] even if their capital structures and PE ratios are very different. Using the unlevered ratio permits us to compare firms when we cannot match on capital structure.

Similarly, PE is sensitive to some accounting method differences. Instead of using PE when accounting methods are very different, we might use the price/sales (PS) ratio, which is less sensitive to accounting method differences. Again, we have redefined the multiple that we are using to be less sensitive to variables on which we cannot match.

Adjusting the Value Driver

A final strategy is to adjust the value driver itself to achieve comparability. Consider again how we might deal with a situation in which accounting methods differ. We might not want to switch to a PS ratio because, even though that will control for differences in accounting that affect expense recognition, sales amounts might still depend on revenue recognition methods. Further, the PS ratio, unlike the PE, will depend on differences in margins; that is, high-margin businesses will have a higher PS ratio than low-margin businesses, even if their PEs are the same. By adjusting the value driver for the differences in accounting, we revise the comparable firm's earnings to what it would have been under the target's accounting methods before determining the comparable firm's PE ratio.

---

[2]Ignoring value created by leverage. However, this effect can also be figured into the computation.

SUMMARY

This chapter has introduced the idea of valuations using multiples. We have focused on how to make a multiples valuation most meaningful. In multiples analysis, we use a ratio, such as PE, for a comparable company and multiply it by a value driver, such as the target company's earnings. We are careful to maintain consistency between the value driver and the denominator of the multiple. For example, both must be pretax, or both must be after tax. They also both must be defined using the same level of earnings, such as operating earnings or net earnings. Finally, they must both pertain to the same time period.

Many experts argue that the multiples approach is not valid because it relies on accounting earnings, not cash flows, and because it uses only one year of data rather than all the future flows of the firm. This argument has merit, as we know that value is related to cash flow, not earnings. However, others argue because the multiples approach is used so often, the value of many firms may actually be based on multiples. In reality, some investors use the multiples approach, but they do not use it in a simple mechanistic way. These investors consider the same factors we consider in a discounted cash flow analysis and incorporate these factors into the multiple. These investors use multiples as a shortcut to a discounted cash flow valuation. This is acceptable if we carefully select multiples appropriate for the underlying value drivers, taking into account accounting methods, earnings growth, and capital structure of the firm.

A multiples analysis requires comparability of the firms in the analysis. Unless the characteristics of the firms in the analysis are similar enough that we expect them to have approximately the same multiple, our analysis will be flawed. Thus, finding comparable firms is an important step in the analysis. When we are unable to find perfectly comparable firms for the analysis, which is usually the case, we must consider how the multiples of the firms in the analysis are likely to differ, and how to factor those differences into our valuation analysis. We must (1) adjust the multiple of the comparable firm before applying it to the target firm's value driver, to account for the expected difference in their multiples; (2) redefine the multiple we are using so it is less sensitive to the differences between the firms; or (3) adjust the value driver of one of the firms to be on a similar accounting basis to the other.

SUGGESTED READINGS

Cornell, Bradford. *Corporate Valuation: Tools for Effective Appraisal and Decision Making.* Homewood, IL: Business One Irwin, 1993, Chapter 4: The Direct Comparison Approach.

Hickman, Kent and Glenn H. Petry. "A Comparison of Stock Price Predictions Using Court Accepted Formulas, Dividend Discount, and P/E Models Applications." *Financial Management* 19, 2 (1990):76–87.

Liu, Jing, Doron Nissim, and Jacob Thomas. "Equity Valuation Using Multiples." Working paper, October 18, 2000.

Park, Sangkyun. "What Does the P-E Ratio Mean?" *Journal of Investing* 9, 3 (2000):27–34.

REVIEW QUESTIONS

1. Explain the terms *multiple* and *value driver* and provide an example of each.

2. In multiples analysis, we use the term *comparable*. What does this mean and why is it important?

3. When we perform multiples analysis, we need consistency between the multiple and the value driver. What are the requirements for consistency?

4. Why do many academics feel the multiples approach is not valid? Provide examples of problems with multiples valuation to illustrate the point. Why do many practitioners prefer the multiples approach?

5. How do earnings quality issues affect the multiples aproach?

6. Why is it important to use truly comparable firms in a multiples analysis?

7. How can the multiples approach be an acceptable shortcut to discounted cash flow valuation?

8. Is it necessary to match on size in a multiples analysis?

9. Suppose you are using the PE method to value a target firm with EPS of $2. You have identified three comparable companies. Their PE ratios are 10, 10.5, and 12. How would you value the target firm?

10. Do we avoid the discounted cash flow assumptions by using the PE method?

PROBLEMS

1. How should analysts go about finding comparable companies? Include an explanation of the difficulties in identifying comparable companies.

2. You are working on a PE analysis. You have analyzed the target company's business prospects and identified four comparable firms. Here is the information you have collected. Complete the analysis and determine a value for the target, Sosa, Inc.

	Price per Share	2001 EPS	2002(E) EPS
Aaron Co.	$ 102.00	$ 5.12	$ 5.71
Banks, Inc.	$ 55.50	$ 2.79	$ 3.13
Cepeda Corp.	$ 87.25	$ 4.36	$ 4.82
DiMaggio Co.	$ 75.00	$ 3.75	$ 4.21
Target:			
Sosa, Inc.		$ 2.21	$ 2.45

3. You have obtained the following information about five companies and a target you wish to value, Bakal Distributing. Additional information:

- Bakal had earnings of $751 million in 2000. Earnings were not unusual in this year.
- Expected earnings growth is similar for Bakal and the five comparable companies, all of which distribute computer components.

	Price per Share	2000 EPS
Robinson Co.	$ 15.00	$ 1.01
Jordan Corp.	$ 30.00	$ 2.85
Ewing, Inc.	$ 27.50	$ 1.73
Barkley Co.	$ 17.00	$ 0.78
Pippen Co.	$ 100.00	$ 7.21

As part of the analysis, you discover that Jordan has a long-term sales agreement with a major computer components manufacturer, which significantly affects the economics of the business. Neither Bakal nor the other comparable firms have a similar agreement. Barkley's EPS is after an extraordinary loss from Hurricane Charles. The loss came to $0.33 per share after taxes.

Use a PE analysis to estimate Bakal's value.

4. You are reviewing the work of an analyst who has valued McCahill Corporation, an electronics manufacturer, using three comparable firms and a PE ratio approach. The analysis follows:

	Current Price	2002 Earnings per Share	PE Ratio
Spengler Corporation	$ 84.00	$ 4.15	20.2
Sier Company	$ 47.00	$ (1.80)	(26.1)
Riff, Inc.	$ 25.00	$ 0.51	49.0
Average of comparable firms' PE ratios			14.4
McCahill's forecasted 2003 earnings per share		$	3.20
Value of McCahill, per share		$	46.08

Comment on the analyst's work.

5. You are analyzing retail discount & variety stores and have obtained the following information:

	Recent Price	Earnings per Share Latest 12 months	PE Ratio
BJ's Wholesale Club, Inc.	47.61	1.94	25
Children's Place Retail Stores, Inc.	17.93	1.78	10
Dollar Tree Stores Inc.	18.89	1.08	17
Family Dollar Stores, Inc.	27.52	1.08	25
Pantry Inc.	6.97	.48	15
Ross Stores, Inc.	29.25	1.80	16
Tuesday Morning Corp.	9.18	.56	16
Venator Group Inc.	15.25	.86	18
Wal-Mart Stores, Inc.	49.50	1.42	35

Source: Mergent Industry Review, Volume 22, No 7, October 26, 2001.

You are attempting to determine which of the stocks in this group might be undervalued. Discuss what questions you would like to have answered before you can make a conclusion.

6. You are analyzing Laverne Company, a Milwaukee, Wisconsin–based beverage company. You have identified four possible comparable companies, with the current market value of each shown here:

Company	Market Value
Shirley, Inc.	$ 378,000
Lenny Corporation	$ 141,750
Squiggy Company	$ 513,000
Carmine, Inc.	$ 1,271,000

Next are the income statement and other information for Laverne and each of the possible comparable companies. Consider whether each of these firms is truly comparable to Laverne. Identify issues that might influence your ability to use each firm as a comparable. Also, suggest what you might do to adjust the results so the income numbers could be used in a multiples analysis. (Note: You need not value Laverne. Just explain all of the important issues in using these firms as comparables.)

Laverne Company Income Statement

For the Year Ended ($ thousands)	2001	2000	1999
Sales	$ 120,000	$ 109,000	$ 98,000
Cost of goods sold	79,200	71,395	65,170
Gross profit	40,800	37,605	32,830
Selling, general, and administrative	14,400	14,170	13,230
Income before tax	26,400	23,435	19,600
Tax	10,560	9,374	7,840
Net Income	$ 15,840	$ 14,061	$ 11,760

DESCRIPTION OF BUSINESS:

Laverne Company is a manufacturer and marketer of bottled water beverages. Laverne's products include carbonated, noncarbonated, and flavored waters. Products are sold through grocery stores, convenience stores, liquor stores, and gourmet shops. Most of Laverne's product is sold in Wisconsin with some additional business in neighboring states.

EXCERPTS FROM FOOTNOTES:

Property, Plant, and Equipment: Property, plant, and equipment are recorded at cost. Depreciation is on a straight-line basis with lives of 15 years for buildings and 2–7 years for equipment.

INVENTORY:

Inventory is stated at lower of cost (LIFO) or market.

Shirley, Inc. Income Statement

For the Year Ended ($ thousands)	2001	2000	1999
Sales	$ 200,000	$ 190,000	$ 180,000
Cost of goods sold	134,000	123,500	120,600
Gross profit	66,000	66,500	59,400
Selling, general, and administrative	24,000	22,800	20,200
Income before tax	42,000	43,700	39,200
Tax	16,800	17,480	15,680
Net Income	$ 25,200	$ 26,220	$ 23,520

DESCRIPTION OF BUSINESS:

Shirley, Inc. manufactures and sells bottled water products. Shirley's products are sold in grocery stores, convenience stores, and smaller independent stores in California.

EXCERPTS FROM FOOTNOTES:

Property, Plant, and Equipment: Property, plant, and equipment are recorded at cost. Depreciation is on a straight-line basis with lives of 16 years for buildings and 2–7 years for equipment.

INVENTORY:

Inventory is stated at lower of cost (LIFO) or market.

Lenny Corporation Income Statement

For the Year Ended ($ thousands)	2001	2000	1999
Sales	$ 5,250,000	$ 4,725,000	$ 4,253,000
Cost of goods sold	3,475,500	3,142,125	2,845,000
Gross profit	1,774,500	1,582,875	1,408,000
Selling, general, and administrative	420,000	472,500	425,300
Interest expense	500,000	450,000	400,000
Income before tax	854,500	660,375	582,700
Tax	341,800	264,150	233,080
Net Income	$ 512,700	$ 396,225	$ 349,620

DESCRIPTION OF BUSINESS:

Lenny Corporation manufactures and markets bottled waters, with and without flavors. Lenny's products are sold throughout New England and in New York and Florida to grocery chains, convenience stores, club stores, and smaller independent stores such as gourmet and liquor shops.

EXCERPTS FROM FOOTNOTES:

Property, Plant, and Equipment: Property, plant, and equipment are recorded at cost. Depreciation is on a straight-line basis with lives of 15 years for buildings and 3–7 years for equipment.

INVENTORY:

Inventory is stated at lower of cost (LIFO) or market.

Squiggy Company Income Statement

For the Year Ended ($ thousands)	2001	2000	1999
Sales	$ 300,000	$ 295,000	$ 301,000
Cost of goods sold	201,000	197,650	204,680
Gross profit	99,000	97,350	96,320
Selling, general, and administrative	40,000	39,500	40,100
Interest expense			18,000
Income before tax	59,000	57,850	38,220
Tax	23,600	23,140	15,288
Net Income before extraordinary item	35,400	34,710	22,932
Extraordinary loss	30,000		
Net income	$ 5,400	$ 34,710	$ 22,932

DESCRIPTION OF BUSINESS:

Squiggy Company is a manufacturer and marketer of bottled water products. Squiggy's products are sold in grocery stores, convenience stores, and smaller independent stores in California.

EXCERPTS FROM FOOTNOTES:

Property, Plant, and Equipment: Property, plant, and equipment are recorded at cost. Depreciation is as follows:

Buildings: 15-year lives, double declining depreciation. Equipment 2–7 year lives, double declining depreciation.

INVENTORY:

Inventory is stated at lower of cost (LIFO) or market.

Carmine, Inc. Income Statement

For the Year Ended ($ thousands)	2001	2000	1999
Sales	$ 600,000	$ 540,000	$ 491,400
Cost of goods sold	390,000	348,300	319,410
Gross profit	210,000	191,700	171,990
Selling, general, and administrative	60,000	54,000	49,140
Gain on sale of plant	25,000		
Income before tax	175,000	137,700	122,850
Tax	70,000	55,080	49,140
Net Income	$ 105,000	$ 82,620	$ 73,710

DESCRIPTION OF BUSINESS:

Carmine, Inc. is a manufacturer and marketer of bottled water products. Carmine's products are sold in grocery stores, convenience stores, and smaller independent stores in Illinois and Indiana.

EXCERPTS FROM FOOTNOTES:

Property, Plant, and Equipment: Property, plant, and equipment are recorded at cost. Depreciation is on a straight-line basis with lives of 16 years for buildings and 2–7 years for equipment.

INVENTORY

Inventory is stated at lower of cost (FIFO) or market.

My Case

a. Find several firms that can serve as comparables for your firm. Review these companies to make sure they are similar in terms of their business. Prepare a written summary of why you selected these firms. Because no firms are perfectly comparable, make sure you discuss the ways the comparables are not truly similar to your firm.

b. Calculate the PE ratio for each of your comparables and your firm.

APPENDIX 16.1 EXCERPTS FROM MERRILL LYNCH FOOD INDUSTRY REPORT (SEPTEMBER 9, 1999)

Excerpts from Investment Highlights:

- Modest category growth was achieved for the 4-week period (ending 8/15/99) as volumes grew 0.8% and dollar sales were up 2.1%. Overall promotional spending was up versus a year ago, possibly helping growth.
- Cold cereal stocks, on average, continue to enjoy a significant premium multiple (10%+) to the food industry, including valuation measures on calendar 2000E such as P/E (21.1x), market cap/EBIT (14.5x), and market cap/EBITDA (11.9x).
- Although food stocks have continued to perform poorly versus the S&P 500, selected cold cereal stocks have done somewhat better. This may reflect more on the leader's changing strategy and less on category volumes.

Excerpts from Exhibits:

Cold Cereal Category—Valuation Analysis [Part 1 of 2]

Company	9/7/99 Price	Calendar EPS 1999E	Calendar EPS 2000E	Relative P/E 1999E	Relative P/E 2000E
General Mills	$ 84.13	$ 3.81	$ 4.19	0.81	0.79
Kellogg	$ 37.94	$ 1.49	$ 1.63	0.93	0.91
Quaker Oats	$ 65.75	$ 2.67	$ 2.96	0.90	0.87
Ralcorp	$ 16.94	$ 1.18	$ 1.38	0.53	0.48
Cold Cereal	—	—	—	0.88	0.86
ML Food	$ 34.30	$ 1.49	$ 1.74	0.84	0.77
S&P500	$ 1,350.45	$ 49.50	$ 53.00	1.00	1.00

Cold Cereal Category—Valuation Analysis [Part 2 of 2]

Company	Market Capitalization/2000E Sales	EBIT	EBITDA
General Mills	2.3	13.6	11.6
Kellogg	2.4	15.3	12.3
Quaker Oats	2.1	14.8	12.3
Ralcorp	0.8	9.0	6.7
Cold Cereal	2.2	14.5	11.9
ML Food	1.4	12.5	9.8
S&P500	—	—	—

Cold Cereal Stock Performance versus Indices

	August 1999	1998	Last Quarter [*]	Last 12 Months
Cold Cereal Index	1%	−10%	2%	21%
S&P 500	−1%	26%	1%	38%
ML Food Composite	−2%	−3%	−4%	−2%

[*]Last Rolling three-month period.
Source: Merrill Lynch Research. Food Industry Report. September 9, 1999.
Note on abbreviations:
EBIT — earnings before interest and taxes
EBITDA — earnings before interest, taxes, depreciation and amortization

17

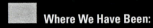

Where We Have Been:

In Chapter 16, we introduced the multiples approach to valuation.

Where We Are:

In this chapter, we examine the effect of earnings growth on the price/earnings ratio. We show how to use the price/earnings to growth ratio in a multiples valuation to adjust the price/earnings ratio for growth rate differences between the target and comparable firms.

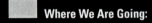

Where We Are Going:

Chapter 18 examines the market/book ratio and other special issues in multiples valuation.

PE Ratios and Earnings Growth

LEARNING OBJECTIVES:

After studying this chapter, you will understand:

- How expected earnings growth affects price/earnings ratios.
- Why we distinguish between supernormal and long-term growth rates.
- How to use the price/earnings to growth ratio to adjust for supernormal growth differences.

In Chapter 16, we saw that the basic premise of a multiples-based valuation is that if two firms are similar, then their ratios of value to some value driver should be the same. When we use the price/earnings (PE) ratio, earnings is the value driver, and the valuation of a target firm's equity, based on the PE of a comparable firm, is

$$P_{TARGET} = PE_{COMP} \cdot E_{TARGET} \qquad (17.1)$$

where P is the market value of the firm's equity, E is earnings, and PE is equity value divided by earnings.

We also saw in Chapter 16 that in a multiples valuation, we must match on, or otherwise control for, variables that affect the valuation ratio. This is to avoid situations in which we expect the target and comparable firms to have different multiples and therefore do not expect (17.1) to be true (even approximately). We usually cannot match perfectly. Instead, we match as closely as possible and then adjust for any differences that remain. To understand how to do this, we examine how the PE ratio *should* behave, based on the assumption that firm value is actually the present value of the expected cash flow stream. We use this knowledge to adjust multiples when it is not possible to match perfectly on key characteristics.

In this chapter, we examine one of the most influential factors on the PE ratio, the expected earnings growth. We develop a means to adjust for different earnings growth rates in a PE valuation. Section 17.1 shows how expected short-term, or "supernormal," earnings growth affects PE ratios, and Section 17.2 illustrates how to adjust a PE analysis to control for a difference in supernormal growth rates.

17.1 How Expected Earnings Growth Affects PE Ratios

In Chapter 16, we learned that to use a multiple to value a company we need to find comparable firms. In PE analysis, these firms must be comparable in characteristics that affect the PE ratio. Often it is difficult to find firms that are alike in all the necessary ways. For example, industry and accounting methods may match, but the expected growth rates of the comparable firms may be different from the target's expected growth rate. We need to find a way to adjust an otherwise comparable firm's PE so we can use the adjusted PE despite the firms' different expected growth rates. To do this, it is necessary first to understand how the PE varies with the expected earnings growth rate.

In order to isolate the effect of expected earnings growth on the PE ratio, we assume that earnings and cash flow are equal.[1] When earnings and cash flow are equal, the PE ratio (using forecasted current-period earnings as the value driver) is given by

$$PE = \frac{\displaystyle\sum_{t=1}^{\infty} \frac{E_t}{(1 + k_e)^t}}{E_1} \qquad (17.2)$$

> Firm's value is net present value of all future earnings (cash flows)

[1] For now, we are ignoring differences in financial reporting methods and aggressiveness of reporting choices, which are examined in Chapter 18.

where k_e is the cost of equity and E_t is the market's current expectation of earnings in period t. Because we have assumed earnings equal cash flow, the numerator in (17.2) is the present value of all cash flows to equityholders, or the value of the firm's equity. The denominator is period 1's earnings.

The higher the expected growth in the earnings series, the higher the PE. This is so because as a greater proportion of the firm's value comes from future periods, the higher is the firm's value *relative to current period earnings* and the higher the PE. As earnings growth increases, the numerator in (17.2) increases, while the denominator is unchanged. Therefore, the PE increases.

There are infinitely many variations in earnings growth patterns. To simplify our analysis of earnings growth and PE ratios, we will assume earnings will grow at one rate for a few years and then at another rate for all remaining years. This breaks the earnings series into two parts: a short-term period of "supernormal" growth and a long-term period of "sustainable" growth. For example, Wal-Mart had a compound annual average earnings growth rate of 17.5% during 1990–2000. In the last two years of this period, earnings growth was over 20%. Although Wal-Mart may continue to grow at high rates for some time, this is unlikely to continue over the long term. At some point, Wal-Mart's growth rate is likely to decrease. Starbucks has also experienced tremendous growth, increasing from earnings of $10 million in 1994 to $181 million in 2001. Starbucks opened over 1,200 stores in 2001. Even though this growth may continue for some time, we would expect lower growth rates at some future date. At some point, there simply will not be 1,200 good locations for new Starbucks stores.

Although we do not expect earnings to follow exactly the pattern assumed in this two-period model, the model still captures an important aspect of earnings expectations: High-growth firms cannot sustain their growth levels indefinitely. After all, if a firm could grow 30% to 40% per year over a long period, eventually it would account for most of the economy! Thus, even if the model is not literally true, it is still a useful way to think about what determines PE ratios.

In this two-period model, the PE ratio is the following:

Value of earnings during supernormal growth period	Value of earnings during normal growth period

$$PE = \frac{\overbrace{\sum_{t=1}^{n} \frac{E_t}{(1+k_e)^t}}^{n} + \overbrace{\sum_{t=n+1}^{\infty} \frac{E_t}{(1+k_e)^t}}^{\infty}}{E_1} \qquad (17.3)$$

In (17.3), the numerator is the value of the firm's equity, which is the sum of the value of earnings during the supernormal growth period and the value of earnings during the normal growth period. The denominator is earnings in the first year. We can rewrite this definition of PE in a format to help us understand PE in terms of growth rates and cost of equity. We assume earnings are expected to grow first at the supernormal growth rate, g_{SN}, for n periods and then at a long-term sustainable rate, g_N, thereafter. The first summation term in (17.3) becomes a growing annuity, and the second summation term is a growing perpetuity. This allows us to rewrite (17.3) as

Value per dollar of earnings in first n periods (supernormal growth period)	Value per dollar of earnings beginning in period $n+1$ (sustainable growth period)

$$PE = \frac{1 - \left[\frac{1+g_{SN}}{1+k_e}\right]^n}{k_e - g_{SN}} + \frac{(1+g_{SN})^{n-1} \cdot (1+g_N)}{(k_e - g_N) \cdot (1+k_e)^n} \qquad (17.4)$$

EXHIBIT 17.1   Calculation of PE Ratio with Varying Expected Supernormal Growth Rates

Expected Supernormal Growth	PE Ratio
10%	13.8
20%	18.6
30%	24.7
40%	32.3
50%	41.6
60%	52.9

Cost of equity = 12%
Normal growth rate = 3%
5 years at supernormal growth rate

We will use this expression to see how growth affects the PE ratio. Exhibit 17.1 shows the PE ratio for various levels of supernormal growth, holding long-term growth in earnings at 3% and cost of equity at 12%. We see the PE ratio changes significantly with changes in expected supernormal growth. For example, the PE is 13.8 when the expected supernormal growth rate is 10% and 24.7 when the expected supernormal growth rate is 30%.

The relationships described in equation (17.4) can help us understand how differences in expected earnings growth affect the PE ratio. This knowledge will allow us to adjust a comparable firm's PE for differences in expected earnings growth before using the comparable firm's PE to value a target firm.

PE and Supernormal Growth Rates—Theoretical Relationship

To see how supernormal earnings growth affects the PE, we plot the PE ratio implied by (17.4) against expected supernormal growth rates. Exhibit 17.2 shows this plot for a typical range of values.

EXHIBIT 17.2   PE Ratio versus Expected Supernormal Growth (g_{SN})

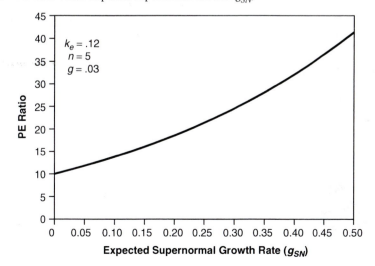

Just as we saw in terms of numbers in Exhibit 17.1, this graph shows the PE ratio changes significantly with varying supernormal earnings growth expectations. Exhibit 17.2 shows us that, as we learned in Chapter 16, a PE analysis must either match closely on expected earnings growth or adjust for the effects of differences in expected earnings growth on the PE ratio in some other way. Failure to do either of these things will cause a potentially large valuation error.

Exhibit 17.3 is the same as Exhibit 17.2, except it also shows how a valuation error occurs if we do not match perfectly on expected supernormal growth. In our example, when the expected supernormal growth rate, g_{SN}, is 20%, the PE ratio is 18.6. When the expected supernormal growth rate is 30%, the PE ratio is 24.7. Suppose we are valuing a company whose expected supernormal growth rate is only 20%. We find a comparable firm in the same industry that is similar in terms of business and profitability, but do not check the expected growth rates to see if they are comparable. The comparable firm actually has a 30% supernormal growth rate. Even though the correct PE for a firm with 20% supernormal growth is 18.6, we will apply a PE of 24.7 to value our firm. The resulting valuation error, which is illustrated by the distance between the two horizontal lines in Exhibit 17.3, is $24.7 - 18.6 = 6.1$ times earnings, or $6.1/18.6 = 33\%$ of value.

Actual PE Ratios and Supernormal Growth Rates

Exhibits 17.2 and 17.3 show how the PE ratio *should* behave, but do PEs really behave this way? To answer this question, we use Exhibit 17.4, a scatter diagram showing actual industry PE ratios plotted against forecasted earnings growth. This data, provided by the American Association of Individual Investors (AAII), show supernormal growth rates do affect PE.

Each dot in Exhibit 17.4 represents an industry. The vertical axis is the industry median PE ratio and the horizontal axis is the industry median of analysts' long-term earnings growth estimates reported by the Institutional Brokers Estimate System (I/B/E/S). AAII labels the growth estimates "long-term." Although AAII does not define long-term explicitly, the magnitudes of the forecasted growth rates suggest that in our terms they are supernormal growth rates and are not intended to represent sustainable growth. The distribution of points in Exhibit 17.4 follows fairly closely the shape of the hypothetical plots in Exhibits 17.2 and 17.3. The graph thus shows that actual PE ratios are related to supernormal growth, just as in the theoretical graphs in Exhibits 17.2 and 17.3.

EXHIBIT 17.3   Valuation Error Using PE Ratio When Expected Supernormal Growth Rates Are Not Equal

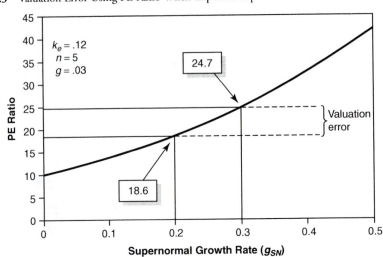

EXHIBIT 17.4   AAII Industry PE Ratios and Growth Forecasts

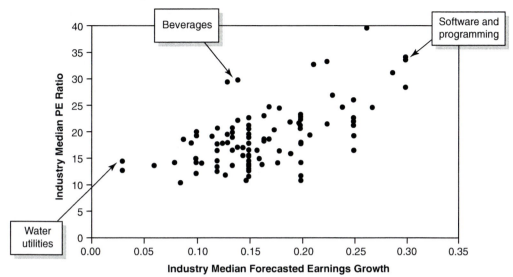

Source: American Association of Individual Investors. *AAII Journal*, September 1998.

17.2 CONTROLLING FOR THE EFFECT OF SUPERNORMAL EARNINGS GROWTH RATES ON PE ANALYSES

Because expected supernormal growth affects the PE ratio, we must control for it in any PE analysis. There are two ways to do so. First, we can try to find comparable firms whose growth characteristics are similar. Firms would then be close to each other on the horizontal axis in Exhibit 17.3, and the distance between the two horizontal lines would be small. If we assume their PE ratios should be the same, there will be only a minor valuation error. Second, we can control for the effect of the difference in the supernormal growth rates by adjusting the comparable firm's PE ratio for the effect of the difference in growth rates.

Matching to Control for PE Differences

Because we know growth rates significantly affect PE, we might try to find a comparable firm with growth prospects that are as similar as possible to the target firm's. One way to try to achieve this comparability is to match on industry. The idea is that two firms in the same industry should have similar growth prospects. Within most industries, however, there is still a wide range of growth expectations across firms. Not every firm in an industry will fall on the industry median dot in Exhibit 17.4. This may occur because different sectors of an industry face different earnings growth expectations. For example, computer manufacturers that make both mainframes and personal computers, such as IBM, and manufacturers focusing only on personal computers, such as Dell, have faced very different growth prospects, even though they are in the same industry. This suggests we should match not on broad industry definitions, but rather on narrow definitions of industry sector. But if we narrow our industry definition, we will reduce (perhaps down to zero) the number of potential comparable firms. If the few remaining firms differ from the target firm in other ways that also affect the PE ratio, then little has been accomplished by using the narrower industry definition.

Different corporate strategies within the same industry sector may also result in different earnings growth expectations and different PE ratios. For example, Pfizer invests heavily in research and development. As a result, its current earnings will be lower but it will likely have higher earnings growth expectations. This may increase its PE relative to that of a competitor that chooses to invest less heavily in research and development. Thus, it is very difficult to find a comparable firm that matches on growth characteristics perfectly, and so we need a technique to adjust PEs for expected growth rate differences.

Adjusting for Supernormal Growth Rate Differences: The PEG Ratio

Even after matching on industry we may never find a firm with exactly the same growth prospects as the target we are trying to value, and we have seen that the difference in growth prospects can have a large effect on PE. We can deal with these growth rate differences by adjusting the comparable firm's PE for the difference in growth rates. That is, we can apply a PE to the target firm based on the comparable firm's PE, adjusted for the difference in the expected earnings growth rates. There are pros and cons to doing this. On the one hand, adjusting the PE for earnings growth differences should result in a more accurate estimate of the target's value. On the other hand, we need more information to do the analysis. With a simple PE approach, we need not estimate growth rates. We assume implicitly the two firms' growth rates are the same, but we never actually estimate them. To factor in growth differences, we need estimates of the growth rates of the two firms.

The **PE-to-growth ratio**, also known as the **PEG ratio**, allows us to factor the differences in growth rates into a PE analysis. Rather than assuming PE ratios are equal across firms, the PEG approach assumes the ratio of the *PE to the growth rate* is the same across firms. Thus, it allows PE ratios to vary with growth. The PEG approach (using the expected supernormal growth rate in the ratio) assumes that

$$\frac{PE_{TARGET}}{g_{SN\ TARGET}} = \frac{PE_{COMP}}{g_{SN\ COMP}} \tag{17.5}$$

This allows us to estimate the appropriate PE ratio for the target firm with the following equation:

$$PE_{TARGET} = PEG_{COMP} \cdot g_{SN\ TARGET} \tag{17.6}$$

where $PEG = PE/g_{SN}$. So, the target's value would be estimated by

$$P_{TARGET} = PEG_{COMP} \cdot g_{SN\ TARGET} \cdot E_{TARGET} \tag{17.7}$$

For example, suppose you are trying to value a privately held bicycle manufacturer, Mavrogenes Company. You have found only one publicly held comparable bicycle business, Hoosier Cyclers. Hoosier is very similar to Mavrogenes except Hoosier has a lower expected growth rate. Exhibit 17.5 shows the assumptions in this example and a PEG-based valuation of Mavrogenes.

EXHIBIT 17.5   PEG Valuation of Mavrogenes Company

	EPS	Expected Growth	Price per Share	PE	PEG
Hoosier Cyclers	$ 4.00	20%	$ 74.40	18.6	0.93
Mavrogenes	$ 2.50	30%			

Estimated value of Mavrogenes = 0.93 × 30 × $2.50 = $69.75

The PEG approach effectively results in the use of a PE of $.93 \times 30$, or 27.9, for Mavrogenes, rather than simply applying Hoosier's PE of 18.6. This results in a valuation of Mavrogenes at $69.75. We would have obtained $61.75 had we used the 24.7 PE that Exhibit 17.3 shows for a 30% growth firm. In contrast, a straight PE valuation of Mavrogenes would have valued Mavrogenes at $18.6 \times \$2.50 = \$46.50$, well below its true value.

The PEG ratio will be useful for valuing otherwise comparable firms with different supernormal growth rates as long as it is roughly constant across the different values of supernormal growth. Under the same assumptions as in Exhibit 17.3, Exhibit 17.6 shows how the PEG ratio varies with the expected supernormal growth rate in earnings.

Exhibit 17.6 shows PEG ratios for various levels of supernormal growth assuming a long-term sustainable growth rate of 3%. For example, at a supernormal growth rate of 20%, the PEG ratio is 0.93. Note that the PEG curve gets very flat above g_{SN} of about 20%. Recall again from Chapter 16 when a curve describing how a valuation ratio varies with some variable is flatter, we expect smaller valuation errors from imperfect matching. By assuming Mavrogenes should have the same PEG ratio as Hoosier, the valuation error was relatively small. In contrast, we saw that had we assumed their PEs were equal, we would have had a larger error. By using the PEG ratio, we can reduce the errors we make in valuing high-growth firms.

Because the PEG ratio adjusts for growth differences, it significantly reduces the error caused by selecting comparable firms with different growth rates. We can select firms comparable in other ways, such as industry, and not limit our comparable firms to those with similar growth rates.

PEG Ratio Not Helpful in Low-Growth Industries

Although the PEG ratio was a more accurate valuation technique in the preceding example, it is prone to large valuation errors in low-growth industries such as electric utilities or food manufacturing. We can see this by noting the steepness of the PEG curve at lower levels of g_{SN} in Exhibit 17.6. The PEG ratios of two firms with 20% and 30% supernormal growth rates should be about the same, even though their PEs will be different. However, the PEGs of firms with supernormal growth rates of 2% and 5% will be very different. Let us consider such an example. We want to value a firm in the lower-growth food manufacturing industry. Our target firm has an expected supernormal growth rate of 5%. We choose a comparable firm whose estimated supernormal growth rate is 2% and do a PE analysis. We incorrectly assume the two firms' supernormal growth rates are the same.

EXHIBIT 17.6   PEG Ratio versus Supernormal Growth (g_{SN}) and Normal Growth (g_N)

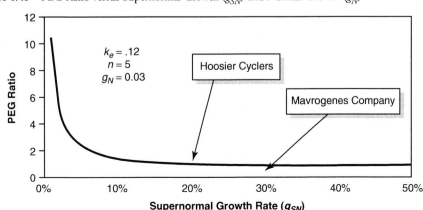

A CLOSER LOOK

Merrill Lynch PEG Example

U.S. BEVERAGES
PRICES, EARNINGS, AND VALUATION DATA
APRIL 6, 2001

	PRICE	Earnings per Share			PE Ratio		EPS GROWTH	PE TO GROWTH
		1999A	2000E	2001E	2000E	2001E		
Large Cap Brands								
Coca-Cola	$44.70	$1.31	$1.43	$1.63	31.3	27.4	16.0%	1.7
PepsiCo	$43.40	$1.24	$1.45	$1.64	29.9	26.5	13.0%	2.0
Anheuser-Busch	$43.65	$1.47	$1.69	$1.90	25.8	23.0	11.0%	2.1
SUBTOTAL					29.7	26.2	14.2%	1.8
Mid-Cap Brands								
Coors (Adolph)	$64.29	$2.56	$3.06	$3.40	21.0	18.9	11.5%	1.6
Robert Mondavi	$49.06	$2.42	$2.77	$3.28	17.7	15.0	16.5%	0.9
Brown-Forman	$62.60	$3.10	$3.33	$3.57	18.8	17.5	9.0%	1.9
Constellation Brands	$73.05	$4.20	$5.06	$5.91	14.4	12.4	17.5%	0.7
SUBTOTAL					18.3	16.4	11.7%	1.4
Soft Drink Bottlers*								
Coca-Cola Enterprises	$16.12	$0.93	$1.16	$1.12	13.9	14.4	13.5%	1.1
Pepsi Bottling Group	$37.00	$1.31	$2.11	$2.42	17.5	15.3	15.0%	1.0
PepsiAmericas	$15.04	$0.67	$0.78	$0.88	19.3	17.1	13.0%	1.3
SUBTOTAL					15.8	15.1	14.0%	1.1
Beverage Composite					27.6	24.5	14.1%	1.7

EPS are calendar year estimates.

*Bottler EPS is cash EPS, which adds back tax adjusted amortization expense.

2000 estimates for PepsiCo and Pepsi Bottling Group are comparable 52 weeks.

Source: Adapted from Merrill Lynch Report. U.S. Beverages. April 6, 2001.

As Exhibit 17.7 shows, we observe a comparable firm PE of 10.8. We observed this because the comparable firm's supernormal growth rate, which we did not consider, is 2%. We apply the comparable firm's PE to the target's earnings. The target's supernormal growth rate, which we also did not consider, is only 5%, so its PE should be only 11.8. We undervalue the target by 11.8 − 10.8 = 1.0 times its earnings, or 8%.

If we instead used a PEG ratio approach, we would observe a comparable firm PEG of 10.8/2 = 5.40. Based on a target growth rate of 5%, we would use a PE of 5.40 × 5 = 27.0 to value the target, compared to the appropriate PE of 11.8. This results in an overvaluation of the firm by 15.2

EXHIBIT 17.7   Valuation Error Using PE Ratio When Supernormal Growth Rates Differ

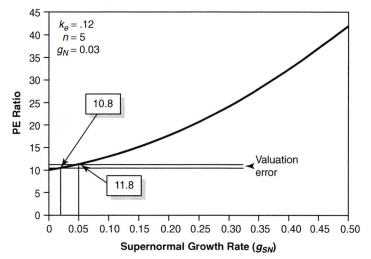

times its earnings, or 129%. In this case, switching from a PE ratio to a PEG ratio significantly increased the valuation error.

In the Hoosier/Mavrogenes example, the PEG improved the accuracy of the analysis relative to the PE; in the current example, the PEG reduced the accuracy of the analysis. Why did switching from a PE to a PEG have different effects in the two cases? In the first example, in which supernormal growth is high, the PE is very sensitive to earnings growth. If we ignore earnings growth differences when the sensitivity to them is high and choose a comparable firm with a substantially different growth rate, we get a serious valuation error. The PEG ratio is almost completely insensitive to growth rate differences when growth rates are high, so choosing a firm with a different growth rate will cause only a small valuation error. The adjustment to the comparable firm's PE ratio that is made by use of the PEG ratio ($PE_{TARGET} = PEG_{COMP} \cdot g_{SN\ TARGET}$) is a fairly good substitute for the way the PE actually reacts to earnings growth differences in this range of growth rates.

In the second example, in which supernormal growth is low, the PEG is very sensitive to the growth rate. As a result, using PEGs causes a significantly larger valuation error than does the PE. The PE adjustment implicit in the use of the PEG ratio is not a very good substitute for the actual relationship between the PE and the growth rate in this region.

Actual PEGs and Supernormal Growth Rates

Actual data confirm that using PEG ratios is a good approach in higher growth rate situations. Exhibit 17.8 shows the PEG ratio plotted against the forecasted growth rate in earnings for the AAII industry data from Exhibit 17.4. Each dot represents an industry. The vertical axis is the industry median PEG ratio and the horizontal axis is the industry median earnings growth estimate. As with the PE ratio, the actual data are consistent with our theoretical graph. The data points form a curve shaped just like the curve in Exhibit 17.6. This means PEG ratios are fairly constant at higher growth rates. Using PEG ratios rather than PEs in higher supernormal growth situations is thus an appropriate approach.

Considering the Effect of the Long-Term Sustainable Growth Rate on PE Analysis

So far, we have focused on the effect of supernormal growth rates on PE. We have determined supernormal growth rates have a large effect on PE, and we must therefore control for supernormal

EXHIBIT 17.8   AAII Industry PEG Ratios and Growth Forecasts

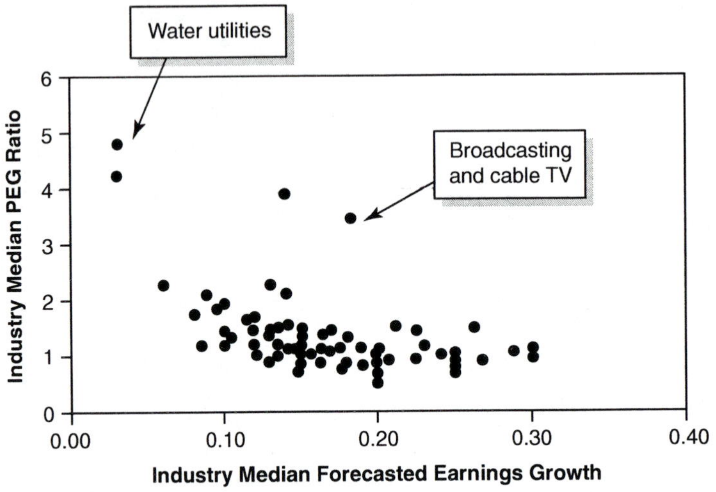

Source: American Association of Individual Investors. *AAII Journal*, September 1998.

growth rates when using PE in a valuation. What about differences in the long-term sustainable, or normal, growth rate? Do we need to adjust for these in a multiples valuation?

Because the long-term growth rate must be sustainable indefinitely, we expect most firms would fall in a fairly narrow range close to the expected long-term growth rate in the economy, say from 2% to 4%. Within such a narrow range of long-term growth rates, the PE ratio is not very sensitive to the long-term sustainable earnings growth rate. This suggests we do not need to worry about matching on or adjusting for differences in the long-term growth rate. The more important matching and control consideration is the supernormal growth rate, not the sustainable growth rate.

Pitfalls in PEG Analysis

Although many analysts use the PEG ratio for comparables valuation, they do not define the ratio in a consistent way. For example, some analysts use a long-term sustainable growth rate, whereas others use a short-term supernormal growth rate. Still others use an historical rate or are not clear about what growth rate they use. Obviously, the way the PEG ratio is defined will affect its desirability as a valuation tool. When we evaluate an analyst's valuation using PEGs, it is important to consider how the ratio is defined and how the PEG varies with the growth rate used in the PEG definition. The PEG ratio is a good valuation tool only if it is roughly constant across growth rates. Only then does it actually control for the differences in growth.

SUMMARY

This chapter has explored one of the practical problems involved in doing a PE-based valuation: how to deal with differences in expected earnings growth between target firms and comparable firms. When firms have different growth rates, they should not have the same PE ratio. The higher the expected growth in earnings, the higher the PE ratio. Thus, the fundamental assumption in PE valuation is violated, and the analysis must be modified to account for the difference. In particular, something has to change about the way the valuation multiple is computed, so the assumption that the two multiples are the same is once again valid. The PEG ratio allows us to start with a comparable-firm PE ratio, but then adjust it for the effect on the PE of differences in expected earnings growth rates.

To simplify our analysis of earnings growth and PE ratios, we assume that earnings grow at a supernormal growth rate for a few years and then at a normal growth rate for all remaining years. The PEG ratio, the PE divided by the growth rate, is preferred to PE ratios when firms are not matched on supernormal growth and the supernormal growth rates are high. When the supernormal growth rates are low, the PE ratio is a better choice than the PEG ratio. When firms are not matched on long-term sustainable growth, the PE ratio can be used because it will usually not produce a large valuation error. To calculate value using the PEG ratio, we multiply the PEG of the comparable firm by the product of the target's earnings and the target's growth rate.

The quality of PE analyses varies considerably. When we evaluate such an analysis, it is important to look for the way the analysis either controls for or adjusts for expected earnings growth differences. Without some sort of mechanism to deal with earnings growth differences, the analysis is bound to have large errors.

SUGGESTED READINGS

Beaver, William and Dale Morse. "What Determines Price-Earnings Ratios?" *Financial Analysts Journal* 34 (July–August 1978):65–76.

Easton, Peter. "Does the PEG Ratio Rank Stocks According to the Market's Expected Rate of Return on Equity Capital?" (January 2002) Working paper.

REVIEW QUESTIONS

1. What is the difference between supernormal growth and normal growth? Why is this distinction important?

2. Describe how PE changes with changes in supernormal growth rates.

3. In a PE valuation, why do we need to have a way to adjust for differences in supernormal growth rates?

4. What is the PEG ratio and how would you use it in valuation?

5. Calculate the PEG ratios relative to the expected supernormal growth rate for these companies.

Company	EPS	Price	Expected Supernormal Growth
Company 1	$ 5.12	$ 50.00	10%
Company 2	$ 10.33	$ 45.75	20%
Company 3	$ 2.56	$ 37.50	30%
Company 4	$ 4.33	$ 48.00	15%
Company 5	$ 15.20	$ 65.00	10%

6. Using Exhibit 17.1, estimate the valuation error (as a percentage of the correct value) in a PE analysis if you used a comparable firm with an expected supernormal growth rate of 40% to value a target firm with an expected supernormal growth rate of 30%.

7. Using Exhibit 17.1, estimate the valuation error (as a percentage of the correct value) in a PEG analysis if you used a comparable firm with an expected supernormal growth rate of 40% to value a target firm with an expected supernormal growth rate of 30%.

8. We know that matching on or adjusting for growth rates is very important in a PE valuation. Why not just match on growth rates instead of trying to adjust the PE ratio using a PEG ratio?

9. If a firm's supernormal growth rate were 4%, and the comparable firm's supernormal growth rate were 8%, what issues would you face in a PE valuation?

10. When is PE a better choice of valuation technique than PEG? Why?

PROBLEMS

1. You are valuing a privately held firm, Staffservice, in the professional employer business. Staffservice serves as the outsourced human resource department for small businesses. After studying the industry, you have determined that Administaff is the most comparable company in terms of business and accounting methods. You expect Administaff's EPS to grow at about 25% per year over the next five years. After that, long-term growth is expected to be about 2%. Administaff's stock price is $27.41.

   Using the following information, calculate a value for Staffservice using the PEG approach.

Administaff Financial Data

Year Ending 12/31	2001	2000	1999	1998
Revenues (000,000)	$ 4,373.2	$ 3,708.5	$ 2,260.7	$ 1,683.1
EPS*	$ 0.62	$ 0.58	$ 0.34	$ 0.31

*Excludes nonrecurring items.

Staffservice Data

Year Ending 12/31	2001	2000
Sales	$ 78,451,200	$ 68,591,213
Earnings	$ 5,230,080	$ 4,286,951

Expected earnings growth for the next five years is 20%.
Expected long-term growth is 2%.

2. Given the following information about target company Ellyn Corporation and comparable company Wolverine, Inc., show how you might calculate a value for Ellyn using the PEG approach. You can assume Ellyn and Wolverine are comparable in terms of business and accounting methods.

Company		EPS	Expected Supernormal Growth	Expected Normal Growth	PE
Ellyn	$	5.55	25%	2%	
Wolverine	$	2.02	30%	2%	14

3. Consider Exhibit 17.2. Draw a line from the origin through the point on the curve that would depict a firm with a 10% expected supernormal earnings growth rate. Now draw a line from the origin to the point on the curve representing a 50% growth rate. Interpret these two lines in the context of the PEG ratio.

4. The following information was taken from an analyst report from the Bilosellhi investment banking firm.

Industry Overview

	Current Price	EPS 2001	EPS 2002E	Projected Supernormal EPS Growth
Wally Industries	$ 35	$ 1.43	$ 1.72	20%
The Beaver Company	$ 48	$ 1.47	$ 1.84	25%
June, Inc.	$ 23	$ 2.30	$ 2.41	5%
Haskell Co.	$ 41	$ 1.05	$ 1.37	30%

a. Calculate the PE ratio for each company relative to estimated 2002 earnings per share.

b. Calculate the PE ratio for each company relative to actual 2001 earnings per share.

c. Calculate the PEG ratio for each company relative to estimated 2002 earnings per share.

d. Calculate the PEG ratio for each company relative to actual 2001 earnings per share.

e. If you were going to use the PEG ratios from these companies to help value a target firm in the same industry, what issues or questions would you consider?

 5. You have been retained to value the privately held Forest Chocolate Company using a PE approach. Forest manufactures and markets candy throughout the East Coast. The candy is priced and marketed similarly to the national brands. Financial information for Forest is shown below. You have collected the following information on

Tootsie Roll, a comparable candy company. You can assume, except as noted for 2001, Tootsie Roll has not had any unusual items in the recent past and that Tootsie Roll and Forest use similar accounting methods. Use this information to create a valuation range for Forest. Then prepare a memo for the CEO of Forest, explaining your analysis and results.

Forest Financial Data

(000)	1999	2000	2001	2002E	2003E	2004E
Sales	$ 19,315	$ 23,555	$ 30,386	$ 38,894	$ 50,173	$ 65,225
Operating Income	$ 2,897	$ 4,004	$ 5,166	$ 6,612	$ 8,529	$ 11,088
Net Income	$ 1,680	$ 2,323	$ 2,996	$ 3,835	$ 4,947	$ 6,431

Note: Management feels that earnings growth after 2004 will be limited because the company will have achieved full distribution on the East Coast.

Tootsie Roll Industries

Year ending 12/31	1998	1999	2000	2001*
Sales (000)	$ 388,659	$ 396,750	$ 427,054	$ 423,496
EPS	$ 1.29	$ 1.37	$ 1.49	$ 1.30

Assume earnings is expected to grow at 25% for the next several years.

Price per share at 12/31/01 was $39.08.

*Includes nonrecurring inventory adjustment and plant closing charges of $.04 per share.

6. Here are four comparable companies in the droid business. This new high-tech business has large growth potential over the next several years. You can assume these companies are all comparable in terms of business and accounting methods and that none has any unusual items in earnings.

	2001 EPS	Price per Share	Expected Growth 2002–2006	Expected Growth After 2006
R2D2, Inc.	$ 3.71	$ 74.20	20%	2%
Skywalker Robots	$ 1.01	$ 26.51	25%	3%
C3PO Inventions	$ 3.54	$ 104.08	30%	1%
The Vader Corporation	$ 4.01	$ 180.45	45%	0%

The target, H. Solo Company, has 2001 net earnings of $1,357,000. Management predicts growth of 40% for the next five years as the business expands distribution. After that, a more modest growth rate of 2% to 4% is planned.

a. Calculate the PE ratios for the four comparable companies.
b. Calculate the PEG ratios for the four comparable companies.
c. Value the target using the PE approach.
d. Value the target using the PEG approach.
e. What is the percentage difference in value between the PE and PEG approaches?
f. Which valuation method, PE or PEG, would you prefer in this situation? Why?

7. You have been hired to value a regional bottling company, ABC Bottlers. The company is significantly smaller than the bottlers in the Merrill Lynch U.S. Beverage report shown in this chapter, but is otherwise similar in business.

ABC Bottlers Financial Data

$ millions		1998		1999		2000E		2001E		2002E
Sales	$	598.0	$	717.6	$	861.1	$	1,040.2	$	1,248.2
Earnings*	$	1.57	$	1.96	$	2.32	$	2.76	$	3.24

*Cash EPS which adds back tax adjusted amortization expense.

Expected earnings growth in the next five years is about 10%.

    a. Suppose you had the opportunity to discuss the Merrill Lynch analysis with the analyst who prepared it. What information would you need about this analysis?

    b. Based on the information you have, value ABC.

 ## My Case

    a. Determine the expected supernormal earnings growth rates for your firm and the comparable firms. You may find such information in analyst reports, in the business press, in trade publications, in the firms' disclosures, and on Web sites such as Yahoo!-Finance. Using this information and your own business analysis, develop a range of supernormal growth rates for your firm and the comparable firms. Prepare a memo summarizing your findings.

    b. Calculate the PEG ratio for each of your comparables and your firm.

18

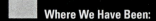 **Where We Have Been:**

In Chapter 16, we learned how to use the multiples approach to valuation. We discussed the importance of matching on key characteristics of the target and comparable firms. In Chapter 17, we learned how to use the PEG ratio to adjust for differences in supernormal growth rates.

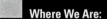 **Where We Are:**

In this chapter, we will explore other situations in which the multiples approach requires us to deal with noncomparability of firms. We will learn how to adjust for differences in capital structure and financial reporting between target and comparable firms and how to use the multiples approach when the target has near-zero earnings or losses. We will show how to adapt the multiples approach for a firm that has several lines of business with different multiples. We will also learn how analysts use the market/book ratio to value firms.

Additional Issues in Multiples Analysis

LEARNING OBJECTIVES:

After studying this chapter, you will understand:

- How capital structure affects the PE ratio and how to adjust for this difference in a PE valuation.

- How to adjust for accounting differences in a PE valuation.

- How to perform multiples valuation on a firm with losses or near-zero earnings.

- How to use multiples valuation on firms with several lines of business.

- How analysts use the market/book ratio to value firms.

Many factors affect PE ratios and all of these must be considered in a multiples analysis. When it is not possible to find a perfectly comparable firm, we must control for any differences that exist. In Section 18.1, we explore the relationship between the PE ratio and capital structure, and how to adjust for the effects of this relationship. Section 18.2 examines the PE and financial reporting differences. Section 18.3 explains how to do multiples analysis when earnings are near zero or negative. Section 18.4 explores PE analyses involving companies in two or more lines of business, whereby the appropriate PE might be different in the various parts of the business. We also apply the technique discussed in this section to firms with discontinued operations. Section 18.5 covers the market/book ratio.

18.1 Capital Structure and PE Ratios

Suppose you are valuing a privately held firm in the candy business. This firm has been in the same family for years and the family does not believe in debt financing. As a result, the firm has virtually no debt. You select a comparable public company. The comparable company is in the same business and has similar growth expectations, similar accounting methods, and even similar operating profitability. However, it uses a combination of debt and equity in its capital structure. Could you use this comparable firm in a PE analysis to value the family business? Not without adjusting for the effect of the difference between their capital structures. In general, two otherwise similar firms with different capital structures will have different PE ratios. As we did when we studied the effects of earnings growth, we will need a way to adjust our analysis for the difference. To find an adjustment mechanism, we will examine how we expect the PE ratio to vary with capital structure. We will assume away all other differences that might affect the PE ratio, in order to focus on the effect of this one variable. We will also construct a ratio that is not sensitive to capital structure differences.

How Does Capital Structure Affect PE?

To determine how capital structure affects PE, we will express PE as a function of financial leverage. Initially, we will assume financial leverage has no effect on the total value of the firm's debt and equity. We also assume because leverage provides no operating efficiencies, earnings before interest and taxes (EBIT) is unaffected by capital structure. These assumptions are essentially the original Modigliani and Miller capital structure irrelevance assumptions discussed in Chapter 11. Capital structure differences affect the division of value among the various claimants, but not the total value they have to divide. We will then apply the Modigliani-Miller Proposition (MM) with taxes to see how to adjust for capital structure while allowing for leverage to create value through debt tax shields, similar to the structure of the adjusted present value model discussed in Chapter 11.

PE Ratio and Leverage Under Original Modigliani-Miller Proposition

Under the original MM Proposition, neither EBIT nor the combined value of debt and equity varies with leverage, so the ratio of these two values, debt plus equity divided by EBIT, also will not vary with leverage. Let us call this ratio PE_U, for unlevered PE ratio. The ratio is unlevered because it is based on value and earnings as if the firm had no debt. Assuming the firm has no nonoperating net assets or other capital claims, the unlevered, pretax PE ratio is equal to the following:

$$PE_U = \frac{COMEQUITY + DEBT}{EBIT} \qquad (18.1)$$

where *COMEQUITY* and *DEBT* are the market values of equity and debt, respectively, and *EBIT* is earnings before interest and taxes.

We also define the pretax equity PE ratio, PE_E, to be the value of equity divided by earnings before taxes, which is equal to *EBIT* less interest expense (*INT*).

$$PE_E = \frac{COMEQUITY}{EBIT - INT} \qquad (18.2)$$

Finally, we define PE_D to be the value of debt divided by the pretax earnings attributable to the debtholders, which is interest. This is essentially a pretax PE ratio for the debt.

$$PE_D = \frac{DEBT}{INT} \qquad (18.3)$$

To determine how differences in capital structure affect the pretax equity PE, we will substitute equivalent expressions for the variables in (18.1). This will provide an equation that relates the firm's pretax equity PE ratio to leverage and the unlevered, pretax PE ratio.

From (18.2), we know the value of equity is the pretax equity PE ratio multiplied by earnings after interest but before taxes, $EBIT - INT$. From (18.3), we know the value of debt is the pretax debt PE multiplied by interest. So, we can rewrite (18.1) as follows:

$$PE_U = \frac{COMEQUITY + DEBT}{EBIT}$$
$$= \frac{PE_E \cdot (EBIT - INT) + PE_D \cdot INT}{EBIT} \qquad (18.4)$$

We define λ to be the proportion of pretax income attributable to the debtholders. This is a measure of leverage.

$$\lambda = \frac{INT}{EBIT} \qquad (18.5)$$

Substituting this expression into (18.4),

$$\qquad (18.6)$$
$$PE_U = PE_E \cdot (1 - \lambda) + PE_D \cdot \lambda$$

(18.6) shows that the unlevered, pretax PE is a weighted average of the pretax debt and equity PEs. We can now rearrange terms to write an expression for the equity PE ratio:

$$PE_E = \frac{PE_U - PE_D \cdot \lambda}{1 - \lambda} \qquad (18.7)$$

Because $PE_D = DEBT/INT$ and the pretax cost of debt, k_d, is equal to $INT/DEBT$, $PE_D = 1/k_d$. Substituting this expression into (18.7),

$$PE_E = \frac{PE_U - \dfrac{\lambda}{k_d}}{1 - \lambda} \tag{18.8}$$

We now have a formula that explains equity PE ratios in terms of leverage and the unlevered PE. We can use this formula to investigate how PE ratios change with changes in leverage. Exhibit 18.1 is a graphical representation of (18.8). Each curve in Exhibit 18.1 represents a firm with a particular unlevered, pretax PE. For example, the top curve represents a firm with an unlevered, pretax PE of 30, and shows how the equity PE changes for this firm as leverage increases from 0% to 75%.

The point at which each curve hits the vertical axis is the unlevered PE ratio, because it represents the PE ratio when leverage is zero. In most cases, the equity PE ratio changes significantly with leverage. Whether PE increases or decreases with leverage depends on the relative values of PE_U and $1/k_d$. In this particular example, the cost of debt is 5%, so $1/k_d$ is 20. If $PE_U > 20$, which is the case for the top curve, then PE_E increases as the firm increases its leverage. If $PE_U < 20$, which is the case for the bottom curve, then PE_E decreases as the firm increases its leverage. When $PE_U = 20$, then the equity PE is the same as the unlevered PE, or $PE_E = PE_U$, regardless of leverage. This is the case for the horizontal dashed line. Note these relationships do not make any statement about whether leverage is good or bad; they only describe how the observed equity PE ratio varies with leverage. This means that unless the unlevered PE equals $1/k_d$, which is not typical, we must adjust for capital structure differences in a PE valuation.

PE Ratio and Leverage Under Modigliani-Miller Proposition with Taxes

In Chapter 11, we discussed how leverage could affect the total value of debt and equity through its effect on taxes. We showed that under the assumptions employed in the Modigliani-Miller Proposition with taxes, the total value of debt and equity increases by

$$VL = DEBT \cdot \tau^* \tag{18.9}$$

EXHIBIT 18.1 Levered PE Ratio versus *INT/EBIT* for Various Unlevered PE Ratios Assuming Original Modigliani-Miller Proposition

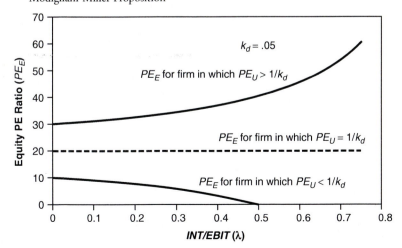

where $\tau^* = 1 - \dfrac{(1 - \tau_c) \cdot (1 - \tau_e)}{(1 - \tau_d)}$, τ_c is the marginal corporate tax rate, τ_e is the marginal tax rate on personal income derived from equity, and τ_d is the marginal tax rate on personal interest deductions. For reasonable assumptions using current tax rates, τ^* is about 14%.

The observed value of equity includes this additional value. So, to obtain the unlevered PE, we must subtract the value of leverage from the numerator. Thus, under the MM Proposition with taxes,

$$PE_U^* = \frac{COMEQUITY + DEBT \cdot (1 - \tau^*)}{EBIT} \tag{18.10}$$

Equation (18.8), which related equity PE to the unlevered PE and leverage, becomes (18.11) under MM with taxes.

$$PE_E = \frac{PE_U^* - \dfrac{\lambda}{k_d} \cdot (1 - \tau^*)}{1 - \lambda} \tag{18.11}$$

Note that if $\tau^* = 0$, meaning leverage does not create any value, then (18.11) is identical to (18.8).

How to Adjust for Capital Structure Differences in a PE Valuation

As covered in the last two chapters, if a variable affects the PE ratio, we must either match on it or adjust for its effect. Because financial policies differ so much, it often is difficult to find firms comparable in terms of their operating characteristics and that also match on capital structure. So, we must find a way to control for the differences in PE caused by differences in capital structure.

The simplest way to deal with differences in capital structure is often to use the unlevered, pretax PE ratio in our multiples valuation. The numerator of the unlevered, pretax PE will be the total value of debt and equity, less the value created by leverage. This gives us what the value of the equity would be if the firm had no leverage in its capital structure. The denominator will be EBIT. When we multiply the comparable firm's unlevered, pretax PE by the target's EBIT, we get an estimate of the unlevered value of the target firm. To get the value of the target's equity, we take this estimate of the unlevered value, subtract the value of its debt, and add the value created by its leverage. Because the unlevered, pretax PE is insensitive to leverage, we can compare multiples of firms with different capital structures, *eliminating the need to match on this variable*. If two firms are comparable in all respects other than capital structure, then their unlevered, pretax PE ratios should be the same:

$$PE_{U,TARGET}^* = PE_{U,COMP}^* \tag{18.12}$$

Substituting the definition of the unlevered PE (18.10) into (18.12) for the target firm, we find that the value of the target firm's equity, based on the unlevered PE approach, is

$$COMEQUITY_{TARGET} = PE_{U,COMP}^* \cdot EBIT_{TARGET} - DEBT_{TARGET} \cdot (1 - \tau^*) \tag{18.13}$$

As you recall, the denominator of any valuation multiple must be the same measure as the value driver by which it is multiplied. Note the consistency between the PE ratio we use and the earnings by which we multiply it. The *unlevered, pretax PE ratio*, which we obtain from the comparable firm, is multiplied by the target firm's *unlevered, pretax measure of income*.

To illustrate a valuation controlling for leverage, consider the following example. We want to value Scarlett Company. It is identical to Butler Industries, except for capital structure and size. We assume $\tau^* = 14\%$.

EXHIBIT 18.2   PE Analysis with Leverage Differences

	Butler Industries		Scarlett Company	
Debt	$	4,000.0	$	200.0
Equity		6,560.0		828.0
Total capital	$	10,560.0	$	1,028.0
Interest rate		0.06		0.06
Tax rate		0.35		0.35
EBIT	$	1,000.0	$	100.0
Interest		(240.0)		(12.0)
EBT		760.0		88.0
Income taxes		(266.0)		(30.8)
Net income	$	494.0	$	57.2
PE ratios:				
Standard (equity) PE		13.28		14.48
Pretax equity PE		8.63		9.41
Pretax unlevered PE:				
Debt $\times (1 - \tau^*)$	$	3,440.0	$	172.0
Equity		6,560.0		828.0
Total		10,000.0		1,000.0
EBIT	$	1,000.0	$	100.0
Pretax unlevered PE		10.00		10.00

The first column of Exhibit 18.2 shows the values of the debt and equity for Butler Industries, along with assumptions for interest and tax rates, and the resulting income statement and PE multiples. Given $4,000 of debt and a 6% interest rate, Butler has $240 of interest expense, and earnings before taxes (EBT) is $760. The firm pays 35% ($266) in income taxes, leaving $494 in net income. Butler has a PE of $6,560/$494 = 13.28, a pretax PE of $6,560/$760 = 8.63, and an unlevered, pretax PE of $10,000/$1,000 = 10.

Scarlett Company, shown in the right column of Exhibit 18.2, is the same as Butler except for its capital structure and size. Its EBT is $88 and net income is $57.2. Scarlett's standard PE is $828/$57.2 = 14.48, while its pretax PE is $828/$88 = 9.41. Its unlevered, pretax PE, like Butler's, is 10. Of the three PE ratios, only the unlevered, pretax PE is the same for the two firms, so only this ratio can be used to compare the two firms without causing a valuation error.

If we value Scarlett using Butler's equity PE, we get 13.28 × $57.2 = $760. Using the pretax PE, Scarlett is valued at $759, computed as 8.63 × $88. In either case, Scarlett is undervalued by about 8% relative to the actual value of $828.

Using the unlevered, pretax PE approach, Scarlett is valued as follows:

$$COMEQUITY_{SCARLETT} = PE^*_{U,BUTLER} \cdot EBIT_{SCARLETT} - DEBT_{SCARLETT} \cdot (1 - \tau^*)$$
$$= 10 \times \$100 - \$200 \times (1 - 0.14)$$
$$= \$828$$

This analysis works because these firms are identical except for capital structure and size.

18.2 FINANCIAL REPORTING DIFFERENCES AND PE RATIOS

Up until now, we have focused on economic differences across firms. Different underlying economics, such as expected earnings growth rates or leverage, lead to different PE ratios. However, financial reporting differences across firms that are unrelated to the underlying economic differences can also produce different PE ratios.[1] Accounting method choices such as straight-line versus accelerated depreciation and revenue recognition criteria can affect PE, as can choices of estimates such as the length of depreciable lives and the amounts of allowances for uncollectible accounts. To be comparable, two firms must use the same financial reporting methods and make similar choices for estimates that affect reported earnings. If the two firms are not similar in terms of reporting choices, then a PE valuation can be severely flawed.

Throughout this book, we have discussed issues related to earnings quality. Earnings quality is especially important in multiples valuation because earnings (or some other financial statement amount) directly drives the valuation. As discussed in Chapter 4, there are three definitions of earnings quality: earnings measured under more conservative accounting methods, earnings that are free from manipulation, and earnings that do not include any nonrecurring items. More conservative accounting methods generally result in lower reported earnings during a firm's earlier years, which results in a higher multiple. Earnings subject to manipulation are more likely to be overstated than to be understated, resulting in lower multiples. Nonrecurring components of income are likely to have a much lower multiple associated with them than income that will recur. Thus, as we consider how to do a multiples valuation, we must consider the firm's accounting. Earnings quality will play a central role in that analysis.

EXHIBIT 18.3 Adjusting for Accounting Differences

($ millions)	Comparable: Anthony, Inc.			
	Reported		Proforma	
Earnings before taxes and depreciation	$	10.0	$	10.0
Depreciation expense		3.0		4.8 [*]
Earnings before taxes (EBT)	$	7.0	$	5.2
Gross fixed asset value	$	60.0	$	60.0
Depreciation as % of gross fixed asset value		0.05		0.08
Equity	$	105.0	$	105.0
Equity/EBT		15.0		20.19

[*]Estimated by actual gross fixed assets × assumed depreciation rate of 8%.

---

[1]The phrase "Accounting doesn't matter" is often used to justify ignoring reporting differences in multiples valuation. This argument could not be more wrong. In an efficient market, accounting choices do not affect share prices, which always reflect expected future cash flows. This implies that PE ratios will differ across firms with different accounting methods, because although price is unaffected, reported earnings surely are not. Reporting differences could be ignored only if accounting did matter. If choosing an accounting method to report higher earnings by 20% (despite no change in expected cash flows) resulted in a 20% higher valuation, then accounting would matter, and only then would accounting differences not create differences in the PE ratio.

Adjusting Earnings for Accounting Differences

One way to deal with accounting differences is to adjust the comparable firm's reported earnings as if the firm used the target's reporting choices. (Alternatively, we can adjust the target to the comparable firm's reporting choices.) It is not always possible to do this precisely, but with some assumptions and estimates, we can reduce the valuation error caused by ignoring the differences altogether.

Consider the firm, Anthony, Inc., which is similar to the target, Cleopatra Company, except that Anthony's depreciation is less accelerated than Cleopatra's. This may be due to the use of straight-line depreciation rather than an accelerated method, or to different estimates of assets' useful lives. Although we probably will not have all the information necessary in the financial statements to compute what depreciation expense would have been under a different method, we can estimate that amount by relating depreciation expense to some other variable. A reasonable variable to use is gross (before accumulated depreciation) fixed assets. We expect depreciation expense to be related to this amount. Further, we expect the ratio of depreciation expense to gross fixed assets to be the same for similar firms that use the same depreciation methods and useful lives. Exhibit 18.3 provides an example.

Suppose earnings before taxes, EBT, is the value driver in our analysis. Anthony, Inc. reports $7.0 million of earnings before taxes, after a $3.0 million depreciation charge. The depreciation charge is 5% of the firm's $60.0 million gross fixed asset value. Assume Cleopatra Company's more accelerated depreciation policy results in a depreciation charge of 8% of gross fixed assets. To do a PE analysis, we need to convert Anthony's reported earnings to what it would have been under Cleopatra's more conservative accounting method. If Anthony had used the more accelerated depreciation, it would have recorded depreciation of $4.8 million ($60 million × 8%) and EBT of only $5.2 million. Assuming equity value of $105.0 million, the depreciation change would increase Anthony's pretax PE from 15.0 ($105.0 million/$7.0 million) to 20.19 ($105.0 million/$5.2 million). The appropriate PE to apply to Cleopatra's EBT is thus 20.19.

Exhibit 18.4 shows Cleopatra's income statement and valuation using Anthony's adjusted PE. Cleopatra's value is computed by taking Anthony's pretax PE after adjusting for the accounting difference (20.19) and multiplying it by Cleopatra's EBT of $13.0 million. The resulting value is $262.5 million. Alternatively, Cleopatra's earnings could have been recomputed under the less accelerated depreciation employed by Anthony, Inc. In that case, Cleopatra's depreciation would have been only 5% × ($12.0 million/.08) = $7.5 million, and EBT would have been $17.5 million. This higher EBT amount is then multiplied by 15.0, to arrive at $262.5. The two approaches are equally acceptable. The important thing is to use an earnings number and a PE that are determined using the *same* reporting choices for both firms.

EXHIBIT 18.4   Adjusting for Accounting Differences—Applying PE Adjusted for Accounting Difference

($ millions)	Cleopatra
Earnings before taxes and depreciation	$ 25.0
Depreciation expense	12.0
Earnings before taxes	$ 13.0
Pretax PE	20.19
Estimated value of Cleopatra's equity	$ 262.5

Reducing Accounting Differences Using the Price/Sales Ratio

Another approach to dealing with reporting differences is to use a price/sales (PS) ratio rather than a PE. This approach eliminates most (but not all) reporting differences because most reporting method and estimate choices affect the timing of expense recognition and thus do not affect sales. While some revenue recognition choices may differ across firms, using the PS ratio eliminates the effect of most reporting choice differences.

While using the PS ratio eliminates some problems, it creates others. If two firms have different operating margins or tax rates, we would expect their PS ratios to differ. Applying the PS ratio of one firm to another with a different operating margin or tax rate will result in a valuation error. The PS ratio is also likely to vary with leverage. Clearly, two otherwise identical firms with different capital structures would have different PS ratios. Therefore, it is best to use an unlevered PS ratio; that is, *equity plus debt* (less value created by leverage) divided by sales.

Using Cash Flow Instead of Earnings as the Value Driver

Because of the wide variety of acceptable reporting options, some analysts have suggested using cash flow instead of earnings as the value driver in a multiples valuation. The multiple could be computed as value divided by some measure of cash flow rather than earnings. Although this would eliminate differences that arise due to accounting choices, it does not necessarily make multiples more comparable. In fact, using cash flow as a value driver may even be worse. Cash flow varies significantly from year to year. In an unusually high-performance year, multiples are lower. In an unusually low-performance year, multiples are higher. Cash flow tends to be even more volatile from year to year than does earnings. As a result, cash flow multiples may vary from year to year even more than earnings multiples. It is therefore likely that assuming two firms have the same multiple to cash flow will introduce a large valuation error.[2]

Research has shown that current period *earnings* is actually a better predictor of future cash flows than is current period *cash flow*.[3] If your goal is to determine the future cash flow stream as

A CLOSER LOOK

Value Drivers and Hollywood

The use of a value driver that is unaffected by reporting choice is especially important if the person who makes the reporting choice can be affected by the valuation. In that case, reporting choices are likely to be more extreme. For example, movie stars and directors often get a percentage interest in a film and are entitled to a payment based on some formula to determine the film's value. When the valuation is based on profits, it is common for the studio to allocate as much of its overhead as possible to the film in an effort to reduce the reported profit (and hence the amount paid to the star/director). The more astute in Hollywood know they should negotiate a contract that names box office receipts as the variable determining the payment, because these are less affected by reporting choices made by the studios.

---

[2]In certain industries in which cash flows are very stable, such as rental properties, multiples of cash flow are more common.
[3]See, for example, Catherine Finger, "The Ability of Earnings to Predict Future Earnings and Cash Flow," *Journal of Accounting Research* 32 (1994):210–223.

accurately as possible, and you can have only one piece of information, either current period earnings or current period cash flow, you are better off knowing current period earnings. This suggests using earnings multiples will be more accurate than using cash flow multiples.

18.3 PE Ratios and Firms with Near-Zero Earnings or Losses

For firms with losses or near-zero earnings, the usual PE and PEG ratios are virtually meaningless. One way to deal with this situation is to redefine the PE ratio using a forecasted earnings number from some future period, say two or three years out, assuming earnings are expected to reach a normal level by then. Sometimes that is not possible. For example, sometimes start-up companies are incurring losses while experiencing incredibly high growth in revenues. Eventually these companies will be profitable, but not soon. For example, Amazon.com reported its first quarterly profit ever in the fourth quarter of 2001, but has never reported an annual profit. Still, its value has been as high as $106 per share.

A common multiples-based valuation approach for these kinds of companies is to use some other factor as the value driver. It need not be an earnings number per se. For example, the number of subscribers to a cable service or the number of "hits" on an Internet site might be used as the value driver. The idea is that each subscriber or "pair of eyeballs" translates into a future cash flow stream having some value. There are two major factors in determining the ratio of value to one of these value drivers: (1) the value of the cash flow stream per unit of the value driver and (2) the expected growth in the number of units of the value driver.

For example, suppose that because of the relative prices allowed by regulators in different areas, each subscriber to a target cable television franchise represents a cash flow stream worth only half that of the comparable firm. In that case, the ratio of value to subscribers for the target firm

A CLOSER LOOK

Multiples Valuation for Firms with No Earnings

Multiples valuation is very difficult for firms with zero earnings or losses, or for start-up firms whose earnings are extremely low and not indicative of long-term profit levels. Eli Amir and Baruch Lev tested whether financial information was useful for valuing cellular phone companies. They found both earnings and book values were largely irrelevant for valuation. In contrast, nonfinancial measures were quite useful in explaining price differences across firms. This research suggests that in using multiples to value firms with no earnings, indicators of future profit potential, such as revenues, number of customers, page views for Internet sites, and so on, are more likely to provide reasonable valuations than are traditional multiples of earnings or book values.

Source: Eli Amir and Baruch Lev, "Value-Relevance of Nonfinancial Information: The Wireless Communications Industry," *Journal of Accounting and Economics* (1996):3–30.

would be only half the comparable firm's ratio. Similarly, if the two firms' prospects for growth in the number of subscribers were substantially different, their multiples of value to current subscribers would also be different. The analyst might adjust them in a manner similar to the PEG ratio adjustment. For example, multiplying the price/subscribers ratio of the comparable firm by the ratio of target subscriber growth to comparable firm subscriber growth would produce a target price/subscribers ratio that adjusts for the different expected growth rates. Whether this adjustment is a reasonable way to deal with the growth differences depends on the rates of growth, much as it did for the PEG ratio.

18.4 VALUING FIRMS IN SEVERAL LINES OF BUSINESS

Many firms operate in more than one line of business, each of which is likely to command a different PE ratio. For example, General Electric makes aircraft engines, appliances, lighting, and medical systems. It also operates the NBC television network and a consumer finance business, among others. Finding a comparable firm with a mix of operations similar to GE would be a daunting, if not impossible, task. In such a case, we may be able to do a better job in a PE valuation by separating the earnings streams and applying different PEs to each component. This process is called **PE decomposition**. Because the various comparable firms we find for each of our business units are likely to have different capital structures, we would probably use an unlevered valuation approach. Thus,

$$COMEQUITY_{TARGET} = EBIT_{TARGET,1} \cdot PE^*_{U,COMP,1} + EBIT_{TARGET,2} \cdot PE^*_{U,COMP,2} + \cdots$$
$$- DEBT_{TARGET} \cdot (1 - \tau^*) \qquad \textbf{(18.14)}$$

where the subscripts ($TARGET$,1; $TARGET$,2; . . .) refer to the target's businesses and the subscripts ($COMP$,1; $COMP$,2; . . .) refer to comparable firms for each of the target's businesses. The U is included in the PE subscript to indicate an unlevered, pretax PE ratio, and the superscript indicates the ratio adjusts for the value created by leverage. Additional refinements, such as using PEGs for one or more of the businesses, can also be applied to each of the component PEs.

Suppose Benjamin Braddock Plastics Corporation has three divisions. Although all three are in the broad industry classification of "plastics," they are in sufficiently different markets that the multiples in each are likely to differ. The plastic toys division manufactures and sells toys to retailers such as Toys "R" Us. The outdoor furniture division manufactures and sells to furniture retailers and catalogs. The office accessories division manufactures and sells to office supply chains such as OfficeMax.

An analyst has found comparable firms for each of the three divisions. To eliminate potential leverage differences, she has determined the unlevered, pretax PE ratios for each of the comparable firms. Her analysis indicates the appropriate multiples for Braddock's three divisions are as follows:

Division	Multiple of EBIT
Plastic toys	27
Outdoor furniture	18
Office accessories	22

A summary of Braddock's income statement by division is as follows:

($ millions)		Sales		EBIT
Plastic toys	$	2,000	$	200
Outdoor furniture		1500		100
Office accessories		700		50
	$	4,200	$	350

Assuming that Braddock has $500 million of debt, its value would be estimated based on the above multiples as shown in Exhibit 18.5. Note that the analyst used the unlevered, pretax multiple and EBIT, which is an unlevered, pretax measure of income. To estimate the value of equity, she subtracted the value of debt, after reducing it for the estimated value created by leverage. PE decomposition can also be used to value firms with marketable securities, by adding in the value of the securities in the same way we subtract the value of debt.

PE Decomposition and Discontinued Operations

Another concern in multiples valuation occurs when the target has discontinued operations. Which earnings should be used in the valuation calculation: earnings from continuing operations or net earnings, including those from discontinued operations? We can apply the principles of PE decomposition to deal with this situation.

Once a firm decides to divest or discontinue a business unit, it segregates the income or loss of the discontinued unit on the income statement from the income or loss of the rest of the firm. The two components are labeled "discontinued operations" and "continuing operations." This separation occurs even before the firm has actually divested itself of the division. Once it has adopted a formal plan to dispose of the division, the division is considered a discontinued operation. The same segregation occurs on the balance sheet. The net assets of the discontinued operations are shown as a separate item on the balance sheet.

The separation of discontinued operations from continuing operations applies to all periods presented in financial statements, including those prior periods that predate the decision to dispose. For example, during 2000, Gannett Company, Inc. a large, diversified news and information company and publisher of *USA Today*, announced plans to sell a business. Gannett reported the 2000 gain on the sale and the income from prior years, as separate items on its income statement as shown on Exhibit 18.6.

We separate the valuation into two pieces, the value of the continuing operations and the value of the discontinued operations. We value the continuing operations by applying an appropriate

EXHIBIT 18.5   Braddock Valuation

($ millions)		EBIT	Multiple		Value	
Plastic toys	$	200	27	$		5,400
Outdoor furniture		100	18			1,800
Office accessories		50	22			1,100
	$	350				8,300
Debt				500		
$1-\tau^*$				0.86		(430)
Value of equity					$	7,870

multiple to earnings from continuing operations. We value the discontinued operations either using an appropriate multiple for the industries the discontinued units are in, or from estimates of the selling prices (net of taxes and transaction costs) if they are available.

18.5   USING THE MARKET/BOOK RATIO

Analysts sometimes use the market/book (MB) ratio to value firms. Valuing a firm using the MB ratio is very similar to using a PE ratio; it simply entails using a different multiple and a different value driver. We estimate value by multiplying a comparable firm's MB ratio by the target firm's book value.

When we used the PE ratio, we assumed that any variables that should affect the PE ratio were the same across firms. If they were not, we had to control for the effect of differences on the PE ratio to avoid a valuation error. So, we had to understand what variables affect the PE ratio. Similarly, we now must consider what variables affect the MB ratio.

We first examine the relationship between the PE and MB ratios. We expect the two ratios to be related to each other because both have market value in the numerator. Further, both ratios have an accounting measure in the denominator, and those two accounting measures (earnings and book value) are related to each other as well.

The MB ratio is simply the market value of the firm's equity divided by the book value of the firm's equity, or, $MB = \dfrac{COMEQUITY}{BV}$, where BV is the firm's book value. We can see exactly how the PE and MB ratios relate to each other by breaking the MB ratio into two components.

$$MB = \frac{COMEQUITY}{BV} = \overbrace{\left(\frac{COMEQUITY}{E}\right)}^{\text{PE ratio}} \cdot \overbrace{\left(\frac{E}{BV}\right)}^{\text{ROE}} \tag{18.15}$$

E is the firm's earnings. (18.15) shows that the MB ratio depends on the PE ratio, and E/BV, which is a common financial ratio called return on equity (ROE). The MB ratio is the product of the PE ratio and ROE. Because the PE and ROE are components of MB, we expect factors that influence either the PE or ROE to influence the MB ratio.[4] This suggests that a MB analysis must match on, or otherwise control for, growth rates, capital structure, accounting methods, and any additional variables that affect the ROE.

Earnings Growth and the MB Ratio

We saw in Chapter 17 that the PE ratio is positively related to earnings growth. Because PE is a component of MB, earnings growth also affects the MB ratio. We therefore need to control for differ-

---

[4]Technically, a variable could affect both the PE and ROE without affecting the MB ratio. Anything that affects current period earnings, but has no impact on either the market value or the book value of the firm's equity, would not affect the MB, despite affecting both components. However, it is unlikely that we would find any such variable. Something that affects earnings but not market value would undoubtedly be some kind of accounting choice that has no cash flow implications. However, this accounting choice is likely to affect the book value as well.

EXHIBIT 18.6   Excerpt from Gannett Annual Report

Gannett Co., Inc. and Subsidiaries Consolidated Statements of Income			
	Fiscal Year Ended		
$ thousands	December 31, 2000	December 26, 1999	December 27, 1998
Net operating revenues:			
Newspaper advertising	$ 3,972,936	$ 3,115,250	$ 2,773,247
Newspaper circulation	1,120,991	971,114	958,456
Broadcasting	788,767	728,642	721,298
All other	339,624	280,356	256,030
Total	6,222,318	5,095,362	4,709,031
Operating expenses:			
Cost of sales and operating expenses, exclusive of depreciation	3,057,252	2,459,749	2,364,338
Selling, general, and administrative expenses, exclusive of depreciation	971,895	792,421	705,416
Depreciation	195,428	169,460	163,776
Amortization of intangible assets	180,487	110,631	89,687
Total	4,405,062	3,532,261	3,323,217
Operating income:	1,817,256	1,563,101	1,385,814
Nonoperating income (expense)			
Interest expense	(219,228)	(94,619)	(79,412)
Interest income	27,209	5,739	19,318
Other	(16,397)	52,966	286,005
Total	(208,416)	(35,914)	225,911
Income before income taxes	1,608,840	1,527,187	1,611,725
Provision for income taxes	636,900	607,800	645,300
Income from continuing operations	971,940	919,387	966,425
Discontinued operations:			
Income from the operation of discontinued operations net of income taxes	2,437	38,541	33,488
Gain on sale of cable business, net of income taxes	744,700		
Net income	$ 1,719,077	$ 957,928	$ 999,913

ences in earnings growth when comparing MB ratios. In a PE analysis, we can use the PEG ratio to adjust for differences in expected earnings growth. Unfortunately, we do not have a similar, simple adjustment for MB. So, in cases in which we cannot find a comparable firm that matches on growth rates, it is better to use the PEG ratio rather than the MB ratio for valuation.

Leverage and the MB Ratio

We know that differences in capital structure affect the PE ratio and they likewise affect the MB ratio. Two otherwise similar firms with different capital structures will also have different MB ratios. Consider the firm Hawkeye's Hospital Supply. This firm has assets with a book value of $100 million and a market value of $250 million. If Hawkeye is unlevered, its MB ratio will be $250 million/ $100 million = 2.5. Suppose, however, that it has debt of $40 million. Assuming $\tau^* = 14\%$, this debt creates $5.6 million of value. In this case its MB ratio will be ($250 million + $5.6 million − $40 million)/$60 million = 3.6. Exhibit 18.7 shows the balance sheet and MB ratios for Hawkeye's Hospital Supply if the firm is levered and unlevered.

Because leverage affects the MB ratio, it is important to match on this variable. If we cannot find a comparable firm with similar capital structure, we can use an unlevered MB ratio. As we do with the unlevered PE ratio, we equate the MB ratios of all capital of the two firms.

$$MB^*_U = \frac{COMEQUITY + DEBT \cdot (1 - \tau^*)}{BV(EQUITY) + DEBT} \qquad (18.16)$$

Thus, a target firm is valued as follows:

$$COMEQUITY_{TARGET} = MB^*_{U,COMP} \cdot [BV(EQUITY_{TARGET}) + DEBT_{TARGET}] \\ - DEBT_{TARGET} \cdot (1 - \tau^*) \qquad (18.17)$$

Accounting Differences and the MB Ratio

Accounting differences also affect the MB ratio. Two otherwise identical firms using different accounting methods should have the same market value, but in all likelihood they will have different book values.[5] Once again, we must match on or control for the differences. We do this either by selecting comparable firms that use the same accounting methods or by adjusting the book value of one of the firms to be the same as the other. Once we eliminate accounting differences, the MB ratios of the two firms should be the same.

MB Ratio and Return on Equity

We saw in (18.15) the MB ratio is equal to the PE ratio times ROE. The factors that influence ROE therefore also affect the MB ratio. We must match on any factor that affects the ROE. It is easier to find firms that match on ROE because we can directly observe the ROE. We simply look for firms within the industry that have the same reported ROE.

Suppose we have matched on ROE perfectly; that is, every comparable firm in our analysis has exactly the same ROE. For that group of firms, ROE is a constant. Then, the MB ratio is simply a constant times the PE ratio, and assuming two firms' MB ratios are the same is equivalent to assum-

EXHIBIT 18.7   GAAP Balance Sheet, MB Ratios, and Leverage

($ millions)	Levered		Unlevered	
	Hawkeye's Hospital Supply Balance Sheet			
Assets	$	100	$	100 market value of assets = $ 250
Debt	$	40	$	0
Equity		60		100
	$	100	$	100
MB		3.6		2.5

---

[5]We assume here that the accounting differences do not affect cash flow. If the accounting differences affect taxes, they will affect cash flow and have an impact on market value.

ing their PEs are the same. Under perfect matching on ROE, therefore, the MB analysis becomes nothing more than a PE analysis.

Now suppose that we could not match perfectly on ROE. As a result, we are concerned about the comparability of the firms in our study. We decide to control for ROE differences, much the same way we controlled for the effect of earnings growth on the PE by using the PEG ratio instead. We could assume that instead of MB ratios being equal, the ratio of MB to ROE is equal across firms. This equality allows for firms with higher ROEs to have proportionally higher MB ratios. If we then examine the *MB/ROE* ratio, we find that it is $\dfrac{MB}{ROE} = \dfrac{P/BV}{E/BV} = \dfrac{P}{E}$. Like matching on ROE, controlling for ROE differences reduced our analysis to a PE analysis. This shows that while we must match on or control for ROE because it affects the MB ratio, once we do so, we are really just using a PE ratio.

MB Ratio and Normalized Earnings Multiples

We have learned that once we control for differences in the ROE, the analysis is nothing more than a PE study. This suggests that we might as well use PEs. Is the MB ratio ever useful for doing valuations? At first glance, it would appear not. If a MB analysis under proper controls always reduces to a PE analysis, then the best way to control for factors affecting the MB ratio (that do not also affect the PE) is to use the PE ratio. However, we should bear in mind that our analysis of PE and MB ratios was based on the implicit assumption that earnings are at a normal level. That is, earnings are not unusually high or low in the year for which the PE is computed. When earnings are unusually high or low, we may want to use a **normalized** level of earnings to determine the PE ratio. (A normalized earnings level is the level earnings would be if not for the aberration in the particular year.) Once earnings are normalized, the PE ratio is more stable across firms.

Using book value rather than earnings as the value driver is very much like normalizing the earnings level. To see why this is so, consider a situation in which two firms have the same PE ratio, relative to a "normal" level of earnings. However, their PEs relative to actual earnings differ because one of the firms had an unusual item in its earnings in the current year. Exhibit 18.8 describes such an example.

EXHIBIT 18.8   Market/Book Analysis as a Way to Normalize Earnings

	Darrin Company	Samantha Company
Market value	$ 20,000	$ 2,000
Book value	$ 10,000	$ 1,000
ROE	0.05	0.15
Normal ROE	0.15	0.15
Earnings	$ 500	$ 150
Normal Earnings	$ 1,500	$ 150
PE	40.0	13.3
PE versus normal earnings	13.3	13.3
MB	2.0	2.0

In Exhibit 18.8, Darrin and Samantha have different earnings levels in the current year and ROEs of 5% and 15%, respectively. However, Darrin's earnings are unusually low; its normal ROE level would have been 15%. The market prices these two firms at about the same multiple of normalized earnings, on the assumption that Darrin will return to its normal level of profitability next year. Still, its PE is unusually high because its earnings level is unusually low; and the PE ratios of the two firms are therefore different (40.0 versus 13.3). However, if Darrin's earnings were first normalized, the PE ratios would both be 13.3. Similarly, the MB ratios are the same. By using book value in the denominator, the MB ratio assumes ROEs will be the same for the two firms. This, in effect, normalizes the earnings of Darrin. So, market/book analysis can be a useful approach when earnings need to be normalized.

SUMMARY

In this chapter, we reviewed four issues in PE valuation and the market/book ratio. First, we saw that leverage affects PE ratios, so we must either match on leverage or adjust for leverage differences in some other way. Because it is usually difficult to match on both operating characteristics and capital structure, we often want to match on the operating characteristics and adjust for leverage by applying an unlevered PE ratio. In doing so, we must be sure we apply the PE to a similarly defined earnings amount. For example, an unlevered, pretax PE is applied to EBIT, the unlevered, pretax measure of earnings.

Second, earnings quality and other financial reporting differences affect the PE. Because financial reporting differences generally have no cash flow implications, they do not affect the fair value of the firm. So, accounting differences affect the PE because they affect the denominator of the ratio, earnings, but not the numerator. We can control for this effect by adjusting earnings for the difference in reporting methods before applying the PE in a valuation. Or, in some circumstances, the analyst may choose to use a ratio that is less sensitive to most accounting choices, such as the PS ratio. Using cash flow as the value driver eliminates the financial reporting difference problem. However, cash flow is more volatile from one year to the next than is earnings. So, it is actually less suitable as a value driver in a multiples analysis, except in certain industries in which cash flows are relatively stable, such as real estate management.

Third, firms with near-zero earnings pose a problem for a multiples valuation. One alternative is to use a "normal" level of earnings, or a level the analyst feels the firm can achieve at some point in the future. Another option is to use a different kind of multiple altogether. Such a multiple might be based on the number of customers, or some other non-financial statement indicator of value.

Fourth, when valuing firms in several lines of business, we can decompose the firm into its various units and apply different multiples to the various components. Then, the firm's total value is the sum of the individual unit values. This technique also applies to valuations involving firms with discontinued operations.

The market/book ratio is another valuation approach. We saw, however, that the market/book ratio is equal to the PE ratio multiplied by ROE. When using the MB ratio, we must match on or adjust for variables that affect PE such as earnings growth, leverage, and accounting differences. In addition, we must also match on ROE. But, once we match on ROE, we are left with a PE analysis. Nevertheless, the MB approach is useful in situations in which earnings need to be normalized.

SUGGESTED READINGS

Amir, Eli and Baruch Lev. "Value-Relevance of Nonfinancial Information: The Wireless Communications Industry." *Journal of Accounting and Economics* 22 (1996):3–30.

Beaver, W. and R. Dukes. Interperiod tax allocation and delta-depreciation methods: Some empirical results. *The Accounting Review* (July 1973):549–559.

Dhaliwal, Dan, David Guenther, and Mark Trombley. "Inventory Accounting Method and Earnings-Price Ratios." *Contemporary Accounting Research* 16, 3 (1999):419–436.

Finger, Catherine. "The Ability of Earnings to Predict Future Earnings and Cash Flow." *Journal of Accounting Research* 32 (1994):210–223.

REVIEW QUESTIONS

1. Suppose you are valuing a target company using the PE method. You have found several comparable firms that are similar in terms of business and accounting methods. However, the target company uses almost no debt and the comparable firms have substantial debt in their capital structures. Could you use these comparables in your PE analysis? Explain.

2. Describe how PE varies with leverage under the original Modigliani-Miller Proposition.

3. How do we adjust for capital structure differences in a PE analysis?

4. How do we adjust for accounting differences in a PE analysis?

5. What is the price/sales ratio? What are the pros and cons of using it as a valuation tool?

6. Because of the variety of acceptable reporting methods, some analysts suggest using cash flow instead of earnings as a value driver in a multiples valuation. Is this an appropriate approach? Explain.

7. How can you apply a multiples approach if a firm has near-zero earnings or losses?

8. What is PE decomposition? How do we apply PE decomposition to firms with several lines of business? How do we apply PE decomposition to firms with discontinued operations?

9. When is PE decomposition necessary?

10. Certain characteristics of a firm affect the market/book ratio enough that we must match on them to use the market/book ratio. What are these characteristics?

11. Under what circumstances is the market/book approach most useful?

12. Assume a company's pretax cost of debt is 6%. The firm's λ, its proportion of pretax income attributable to debtholders, is 0.40. The company's unlevered PE ratio is 10. τ^* is 14%. Under the MM Proposition with taxes, what will the firm's pretax equity PE ratio be?

PROBLEMS

1. Consider three firms, Phoebe Corporation, Monica, Inc., and Rachel Company, which all run coffee shops in New York City. They are identical except for their inventory accounting methods.

    Phoebe used LIFO for tax purposes and, due to the book/tax conformity rules in the Internal Revenue Code, also uses LIFO for financial reporting.

    Monica has foregone the tax benefits of LIFO and uses FIFO for tax purposes so that it may also use FIFO for financial reporting.

    Rachel has received special permission to use LIFO for tax purposes and FIFO for financial reporting. (This is not possible but is presented in this problem for illustrative purposes.)

Assume that per unit inventory costs are rising and the firms are increasing their physical inventories each year. All three firms are profitable, and the market is informationally efficient, properly valuing all firms at the present value of their expected cash flow streams.

a. Rank the three firms by price/earnings ratio from smallest to largest. Note ties, if any.
b. Rank the three firms by price/sales ratio from smallest to largest. Note ties, if any.

2. Suppose Latter Corporation has a market/book ratio of 2.0 and that markets are efficient.

a. If Latter were to write off some of its assets for financial reporting purposes, there were no tax deduction allowed for the write-off, and the write-off provided no new information to the market about the value of Latter's assets, what would happen to its market/book ratio?

b. Make all the same assumptions as in (a), except that the write-off signals investors that Latter's assets are less valuable than they previously thought. Now what would happen to the market/book ratio?

3. Discuss matching issues when doing a valuation using market/book ratios of comparable firms.

4. Describe the sensitivities of the market/book ratio to ROE and earnings growth.

5. **a.** How does a ratio of market/book ratio divided by ROE control for cross-firm differences in the market/book ratio in a way that is similar to the way the PEG ratio controls for cross-firm differences in PE?

b. What does the market/book ratio divided by ROE reduce to?

6. You are trying to value Andrew's Computer Company, a company that sells and repairs computers. Andrew has debt of $2 million. Here is an excerpt from Andrew's income statement:

Andrew's Computer Company
Summary of Income Statement

For the year ended December 31, ($000)	2002	2001
Net sales	$ 4,335.00	$ 4,128.57
Operating expenses	3,901.66	3,715.87
Earnings before interest and taxes	433.34	412.70
Interest expense	100.00	100.00
Earnings before taxes	333.34	312.70
Taxes	116.67	109.45
Net Income	$ 216.67	$ 203.25

You have identified two similar computer companies, Elbo Services and GSM Computer Associates. These companies are comparable to Andrew in terms of accounting methods, growth, and business. You have the following information about these firms.

Income Statement Information
Year ended December 31, 2002

($000)	Elbo Services	GSM Associates
Net sales	$ 750.00	$ 6,000.00
Operating expenses	675.00	5,480.00
Earnings before interest and taxes	75.00	520.00
Interest	25.00	25.00
Earnings before taxes	50.00	495.00
Taxes	17.50	183.15
Net Income	$ 32.50	$ 311.85

Market Value Information
12/31/02

Debt	$ 500.00	$ 500.00
Equity	500.00	6,122.00
Total capital	$ 1,000.00	$ 6,622.00

Assuming τ^* is 14%, value Andrew using a PE analysis.

7. A few years ago, your Aunt Sheila started an Internet-based business called Athletic Apparel, which sells high-quality exercise clothing at discounted prices. All of Athletic Apparel's historical income statements are shown below. Going forward, she expects growth to be about 10%.

Athletic Apparel Income Statement

For the Year Ended December 31,	2001	2002	2003E
Sales	$ 177,991	$ 250,003	$ 355,111
Cost of goods sold	133,493	187,502	266,333
Gross profit	44,498	62,501	88,778
Advertising expense	50,000	50,000	30,000
Depreciation	11,840	12,472	9,978
Administrative expenses	35,000	42,000	43,260
Operating income	(52,342)	(41,971)	5,540
Income taxes	0	0	0
Net income	$ (52,342)	$ (41,971)	$ 5,540

Athletic Apparel is using accelerated depreciation for book purposes. The company is currently using a 20% declining balance method of depreciation. For inventory, Athletic Apparel uses the FIFO method. Aunt Sheila owns 100% of Athletic Apparel and the firm has no debt.

A similar business, Exercise Outfitters recently sold for $3 million. Historical income statements are shown below. Exercise Outfitters expects earnings to grow at about 10% after 2003. This firm carries no debt. Exercise Outfitters uses straight-line depreciation for book purposes. Assets are depreciated over a 10-year life. Exercise Outfitters uses the FIFO inventory method.

Exercise Outfitters Income Statement

For the Year Ended 12/31	2001	2002	2003E
Sales	$ 559,872	$ 604,662	$ 653,035
Cost of goods sold	363,917	393,030	424,473
Operating expenses, excluding depreciation	55,987	60,466	65,303
Depreciation	16,000	18,000	18,000
Operating income	123,968	133,166	145,259
Income taxes	43,389	46,608	50,841
Net income	$ 80,579	$ 86,558	$ 94,418

Discuss any issues and concerns about the use of a multiple to estimate the value of Aunt Sheila.

My Case

a. Review the financial statements and disclosures for the comparable firms, looking for financial statement quality issues, including accounting method differences, as well as any other differences that would affect comparability. (You have already done this on your target firm in Chapter 4.) Make any necessary adjustments and document the reasons for your adjustments. Record any other financial statement quality concerns.

b. Calculate the PE ratios based on the proforma earnings.

c. Calculate the PEG ratios based on the proforma earnings.

Index

A

A&P, 54,59,102
Abbott Laboratories, 155
Abnormal returns, 22
Accounting
  Analysis, 15, 67-87
    Of balance sheet, 70-72
    Of cash flow statement, 78
    Of income statement, 75-76
  Consistency, 13
  Disclosures, 10-11, 114
  Engineering, 76
  Equation, 68
  Estimates, 10, 114
  For contingencies, 71, 96-97
  For investments, 93-96
  Methods, 10, 70-71, 112
  Standard setting, 326-327
Accounting Principles Board, 69
  Opinion No. 25 "Accounting
    for Stock Issued to
    Employees", 325-326
Accruals management, 71
Accumulated postemployment
  benefit obligation, 357n,
  378-382
Ackerman, Alan R., 76
ACNielsen, 52-53
Active investment strategies, 31
Actuarial gains and losses, 360,
  362, 382
Adjusted present value model, 16,
  134, 136-137, 251-261
  Compared to free cash flow
    model, 252-254
Agency cost of free cash flow, 258
Albertson's, Inc., 155

*Almanac of Business and Industrial
  Financial Ratios*, 103-105, 111
Amazon.com, 55-56, 58, 107,
  129, 149, 149n, 179, 222,
  229, 431
American Association of Individual
  Investors, 410-411, 415-416
American Express Company, 155
American Institute of Certified
  Public Accountants, 8n, 69
Amir, Eli, 431
Amortization of bond discount
  or premium, 199-200
Anheuser-Busch, 414
Annual Statement Studies, 111
AOL Time Warner, 155
APBO, *See* Accumulated
  Postemployment Benefit
  Obligation
APV model, *See* Adjusted present
  value model
Aquafina, 47
Arthur Andersen, 12
Assets
  Current and noncurrent, 81
  Defined, 68
Asymmetric information, 7, 12-13
AT&T, 68, 79, 85
At the money stock option, 321
Auditors, 8, 12
Audits, 13
Available-for-sale securities, 94-96

B

Balance sheet, 68-72
Balance sheet equation, 68
Ball, Ray, 32

Note: Any page number followed by an n means that topic is found in a footnote.

Bankruptcy, 11
Barriers to entry, 46
Barry, Marc, 50
Base income, defined, 138
Bear Stearns, 155
Behavioral finance, 33
Beresford, Dennis, 326
Berkshire Hathaway, 49, 58-59, 179-180, 327
Bernard, Vic, 32
Best Buy Co., 155
Beta, 146, 149-155
    Estimating, 152-155
    Unlevered, 160-161
Bethlehem Steel, 260
Beverage Industry, 47
Big bath, 76
Black, Fischer, 319n
Black-Scholes option pricing formula, 132, 319-321, 323, 325, 335-336
    With dividends, 320n
Boeing, 155
Book-tax conformity, 297n
Bottled water, 47
Brewer, Karl, 6
Bridgestone/Firestone, 128
Brown-Forman, 414
Brown, Philip, 32
Buffett, Warren, 49, 58-59, 327
Bureau of Economic Analysis, 45
Bush, George W., 26
Business analysis, 14-15, 41-60
Buy-side analysts, 3
Buyers, 48

C

C3I Analytics, 50
California power crisis, 51
California Public Employees' Retirement System, 3
Call options, 317n, 320
CalPers, *See* California Public Employees' Retirement System
Cannibalization of revenues, 107
Capital asset pricing model, 146
Capital expenditures
    Expansion, 217-219, 227
    Lumpy vs. smooth, 218

Maintenance, 217-218, 227
Capitalized interest, 201-202
CAPM, *See* Capital asset pricing model
Cash flow from financing, 77
Cash flow from investing, 77
Cash flow from operations, 77
Cash flow statement, 77-79
    Defined benefit plans and, 364
    Direct method, 77n
    Indirect method, 77
Cause of change analysis, 109
Census, U.S., 45
Center for Research in Security Prices, 153-154
Cereal (hot) market, 52-53
Changes in accounting principles, 74
Charles & Colvard Ltd, 113
Chicago Board Options Exchange, 317
Chicago Tribune, 50-51
Circuit City Group, 355-364, 366-371
Cisco Systems, 115
Claus, J., 149n
CNN Money, 211n
Coca-Cola, 47, 59, 155, 414
Coca-Cola Enterprises, 414
Collins, Daniel, 297n, 357n
Combined income statement and cash flow statement, 78-79
Common equity, as residual claim, 83, 128
Common-sized income statement, 112, 114
Comparable store sales, 107
Comparative advantage, 29-30
Competitive rivalry, existing, 44-46
Complementary products, 49
Compustat, 394
Concorde, 56-57
Conference calls, 4-5
Confidence intervals, 154-155
Conservatism, 10, 13, 75-76
Consolidation, 93
Constellation Brands, 414
Construction in progress, 201-202
Contingent liabilities, 71, 96-97
Cooking.com, 81

Coors, Adolph, 414
Core competencies, 59
Core operations
    Defined, 127
    Valuing with free cash flow model, 220
Corporate Executives' Stock Option Accountability Act, 326
Corporate finance specialists, 4
Cost of equity, 145-155
Credit ratios, 100, 103-104
Credit Suisse First Boston, 42
Cross-sectional analysis, 112
Current assets, defined, 81
Current liabilities, defined, 82
Current ratio, 100, 103
Curtailments, 360, 360n
Customer analysis, 49-51

D

Dasani, 47
Days payables outstanding, 100, 102
Days receivables outstanding, 100-102
Dean Foods, 155
Debt claims, defined, 128
Debt covenants, 10
Debt service, defined, 132-133
Debt to capital ratio, 100, 103
Deferred tax asset, 303, 306, 308-310
Deferred tax liability, 300, 306, 308-310
Defined benefit plans, 349, 351-354
    Accounting for, 355-364
    Economic amounts and, 357-360
    Economic cost of, 355-357, 361
    Employer contributions to, 359
    Footnote disclosures, 366-369
    Pension plans, 351-354
    Valuing firms with, 364-371
        Income tax considerations, 365-366, 368-369
Defined contribution pension plans, 349-351, 354
    Accounting for, 354-355
    Valuing firms with, 355

Dell Computer Corporation, 411
Department of Commerce, 45
Department of Labor
     Private Pension Plan
         Bulletin, 350
Discontinued operations, 74, 85
Discounted cash flow analysis,
     11-12
Disqualifying disposition, 327
Dividend discount model, 16,
     134-135, 171-179
     Assumptions of, 172-176
     Circularity of, 184-185
     Firms not paying dividends
         and, 179
     Gordon Growth Model, 173,
         178, 219
     Just barely sustainable dividend
         growth rate, 173-180,
         184-185
     Normal dividend growth rate,
         176-179
     Supernormal dividend growth
         rate, 176-179
     Two-stage model, 176-178
Dividend exclusion, inter-corporate,
     296-297, 307-308
Dividends, defined, 133
Dodd, Christopher, 327
Donaldson, Lufkin and Jenrette
     Securities Corporation, 237
drugstore.com, 129
Dun & Bradstreet, 111
Duration, 146, 146n

E

Earnings per share
     Antidilutive securities and, 84
     Basic, 83-84
     Convertible securities and, 84,
         84n
     Diluted, 84-85
     Warrants and options and, 84,
         84n
Earnings quality, 15, 75-76, 325,
     389-390, 428-431
     See also Accounting analysis and
         Financial statement quality
Economic balance sheet, 127-133

Economic ownership of retirement
     plans, 353-354
Economic position of pension
     plan, *See* Funded status
Economic structure of an industry,
     43-48
EDGAR, *See* Securities and
     Exchange Commission
Effective income tax rate, 100,102,
     110, 296
     On core operations, 226, 296,
         307-312
     Reconciled from statutory tax
         rate, 306, 308-309
Effective interest rate method, 82
Efficient market hypothesis, 21
     Anomalies, 32, 33
     Defined, 22-23
     Empirical evidence, 31-34
     Implications for behavior of
         security prices, 23-27
     Implications for security analysis,
         29-31
     Information costs and, 31
     Information sets and, 22-23
     Paradox of, 28
     Role of investors in, 28-29
     Semistrong-form, 22-23
     Strong-form, 22-23
     Weak-form, 22-23
EITF, *See* Emerging Issues Task
     Force
El Paso Electric, 97
Emerging Issues Task Force, 69, 75
     Consensus 00-15, 331n
Employee Retirement Income
     Security Act, 359n
Employee stock options, 317-342
     Accounting and, 325, 328-329
     Differences versus publicly
         traded options, 321-324
     Earnings quality and, 327
     Forfeitures of, 321
     Grants of, 321
     Incentive alignment and, 321
     Income tax law and, 327-329
     Intrinsic value method of
         accounting, 325
     Marginal tax rate on, 330-331
     Outstanding, 335
     Restrictions on, 321-323

Valuation analysis and, 329-341
     Vesting period for, 321
     Yet to be granted, 330-335
Entrants, potential, 46
Enron Corporation, 9n, 11, 12,
     76, 392
EPS, *See* Earnings per share
Equity, defined, 83
Equity Expansion Act of 1993, 326
Equity method, 81, 93-94
Equity risk premium, 146-149
     Historical, 148-149
ERISA, *See* Employee Retirement
     Income Security Act
ESOs, *See* Employee stock options
Expenses, defined, 74
Expiration date (of stock option),
     317
External analysis, 43-53
Extraordinary items, 74, 85
     Early extinguishment of debt
         and, 85n
     Terrorist attacks and, 75
Exxon *Valdez*, 96

F

Fahnestock & Co., 76
Fair value, defined, 129
Fama, Eugene, 22, 22n
FASB, *See* Financial Accounting
     Standards Board
Federal Reserve Bank, 45
Federal Reserve Bulletin, 45
Federated Department Stores,
     105-106
Fidelity Investments, 3
Financial Accounting Standards
     Board, 8-9, 8n, 13, 69-70,
     93n
     Due process, 9, 69-70
     Political pressure and, 9, 69
     See also, Emerging Issues Task
         Force, Statements of
         Financial Accounting
         Concepts, Statements of
         Financial Accounting
         Standards
Financial leverage, *See* leverage
Financial statement analysis, 15-16

Financial statement quality,
    9-12, 222
    See also Earnings quality
Financial statements, 67-89
    Management influence over, 9-12
Finger, Catherine, 430n
Finlay Enterprises, Inc., 113
Fisher-Price, 74
Five forces framework, 44-48
Flows to equity model, 16, 134-135,
    179-181
Food and Drug Administration, 51
Ford Motor Company, 392
Forecasting, 14, 16, 211-244
    During forecast horizon, 221-222
    Internal consistency of, 213,
        215, 219
    Reasonableness of, 213, 219
Form 8-K, 82
Form 10-K, 82
Form 10-Q, 82
Fortune, 50
Forward-looking statements, 221
Frank, David, 11
Free cash flow
    Defined, 132
    Differences versus GAAP cash
        flow, 189-192
    Equivalents, 190
    Modeling, 213-219
        Cause and effect relationships
            in, 213-216, 219
        Fixed and variable costs in,
            215-216
        Forecast horizon and, 219-222
        Refining, 229-236
        Setting assumptions in,
            219-229
        Terminal value (perpetuity)
            and, 219-220, 227-228
        Valuation spreadsheet,
            224-225
    Pension plans and, 357
Free cash flow model, 14, 16,
    134-137, 187-189, 211
    Compared to residual income
        model, 278-285
    Generalized for defined benefit
        plans, 364-371
    Generalized for employee stock
        options, 329-341

Free cash flow statement, 189-192
Free cash flow worksheet, 192-202
    Defined benefit plans and,
        366-370
    Income tax effects in, 195
Friedman's Inc., 113
Fundamental analysis, 31
Funded status, 355-357, 359
    Overfunded plans, 359
    Underfunded plans, 359
    Volatility of, 355-356
    See also Transition asset
        or obligation

G

GAAP, *See* Generally accepted
    accounting principles
Gains, defined, 74
Gannett Company, Inc., 433, 435
Gatorade, 41, 137
General Electric, 211, 432
General Mills, 395, 404
General Motors, 150, 349
Generally accepted accounting
    principles, 4, 8
    Decision usefulness and, 8
    Hierarchy of, 69-70
    Historical cost and, 13
    Limitations of, 12-14
Governmental Accounting
    Standards Board, 69
Governmental and regulatory
    analysis, 51
Green Bay Packers, Inc., 180
Gross margin percentage, 101-102,
    108-109
Grossman, Sanford, 28n
Guidera, Jerry, 76n

H

Handy and Harman, 349
Held-to-maturity securities, 94-96,
    95n
Helene Curtis Industries Inc., 51
Historical cost, 13
Holland Capital Management, 11
Hollywood, 430
Human resources, 58-59

I

I/B/E/S, *See* Institutional Brokers
    Estimate System
IHOP Corporation, 114
In the money stock option,
    317, 320
Incentive stock options, 327, 327n
Income statement, 72-76
    Content of, 73-74
    Relationship to balance sheet,
        72-73
Income taxes, 295-312
    Accounting for, 297-304
    Footnote disclosure, 304-307
    Foreign operations and,
        310-311
    Free cash flow worksheet and,
        310-311
    Provision for, 299-300, 304,
        308-309
    Rates, 295-297
Individual competitor assessment,
    48-49
Information Resources Inc., 47
Institutional Brokers Estimate
    System, 410
Intel Corporation, 127-128
Interest cost, 359, 380-381, 380n
Interest coverage ratio, 100,
    103-104
Internal analysis, 54-59
International Accounting
    Standards Committee, 69
International Business
    Machines, 411
Intrinsic value
    (of stock option), 317
Inventory turnover ratio, 100, 102
Investment bankers, 4
Investment priorities, 59
Investment ratios, 100, 104-106
Investment strategies, 31
Iowa Electronic Market, 26

J

Job Creation and Worker
    Assistance Act of 2002, 301n
Johnson, Bruce, 297n, 357n
Johnson Controls, 232

K

Kellogg, 395, 404
Kellogg Graduate School
    of Management, 6
Key Business Ratios, 111
Kozmo.com, 81
Kraft Foods Inc., 50
Krispy Kreme Doughnuts, Inc., 114

L

L.L. Bean, 51
Lafarge North America Inc., 232
Lagrangian multiplier method, 168n
Land's End, 155
Lazare Kaplan International,
    Inc., 113
Legal ownership of retirement plans
    contrasted with economic
    ownership, 354
Lehman Brothers Inc., 6, 237, 349
Leisenring, James, 326
Lev, Baruch, 431
Leverage
    Cost of capital and, 258-260
    Defined, 251
    Financial distress costs and,
      257-258
    Operating decisions and, 258
    Taxes and, 255-256
    Value created by, 252-258
Levin, Carl, 326
Liabilities
    Current and noncurrent, 82
    Defined, 68
Lieberman, Joseph, 326
LIFO conformity rule, 299
Lipshitz, Clive, 6
living.com, 81
Log-normal distribution, 319
Lone Star Technologies, 232
Long bonds, 148
Loss carrybacks, 301-304
Loss carryforwards, 301-304
    Accounting for, 302-304
    Valuations and, 304
Losses, defined, 74
Lucas, Tim, 75
Lucent Technologies, 115

M

Major League Baseball Players
    Association, 48
Malone, Michael, 326
Manipulation, freedom from, 75-76
Maremont, Mark, 76n
Marginal tax rate, 296, 307
Market-to-book ratio, 33, 100,
    104-105, 386, 434-438
    Accounting differences and, 436
    Capital structure and, 435-436
    Expected earnings growth and,
      434-435
    Normalized earnings multiple
      and, 437-438
    Relationship to PE ratio, 434,
      436-437
    Return on equity and, 434,
      436-437
Marketing and selling strategies, 57
Matching principle, 297, 329
Materiality of errors, 12, 12n
Mattel, 49, 54-55, 101
Mauboussin, Michael,
    42, 243, 243n
Mayors Jewelers Inc, 113
McCain, John, 26
McDonald's Corporation, 48, 59,
    76, 114, 392
Merger and acquisition analysts, 4
Merrill Lynch & Company, 3, 237,
    395, 404-405, 414
Michael Anthony Jewelers, Inc., 113
Microsoft Corporation, 50, 96,
    129, 317
Milton, Stephen, 50-51
Minority interest, 82-83, 93
Mission, corporate, 54
Modigliani-Miller Propositions on
    Capital Structure Irrelevance,
    254-258, 423-426
*Moody's Handbook of Common
    Stocks*, 111
Moody's Industry Review, 111-113
Moody's/Mergents, 111
Morgan Stanley, 155
Movado Group, Inc., 113
Multiple, 386

Multiples analysis, 11-12, 16,
    385-398
    Adjusting multiples, 396,
      412-416
    Adjusting value drivers,
      397, 429
    Arguments for and against use of,
      389-391
    As shortcut for discounted cash
      flow analysis, 391
    Comparability in, 386, 391-394,
      411-412
      When not necessary, 393
      When not possible, 396-397
    Diversified firms and, 432-434
    Implicit discounted cash flow
      assumptions and, 389
    Matching in,
      See Comparability in
    Redefining multiples, 396-397,
      430-432

N

Nasdaq, 4n
NBC, 211, 432
Negative debt, 157
Net assets, defined, 68
Net operating profit after tax, 191
New York Stock Exchange, 4n
Nobel Prize, 319, 319n
Noncontrolling interest,
    See minority interest
Noncurrent assets, defined, 81
Noncurrent liabilities, defined, 82
Nonfinancial information, 13
Nonoperating cash flows,
    defined, 132
Nonoperating net assets
    As negative debt, 157
    Defined, 128
Nonqualified stock options,
    327, 327n
Nonrecurring items, exclusion of,
    75-76
NOPAT, *See* Net operating profit
    after tax
Nordstrom, 57
Normal return, 29
Normalized earnings, 437

O

Occupational Safety and Health Administration, 51
OfficeMax, 432
OPEB plans, *See* Other postemployment benefit plans
Operating margin percentage, 100-102, 109
Operating ratios, 100-102
Option holder, 317
Option premium, 319, 321, 323
Option writer, 317
    Firm as, 323-324
Oracle Corporation, 50
Other capital cash flows, defined, 133
Other capital claims, defined, 128
Other postemployment benefit plans, 353-354, 357n, 364-371
    See also Defined benefit plans
Out of the money stock option, 319-320

P

p-value, 154, 154n
PaineWebber, 6
Passive investment strategies, 31
Pay as you go funding of other postemployment benefit plans, 353
PBO, *See* Projected benefit obligation
PE ratio, *See* Price to earnings ratio
PE to growth ratio, 412-416, 432, 435
    Errors in low-growth industries, 413-415
Peapod, 58
PEG ratio, *See* PE to growth ratio
Pennzoil, 129
Pension plans,
    Growth in contributions and assets, 350
    Relative use of defined benefit and defined contribution plans, 352
    See also Defined benefit plans and Defined contribution plans

Pepsi Bottling Group, 414
PepsiAmericas, 414
PepsiCo, 47, 59, 414
Permanent differences, 298, 307
Perpetuity value, *See* Free cash flow modeling, terminal value and
Pfizer, 58, 412
Plan amendments, 360, 362
Plan assets, 357, 365-366
Polaroid, 260
Pooling of interests, 71
Porter, Michael, 44
Portfolio managers, 6
Post-earnings announcement drift, 32-33
Potential employees, 4
Precision, 162, 168-169
Preferred stock, 83
Prentice Hall, 111
Pretax income, 296
    Reconciled to taxable income, 298-299
    That will ever be taxed, 298-300
Price path, 24
Price-to-earnings ratio, 33, 100, 104-105, 386
    Capital structure and, 423-427
    Decomposition, 432-434
    Discontinued operations and, 433-434
    Expected earnings growth and, 392-393, 407-416
    Financial reporting differences and, 428-431
    High or low earnings years and, 392
    Near-zero earnings and loss firms and, 431-432
    Unlevered, 423-427
Price-to-sales ratio, 386, 430
Price tree, 318-319
Price Waterhouse, 6
Pricing, 56-57
Private equity investors, 6
Private label, 395
Private Securities Litigation Reform Act, 221
Procter & Gamble, 50-51
Product differentiation, 56-57
Product life cycle, 54-56
Product positioning, 57

Products and services, 54-55
Projected benefit obligation, 357, 359-360, 365-366, 378-382
Proxy statement, 394
Put options, 317n

Q

Quaker Oats Company, The, 41, 74, 395, 404
    Acquisition of Stokely-Van Camp, 137
Quality of earnings, *See* Earnings quality
Quick ratio, 100, 103
Qwest Communications International Inc., 237

R

R. J. Reynolds Tobacco Holdings, Inc., 97
Ralcorp, 395, 404
Rappaport, Alfred, 243, 243n
Ratio analysis, 106-115
Ready-to-eat cereal industry, 395-396, 404
Recognition criteria, 70-71
Reeds Jewelers, Inc., 113
Regulation, 13
Regulation Fair Disclosure (FD), 7
Regulators, 8-9
Related-party transactions, 11
Representational faithfulness, 326-327
Residual income, defined, 138, 268
Residual income model, 16, 134, 138, 267-286
    Accounting differences and, 278-279
    Cash flow differences and, 279
    Clean surplus assumption, 268n
    Compared to free cash flow model, 278-285
    Defined, 267-269
    Derivation of, 289-290
    Equity level, 267-268
    ESO valuation in a, 336-337
    Operating level, 268-269
    Terminal value assumption in, 269-279, 290-291

Return on assets, 105
Return on capital, 100, 105-106
Return on common equity, 100, 105-106
Return on plan assets, 359, 361-362
Returns momentum and reversals, 33
Revenue growth rate, 101-102, 107
Revenues, defined, 74
Reverse valuation, 243
Revsine, Lawrence, 297n, 357n
Risk-free interest rate, 146-148
Robert Mondavi, 414
Robert Morris and Associates, 111

S

Salomon Smith Barney, 6
Scenario analysis, *See* Sensitivity analysis
Scholes, Myron, 319, 319n
Schroders, 6
Schroeder, Michael, 76n
Schwan's Sales Enterprises, 50
SEC, *See* Securities and Exchange Commission
Securities Act of 1933, 8, 8n
Securities and Exchange Commission, 4n, 13, 45
  Accounting methods and, 7-8, 8n
  Composition of, 9
  Disclosure requirements and, 7-8
  Division of Corporate Finance, 9
  Division of Enforcement, 9
  Electronic Data Gathering, Analysis and Retrieval (EDGAR), 45, 82
    Accessing via World Wide Web, 82
  Filings submitted electronically, 5, 82
  Office of the Chief Accountant, 9
Securities Exchange Act of 1934, 8n, 9
Security analysis
  Beliefs about market efficiency and, 30-31

Comparative advantage and, 29-30
  Goal of, 21-22
Segment reporting, *See* Statement of Financial Accounting Standards No. 131
Sell-side analysts, 3-5, 7
Selling short, 21, 321
Semistrong-form market efficiency, 22-23
Senate Committee on Banking, Housing and Urban Affairs, 327
Sensitivity analysis, 236-243
Service cost, 359, 366, 380-382
  As free cash flow equivalent, 365
Settlement rate, 378
Seven-Eleven, 57
Shareholders' equity, defined, 68
Smoothing adjustments in pension plan accounting, 355-357, 360-364
Snapple, 41
Special items, 74, 85
Special purpose entities, 11
Standard & Poor's, 111
Standard Industrial Classification, 394
Starbucks Coffee Company, 67, 408
  Beta, 150-151, 153-155
  Cautionary statement pursuant to the Private Securities Litigation Reform Act of 1995, 221
  Cost of equity, 155
  Credit ratios, 103-104
  Defined contribution plan, 349-351
  Economic balance sheet, 129-133
  Employee stock options, 323-324, 335-336
  Financial statements, 79-87
  Finding information on, 223
  Free cash flow, 194-199
  Free cash flow model, 213-219
  Income tax footnote, 307-310
  Investment ratios, 100, 104-105

Marginal tax rate on employee stock options, 331
  Operating ratios, 100-102, 106-108
  PE ratios over time, 392
  Refining the forecast, 232-236
  Residual income valuation, 269-278
  Valuation, 222-229
  Weighted-average cost of capital, 159-160
  Yet-to-be-granted employee stock options, 333-335
Statement on Auditing Standards No. 69, 69
Statements of Financial Accounting Concepts, 9, 69
  No. 1, 72, 72n
  No. 6, 68, 68n, 72
Statements of Financial Accounting Standards, 9, 69-70
  No. 5, 96-97
  No. 87, 355
  No. 106, 9, 69, 355, 360n, 362n
  No. 109, 303
  No. 115, 93-96, 95n
  No. 123, 9, 69-70, 325-327, 331, 333, 335
  No. 131, 230-231, 233, 233n
  No. 132, 355
Statutory tax rate, 295
  Net effect of state, 295
  Reconciled to effective tax rate, 306, 308-309
Stiglitz, Joseph, 28n
Stock option overhang, 322
Stock options, *See* Employee stock options
Stokely-Van Camp, 41, 137
Strike price, 317
Strong-form market efficiency, 22-23
Substitute products, 46
Super Bowl, 34, 34n
Suppliers, 48
Supply chain, 57-58
Survey of Current Business, 45
Sweeteners, 360
Systematic risk, 146, 150-152
  See also Beta

T

t-statistic, 154, 154n
Taggart, Robert, 160n
Tau-star (τ*), 160-162, 255-256, 425-426
Taxable income, 296
    Reconciled to GAAP pretax income, 298-299
Technical analysis, 31
Tel Aviv University, 6
Telemundo Telcommunications Group, 211
Temporary differences, 298, 306
Texaco, 129
Thomas, Jacob, 32, 149n
Tiffany & Co., 102, 113
Tippie Graduate School of Business, 26
Toys "R" Us, 49, 432
Trading rules, 30
Trading securities, 94-95
Transition asset or obligation, 362, 362n
Treasury bonds, 146-148, 146n
Treasury Department, 146n, 148
Trend analysis, 106-112

U

U S West, 237
Unilever, 50-51
Unitil Corporation, 177-178, 181

Universal Card Services, Inc., 85
University of Iowa, 26
Unlevered beta, *See* Beta, unlevered
Unlevered cost of equity, 160-161, 252
Unrecognized assets and liabilities, 72
Unsystematic risk, 150-152
Upside, 326
USA Today, 433
USG Corporation, 257
USX Corporation, 229

V

Valuation, 14, 16
Valuation allowance, 303, 310
Valuation rules (under GAAP), 70
Value driver, 386
Value Line Investment Survey, 111, 223
Value strategy, 104
Venture capitalists, 4

W

W. W. Grainger, 256
WACC, *See* Weighted-average cost of capital
Wal-Mart Stores, Inc., 57-58, 107, 311-312, 408
Wall Street Journal, The, 76
Washington and Lee University, 6

Washington Post, 155
Watson Wyatt Worldwide, 322
Weak-form market efficiency, 22-23
Weighted-average cost of capital, 155-160
    Contrasted with return on capital, 273-276
    Division specific, 163
    Leverage and, 258-260
White Hen Pantry, 57
Whitehall Jewellers Inc, 113
Whole Foods Market, 57
WHX Corporation, 349
William Blair, 6
William Wrigley Jr. Company, 55
Wolf Brand, 137
Working capital ratios, 112

Y

Yield curve, 148

Z

Zale Corp., 113